MW01076064

MARCEL
MAUSS

Marcel Fournier

MARCEL
MAUSS

A BIOGRAPHY

Translated by Jane Marie Todd

PRINCETON UNIVERSITY PRESS

PRINCETON AND OXFORD

2006

FIRST PUBLISHED IN FRANCE UNDER THE TITLE *MARCEL MAUSS* © LIBRAIRIE
ARTHÈME FAYARD, 1994.

ENGLISH TRANSLATION © 2006 BY PRINCETON UNIVERSITY PRESS
PUBLISHED BY PRINCETON UNIVERSITY PRESS, 41 WILLIAM STREET, PRINCETON,
NEW JERSEY 08540
IN THE UNITED KINGDOM: PRINCETON UNIVERSITY PRESS, 3 MARKET PLACE,
WOODSTOCK, OXFORDSHIRE OX20 1SY

ALL RIGHTS RESERVED

LIBRARY OF CONGRESS CATALOGING-IN-PUBLICATION DATA

FOURNIER, MARCEL, 1945–

[MARCEL MAUSS. ENGLISH]

MARCEL MAUSS : A BIOGRAPHY / MARCEL FOURNIER ; TRANSLATED BY JANE MARIE TODD.

P. CM.

INCLUDES BIBLIOGRAPHICAL REFERENCES AND INDEX.

ISBN-13: 978-0-691-11777-5 (CLOTH : ALK. PAPER)

ISBN-10: 0-691-11777-2 (CLOTH : ALK. PAPER)

1. MAUSS, MARCEL, 1872–1950. 2. ETHNOLOGISTS—FRANCE—BIOGRAPHY. 3.
ETHNOLOGY—FRANCE—HISTORY. 4. SOCIOLOGY—FRANCE—HISTORY. I. TITLE.

GN21.M38F6813 2005

305.8'0092—DC22

[B]   2004061957

BRITISH LIBRARY CATALOGING-IN-PUBLICATION DATA IS AVAILABLE

PUBLICATION OF THIS BOOK HAS BEEN AIDED BY THE FRENCH MINISTRY OF CULTURE—
CENTRE NATIONAL DE LIVRE.

THIS BOOK HAS BEEN COMPOSED IN 10/12 BERKELEY MEDIUM
PRINTED ON ACID-FREE PAPER.
PUP.PRINCETON.EDU
PRINTED IN THE UNITED STATES OF AMERICA

1 3 5 7 9 10 8 6 4 2

CONTENTS

INTRODUCTION

MARCEL MAUSS is the object of great admiration. Georges Condominas called him "the father of French ethnography."[1] "The Gift," required reading for any anthropology student, is his "most deservedly famous" work, as Claude Lévi-Strauss has noted.[2] It is, in Georges Gurvitch's words, a "true masterpiece."[3]

The intellectual legacy bequeathed by this great scholar, long unappreciated by everyone but anthropologists, is now available to the academic community. *Sociologie et anthropologie* (Sociology and anthropology), a collection of half a dozen of Mauss's writings, was published in 1950, the year he died. In the late 1960s, Presses Universitaires de France brought out selected works under the title *Mauss*;[4] and, more important, a three-volume edition of his works was issued by Minuit in those same years.[5] These editions, however, include only the scholarly works. His many political works, which, as Denis Hollier lamented, were extremely dispersed, have also recently been collected.[6]

In a few sentences, Henri Lévy-Bruhl expresses the essence of what we need to know about a man who was his teacher and friend: "Mauss is known primarily as an ethnologist and a historian of religion"; "Mauss despised all dogmatism"; "Mauss knew everything"; "Mauss was teeming with ideas"; "Mauss was the epitome of dedication"; "Mauss did not leave behind any general overview." And in only a few lines he retraces Mauss's "original and attractive physiognomy": "Physically large and with a good build, his face framed by a light brown beard; regular features; sharp, shining eyes. His conversation was sparkling, though his voice was somewhat hollow and his manner of speaking slow. In his remarks there was often some paradox by which he himself was sometimes taken in."[7]

Lévy-Bruhl is discreet about Mauss's personal life: "His was a scholar's life and displays few prominent traits."[8] But he immediately adds: "This is not the place to talk about the man his friends and loved ones will forever mourn for his great kindness, sensitivity, and gentleness. . . . It is fitting to say, however, that his kind-heartedness was to some extent prejudicial to his scholarly output."[9] Little is known about the man: a few short biographical accounts are devoted to him but he has never been the object of a true intellectual biography.[10]

To write the intellectual biography of a scientist is to focus on his character—a unique set of abilities, habits, temperaments, and physical and mental strengths[11]—but also to write the history of the people and disciplines associated with him (in this case, the history of religion, ethnology, and sociology). In addition, as Mauss's former student André-Georges Haudricourt suggests, it is to grasp the subject's work in its context.[12] Such a project is ambitious, not to say perilous, especially if we wish to be complete. This was the wish Mauss himself formulated when he wrote an obituary for the English anthropologist James Frazer: "A work of art may be merely suggestive. The history of a scientist, however, must be truthful and everything must be said in it."[13]

One's interest in Mauss's life increases as one moves away from the man and toward his environment and his age. The environment was made up of new academic disciplines (ethnology and sociology) and of a school of thought, the Durkheim school; the age was the long period extending from 1872 to 1950 and marked by two major wars. Through his writings, his teachings, and his political action, Mauss found himself at the center of the intellectual and political life of his country and of Europe—in the "witch's cauldron," to use his expression.

One cannot speak of Mauss without mentioning his uncle Émile Durkheim, head of the French school of sociology:[14] Mauss himself acknowledged that it was impossible to separate himself from the work of the school. "If there is any personality, it is submerged in an intentional impersonalism. The sense of work in common, as a team, the conviction that collaboration is a counterforce to isolation, to the pretentious search for originality, may be what characterizes my scientific career."[15]

Mauss embodied better than anyone that ethic of research characteristic of all who participated in the great collective adventure of *Année Sociologique*. His entire scientific life was organized around the journal, and most of his large body of writings took the form of notes, notices, and book reviews. Little has been known about the dynamic of the team of young researchers surrounding Durkheim, a group usually portrayed as a cult. Access to Mauss's personal archives, and in particular to his correspondence, now makes it possible to shed light on this founding moment in the history of the human sciences.[16]

In observing the exchanges, arguments, and differences of opinion Mauss had with all concerned, we may draw a more accurate portrait of the Durkheim school and present the specific contribution of each of its members. It is true that more than the others, Mauss found himself in a position of dependence, "in Durkheim's shadow," as Condominas writes.[17] His works, particularly his early writings, seem to be an "integral part of the collective work accomplished by the school of sociology."[18] But when we read Mauss's writings as a whole, including the unpublished texts, we are led to qualify that assertion of his orthodoxy: the nephew always called himself a Durkheimian, but he was one in his own way.

Mauss had little interest in developing systematic theories but preferred "to work on his materials," to establish a few valid generalizations, and then "go on to something else."[19] Like Durkheim, Mauss was an ardent defender of positive science, believing *only in the facts*. He shared an evolutionist conception of history and attributed a heuristic value to the study of the elementary (or primitive) forms of social facts. He applied himself to the analysis of the social functions of institutions and to the study of the mechanisms of social cohesion. And through his work on the ritual manifestations of religious life, he contributed toward a theory of the sacred. He acknowledged that "the innermost fount of social life is a set of representations"; he joined the vast Durkheimian enterprise whose object was to study the "human mentality."

And yet Mauss cannot be easily confined to a single category. He moved from one discipline to another, took an interest in a host of questions, and, though following in his uncle's footsteps, also managed cautiously to mark himself off from him. He acknowledged that society is built on solidarity; but he believed that it also requires reciprocity for its survival. And though maintenance of the social order requires consensus, it also depends on the interpenetration of different social groups.

Mauss's position as nephew, disciple, and successor had one advantage: he was not compelled to lead the major battles, though there was no dearth of adversaries in academia. He could allow himself to open a dialogue with former enemies and attempt compromises, especially with psychologists. He was more interested in furthering knowledge than in defending a doctrine, and his attitude toward science—always both rationalist and empiricist— was less that of a professor who wants to transmit a body of codified knowledge than that of a researcher aware of the limits of his methods who wants to collect new data and reduce ignorance about reality. As he liked to remind us, it is "the unknown that must be unveiled." Even though Mauss never did fieldwork, he was mindful of reality and familiar with all the ethnological research.

It would be a distortion to see Mauss merely as the heir to the Durkheim legacy. After World War I, the burden of editing the vast and previously unpublished work of Durkheim and his collaborators did fall on his shoulders. But he also pursued his own research in every direction, from the gift of "bodily techniques" to the idea of civilization and the notion of person. And though he relaunched *Année Sociologique* primarily out of a sense of obligation to Durkheim's memory, the Institut d'Ethnologie, which he helped to found in 1925, was not a specifically Durkheimian enterprise.

There is a great temptation to seek a unifying principle in Mauss's writings. Victor Karady claims that his work holds together more as a result of "contingent circumstances than as the dialectic of a creative project and its realization."[20] This is a harsh judgment, since it assumes that the realization of a creative project owes nothing to circumstance. Yet it is true Mauss was often sorely tested by the death of Durkheim and of Henri Hubert and by his own illnesses, for example—and faced many professional and personal obligations. As a result he left several projects unfinished: a thesis on prayer, a masterwork on the nation, a small book on Bolshevism, a study of technology.

What remains of that life devoted to science and marked by the spirit of the gift? Maurice Leenhardt replies succinctly: "Few books, articles dispersed everywhere, an enormous influence."[21] As a teacher, he was dear to his students, but he acted primarily as guide, companion, motivator. He remained a student at heart throughout his life and at the end of his career wanted to become the pupil of his pupils. "Mauss was never a big shot," notes Jean Cazeneuve. "There was always something young and a little bohemian about him, and even as a teacher he seems to have secretly remained an eternal student."[22]

Marcel Mauss was foremost a scholar, but a scholar who never lost interest in what was happening around him. Unlike his uncle, he was actively engaged in politics from his university days. A member of the Groupe des Étudiants Collectivistes (Collectivist student group), of the Parti Ouvrier Français (French workers party), and of the Parti Ouvrier Socialiste Révolutionnaire (Revolutionary socialist workers party), he supported Émile Zola during the Dreyfus Affair, was a contributor to *Devenir Social* and *Mouvement Socialiste*, became a reporter for *Humanité*, and published articles in *Populaire* and *Vie Socialiste*. Little is known about the role political activity played in his life, particularly the place of the cooperative and socialist movements he participated in. Mauss could have run for national office. He preferred to remain merely a militant, faithful to his convictions and to his friends but intent on adapting to new realities.

Such political involvement, one suspects, influenced his work: after World War I, Mauss wrote a long series of article on violence, published an important piece entitled "A Sociological Appreciation of Bolshevism," and began a book on the nation. It was also at that time that he composed "The Gift" for the journal *Année Sociologique*, an essay that attests not only to the research concerns of a specialist in the history of religion and in ethnology but also to the sensibility of a politically engaged intellectual. A sociologist, ethnologist, and Jewish militant committed to socialism, Mauss felt the ambivalence specific to his position and his milieu. His reflections on World War I, the Russian Revolution, the nation, Nazism, and other matters were those of a man who, one way or another, knew how to steer the leftist course through the storm. It is in reading his "Sociological Appreciation of Bolshevism" that we grasp the power of his thought, his capacity to draw immediate political and moral conclusions from one of the twentieth century's great human tragedies.

At the start of this research, I shared my plan to write Mauss's intellectual biography with some of my colleagues. Some reactions were positive:

"Now that's an interesting project, no one's done it yet!" But those most familiar with the question proved somewhat skeptical. "It won't be easy," they warned me.

They were right. Carrying out this project required considerable research and documentation, made possible by the conjunction of several favorable circumstances. I received research grants and invitations to the École des Hautes Études en Sciences Sociales (School of higher studies in the social sciences) and to the Maison des Sciences de l'Homme (Institution for the human sciences); I benefited from the collaboration of members of the Mauss family and of people who knew Marcel Mauss personally; and I enjoyed the support of Pierre Bourdieu and Maurice Agulhon, professors at the Collège de France. I also had access to the Hubert-Mauss collection, a necessary condition for completing this book. The documents the Hubert and Mauss families deposited in the archives of the Collège de France constitute a valuable source of information for anyone interested in the history of the French school of sociology. They include correspondence between Durkheim and Mauss, a set of letters received by Mauss, manuscripts (some unpublished), notes on the courses Mauss took and offered, notes on his readings, and various documents relating to *Année Sociologique*, the Institut Français de Sociologie, and *Annales Sociologiques*.

Although the letters opened countless avenues, I had to broaden the investigation by examining other archives, by interviewing Mauss's nephews, niece, and former students, and by taking a complete inventory of his political writings. The support and kindness that were lavished on me by many different people, and in particular by the members of the Mauss family, were not only greatly appreciated but decisive in enabling me to complete the project.

Gradually the figure of the great man faded away, to be replaced by a rich and complex personality, that of a kind-hearted and thoughtful man.[23] That personality is particularly engaging in that, to use Henri Lévy-Bruhl's expression, it is the "seat" of a series of important historical events and bears the mark of a unique intellectual and social itinerary that would carry Durkheim's nephew, born into a provincial Jewish family, to the Collège de France.

This study follows chronologically the major stages of Mauss's life and comprises four parts: (I) Durkheim's Nephew; (II) The Totem and Taboo Clan; (III) The Heir; and (IV) Recognition. The epilogue covers World War II and the postwar years. This book is part of a triptych that also includes the publication (in collaboration with Philippe Besnard) of the correspondence between Durkheim and Mauss[24] and of Mauss's collected political writings.[25] It will become clear that in this book I seek to present an overview of Mauss's writings through an account of his life: in short, a key moment in the history of the constitution of the human sciences. In this way we may gain a clearer understanding of the scope and breadth of Mauss's influence, which was significant not only on the generation of researchers he trained—Denise Paulme, Louis Dumont, André-Georges Haudricourt, and others—but also on Claude Lévi-Strauss, Georges Condominas, and Pierre Bourdieu, to mention only a few.

PART I

DURKHEIM'S NEPHEW

Most children resemble their mother's brothers.

—*Talmud*

I

ÉPINAL, BORDEAUX, PARIS

E VEN IN HIS EARLY YEARS, everyone automatically associated Marcel
Mauss with Émile Durkheim, whom Mauss's classmates mischievously
called "the uncle." As Henri Lévy-Bruhl notes, Durkheim not only
was Mauss's teacher and a "wonderful professor" but was also his mother's
brother.[1] In his correspondence with his friends, Mauss presented himself as
"the nephew" and referred constantly to "the uncle," "Durkheim," or simply "D." "The uncle is continuing his courses . . . he gets tired and is tired";
"the uncle is doing much better but is still nervous." The bond between the
nephew and his "good uncle" was solid, based on kinship, intellectual affinities, and work in common.

In the "Vôôôges"

Like Durkheim, Marcel Mauss was born in the town of Épinal. They were
fourteen years apart: the uncle was born April 15, 1858; the nephew, May
10, 1872. Mauss's father, Gerson, born in Hatten in the Bas-Rhin in 1834,
married Durkheim's elder sister, Rosine, born in Épinal in 1848, and the
couple settled in Épinal. They had two children: Marcel Israël and Camille
Henri (b. June 10, 1876). When Marcel was born, his father was thirty-seven
and his wife was twenty-three. The family surname is undoubtedly German.
It is said that one of Marcel's great-grandparents, not wanting his family to
bear the name of an animal—*Maus* means "mouse" in German—went to
city hall and did what was required to add an *s* to his name.

In the "information on [his] origins" he provided to the Collège de France,
probably in November 1940, Mauss gave a detailed genealogy of his family
going back several generations: "All my grandparents' relations were born of
French parents. The ancestors of my grandfather Durkheim's mother surely
came from the region of Mutzig, dating back to at least the fifteenth century.
My father served his country for seven years (including leaves), participated
in the Italian campaign, and was saved from typhus by a nun from his home
region of Epfig." And he added: "The family opted for France in 1872 and
resettled from Bischwiller to Épinal."[2]

Even as he went on to reveal his Jewish identity—a rabbi grandfather, a
Jewish given name—Mauss wanted to show that his origins and his allegiance were French. In this case, the notion of allegiance acquired a patriotic

dimension: his father had participated in France's Italian campaign during the Franco-Prussian War, and at its conclusion the family had opted for France. The Frankfurt Treaty, which in 1871 ratified Germany's annexation of Alsace, allowed its residents to choose French nationality, but if they did so they had to leave Alsatian territory.

The history of the Mauss and Durkheim families was closely tied to that of the Alsace-Lorraine region. Épinal is a small town covering three kilometers in the Moselle Valley, close to Alsace. It is the capital of the department of Vosges and in the early 1870s had slightly more than ten thousand residents. The Mauss family occupied a house in the central city at 2, rue Sadi-Carnot, facing the Moselle River.

The region, well known for mineral water and hot springs resorts that developed over the course of the nineteenth century, is agricultural in the west and industrial in the east. Textiles are the most important industry. Spinning and weaving mills, established in the early nineteenth century, multiplied quickly. In 1871 there were 150 such mills, with more than 500,000 spindles and 16,800 power looms. At the time, the manufacture of linen (the famous "Vosges cloth") was concentrated in Gérardmer, where eighty such factories employed more than 3,000 people. Yet the industry remained fragile throughout the century, shaken by many crises: fluctuations in the price of cotton, steep competition from English manufacturers after the free trade treaty between France and England was signed in 1860, a fall in the price of raw cotton during the American Civil War, fires in several factories in the 1880s.

The Mauss family worked in the textile sector. Marcel's father was the "busiest man in France," according to his wife; his son's birth certificate indicates he was a merchant.[3] A sales representative for a drapery company, he also worked with his brothers to set up a small business in Elbeuf called "Mauss et Frères," which specialized in the manufacture of black and figured fabric. Rosine Durkheim was very familiar with that production sector, since she had worked with her sister Céline in a cottage industry, an embroidery shop. Their mother, Mélanie Durkheim, the daughter of a livestock merchant, had opened the shop to supplement her husband's meager income. After their wedding, Rosine Durkheim and Gerson Mauss took over the Mauss family business, whose company name became Fabrique de Broderie à Main, Mauss-Durkheim (Mauss-Durkheim handmade embroidery). Like several other families from the Vosges, they thus set out to produce embroidery. Most of the labor was assigned to women from the countryside who worked at home. True to family tradition, Marcel's younger brother, Camille, joined his parents' business, which, according to one member of the family, was "doomed by the course of history." Marcel's mother regularly complained that business was "deplorable," "as bad as it gets," in a "total slump." It reached the point where she thought of "closing up shop": "I am completely out of work and am much more sorry for the workers than for myself. I've had it up to here with this business."[4]

Marcel never joined the family business. During visits to Épinal in his adulthood, however, he worried about the future of the little factory and also about the economic situation of the region and the fate of the workers. He took out subscriptions for his "comrades from Épinal" to the journal *Mouvement Socialiste*, closely followed the activities of the socialist and co-operative movement in the Vosges, and sought to sensitize Parisian militants to the struggles of striking workers in the Meurthe Valley. Épinal would also provide concrete examples for an article Mauss published in *Humanité* on "employer mutualism."[5]

Marcel loved the region of Vosges, where he spent his entire childhood and adolescence. In this he resembled Émile Durkheim, who as an adult wanted to move closer to Épinal. In 1884, at the age of twenty-six, Durkheim left Sens for Saint-Quentin; in 1893, while a professor at Bordeaux, he expressed the wish to find a position in Nancy where, "as a Lorrainian, [he] would be near his family. . . . [He] would be in his home environment."[6] Once settled in Paris, Durkheim regularly returned to Épinal for holidays and summer vacations.

Marcel was very attached to his family and followed the same pattern. His visits to the countryside were particularly agreeable because he was athletic: he enjoyed swimming, running, boxing, and, after he moved to Paris, fencing. But what Mauss liked more than all those athletic activities was "to roam the woods." A great lover of mountain hiking and climbing, he returned when he could to the "Vôôôges," as his English friend Mabel Bode put it, to breathe the pure air and to rest. As a youngster, that "big animal," as his eighth-grade teacher had called him, dreamed of becoming a lumberjack, perhaps so he would not have to leave the wide open spaces and freedom of the Vosges forests.[7]

In this "world apart" that stands between the Alsatian plain and the Lorrainian plateaus, the price of freedom was well known: from 1870 to World War I, the region suffered direct repercussions from the face-off between Germany and France. In October 1870, General von Werder entered Épinal at the head of an army of fifteen thousand. The Frankfurt Treaty, signed on May 10, 1871, put an end to the war, but Alsace and several communes in the Vosges were reunited with Germany. Theoretically, the new border imposed by Otto von Bismarck was drawn to include only those regions where German was spoken; but for strategic and economic reasons, it extended far beyond them. For France it was a humiliating defeat. For the Vosges communes that remained French it was the starting point for a broad demographic and economic expansion. Nancy became the chief French city in the east, Belfort experienced a major boom, and Épinal, spurred by the construction of large coal-burning factories, saw its population triple in fifty years and became known as the "only major center in the Vosges." After the war, the strategic location of the Vosges region led to its militarization. Many forts were built and large garrisons were located there. A narrow-track railroad several dozen kilometers long connected Épinal's armories to the different forts surrounding the city. This massive presence, punctuated by frequent military parades and reviews, turned residents' lives upside down. At the start of World War I, Épinal would be one of four major retrenched camps in eastern France, and General Dubail, head of the First Army, would install his headquarters in the local Church of Notre-Dame.

When the Franco-Prussian War broke out in 1870, Émile Durkheim was twelve years old. "We were sure of victory, I remember it very well," he would later write. The painful experience of defeat produced a strong burst of patriotic feeling in him and in the members of his family. In the face of national decline, he declared himself an advocate of regenerating France. And, though aware that war was a "historical necessity" and would "always exist," he hoped it would hold "an ever diminishing place in the lives of peoples."[8]

On that last point, Durkheim was mistaken. In his life and that of his family, war would hold a central place. Marcel Mauss, though born after the end of hostilities, retained "from his Vosges forebears and the still-raw memories of the Franco-Prussian War a prickly patriotism and a somewhat military demeanor."[9] He would even have liked to pursue a military career, were it not for the difficulty a Jew would have had realizing such professional aspirations. Later, in World War I, the army did not overlook him: Marcel wore a military uniform for more than three years.

A Jewish Education

Alsace and Lorraine were the cradles of French Judaism. In 1808 they were home to thirty-six thousand Jews, accounting for 80 percent of the Jewish population in France. These eastern communities were significant not only in number but also because of their religious and community cohesion.[10] The proportion of Jews living in the region gradually dropped, however, to 70 percent in 1841 and to 56 percent in 1861. What Alsace and Lorraine lost, Paris gained. In his 1886 novel *Au pays du Rhin* (In the Rhineland), J.-J. Weiss writes: "They've barely turned sixteen and they leave Alsace. . . . So what? Young people are right to leave. In Paris, the Jew is equal to everyone else."[11]

To be a Jew in Alsace and Lorraine was to live as a minority surrounded by a Catholic majority and a large number of Protestants. The Christian tradition was solid. Relations between the various religious groups were not always easy. In 1789, 1830–1832, and 1848, the Jews of Alsace were the victims of exactions and violence. This traditional anti-Semitism was often expressed in legends and songs: In the popular imagination, the Jew was associated with the thief.[12] "The Jews are not popular in Alsace-Lorraine," observed Reybell early in the nineteenth century. "Especially in the country-side, they are hated; some criticize their business practices, others display a racial and religious hatred that is all the more violent for being blind. Hence we find that some political parties take on the coloring of anti-Semitism to gain the sympathies of the rural masses."[13] Referring to the period of the Franco-Prussian War, Durkheim himself noted: "Being from a Jewish back-ground myself, I was able to observe it closely. It was the Jews who were blamed for the defeats." And he added: "When a society suffers, it feels the need to find someone to whom it can impute its pain, on whom it can take revenge for its disappointments; and those to whom some disfavor on the public's part is already attached are naturally designated for that role. It is the pariahs who serve as scapegoats."[14]

In the late nineteenth century French Judaism underwent a change that "was to make a population divided into scattered communities into a body united by an administrative structure whose center was located in the capi-tal."[15] The Jewish community became a more open society and membership in it a matter of conscience and an act of will. Both Durkheim's and Mauss's intellectual journeys would be marked by these transformations. Although they distanced themselves from religion, this stance did not necessarily entail breaking off from the community. Their most fundamental experience of Judaism was of a closed community that, pressured by events to be more open, became integrated and adopted the values of the surrounding society.

Durkheim saw Judaism as "a collection of practices meticulously gov-erning all the details of life and leaving little freedom for individual judg-ment."[16] In his study of suicide, he explained the attitude of Jews in terms of "the reprobation with which Christianity long assailed them" and which created "feelings of a particular energy" among them. And he added: "The need to struggle against universal animosity, the very impossibility of com-municating with the rest of the population, obliged them to stand shoulder to shoulder. As a result, each community became a small, compact, and coherent society with a very keen sense of itself and of its unity. Everyone there thought and lived the same way; individual differences were made nearly impossible by communal life and the close and constant surveillance everyone practiced on everyone else."[17]

For the Durkheims more than for most other Jewish families, tradition was religious. "In that family," Henri Durkheim recalled, "we were rabbis from father to son for eight generations."[18] Émile Durkheim's grandfather Israël David was a rabbi in Mutzig, Alsace. His father, Moïse (1805–1896), was the rabbi of Épinal and chief rabbi of Vosges and Haute-Marne. While presiding over the fate of the community, he also became a prominent local

personality whose power was recognized and appreciated by the administrative authorities. It is not surprising that the rabbi of Épinal had a "home
where it was austerity more than opulence that reigned, where observance
of the law was a precept and an example, where nothing came about to distract one from one's duty."[19] The education the young Durkheim received
focused on duty and responsibility and inculcated the value of work, with
nothing but contempt for easy success. One of his collaborators would say
that Durkheim could never feel pleasure without experiencing remorse as a
result.[20] Durkheim was groomed by his father to continue the family rabbinical tradition; he learned Hebrew and was conversant with the Pentateuch
and the Talmud.

But the young Durkheim refused to pursue the career of rabbi and during
his first year at the École Normale Supérieure broke away from Judaism.
Some characterize Durkheim's attitude toward the Jewish religion as "agnos-
ticism"[21]; others speak of a lack of "express commitment to any established
religious institution."[22] Étienne Halphen would say that his maternal grandfather "was always areligious with a capital and privative A; anyone wanting
to find a whiff of Judaism in his works is on the wrong track."[23]

Durkheim took his leave from Judaism within a particularly difficult
context and personal situation. He continued to feel remorse, like "the Jew
who eats pork flesh for the first time."[24] Émile was a tormented man, torn
between his allegiance to two different histories, two cultures—the Jewish
Diaspora and the richness of the Bible and Talmud on the one hand, Western
humanism and classical culture on the other. He felt guilty for not continuing the family tradition. It was as if the son (Émile-David) admitted he was
the murderer of the father (Moïse).[25]

Throughout his life, Durkheim would remain the "rabbi's son" and at
a professional level would often be perceived as a religious leader. Hubert
Bourgin described meeting "the Master" Durkheim as he was leaving the
École Normale Supérieure in 1899:

> His long skinny body was enveloped in an ample dressing gown, a plush cas-
> sock concealing his bony and muscular frame, the fragile support of thought.
> His face emerged pale, ascetic, with its high bald forehead, short beard, thick
> mustache, and prominent rabbi's nose; but his whole hard dry face, magnifi-
> cently illuminated by two deep-set eyes with an intense and gentle power that
> imposed respect, attention, even submission, and which required a serious sim-
> plicity, an utterly bare simplicity such as you saw before you, like imperious
> sovereigns—that face inspired confidence.

Bourgin presented Durkheim as a "priest": "He was a hieratic figure.
His mission was religious."[26] That image of Durkheim as a "lay priest" or
"prophet of some nascent religion" quickly took root and became legendary.
According to a well-known witticism, as he passed in front of Notre-Dame

Cathedral, the rabbi's son said with a smile: "It's in such a pulpit that I ought to have spoken."[27] "Heir to the prophets," Durkheim felt an ardent faith; he passionately wanted to "forge and fashion his listeners' convictions."[28] He cut an impressive figure: "Long and intense reflection; an unusual capacity for abstraction; assiduous, constant labor attentive to both the details and the whole picture; a forceful, heroic obstinacy focused on the task at hand; extreme rigor in his method."[29] But "under the unpolished and somewhat cantankerous-looking envelope," his friends and relations discovered "an ardent, impassioned, generous, and, at the same time, clearly real soul. A true Jewish type, since, whether one laments it or celebrates it, one does not find the likes of him anywhere else."[30] Georges Davy also wanted to correct the "false image" of Durkheim: "His ascetic profile, his emaciated face, his brusqueness, his eloquence and his gaze were imposing. They sparked both the enthusiasm of enraptured audiences and the terror of [degree] candidates backed into a corner. How could anyone guess at the tender heart and worried soul that this inspired prophet concealed?"[31]

When Mauss's grandfather died, it was the women—first the grandmother, then her two daughters, Rosine (Mauss) and Céline (Cahen)—who continued the family traditions. The two families were very close. They lived in the same house, one on the ground floor, the other upstairs. The holidays were usually celebrated together at Céline's. Marcel Mauss's mother was "fairly religious, she prayed alone, went to synagogue."[32] Her husband, Gerson, was also religious. He wrote to Marcel: "Don't neglect to go to the Schul in your neighborhood. As for fasting, I have no doubts about it. . . . My success in business I have always attributed to the will of God."[33]

The young Mauss's studies and the activities of the family business quickly put him in contact with the "outside world." Concerned about his education, his mother made every effort to stimulate him intellectually. For example, when Marcel was only twelve, she gave him a book containing selections from the works of the literary historian and critic Charles Augustin Sainte-Beuve as a New Year's present. Mauss found the engravings so beautiful that he always kept the book; he also made it "the foundation of his literary knowledge from seventh grade on."[34]

Like the young Jews of his generation, Marcel had a religious education, learned Hebrew, and was bar mitzvahed. He received a Jewish given name, Israël, but never used it. In Jewish families, the choice of given name often obeys fixed rules. It is taken alternately from paternal and maternal ancestors and always from a deceased relative. There is also a belief that the name expresses the very essence of the person, so much so that knowing someone's name may give you power over that individual. In the only study he would publish in *Revue d'Études Juives*, Mauss looked into the etymology of his given name: "It is rather generally acknowledged that Israël is an artificial name. . . . For my part, I see no linguistic difficulty in granting the etymology Is-Rahel, and the only problem I see is that the children of Rachel are Joseph and Benjamin, not Israel. But these name changes from phratry to tribe, from tribe to nation, then from nation to nation subsection are a normal thing and are often even the best indicators of historical events. It is possible that all these things conceal a very distant and very hazy past."[35]

Marcel stopped practicing his religion early on, at about age eighteen, notes Steven Lukes.[36] But is it really true, as Lukes goes on to say, that the break came about "without a rift or any tension, in a family environment that was very strongly dominated by Durkheim's influence"?[37] Mauss respected his family's convictions but refused, sometimes in a "finicky" and "overbearing" way, to make "demonstrations of piety."[38]

As adults, Durkheim and Mauss usually went to Épinal for the religious holidays. Their presence created problems for their parents. "I must admit to you," Rosine Mauss wrote her son, "that I am absolutely determined to do Passover as I have always done it. What upsets me is that I would like Émile [Durkheim] to come and I don't know how to reconcile the demands of his stomach with the ritual obligations of Passover. If he wants bread anywhere but in his room, I'll never be able to sit at a table next to bread."[39]

Marcel also participated in the holidays, but family obligations irritated him. He confided to his friend Henri Hubert: "The ceremonies begin today and go on until at least Tuesday. . . . There's absolutely nothing good about the fuss and the feasts, nothing. There's very little sense left in that whole family system."[40] This attitude annoyed his mother: "Let me admit that I don't like the two of you here for the high holidays. I don't want to be shocked or embarrassed about following our old traditions. . . . I cling to them, first, because I'm too old to change and, second, because you've offered me nothing to put in their place."[41] The mother always reminded her son of his religious duties: "If you wanted to please me, you'd observe Passover the best you can. It begins tomorrow evening."[42]

The knowledge Mauss acquired of Judaism in his youth and his mastery of Hebrew were later useful to him in his work on sacrifice and prayer. While pursuing his studies in Holland, he got in touch with the rabbinate of Amsterdam, and he would sometimes go to Épinal for the express purpose of consulting "the chief rabbi, formerly one of the good Talmudists." "I'm on the best of terms with him," he confided to Hubert at the time, "I hope he'll do this thing for me."[43]

Student and Disciple at Bordeaux

Advanced studies and a university career were excellent prospects for a young Jew from Épinal. Marcel's uncle was well aware of this. In his classic work *Suicide*, Durkheim established as a general law that "religious minorities, to be able more surely to withstand the hatred of which they are the object, or simply as a result of emulation, strive to be superior in knowledge to the populations around them." And, to make himself clear, he added:

> Thus the Jew seeks to educate himself, not to replace his collective prejudices with well-considered notions, but simply to be better armed for the struggle. For him it is a way of compensating for the disadvantaged situation created by public opinion and sometimes by the law as well. And since science on its own has no power over tradition, which has retained all its force, he superimposes that intellectual life on his usual activities without the former undermining the latter. Therein lies the complexity of his physiognomy. Primitive in certain ways, in others he is cerebral and refined. He thus combines the advantages of strong discipline, which characterized small groups of earlier times, with the benefits of the intense culture with which our large societies are privileged. He has all the intelligence of the moderns without sharing their despair.[44]

Mauss received an excellent classical secondary education at the Épinal *lycée*, but did not, as might have been expected, go on to the École Normale Supérieure—one of the so-called *grandes écoles*, elite institutions of higher education. In the autumn of 1890 he joined his uncle Émile in Bordeaux. That city, a true geographical crossroads and an active port, was at the time a lively center of trade and was closely associated with prestigious vineyards. It was also a center of knowledge and culture. In addition to the *collèges, lycées*, and many other schools (of hydrography, commerce, and agriculture, for example), there was the "great and venerable" university, where four thousand students were welcomed by Montaigne "smiling from his tomb."[45]

The decision not to become a Normalian may seem surprising, but Mauss was not fond of the boarding school life. Durkheim did not insist; he himself had suffered from school competition and the fear of failure. Moreover, he was disappointed by the education dispensed at the École Normale, with what he saw as its overly literary curriculum, its dilettantism, and its superficiality.

Over the summer, after reading "little books" by the philosopher Théodule Ribot, Marcel had decided to embark on an academic career. He also devoured the texts *La psychologie anglaise contemporaine* and *La psychologie allemande contemporaine* (Contemporary English psychology; Contemporary German psychology); and, like Durkheim in the early 1880s, he was "won over."[46] He thus chose to pursue sociology, a discipline still "rather unfashionable, especially in France, where the excesses of the late Comtists had exposed it to ridicule. It was also far from fully constituted."[47] His uncle's success served as an example and eliminated any resistance the family might have mounted at the time.

After passing his *agrégation* in 1882,[48] Durkheim had become a secondary school philosophy teacher, working in Le Puy, Sens, and Saint-Quentin, and

later in Troyes, after time spent in German universities analyzing the status
of philosophy and particularly ethics. His plan for a "true science of mores"
took shape. "The day will no doubt come," he wrote, "when the science
of ethics will be so advanced that theory will be able to govern practice.
But we are far from that point."[49] He was appointed as *chargé de cours*[50] in
1887 at the Université de Bordeaux, succeeding Alfred Espinas, who had
recently been promoted to dean of the faculty of letters. Espinas was probably responsible for the transfer. The position Durkheim held, which would
become "chair of social sciences" in 1896, was created especially for him by
Louis Liard, director of higher education, who was reorganizing the French
university curriculum. Durkheim was also responsible for a class in pedagogy; when he was hired, the title of the course included the words "social
science."

Durkheim was twenty-nine when he arrived in Bordeaux and had just gotten married in Paris. On October 17, 1887, he had wed Louise Dreyfus, the
daughter of a Parisian entrepreneur whose family was from Wissembourg,
Alsace. He married well, according to contemporaries: Louise was a devoted
wife with a dowry of 100,000 francs.[51] They had two children, Marie in 1888
and André in 1892. Mauss spoke of his aunt with great admiration: "She
always knew how to provide her husband with the most favorable working
conditions. She was very well educated and eventually able to collaborate on
his work. For many years she copied some of his manuscripts, corrected all
his proofs; without her, *Année Sociologique* would have been an overwhelming burden for Durkheim."[52] Georges Davy, one of the contributors to *Année
Sociologique*, called her an "admirable partner" who "devoted her life fully
and joyfully to her husband's austere life as a scholar."[53]

It was a challenge to introduce sociology into the university. As Durkheim
acknowledged at the start of the 1887 school year, sociology was a "young
science." Its history had to be retraced, its objects (social facts) and its methods (observation and experimentation) defined, and the theoretical and
practical "services" it could render had to be identified. Durkheim sought to
be convincing; his tone was sober, free of artifice and rhetoric.

Durkheim was "very anxious about the success of his courses," working from morning till night preparing each of them.[54] The young "scholar
of great value" was already perceived as a master. According to the rector's
reports, he was "a zealous professor who has an enormous influence on
his disciples. . . . No professor gives more of himself." Henri Durkheim, a
nephew who lived with him in Bordeaux, recounted: "He was in his office
all the time, but also worked everywhere else. Wherever he was, he was
working. His wife was extraordinarily devoted to him, she respected his job
and suffered because of it, especially because he got very tired. Whenever
she scolded him, he replied that one has to do what one has to do. She also
attended his public courses."[55]

Intellectually, the fifteen years Durkheim spent in Bordeaux were intense. Mauss noted: "I don't know if my readers realize how much work was required for that young professor in Bordeaux, essentially solitary and without support, to be so productive. All this was done in fifteen years, between 1887 and 1902, when Durkheim was between twenty-nine and forty-four. During that period, Durkheim published *The Division of Labor in Society*, *The Rules of Sociological Method*, and *Suicide*, and organized, edited, and wrote the first four volumes of *Année*. Not to mention his essays and his intense collaboration with each of us."[56]

The uncle's first major work was published by Alcan in 1893. It was his doctoral thesis, *The Division of Labor in Society*, a study of the organization of advanced societies. It took nearly ten years to complete and its aim—to found a science of ethics—was ambitious. What is the nature of social solidarity? How is it that the individual, even while becoming more autonomous, grows more dependent on society? These questions led Durkheim to distinguish between two historical forms of social solidarity, mechanical and organic, through the study of legal rules. Mechanical solidarity, characteristic of so-called primitive or backward societies, relies on resemblances and links the individual directly to society. Organic solidarity, characteristic of so-called industrialized or advanced societies, results from a long process of social differentiation. In modern society, the division of social labor performs the function previously fulfilled by the *conscience collective*.[57] This can be problematic, since when changes are rapid and conflicting interests have not had time to stabilize, society can find itself in a state of anomie, unable to regulate itself.

The book had a political dimension, as Durkheim acknowledged: "I would claim that my research does not deserve an hour's trouble if its interest are only speculative."[58] What to do about anomie, that ill of modern societies? Durkheim sought greater social justice and, to counter the laxity of morals he had observed, hoped that "discipline would be established and consolidated." He concluded, "Our first duty is to fashion an ethics for ourselves."[59] Durkheim made a strong impression at his thesis defense. "That one will be a master," noted Lucien Muhlfeld.[60] Léon Brunschvicg and Élie Halévy acknowledged it was a remarkable thesis, but Durkheim's approach was "so audacious and original" that the "keenness of the opposition" could be anticipated in advance. Philosophers found it unacceptable to introduce "sociological positivism" into the realm of ethics.[61]

The next year Durkheim published a series of articles in *Revue Philosophique*. In 1895 they would become *The Rules of Sociological Method*. This book marked the birth of sociology as a positive science. "One must treat social facts as things," declared Durkheim. *Rules* contained everything: a definition of the object (the social fact), rules for observing (eliminate all "prenotions" from science) and explaining social facts, a presentation of the comparative method, especially the method of concomitant variation as the instrument par excellence for establishing proof in sociology. The tone is often polemical and the book reads like a manifesto. Sociology, Durkheim concludes, must be "independent of philosophy."

Charles Andler, a philosopher by training, became the spokesperson for philosophers in *Revue de Métaphysique et de Morale*, denouncing "that so-called science known as sociology," which he saw as nothing more than a trend. He wrote ironically: "No one has ever seen the 'collective mind' as such speak and dictate ideas to secretaries of deliberative assemblies."[62]

Durkheim, isolated in Bordeaux, felt "the enormity of his task" and his relative powerlessness.[63] He was also annoyed by the resistance his books encountered. His only ambition, he said, was to "see that [his] work does not remain fruitless." He confided to his nephew Marcel: "I am not interested in being praised for my talent or style. I only want to feel that the trouble I've taken has been of some use."[64] From the time he started publishing, Durkheim was the object of lively controversy, which continued throughout his life. Critics targeted both his methodological principles and his analysis of morality, cognition, and religion. His opponents, including rivals (such as Gabriel Tarde and René Worms), reproached him for his sociological "imperialism" and for the set of issues he tackled, which they identified with "social realism."[65] Mauss said that Durkheim was accused of "collectivism, a charge thrown at him by thin-skinned moralists and several classic and Christian economists on the basis of *The Division of Labor in Society*. As a result of rumors of that sort, academic chairs in Paris were denied him."[66]

Mauss later said that his own life "was enriched by several unmatched strokes of luck," and that he "lived the whole first part of it in the proximity of three great men," to whom he devoted himself: Durkheim, the socialist leader Jean Jaurès, and his professor and later colleague Sylvain Lévi.[67] Durkheim's intellectual power and moral ideals quickly made him a master and model for his nephew. The uncle acknowledged his responsibility: "I'm the one [your mother] asked to train you. I trained you according to my ideals. One must accept the consequences of what one desired. She is free to regret it, but she cannot hold it against you."[68] At that point in Mauss's life, Durkheim's influence was a determining factor, so much so that, in his academic work, the nephew was sometimes "inhibited . . . by a life spent in the shadow of his more famous uncle."[69] Marcel was Durkheim's student, first disciple, and closest collaborator. The founder of French sociology would say that his nephew was "almost my alter ego."

Mauss enjoyed a certain freedom in Bordeaux. He lived at 51, rue de la Teste, and paid 1.50 francs for his meals at the Pension Bourgeoise at 17, rue Mably. His financial resources consisted of a scholarship and help from his family. At the Université de Bordeaux he enrolled at the faculty of letters to earn his *licence* (bachelor's degree) in philosophy and also took law courses for a year (1891–1892). The next year, he interrupted his studies to do his military service and went to Neufchâteau in his native region, where he was placed in the noncombatant services.[70]

Durkheim played the role of vigilant guardian to his nephew. He guided him in his studies and helped him organize his life. Mauss naturally attended his uncle's classes and considered him "the most reliable and agreeable of orators." In class, Durkheim used clear language and presented concrete data—official statistics on suicide, for example. He was eloquent and always rigorous, seeking to convince rather than to persuade; he appealed "less to the feelings than to the reason."[71] In his courses on pedagogy, "a discipline within his field of expertise," Durkheim brought "the same spirit, the same originality, the same simultaneously personal and exclusively positivist reflection that he brought to everything."[72]

The subjects were entirely new; the problems had not been touched on by anyone else; the method was wholly innovative; and the facts had never before been studied. On the efforts Durkheim took in preparing and teaching his courses, Mauss wrote: "Not only was Durkheim a wonderful professor, he truly loved to teach. He sought both scientific truth and pedagogical effectiveness, which took a great deal of effort. Just imagine that overwhelming task. . . . Durkheim never faltered."[73]

As soon as he arrived in Bordeaux, Durkheim, assigned the task of teaching "social science and pedagogy," sought to separate the two fields and "give a public course in social sciences and a series of lectures on pedagogy." The class on pedagogy, which met on Thursdays, was offered to a small group of men and women teachers and later to candidates for the *licence* in literature and for the *agrégation*. The social science class met on Saturdays and was open to the public. Durkheim's courses at the Université de Bordeaux between 1888 and 1895 were as follows:

Social Science	Pedagogy
1888–1889	
Family, Origins, Principal Types	Explication of Authors
Morals and the Philosophy of Law in Kant	Education of the Intelligence
1889–1890	
Suicide	History of Pedagogy
	Moral Education
1890–1891	
Physiology of Law and Mores (The Family)	French Pedagogy in the Eighteenth and Nineteenth Centuries
	Intellectual Education

(Continued)

(Continued)

Social Science	Pedagogy
1891–1892	
The Family (from the Patriarchal Family On)	Education and Pedagogy in Antiquity
	Practical Pedagogy
1892–1893	
Criminal Sociology	Nineteenth-Century Pedagogy
	Psychology Applied to Education
1893–1894	
Criminal Sociology (continued) Punishment, Responsibility: Procedures	Psychology Applied to Education
1894–1895	
Religion	Conference on Psychology

Beginning in 1893–1894, practical exercises for *agrégation* candidates in philosophy were added to his course load.

As Mauss notes, all this teaching became a burden for his uncle: "You can understand why he felt rather torn by that lifelong obligation to interrupt his favorite studies, those he felt solely responsible for, where he was ahead of everyone else, for less urgent, less important, work."[74] Durkheim himself complained: "If I could just find some good little spot in Paris where I could work in peace, learn what I don't know, that would be ideal. But it's a very difficult thing to find."[75]

The first classes Mauss took from Durkheim in Bordeaux dealt with "the physiology of law and mores." At the time his uncle was beginning to glimpse one of his most profound general ideas, "the disappearance of nature and of the politico-familial role of ancient groups—clans, extended families, and so on—and the need to reestablish new subgroups that are no longer family groups at all."[76] Durkheim thus elaborated a sociology of moral and juridical facts, but this was not his only aim. He also hoped "to find solutions to practical problems based on solutions to general and theoretical problems"[77] and to propose new forms of action and organization. Mauss was taken by his uncle, impressed by "his Cartesianism, his always realistic and rationalist search for the facts, his capacity to know and embrace them." "It is these qualities," he acknowledged, "that I believe I have consciously and conscientiously developed in myself."[78]

Other Influences

At the Université de Bordeaux Mauss received training in philosophy, which included psychology and sociology, as we find in the essays he composed and the oral presentations he gave in front of his professors. The questions Mauss had to answer were: "Is it true that a law can be posited on the basis of a single experiment?"; "Is consciousness an epiphenomenon?"; "How is it possible to substitute the notion of law for the notion of substance?"; "What is the relationship between representation and religious life?" In May and June 1893, Mauss gave reports to Durkheim, Octave Hamelin, and Marcel Cachin on topics as varied as "the unknowable," "progress and impartiality," "cosmopolitanism," and "the so-called unconscious psychological phenomena."

Aside from Durkheim, the professors who had a profound intellectual influence on the young scholar were Alfred Espinas and Octave Hamelin. Espinas (1844–1922), a graduate of the École Normale Supérieure (class of 1864), an *agrégé* in philosophy (1871) with a doctorate in letters (1877), taught at the faculty of letters in Bordeaux beginning in 1878.

A disciple of Herbert Spencer, Espinas made sociology subservient to biology, but he can still be considered a precursor in the field of sociology: he defined "its positivity and essential spirit."[79] His most important work was his thesis, *Les sociétés animales* (1877; Animal societies), in which he analyzed the various types of association—from parasitism to mutualism—found in the animal world. Rumored to be a staunch Lamarckian,[80] he introduced the idea of *conscience collective* to sociology by assimilating society to a living organism. He did not pursue his reflections on the matter, however. Although he did precise research in psychology, on the sense of color, for example, on the sense of space, and on sleep among hysterics, he was also interested in the history of ideas and doctrines and devoted himself to making "the state of European thought" better known. In 1880 he published *La philosophie expérimentale en Italie* (Experimental philosophy in Italy); in 1891, *Histoire des doctrines économiques* (History of economic doctrines); and in 1887, with the collaboration of Théodule Ribot, he translated Spencer's *Principles of Psychology*.

Espinas belonged to a group of thinkers who, after the Franco-Prussian War, had aspired to "regenerate their country" and ground politics in science. In an article titled "To Be or Not to Be, or the Postulate of Sociology," which he published in 1901, he rejected transcendence and adopted science at its most positivistic as his guide: "If the future vicissitudes of a society can be predicted, then societies must be an object of nature, subject to laws like other objects, an object that can be known scientifically."[81] For Espinas, if politics is to avoid being driven by moral feelings or passion, it must find support in precisely calculated facts: "The time is near when all enlightened minds capable of manly labor will be able to refer to precise data to justify their doctrines, data we will not fail to possess on every point essential to men of goodwill."[82]

Espinas, later influenced by his colleague Durkheim, seemed to be an "impenitent sociologist" but remained "jealously aloof from any school."[83] Relations between the two colleagues deteriorated when Espinas agreed in 1894 to take over a class on social economic history at the faculty of letters in Paris. Durkheim had wanted to apply for the same position. He advised his nephew to keep his distance from Espinas.[84]

But Mauss continued to have great admiration for Espinas. He sent him his published works, kept him informed of his interests, and even asked for advice, especially when he was considering a position in secondary education. The "old overworked teacher" displayed great affection for his student and enthusiastically supported him, but without seeking to influence him. For example, he sent his warm congratulations when Mauss published his study on sacrifice: "Your work surpasses my expectations. It is very vigorous and original. It's what I would have dreamed of doing if my intellectual life had not been fragmented by professional obligations."[85]

The relationship between Mauss and his other philosophy professor, Octave Hamelin (1856–1907), was particularly close, since Hamelin was "an irreplaceable friend" to his uncle. Durkheim had great admiration for the man he characterized as "a pure rationalist, an austere lover of right reason, enemy of every form of dilettantism. Thinking was the most serious thing in his life." Hamelin was a "great mind" but was not well known to the general public. In fact, he "sacrificed himself completely for his students. It was for them that he reserved the nuggets of his incomparable science."[86] In the preface to Hamelin's *Système de Descartes* (Descartes's system), published posthumously by Alcan in 1911, Durkheim reiterated his admiration for the man, saying he worshipped his memory, citing his noble character and intelligence, his lofty reason and firm will, his tenderness and sensitivity.[87]

At a philosophical level, Hamelin was a disciple of Charles Renouvier, the author of *Science de la morale* (1869; Science of morals), which greatly influenced republican intellectuals of the late nineteenth century. Like Durkheim, Renouvier favored the spread of an uncompromising rationalism, encouraged interest in the scientific study of ethics, had a sense of social justice, defended republican education and the public schools, and tried to reconcile the individual and social solidarity.

Hamelin belonged to the group associated with the journal *Année Philosophique*, directed by Édouard Pillon, which was developing a neo-Kantian or "neo-criticist" doctrine. The scientists behind the group, rather than consider known objects directly, first asked how we know what we are able to know. Hamelin's most important contribution was his theory of cognition. Rejecting all forms of intuition or transcendent reason, he claimed that cognition was built solely on "sharp, precise, clearly defined concepts."[88] His aim was to elaborate a system of categories based on the central idea that every representation, like the world itself, is a relationship. "Thesis, synthesis, antithesis, such is the simplest law of things in its three phases," wrote Hamelin. "We will name it with a single word: relationship." In his *Éléments principaux de la représentation* (Principal elements of representation), "the result of thirty years of meditation and research," he argued that "correlation is the first fact of cognition or the supreme law of being, its immediate character. The world is a hierarchy of relationships: every notion summons up and thereby defines its opposite; being is conceived only in opposition to nonbeing. It therefore appears that the relationship is a more fundamental and primitive notion than being itself."[89] Things had to be constituted through relationships.

The method Hamelin developed was to synthesize antithetical notions, then elaborate other notions: time, number, space, causality, finality, and so on. His philosophy was pure idealism and constructed a priori categories. As Dominique Parodi pointed out, though it was guided by experience, it claimed to rise above all forms of empiricism, above positive science. Hamelin would write: "The theory of cognition is one thing, psychology is another." It may be possible to establish a link between the ideas of Hamelin and Mauss—around the notions of relationship and the whole—but the student's approach would be resolutely sociological. Nevertheless, Mauss remained good friends with his professor, even putting him up in his apartment when Hamelin came to Paris, and always defended him. Some ten years later, Hamelin died in an accident, carried off by a wave on a beach in Les Landes while trying to save two others who were drowning. He was a "victim of his devotion," Durkheim said. Mauss, on learning of his death, expressed his anger and sadness to his friend Hubert: "You know about poor Hamelin's death, the historic death of that brave man and the stupidity of the people who pulled him out after a few minutes and didn't even try to resuscitate him. The country has lost one of its exceptional men and I have lost a friend who was devoted to the point of being biased in my favor!"[90]

First Political Activities

Around the turn of the century, the socialist movement made important inroads. The newspaper *Petite République* was created, a minimal platform elaborated, and in 1893 Jean Jaurès was elected to the Chamber of Deputies. In June of the same year, fifty more socialist deputies were elected. The political balance shifted significantly. The propaganda campaigns of the socialist Jules Guesde had a major impact, especially in the industrial regions of northern France, and his Parti Ouvrier Français (POF) grew rapidly, its membership rising from two thousand to more than ten thousand between 1890 and 1893.[91] During the same period, the syndicalist movement also grew in influence and became more radical, adopting the principle of the general strike. Trade union meetings multiplied, and in 1895 the Confédération Générale du Travail (General labor confederation) was formed with Fernand Pelloutier at the helm. More than ever before, the "social question" was central to political debates.

Durkheim was well acquainted with these ideas and men. A friend of Jaurès since his student days at the École Normale, he had diverted the future socialist leader "from the Radicals' formalism and empty philosophy."[92] He had an obvious interest in socialist ideas: he mastered "the sources" (Saint-Simon and Marx) early on and in 1892 published "Note on the Definition of Socialism" in *Revue Philosophique*. In 1895–1896 he devoted his sociology course in Bordeaux to the history of socialism, and in 1897 did a critical evaluation of Gaston Richard's *Le socialisme et la science sociale* (Socialism and social science) and Antonio Labriola's *Essais sur la conception matérialiste de l'histoire* (On the materialist conception of history). Durkheim's definition of socialism made a deep impression on Guesde and Jaurès, who claimed to agree with him. "Socialism," wrote Durkheim, "is a tendency to move economic functions, abruptly or gradually, from their current state of diffusion to the state of organization. One may say it is also an aspiration toward the more or less complete socialization of the forces of production."[93]

Although he was convinced that history was evolving toward increasing socialization, Durkheim bristled at embracing socialism as it was practiced. When his nephew tried to convince him otherwise, he replied: "As far as I'm concerned, you're beating down an open door and preaching is pointless. I'm ready to embrace socialism when it has changed its methods, that is, when it has ceased to be exclusively a party of class. . . . Many of us would join under those conditions."[94] Mauss was well aware of his uncle's reluctance, stemming from his opposition on principle to any "political or politicking" activity or to any "class- or worker-based" action of a violent nature.

> Durkheim was strongly opposed to any war between classes or nations. He wanted change only for the benefit of society as a whole and not for one of its factions, even if that faction had the power and the numbers. He considered political revolutions and parliamentary evolutions superficial, costly, and more theatrical than serious. He thus always resisted the idea of bowing to a party's discipline, especially if the party was international. Even the social and moral crisis of the Dreyfus Affair, in which he played a major role, did not change his opinion. . . . He thus continued to occupy the middle ground; he "sympathized" as we now say, with the socialists, with Jaurès, with socialism. But he never devoted himself to it.[95]

Durkheim's work interested the socialists, however, although some of the most revolutionary perceived him as a major adversary of socialism. Far from "crossing over," Durkheim returned to "pure science" when he began publishing *Année Sociologique* in 1896, leaving his history of socialism unfinished. Although he remained faithful to the republican creed and was concerned with social questions and the role of professional groups, he identified at the deepest level with the social figure of the scientist. The scientific method he practiced accustomed him to reserve judgment until he felt well informed, and he did not want to give in to the "pressure of the mob and the prestige of authority."[96] From his perspective, the sociologist's aim should not be to have a "political career in the strict sense"—he would be a "very inadequate statesman" in any case—but, more modestly, to be an "adviser, an educator." "It is primarily . . . through books, lectures, popular education that we should act. . . . We are much better suited for helping our contemporaries clarify their ideas and feelings than for governing them."[97] Durkheim would restate his rejection of partisanship every time he saw his nephew "distracted" by various political commitments.

Unlike his uncle, who refused to participate directly in socialist debates, Mauss became a militant and a "party man." At the Université de Bordeaux, a few of the most brilliant students were converted to socialism, specifically its Marxist or Guesdist forms, and they discussed Marx's *Capital* at meetings of the social studies club. In collaboration with the Parti Ouvrier Français, these politically involved students invited Jaurès to give a lecture in 1893, on which occasion "he spoke glowingly of Durkheim's works."[98]

While studying at the university, Mauss met Marcel Cachin (1869–1959), who was a few years his senior. Originally from Paimpol, Cachin arrived in Bordeaux in 1890 to earn his *licence* in philosophy. His professors were Espinas, Hamelin, and Durkheim. On his arrival, the young man from Brittany joined the Groupe des Étudiants Socialistes (Socialist student group) and participated in their activities—public meetings, demonstrations, drafting of tracts—and in March 1892 became a member of the Parti Ouvrier Français.[99] Once he had earned his *licence*, Cachin became a kind of "permanent volunteer" and devoted his time to militant action.[100] He supported himself by tutoring young people belonging to Bordeaux's upper middle class. As a result of his political activities, Cachin was denied his scholarship in 1895 and could not go on to study for the *agrégation*. A contributor to the journal *Socialiste de la Gironde*, he got involved in propaganda work, crisscrossing the provinces and forming branches of the POF everywhere. In 1900 he became deputy mayor of Bordeaux, in charge of public health, sanitation, and public transportation.

In Bordeaux, Mauss associated with the Groupe des Étudiants Socialistes and he too joined the Parti Ouvrier Français. His classmates consulted him and sought his help in composing tracts. One of them wrote him: "As for me, I want only to shed light on a few facts, a few statistics, which will make the feeling of personal dignity, etc., ring in the hearts of those who read me. But you'll understand why I want to appeal to your insight."[101]

The *Agrégation*

After earning his *licence* in letters, Mauss went to Paris to study for his *agrégation* in philosophy, which he called that "other initiation rite of civilized beings."[102] He was living with his cousin Albert Cahen, a medical student. In 1893–1894, he had what was called an "*agrégation* scholarship,"[103] but he still had to depend on monetary aid from his parents to make ends meet, as his uncle never failed to remind him: "You've got to stop this perpetual criticism of our family communism. You benefit from it, in any case, since thanks to it you can devote yourself to your favorite studies without worrying about money."[104] The next year Marcel returned to Bordeaux, where he could count on hearing advice from his uncle and philosophy professors. The syllabus for the 1895 *agrégation* exam included the following authors: Aristotle, *Physics*, book 7; Diogenes Laertius, book 10; Cicero, *De natura deorum*; Hobbes, *De cive*; Descartes, *Meditations and Reply to Objections IV*; Bossuet, *Traité du libre arbitre* (Treatise on free will); Berkeley, *Three Dialogues between Hylas and Philonous*; and Taine, *On Intelligence*, books 1, 2, and 3.[105]

Was this simply an "obligatory rite of passage" for Mauss, of which he acquitted himself "brilliantly, as a duty, only to turn immediately to specialized studies"?[106] The *agrégation*, a difficult ordeal, was indispensable for anyone wanting to make a career in secondary and university education. The best way to prepare for it was to be admitted to the École Normale Supérieure. Although scholarships for the *licence* and the *agrégation* were created in 1877 and 1880, respectively, allowing non-Normalians to qualify for the exam, the school on rue d'Ulm was still preeminent: a high percentage of the *agrégés* were Normalians and an even higher percentage of Normalians ranked in the top five every year.[107]

As a non-Normalian living in the provinces, Mauss was at a double disadvantage. But he was serious about his preparation. He benefited from the help of his Bordeaux professors, particularly Hamelin and his uncle. Durkheim, a philosophy *agrégé* and member of the board of examiners for the *agrégation* from 1881 on, knew the ins and outs of the test, and had in fact denounced some of its weaknesses. In an 1895 article titled "Philosophical Education and Philosophy *Agrégation*," he lamented that the exam, in valuing "wholly formal talent" and "the quest for distinction and originality," led candidates away from "all positive data and definite knowledge." In the exams he corrected, moreover, Durkheim observed a "vagueness in the language" and a "corresponding vagueness in the ideas." Hence he feared that philosophy would become "a form of symbolism and impressionism." This fear seemed well founded in that the rise of neo-mysticism among students left "the door wide open to every sort of fantasy."

Durkheim preferred the "solid" to the "brilliant." His objective was to "equip young people with complete knowledge so that they are one day in a position to examine doctrines intelligently and to form an enlightened opinion on their own."[108] After staking out that position, Durkheim met with an almost immediate reaction from philosophers: he was criticized for wanting to reduce philosophy to the logic of the sciences and for conceiving of philosophy education at the secondary school level as a "purely sociological and practical education." The philosophers were particularly irritated because his criticism of students' "foolhardy essays" exposed the incompetence of their teachers. Perceived as someone who wanted to bury philosophy, Durkheim was then easily categorized as a belated positivist, a dogmatic reductionist. Some said it was dangerous to have Durkheim as an ally.[109]

While his students were preparing for the *agrégation*, Durkheim played an active role. As Mauss would recall, he never failed "to prepare what is called 'the author,' in other words, the book by the Greek, English, French, or Latin philosopher whose piece on ethics or politics was on the syllabus."[110] Throughout 1894 Mauss wrote several essays, in particular, "The Role of the Imagination in External Perception," "Nature and Role of the Image," and "To What Extent Is Morality an Internal Matter?" His teachers advised him, guided his readings, and commented on his essays.

In what he called a regular exchange of letters, Durkheim sought to keep tabs on his nephew to "prevent him from working without purpose." He added: "One must always have a plan in mind. I don't sense from your letter that you are concerned enough with that." He gave precise counsels: "Work steadily and not immoderately. If you pay more attention to being rigorous, to filling your schedule, there will be no point to being immoderate"; "Don't be satisfied with intuitive and muddled syntheses." Marcel earned congratulations: "Good essay"; "This may be the best thing you've done"; "There's notable progress." He also earned criticism: "In terms of form, a certain inclination toward tasteless extravagance"; "In terms of content, still too much padding of the thought." And so forth. Durkheim was not always satisfied: "I wonder what this progress of yours can consist of, given that from what you tell me, you've done nothing new this year except your work on Kant, since . . . your essay and your work on Spinoza are leftovers from last year. If you've acquired more dexterity in form and thought through contact with your new environment, you won't have wasted your time and maybe that's all you can get from it."[111]

That "new environment" was the Sorbonne and the courses and lectures Mauss attended there in preparation for the exam. It was also his new friends—Edgar Milhaud, Abel Rey, and Paul Fauconnet (Milhaud had introduced him to Fauconnet in 1893). Indeed, during the "ordeal," Mauss formed what he and his friends—"good trade unionists" that they were—called a "syndicate." Nothing short of death would come between them.[112] Fauconnet was noted for his sense of calm and self-control and was a model student. The teachers he and Mauss shared were Émile Boutroux, Gabriel Séailles, and Victor Brochard, all professors of philosophy at the faculty of letters in Paris. Boutroux (1845–1921), an *agrégé* in philosophy, a doctor of letters, and as of 1888 a professor in the history of philosophy, was completing L'idée de loi naturelle dans la science et la philosophie contemporaine (1895; The idea of natural law in science and contemporary philosophy). Brochard (1848–1907), three years his junior, followed the same career path: *agrégation*, doctoral thesis, *chargé de cours*, and beginning in 1849 professor of history of ancient philosophy. In addition to writing his own books, *L'erreur* (Error) and *Les sceptiques grecs* (1887; The Greek skeptics), Brochard was responsible for editing Descartes's *Discourse on Method* and *Principles of Philosophy* and was on the editorial board of *Revue Philosophique*. Séailles (1852–1922), the youngest of the three, was also an *agrégé* in philosophy and a doctor of letters. He became a *maître de conférence* of philosophy in 1886, and in 1893 was named *directeur de conférences* in philosophy at the faculty of letters.[113] A free thinker and an apostle of secular education, he subsequently participated in the founding of the Ligue des Droits de l'Homme (League of human rights). In addition to writing *Histoire de la philosophie* (1887; History of philosophy) with Paul Janet, Séailles completed a short "psychological biography" of Ernest Renan in 1895.

According to his uncle, Mauss was at that time "a man of excessive outbursts and prejudices." Durkheim added that Mauss was too easily impressed. For example, he was enthusiastic about Théodule Ribot, one of the pioneers in French psychology, and admired his "perfect eclecticism." Along with Milhaud, Fauconnet, and Alfred Bonnet, Marcel took classes from Ribot, director and founder of *Revue Philosophique* at the Collège de France. They all found him "a model of clarity, precision, and fairness."[114] Also attending classes was Georges Sorel, "an older comrade, an astute critic of everything but himself."

Mauss's mother anxiously followed her son's "preparation," writing, "I won't talk about your *agrégation*. It's like revenge: Think about it constantly, never talk about it."[115] She gave a great deal of advice: "Work regularly but not excessively"; "Go to bed at ten, get up at seven, and plan your day well"; "For the moment, don't be concerned about anything but your exam. Stay away from your friends." But she was not stingy with her encouragement: "If you succeed with the help of God, it will be the best day of my life. If it so happens that you don't succeed, you'll have lost nothing and we'll do everything possible to make you forget the failure and help you remedy it."[116]

When he took the exam in May 1895, Mauss was well prepared. He was so encouraged by the first rounds that he went from a "state of pessimistic agitation to a state of optimistic agitation." His uncle had to remind him "that there are still serious obstacles" and identified the "little flaws" to beware of: "Say everything you have to say, but take your time and show the necessary courtesy. Don't be aggressive. It's possible to say everything you want without offending anyone. . . . One must be moderate in form without yielding anything in terms of content. . . . Finally, go for the essential and don't get bogged down in digressions that would prolong your presentation. . . . And then, between each round, get plenty of rest. Don't get worked up about the Sorbonne. Best of luck."[117]

The question on the history of philosophy had to do with "the theory of will in Descartes." Descartes was a philosopher Mauss knew well, having taken Hamelin's course on him. The philosophy question was difficult: "On probability. Is probabilism necessarily indistinguishable from skepticism?" Mauss knew all about the reflections on scientific method (and the use of statistics) that his uncle had just published in *The Rules of Sociological Method*. If we can rely on the twenty-page draft that has survived, in his response he established a relationship between philosophy and mathematics, between science and common sense. He distanced himself somewhat from positivistic epistemology and asserted the force of belief: "Th[ings] are probable insofar as they are believed, insofar as we act in relation to them. . . . Hence the most erroneous, the most unreasonable ideas were objects of belief, were things for those who acted on them." Mauss pursued his argument not by quoting Aristotle, Plato, Hume, or John Stuart Mill, but by describing the beliefs of the Australian "savage": "If a snake kills a man, it is not the snake who is blamed but the man. He is considered unclean within the clan." The candidate for the *agrégation* called himself a "relativist" and already displayed an interest in linguistic and ethnological questions.[118]

Mauss passed the *agrégation*, placing third (of eight) behind Marcel Drouin and Milhaud, but just ahead of Fauconnet. Drouin was a Normalian, Milhaud and Fauconnet students at the Sorbonne. The evaluation of Mauss's performance was extremely positive. The members of the board of examiners said he was "an outstanding student for whom they had great hopes and about whom only a single fear was expressed: that he not work too hard. Earned only marks far above the average."[119]

After a short delay, his philosophy professor Hamelin sent his congratulations: "You're very kind to have thought of me while applying all your efforts to doing well on the exam. I'm so grateful for how you exaggerate the effectiveness of the few bits of advice I was able to give you now and again."[120] Mauss, apologizing for "being the worst procrastinator in the world," replied five months later and thanked Hamelin for "showing his satisfaction at the time of his success." "I'm afraid, dear teacher, that you're mistaken about your student's positive qualities. In the first place, if he has any mind for philosophy, he owes it to the education that you and my uncle gave him."[121]

The board of examiners also noticed the student's loyalty to his professors; they told him they had recognized him as Hamelin's and Durkheim's student. "I am sure," Mauss continued, "that they're telling the truth, since throughout the exam I never thought of any judges but my uncle and you. I acted as if you alone were the entire board." As for his ranking, Mauss had predicted it and said he was very happy with it, especially when he compared himself with his friends Drouin and Milhaud. The new *agrégé* also acknowledged he had made "a few blunders" that "certainly marred the exam." What did it matter? The board treated him as if he had been "among the very best" and "very sincerely" supported his scholarship application, support that was particularly important since Mauss intended to go on for his doctorate, as his uncle had done. "Even before my *agrégation*, I was preparing myself [to study oral ritual and religious ideation] through good historical and philological studies, in addition to my philosophy *agrégation*. The subjects of my thesis were fixed at that time: Leo Hebraeus and Spinoza, whose close connection to each other I discovered in 1893."[122]

Mauss thought seriously about pursuing a career in secondary education; he also imagined the possibility of taking a position at the University of Algiers. His mother wrote: "You can't sit on a branch like a bird for five years." She therefore advised him to "seize the opportunity" and go to Algeria if he felt up to the trip. She added: "It would be a tremendous stroke of luck for an active, inquisitive man to get his start in a place like Algiers."[123]

The Revolutionary Student

The time Mauss spent preparing for and passing his *agrégation* was also a time of political involvement and dreams. Milhaud would recall: "We had dreams, few of which came true."[124]

When he arrived in Paris to prepare for the *agrégation*, Mauss found a city still shaken by anarchists' terrorist attacks: the Chamber of Deputies was bombed in 1893; repressive measures, known as the "scoundrelly laws" (*lois scélérates*), were adopted; and many people were arrested. Sadi Carnot, president of the Third Republic, was assassinated by an Italian anarchist in June 1894, and the trial in Trent of nineteen anarchist writers, artists, and theoreticians alongside eleven thieves was held in August of the same year. The anarchist movement was very active and enjoyed a certain vogue among a new generation of intellectuals and artists. As Maurice Barrès describes them in *Les déracinés* (The uprooted), they constituted a sort of "intellectual proletariat" whose loss of class standing made them receptive to criticisms of bourgeois society.[125] They wanted to replace love of country with egoism. Revolt ensued: the literary avant-garde moved closer to the political avant-garde. The new journals—*Revue Blanche, Entretiens Littéraires, Art Social*—granted more and more space to ideological and political questions: individual or collectivity? spontaneity or constraint (and conspiracy)? nostalgia or hope for an imminent renaissance? art for art's sake or political engagement?[126] Gradually, the neologism "intellectual" and the images associated with it spread. As Bernard Lazare proclaimed in *Révolte* in March 1894, the new role of intellectuals was "to act," not by wielding a gun, a dagger, or dynamite, but with the pen, by performing an "intellectual action."

The Latin Quarter was in an uproar. Politics again captivated students who had been pacified for a time by reforms in higher education. Then the first political groups appeared, such as Étudiants Socialistes Révolutionnaires Internationalistes (Internationalist revolutionary socialist students). Members' objectives were "study, propaganda, and socialist action." They had little influence at first but grew in strength after riots in the Latin Quarter were set off by a minor incident, a conviction on morals charges of a student from the School of Fine Arts. In July 1893 police intervened to stop the demonstrations, and pitched battles ensued. Confrontations with the authorities drew the student movement closer to worker-controlled political organizations, the only ones that could wage war against the government.[127] Things got even hotter the next year. In the provinces and in Paris, socialist students held meetings and lectures; they published brochures and magazines, including *Ère Nouvelle*. Public lectures, such as "Idealism and Materialism in the Conception of History," which Jaurès delivered to collectivist students meeting in the hall of Sociétés Savantes (Scholarly societies), drew between 1,500 and 2,000 young people. Even the École Normale Supérieure was affected: the literature students who graduated in 1894, including Charles Péguy, Paul Mantoux, Félicien Challaye, and Albert Mathiez, rallied behind socialism.

The newly constituted Groupe des Étudiants Collectivistes wanted to define not only the place of students in the socialist parties but also the form socialism ought to take. That movement, which opposed both the Guesdists and the anarchists, sought, though still obscurely, "a third path to socialism, humanistic but scientific." Péguy would remember with delight the attraction of socialism at the time: "A young socialism, a new socialism, a grave, somewhat childish socialism—that's what you need when you're young—a youthful socialism had just come into being."[128]

In Paris, where he sought to "make the most of things," Mauss reestablished ties with student and socialist political circles. Edgar Milhaud (1872–1964) and his brother Albert, who came from a well off, educated Jewish family in Paris, were active members of the Ligue Démocratique des Écoles

(Democratic league of schools) founded in 1893. They fought for the "defense and progress of the Republic." Durkheim advised his nephew, who informed him of his new contacts and "discoveries," to be cautious: "Go see what it's all about before joining. I don't know much about it."[129]

In 1895 Mauss and the Milhaud brothers were the leaders of the Ligue Démocratique des Écoles, with Franklin-Bouillon as secretary; Mauss was also a member of the Groupe des Étudiants Collectivistes. This was an entirely natural choice for someone who, like other students, had left the Parti Ouvrier to join the Parti Ouvrier Socialiste Révolutionnaire (POSR). That party, headed by Jean Allemane, a Communard typographer who was elected to represent Paris in the Chamber of Deputies, declared itself "atheistic, republican, communist, and internationalist." Its doctrine was class struggle; it called for general strikes and distrusted parliamentary action. In some sense, it was the radical worker faction of the socialist movement, and anyone who was not a manual laborer was viewed with suspicion.

Mauss, the delegate of the Groupe des Étudiants Collectivistes at various congresses of the socialist and cooperative movement, "personified the alliance of intellectual workers and manual laborers."[130] He was one of the militant students who wished to deal "a fatal blow to the intellectual dictatorship of the bourgeoisie." To borrow Hubert Lagardelle's motto for the first issue of the magazine *Jeunesse Socialiste* (Socialist youth) in January 1895, such students wanted "to develop a socialist consciousness in students and teachers." The mode of action Mauss would favor while at the École Pratique des Hautes Études was participation in *Devenir Social* (Social change), an international journal of economics, history, and philosophy published in Paris. Founded in 1895 by Alfred Bonnet, it patterned itself on the Toulouse journal *Jeunesse Socialiste*. This new review, with offices at 16, rue du Soufflot, published texts by Friedrich Engels—on the history of early Christianity—and by Karl Kautsky, Georgi Plekhanov, Émile Vandervelde, Antonio Labriola, and Paul Lafargue. Sociology, a "perfectly distinct science," played a large role in *Devenir Social*: the works of Durkheim, Gustave Le Bon, Tarde, and Gaston Richard were the subject of long discussions. Hubert and Fauconnet also contributed to the journal, where science and politics were so intertwined that Hubert Bourgin called it "socialo-sociology."

In the first two issues of the journal (April and May 1895), Sorel published a long article titled "Mr. Durkheim's Theories." At the time, Mauss thought Sorel had "a penetrating mind, if not a learned and judicious one."[131] Against the "babblers who rant about social questions," Mauss was to side with the "(overly) scientific minds." The tone of Sorel's articles was respectful, except when he evaluated the political ideas of the author of *The Rules of Sociological Method* and *The Division of Labor in Society*: "The author takes a forceful stand against socialism. He maintains that all the research done heretofore on value is not truly scientific. . . . One must not conceal the fact that socialism is facing an adversary of the first order." This criticism did not prevent Sorel from inviting Durkheim to "embrace socialism": "Perhaps he will manage to cross the line separating him from us: It would be a happy event for social philosophy; I would be the first to acclaim him as my master. No scientist is better prepared than he to bring Marx's theories to higher education."[132]

Mauss published two long book reviews in *Devenir Social*.[133] The first, in April 1896, was a critique of G. de Greef's *Évolution des croyances et des doctrines politiques dans trois sociétés: L'ancien Pérou, l'ancien Mexique et l'Égypte* (Evolution of political beliefs and doctrines in three societies: Ancient Peru, ancient Mexico, and Egypt). While acknowledging the study's historical aspects, Mauss pointed out several methodological errors, primarily in the treatment of sources (misquotations, incomplete bibliography), and criticized it for neglecting the religious dimension of all political beliefs in primitive societies. Aware that "the difficulties of such a science are infinite," Mauss concluded that "sociology, more than any other science, needs specialized and positivistic studies."[134]

The second book review, published in April 1897, was of Célestin Bouglé's *Les sciences sociales en Allemagne* (The social sciences in Germany). Bouglé, two years Mauss's senior, would become one of the first contributors to *Année Sociologique* and later one of the most visible and influential members of the Durkheim group.[135] A young and promising *agrégé* (he ranked first in 1893), Bouglé had returned from a year's study in Germany and now taught philosophy at the Saint-Brieuc *lycée*. His first book not only presented "the social science movements in Germany" and, in particular, four professors (Lazarus, G. Simmel, A.H.G. Wagner, and R. von Jhering), but also proposed a criticism of Durkheim's work. He rejected the notion of methodological unity in the social and natural sciences; he denied that social facts could be understood solely by studying them from the outside; he maintained that introspection and psychology were fundamental for the social sciences and that social science was not directly useful in determining the ends human beings ought to pursue.[136]

According to Mauss, Bouglé's book had undeniable positive qualities: beautiful and sound exposition, order, and clarity; a conscientious collection and classification of information; elegant and useful studies. His chief reservation concerned the selection of German authors: why Simmel and not W. Wundt? Simmel was "still only starting out," whereas Wundt had had a major influence on sociology as a whole. In addition, Mauss criticized Bouglé for adopting a psychological point of view and for defending introspection as a method for understanding social facts. In any case, he did not want to "intervene too much in the debate" between Bouglé and his uncle:

Let us try rather to smooth over the debate between Bouglé and Durkheim. When Durkheim speaks of the objectivity and specificity of social facts, he does not mean they are outside consciousness or that they are not themselves facts of consciousness, and as such stemming from the general laws of representation that psychology is seeking. He says they are psychological phenomena of a special kind, that there is no continuity between a fact of individual consciousness and a social law or social movement of any kind. Something specific always intervenes, something that only sociology can study and explain. Psychology is more general than sociology, and generality does not explain specific differences. The movement is thus unanimous in distancing French sociology from biological and ontological metaphors.[137]

Durkheim also wanted to reduce the distance separating him, or appearing to separate him, from Bouglé.[138] But when he read his nephew's review, he was rather surprised: "[Your article] is very good and Bouglé has asked me to thank you."[139]

True to his political convictions, Mauss maintained his ties with socialist organizations and was inclined to "give his savings to the Party,"[140] but he preferred "the indirect action of science, the action of the socialist," to "public action." He defined his "socialist duties": "It seemed to me that increasing [human] rationality, as far as it was within my means, . . . and making others aware of the profound things inside us, the laws of our actions, were sufficient."[141]

As he completed his education, Mauss would identify with "those who have left the socialist movement either because their work does not allow them to stay or because their somewhat bourgeois nerves make them find some of the excesses unbearable." The actions of the scientist and those of the militant would intersect again only with the Dreyfus Affair, that is, in response to the "needs of the hour and the demands of the socialist movement."

STUDENT AT THE ÉCOLE PRATIQUE

DES HAUTES ÉTUDES

RATHER than commit himself immediately to a career in secondary education, Mauss decided to complete his training. In the autumn of 1895, he found his way to the École Pratique des Hautes Études (Practical School of Higher Studies), another of the *grandes écoles*, and enrolled as a scholarship student in the fourth and fifth sections of the school, the fourth focusing on the science of history and philology, and the fifth on religious science. The choice of this elite school was inevitable for someone who wanted to enter a brand-new field, "oral ritual and religious ideation," while pursuing studies in philology.

Mauss had been interested in the study of religion for several years: "As a student, I wavered between what are now called quantitative studies (my collaboration with Durkheim)—suicide, the history of cities, human settlement— . . . law studies (for three years), and religious sociology. It was my attraction to philosophy and a conscious decision that, on Durkheim's recommendation, led me to specialize in the study of religious facts and to devote myself to them almost wholly and for all time. Durkheim taught his course in Bordeaux on the origins of religion (1894–1895) for me and for himself. Together we sought the best way to use my strengths in the service of the nascent science and to fill the most serious gaps."[1]

In 1886 Durkheim identified religion as one of the "major regulating organs of society," along with law and morals, and expressed the wish "that we begin to study religion as a social phenomenon." But it was a field in which he still did not feel competent.[2] The next year, in a critical note on Jean-Marie Guyau's *L'irreligion de l'avenir* (The irreligion of the future), he reasserted that "religion is on the whole or in great part a sociological phenomenon; to study it one must first adopt a social perspective."[3] In his own view, however, "it was only in 1895 that I had a clear sense of the key role played by religion in social life." He added: "It was then that for the first time I found the way to approach the study of religion sociologically. For me it was a revelation. That 1895 course stands as a line of demarcation in the development of my thought."[4]

Année Sociologique would devote a great deal of attention to the study of "religious phenomena." When the first volume appeared in 1898, Durkheim acknowledged that "everything concerning the history of religion holds an important place in our compilation."[5] He confided to his nephew: "Apart from its documentary interest, *Année Sociologique* must establish an orientation. Fundamentally, the sociological importance of the religious phenomenon is the culmination of everything I've done; and it has the advantage of concretely recapitulating our entire orientation, more concretely than the formulations I have used up till now."[6]

The Question of Religion

The history of religion was a discipline in turmoil in the second half of the nineteenth century. Texts from the Eastern religions were being published: the most significant in this respect were the writings of Brahmanism, particularly the translation of the Vedas under Max Müller's direction. Archaeological research had also led to the discovery of many other texts from Babylon-Assyria and Egypt and from Asia Minor and Syria. These discoveries revolutionized the understanding of the Old Testament, suggesting that Jewish traditions derived for the most part from Babylon. The pan-Babylonianist thesis defended by some researchers went even further: all myths throughout the world were said to have a single and unique origin.

In addition, the growth of colonization and evangelism called for a better knowledge of so-called primitive peoples and their religions. Anxious to study these peoples before they vanished as a result of contact with Western civilization, specialized researchers tried methodically to collect information on tribal ways of life and thought. With the development of anthropology, mythological and sociohistorical studies no longer confined themselves to Indo-European traditions: any reflection on the evolution of religion could now look to ethnographic data for supporting evidence.[7]

At the turn of the twentieth century, religion, which had previously been the domain of a few scientists and scholars, became the subject of political debates. The Third Republic embraced political liberalism and wanted "to free the conscience." It adopted major measures to that end: freedom of the press and of assembly in 1881; secularization of the public schools in 1882–1886; freedom of the communes, bringing about more local control, in 1882–1886; freedom to form labor unions in 1884; freedom of association in 1901; freedom of worship guaranteed in 1905 with the separation of church and state. There was a great deal of unease in Catholic circles, and the episcopate intervened repeatedly, for example, with the *Providentissimus* encyclical in 1893 and the encyclical addressed to the French clergy in 1899. The clergy obviously feared that the neutrality imposed on teachers in the classroom would bar any reference to God and that universities would eliminate theology from their curricula. The history of religion looked like a "dangerous and misguided idea."[8]

In France as in other European countries—the Netherlands, for example, where the movement originated—the idea of making the study of religion a matter of scientific research slowly took hold. Ernest Renan (1823–1893), a former seminarian turned philologist and a specialist in Semitic languages, popularized the idea of a scientific, nondenominational study of religion, and especially of Christianity. His *Life of Jesus* (1863) was a great success.

The Catholic church was extremely nervous about this new discipline. Those studying the history of religion taught that infallibility did not exist, that orthodoxy was a chimera. Far from remaining inactive, members of the clergy came up with various initiatives aimed at retaining a foothold. In 1884, abbé de Broglie introduced a course in the history of religion at the Institut Catholique; in 1889 abbé Poisson created the journal *Revue des Religions*; and a group of Catholic ecclesiastics founded *Revue d'Histoire et de Littérature Religieuses*. As several people pointed out at the international congress on the history of religion held in Paris as part of the 1900 Universal Exposition, the science of religion, though gaining ground, was "still far from acquiring its legitimate and necessary place in public education."[9]

Protestant academics proved to be less reluctant than their Catholic colleagues to undertake the study of religion, since, unlike the Catholics, Protestants were not persuaded that they alone had a full understanding of the scriptures. In *Revue Scientifique* of 1879, Maurice Vernes, a specialist in the religion of Israel, argued for the possibility and necessity of teaching the history of religion. The next year he published the first issue of *Revue de l'Histoire des Religions* with the cooperation of Émile Guimet (1836–1918), a wealthy industrialist from Lyons and a great lover of Asian art. Guimet had founded a museum the previous year devoted to Far Eastern religion. Vernes (1845–1923) was one of the "most qualified scholarly authorities" in the late nineteenth century and actively participated in "propaganda promoting the history of religion."[10] He was among the first group of professors in the fifth section of the École Pratique des Hautes Études, where he taught the "religions of Semitic peoples."

Jews were also involved in this "scientific and intellectual movement." In 1879, anxious to "hold on to his place in the chorus of the human sciences," Baron James de Rothschild took the initiative of creating a Société d'Études Juives (Society of Jewish studies). The objective of the new scholarly society was "to promote the development of studies relating to Judaism; it confines itself exclusively to the field of science."[11] That "concern for truth" guided *Revue d'Études Juives*, which the society published from 1880 on. "We do not want to engage in religious propaganda," it explained, "and we are not pursuing a goal of edification."

For those identified as "Israelites," the "Jewish question" was doubly complex, since it was posed in ethnic and racial as well as in religious terms. Although Zionism had great difficulty taking root in France and was for the most part the monopoly of the new Jewish European émigrés, the plan to create a Jewish state nevertheless represented a challenge to the French Jewish community's desire for integration.[12] Two opposing views of Judaism took shape. For some, it was primarily a religion; for others, the Jews constituted a people or an ethnic group. Specialists in the history of religion could not ignore that debate. Religion or race? wondered Ernest Renan. For the former seminarian, now a professor of Hebrew at the Collège de France, Judaism was a religion and not an ethnographic fact. Sylvain Lévi, a professor of Sanskrit and of East Indian religions at the École Pratique des Hautes Études who also held a chair at the Collège de France, read Renan's books and, like other Jewish intellectuals, drew many ideas on Judaism from them.

In the late nineteenth century, on the recommendation of Chief Rabbi Zadoc-Kahn, Lévi joined the central committee of the Alliance Israélite Universelle (Universal Israelite alliance). With the outbreak of World War I he became the official spokesperson for French Judaism on the Zionist question. For him, the debate that divided his community took the following form: "Throughout its crises, Judaism has always been torn between two currents: the first, inspired by Moses, tends to drive the chosen people back into ethnic isolation, to multiply the barriers that separate them from other nations; the second, the legacy of the prophets, extends a fraternal hand to humanity and advances beside it toward triumphant justice."[13] Lévi felt he was being faithful to the France of 1789, the nation of human rights, and to the France represented by the heroes of the Dreyfus Affair, Zola's France. The affair began in 1894 with the treason conviction, largely based on forged evidence, of Captain Alfred Dreyfus, a French general staff officer and a Jew. The case and subsequent developments divided France and dominated French life for a decade. Although ultimately the affair united and brought to power the French Left, the rise of anti-Semitism accompanying it added a tragic dimension to the already controversial and politicized question of Jewish identity.

The Section of Religious Science

Charles Péguy commented ironically on the École Pratique des Hautes Études: "The (practical?!) school of higher studies. Fourth section. Or fifth. Or third. Well, the section of religious SCIENCE. At the Sorbonne, at the end of the science hall, stairway 1, second floor."[14] Along with the Collège de France, the École Pratique des Hautes Études was one of the first institutions to open its doors to the "new religious science."

Founded in 1868 by Victor Duruy, minister of public education, the École was originally divided into four fields: mathematics; physics and chemistry; natural history and physiology; and the science of history and philology.

As a scholarly institution it occupied a somewhat marginal position in the system of higher education. Its specific mission was to "set in place, next to a theoretical education, exercises that can strengthen and expand it." The designers of the curriculum not only had to give a full accounting of acquired knowledge but also and above all had to show how knowledge is acquired and how it advances. In short, they had to link education closely to research. The École did not require students to have a degree to attend and did not administer exams. Given the paltry salaries of the professors, the purely honorary degrees bestowed on the students, and the lack of specific career opportunities provided, relations between the school and its members were based on a sense of vocation and the objective pursuit of knowledge.

The fifth section, called "religious science," was created in 1886. The initiative came from Louis Liard, the new director of higher education.[15] The section was established in a polemical climate coinciding with the elimination of the faculty of Catholic theology at the Sorbonne. As Vernes put it, sacred history was thereby secularized. Eleven professors were appointed and the same number of chairs founded: five Christian chairs and six chairs divided between the classical world (Greece and Rome), the religions of Semitic peoples (two chairs), Egypt, India, and the Far East. It was all a question of balance: Christianity on one side and, enjoying equal status, all the rest on the other.[16] Christianity no longer stood for religion as such; it was only one of the religions that the professors, true scholars that they were, deciphered and analyzed with the methods provided by history, archaeology, and especially philology.

From the moment it was founded, the fifth section provoked intense resentment. As Sylvain Lévi recalled, the new creation was seen as "a diabolical machine destined to combat belief and to propagate one official atheist doctrine or another."[17] The section was part of the sciences and considered itself resolutely secular, but without being antireligious or irreligious. Its entire faculty was convinced of the need to "maintain full spiritual freedom, generous tolerance, a disinterested passion for truth, and a scrupulous fidelity to scientific integrity."[18] The aim of all their efforts was to separate the history of religion from apologetics or theology, without taking an aggressive attitude.

As the Dutch historian P. D. Chantepie de la Saussaye said at the 1897 congress of religious science in Stockholm, there was no longer a legitimate place within the field of science for the old apologetic method; it had to be replaced by the "impartial and free search for truth."[19] Henri Hubert, in the introduction to the French translation of Chantepie de la Saussaye's *Manual of the History of Religion*, was very clear: no fraternization was possible between the science of religion and theology. It was open conflict. It is therefore clear what was at stake in 1900 when abbé Loisy was invited to teach a course at the École Pratique des Hautes Études. The section, sensitive to the difficult situation created by the church for the "modernist" Catholic priest, agreed to offer him refuge so that he could continue his work in complete freedom.[20]

When Mauss arrived at the École Pratique, the luminaries of the fifth section were Protestant: Albert Réville and his son Jean, Maurice Vernes, and Auguste Sabatier. The two Révilles held the positions of chairman and secretary. Albert Réville (1826–1906), the son and grandson of pastors, had himself served as a minister in the Netherlands before returning to France in 1873 to defend liberal ideas in religion and politics. A professor at the Collège de France beginning in 1880 and a specialist in the history of dogmas, he was one of the most eloquent and influential representatives of Protestantism's liberal tendencies. The author of *Manuel d'instruction religieuse* (1863; Manual of religious instruction) and the popular *Histoire du dogme de la divinité de Jésus-Christ* (1869; History of the dogma of Jesus Christ's divinity), he published a history of religion whose first two volumes dealt with the "religions of uncivilized peoples" (1883; *Histoire des religions*).[21] His *Jésus de Nazareth* (1897) was hailed as "the most objective result of all the truly objective work yet accomplished in this field, which has been a never-ending theater of passionate controversies and fantastic inventions." It was believed the book marked the end of "historical dilettantism."[22]

Albert Réville was an exegete, historian of religion, and religious philosopher; his son Jean Réville (1845–1908) followed in his footsteps. Before earning a doctorate in theology and pursuing an academic career, he too had been a minister. In 1880 he took charge of *Revue de l'Histoire des Religions*, and when the section of religious science at the École was created he was hired as a *maître de conférence* in the history of the church and Christian literature.

The orientation of the fifth section was deeply influenced by the new Dutch "religious science" represented by professors at the University of Leiden, especially C. P. Tiele and Chantepie de la Saussaye. Albert Réville and Jean Réville studied under them and wanted to be both liberal theologians and academic researchers. They claimed that the researcher's task was to prove the existence of a "natural religion," an innate need for religion. They opposed the doctrine of predestination and stressed the individual's autonomy and dignity. Such individualist thinking was very much in step with the political climate of the Third Republic.[23]

The various religious denominations maintained a precarious balance in the fifth section. When the section was created, the Catholics kept their distance, but at the last minute, a "representative" of that denomination was added: Adhémar Esmein, professor at the law faculty, was assigned to teach the history of canonical law. From the section's early years, the École sought to broaden the denominational base of the faculty, hiring two Jewish professors: Sylvain Lévi in 1887 for the religions of India, and Israël Lévi in 1896 for Talmudic and rabbinical Judaism. In 1887–1888 it also invited Isidore Loeb, one of the editors at *Revue des Études Juives*, to teach a course. Representation of the different religious denominations was still an issue. But, as Sylvain Lévi noted, tensions at the school never turned into open conflict: "It was everywhere acknowledged and understood that except in the area reserved for faith, which commands respect, the study of religions, facts, and doctrines can and must be treated with the same freedom, the same independence of mind, as the study of history, archaeology, and sociology, with which it is so closely associated."[24]

A "Second Uncle": Sylvain Lévi

Mauss chose the École Pratique not to complete his education but to "gather material." "With the obliviousness of youth and an obliviousness to philosophy," the young *agrégé* hoped that within two years he would know "all I needed to know about prayer in the past and present world and, a year after that, would write a doctoral thesis on the subject."[25] He immediately decided to meet with Sylvain Lévi (1863–1935). As Lévi's collaborator Alfred Foucher would note, this young intellectual, the descendant of Alsatian Jews and the undisputed leader in the field of Eastern studies in France, had a magnificent—indeed, meteoric—early career. At twenty-three, he was a professor at the École Pratique; at twenty-seven, doctor of letters; and at thirty-one, professor at the Collège de France.[26] The first exchanges between Lévi and Mauss, just before the start of the 1895 school year, were testy, since the professor did not take his visitor seriously: "Sanskrit alone will take you three years, Vedic Sanskrit at least another year, and your subject does not allow for a mediocre range of knowledge. Jettison the secondary authors, starting with Max Müller, and all comparative ethnography." At thirty, Lévi, who had been Abel Berdaigne's favorite student, was "a scholar of exquisite culture"; he was preparing to publish his *Doctrine du sacrifice dans les Brahmanas* (1898; Doctrine of sacrifice in the Brahmanas), a book remarkable for the rigor of its analyses and the lucidity of its translations. But Lévi, far from discouraging his visitor, issued a challenge: "Here, then, let's give it a try, take Berdaigne's *Vedic Religion* and tell me what you think of it."[27] Mauss read the book in three days and returned to tell his future teacher: "If Berdaigne is right, all the others are wrong. I'm resolved to find out." More than satisfied with that reaction, Lévi wished him luck and invited him to take his classes.

Mauss thus again found himself, with a few other students, on the "benches marked by countless gashes," "amid old books," in the "old rooms of the old library of the old Sorbonne."[28] His concerns were twofold: to study languages (Indo-European comparative linguistics with Antoine Meillet,

Sanskrit with Louis Finot, Hebrew with Israël Lévi) and to study religion (the ancient religions of India with Lévi and his close collaborator, Foucher, and primitive religions with Léon Marillier). He studied with the following professors between 1895 and 1902:

> *Fourth section (science of history and philology)*
> 1895–1896: Sylvain Lévi, Louis Finot
> 1896–1897: Sylvain Lévi, Louis Finot
> 1897–1898: Louis Finot (three conferences a week)
> 1898–1899: Study abroad in Holland and England
> 1899–1900: Sylvain Lévi, Carrière, Antoine Meillet
> 1900–1901: Sylvain Lévi, Antoine Meillet
> 1901–1902: Sylvain Lévi, Antoine Meillet
>
> *Fifth section (religious science)*
> 1895–1896: Léon Marillier, Alfred Foucher
> 1896–1897: Léon Marillier, Israël Lévi, Alfred Foucher
> 1897–1898: Léon Marillier, Israël Lévi, Alfred Foucher
> 1899–1900: Israël Lévi, Alfred Foucher, Isidore Lévy

As Mauss noted, only a "handful of young people" actively and regularly attended Sylvain Lévi's classes at the École Pratique. There were about fifteen registered students. Those attending the École Pratique would become Mauss's colleagues, collaborators, or friends (if they were not so already): Henri Hubert, Henri Beuchat, Arnold Van Gennep, Paul Fauconnet, Daniel Halévy, Isidore Lévy.

Mauss also made friends with two English-speaking colleagues, Joe Stickney and Mabel Bode. Stickney, an American, was greatly admired at the time. In Mauss's eyes, he embodied "everything Old New England has to offer. He has beauty, elegance, and charm; and under that charm he is full of delicacy and strength."[29] After writing a thesis titled "Gnomic Poetry in Greece Compared to Gnomic Poetry in India"—a "masterpiece of comparative literature," Mauss would say—Stickney would pursue an academic career at Harvard. Mabel Bode, an Englishwoman born in Ivry-sur-Seine in 1871, held a doctorate in philosophy. Already trained in Burmese and Pali, she returned to France on the advice of her professor to take history courses in the fourth section ("France in the Thirteenth and Fourteenth Centuries," "The Monastic Rules of the Middle Ages," and others) and to learn Sanskrit with Sylvain Lévi. The subject of her thesis was a history of Buddhism written by a Burmese monk. Bode, a "lovely, kind, frail, but hard-working" woman, had great admiration for her teacher; according to Mauss, she "totally loved" Lévi. She was proud to take his teachings to the University of London, where she would teach Pali. Bode corresponded regularly with Mauss beginning in the summer of 1896, and they often saw each other in Paris. When Mauss visited England, he would not neglect "the rite of lunching" with his old friend, as she liked to call it.

Mauss discovered "guides" at the École Pratique, some of whom would also become colleagues and friends. Among his teachers were Léon Marillier, Antoine Meillet, Israël Lévi, and Sylvain Lévi. Antoine Meillet (1866–1937), born in Moulins, was the son of a notary living in Châteaumeillant in central France, and was only six years older than Mauss. After passing his *agrégation*, he studied at the École Pratique des Hautes Études with Ferdinand de Saussure. He would replace Saussure during his leaves and would later succeed him in the fourth section. The philologist, linguist, and historian was a modest man with a perpetually surprised look on his face. He inspired a "worshipful tenderness" and was a "prodigious scholar," a "sort of magus" for his students.[30] His mind was "open to anything" and he passionately loved taking walks and listening to music, especially Mozart and Wagner but also Debussy and Ravel. The time he did not devote to music he spent with his friends.

Mauss fondly remembered the years when he was often the only one at Meillet's lecture at the École Pratique: "Over several years [Meillet] taught me what I know of Zend and the Avesta."[31] His professor spoke highly of him: "Thanks to his learning and his mastery of philological methods," he made rapid progress in Zend, which was new to him.[32] Mauss continued his training with Meillet and learned the comparative method. A solid friendship developed between master and student, founded on "wide-ranging trust" and "absolute openness," attested in the regular correspondence they maintained. Their relationship was particularly close because Meillet was soon to become a sociologist and would collaborate with Durkheim on *Année Sociologique*.

Léon Marillier (1863–1901) was a professor in the section of religious science beginning in 1888. He was also codirector of the *Revue de l'Histoire des Religions*. An *agrégé* in philosophy, he was interested in biology and psychology and did training at the medical school laboratory and in mental hospitals. His classes dealt primarily with religious psychology and, beginning in 1890, with the "religions of uncivilized peoples." In the academic world, Marillier was admired for his impartiality and scientific integrity. He and his wife were also passionate defenders of various causes: international peace, the defense of oppressed peoples, social justice, the fight against alcoholism.

Marillier was convinced of the "utmost importance" of research on the early periods of social development. For some historians of religion, a methodical study of the religions of uncivilized peoples represented a great danger, that of "misunderstanding the originality of the major historical religions and what they owe to the very persons of their founders." Hence the "very keen resistance" that theologians, Orientalists, archaeologists, and mythologists mounted against ethnographers' and sociologists' efforts at encroachment. Marillier, lauding James Frazer, Andrew Lang, William

Robertson Smith, and Edward Burnett Tylor, invited his colleagues "not to engage in endless polemics." What was needed was "a more productive task." His recurring theme: "Only the facts convince."[33]

In his long review of a book by S. R. Steinmetz, Mauss acknowledged his debt to Marillier, "who was kind enough to share his bibliography and the notes from his different courses on taboo, funerary rites, worship of the dead, and marriage." Mauss borrowed his critical method from the "scientific personality" of a man he considered a psychologist and an anthropologist. "M. Marillier taught us to critique the facts before anything else. Every traveler's account or ethnography book was rigorously debated." That "significant work of scrutiny" became a model of sorts for Mauss.[34]

In 1897 in *Année Sociologique*, Mauss reviewed two of Marillier's essays: "The Place of Totemism in Religious Evolution" and "The Origin of the Gods." According to him, they were fine examples of "serious scholarship."[35] Mauss would be harsh toward Marillier when the latter published his "testament" on religion in the *Grande Encyclopédie*: disappointed to find a "certain theological residue" in that analysis, he expressed reservations about the thesis, which concealed a sort of "internal God" under the name "religious emotion" and made religion an essentially nonsocial phenomenon.[36]

It is hardly surprising that Mauss ultimately established a special relationship with the two Lévis, Israël and Sylvain: intellectual affinities combined with a sense that they belonged to the same community and culture. Mauss turned "instinctively" to Israël Lévi (1856–1938) and found him to be a "teacher as perfect as he is devoted," a man of "rigorous method, vast science, absolute precision, steady effort, and a promising vision." His "modesty is equal to his worth." Israël Lévi rarely used the comparative method or the resources sociology provided for the history of religion. As one of his colleagues later explained, he confined himself to the texts, which he examined with scrupulous rigor. His work was a "monument of intellectual honesty."[37] For Mauss's benefit, this "pure historian," who helped his students "serenely, moderately, and firmly," studied "the principles for constructing rabbinical prayer: eighteen benedictions and a prayer for the dead."[38]

Sylvain Lévi, a professor of Sanskrit in the fourth section and of the religions of India in the fifth, was assisted in the classroom by two of his former students, Louis Finot and Alfred Foucher. Mauss and his "peers and study partners" were put through a grueling ordeal: a course in Sanskrit grammar, a course in metrics, translations from and into the original language, an introduction to Pali, and Buddhist translation.[39]

In his first year, Mauss earned a positive evaluation from his professors. Finot invited him to present an "interesting study on the state of ethnographic research on India" and congratulated him for managing to "familiarize himself with all the difficulties of the Sanskrit language" and for henceforth being able to study on his own. In Sylvain Lévi's course, Mauss earned an "honorable mention" for his "rapid and steady progress" and was invited to "play an active role" in the lessons for second- and third-year students.[40]

Mauss also took Sylvain Lévi's courses at the Collège de France on the Vedas and the Brahmanas. The few students who came called Lévi their guru, the fashionable term in India. Observers said he had an intense gaze and always a resonant voice. He was heir to the humanists and, according to Paul Masson-Oursel—who would succeed him at the École Pratique—he possessed "the active sanctity and pure impartiality of the Eastern sages." He was someone who led others to "recognize their vocation."[41]

For all who knew him well, Sylvain Lévi was a great scholar, a good man of noble character enlivened by a spark of genius. For his students, he was a "charmer of souls, a source of inspiration and of life."[42] Mauss was not slow to praise his master: "His phenomenal memory, his talent, his sharpness, his knowledge, his impeccable attitude, his perfect awareness of every step in his thought process, his infallible clear-sightedness . . . his good sense and discerning reason, his deliciously precise mode of expression, his perpetual enthusiasm, the intact flame of his scientific youth, these marks, these *laksana*, these signs of a great man, he had them all." Finally, this specialist in India distinguished himself from most of his colleagues by his profound intellectual and moral integrity. His rule was to "publish nothing but original things, to teach nothing that is not worthy of publication, to immediately publish every completed study, to do nothing that is not useful to his current students and, over and above his students, to science."[43]

For Mauss, this "exceptional man" immediately became his "second uncle," uniting in one person "what everyone else can only dream of being in part: he is great, wise, good, strong, powerful, and saintly." He was not only a model but also "the most affectionate, the friendliest of men." He kept each of his students in his thoughts and followed them "closely, the way a father follows his son." A filial relationship formed immediately between Sylvain Lévi and Mauss. Over the years, it turned into a solid friendship. The professor lavished advice and encouragement on his student and "dear friend." The qualities that appealed to Sylvain Lévi and his wife the first time they met Marcel were "his candor, his intellectual curiosity, his general kindness, the straightforwardness of his character, his sense of family, the warmth of his friendships, and the sharpness of his antipathies."[44]

Sylvain Lévi showed Mauss great affection and great respect: "Two years of continuous contact has allowed me to appreciate the qualities of your mind and to get a sense of the qualities of your heart. I am proud to have counted you among my students and very happy to count you among my friends."[45] Mauss would note that one of Lévi's great merits was to think of each of his students "materially, paternally, fraternally."[46] On a trip to Nepal in early 1898, he wrote Mauss: "Around the house my wife and I have adopted the very good habit of regarding you—how shall I say?—as a nephew. I mean that our friendship for you is combined with something more intimate and more instinctive, a community of race and education no doubt. And the only too legitimate affection and respect produced by your loyalty, your openness, your hunger for knowledge mingle with a hint of pride at the idea that you were my student and would not be embarrassed [that I am] your teacher."[47]

Mauss became one of Sylvain Lévi's "treasures." Throughout his career, he benefited from his professor's support as well as his advice. It was Lévi who advised him to study in the Netherlands and Great Britain in 1897–1898, a trip that gave him the idea for his study on sacrifice. The two met regularly to discuss their respective work, academic strategies, and various questions regarding religion and the state of the world. During these discussions, they analyzed the "profound difference" that separated them. Mauss would defend reason and science, taking issue with Lévi, "a mystic from a family of mystics." But "partly out of sympathy for a good cause . . . but especially to help him," in 1931 Mauss agreed to join Sylvain Lévi on the central committee of the Alliance Israélite Universelle, an organization to which his own predilections would have been unlikely to lead him.[48]

Much more than Mauss, Lévi remained attached to his "race," not wanting to emancipate himself completely from his traditional milieu. He was a man of action as well as study. Driven by a deep sympathy for "any enterprise that seems well suited to serve and honor Judaism," he devoted himself to the Alliance Israélite Universelle, the *Revue d'Études Juives*, the Zadoc-Kahn association, and the Fonds des Étudiants Étrangers (Foreign students fund).[49] For over thirty years, Sylvain Lévi participated in the debates dividing the French Jewish community. He did not support the creation of a Jewish state. In 1919 he said: "France need not go so far as to let a new state be constituted, a state corrupted at its root by a misunderstanding about religion and race and with weighty consequences for international politics."[50]

Henri Hubert, the Twin Brother

Mauss met Henri Hubert in 1896 when they were taking the same courses at the École Pratique des Hautes Études. As Mauss liked to remind him, they were "work twins," "Siamese twins," but their social and scholarly paths were different. Hubert, born in 1872, the same year as Marcel, came from a well-off Parisian family. His father had retired early from the hosiery business and devoted his free time to "intellectual distractions" (courses at the Sorbonne, visits to museums). The young Hubert pursued his studies at Louis-le-Grand *lycée* and ranked first in the *concours général*, the competition among all *lycée* students. He was an "excellent student in every area, with no gaps." He had an enormous intellectual curiosity, "considered everything, read everything, knew everything." He was not overly concerned about taking the shortest route to the *agrégation* and first enrolled at the Sorbonne. After earning his *licence* in 1892, he went on to the École Normale Supérieure, where he secured a position as assistant librarian so that he could "work more freely."

In 1895, "like a Benedictine monk at work" amid a pile of volumes and slips of paper covered with his tiny and rushed handwriting, he prepared for the *agrégation* in history and geography (he would rank third out of fifteen).[51] Of his interests at the time, Hubert would say: "I was drawn to art." As a student he enjoyed doing caricatures of his professors, and his friends fought over his many sketches. He also illustrated the album marking the centenary of the École Normale Supérieure. As an adult, Hubert distinguished himself from his colleagues by his "artistic tastes." He spent his leisure time doing drawings and watercolors—usually landscapes—and collected artworks, primarily Far Eastern art. Mauss told him: "I don't have your delightful joy for artistic beauty."[52]

Like other students of his generation, Hubert got to know the school's librarian, Lucien Herr. Herr was a socialist militant, a sort of "Titan" with "piercing eyes" who, "from on high, behind the massive desk—tall, long, wide, towering—reigned over books and visitors." Initially a member of the Fédération des Travailleurs Socialistes (Federation of socialist laborers) and of the Parti Socialiste Ouvrier Révolutionnaire, he joined the Parti Socialiste Français at its creation. In 1899 Herr became one of the organizers and administrators of the Société Nouvelle de Librairie et d'Éditions (New publishing and bookselling society) to which several contributors to *Année Sociologique* would gravitate.[53] Hubert shared Herr's socialist ideals but kept his distance from militancy. As Bourgin later explained, Hubert, to serve the cause that he "discreetly and seriously" embraced, did not anticipate "using any means other than those of his profession." This principle is illustrated by his participation in the journal *Notes Critiques: Sciences Sociales*, for which he would write more than twenty book reviews between 1901 and 1903. Hubert's lack of activism did not, however, prevent him from being sensitive to the dangers represented by anti-Semitism in France at the time of the Dreyfus Affair.[54] "What a country!" he exclaimed, referring to the "disgraceful judgment by the war council" and the charges of libel brought against Zola after his open letter of protest to the president of the Republic.[55]

Like Mauss, Hubert did not turn to teaching after passing his *agrégation*. He was free from financial worries and devoted himself to studying Semitic languages and Byzantine culture.[56] At the École Pratique des Hautes Études, where he enrolled in the autumn of 1895, Hubert took the fifth section course offered by abbé Quentin, a doctor in theology and specialist in Assyro-Babylonian religion. The next year, his course load was much heavier: classes in the fifth section from Quentin and Israël Lévi and in the fourth from V. Bérard (comparative grammar), R. P. Scheil (Assyrian philology), Carrière (Hebrew), and J. Halévy (Abyssinia). It was then that Hubert got to know Mauss, who was also taking the class taught by Israël Lévi, the new professor of Talmudic and rabbinical Judaism.[57]

On a personal level, Hubert was "marked by Jansenism." But as his friend and fellow student Marcel Drouin explained, there was in him "no austerity, simply the traditions of a wholesome bourgeoisie ready to use all its resources to better fulfill its duties."[58] His manner was "both courteous and reserved." Salomon Reinach, his superior at the Musée des Antiquités Nationales in Saint-Germain, said, "He blushed easily. Neither the École Normale nor the army had taught him to talk dirty and I never heard an indecent word from him."[59] At an intellectual level, Hubert's "hard-working and sweet" nature inspired sympathy and confidence: "With his enormous head, his high bulging forehead, his grave or smiling mouth, his pale complexion, his bright eyes, his clear and understated voice, and his restrained gestures," he was "typical of his profession and his vocation."[60] In short, he was the exact opposite of a dilettante. Demanding of others, he was much more so of himself.

When they met in class for the first time, Hubert and Mauss discovered real intellectual affinities and became close friends right away. Shortly thereafter, while staying in the Netherlands, Mauss wrote Hubert: "First, I would like to express (it's easier to say at a distance) the profound friendship I feel for you. The connection between us is not only intellectual; and (I like to please people I like) your extreme refinement has given me real respect for you and complete confidence in your character."[61]

It was the beginning of a long and fruitful collaboration. As Mauss later said, "I have generally participated in everything [Hubert] did that was not strictly critical or archaeological. He always checked what I wrote." He remembered fondly the first years of their friendship: "At the time we first met and discovered common ground, H.H. and I lived in a sort of enthusiasm. Together we were discovering the world, humanity—prehistoric, primitive, exotic—the Semitic world and the Indian world, in addition to the ancient world and Christian world we already knew. . . . It was a constant joy of discovery and novelty."[62]

Mauss drew Hubert into the sociologists' camp and introduced him to his uncle Émile. Hubert was one of the first to be connected with Durkheim and "became one of the most fervent and simultaneously one of the most independent of his disciples."[63] Durkheim thought he could get along with Hubert as easily as with Mauss. He had the impression that "of all [his] collaborators, he was among those with whom agreement would be easiest and fullest."[64] Hubert was quickly considered "one of the family"; he was welcome in Bordeaux and Épinal, where he participated in the Durkheim-Mauss family celebrations.

Associated from the start with the publication of *Année Sociologique*, where he was a central figure, Hubert soon became aware of how important his participation in the review and his collaboration with Mauss were: "Don't forget we are called upon—at least I hope we are—to make a difference, that we must make those around us work, that we will act less through the perfection of our works than through the activities of our minds, through the need, the desire, the sacred fire of organized labor that will emanate from us. We must percolate, my dear friend. In the meantime, let's try to live simply, pleasantly."[65]

The first thing Hubert and Mauss wrote together was for *Année Sociologique* under Durkheim's supervision: they began their "Essay on the Nature and Function of Sacrifice" while Mauss was studying in the Netherlands and Great Britain.

1896: A Difficult Year

The already close relationship between Mauss and his uncle would be strengthened by the ordeals they endured together in 1896. That year Durkheim's father died (at age ninety-one) in Épinal, as did Mauss's (at age sixty-two) during a trip to Paris to meet with a doctor specializing in heart ailments. The two deaths—the "double blow," to use Sylvain Lévi's expression—shook Mauss profoundly, even more than he realized.

Durkheim too was deeply affected and went through a period of intellectual and moral confusion at a time when he was very busy writing *Suicide*. Already responsible for the education of two of his nephews—Mauss and Henri Durkheim, whom he took in after the death of the latter's father, Félix, in 1889—he now became head of the family. It was with him that his elder sister discussed the choices open to her son Marcel. Yet Rosine Mauss, living in Épinal, was the family's true center. According to her friends, she was a strong woman who energetically managed the family business and attentively followed her son's education and professional career. Although his relationship with his mother was excellent—she wrote him almost every week—Marcel usually asked his uncle for advice, except in political matters. At difficult times, he also asked Émile to act as intermediary between him and his mother.

Mauss was twenty-four when he lost both his father and his maternal grandfather; he had his *agrégation* certificate in hand but little money. During the previous year (1895–1896), he had had a doctoral scholarship, but to survive he had had to rely on his family as well, that is, on the help of his mother, who still had her little embroidery business. He found it embarrassing to be supported by his mother. He even thought of inviting her to join him in Paris. "That would compensate her for her sacrifices and

reduce her solitude and definitely make me settle down."[66] To reduce expenses, Mauss shared his apartment with his cousins for several years and
bore the inconvenience with relative ease.

For Mauss, these years of study were "years of sacrifice," in Sylvain Lévi's
words. His teacher and friend wrote, "As for those who blame and ridicule the Jews, they must not know them very well! You left your mother
in mourning, you delayed getting married, you had the courage to remain
a student when you were in a position to become a teacher, and, as for me,
you know the even more painful sacrifice I agreed to impose on myself. And
what reward does each of us hope to get other than to serve our country and
science as far as we are able?"[67]

Student life in Paris did not disagree with Mauss. He discovered a city dis-
rupted, first, by anarchist attacks in 1893, then by student demonstrations,
and finally by the Dreyfus Affair. At a time of "historical crisis," the city,
"light-hearted on the surface, suddenly hot as an oven, flamed up, revealing
its deep core. . . . Anyone who did not live through that astonishing civil
war conducted without a brutal act, without a drop of blood shed, but with
an intellectual passion so fierce that men died of exhaustion, of sadness,
of sorrow, of anger; anyone who did not go through it, did not fight in it,
however Parisian he may be, does not totally know his city. There is a secret
within it that has not been shown him."[68]

The young provincial Mauss knew Paris much better than the Parisians.
Hubert criticized him for his "Boul'Mich pals," referring to the trendy
Boulevard Saint-Michel, full of colorful boutiques, cafés, and bars. When
he was abroad, Marcel felt bored. Comparing the Netherlands to France,
he would say: "If you only knew how far it is from the hotbed of ideas in
Paris!"[69] To his friend, who did not like "palling around" and "sometimes
suffered from loneliness," Mauss advised "outings, which teach more about
life than any reflection. The time you're wasting right now by not taking
advantage of your youth will never come again." As their mutual friend
Fauconnet would note, Mauss and Hubert had different lifestyles: "I'm
afraid you exaggerate the importance of the way Durkheim and Hubert criticize your way of working. Hubert really understands life too intellectually,
which I don't think you'll ever get used to."[70] Mauss called himself "pleasure-seeking": "There's nothing like long conversations, nice walks, pouring
out your feelings at dusk, to give relationships that extra dash of sentiment
that makes them linger in your mind and memory."[71] And referring to a
four-day fling in Brussels with a "little woman from Paris," he confessed to
Hubert: "Don't tell anyone, it's a necessary weakness that embarrasses me.
My friend, I believe that an agreeable mistress, not virtuous but earnest . . .
is an important element of happiness at our age."[72]

Mauss worked slowly, as he himself acknowledged: "The nephew is loafing
about half-asleep, dragging his relative intelligence behind him." He worked

"lifelessly, loafing."[73] His slowness would drive Durkheim and his friends to despair. Uncertain about his resolve, they had trouble putting up with his delays. His Aunt Louise advised: "Watch what you say in your letters so as not to feed [Durkheim's] anxiety." That piece of advice was appended to a long letter Durkheim wrote his nephew to encourage him to overcome the obstacles he faced in writing the "Essay on Sacrifice," in which the uncle said: "To be a man means to have an inclination for noble concerns, and if I did not pay heed to your shortcomings, your aversion to worrying and planning ahead, it would be a sign that I was growing less fond of you. . . . I'm afraid you're amusing yourself with a lot of pointless curiosities. Be careful not to go as quickly as I do, what is explicable for me would be inexplicable for you. But that's no reason to dawdle."[74]

Mauss, still interested in writing a thesis that, as a result of "naïveté and intrepidness," would come to be on prayer, became more intellectual and scholarly between 1895 and 1900. While continuing his studies in the history of religion and writing his first book reviews, he became his uncle's research assistant and a valuable collaborator. Durkheim was at a turning point in his career, both at an intellectual and at a professional level. In 1896, nine years after coming to the Université de Bordeaux, he was named to a permanent chair in social science. When he completed *Suicide* (published in 1897), he founded the journal *Année Sociologique*. Mauss said of his work relationship with Durkheim: "I collaborated on everything he did, just as he collaborated on my work and even rewrote entire pages of it."[75]

The nephew's collaboration took up most of his time and was indispensable to his uncle. Merely to compose the tables that appear in *Suicide*, Mauss examined vast numbers of files on suicides recorded in France between 1889 and 1891, using "the quantitative method to classify 26,000 suicides listed individually on index cards and distributed among 75 boxes."[76] (These files were made available to Durkheim by Gabriel Tarde while he was in charge of judicial statistics.) The volume alone indicates the scope of the work, "especially if one considers the number of variables at play in the analysis: age, sex, marital status, province, presence or absence of children."[77]

Émile asked his nephew to read articles relating to suicides in the German army, in Great Britain, and in Spain. Mauss also did documentary research on the question of suicide among the Hindus. He consulted Sylvain Lévi, who said he was willing "to take the question as the subject of a course next year" and to bring him texts they could discuss together. Lévi quickly transmitted information to Mauss.

As Durkheim was writing *Suicide*, he asked his nephew to reread the manuscript, to gather the crucial bibliographical references, and to finish the last statistical tables. He was nervous about Mauss's performance: "In two days you've gone over twelve pages; there are a hundred, figure it out.

Yet you're embellishing the notes; you're having fun instead of confining yourself to simple, indispensable references. . . . What a mess you're making for us!"[78]

Suicide adopts a dual strategy. Not only does Durkheim apply, within the framework of empirical research, the principles he developed in *The Rules of Sociological Method*; he also studies from a sociological point of view the most individual, private act possible. The dazzling demonstration relies on a carefully argued critique of other approaches (including psychopathological, psychological, and biological perspectives), and on the meticulous analysis of a mass of statistics: suicide rates by religious denomination, age, sex, marital status, and so on.

Durkheim was still concerned with the question of "social dissolution." The two axes of his analytical model were integration and regulation. The "middle course" would be a situation where the individual was sufficiently but not excessively integrated and was adequately constrained by rules. Since that "middle course" does not exist in modern societies, two major types of suicide exist in them: first, egoistic suicide, which results from too pronounced individualization; and second, anomic suicide, seen in periods of rapid change (economic crisis or prosperity, for example),[79] which can be explained by the absence of rules or norms.[80] Whether the suicide is egoistic or anomic, the individual is suffering from the same sickness, known as infinity sickness, which takes different forms: some lose themselves in the "infinity of the dream," others in "the infinity of desire."[81]

Once the variables governing the suicide rate were known and it had been established that the current suicide rate among European peoples was an indication of a pathological state, Durkheim wondered what needed to be done to remedy it. As Mauss noted, "social questions are fundamental to his concerns." That is why, like *The Division of Labor in Society*, *Suicide* concludes with moral and political considerations. Durkheim believed that since neither repressive legislation nor education appeared effective or even possible, the autonomous life of professional groups had to be set up to provide individuals with both a social environment and a discipline.

The philosopher Gustave Belot proclaimed it "a fine book."[82] The source of Durkheim's originality, as his collaborator Fauconnet emphasized, lay in the fact that he was "both scientific and sociological. . . . The monograph on suicide is an attempt to raise a precise problem and give its sociological solution based on the observation of all the known facts." Fauconnet added: "*Suicide* must be considered a new exposition and illustration of the rules of sociological method recommended by M. Durkheim." The method, applied to the question of suicide, "gets results" and shows that "an inductive sociology is possible." Of course, Fauconnet was convinced that the book would not fail to elicit objections, and that its author risked being accused of dogmatism. But he warned the contrarians: "It will not be enough to make a few dialectical arguments: you will have to provide new facts or interpret the statistics in a new way."[83]

Unlike Maurice Halbwachs, one of the contributors to *Année Sociologique*, Mauss did not return to the study of suicide, but he later used it as an example. "Directly inspired by the ideas Durkheim expressed," he defined the specific character of social phenomena: "It would be impossible to understand why the suicide rate is uniformly higher in Protestant societies than in Catholic societies, in the world of business than in the world of agriculture, if we did not concede that a collective tendency toward suicide manifests itself in Protestant environments and in business environments by virtue of their organization itself."[84] The experiment in empirical research that *Suicide* represented also allowed him to become aware of the need "to examine official documents" (judicial, economic, and demographic statistics, for example) "in every detail." "Like any scientific observation, statistical observation must aim to be as accurate and as detailed as possible." Mauss added: "In the absence of meticulous precautions, one runs the risk of obtaining false data."[85]

3

RITES OF INSTITUTION:

EARLY PUBLICATIONS AND
TRAVEL ABROAD

EVEN before finishing his training at the École Pratique, Mauss published his first writings: book reviews he submitted to *Revue de l'Histoire des Religions* in 1896. The prestigious periodical was devoted to the science of religion but was open to ethnology. It was closely associated with the fifth section of the École, where its founder, Maurice Vernes, its two codirectors, Jean Réville and Léon Marillier, and its main contributors were all professors. The first review Mauss published was of a book by Adolf Bastian. The author, a German doctor, was in the forefront of ethnographic studies in Germany: he had done a major survey of the populations of Indochina and the Brahmaputra Valley; had published a general overview of man in history; had founded an ethnographic museum; and had organized the Berlin Ethnology Society, one of the largest in Germany.

Bastian's work belonged more to ethnology than to the history of religion. Mauss's criticism was harsh: "No order, no guiding thought . . .; paragraphs that don't go together are placed one after the other; a useless index." Mauss rejected the many "speculations" and took an interest only in the tangled "vegetation of facts." Even at that level the book was disappointing, since it added a "very limited . . . amount of new knowledge" and included several errors.[1]

The same year, Mauss also published a fifty-page critical study in two parts in *Revue de l'Histoire des Religions*. It examined another book written in German, S. R. Steinmetz's study of "religion and the origins of penal law," which presented observations of 197 different peoples. Mauss's article is well documented, including nearly two hundred footnotes, citations of French studies but also of English, German, and American ones, and an analysis of Hebraic law with several references to Genesis and Deuteronomy. Mauss gave an in-depth reading of Steinmetz's book: Mauss's analysis of the "same materials" allowed him to do new research and to give a sociological explanation of primitive punishment (the vendetta). In his view, a book review had to be "dogmatic," had to seek to "elicit the search for new facts" or to reclassify "misclassified facts," and had to give a new analysis of "those [facts] that have been wrongly described."[2]

At that time, Mauss began to be convinced of the benefits for the science of religion of "sociological" or "social" ethnology. As a "study of social
phenomena among primitive peoples," ethnology had an advantage over
general sociology in that it studied "more simple phenomena" "closer to
their origin" and "in a more immediate relationship with one another."[3]
Tired of philosophical generalizations, Mauss discovered a new methodology whose great strength was to "give the exact physiognomy of the facts assembled" and, with due vigilance, to invite others to "search constantly for
contradicting facts." As the English anthropologist Edward Tylor suggested,
it was more important to take into account "deviations from, rather than
coincidences with, the typical phenomenon." In his article on Steinmetz's
book, Mauss managed to grant a religious origin, and thereby a social dimension, to punishment and private revenge. His analysis was an extension
of Durkheim's *Division of Labor in Society*, which granted a central place
to the various kinds of legal sanctions and rules that determine the different forms of social solidarity. Durkheim concluded, "One cannot point to
a single society where the vendetta was the primitive form of punishment.
On the contrary, it is clear that, in the beginning, penal law was essentially
religious."[4]

Mauss referred many times to Durkheim's writings. The nephew relied
on *The Rules of Sociological Method* to criticize Steinmetz for not having
defined his object, for having poorly identified his population—"What is a
primitive people?"—for having based his classifications on commonplace
notions, and finally, for having been too trusting of "either indigenous or
ethnographic interpretations, whose usual incompetence is well known."

Mauss, identifying problems he would subsequently make into objects of
study—sacrifice, magical power or mana, and more generally, the sacred—
raised the major questions that would orient his work. How to explain a
social fact completely? What is the relationship between psychology and
sociology? In what way is functional analysis compatible with an evolutionist approach?

Mauss sent his review to Gabriel Tarde, head of statistics at the Ministry of
Justice. Tarde judged the study "very interesting." Its value lay both in "the
critic's insight and the scholar's precision and breadth of knowledge."[5] In response to Mauss's critique, the book's author wrote that his intention was to
provide "studies based on ethnographic data and not a complete history of
punishment." He protested the assertion that "he had naïvely accepted the
interpretation of ethnographers." But on the whole, he seemed happy with
how Mauss had treated him and thanked him, expressing the wish to meet
him soon at a conference in Paris.[6]

Mauss's article greatly pleased Durkheim: "I see your erudition has developed enormously, and yet you remain in control of it. All that—and the form
as well—is beginning to show signs of maturity. . . . I'm obliged to you for

making me become more completely cognizant of my own thinking by reading your work and talking to you, and that is the greatest service you could
render."[7] The uncle greatly respected Steinmetz as "someone we'll be able
to get along with."[8] His nephew's reflections were important enough to him
that, two years later, in the first volume of *Année Sociologique*, he personally
summarized the "well-documented" article on Steinmetz. For Durkheim,
that was a way of congratulating his nephew, who was able skillfully to put
to use the lessons he had learned.[9]

Holland and England

For young *agrégés* intending to pursue a career in teaching and research,
spending time abroad was an obligatory "rite of passage" or better, a "rite
of institution." During the school year 1885–1886, at the invitation of the
minister of public education, Durkheim had gone to Germany to study the
teaching of philosophy and the state of the social sciences. In the late nineteenth century Germany was a privileged destination, because of the superiority (or imagined superiority) of its education and research system.

Rather than study abroad, for a time Mauss toyed with the idea of applying
to the Institut Thiers. The institute, founded in 1893 by the wife of the historian and statesman Adolphe Thiers, provided a place to live and financial aid
to promising students, allowing them to prepare their doctoral theses. Every
year five candidates, often Normalians, were chosen for a scholarship lasting a maximum of three years. Mauss's mother did not understand her son's
choice: "I don't see where that private institution can lead."[10] Durkheim was
scandalized: "You must have given some thought to how strange it would be
for a wealthy young man to ask for a place in a charity institution, possibly
at the expense of some penniless laborer."[11] The uncle was surprised that his
nephew wanted to "end [his] student career with an internship . . . after doing everything to avoid it." His advice was as follows: "If you must hold on
to your freedom for another year, with its advantages and disadvantages, at
least let it be with a precise goal in mind, like a trip to England and Holland.
That trip should be made and must be made."[12]

When he decided to go on a "scientific expedition" to Holland and
England, Mauss was interested in "studying the state of the science of religion," as the letter of recommendation from the Ministry of Foreign Affairs
indicates (Office of the Consulates and Business Affairs, November 20,
1897). He wanted to meet researchers and professors: H. Kern, C. P. Tiele,
and Oort in Leiden; Willem Caland in Breda; and Tylor and Moriz Winternitz
in Oxford. He would thus "come into direct contact with these scholars" and
also, in the case of the English anthropologists (James Frazer, Andrew Lang,
E. Sidney Hartland, and so on), "make that important [research] movement

known in France."[13] Mauss was thinking of writing a book on the English school of anthropology.

For anyone who was interested in the study of religion, the choice of Holland and England is easy to understand. Mauss intended to devote himself entirely to writing his thesis on the origins of prayer, but he first wanted to further the dual training he had received at the École Pratique: in ancient languages, including Sanskrit, and in the study of so-called primitive peoples. As he confided to one of his friends, "one must be a good philologist to be a good sociologist."[14] A knowledge of ancient languages seemed especially important because, at the time, language was considered the best source for learning the specific traits of a people. And for those in search of the "languages of paradise," to borrow Maurice Olender's expression, the vogue in the human sciences was for Sanskrit, which usurped the former privilege granted to Hebrew. In the salons and academies of France, England, and Germany, discussions of the Vedic idiom hastened the establishment of comparative language studies by legitimating the Indo-European hypothesis, which posited a close kinship between the Indo-European language and the idioms of the chief European ethnicities.[15] This discovery of a kinship led to a "complete revolution in how the early history of the world was studied."[16] Although Mauss harshly criticized the ideas of the school of comparative mythology,[17] he joined the comparative philology movement and in his imagination invented a "providential couple": the Semite and the Aryan.

Mauss was supposed to leave in early autumn, but a bad abscess forced him to postpone his departure until late December 1897. His stay in Holland was brief, lasting from December to the following April. His mother hoped he would take full advantage of his trip: "I'll get my money's worth, as you say, if you come back, God willing, healthy and even more learned. But I'd like all that science to get you set up in life, since I'd so love to see you start a family before I make my final journey."[18]

In Leiden, Mauss met Kern and Tiele, who were "utterly kind" to him, but he worked primarily with Caland, whose work he knew well and whom he respected for his great proficiency.[19] He confided to Hubert: "He's the best of men, with a good and solid intelligence. And a very open mind."[20] Caland was a specialist in the worship of the dead in ancient India and his work was well received in Paris. Out of modesty and a lack of time, Caland was at first reluctant to receive his young French visitor, but finally agreed "willingly to help him."[21]

The life Mauss led in Holland was rather "drowsy," punctuated by "long and depressing daydreams." Initially the country bored him, as he wrote Hubert: "As a country it's a complete nonentity. . . . It's flat, sodden, with no irregularities, no hills and valleys, no life. . . . The things are just like the people. Life as a whole is ordered by the movement of slow boats that take the place of our haulers."[22] Intellectual life was disappointing as well.

In Holland, "no one thinks, no one invents. No philosophical excitement. They [put] good German essays into a clear style; they slowly adapt their country to English utilitarianism, to European progressivism. . . . If you only knew how far it is from the hotbed of ideas in Paris."[23]

A few weeks sufficed to correct some of his first impressions: "I now love the milky sky of Holland and its pale women."[24] His stay, devoted primarily to study, was demanding. As one of his correspondents said, it transformed Mauss into a "French scholar." Not only did he start writing book reviews for *Année Sociologique*—to the first volume, published in 1898, he contributed more than twenty reviews and close to two hundred notices—but he let himself become completely absorbed in his "mechanical work" translating sutras. At the end of his stay, when he was "in a real fever of work and sadness," Mauss felt tortured by "time slipping away" and the "need . . . to finish up." Without "anything to distract him," he sought to finish his Spinoza and "not to drop the sutras."[25]

For a time Mauss considered going to Germany to complete his work with Hubert; but, keeping to his schedule, he went to England in June. Such a "detour" was obligatory for someone whose study of sacrifice would lead "to the heart of primitive societies." England meant Edward Tylor, author of *Primitive Culture* (1871) and editor of the important guide *Notes and Queries on Anthropology* (1st edition, 1874). It meant Max Müller, a German scholar who taught at Oxford. And finally, it meant James Frazer, who was busy at the time preparing a new edition of his already famous *Golden Bough* (1890).[26]

None of these scholars had ever gone near a primitive society, but their works assembled a vast quantity of information on all regions of the world and raised the controversial question of the "origins of religion." It is possible to speak, as Mauss did, of an English school of religious anthropology: "After the instigator, Tylor, after MacLennan, after A. Lang, after the early R. Smith, after the early Frazer, came the definitive works, which show the results of work by a school, the consequences of a method."[27] These "definitive studies" were by Dr. Alfred C. Haddon, who in 1898–1899 led a second major expedition to the Torres Strait in New Guinea; by the Reverend Lorimer Fison and Alfred William Howitt (*Kamilaroi and Kurnal*); and by the Australian anthropologist Baldwin Spencer who, in collaboration with F. J. Gillen, made various observations in central Australia (*The Native Tribes of Central Australia*).

According to the anthropologist E. Sidney Hartland, all these studies revealed "a new world of the primitive mind." He added: "The discoveries thus made were promptly seized by inquirers into the history of human institutions and beliefs with the daring, but not always the success, of a Cortés or a Pizarro."[28] It was no longer enough for anthropologists to read books in the library and formulate coherent hypotheses; they had to go out into the field and collect new data. That radical change in ethnography was the occasion for many lively polemics: "The quiet noncombattant student is astonished to find himself in the theater of war, and hardly knows where to seek a bomb-proof burrow that he may hide his head from the shells of the polemics."[29]

Totemism, a "Scottish invention" along with radar, whiskey, and marmalade, was central to every discussion.[30] Although the theory of totemism, focusing on the importance of belief in the magical properties of an object, usually an animal or plant, for a clan or tribe, seemed to be well established in the works of McLennan, Frazer, Smith, and Jevons, two "smashing blows," in Hartland's expression, were dealt: first by Franz Boas, with the remarkable Jesup Expedition to tribes in northwestern Canada; and then by Spencer and Gillen, in their meticulous description of the Arunta of central Australia. Everyone was full of hope: "The coming century has doubtless many surprises in store for us and our children. It will be no surprise for students of anthropology if the progress of discovery enables us by-and-by to reconstitute the history of humanity to an extent of which . . . all the generations of learned of the past never so much as dreamed."[31]

As he set out for England, Marcel had no precise plan. "Where should I go?" he wondered. "I'm somewhat drawn to Frazer. I find the classes annoying and M. Müller disgusts me."[32] He first thought of going to Cambridge, "because of the anthropologists and the library Frazer's set up there," but his work on the sutras was leading him to Oxford, where Moriz Winternitz could help and supervise his work.[33] It was a decision one of his professors at the École Pratique approved of. While providing his former student with a little information on how to find a place to stay in England, he advised him to give priority to "personal work." "Just like here, one does one's little bit of science abroad only through personal work and everyday conversation; classes are the least important and their role, essential at first, afterward becomes rather minor."[34] Hubert had the same attitude, advising his friend to study Sanskrit or Talmudic Hebrew instead of taking Frazer's classes.

As in Holland, in England Mauss led "too regular, too mechanical, too sober, and too chaste a life" and succumbed to "melancholy at the sight of the vast expanses," to the point of feeling curiously "old and sad." His mental state worried his family: "You feel off kilter at a physical as well as a moral level. . . . Put away your work and try to get outdoors, try to exercise."[35] Durkheim also sought to cheer up his nephew: "For the first time in your life, a few bad things have happened to you this year. I'm expecting a great deal of good to come from that experience. For the first time you agreed to work to a deadline and I hope you'll honor your commitment. That exercise . . . will be painful, but will prove beneficial to you. Don't lose your footing, learn to enjoy the pain a little. I know what it is to be in a foreign country. It's always painful. But it's always beneficial."[36]

Mauss complained of his unfitness for travel; he found it difficult to leave the people he loved and did not like new faces.[37] But his poor ability to adapt, as he recognized, did not prevent him from at one point considering requesting a 15,000-franc grant to take a long trip: "It would be a splendid opportunity to see things I could talk [about] my whole life, and for some time I've dreamt of Mesopotamia, India, Tibet, Melanesia, without wishing to give my dreams a clear form." He abandoned the idea so as not to put off indefinitely his present work, and especially so as not to abandon *Année*. He added: "The wanderer's life suits me only in small doses."[38]

Despite his "internationalism," in his first weeks in England Mauss felt "compulsorily" French and, "for lack of curiosity and time," spoke little English: "Not ten words a day." In the end, however, he "acclimated himself a little," gradually mastering English and recovering his taste for life. His work put him in touch primarily with Moriz Winternitz, "one of the most proficient in the sutras" but "a poor fellow . . . marginalized by anti-Semitism, an Austrian denounced by Müller who, after working him like a nigger, dumped him."[39] Mauss also met Edward Tylor and James Frazer, who invited him to dinner. He presented them with his article "Religion and Penal Law" as well as with the first volume of *Année Sociologique*.

Although he was busy with a heavy work schedule and "very stingy with his time," the author of *The Golden Bough* received his young French visitor warmly.[40] As Mauss would say, there were many affinities between the Cambridge scholar and French sociologists and anthropologists. In 1886, at Lucien Herr's suggestion, Durkheim had read Frazer's "admirable article" on totemism.[41] Mauss remembered with delight the first edition of *The Golden Bough*. It was, he said, a "masterpiece of literary art and, for the time, a masterpiece of mythological thought and religious science, and of empathy." In 1901, when the second edition was published, Mauss praised the "literary form" and "scientific value" of that "fascinating book."[42]

James Frazer was both a scientist and a humanist seeking to satisfy his taste for the beautiful, his empathy toward human beings, and his hunger for truth and goodness. He devoted himself to science and wanted to make it appealing. Mauss very much liked the "candor, altogether Gaelic, or British if you like," of the man he called Sir James. If we are to believe him, Mauss never broke off his "intimate relationship" with Frazer's work, thought, and person.[43] The relationship between Mauss and Frazer, professional at first, became friendly. Frazer's wife (his "formidable partner," Bronislaw Malinowski would say), née Adelsdorfer, was French, from an Alsatian and probably Jewish family.[44] As soon as he returned to France, Mauss sent Lilly Frazer "specimens of Épinal prints" and invited her to visit along with her husband.[45] The friendship, however, never prevented Mauss from criticizing Frazer, sometimes harshly, on, for example, the controversial question of the origin of sacrifice.

A New Review: *Année Sociologique*

Whether in Holland or in England, the student Marcel Mauss hardly behaved like a dilettante in search of distractions and spiritual nourishment. He lived like a researcher. He complained to Hubert: "This work on sacrifice will have ruined the year for me. . . . I've led a ghostly life in a Sanskrit dream, slaving away at texts too difficult for me, having nightmares that I'll never finish, seeing my ambitions wither every day, my ignorance grow, with the horrible idea of another failure." Mauss had dreamed of a year abroad that would be "a year of life, of distraction, of studying people and things, of pleasant and free travel, of almost artistic reflection." He concluded that it had turned out to be "drab, abstruse, lonely, and nauseating."[46]

Mauss had a full schedule. In addition to the sutras, he had to read a great deal, primarily for book reviews and notices to be published in the first volume of *Année Sociologique* (Caland, W. Crooke, P. Gardner, A. Hillebrandt, F. B. Jevons, Mary H. Kingsley, Müller, Steinmetz, H. Usener, and so on).

Mauss's role in that new undertaking cannot be overstated. Durkheim himself congratulated him for the "spontaneity with which [his nephew] followed and pushed him into the adventure of *Année Sociologique*."[47]

It was an ambitious project. Inspired by the review *Année Psychologique*, directed by Alfred Binet and first published by Alcan in 1895, Durkheim intended both to publish his collaborators' studies ("original essays") and to review the international sociological literature year by year. The title of the review (The year in sociology) was taken from an annual section of *Revue de Métaphysique et de Morale*, founded in 1893 by Xavier Léon, the "sociable philosopher par excellence."[48] Durkheim's future collaborators played an active role in the review, particularly Célestin Bouglé, who in 1894 published articles on Simmel, Warner, Paul Lapie, and François Simiand.[49]

In the spring of 1896 Durkheim began the first negotiations with Alcan: "I'm going to see Alcan shortly," he wrote Bouglé, "and as soon as a solution has been found, I'll share it with you."[50] He was full of hope: "The publication of *Année* will be an event—because for the first time a group of sociologists will set a single task and work together."[51] To create such a group, however, he had to convince everyone. In addition to approaching many French and foreign publishers to obtain books for review, Durkheim maintained a regular correspondence with his future collaborators, which included three *agrégés* in philosophy (class of 1893): Célestin Bouglé, Paul Lapie, and Dominique Parodi. Bouglé, though he did not conceal his reservations about *The Rules of Sociological Method*, was one of the first to express his interest in the project and played an important role in bringing the team together. Lapie and Parodi were his friends; another contributor, Henri Muffang, an *agrégé* in grammar (1890), was his colleague at the *lycée* in Saint-Brieuc.

Mauss did not hesitate to support his uncle, who was apparently over-whelmed by the "enormity of his task." Mauss later recalled: "I was his recruiter in Paris from 1895 to 1902. That's how we formed the group of competent and specialized scientists and overcame the first difficulties of our science in an atmosphere of trust."[52] Among the first contributors to *Année* were three of his best friends: Paul Fauconnet, Henri Hubert, and Albert Milhaud.[53] The first was an *agrégé* in philosophy, the others *agrégés* in history. In October 1895 Mauss introduced Fauconnet to his uncle, and the next year, when he got out of the army, the young *agrégé* was recruited to join the *Année Sociologique* team, where he wrote the column on "moral facts" with Durkheim and Emmanuel Lévy. As a schoolboy, Fauconnet had had "a passion for history," but his interest in politics led him to sociology. "He wants to be a socialist but also wants to back up his political beliefs with science, the science of societies," Durkheim said of him. With Durkheim's consent, he chose "Responsibility" as the subject for his thesis. Then he accepted the delicate task of writing a long review of Durkheim's *Suicide* for *Revue Philosophique*. In concluding he wrote: "There is no sociology, but only a sociological way of studying economic, legal, religious, and demographic phenomena. It is characterized by the use of the comparative method, which can apply only to social facts having a reality of their own."[54]

Like Fauconnet, François Simiand published a lengthy review of *Suicide*, this one in *Revue de Métaphysique et de Morale*, and did not hesitate to question the value of certain statistical data and to reject what he called a "metaphysics of sociology," a "sociological realism."[55] This brilliant young Normalian ("one of our best," Mauss would say), born in Gières, in southeastern France in 1873, distinguished himself by his curiosity, his erudition, and the audacity of his analyses and syntheses. An *agrégé* in philosophy (ranked first in 1896), he joined the team at *Année* "in full independence." The vast majority of the first contributors were young *agrégés* like him.[56]

In the early years, Bouglé, Fauconnet, Hubert, and Simiand, along with Durkheim and Mauss, were the main figures behind *Année Sociologique*.[57] In the operations of the collective enterprise, Hubert rapidly came to occupy a central place. He was a "linchpin."[58] Durkheim told him, "*Année* is impossible without you." Hubert had what he called a true "devotion" to the review. Mauss dreaded it: "*Année* . . . is a true poison, worse than the flu."[59]

As Durkheim was well aware, the publication of such a review was a "burdensome task" and required "thankless work," often at the expense of other, more gratifying intellectual activities. He wrote his nephew: "Do you feel you got stuck with that bibliographical labor? By you, I mean all you young people. I feel we have to produce, we will matter only insofar as we produce."[60] Hubert complained that *Année Sociologique* yielded him little, "scientifically speaking." Mauss struck the same note: "I believe it's time we all add dogmatic [i.e., theoretical] publications to our work at *Année*."[61] "In that workshop of sorts," Mauss would say, "one must have great self-abnegation."[62]

To judge by the preface to the first volume, which appeared in 1898, the founder's intention in *Année Sociologique* was to inform sociologists regularly "of the research being done in the specialized sciences, the history of law, of mores, of religion, moral statistics, economics, and so on, since it is there that the materials are found from which sociology must construct itself."[63] Durkheim also hoped "to interest readers who are not professionals in sociology"; he wanted to give them "the sense of what sociology ought to be and what they ought to require of sociologists."[64] In contrast to too many sociologists, who "dogmatize on a daily basis," Durkheim intended to do useful work by reviewing recent books in the social sciences, not only in French but in foreign languages as well, and by "indicating, at least summarily, what benefit sociology can draw from them." In some sense, it was "an up-to-date handbook for one of the newest and most important sciences," but a special handbook because, "under Durkheim's direction . . . and somewhat at [Mauss's] urging," the review sought to "organize not merely ideas, but especially facts." Durkheim gave his nephew precise advice on how to compose book reviews, told him not to analyze each work individually but to do an overall plan to avoid repetition, to present things in the most interesting form, to identify and point out "all the residue," to confine himself to the important works, to dot all the i's. He thought that would be an "excellent exercise" for his nephew.[65]

With the second volume, the review became a "sort of catalog, kept sufficiently up to date, of the various specialized sociologies."[66] It was supposed to make for positive, constructive reading: "Our role must be to extract the objective residue from the works we are studying, that is, the suggestive facts, the fruitful views." Durkheim liked to say that "the little things that remain of a book are so many achievements for science."

But when he was weary or discouraged, Durkheim expressed his anxiety. Hence, shortly before the first volume of *Année Sociologique* was published, he confided his dismay to his nephew: "I thought that my *Suicide* was going to clear up the misunderstandings, to lead to understanding. I expect that will not be the case at all. . . . I see I have no power against reigning opinion. Under such conditions, what's the point of *Année Sociologique*? It's already caused me sleepless nights, and what for?"[67] One of his main fears was that it was a "pure bibliographical study": "So what's the point of so much trouble? . . . Or maybe the time's not yet ripe?"[68]

Despite his fatigue and irritation, Durkheim did not hand over the reins. In the end, he declared himself "ready to do anything in [his] power to keep *Année* alive." He was still the one who "supervised everything," responsible for "a whole organization effort [his collaborators] did not suspect."[69]

In his report on the first issue of *Année*, Mauss recalled the objectives of the review. On the one hand, it was "to inform the sociological public, which is very vast, still too worldly but very important, of the major ethnographic, historical, and legal studies." On the other, it was "to clarify for ethnographers and ethnologists, historians of religion, and so on, sociologists' desiderata." To justify the "large place" occupied by ethnography books and questions, he added: "Every social fact must above all be studied in its roughest state. . . . In addition, for the editors of *Année*, ethnography has the greatest importance. Sociology can only be comparative; and, as with ethnologists, the basis of comparison will necessarily be ethnographic facts."[70]

Aware of the "flaws" of the first volume—typographical errors, arbitrary choices, overly detailed study of some books—Mauss recognized that the "goal is difficult to achieve." "We cannot think of being complete. We'll have to feel our way for a few more years. But even this year, we've made an effort to do objective, disinterested work, to present in a handy form the many results of a host of studies." Hubert was more severe: "The big problem with *Année* is that it's good work bungled. That's sad."[71]

Année Sociologique inaugurated a new type of intellectual study. Whether because of "the scientific division of labor among a team with various areas of competence, the collaboration on authoritative works, the imposition of a strict schedule of scientific production based on the deadlines set for issues of the review, the obligation for each contributor to cover accurately a delimited field of research, or the communion of companions in the doctrine of a master, first among equals," *Année Sociologique* looked like a "revolutionary enterprise."[72] Its mode of operation made it akin to a research institute.[73] Durkheim believed that "science, because it is objective, is essentially an impersonal thing and can progress only by collective effort."[74] Mauss held the same view: "Every science is the result of work in common."[75]

From the outside, the *Année Sociologique* group might easily look like a cult or a militia. Mauss would say that Fauconnet "was recruited for the team at once. . . . He devoted himself to the study of moral facts."[76] All the collaborators, Mauss in the lead, acknowledged Durkheim as the true master: "What brought us all to him was that we knew he was a scientist, that his method was very reliable, that his knowledge was very vast and scrupulously verified."[77] Durkheim's ambition was to "see a few young people of value" "not follow [him] slavishly but use [his] results openly."[78] He was extremely satisfied with the work done by his young collaborators, as he told Mauss when the manuscript of the first volume of *Année* was sent to the printer: "My relations with my collaborators have been pleasurable and among them all I found a very touching devotion to the common task."

Durkheim suggested readings, corrected essays, and gave studies a particular orientation. He attended to everything and everyone. His student

Georges Davy noted, "even in memos of instruction or scientific advice, one feels the presence of affection." *Année Sociologique* cannot be reduced to a philosophical cult, however. At most, Mauss would say, there was "an understanding and a group."[79] Although the spirit of collaboration ruled, integration was very weak—"there were no conferences, no meetings, no motto"—because the team was dispersed.[80] Durkheim was in Bordeaux those first years; Bouglé lived in Montpellier, then in Toulouse till 1907; Fauconnet replaced Bouglé from 1907 to 1920. Within the *Année* team, it is possible to identify subgroups based on affinities or networks. For example, there was the Bouglé-Lapie-Parodi subgroup, the Hubert-Mauss subgroup, and later one consisting of their students (Antoine Bianconi, Henri Beuchat, Philippe de Felice, Jean Reynier). These were not cliques, however.[81] Mauss met frequently with most of the early contributors to *Année* and corresponded regularly with them: not only Fauconnet and Hubert but also Bouglé, Lapie, Lévy, and Simiand. "We were lost souls," he said, "who managed to find our way [exploring the social phenomenon] only by calling out to one another in the forest."[82]

The review covered a vast area: general sociology, moral and legal sociology, criminal sociology, economic sociology, social morphology, and so on. The work was often tedious and presupposed a knowledge of the entire scientific output of the time and the mastery of foreign languages, primarily English, German, and Italian. It also obliged contributors to maintain contact with a large number of publishing houses. Durkheim was "entirely absorbed" in his work as director of the review;[83] just to get review copies of books, he had to write hundreds of letters.[84] And then there was the extensive correspondence he maintained with the contributors, sending out books, correcting reviews, and providing encouragement.

It was a courageous enterprise and seemed to be very useful. Gustave Belot noted in *Revue Philosophique*: "That service is particularly noticeable in a science whose field is at once so vast, whose aspects are so varied, and whose elements are so intimately connected."[85] Some might have feared that Durkheim, who seemed "predisposed by temperament to systematic constructions and absolute assertions," would have wanted to "produce a doctrine and turn his *Année Sociologique* into the manifesto of a school." But that was not the case. Belot continued: "His first goal is precisely to provide a glimpse of the richness of the materials available or to constitute a collection, to counter sociologists' temptation to 'dogmatize.'"[86]

In the first series, which appeared between 1898 and 1913 and comprised twelve volumes, *Année Sociologique* published 18 essays, analyzed no fewer than 4,800 books or articles, and mentioned (without comment) 4,200 others. These were not always just book reviews or summaries; 1,767 "analyses" exceeded one journal page, sometimes reaching as many as ten or even twenty pages. Durkheim was aware that his nephew's participation in the review was "burdensome" since "beginner that he is, [he] puts in an enormous amount of time on his reviews."[87] Mauss later evaluated his contribution this way: "To measure things by volume, the largest part of my, or of our, work was devoted to writing, editing, and publishing *Année Sociologique*. I published about twenty-five hundred octavo pages of the ten or eleven thousand pages in the fourteen volumes already published or now being published."[88] Emphasizing the scope of that collaboration, Henri Lévy-Bruhl would write: "[Mauss] scattered a large part of his knowledge and thinking among the many book reviews he wrote for *Année*. . . . It was to *Année Sociologique* that he gave the best of himself."[89]

In analyzing the some 2,800 book reviews of at least six lines, we can identify the chief contributors to *Année*.[90] In order of importance, they are: Durkheim (498 reviews), Marcel Mauss (464 reviews), Henri Hubert (396 reviews), and François Simiand (254 reviews). And if we consider not the number of reviews but the number of books and articles reviewed and analyzed, Mauss's role is even greater than Durkheim's.

Corresponding to the central place occupied by Durkheim, Mauss, and Hubert at the review was the importance granted religious sociology as "the keystone of social theory." In the first three issues, the "religious sociology" section was the most voluminous, occupying a quarter of the pages devoted to book reviews.[91] In the preface to the second volume of *Année*, Durkheim justified the primacy granted to the field of religion: "From the beginning, but in a confused state, religion contained all the elements that, by becoming separate and determinate, by combining with one another in a thousand ways, gave birth to the various manifestations of collective life!"[92]

Mauss was responsible for the religious sociology section, but, in the case of the subsection "myths," he shared that responsibility with Hubert from the beginning. With the third volume in 1900, Hubert would become jointly responsible for the section as a whole. It represented a significant part of *Année*: more than 100 pages of the 560 that made up the first volume, with about 20 long book reviews and more than 200 notices. A summary of the religious sociology section indicates the scope of Mauss's concerns:

1. General treatises, philosophy, method.
2. Primitive religions in general. Monographs of tribes.
   A. Malaya;
   B. Uncivilized tribes of India and Indochina;
   C. Africa;
   D. Oceania;
   E. North Asia. Ancient Indo-European peoples. Relics of primitive religions among civilized peoples.
3. Domestic cults.

4. Beliefs and practices concerning the dead.
   A. Prehistory;
   B. Uncivilized peoples;
   C. Religious anthropology;
   D. Greek antiquity;
   E. China.
5. Popular cults in general, and especially agrarian cults.
6. Ritual.
   A. Prayers and ritual;
   B. Magic.
7. Myth
   A. Comparative mythology;
   B. Primitive peoples;
   C. Relics of myths;
   D. Myths proper;
   E. Popular legends;
   F. Christian mythology.
8. Organized worship. Monasticism.
   A. Constitution and development of Hebraic and Israelite dogma. Constitution of the synagogue;
   B. Christianity. Formation of dogma;
   C. Formation and establishment of the Churches;
   D. Birth and expansion of Christianity. Baptism;
   E. Buddhism;
   F. Mohammedanism.

At *Année Sociologique* as it was organized, Mauss's participation was crucial. Durkheim wrote: "You are one of the linchpins of the operation and altogether essential, not only because you're in Paris but also because, as I anticipate and hope, a theory will emerge from *Année Sociologique*. That theory, the exact opposite of historical materialism, which is so crude and simplistic despite its objectivist current, will make religion rather than economics the matrix of social facts. The role of the person involved in religious studies—even though, or rather because, religion is now to be found everywhere—will thus be significant."[93]

For Durkheim, however, "that cooperation is an occasion for moral suffering: The most unbelievable irregularities are removing all reliability from a collaboration in need of it."[94] There were many calls to order. Mauss was not punctual and his delays were a constant source of frustration for his uncle. Durkheim wrote Hubert, "I fear delays and procrastination, which are only too common from my nephew."[95] Nervous and prone to extreme anxiety, Durkheim was easily exasperated. One day, worried that he had not received a letter as early as he was expecting it, he took a sterner tone with Mauss: "You're a barbarian." Sometimes he grew sad: "You break my heart"; "You're hurting us." He would complain about his nephew to Mauss's mother: "My dear Rose, it's impossible for me to accept in silence Marcel's attitude toward me. . . . In the space of seven, almost eight weeks, Marcel has produced nothing appreciable. There's no reason to think he'll produce anything more in forty weeks."[96]

Durkheim used every means possible to "shake him out of that lovely insouciance, which could quickly turn to apathy or complacency."[97] He could not understand why Mauss had so much trouble writing an essay that did not call for any particular effort at analysis: "I find that helplessness disconcerting."[98] Seeking "the cause of that fundamental flaw," he gave the following explanation: "On the one hand, there's an idealism that demands . . . he do well; on the other, a need to indulge in the sweetness of life, to not torment himself or others, and as a result to not earnestly look ahead."[99] The uncle seemed discouraged with his nephew, who "thereby finds a justification for not doing anything," defending "the fine theory of [his] sacred peace of mind."[100] He asked Hubert to "help him in this rescue operation."

Apparently there was little success, since two years later Durkheim would have to admit that "there is no cure for the illness; we are dealing with a hopeless case. To palliate the effects of that illness, I can do nothing more than what I'm doing, which is to remind him constantly of his obligation and do part of his work."[101] It is true that Mauss set to work only when goaded by necessity, that is, at the last minute. Some said that "the uncle sometimes locked the nephew in a room above his study so that he could hear whether he was pacing up and down instead of writing."[102]

Marcel was extremely sociable and valued friendship a great deal. He found pleasure in life. Impulsive, not to say impetuous, he got stirred up over nothing and was always ready to spring into action. Nothing really predisposed this strapping young man to an academic career. He would confide to his mother, "I was utterly ill suited for the intellectual life."[103]

Sacrifice

For the second volume of *Année Sociologique*, Mauss began his first major study in collaboration with Henri Hubert, "Essay on the Nature and Function of Sacrifice." In so doing, he risked relegating his thesis to the background. Durkheim wrote him: "I believe the study [on sacrifice] is altogether important and that you must devote yourself entirely to it. Your thesis and the rest will come in its time. Let's not rush things. Also, it's no bad thing to arrive at the Sorbonne with a certain authority."[104]

The idea came from Sylvain Lévi, his professor at the École Pratique, who in 1898 would publish *La doctrine du sacrifice dans les Brahmanas*. Mauss said of that book, which he considered a masterpiece: "[It] was made for me. From the first words it gave me the joy of a decisive discovery. 'Entry into the world of the gods . . .': There it was right in front of us, the beginning of our study on 'sacrifice,' the one by Hubert and me. We had only to provide proof."[105] In *Année Sociologique* he wrote a positive critique of his teacher's work: "This book is of the greatest interest for sociologists, and we have drawn from it generously in the study we have published in these pages."[106]

In tackling sacrifice, Mauss and Hubert were approaching a delicate question of interest to anthropologists, historians of religion, and obviously Christian theologians, who were afraid that the dogma of the Eucharist would be tampered with. Sacrifice was part of almost every religion, even a central part. Father Marie-Joseph Lagrange called it "the religious act par excellence."[107] For some researchers, including Renan, sacrifice was "the oldest and most serious error, the one most difficult to uproot of those bequeathed to us by the state of madness humanity passed through in its early periods." Renan thought it was a way for primitive man to "appease the unknown forces surrounding him" and to "win them over as one wins over a person by giving him something."[108]

From the beginning of his research, Hubert perceived the impact their study could have: "Now, my friend, we are condemned to engage in religious polemic. . . . Onward, I like combat. Let it spur us on."[109] "Essay on the Nature and Function of Sacrifice" has a deliberately polemical dimension. In it Hubert and Mauss criticize various authors and assert, as Hubert would say elsewhere, that science "must extirpate from its own domain the unknowable and banish theology."[110] The mere fact of linking "the ceremonies of Christian sacrifice and those [they] had studied" was scandalous. What Christian was not shocked to read: "The Christian imagination, built from ancient blueprints . . ." or "the conception of a god sacrificing himself for the world . . . became, even for the most civilized peoples, the loftiest expression and the ideal limit of pure abnegation"?[111]

Hubert and Mauss did not wage battle alone, however. In the same volume of *Année*, Durkheim acknowledged in a preface "the sort of primacy" the review granted to religious sociology. Defending the perspective adopted in his own study and in Hubert's and Mauss's, he wrote: "To be able to say with some chance of success what the society of tomorrow will be, what it must be, it is indispensable to have studied the most remote forms of past societies. To understand the present, one must take leave of it."[112]

Also in that volume, Durkheim devoted a short essay to the "definition of religious phenomena," arguing for the obligatory—and thereby social—character of religious beliefs and practices. His conclusion intersected that of his two close collaborators: "The notion of the sacred is social in origin and can be explained only sociologically."[113] It is no accident that the two essays were published in the same volume. Durkheim was afraid that, "when people read the book reviews, the connection between the facts [Mauss] speaks of and the social order will not always appear clearly enough." He explained to Mauss: "After thinking about it a great deal, I believe it preferable to offer my essay on religion along with your own. That's the only way to show in general that religion is a sociological matter. . . . It's therefore not a bad thing to indicate in a general way how and in what sense there is a religious sociology."[114]

"Essay on Sacrifice" was an ambitious project: as Tylor pointed out in a letter to Marcel Mauss, the subject was "difficult." In *Primitive Culture*, published the same year as Darwin's *Descent of Man* (1871), Tylor elaborated a theory of religion—animism—and, convinced that even early man shared a few forms of religious belief, described the evolution of religions by their degree of intellectual sophistication. The most recent derived from primitive religious systems and conserved traces—relics—of their origins. There is also an interpretation of sacrifice in Tylor's book: sacrifice is a gift given to the gods with the aim of winning their favor or diverting their anger. The theses had an immediate success. Tylor was elected to the Royal Society and named professor at Oxford. For some people, anthropology became "Mr. Tylor's science."

Mauss was interested in Tylor's work but could not ignore that of other English anthropologists—James Frazer, of course, but also the theologian W. Robertson Smith, who died in 1894. Smith, a friend of the lawyer John Ferguson McLennan, was coeditor of the *Encyclopedia Britannica* and a professor at Cambridge beginning in 1883. He was attempting to apply the theory of totemism to the Bible. In his last book, *Lectures on the Religion of Semites* (1889), he presented totemic sacrifice as the first phase of religious evolution. In general, the totemic animal is taboo for members of its clan, but on certain occasions it is eaten: the ritual ceremony ends with a meal that sanctifies the unity between the totem and the clan and ensures the well-being of its members. Smith concluded from this that the animal sacrifice is not a self-interested gift. The theory that claimed otherwise, he believed, was inadequate not only because it conceived of God as a king or lord who expected only fidelity and tribute from his subjects, but also because it could not take into account burnt offerings and, in particular, human sacrifice. Such an interpretation, exclaimed Smith, was "absurd and revolting."[115] From his point of view, sacrifice was essentially a communion, and some of its characteristics could still be found in the most advanced forms of sacrifice.

Hubert and Mauss acknowledged their debt to Smith: "We have indicated . . . how our theory is connected to Smith's. Everything he said about the sacred, the taboo, the pure and the impure, we have put to good use." This tribute did not rule out criticism: "We have rejected his genealogical explanation of sacrifices. As is well known, he had them all derive from totemic communion."[116] Such criticism was addressed to Frazer as well, wrongly perhaps, in that Frazer seems to have been distancing himself from the theses of his friend Smith. When "Essay on the Nature and Function of Sacrifice" was published, Frazer criticized Mauss for "making the mistake of thinking that he and Smith were in agreement," since that was far from the case. "I have never accepted his derivation of sacrifice in general from totemism. The theory has always seemed to me artificial and destitute of adequate evidence. . . . In fact he and I approached religion from different, almost opposite standpoints." If the differences were not obvious, it was because, out of "mutual affection," they preferred to emphasize "the points of agreement and to pass over in silence the points of disagreement."[117] Frazer suggested that Mauss consider him and Smith writers "who, even though they have many things in common, also have differences, which are major but which they keep concealed."[118] In the preface to the second edition of *The Golden Bough*, published in 1900, Frazer explicitly objected to Smith's theses: "I never assented to my friend's theory, and, so far as I can remember, he never gave me a hint he assented to mine."[119]

Hubert and Mauss wanted "as much as possible to intermingle and compare and differentiate the facts" they had available. The two friends began from different standpoints, but their concerns intersected. As Mauss acknowledged, "[Hubert] wanted to understand the sacrifice of the god, which was the aim of his research on the Semitic origins of Christian myth, and I wanted to see if the ritual formula of sacrifice really depended so closely on Christian myth that the ritual was derived from it."[120] What led Hubert to the study of sacrifice was "his research on the cult of the Syrian Goddess, in which the sacrifice of God—the rite and the myth—plays a major role."[121]

There were so many difficulties that Mauss became somewhat discouraged: "Work is going slowly. I feel my machinery getting jammed up!"[122] Distressed at the state of their work or, rather, at his nephew's work, Durkheim wondered "whether you ought not to give up."[123]

The "Essay on Sacrifice" was written under the watchful eye of the "impatient, fearful" Durkheim[124]—to use his nephew's words—who, from Bordeaux, was following its progress "in his own mind." He gave much advice and encouragement: "The first draft does not need to be written carefully"; "Don't waste your time writing me long letters on the plan. Execute it, that's more urgent"; "I'm convinced you can do something very good that will do you great credit"; "I'm afraid there may be . . . a little verbosity." Durkheim offered his collaboration and then, afraid "to exert control, even in appearance, or to look like a schoolmaster," he became more discreet: "If you believe I can serve you in any way, I am yours completely; it will be delightful for me merely to collaborate with you."[125] Hubert agreed to "have a long talk" with Durkheim when he came to Paris: "It's done me a great deal of good. We didn't come to an understanding right away, because we have different starting points. He started from the idea of punishment. . . . Then, with goodwill, we ultimately understood each other."[126]

Everything was done through the mail. Hubert and Mauss wrote and rewrote the outline, exchanged their note cards, discussed one question or another in their letters, added information, and corrected the preliminary versions. They had to learn to work together, divide up the task while taking each other's area of competence into account. "We worked very seriously," Mauss would say. To compose the final version of the text, the "original plan" was "July in Paris; then half Switzerland half Épinal—we were to have wound things up by September," with possibly a short stay in Bordeaux. But under pressure to meet the deadline, Mauss did the final revisions by himself in summer 1889 when he joined his uncle in Épinal: "All right! I say that once more to annoy you [Hubert]. It'll go out as it is. We don't have time to send you the rest. It'll be printed as is."

The comparative method obliged them to bring together often diverse facts chosen from various regions and eras, but Mauss and Hubert did not deny their specificity. Mauss wanted "to do the least superficial work possible." He feared "too hasty an edit," which "could have serious drawbacks."[127] Hubert was aware that "a study of every type of sacrifice in all the important religions [was] impossible" because of a lack of time and space. He invited his friend to "stick to the facts" they already knew well, to critique them, and to probe deeper in the analysis. In a letter he wrote to Durkheim, Hubert indicated the limitations of their work: "We do not claim to do a scientific, exhaustive study; we set out a hypothesis constructed with the help of a certain number of facts. No one could have done a definitive study in 150 pages and after only a year."[128]

Mauss agreed to present their work as a "provisional hypothesis" but only on the condition that they "bring together a larger number of facts than previous hypotheses." For the two friends, completing a joint study was a challenge and an ordeal. The initial idea was to give "real unity" to their study and to write in each other's presence as much as possible.[129] There was an asymmetrical relationship between Mauss and his friend, since Mauss knew the texts better, particularly the Sanskrit texts. But Hubert demanded "the right to work." He insisted: "A collaboration where one of the two does everything isn't fair."[130] His collaboration quickly became indispensable, because he was responsible for the part devoted to the "sacrifice of the god." When Mauss submitted the outline to Sylvain Lévi, the latter criticized his "inclination toward abstraction" but set his mind at ease because "the auspicious idea of collaborating with . . . Hubert ensures a solid framework of facts." "You'll be precursors," he added.[131] The historian Hubert could correct the philosophy *agrégé*: "Let's be wary of jargon and abstract terms," he wrote. "Your draft is full of clichés of that kind. I'll slash them ruthlessly. I find nothing emptier or more illusory than such philosophical language."[132]

Hubert and Mauss focused their "brilliant and suggestive analysis"[133] on two different religions, Hinduism and Judaism, in the hope that by comparing them they would reach "sufficiently general conclusions." The well-documented study—"very detailed, very polished," Alfred Loisy would say[134]—had more than five hundred footnotes and references to many authors. It relied on a reading of written texts—the Vedas, the Brahmanas, and the sutras for Vedic ritual, the Pentateuch for Hebrew—and on collections of hymns, methodological and theological glosses, and manuals of rituals. In addition to these Sanskrit and Hebrew texts, but in the background, were texts drawn from classical antiquity and early Christianity. There was no question of relying on ethnographic data: "The facts recorded by ethnographers, generally truncated by hasty observation, assume their value only if they are linked to more precise and more complete documents."[135] Mauss was aware of the limits of his knowledge: "As for the ethnographic documents, they'll be very limited. Apart from the fact that my knowledge of them has not increased this year, such arguments provide proof only if they are complete (or nearly so)."[136]

True to Durkheim's directives, Hubert and Mauss began their study only after they had defined the facts they designated by the term "sacrifice." Durkheim suggested a definition: "An operation, or set of operations, that is part of a system of religious rites and whose result is to destroy (through manducation, punishment, sacrifice by fire, etc.) or to put out of common use (offering) one or several animate or inanimate objects."[137] Hubert and Mauss put the emphasis on consecration: "Sacrifice is a religious act that, by consecrating a victim, modifies the state of the moral person who performs it or of certain objects in which he is invested."[138]

The objective of their work was to "demonstrate and describe the externalities of a single mechanism," to find a single "kernel" in the various forms of sacrifice. As Mauss claimed, it was a matter of "seeking the general and profound nature beyond its forms, which are more or less isolated from one another."[139] What is a sacrificial ritual? It is "a way for the profane to communicate with the sacred through the intermediary of a victim, that is, a thing destroyed during a ceremony."[140]

Their meticulous and rigorous approach made it possible to extract the general schema of sacrifice—its grammar, E. E. Evans-Pritchard would say. As Mauss would later reaffirm, the sacrifice entailed "a prelude, the entrée; a drama, the destruction of the victim; a conclusion, the exit."[141] Also precisely identified were the various elements that compose the sacrifice: the sacrificed, the sacrificer, the places and instruments, the sequences. Using different examples, Hubert and Mauss explained how the schema varies according to the intention behind the sacrifice. The part of the study devoted to the sacrifice of the god, "one of the most accomplished forms in the historical development of the sacrificial system," included a thorough analysis of the relation between rituals and myths.

Hubert and Mauss's audacity consisted of conferring a social dimension and a social function on religion. As they stated explicitly in the conclusion: "Religious notions *are* because they are believed; they exist objectively as social facts. The sacred things in relation to which sacrifice functions are social things." When they reevaluated their first studies, Hubert and Mauss would go further: "In our view, everything that characterizes society for the group and its members is conceived as sacred. If the gods are leaving the temple and becoming profane, each at their appointed hour, by contrast we now see human but social things—the nation, property, work, the human person—enter it one after another."[142] They would acknowledge that "the ultimate goal of [their] joint research was to study the sacred" and for them, that was "the clearest benefit of [their] work on sacrifice."[143] They were proud "to have shown a clear case where the idea of the sacred was operating," a forceful idea that was "the first central phenomenon of religious phenomena."[144]

As he was composing the "Essay on Sacrifice," Mauss had the feeling that, by showing that "the religious act's aim is to place the individual at the center of the collectivity," he had discovered one of the essential factors of social and religious life. The themes he wanted to address in what he saw as a "sociological and moral" conclusion were: "Relation between the individual and society in sacrifice. Sacred things, creation of social conscience. The need for the individual and society to move closer—during grave circumstances for the individual, for society, and for nature—to that central system of the individual's and of society's inner life. Relation between the sacrifice and prayer."[145]

Durkheim dreaded the "dialectical subtleties" that were "customary" in his nephew.[146] In the end, however, the conclusion Mauss wrote with Hubert, even reduced to more modest proportions, provided elements for reflection in what would be called "sociological metaphysics": how individuals acquire "the social force as a whole"; how a balance that has been threatened is reestablished; how the social norm is maintained.[147]

In the same volume of *Année*, Mauss published more than twenty book reviews and over eighty short notices on works in religious sociology. In his critique of Tiele's *Elements of the Science of Religion*, he gave an idea of what a "science of religion" might be. That science, clearly distinct from the philosophy of religion, "studies an order of facts defined with the help of a definite method." This was the sociological method: "Thanks to it, facts of a religious nature stand as objective and natural things. They have an existence outside the fleeting instants when the individual thinks them and acts on them. They are part of a real whole, the one formed by social things, and they have a useful function to perform there. Thanks to sociology, one can study them comparatively even while pursuing detailed analyses as far as possible, and these analyses retain all their value." Mauss added: "The future seems to lie with comparative and in-depth monographs."[148]

This project was a true research program in that Hubert and Mauss offered up for sociological analysis a set of social beliefs and practices that were not religious. In "Essay on Sacrifice," the contract, atonement, punishment, the gift, abnegation, and ideas relating to the soul and immortality were considered one by one. The scope of these topics shows "how important the notion of sacrifice is for sociology."[149] The philosopher Gustave Belot called it "an unusual and forceful study."[150]

When the essay appeared, Alfred Espinas congratulated his former student: "It is a great and beautiful construction, gilded with a respectable objectivity by the erudition of you and your collaborator." He very much liked the text, which took him back to a time when he "was serving mass." "It's all true . . . the theory is correct," he said. But he criticized his former student for wanting "to rival the metaphysicians in dialectical refinement, when you are, in fact, a good and honest and loyal organizer of facts."[151] Octave Hamelin, another of his philosophy professors, appreciated "the intimate union of history and the idea: It is only through it that one reaches the concrete notion." But he said he was somewhat surprised by the content. He immediately corrected himself: his surprise was "perfectly unjustifiable" since he "understood for the first time the dogma of real presence" and "saw the entire outcome of the evolution of sacrifice."[152]

In Great Britain, people were attentively following the work of Durkheim's young collaborators. The journal *Folk-lore* pointed out the importance of the first volume of *Année Sociologique*: "We wish well to the new venture; and we gladly hail the [rise] of a French critical and constructive school of enquirers into the savage custom."[153] In his review of the second volume, E. Sidney Hartland restated his admiration for the journal: "high quality"; "a truly scientific spirit"; "subtlety, precision, and sound judgment in the book reviews." He concluded: "We can expect only solid results from it."[154] The importance of the "Essay on Sacrifice" for specialists in the history of religion did not escape the vigilant eye of the president of the Folklore Society: "It is quite certain that we could not have advanced towards the solution of the problems involved without a methodical consideration of the mechanism of sacrifice. Messr. Hubert et Mauss have not merely pointed this out, they have shown the way. Progress will follow by an adaptation of their method to inquiries concerning other religions and among peoples."[155] By that means, what could already be called the French school of sociology found affirmation.

The Dreyfus Affair Seen from Afar

In January 1898, Émile Zola's "J'accuse," published in *Aurore*, sent out "a cry from the soul": "I have only one passion—for light, in the name of humanity, which has suffered so much and has the right to happiness." The public was thrown into turmoil. Dreyfus's supporters had been desperate for some time, but now recovered their strength and confidence. The day after the article appeared, a first petition circulated for a "revision" (that is, a new trial for Dreyfus), and several hundred people signed within a few days. They would be called "intellectuals"—primarily academics, writers, scholars, artists, and poets. Among those protesting the "violation of due process in the 1894 trial and the iniquities surrounding the Esterhazy affair" were several university *agrégés*: Lucien Herr, Charles Andler, Célestin Bouglé, François Perrin, Élie Halévy, and François Simiand.

The Dreyfus Affair unleashed a wave of anti-Semitism. In various cities, including Bordeaux, thousands demonstrated in the streets, shouting "Death to the Jews, death to Zola, death to Dreyfus." All of Lorraine was affected. In Épinal, Nancy, and Bar-le-Duc, people marched and broke windows, cursing Zola and the Jews. Anti-Semitic writings multiplied, attacking *juiverie* and "stock market Jews," symbolized by Rothschild. The Jewish community was dismayed but reacted only rarely and timidly. Léon Blum later recalled: "French Jews avoided the subject. They no longer talked about the Affair among themselves. A great misfortune had befallen Israel. People submitted to it without a word, waiting for time and silence to erase its effects."[156] It is true that French Jews facing adversity tended to place themselves under the protection of the French Revolution's ideals, showing they were more French than the French. If Jews engaged in the debate, it was often less out of solidarity for one of their own than out of a sense of duty, a passion for justice, and a humanitarian impulse.

The "terrible storm" exasperated Rosine Mauss. "I'm afraid to go out, what with all the signs plastered every night on the shutters of Jewish stores. . . . There's not even a bench to sit down on that's not carved with 'Down with the Jews.' Three nights running, kids sent out fire ships on the Moselle, always with the same sign and the same shouting in the streets."[157] Just reading the paper put her "in such a state that it's impossible to talk about anything else but that sad affair."[158] She was especially anxious because she feared that Marcel's involvement with the Dreyfusards "might hurt him in [his] career." She wanted to go live in Alsace, "to have some peace" and so that her sons could "find jobs abroad."[159]

Durkheim was also concerned with the outbreak of anti-Semitism, but he did not attribute it to French racism. Rather, he thought it was a "consequence and superficial manifestation of a state of social malaise."[160] In a letter to Mauss, he spelled out his point of view: "The situation is indeed grave; but it seems to me that anti-Semitism is only a superficial manifestation. What is serious about it is, first of all, that a minor affair—since it's nothing in itself—could have produced such unrest. Because there had to be a profound moral disorganization underneath it all for an incident so unimportant to cause such upheaval." He added: "Never has there been such moral disorder in our country." Durkheim remained worried. He was clearly not optimistic, but at the same time he did not intend "to be discouraged from the fight." "On the contrary," he wrote his nephew, "that is one of the good sides of the situation, to have awakened an inclination toward combativeness that has lain dormant for too long. There is something to do, since there is a battle to be waged, and if we know what we want, we will quickly regain ground. The essential thing is that the elements that have coalesced remain united and that there be no debacle."[161]

Durkheim had Hubert suggest the idea "of a permanent league for respect and legality," and he urged Lucien Herr to talk about it with Émile Duclaux, director of the Institut Pasteur. He quickly spoke to Marcel in more precise terms about this planned league: "For the moment, we're seeking to organize a league under Duclaux's direction for the defense and rights of citizens." Organizing it was far from easy: "Up to now I've gotten five signatures. It's distressing to see the cowardliness that's derailing us. It's all despicable." Durkheim did not have many illusions: "Let's do what we can and resign ourselves about the rest. I feel like I'm in internal exile. So I have withdrawn almost completely from university life. What I see there is too painful a sight."[162]

The Ligue des Droits de l'Homme was founded on February 20, 1898, at the initiative of Senator Ludovic Trarieux. Durkheim, "a member of the league before it even existed,"[163] did not hesitate to confront the "pettiness and cowardliness" of his colleagues and did recruiting for the new organization, becoming secretary of the Bordeaux branch. At a time of intellectual and moral lassitude, he confided to Bouglé that he "had just spent the saddest winter": "All those deplorable events, the impression they give of our moral isolation, the sickening spectacle of so much cowardice, ultimately undermined my courage or at least led me to ease up somewhat in my activities. The state of the Bordeaux atmosphere, I mean the university atmosphere, played a large role in that. . . . Under such conditions one ultimately withdraws into oneself and is discouraged from acting." Durkheim wanted to remain optimistic and asked only to "get back on his feet" so that "the intolerable sense of loneliness" would disappear. His immediate plan was to write an article entitled "On the Individualism of Intellectuals." "That is the heart of the debate," he explained to his collaborator. "One would have to show that individualism in everything we might do is our only collective aim; that, far from dispersing us, it is the only possible rallying point."[164]

Durkheim thus joined the battle in the name of moral, not political, imperatives, and even less as a Jew. His primary concern, he wrote, was to "save our moral heritage."[165]

The socialists were hesitant to become openly involved. Even after Jaurès rallied the troops, some, such as Gabriel Deville at *Devenir Social*, asked: "Was the party qua party supposed to pronounce Dreyfus's innocence and lead a campaign in his favor?"[166] "Not seeing what benefit the proletariat, unjustly condemned to poverty, could draw from that affair of a rich captain illegitimately condemned of treason," a certain Charles Rappoport refused to sign any petition in support of Dreyfus or Émile Zola.[167]

From Leiden and Oxford, Mauss observed "that astonishing civil war conducted without a brutal act, without a drop of blood shed, but with an intellectual passion so fierce that men died of exhaustion, of sadness, of sorrow, of anger."[168] The affair deeply saddened him. He wrote to Hubert: "There is no pleasure in thinking of my country. . . . The moral fog that hangs over France is making me forget its beauties."[169] And he was outraged: "As for things in France, instead of being sickened, I'm in revolt."[170] His friend, his uncle, and his mother kept him informed of the events.

In the midst of writing the essay on sacrifice, Mauss declared that he wanted, by way of conclusion, to address the question of sacrifice to the nation as it was instituted by obligatory military service. Although Hubert and Mauss finally decided not to give an explicitly political dimension to their analysis, they would become the advocates of a middle ground between individualism and altruism, arguing that an individual must never completely efface himself in favor of the nation. In other words, the defense of a new secular and republican ethics did not necessarily lead to self-surrender, civil sacrifice. There is nothing astonishing in the fact that they were both spontaneously drawn to defend an innocent man who was being sacrificed for reasons of state, albeit in its republican form.

With a few years' hindsight, Mauss would see all that "turmoil, that exasperation," as the sign of a "swaggering, militarist, nationalist madness" that had seized hold of several European democracies, first France, then England: the "nationalist frenzy." "But in our country," he added, "nationalism is complicated by anti-Semitism and, as in Germany, it elaborates the ideas of the petty bourgeois class and of the reactionary castes."[171] He concluded, "We are now witnessing the supreme thrust of what constitutes the form of society that the social revolution will destroy."[172]

PART
II

THE TOTEM AND

TABOO CLAN

IN 1898, at the end of his year abroad and now twenty-six, Mauss found himself facing the same problem: What was his professional future? The job market in social sciences was very tight. Thinking of Paul Fauconnet, whose career "was at times something akin to martyrdom," Mauss later recalled: "Young people today imagine things were easy before the war, with regular promotions and adequate compensation for work with no bumps along the road! What a mistake! I know of very few scholars whose lives back then were not difficult and full of sacrifice for a long period of time."[1]

Two possibilities for Mauss opened up, the first in Bordeaux, where his uncle wanted to bring him, and the second in secondary education. Durkheim brought up the idea of creating a class in the science of religion at the Université de Bordeaux. But his nephew was against it: "As one opposed to other injustices and other favors," he did not want there to be "any appearance, well-founded moreover, of nepotism and coteries."[2] Durkheim abandoned the idea for the same reason: "To bring [the plan] to fruition I would have had to have the faculty's ear completely; there would have had to be no hostility that might lead my colleagues to suspect me of nepotism." The position he had taken in support of Dreyfus had isolated him and obliged him to be more cautious.[3] In fact, when Isidore Lévy shortly thereafter became a candidate to teach a new course at Bordeaux on the ancient Eastern world, Durkheim anticipated that he "would abstain from voting while orally justifying his abstention." He did not "want to seem to be responding to the nepotism" of one of his colleagues (Foucart) "with Semitism."[4] An *agrégé* in history (1894), Lévy pursued his studies at the École Pratique des Hautes Études, where he knew Mauss. After spending two years (1897–1899) at the French Institute for Eastern Archaeology in Cairo, he was assigned to teach a course on the northern Semites in the fifth section of the École and agreed to collaborate on *Année Sociologique* beginning with the second volume.

As for secondary education, Mauss was still thinking seriously about it. His mother did not conceal the fact that "her pleasure, or, to tell the truth, her happiness" would come from seeing her son "with a good job and happily married." She also wanted him to become a teacher, close by if possible. But aware that "no man is a prophet in his own country, especially if he's Jewish,"[5] she came around to her brother's point of view: "It's up to you now to have a goal and to know what you want. If you've set your sights on the university, you must seize the opportunity while you've still got breath and are on your way: Buckle down and finish up your thesis in a hurry so you can get a job in higher education as quickly as possible."[6]

Rosine Mauss agreed to additional "pecuniary sacrifices" to allow her son to "be done with the thesis" and "get a job in higher education more quickly." She did not forget that her brother Émile's thesis "remained on the drawing board for a long time."[7] Under pressure from his uncle and friends, in early summer 1898 Mauss agreed to consider "remaining free to do [his] work for another two years" for "the needs of [his] career and happiness."[8]

His friend Hubert had been hired in 1898 to teach a course at the Musée des Antiquités Nationales in Saint-Germain, about ten miles northwest of Paris. The job, while "leading to new studies and requiring universal competence," also worsened what he called his "doubting disease." He confided to Mauss: "I'm wasting a great deal of time in self-examination, asking myself: What am I? What am I good for? What do I know? What have I done? When I realize I'm ignorant about something, I'm overcome with anxiety."[9] At the museum, his superior—Salomon Reinach, one of the three Reinach brothers—was "extremely sympathetic" toward him.

As a result of their academic success, the Reinachs were held up as models for young Jews. Joseph, the eldest, was a brilliant attorney and deputy associated with the French republican leader Léon Gambetta. Théodore, the middle son, having earned a doctorate in law and another in letters, was a specialist in Hellenic archaeology and numismatics. He pursued two careers, in politics (as a deputy from 1906 to 1914) and in academics, eventually at the Collège de France (1924). Salomon was endowed with an enormous capacity for work and an insatiable curiosity, and was not one to avoid controversy. He devoted himself to Mediterranean archaeology and became enthralled with the history of religion, of philosophy, and with so many other fields that Hubert said he was "a new Pic de La Mirandole or the last of the encyclopedists."[10] In Hubert's eyes, he seemed to be a "very good fellow," "eminently easy to manage," someone he hoped "to convert to [their] ideas" and "make serve [their] plans."[11]

Hubert and Mauss devoted a large share of their time and energy to research and reading. In addition to "Essay on the Nature and Function of Sacrifice," they published many reviews in *Année Sociologique*, for the most part on books in religious sociology. They paid particular attention to the question of totemism and to the ethnological research being done in Australia. Mauss knew personally several of the authors of books he reviewed: Caland, Frazer, Lévi, Marillier, Tiele, Tylor, Winternitz. Mauss began to wonder if it was time to add more theoretical work to *Année*. He appealed to his friend: "Let's keep company, that's fine, but let's not dissipate our energies and let's strike hard."[12]

The historian/archaeologist and the philosopher/ethnologist continued to have interests in common. As the twentieth century began, both lived under the dual sign of intellectual work and political involvement. Mauss especially participated in political congresses, worked with the cooperative movement, and published political articles.

4

IN THE CENACLE

IN EARLY 1900 Durkheim received a telegram from the minister of public education inviting Mauss to "take [a] philosophy *lycée* assignment for [the] school year." Mauss's uncle suggested he "go see M. Lachelier if [he] was inclined to accept," but advised him to refuse: "No point in telling you that you must think of your thesis."[1] Mauss's reply was unambiguous: "I told you my thesis was not hopeless . . . that it didn't seem to me the job would be interesting . . . that it didn't seem like Lachelier would be annoyed if I refused."[2]

Mauss was still available and could "be of service to his teachers," as Sylvain Lévi said. At the end of that year he accepted a teaching assignment at the École Pratique des Hautes Études, where he had been taking classes since his return from England. When Alfred Foucher announced he had to go to Saigon for a year to temporarily replace Louis Finot as director of the Far East School, Sylvain Lévi, who held the chair in the religions of India, asked Mauss to temporarily take over the course Foucher had been teaching. This was one of twelve lecture courses, or conferences, proposed by the section of religious science in 1900–1901.[3]

In putting forth Mauss's name Lévi noted that the candidate had taken the conference in question, that he "was already known for his essay on sacrifice written in collaboration with H. Hubert," and that he had published several reviews in *Revue de l'Histoire des Religions*. Mauss encountered no opposition, and as his professor of Sanskrit, Willem Caland, emphasized, it would be "an honor to be able to replace Foucher."[4]

Durkheim did not entirely approve of his nephew's decision but found it difficult to object, since he was not sure he would be able to find him a position once he had his doctorate. But the uncle feared that his nephew's "work," that is, his thesis, would "forever remain on the drawing board" and that Mauss would be unable to "break the deadlock." Durkheim therefore advised him to "work to make [his] teaching as good as possible" and to "keep an eye out for any spare time that might become available to do [his] own work."[5]

During the school year 1900–1901, Mauss's first conference was a "succinct history of the religions of India" (pre-Buddhist Brahmanism, Buddhism, Jainism, and the various religious movements contemporary with ancient Buddhism) and an "analysis of the various systems of Hindu philosophy and explications of the Vedantic texts." Twenty-four students had signed up, including two graduate students and a few regular auditors. Mauss, some-what disappointed by his students, confided to Hubert at the end of the school year: "I have nothing but crackpots left at my lectures."[6] The next year Mauss was given the same assignment for the first semester; his confer-ence, taken by three students, was devoted to a "history and text explication of Yoga philosophy."[7]

As Sylvain Lévi's protégé, Mauss was thus living in what was then called "the cenacle." But the section of religious science was thrown into up-heaval by the deaths of two professors, Auguste Sabatier and Léon Marillier. Sabatier, who held the chair in Christian literature, died in April 1901. Dean of the faculty of Protestant theology at the Université de Paris and assistant director of the École Pratique des Hautes Études, he was the most famous of the French theologians. The author of books on the life of Jesus, the apostle Paul, and the Apocalypse, he was admired for "the scope and soundness of his knowledge, the rigorous integrity of his criticism, and the admira-bly constructive power of his philosophical thought."[8] In the first volume of *Année Sociologique*, Mauss had given a relatively positive evaluation of Sabatier's last book, *Esquisse d'une philosophie de la religion d'après la psychol-ogie de l'histoire* (Sketch of a philosophy of religion based on the psychology of history). It was, Mauss said, a work of philosophy and not of science; but its author was able to use a method both historical and comparative and had identified "the social element in religion." In addition, he "saw adequately the importance of a theory of prayer for a science of religion."[9]

Mauss considered applying for Sabatier's position, but only on the condi-tion that the name of the chair be changed. Hubert adopted the same posi-tion. The two friends analyzed the situation together, discussed strategy, and evaluated their respective chances. Hubert's first reaction was: "I must tell you I'm not at all set on going there for the moment. . . . Apart from the fact that I'd be very ashamed to go there before all of you." A colleague, Isidore Lévy, pressured him to apply, telling him that being hired by the École would be "the best means to secure his future at that good school." Lévy also thought that the professors were "afraid of hiring another Jew" and that Hubert would be "the only one capable of prying the Protestants at the school away from the Révilles."[10]

"Who should be brought into the place? You or me?" wondered Mauss. He consulted Sylvain Lévi, who believed "that something might be feasible" for him. Mauss, however, thought it would be "more feasible" for Hubert and in his own case "it's better to leave me in a temporary position that they will be forced to make permanent at some point."[11] Lévi finally came around to Mauss's arguments and decided to work toward Hubert's appoint-ment. There was a complex strategy. Lévi first had to approach Louis Liard, director of higher education, to get him to exert "pressure on the school and let Father Réville know he wanted a change" in the chair. Then he had to get the support of the École. Mauss, who "would make arrangements to vote," invited his friend to take "the necessary steps to the extent possible."[12] Hubert asked for letters of recommendation from Ernest Lavisse and Durkheim. Durkheim did not hesitate to support him, making a point to express his "high esteem" for Hubert: "He is one of the rare historians who, without losing his concern for exactitude and precision, has been able to go beyond the narrowly historical point of view and feels the need to break new ground."[13]

Even for Hubert, victory was far from assured. There were two opposing points of view: first, that the chair in Christian literature should be maintained (with Loisy and Monceau as candidates); second, that it should be opened up, either to Assyro-Babylonian religion (Fossey) or to the primitive religions of Europe (Hubert). Several professors defended the idea of keeping the chair in Christian literature; some, including Maurice Vernes and Jean Réville, secretary of the section, supported Loisy.

Alfred Firmin Loisy, though still a priest, was in a delicate situation at the time because of the "theological uproar" his writings had produced. A "modernist" in search of errors in the Bible, he had found himself forced by Cardinal Richard, bishop of Paris, to give up teaching at the Institut Catholique de Paris. Some professors at the École had already shown themselves to be "extremely reserved" about his candidacy, fearing that despite his more liberal views, he "would not be free to treat questions of biblical criticism" and would "subordinate criticism to dogma." Loisy, aware "that he was not yet adequately integrated into the school," knew his chances were poor. He would later say: "I would have been approved if I'd left the Church."[14]

Albert Réville, president of the section, declared his support for "adding the disciplines lacking" but did not make his preferences known.[15] The idea to "open" the chair was gaining ground, but Hubert's chances seemed slim. Adhémar Esmein, professor in the history of canonical law, stepped forward to restate the section's orientation: "We are a section of religious science above all; research on primitive religions serves sociology more than the science of religion. Studying them is interesting to us but not essential."[16]

At the committee meeting, members responsible for examining the candidates proposed creating a new course on Assyro-Babylonian religion and of assigning it to Charles Fossey. Fossey was a serious candidate: born in 1869 and an *agrégé* in letters (1890), he had already conducted archaeological expeditions to the Anti-Lebanon mountains, Syria, and Iraq. But several professors were against the proposal and openly defended Hubert's candidacy: they were Israël Lévi, Sylvain Lévi, Durembourg, Esmein, and Millet. For Sylvain Lévi, "there's a place waiting for Hubert in the section." He added that "not only had he personally appreciated his work, his learning, and his methods for a long time but all his teachers (Perrot, Durkheim, Durembourg, Carrière, S. Reinach, Bérard) were agreed in recognizing him as eminently qualified for teaching at the École."[17] The vote was very close, and Hubert emerged the winner only after three rounds.[18] Charles Fossey, defeated by two votes, was assigned to teach a course in the section; he received a regular teaching appointment only in 1907. In the meantime, he was hired by the Collège de France (in 1906) as professor of philology and Assyrian archaeology. Hubert's victory, as Durkheim pointed out, also belonged to sociology: "From an overall perspective, it is not without interest that sociology is moving into the École des Hautes Études. Though once again it's not on the bill, it's in the choice and in the person. There is reason to celebrate that."[19]

A few months later, in October 1901, the death of Léon Marillier took on the dimensions of a catastrophe for his family and for members of the section of religious science. The event was tragic in itself. A maritime disaster in Port-Béni killed Marillier's wife and sister-in-law in August and put him in the hospital. Marillier escaped almost miraculously, struggled for many long weeks, "wanting to recover so as to devote himself completely to acts of justice and kindness, in memory of vanished happiness," but in the end was "struck down."[20] He was not yet forty years old.

That sad event opened the way for Mauss to join the faculty of the École Pratique. Marillier had praised the section's former student when the first volume of *Année Sociologique* appeared: "The analyses of works related to religious studies have a scope, a precision, and an exactitude that do great honor to our collaborator M. Mauss, who is the author of most of them."[21] In addition Mauss, who was interested both in the history of religion and in the study of uncivilized peoples, appeared to be the heir to Marillier, whose teachings and writings he knew well. In 1901 he also provided three book reviews to *Revue de l'Histoire des Religions* and became one of its regular contributors. Mauss's name seemed unavoidable when considering who would succeed Léon Marillier, who taught the conference on the history of religions of uncivilized peoples. Learning of the tragic death, C. P. Tiele wrote Mauss: "It is a great loss for the school, the journal, and the science of history. I believe you have the right to apply to fill that vacant chair and I hope you'll be successful."[22]

Mauss immediately applied and asked for an interview with Albert Réville, president of the section of religious science. In preparation for that visit, Durkheim gave his nephew some advice: "Watch yourself. Don't let anything slip that will detonate and astonish that old man. . . . Let him lead the conversation. Don't press him pointlessly. You've come so that he can get to know you, not so you can preach to him."[23]

The president of the section did not hide his sympathy for Mauss.[24] But Mauss was not the only one in the race. Abbé Loisy, assigned to teach a course on "Babylonian myths and the first chapters of Genesis," considered for a time reapplying. He finally gave up, convinced "that he would once more be doomed to failure."[25] Two other candidates, Ernest Bertrand and Louis Duvau, asked that the title of the chair be changed, the former proposing it be on the history of Protestant dogmatics, the latter, on Germanic and Scandinavian religions. The problem of "redundancy" was quickly raised.

The idea of devoting a conference to Germanic and Scandinavian religions seemed appealing, as Jean Réville noted. But, he added, "it is not possible to eliminate the direct study of the religions of uncivilized peoples from the curriculum," especially since Hubert's conference would not replace it. His friend's presence, far from hurting Mauss's chances as some might have feared (given his close collaboration with Hubert), actually helped Mauss, in that Hubert's course "was closely related to studies on Germanic and Scandinavian religions."[26]

Durkheim personally intervened with Louis Liard, pointing out that "to eliminate that course is to eliminate a good part of the school of comparative religious science; alongside folklore, religious ethnography is the starting point for that field of research."[27] Saying he was ignorant of protocol, Durkheim did not urge his nephew to introduce himself to Liard. But he dictated his behavior to him: "If you go . . . be more cautious. . . . Don't look like you want a commitment from him. Indicate how you understand your teaching, let him sense the true nature of your work. Don't give the impression you'll move heaven and earth, beware of big words, and by all means don't get carried away."[28]

By a vote of eight to four, the committee members decided to keep the chair on the religions of uncivilized peoples. The way was now clear for Mauss, though some professors were afraid he dealt only with "general questions" and primarily "methodology." An aggressive Jules Toutain quoted a passage from Hubert and Mauss's study on sacrifice to prove that Mauss was "unduly concerned with methodology." Convinced there was no candidate who corresponded "completely to the desired conditions for teaching the religious history of the uncivilized," Toutain suggested creating a course on Assyro-Chaldean religion. But Sylvain Lévi and Israël Lévi came to Mauss's defense and cited Frazer's and Tiele's positive evaluations. Sylvain Lévi added: "Mauss has oriented his studies for many long years toward ethnology. He studied Sanskrit and the Semitic languages just so he could directly study documents that seemed very important for religious ethnography."

Marcel was selected without opposition, with ten votes for and two abstentions. The committee also asked him to "continue his courses on the religions of India as M. Foucher's replacement until the latter returns."

In the institution where he himself had studied, Mauss thus found himself at home with his collaborator and "twin" Henri Hubert and his teacher and "second uncle" Sylvain Lévi. Lévi hurried to write Durkheim and confide he was "happy to have been able to get Marcel a regular position in a place he is made for." And he added: "I don't doubt his genius; rather, I doubt his reliability."[29] As his former teacher Espinas also told him, Mauss was "in the right place": he could now "take on the formidable problems, formidable because of their complexity, and introduce students to them."[30]

The new professor did not hide the fact that "discovering the true nature of religious facts raises real difficulties." In his opening public lecture, the text of which would be published in *Revue de l'Histoire des Religions*, Mauss did not confine himself to praising his predecessor; he also sought to present the main lines of his teaching. The title of the conference, "History of the Religions of Uncivilized Peoples," irritated him. According to him, it conveyed prejudices that were commonly shared, even in educated circles. So-called primitive peoples were usually considered "savages" or "big children" distinguished by their bizarre behavior—cannibalism, deformation of the body, tattooing, totemism, magic, and so on—and peculiar beliefs. They were called naïve and considered devoid of intelligence. Mauss's position was unambiguous:

> There are no uncivilized peoples. There are only peoples from different civilizations. The hypothesis of "natural" man has been definitively abandoned. . . . Let us leave aside these pointless speculations on the paradisiacal man or the horde of pithecanthropines. Let us quite simply understand by "uncivilized peoples" peoples that, in the hierarchy of known societies, occupy a very low place. These are small, sparse social groups with limited habitats even when they are nomadic, with rudimentary languages and technical skills and with sufficiently elementary legal, familial, religious, and economic systems.[31]

There was an "enormous quantity of facts to be studied," with Indonesian and Oceanian populations as the privileged field. Mauss, already familiar with the ethnographic literature, having reviewed it in bulk for *Année Sociologique*, asserted the value of "recent observations by ethnographers" and praised their "precision, richness, reliability, and certainty." On that point, Mauss moderated the views he had expressed in "Essay on the Nature and Function of Sacrifice." Of course he was still critical toward certain witnesses (for their poor observations or untrustworthiness, their prejudices, their vague information), sometimes to the point of losing his temper. "When will the explorers spare us their literature and confine themselves to writing only about what they've seen, or, even better, to publishing only maps, itineraries, and their travel journals?"[32] But his overall evaluation was positive. "There are massive reliable documents, a host of truthful witnesses. Genuine facts are proliferating. They have not failed science; it is the scientists who have failed to observe them."[33] It was time to set to work.

In his conference, Mauss proposed, first, to train his students in "bibliographical research, as exhaustive as possible, fruitful whenever called for," beginning with the study of ethnographic texts on magic among the Melanesians. He then intended to devote himself to "connecting facts, synthesis," by analyzing the "elementary forms of prayer" in Australia and Melanesia. His program, both precise and ambitious, was marked by what he called "methodological caution." Wary of general theories, Mauss wanted "to remain within the area of religious and social facts" and, rather than seek the "general motives that may have inspired religious acts," confine himself to "explaining a religious fact by other religious facts or other social facts."[34]

Teaching

For Mauss, his inaugural lecture was an opportunity to indicate the spirit and aspirations of his future teaching. But was it a "turning point in his thought," as Condominas suggests?[35] The eternal student emerged from his uncle's shadow to begin his career as a professor and researcher and began to surround himself with students, some of whom would become his collaborators. Yet in his lecture he makes no reference to Durkheim. Was he distancing himself or simply exercising caution for tactical reasons? In any case, in 1904–1905 and 1905–1906, the course he would offer on "the relationship between the family and religion in North America" would be inspired by his uncle's unpublished research.

As Jean Réville remarked in his praise of the new professor, Mauss made a name for himself in the scientific world primarily through his active collaboration on *Année Sociologique*. It was "one of the most eloquent proofs of the enormous progress that studies in religious history and psychology made in the last years of the nineteenth century."[36] Mauss was still one of his uncle's closest collaborators. But at the École Pratique he took great care not to proselytize. In order to dispel a prejudice against him, he was later anxious to explain himself: "In my chair in the history of the religions of uncivilized peoples, I was faithful to the baroque title it bore and to the spirit of the École des Hautes Études. I taught only from a rigorously historical, critical, noncomparative point of view, even when the facts I was studying interested me only from a comparative point of view. I never practiced militant sociology."[37]

Twice a week, in an oblong room overlooking rue Saint-Jacques and decorated with aquatints and a few Byzantine mosaics, Mauss met with his students around an enormous rectangular table made of dark wood. The young professor was impressive and attractive: tall, his face framed by a light brown beard, regular features, shining eyes. Despite a somewhat hollow voice and slow speech, his conversation was said to be "sparkling."[38] His students fondly remembered their first contact with him: "Mauss was friendly in a most seductive way. Rather than disciples, he had comrades whom he brought into the movement. You'd have had to know him in his youth. He was older than we were and already famous, and he visited us in our student rooms with the elegant simplicity of an artist. His conversation was literally entrancing; and after he left, we gratefully washed the cup from which he had taken our tea."[39] There was nothing stiff about him; he had "a spontaneity, a gift for improvisation that would have been dangerous if he had not possessed a vast and rich store of knowledge."

The first year, about fifteen students were enrolled in his class. Mauss wrote Hubert, "My teaching is a colossal success. I had as many as fifteen students."[40] Because he abhorred teaching that was too formal, Mauss deviated from the lecture format and adopted that of the seminar. He rarely wrote out the substance of his classes, preferring to use note cards and to discuss books he placed on a table in front of him. His method was inspired by the tradition established by his predecessor, Léon Marillier: the critical study of documents as a group.[41] There was considerable ethnographic documentation. As his students liked to say, Mauss "knew everything." "He has a gift for reading and for retaining what he's read and is interested in the most various questions. . . . He has extensive knowledge not only of history and classical antiquity, but of political economy, law, psychology."[42] Anything was apt to be considered: the sacred texts of India, Germanic or Celtic laws, Gallic customs, Scandinavian myths, and so on. Students learned to respect various authors: Frazer, Eliot Smith, W.H.R. Rivers, Charles Gabriel Seligman, Malinowski, William Armstrong, K.J. Preuss, Richard Thurnwald, and others. There were also studies from the Royal Anthropological Institute and the Smithsonian Institution. And Mauss did not hesitate to cite studies by his colleagues at *Année Sociologique*.

Mauss wanted to expose students to ethnographic facts. He said he was a "positivist who believes only in the facts, even conceding the higher certainty of the descriptive sciences when compared to the theoretical sciences (in the case of complex phenomena)."[43] That orientation was obvious from the early years: "A careful inventory of all the known facts about oral rites among the Australians" (1901–1902); "Determine to what extent the facts reported were accurate" (1903–1904); "Students participated . . . in sociological analysis and classification of facts" (1906–1907). Mauss's pedagogical approach stressed the empirical dimension, because he wanted to develop instruments for data collection in response to requests. In 1903–1904 he composed a folklore questionnaire and a technology questionnaire for a survey to be done in Korea; then, in 1906–1907, he wrote a guide containing ethnographic instructions for directly observing the populations of the French colonies in western Africa and the Congo. That guide, composed at the request of the Comité de l'Afrique Française (Committee on French Africa) was to include "general instructions, directions for collecting objects, and special instructions concerning the main classes of social phenomena."[44]

The connection Mauss established between his teaching and his own research was relatively direct. He would say: "My classes never entirely coincided with my own work." But he added: "I taught the material for the first volume (on prayer) several times."[45] The first two classes he taught dealt with the "elementary forms of prayer" and with documents concerning "magic in Melanesia." These were his two main research concerns.

Nevertheless, in 1903–1904, Mauss was no longer taking prayer as the subject for his Monday conference. Had he set aside his thesis? His mother was worried: "It's already 1903 and I never hear anything about your thesis anymore! Yet you've been working on it for eight full years and I wonder if I'll ever have the joy of seeing you finish it."[46] Mauss would return to it a few years later and in his classes would analyze "the origins of formulary rites in Australia" (1908–1909) and "primitive forms of religious language" (1912–1913). For three years, his Monday conference was devoted to "the analytical and critical study of ethnographic documents concerning relations between the family and religion in North America." That course, inspired by Durkheim's studies on the family and marriage, dealt first with totemism, then, in 1905–1906, with the institution of the potlatch and more generally "primitive forms of collective contracts, exchanges of legal and religious services among groups." In 1904–1905 Mauss also presented the results of the major study he was conducting in collaboration with Henri Beuchat on "relations between the social, seasonal morphology of the Eskimos and their religious and legal phenomena."

Marcel Mauss's Courses at the École Pratique des Hautes Études, 1900–1914

East Indian Religion
   1900–1901
      Concise History of the Religions of India
      Analysis of the Various Systems of Philosophy and Explication of
         Vedantic Texts
   1901–1902
      History and Explication of Yoga Philosophy Texts

The Religions of Uncivilized Peoples
   1901–1902
      Studies in the Elementary Forms of Prayer
      Critical Study of Documents on Magic among the Melanesians
   1902–1903
      Theory of the Elementary Forms of Prayer (Australia, Melanesia)
      Analytical and Critical Explanation of Ethnographic Texts on Magic in
         Melanesia

1903–1904

> Analytical and Critical Study of Ethnographic Documents on the Relationship between the Family and Religion in North America
>
> General Theory of Magic and Its Relation to Religion

1904–1905

> Analytical and Critical Explication of Ethnographic Texts concerning the Relationship between the Family and Religion in North America
>
> Analysis of Basic Notions of Magic

1905–1906

> Analytical and Critical Explication of Ethnographic Texts concerning the Relationship between Religion and the Family in American Societies of the Northwest
>
> Secret Societies in North America

1906–1907

> *First semester*
>
> > Study of Ethnographic Texts concerning Ritual Prohibitions in Polynesia
>
> *Second semester*
>
> > Compilation of Ethnographic Instructions for Observing the Populations of the French Colonies in Western Africa and the Congo
> >
> > Study of African Religious Systems

1907–1908

> *First semester*
>
> > Instructions for Descriptive Sociology (continued)
>
> *Second semester*
>
> > Explication of Ethnographic Documents concerning the Religious Systems of Africa
> >
> > Relations between Religions and Clans among the Pueblo Indians

1908–1909

> *First semester (temporary replacement for R. Hertz's Tuesday conference)*
> > Analytical and Critical Study of Documents concerning Religions in Africa
>
> *Second semester*
>
> > Origins of Formulary Rituals: Australia

1909–1910

> Theory of the Origins of Formulary Ritual
>
> Analytical and Critical Explication of Documents concerning Ritual Prohibitions in New Zealand

1910–1911

> Theory of the Origins of Formulary Ritual
>
> Explication of Documents concerning Religious, Legal, and Economic Services between Clans in the Indian Tribes of the American Northwest

1911–1912

    Religious Language and Secular Language

    Analysis of Ethnographic Documents concerning Religious, Legal, and Economic Services between Phratries and Clans in the American Northwest

1912–1913

    Primitive Forms of Religious Language

    Primitive Forms of Collective Contracts and Exchanges in New Guinea

1913–1914

    Theory of the Origin of the Belief in the Virtue of Formulas: Critical Organization of Documents concerning Relations between Legal and Religious Organization

In his early years at the École Pratique, Mauss was also concerned with the study of magic. It was the subject of his Tuesday conference: "General Theory of Magic and Its Relation to Religion," "Analysis of the Basic Notions of Magic," and so on. He published two major studies on the subject: "The Origin of Magical Powers in Australian Societies" for *Annuaire de l'École Pratique des Hautes Études, Section des Sciences Religieuses* and "Outline of a General Theory of Magic" for *Année Sociologique*. He then diversified his fields of interest, dealing with "secret societies in the American Northwest" (1905–1906), with "relations between religion and clans among the Pueblo Indians" (1907–1908), and with "ritual prohibitions in New Zealand" (1909–1910). With Durkheim he coauthored a long study on "some primitive forms of classifications" for *Année Sociologique* (1903) and in his courses granted particular attention to the analysis of religious representations.

5

CITIZEN MAUSS

W HEN MAUSS returned to Paris in July 1898, he once more found himself in the midst of political turmoil. Jaurès was about to publish a series of articles he called "Proofs" in the newspaper *Petite République*. Things happened in quick succession: with the discovery that evidence against Dreyfus had been forged, Lieutenant Colonel Henry was arrested and then committed suicide; Ferdinand Esterhazy fled.

With Lucien Herr and Charles Andler

The "intellectuals" were still a small group, but they held certain bastions from which they exerted their influence, including the École Normale Supérieure, pro-Dreyfus for the most part, and the publishing house Librairie Bellais, which the poet and writer Charles Péguy had purchased with his wife's dowry in 1898. At twenty-two, Péguy was a "small, ruddy, high-colored man with close-cropped hair; a light brown beard curling at the cheeks and chin; bright, sharp, penetrating, and mischievous brown eyes; a straight nose and delicate mouth; and a flat but engaging voice." Hubert Bourgin recalled that he was "the clearest and staunchest of social-ists."[1] He recruited young socialist Normalians to protect Dreyfusard professors at the Sorbonne—Ferdinand Buisson, Alphonse Aulard, and Charles Seignobos—who were being threatened by anti-Semitic gangs. Péguy was the leader of that "little army of justice and truth" "on days when there was fighting"; Lucien Herr was its leader "on days when there was no fighting."[2] They sometimes had to face mobs of nationalist and anti-Semitic law students.[3] The Librairie Bellais, located on the corner of rue Cujas and rue Victor-Cousin, a short walk from the offices of *Revue Blanche*, became the headquarters for Latin Quarter Dreyfusism.

After returning from abroad, Mauss became one of the regulars at Péguy's publishing house. There he found Lucien Herr, who was more of an activ-ist, more revolutionary than he, and who was attempting to organize young people. A librarian at the École Normale, Herr inspired confidence by his strength, his discretion, and his impartiality. As Bourgin has noted, for stu-dents and all those close to him he was the "great inspiration, the great pro-vider of intellectual nourishment." But the "severe and powerful guard" was also a "passionately verbose" political militant: "All these opinions, all these schools, all these systems, all these parties who raised the flag out in the open or wore the leftist label in the shadows, he served or helped them, or they were able to cite his collaboration, his authority, or simply his name."[4] Herr made the shift from Paul Brousse's possibilism to Allemanism in 1890 and, when the Parti Ouvrier Socialiste Révolutionnaire(POSR) was founded, he participated in the major debates among the different factions surrounding the journal *Mouvement Socialiste.*

Mauss was quite willing to have Herr serve as a "constant and well-heeded adviser." He had known him "forever," as he himself pointed out. "I heard of him through Durkheim. . . . His fame was known to me from the age of fifteen. . . . Even though Herr was still infatuated with metaphysics on the one hand and history and politics on the other and was never a strict sociologist, he was one of the people who had best known, appreciated, popularized, and promoted Durkheim's and his students' work."[5]

When he arrived in Paris, Mauss got in touch with Herr. The first meeting took place at Seignobos's home, where he was taken by his friends Edgar and Albert Milhaud. The young militant, who was preparing for his *agrégation* at the time, was fascinated by the "ideal of force, of learning, of good sense as it were" that the older man seemed to embody. He also shared his political ideas: "Our socialism brought us together. At the time, he was in the POSR like my friends . . . and Allemane often spoke of him with respect and affection." Herr took an interest in Mauss and was utterly frank with him about his work and "adventures." The two traveled together and became friends, though Mauss addressed the older man as "sir" and was never at ease using his name.[6] In 1926, after her husband died, Jeanne L. Herr confided to Mauss: "My husband cared very much for you and your affection was precious to him."[7]

Mauss would say that Herr's authority, enthusiasm, and encouragement led "many of us to recognize our vocation."[8] It was "in great part out of sympathy" for Herr that "Henri Hubert's political views became tinged with socialism" and that Hubert became "one of the most zealous and reliable directors" of Péguy's publishing house. Hubert "really worshipped" the École Normale librarian and had served as his assistant in 1893–1894, considering him "a model, for himself and for others, of moral and scientific [integrity], of disinterested work, teamwork, and impartiality."[9]

Herr was someone who, in friendship and in political action, was unreservedly passionate. According to Mauss, that quality often blinded him. One of his errors was to believe in Péguy, admiring his "frankness, physical vigor, eloquence, and love of grandeur" and picturing him as the "Rousseau of our time." Mauss proved "rather cool" toward Péguy at their first meetings; he did not much like his long poem *Le mystère de la charité de Jeanne d'Arc* (The mystery of the charity of Joan of Arc), which he found "printed brilliantly but poorly thought out and only just poetic enough in its rhythms and images." It took all Herr's influence to convince Mauss to "follow Péguy" and, for example, "be among the troops he commanded" at the funeral in 1899 of Félix Faure, president of the French Republic from 1895 to 1899 and opponent of a new trial for Dreyfus. Péguy did show an interest in sociology: He reviewed *Suicide* in *Revue Socialiste* and, in his "first dialogue on the harmonious society," which he called *Marcel,* he described sociologists who "do their surveys of citizens and of the commonwealth as best they can, and then offer them to the citizens."[10]

Mauss quickly came to despise the young writer's immoderate ambition, lack of caution, and unreasonableness, and was less and less accommodating toward the poet's "unilateral and monolithic thinking," criticizing him for "always being up to his tricks."[11] He wrote Hubert that Péguy was a "dangerous madman."[12]

There was something incendiary in Péguy's nature, notes the historian Daniel Halévy: "Everything was burning around him, friends were consumed, enemies devoured by fire; too often, alas, friendships themselves were singed and damaged by sometimes bitter violence."[13] Because of Péguy's idealism and lack of experience—for example, he optimistically printed more than ten thousand copies of Jaurès's articles under the title *Action Socialiste*—the Librairie Bellais ran into difficulties and, to avoid bankruptcy, had to accept Lucien Herr's financial aid and the creation of a new publishing venture, the Société Nouvelle de Librairie et d'Édition. In January 1900, Péguy finally began to publish *Cahiers de la Quinzaine,* an informational and educational journal that presented itself as a companion to *Mouvement Socialiste* and *Revue Socialiste.*[14]

The Société Nouvelle de Librairie et d'Édition sought to bring together "men wishing to be useful in intellectual labor and popular education" and appealed "to the kindness of all men interested in justice and truth, all those who want to express a useful empathy for an act of disinterested cooperation." These were intellectuals, Normalians, professors who wanted "to do scientific publishing and salubrious commerce, tendentious but scholarly and honest publishing, honest yet remunerative commerce." The administrative board, headed by Lucien Herr, included Léon Blum, Hubert Bourgin, François Simiand, and Mario Roques.

The new board members, coping with Péguy and his "mocking retorts, sudden plans, and sharp-edged paradoxes and formulas," managed to stay together thanks only to Herr's discipline and authority. Misunderstandings multiplied between the society's new administrators and Péguy, who was accorded the title "publisher's representative." After the press declined to publish Antonin Lavergne's *Jean Coste,* these misunderstandings led to legal action and a breakup "under terms in equal parts unpleasant and unexpected." There was no way out, explained Mauss: "Péguy certainly exceeded the limits of acceptable behavior. I have no hesitation in saying so. . . . At that time, I definitively parted ways with Péguy and never said another word to him or even nodded in his direction."[15] The poet would take his revenge for Mauss's abandonment:

> At the École Normale [the Sorbonne], rubbing shoulders with professors led me to hope for a long time, or rather, allowed me to hope, that I too would acquire, would achieve that academic elegance, the only authentic kind. . . . Oh yes, I too hoped that some day I'd have that supreme distinction, that finesse, that supreme elegance of [Marcel] Mauss (not the wine merchant), the diction, the severe, impeccable, implacable diction, the finesse of a file cabinet. . . . But I have to give up. Forty years have gone by. Now I must give up. I must capitulate. That elegance of Mauss's. I can't hide anything from you. The dream of my sleepless nights, the image of my feverish nights. That elegance of Mauss's, mustn't think about it anymore. That elegance of Mauss's, must give it up. That ne plus ultra, that delicate profile, that noble, assured gaze, not loutish at all, that flowery language, those pleasing lips, that jacket, democratic but elegant, democratic but sober, democratic but severe, that beard, curly, fiery red, blond, golden yellow glowing red, golden yellow flaming red, well trimmed four-cornered falling, tapering falling, secretly glowing, that mustache, not precisely, not vulgarly, not crudely swaggering but triumphantly royal in almost the same color, those long sociologist pants, those republican cuffs, that elegant vertical pleat in the pants, so evenly, so equitably remunerative, that elegant High German way of speaking, that lily-and-rose complexion, must give it up.[16]

The Société Nouvelle pursued its activities nonetheless, initially publishing a few quality works: *Revue d'histoire moderne et contemporaine de la France* (Overview of modern and contemporary French history) by Georges Brière, Hubert Bourgin, Paul Caron, and Philippe Sagnac, and *Catalogue bibliographique des sciences sociales* (Bibliographical catalog of the social sciences). They also started a series, "La Bibliothèque socialiste" (The socialist library), which published, notably, Maurice Lauzel's *Manuel du coopérateur socialiste* (Handbook on socialist cooperation) and the Belgian socialist Émile Vandervelde's *Le collectivisme et l'évolution industrielle* (Collectivism and industrial development). Between 1900 and 1906 more than thirty-five titles appeared, including books by Alexandre Millerand, Anatole France, and Léon Blum, and a translation of Karl Marx's *Communist Manifesto* with an introduction and commentary by Charles Andler. Andler, born in Strasbourg in 1866 and an *agrégé* in German (1899), had been a *maître de conférence* since 1893 at the École Normale Supérieure. A possibilist socialist, he wrote his doctoral thesis on the origins of state socialism in Germany (1897).

The publishing house also organized a socialist school, the École Socialiste, whose aim was to "instruct ignorant or indifferent students."[17] The school was set up in the offices of the Union Mouffetard, the people's university in the fifth arrondissement. On the curriculum were courses on the history of socialist doctrines and parties, on economic organization (cooperatives, trade unions), and on social legislation. A place was also made for the lecturers' particular interests. The objective for those such as Fauconnet, Mauss, and Simiand, who were seeking "a foundation for socialism in sociology itself," was "to inform first, then prepare for action." The idea was to present not "pompous lectures" but "simple talks, familiar lessons, followed, if advisable, by discussions or observations."[18] The "talks" Mauss gave usually had to do with the cooperative movement.

Several organizers of the socialist school taught at the École Normale Supérieure, and its hard-core members were part of the journal *Mouvement Socialiste*,[19] whose director was Hubert Lagardelle (1875–1958), founder of the group Jeunesse Socialiste (socialist youth). His managing editor, Jean Longuet (1876–1938), was Karl Marx's grandson and socialist leader Paul Lafargue's nephew. Once a member of the POF, Lagardelle had left it when the Guesdist party refused to commit itself openly to Dreyfusism; he then moved closer to Jaurès and supported his theses at the Japy congress in 1899. In its first issue, *Mouvement Socialiste* published an article by Jaurès on "socialist unity." The journal's objective was to "give an exact representation of the socialist movement as a whole" at both a theoretical and a practical level, whether in the description of experiments done or attempted by the proletariat or in the diffusion of information on politics, economics, statistics, syndicalism, the cooperative movement, or municipal affairs.[20]

Rejecting both "dogmatic oversimplification" and "empirical reformism," *Mouvement Socialiste* wanted to remain faithful to its principles without practicing exclusivism. It intended to devote a large amount of space to discussion, since "the essence of socialist thought is free examination and free criticism." Lagardelle gathered around him the better part of the Groupe des Étudiants Collectivistes, his old friends: Philippe Landrieu, Georges Fauquet, and Louis Révelin. That team expanded during the Dreyfus Affair with the arrival of André Morizet, Jules Ubry, Mauss, and Fauconnet. A connection was also established with other Normalians or former Normalians: Blum, Mario Roques, Simiand, Albert Thomas. In Lafargue's expression, these were "intellectuals comme il faut." The Société Nouvelle de Librairie et d'Édition hailed the journal.

Mauss, aware of the importance "of organizing classes into groups of socialist students to give socialism orators, lecturers, and writers," also played an active role in the new Fédération des Jeunesses Socialistes Révolutionnaires (Federation of revolutionary socialist youth). That federation, created in early 1899 by Jean Longuet following rifts within the student movement, also wanted to mark itself off from the Guesdist influence prominent at the time. Not abandoning his role as a professor, Mauss insisted in his courses on the "necessary study of the facts." He assigned each member a social studies project and, "on the designated day, he collected it and made corrections."[21]

In the lecture he gave to the Groupe des Étudiants Collectivistes in March 1899, Mauss, following Jaurès in *Petite République,* attempted to define "social action," which he saw as "equally distant from pure passivity and blind revolt, as far from empty scholastic disputes as from negation." He said that action was known to be "rational" and "inspired by existing facts explained by a scientific method of observation"; but no one could say "what it is in itself." For Mauss, socialist action was "mental" in the first place, since socialism was itself a "phenomenon of consciousness." The militant drew on Durkheimian sociology to make his argument: "Property, law, and workers' organizations are social facts, real facts corresponding to the real structure of society. But these are not material facts; they exist only in the minds of men assembled into a society. These are mental facts—economic facts themselves are social facts (money, value, etc.) and thus mental facts, just like all the other social facts connected to them, which they determine and which are determined by them, property law for example."[22]

All efforts had to be directed "toward bringing about a new way of seeing, thinking, and acting in the minds of individuals and in the entire social group." What was that "new attitude"? Mauss spoke of a "new way of behaving in relation to the facts," a "new law," a "new social hierarchy," a "new system of values," and a "new moral system of rewards and punishments." That was "the form, the bold framework of steel of the society of tomorrow, which must be forged in our own time." And anyone who wanted to build the "collectivist society" now had to develop "the socialist mind": "What, then, is the socialist mind? . . . It consists of the rational formation of an ideal, a socialist or, if you prefer, collectivist goal. . . . To be socialist is to want to change the legal forms of present-day society in the direction of greater socialization. . . . It is to want an acceleration in social evolution. Socialist action is essentially a conscious action in the interest of the collectivity."[23]

A voluntarist who thought that the will was the dominant force in constituting the world, Mauss distanced himself from economism, the belief that economic interests were the determining factor. And though socialist action was "an action to transform society, a social action," it had to act on "society as a whole" through a social group—the party. "Socialism is a new social fact, historically unique. . . . It is, as it has always been, the agitator of the social question in its entirety. . . . Socialism is even now the agent of the future society. Not only does it want to dissolve present-day society, it wants and can construct the necessary society."[24]

For Mauss, however, the idea was not to "get locked into a Bible": "By what right do our critics limit us to a narrow, distorted, and intentionally diminished Marx?" Aware that "action always precedes theory," he emphasized two fields of action where it was possible to begin "the total emancipation of the proletariat within capitalist society": the trade union and the socialist cooperative. These movements seemed to be purely economic, but "as foundations of the future society," they were the expression of a "new form of social consciousness" with "the advent of a new legal organ, new principles of action, new incentives for sacrifice and solidarity." The trade union had an "awe-inspiring role." Not only did it "improve the individual's fate" but also and above all it asked "for subordination and sacrifice from every person." Mauss placed himself within the tradition of the "best scientists," including Durkheim, who believed the movement was a "new form of acting and thinking," a "new type of life toward which we are moving with all our strength."[25]

The socialist cooperative also represented "more than a powerful, colossal interest group." It was "something infinitely rich, phenomenally fertile," where a great "economic vigor" and an "incomparable force of idealism, justice, impartiality, and intellectual and moral energy manifested itself all at once."

Mauss presented syndicalism and cooperation as ways "to live the socialist life immediately," that is, "to have the proletariat in the capitalist regime live right now, as much as possible, its future life, in the form of the most complete communism, the most rational solidarity, the most conscious and the most autonomous action." In so doing, he relegated political action to a secondary role or, rather, to its "just and legitimate" place, and attributed a much broader aim to socialism, both humanitarian and revolutionary. Socialism was humanitarian because it was steeped in justice, law, and freedom: "Socialism has never been a matter of big money." It was revolutionary, but not in the narrow, anarchical sense of the word: "Social revolution is entirely social and mental; it has already come about in each of us. We all sense the outmoded nature of bourgeois society, the need for the collectivist society, and we feel that in our minds, as it will some day be in actuality, there is no slow transition between the two societies, no simply quantitative modification, but an abrupt transition, an organic modification."[26]

The text of Mauss's lecture on "socialist action" appeared in *Mouvement Socialiste*, which, like other journals and most scientific publications, attested to the originality of French socialism, which was both politically engaged and open to new ideas, without narrow partisanship.

But the socialist movement was in complete turmoil at the time. The actions of intellectuals and, especially, students' newly awakened interest in scientific socialism elicited intense theoretical debates. Like many young intellectuals, Mauss became involved in them and contributed to the emergence of a unified socialism, opposed to the intransigence of the Guesdists, whose platform included opposition to any compromise with the existing government. As Andler noted, these were far from Mauss's usual concerns. Jaurès would be the symbolic figure for that unified socialism.

The Japy Congress

On the eve of the Japy congress in December 1899, Herr, Andler, and other collaborators at the publishing house founded the Groupe d'Unité Socialiste (Group of socialist unity), the militant wing of the Société Nouvelle de Librairie et d'Édition: "We combined action through the book with action through the spoken word," explained Andler. "We did not want to compromise the budding unity. We had great hopes for it. . . . Our group met at the publishing house on Sunday mornings."[27]

More than seven hundred delegates met in Salle Japy—Guesdists, Blanquists, Allemanists, and independents. They included Péguy, from the Groupe d'Études Sociales des Anciens Étudiants du Lycée d'Orléans (Social studies group of the alumni of the Orléans *lycée*); Blum, from the Groupe d'Unité Socialiste (Socialist unity group); and Mauss, from the Groupe des Étudiants Collectivistes de Montpellier (Group of collectivist students from Montpellier). Speaking in the name of *Mouvement Socialiste,* Mauss said he was "completely happy": "No one knows what will come out of the congress, but everyone feels it constitutes an event."[28]

Mouvement Socialiste supported unity. Although a crisis erupted when Alexandre Millerand joined the Republican Union cabinet formed by René Waldeck-Rousseau in June 1899—becoming the first socialist to serve in a bourgeois cabinet—leaders of the socialist movement considered support of the government a "question of tactics" and thus secondary. Priority had to be given to organizing the party. As Mauss explained: "To proceed otherwise is to expose ourselves to the most serious rifts" at a time when unity was necessary at both the national level ("we are burdened with heavy responsibilities in our country") and the international level ("international socialism demands it").[29]

Unity, acquired at a tumultuous time, was fragile. A compromise motion condemned participation in the government while approving it under exceptional circumstances. A resolution adopted by acclamation stipulated the establishment of a permanent general committee combining the five organizations represented and ensuring control of the press. Péguy was poorly received: He was called "Thief! Liar! Bounder! Murderer!" and came away disappointed by the congress. He felt that Jaurès had conceded the battle to Guesde. The congress marked the poet's break with official socialism. Herr notified him that their political and personal relationship was over: "You are an anarchist: We will march against you with all our might."[30]

Although the socialists saw themselves as a party, they were still only a collection of organizations representing various currents. Their splintering was to be expected. But after the congress, Mauss was optimistic: "The Parti Socialiste Français is beginning to unify in peace. . . . Socialism is more alive than ever. Since the congress, the activity of all our organizations has been almost feverish." He saw his party, the party of reform and social revolution, "attracting new militants every day and every day advancing with a more assured step toward its political and economic goal."[31]

He explained that, after dedicating their "forces . . . to the fight for the most mediocre of Republics, for humanity and justice"—in short, after being Dreyfusards—socialists ought to be concerned with their "own action" and "work energetically on propaganda." The circumstances appeared "infinitely favorable": the country was calm, the reactionary parties had been rooted out. But the "reaction" was not dead, nor was anti-Semitism, which had become "the economic and political doctrine of the petty bourgeoisie." According to Mauss, therefore, the socialist party could not "rest on its laurels." He was not opposed to the idea of a form of propaganda that would be "primarily economic, socialist, and revolutionary." "Of course, the class struggle must be directed exclusively against capitalism, which is not one faction or another of the bourgeoisie but the bourgeoisie as a whole (including the petty bourgeoisie, heed me well, citizen candidates!)." But, he added, socialist propaganda was not serious unless it also attacked clericalism, militarism, and nationalism.[32]

But a rift occurred at the following national congress in Salle Wagram in December 1900, when delegates of the Parti Ouvrier walked out. Support of the government was once more the question that pitted the two largest socialist groups against each other. Jaurès's faction supported it; the other faction, led by Guesde and Vaillant, rejected any form of cooperation. Like his friends, Mauss was "saddened by the scission between Jaurès and Guesde and Vaillant."

Durkheim, observing the political intrigues from Bordeaux, had a hard time understanding his nephew's sorrow: "The socialism of socialists like Guesde and all the rest is the worst there is. Those people are lousy politicians, no better than your average opportunist, worse even. It was therefore altogether desirable that the separation should come about. Class socialism, which reduces the social question to the worker question, is produced by the uneducated and the hateful." According to Durkheim, there was "much to do, good things. We must help Jaurès and his friends gradually become aware of who they are and put an end to a misunderstanding that serves to perpetuate bourgeois traditionalism." And he concluded: "For myself, I am ready to do everything I can toward that aim."[33]

Mauss did not need his permission. He was swept along by socialist action: meetings, lectures, articles in *Mouvement Socialiste,* participation at the congresses of the socialist and cooperative movement. Jaurès asked him to come to *Petite République* to meet with him. Jean Longuet urged him to "do whatever is possible, and even what is impossible to come to a meeting" concerning an article written by Péguy for *Revue Blanche.*[34] Lagardelle invited him to dinner at his home with the German socialist Karl Kautsky.[35]

Finally, there was the "socialist project of La Maison du Peuple [People's center] on the Left Bank."[36] Mauss explained that, as in Belgium, it would be "a school with a communist administration, a school of fraternity and law, an example of collective property, an act of worker and popular solidarity."

Mauss was not always at ease in the political circles he frequented. He expected the Lyons congress (July 1901) to be "a hodgepodge. Upstanding men are rare, imbeciles make up the world at large."[37] There were also squabbles, with Hubert Lagardelle, for instance. Disappointed by Millerand, Lagardelle abandoned Jaurès and the Société Nouvelle de Librairie et d'Édition. Mauss reprimanded him: "I find the perpetual criticism of individuals unbearable when I see that the real work is not being done. Around me all efforts are dispersed and scattered. I'm distressed about it but am resolved to do everything to reduce the level of anarchy."[38]

Despite the differences and divisions, Mauss did not forget "the efforts that unite them" and remained associated with *Mouvement Socialiste*, "the only socialist journal he knew." He found "the polemics annoying," but he continued to buy subscriptions for his "Épinal comrades." In 1902 Mauss published an article in that journal on the war in the Transvaal, a war no one was paying any attention to. Deploring the absence of a "true human consciousness, which will one day make men join together in solidarity the way citizens of a single nation do today," he expressed regret that no "serious efforts" were being made in France "to rouse public opinion." "Some organize, others want to reform, still others want to make revolution. No one is educating." There was nothing but verbiage and doctrinarism, ideology. He lamented that "for socialism, human solidarity is a sort of vague formula, it is not yet a traditional and active faith on the part of the universal proletariat."[39]

Mauss publicly distanced himself from Lagardelle when the latter gave a different orientation to *Mouvement Socialiste*, making it a review of new Marxist currents related to the development of revolutionary syndicalism. This new orientation would be made explicit in 1904. Issue 15, with more than fifty pages devoted to "insipid gossip, where slander is confused with documentation," irritated Mauss. Georges Sorel, he wrote, "vents his filthy bile on his best friends, on the people he respects the most."[40]

François Simiand and *Notes Critiques*

In 1900 the Société Nouvelle de Librairie et d'Édition decided to publish a bibliographical bulletin (*Notes Critiques: Sciences Sociales*), and the assistant editor, François Simiand, immediately turned to Mauss. "Fauconnet and Hubert must have spoken to you about our future social science criticism bulletin and I am expecting your cooperation.... As you undoubtedly know, I have Durkheim's approval."[41]

Simiand was one of the young Normalians living in "moral and intellectual intimacy" with Herr. He was at Herr's side during the Dreyfus Affair when Herr launched a revolutionary assault on the army, the church, the reactionary forces, discipline, and tradition. After the Dreyfusard battle, Simiand, the son of a teacher, entered the socialist fray. Bourgin said of him: "He was a sociologist and a socialist, and united in his person science and the apostolate, something [I found] indispensable and almost natural."[42] Simiand, an admirer of Jaurès, was anxious to find practical solutions and leaned toward administration. He did not hesitate to take on practical tasks alongside his "obstinately pursued scientific work": he published propaganda, headed a technical school to train personnel in cooperatives, and so on.[43] Mauss later said that Simiand, who became a librarian at the Ministry of Commerce and Labor, rendered "enormous services to our cause." He conducted countless surveys of the workers' movement, published the "Bibliothèque socialiste," edited many publications, and founded the École Socialiste. "The spirit of his career and of all his actions was that of a socialist entirely devoted to the study of society and, in society, of the interests of the proletariat, of wage labor." His was a spirit of sacrifice. "Whenever there was someplace to go, to make sacrifices, he was there."[44]

Simiand collaborated with the group of sociologists associated with Durkheim, contributing "thirty years of criticism and organization." There were close ties between *Année Sociologique* and *Notes Critiques*. Almost all contributors to *Année,* including Durkheim, analyzed books in *Notes Critiques.*[45] The overlap between the two journals would continue, since "some people would be recruited for *Année* after writing analyses in *Notes Critiques* (Claude E. Maître, Georges Vacher, Georges Gelly, Louis Gernet), whereas, for others, the collaboration began at nearly the same time (Bourgin, Chaillié, Halbwachs, Beuchat, Jean Reynier, Stickney)." Several of those new recruits were Mauss's and Hubert's students at the École Pratique des Hautes Études. Durkheim, overworked editing and organizing *Année,* seriously considered the possibility of "merging *Notes* with *Année*": "I'll do everything possible in that direction."[46]

The two journals did not merge and *Année Sociologique* still had its raison d'être. Fauconnet characterized it as follows: "To apply to the study of social facts the general method of the inductive sciences" and "to ask questions and sort out problems rationally, in short, to develop an 'objective sociology' through book reviews." It was thus out of the question for *Année* to deal with politics proper and review all the books written by socialists or on socialism. "The socialist doctrine and its movement are considered solely as social facts which there are good grounds for explaining."[47]

Between 1901 and 1904 Mauss published about fifteen book reviews in *Notes Critiques,* dealing for the most part with the history of religion and ethnography. He often analyzed the same works in *Année Sociologique.* His critiques were often harsh, focusing on methodological shortcomings and on misquotations.

The only political book Mauss reviewed in *Notes Critiques* was written in English: *The Cooperative Wholesale Societies Limited Annual*. He called it admirable for its many engravings and photoengravings, statistical tables, diagrams, and figures. Such a publication, he concluded, was proof of the "colossal success" of English cooperative federations.[48]

The Cooperator

For Mauss, cooperationism, in offering a limited form of socialism within the context of capitalism, was "one of the ways to have an impact on capitalist society."[49] In 1896–1897, he joined L'Avenir de Plaisance (The future of leisure), a small consumer cooperative, where he met Georges Fauquet, a medical student.

In the 1890s the cooperative movement made significant advances. There was a proliferation of consumer cooperatives: the finest example, Bellevilloise, was the largest cooperative in France. It had seven thousand members and offered various goods (bread, meat, coal, shoes, notions, groceries, wine). In 1896 the Verrerie Ouvrière (Workers' glassworks) in Albi was inaugurated as, in Jaurès's expression, a "true fortress of unionist and political freedom in the face of big management in defeat."

The socialist current that embraced Benoît Malon had "cooperatist sympathies" and, after a strike, created a cooperative in Puteaux called "Revendication."[50] But until the late 1890s the socialist movement opposed the cooperative movement. The Guesdists were not alone in thinking that cooperation diverted the working class from real revolutionary struggle by inadequately elaborating the problem of appropriating the means of production. This critical distance seemed particularly justified, given that a Christian socialist–inspired current—the Nîmes school—was developing within the cooperative movement. For that current, the consumer cooperative was not an instrument for social emancipation. For the economist Charles Gide, one of the chief theorists of the Nîmes school, cooperationism stood as a third way between capitalism and collectivism, and his ultimate objective was to build a "cooperative republic." Jaurès knew Gide and considered him a "free spirit," regretting that he clung to an "anticollectivist prejudice." But he was tempted to say that "despite this aversion or this lapse, he is a collectivist without knowing it."[51]

The cooperative question elicited many interpretations among socialists. In regions such as Nord, where the Parti Ouvrier was well rooted, militants used cooperatives as a place to spread their ideas and as a means for transformation. The intersection between cooperative economics and socialist politics came about only in 1895, with the founding of the Bourse des Coopératives Socialistes, or BCS (Socialist cooperatives center), whose growth would be "magnificent." About sixty "strong workers' societies" participated in what Mauss termed "regular debates, admirable for their wisdom and forcefulness."[52]

Differences of opinion remained great, however. Lagardelle called the consumer cooperative "a dupery born of a gross ignorance of capitalist mechanisms." And after asking if such a cooperative could be a "school for solidarity," he replied: "A disgraceful instrument for bringing people together is a defective school for solidarity." The distance separating revolutionary action from cooperation was the same as that "separating class instinct from class consciousness."[53] For any revolutionary militant, cooperationism appeared "useful to the proletariat only where—and insofar as—a strong syndicalist and political movement already exists."

Mauss closely followed the activities of the cooperative organizations for *Mouvement Socialiste*. He composed the report on the first international congress of socialist cooperatives, organized by the Bourse des Coopératives Socialistes, which was held in Paris from July 7 to July 10, 1900, the same year as the Universal Exposition.

Mauss judged the results of the congress to be largely positive. It created new organizations, clarified principles, and put a large portion of cooperative organizations "on an openly socialist path." In short, it was a "good and serious piece of work." In his summary of the debates, he presented the discussions concerning intercooperation (relations between socialist producer and consumer groups) and cooperative insurance. He focused his attention on "the central debate," namely, how to define a socialist cooperative and the conditions necessary for a cooperative to be considered socialist. A socialist cooperative, he wrote, is "a society whose members are driven not only by the legitimate desire to improve their well-being but also by a wish to abolish wage labor by every path and every means, political and economic, legal and revolutionary."[54]

Jaurès actively participated in the debates of the congress and was enthusiastically applauded several times. He declared: "It is not enough for cooperation to become socialist, socialism must become cooperative. . . . Just as you tell cooperators 'Join socialism,' the socialists must tell workers: 'Join cooperatives!'"[55] The socialist leader was converted to cooperation by Mauss: from his point of view, a threefold action—political, syndicalist, and cooperative—was necessary. Socialists, even while respecting the autonomy of every form of action, had to seek to bring about "a profound harmony between cooperation and socialism."

Mauss, a delegate for the new Coopérative Socialiste he had helped to found, frequently intervened on questions of procedure or on fundamental problems. At the start of the congress, he requested that the studies be published by the Société Nouvelle de Librairie et d'Édition. He also called for the adoption of a different voting method (by cooperative society rather than by delegate). And finally, he took a position in support of founding cooperative workshops run by consumer societies, themselves federated for purposes of production.

On the third day of the congress, Mauss presented a report he had prepared on international relations: "Citizens, if we want to develop the universal workers' organization, it is time to take the federative path. . . . Above all, every workers' cooperative must do what the English cooperatives have done. Let them first form vast federations, let them be 'a state within the state,' and they will be able to become a workers' internationale, a world organization standing up to world capitalism."[56]

Aware that certain matters, though "eminently desirable," were not "immediately practicable," Mauss maintained it was nevertheless possible to "prepare the way." His report included all sorts of proposals whose aim was to develop ties between socialist consumer organizations: representation at the various congresses by members of different federations, exchanges of publications, the creation of an international journal of workers' cooperatives, the establishment of a "permanent office for international socialist cooperatives, an international mutual aid society for moral and commercial support, and an international agreement for certain purchases in common." He also mentioned two ambitious projects: to found an international bank of workers' cooperatives and to arrange for international insurance (fire, accident, life, and medical) for cooperatives and cooperators.

Mauss acknowledged that these measures would take a long time to organize and would require intense militant activity from everyone: "Comrades, we believe we are acting as organizers, as militants, even while encouraging workers to look ahead, seeking to create a little security for them in the uncaring society they live in. We are not making them contented. We are educating them for their revolutionary task by giving them a foretaste, so to speak, of all the advantages the future society will be able to offer them. We are giving them a weapon for struggle by improving their position and ensuring that of their loved ones."[57]

Mauss hoped the socialist cooperative would be able to join "the international federative path" without delay. His concern for the "immediately practicable" may look like a "bourgeois" attitude. He would defend himself against that charge: "Citizen Mauss does not accept the label 'bourgeois cooperator' that has been applied to him. He never looked for anything in cooperation but duties and travails. As for his bourgeois mind, he asks that it be duly noted that since 1890 he has never belonged to any but revolutionary and socialist groups."[58]

A few days later, Mauss, along with Jaurès and other socialist delegates, attended the official congress of the Comité Central des Coopératives (Central committee of cooperatives). The objective was to pass a number of socialist motions (workers' organizations were to be the only owners of the cooperative workshops created by the federations; a normal eight-hour day would be established) and to "fight against a certain nationalist and decentralizing current that had formed on the question of regional federations."[59]

The situation the cooperative movement found itself in was far from heartening. On the one hand, the insufficient number of socialist cooperators were "left to fend for themselves"; on the other, the cooperatives themselves were "abandoned" since socialists "were returning to the narrow and abstract sphere of pure politics" and "stood apart" from the cooperative movement. It is therefore not surprising that the socialist spirit did not permeate the cooperatives quickly enough and that they were "marking time."

Mauss remained optimistic, however, especially after the "felicitous successes" of the Bourse des Coopératives Socialistes: "Above all, we are witnessing the dawn of the federative movement. . . . It is the beginning of colossal businesses, the beginning of proletarian agglomerations, class agglomerations, built on the bedrock of consumption." He concluded: "It is up to the socialists to push faster toward the final goal: the absolute emancipation of the international proletariat as a whole."[60]

La Boulangerie

Mauss was personally involved in cooperatives. In March 1900 he founded a small society with Philippe Landrieu inspired by the Maison du Peuple in Brussels and the Voorult in Ghent. Landrieu, born in Le Havre in 1873 to a family of Protestant republican merchants, pursued studies in agronomy, then medicine, and finally specialized in physics and chemistry. His political choices were close to Mauss's: he was an active member of the Groupe des Étudiants Collectivistes as of 1894, joined the Parti Ouvrier Socialiste Révolutionnaire, participated in *Mouvement Socialiste,* and collaborated with Jaurès. Like Mauss, Landrieu—who later worked as a laboratory assistant at the Collège de France beside chemists Marcelin Berthelot and Charles Moureu and physicist Paul Langevin—saw cooperation as a way to prepare the ground for a new society. He joined the cooperative movement, which he found to be a welcome alternative to the struggles and polemics that were pitting the various factions of the socialist movement against one another. His fondness for concrete accomplishments and his organization skills made the militant cooperator a shrewd administrator.

The new Coopérative Socialiste, called simply La Boulangerie (The bakery), was located at 84, rue Barrault, in the thirteenth arrondissement. There were thirty-eight founding members and its initial assets were 1,900 francs. Its delegates at the first national and international congress of socialist cooperation were Jaurès and Mauss. Landrieu would replace them at the following congresses in Lille (1901) and Amiens (1902). The Coopérative Socialiste intended to cover the entire sector, "breads, pastries, cookies, and petits fours." Mauss was quite satisfied with his involvement: "For my part, I'm becoming entrenched in the working class where I'm the most narrow-minded and the most vulgar. Birds of a feather . . . I'm doing well. I write a lot. I act quite decisively. The cooperative is working, as is the school for laborers."[61] He also tired of it at times, telling Hubert: "The publishing house is limping along, like everything . . . like La Boulangerie . . . like the party . . . like our bland Jacobin republic. You'll find all that very shabby and confining."

The situation of La Boulangerie, which had over 150 members the first year, quickly appeared fragile: bread delivery to distant cooperative societies encountered insurmountable difficulties. Mauss wavered between worry and a reasonable optimism. Landrieu had to devote himself to "incomprehensible tasks and to study" the various problems the socialist Boulangerie encountered in order to find a solution.

Things were "really going badly" in 1901, and in June the cooperative had to borrow 40,000 francs. According to the terms of the contract signed with A. Lainy of Grands Moulins de Corbeil (General mills of Corbeil), Dr. V. Kasimir and Mauss declared "they were jointly guaranteeing the Coopérative Socialiste for up to 20,000 francs." But that was not enough, and the next fall Landrieu sent Mauss a cry for help. "We need you. The Boulangerie's financial situation is critical. Borrowing solved nothing, as might have been expected."[62] A few months later, Dr. Kasimir and Mauss had to honor their financial commitment and pay the 20,000 francs.[63]

For the Coopérative Socialiste, it was still difficult to make ends meet but the funds provided made it possible to manage.[64] Mauss found himself holding four hundred 25-franc notes at 4 percent annual interest. The problem was to "give an accounting" to his family. Durkheim was the first to be informed of his "setbacks": "Please believe I did not make the decision lightly. I knew better than anyone that I was risking that considerable sum, that I was making a commitment. The thing was done, I assure you, with complete awareness. . . . In the current state of affairs, there is some hope that the sacrifice will become an investment some day. But I have no illusions."[65]

Émile was far from happy with his nephew's behavior: "Let this matter serve as a lesson to you, let it teach you to cut back on what you take on, to better understand what you can do before launching some initiative. The things you want to do are too big and there are too many of them." While suggesting he tell his mother "the truth as it is,"[66] he offered to advance him funds: "I would certainly not like you to forget this incident. But you have to work. So for the moment, put it all out of your mind."[67]

Rather than accept his uncle's offer, Mauss preferred to turn directly to his mother. Feeling "guilty for violating the wishes" of his parents by placing a "large amount of money in a risky undertaking and in a cause whose goals [they] would not approve of," he asked his mother to forgive him for "risking a small fortune" that did not belong to him.[68]

Thanks to Mauss's sacrifice, Landrieu was somewhat reassured about the future of the Coopérative Socialiste, even though "the money situation is still difficult." In 1903, it had more than a hundred members and owned a pastry factory, a coffee distillery, and a bakery that produced satisfactory results. But two years later the facts had to be faced: "The situation is not good. We're selling very little. Overall costs have risen. . . . The situation can't go on."[69] Several society members thought there was no advantage to "starting up the business again because of the debts that have to be paid immediately." "May Charles Gide's god come and help us!" one of them exclaimed. During a calm meeting, members of the cooperative agreed "not to mount any opposition" and to facilitate the federation's takeover of La Boulangerie.[70] For Mauss, that decision meant he would have to "voluntarily give up the money [he] had advanced to the cooperative and the notes [he] had signed."[71] The Coopérative Socialiste merged with the Magasin de Gros des Coopératives de France (Wholesale warehouse of French cooperatives), which, created in 1905, already owned warehouses in Paris and a shoe factory in Pas-de-Calais.

This misadventure did not discourage citizen Mauss, who always remained interested in cooperation. When the newspaper *Humanité* was created, he and Landrieu would write the column devoted to cooperatives.

6

RUE SAINT-JACQUES

DURKHEIM was the first to celebrate his nephew's new job at the École Pratique: "I congratulate you and I congratulate us on the fact that your situation is somewhat regularized."[1] His only fear was that his nephew's "new responsibilities at the École des Hautes Études will make him completely unusable for volume 5 [of *Année*] unless we resign ourselves to not publishing till Trinity Sunday."[2]

For several years Durkheim had wanted to find a position in Paris, not so much to be a professional success as to obtain the means for intellectual action and the resources he did not have in Bordeaux.[3] He confided to his nephew: "If only I could find some little corner in Paris that would leave me some leisure time! That's what I need. . . . But that's a very difficult thing to find."[4] His collaborators at *Année Sociologique* shared the same feeling: "What great things could be done if he were a professor in Paris."[5]

Durkheim failed three times in his attempts to leave Bordeaux. First, in 1894, he had a philosophy chair at the Sorbonne "taken away" from him by his colleague and dean Alfred Espinas, who taught sociology in his classes. "His conduct toward me in that whole affair was lacking not only in generosity but in integrity. It was underhanded and evasive in addition to being petty. He swore to me by God almighty that he would never have gone up against me for a class in pure sociology, even though I know he had thought it all through and from the very first considered his course [illegible] to include a sociology course."[6]

Second, in 1897, the minister of public education named Jean Izoulet, author of a recent book called *La cité moderne* (The modern city), to a new chair in social philosophy at the Collège de France. Durkheim called this the "wretched Izoulet affair." Although he had few illusions about his chances, Durkheim felt Izoulet's appointment was a "disgrace."[7] Sociologists believed it was *finis sociologiae* for the Collège: "That traveling sideshow, that absurdity, will be the end of it."[8]

And finally, in 1899 Gabriel Tarde, the author of *Lois de l'imitation* (Laws of imitation), was hired by the Collège de France, also as a philosopher. For several years a lively polemic about sociology had been developing between the learned professor Durkheim and his clever opponent. One emphasized the group and social constraints ("social realism"), the other the individual and interaction; one privileged the methodical observation of facts, the other speculation and imagination. In contrast to Tarde, Durkheim stood as a believer in science. Five years later the two would defend their respective theses in a debate on "Sociology and the Social Sciences" at the École Pratique des Hautes Études Sociales.[9] Durkheim was sorry that Tarde's appointment at the Collège perpetuated the confusion between philosophy and sociology, but he considered the "outcome" altogether normal, since "no one will think of getting me out of [Bordeaux] until [Tarde] has got a good job."[10]

Defense of Sociology

Opposition to sociology remained strong and Durkheim still sensed the "same reluctance" about what he was writing, if not a "stubborn resistance." Even the publication of *Suicide* did not clear up the misunderstandings. Durkheim thought it would be merely "wasted effort. I feel like the doctrinal resistance I thought I'd broken down somewhat is now reforming."[11] In a short posthumously published text titled "Sociology," Durkheim identified the two conditions for the discipline's development: "First, traditionalism had to lose some of its authority. . . . Second, true faith in the power of reason was required if people were going to dare translate the most complex and unstable realities into definite notions." He concluded: "France satisfied that dual condition."[12] Mauss was more dubious and observed that "the old rival forces have not laid down their weapons. Opposition endures and is growing. In France particularly, philosophers have forcefully played their critical role."[13]

The same year Mauss came to the École Pratique, he agreed for the first time to present Durkheim's ideas; with Fauconnet he wrote the "Sociology" entry for *La Grande Encyclopédie*, "with Durkheim's assistance." The uncle, unconvinced of the usefulness of having his collaborators write the article, feared it would distract them both from the work that ought to be their chief objective. He hoped "everyone would waste the least amount of time possible on it." But he composed an outline himself and, noting that the entry would be anonymous, offered his collaboration, especially on the history of sociology ("origins, the eighteenth century, Saint-Simon, Comte, Spencer").[14]

Mauss and Paul Fauconnet knew each other well: they had met the first year Mauss spent in Paris and had prepared the *agrégation* in philosophy together. In the entry they wrote, they attempted to present *Rules of Sociological Method* in clearer language and a less "dogmatic" style. They set aside the section on history—but referred in the bibliography to books by Espinas, Alfred Fouillée, Bouglé, and so on—in order to "determine, first, the object of sociology and then the method it uses." They gave many examples of specifically social facts: the economic life of modern societies (industrial production, division of labor, credit, trade), language acquisition, matrimonial and domestic relations, religion, and statistics on marriage, suicide, and crime. The authors explained that there were easily identifiable social phenomena distinct from those studied by the other human sciences, such as psychology. These were institutions, that is, "sets of already instituted acts or ideas that individuals find before them and that more or less impose themselves."[15] The word *institution* referred both to customs and to fashions, to prejudices and superstitions as well as to political constitutions and legal organizations. The specific object of sociology was institutions.

Once that object was defined, Fauconnet and Mauss summarized Durkheim's discussion of the explanation of social facts: "Sociological explanation proceeds by moving from one social phenomenon to another. It establishes a relationship only between social phenomena."[16] The line of demarcation was clearly drawn: sociology was distinct from the philosophy of history (Condorcet, Comte), which was concerned with "seeking only the goal toward which humanity is heading." It was also opposed to doctrines that would seek the determining causes of social phenomena in the nature of the individual. Spencer, Tarde, the classical economists, and theorists of natural law were all taken to task. General considerations regarding human nature were inadequate for anyone wishing "to explain why, in a particular kind of society at a particular time in its development, one finds a particular institution."[17] Mauss later reaffirmed his opposition to philosophy several times—even the philosophy of the "rigorous scholastic" Kant—and particularly, the "philosophical conception of religion." From the sociological perspective, it was clear "there is not a thing, an essence, called Religion; there are only religious phenomena, more or less incorporated into systems called religions that have a definite historical existence in determinate human groups at determinate times."[18]

Fauconnet and Mauss avoided giving priority to economic or morphological phenomena. The mode of explanation they privileged seemed to be "circular," "since the group's forms are presented sometimes as effects and sometimes as causes of the collective representations." They acknowledged this from the outset: "But that circle, which is real, implies no petitio principii; it is characteristic of the things themselves. There is nothing so pointless as to wonder whether it is ideas that brought forth societies or societies that, once formed, gave birth to collective ideas."[19]

Sociology thus understood assigned a preponderant role to the mental element of social life, collective beliefs and feelings. Fauconnet and Mauss declared: "The deepest core of social life is a set of representations." They immediately added: "In that sense, it is possible to say that sociology is a psychology. We would accept that formulation, but only on the express condition of adding that this psychology is specifically distinct from individual psychology."[20]

There is in this text a desire to attenuate Durkheim's dogmatism. When Fauconnet and Mauss came to the question of method, they abandoned the task of "formulating completely and definitively the rules of sociological method." At most, they wanted to present a certain number of scientific procedures already sanctioned by custom. These were: definition, observation of facts, systematization of facts, and verification of hypotheses. Fauconnet and Mauss ridiculed both "dialectical discussions" and "scholarly encyclopedias"; they warned against not only "abdications of empiricism" but also "hasty generalizations." Objectivity (setting aside one's personal feelings and opinions), harsh critique of sources (statistical or ethnological documents), rigorous comparative approaches, and the rejection of absolute truth were all characteristic of the new ethos of the social science researcher. For science, this was the condition for the "possibility of progress."

In France, which was witnessing the "growth of hasty sociology," these clarifications were welcome since, as Hubert noted, the word "sociology" had become "a magic word that has already produced too many magicians." The "harm is already so great," he said, that an immediate reaction against it was desirable: "True sociological analysis is slow and difficult; it demands meticulous and precise surveys; it can act productively only on very well known facts and, since these are rare, it has everything to gain by doing original historical research designed to tell us about the fleeting signs of social facts, which are difficult to observe because they occur in good part in the unconscious or are translated into consciousness in terms that distort it, in order to make them intelligible to individual reason."[21]

Mauss, ever diligent, did not hesitate in his many book reviews to remind readers of various rules of method and to reprimand even the most renowned specialists in religious history. He did not doubt for an instant that those who wanted to satisfy historical and philological imperatives and the need for scientific explanation had to use the sociological method: "Thanks to it, facts of a religious nature stand as objective and natural things. They have an existence outside the fleeting moments when the individual thinks them and acts on them. They are part of a real whole, the one formed by social things, and they have a useful function to perform there."[22] When he became an advocate of "comparative, in-depth monographs," Mauss sided with science, but a science that, far from being closed, was an "indefinitely perfectible system." He hoped that, between simple history and philosophy, there was a place for a "strict inductive discipline."

The Categories of Understanding

The question of collective representations played a central role for Durkheim and his collaborators. In 1898 Durkheim published an article called "Individual Representations and Collective Representations" in *Revue de Métaphysique et de Morale*. In 1903 he and his nephew published their famous essay "On Some Primitive Forms of Classification" in *Année Sociologique*. Both had been thinking about the subject for a long time. It was easy for them to complete the essay because in 1902 Durkheim had been named a *chargé de cours* in the faculty of letters at the Sorbonne. The uncle, afraid he would come across as someone seeking to "worm his way into Paris" at all costs, had for some time hesitated to apply to the Sorbonne to replace Ferdinand Buisson (1841–1932). Buisson, a former director of primary education (1879–1896) and professor in the science of education from 1896 on, had just been elected as a Radical-Socialist deputy. The faculty finally voted by a very large majority to appoint Durkheim. His sister Rosine was particularly happy but, "like all joys, [hers] was mitigated by the fear that too much work will undermine his health."[23]

For Durkheim, who now felt like a Bordelais, it was difficult to adjust to Paris. "The change has been distressing," he confided to his friend and former colleague Octave Hamelin. After a period of despondency, he had had to remake his life plan and get back on his feet.[24] He wrote of the "partial change of my moral personality" and the "bad moments I had to undergo— partly because of my own imagination."[25] As he indicated in a later letter, he was suffering from clinical depression: "I'm doing better. . . . I feel much less sensitive and unstable, but what a winter I've had here. The worst of it is that my depression had never before taken that form, which led me to believe that it was all moral, and as a result difficult to treat."[26]

In 1902 a new edition of *The Division of Labor in Society* appeared, with a preface entitled "A Few Remarks on Professional Groups." Durkheim was still very involved in publishing *Année Sociologique* and wanted to change its format, reducing the extensive bibliographical work and allowing more space for original studies. Alarmed by the idea that he would have to "take on that enormous bibliographical task for another five years," he wrote Hubert: "I believe that we're of more value than that, that we must and can produce, and that as a result we will have to get away from the exclusively bibliographical phase."[27] Two days later, he added: "We must practice sociology and not constantly collect materials. Yet the years go by; we have acquired the habit of that bibliographical work and have lost that of producing."[28]

Hence there was no question of dropping the essays in *Année Sociologique*, even though they presented certain problems. They had to be "solicited every year and we are beholden to people's goodwill," and they were often "ready only at the last minute."[29] Durkheim wished he could establish a long-term schedule and therefore issued an invitation to his nephew: "Will you be able to do an article with me called 'The Primitive Classifications of Things' (a rough working title) between now and about August?"[30]

This was not their first collaboration. In the previous volume of *Année Sociologique*, Durkheim and Mauss had separately reviewed various aspects of Baldwin Spencer and F. J. Gillen's *Native Tribes of Central Australia* (1899). Durkheim called it "one of the most important books in ethnography and descriptive sociology we know," containing an "enormous volume of infinitely valuable . . . facts."[31] Mauss addressed the part of the book dealing with religious facts, particularly totemism and initiation ceremonies, and Durkheim the part devoted to social and familial organization (territorial groups, matrimonial classes, and totemic groups). In his 1902 *Année* article "On Totemism," the uncle continued his discussion of a discovery by Spencer and Gillen, who "directly observed a totem system in its unity and integrity," the system belonging to the Arunta.[32]

Mauss's collaboration was indispensable in the writing of the essay on classification: "I provided all the facts," he would explain.[33] The essay assembled a mass of ethnographic information on many tribes in Australia and America. In the last part of the essay, the comparative analysis of classification systems was broadened to take into account Chinese divinatory systems (astrology, horoscopes) and Greek and Brahmanic mythologies.

In their 1903 *Année* article, "The Primitive Forms of Classification," the two sociologists examined an old problem of a philosophical nature: the categories of understanding. This subject also preoccupied psychologists, who, during this same period, were uncovering the complexity of mental operations. On the problem of classification—a procedure consisting of "classifying beings, events, facts in the world, into genera and species, of subsuming one under the other, of determining their relationships of inclusion or exclusion"[34]—Durkheim and Mauss rejected both the logicians and the psychologists. They demonstrated that the classification of things in nature and the cosmos did not correspond to an innate property; nor was it a product of individual mental activity. It was a "true social institution."

Durkheim and Mauss first analyzed the "most rudimentary" classifications human beings had made, "the humblest we know of," those of the Australian tribes. They established a correspondence between these classifications and the social organization of the tribes (phratry, matrimonial class, clan). "The classification of things replicates [the] classification of men." It was a daring proposition and opened the vast field of cognition to anthropology and sociology. Durkheim and Mauss, unafraid of accusations of "social realism," asserted the "sociocentrism" of their analysis: "Society has not been simply a model according to which notions of classification have operated: its own frameworks served as frameworks for the system. The first logical categories were social categories; the first classes of things were classes of men into which these things were integrated. It is because men were grouped and thought of themselves as groups that they ideally grouped other beings, and the two modes of grouping were at first confused to the point of being indistinguishable."[35]

The perspective was resolutely evolutionist. It raised the question of the "primitive mentality," which would become the subject of an animated debate when Lucien Lévy-Bruhl's *How Natives Think* was published in 1901. Durkheim and Mauss acknowledged that "primitive classifications do not constitute unique exceptions without any similarity to those in use among the most cultured peoples. On the contrary, they seem to be permanently attached to the first scientific classifications. . . . It is possible to say without error that they belong to science and constitute an early philosophy of nature."[36] Nevertheless, the differences could not be denied, since there had been an evolution: "Not only does our current notion of classification have a history, but that history presupposes a considerable prehistory. It would be impossible to overstate the indistinctness of the human mind at its beginnings."[37] Emotion or social affectivity stand in opposition to the "reflective thought of individuals."

For Durkheim, "The Primitive Forms of Classification" was the culminating point of his reflections on totemism. It was a "fine essay," Salomon Reinach acknowledged. The curator of the museum in Saint-Germain was quick to congratulate the authors as "scientists and thinkers who work firsthand, reflect intensely, and plunge deep into the darkness in order to pierce it." He thanked them for raising a problem "of key importance."[38] For E. Sidney Hartland, who read *Année Sociologique* with interest, there was only one word to describe the 1903 issue: "excellent." In his long review of Durkheim and Mauss's "acute and learned paper," he expressed only one reservation: all generalizations were impossible so long as the data "proving that totemism was universal" had not been collected.[39]

Durkheim and Mauss thus opened a new avenue leading to the sociology of cognition. It was possible to analyze other "functions or fundamental notions of human understanding" as they wished to do (the ideas of space, time, cause, substance, the different forms of reasoning, and so on). As Mauss would point out, this was the mission of *Année Sociologique*: "With Durkheim's agreement, we immediately isolated the problem of reason." Religious representations would be approached from "many sides": number; cause (an essay on the origins of magical powers); space; time (an essay on the origin of the notion of time); soul; world (the notion of orientation); gender; space. Mauss later concluded: "This [was] one of the most philosophical projects ever to be attempted by a school. Durkheim pursued it in depth from a dogmatic standpoint in his 'Elementary Forms of Religious Life.'"[40]

The overall intention was to shed light on an interdependent and interpenetrating relationship between fundamentally different orders of social facts, for example, social organization and collective representations. Mauss continued his studies of these questions in his essay "Seasonal Variations."

Durkheim at the Sorbonne

At the Sorbonne, Durkheim found a large group of students entranced by his intellectual passion, his eloquence, and his dialectics: "He was always grave, he never eased up," wrote Bourgin. "Nevertheless, his voice, always somewhat muffled at the most intense moments, was not without charm; and we felt we were yielding to a sort of incantation."[41] Durkheim, strongly identified with the new Sorbonne, would be the object of admiration but also of many attacks. One of the first and most virulent would come from the Catholic Péguy, who, as a result of associating with the contributors to *Année Sociologique* at the publishing house, feared that in a world without God there would be "regression," that is, the imposition of a government catechism taught by gendarmes with the collaboration of the police.[42] Durkheim stood at the head of a new church or, more precisely, of a new clan: the "totem and taboo clan," Bouglé would say, referring to the close relation between the uncle and the nephew.[43]

Mauss was worried about Durkheim's "wild success." "The uncle began his courses: an enormous crowd, a bad audience. . . . He goes to a tremendous amount of trouble for things that aren't worth it. We must use all our might to keep him at *Année*."[44] "D. has enormous quantitative success, but naturally it would be better for him, and for us, if he would practice sociology exclusively. Apart from being tired, he's basically happy."[45]

The nephew was judging the uncle. But in Paris, Durkheim had more than one reason to be critical of Mauss. The two lived near each other. When he arrived in Paris, Durkheim moved to 250, rue Saint-Jacques. In 1903 Mauss left 21, rue des Gobelins, to move to the seventh floor at 31, rue Saint-Jacques, a "disgracefully modern apartment" where he had "every comfort possible but no space." He set up his office there, furnishing it with a large oak table, an upright piece of furniture with an adjustable writing stand, a file cabinet, and three built-in bookcases. The nephew would have preferred to live with his friend Hubert, since "we might have managed things very well the two of us."[46] But he found himself back with his cousins and his new apartment quickly came to give him "less and less satisfaction."

Tensions developed between Durkheim and Mauss, who did not want "to be led by force." Mauss's behavior, with its "mysteries" and long silences, irritated his uncle. In the first place, at age thirty he was still single and observed his friends' "family life" with a certain irony, particularly the "Fauconnets, [who] are probably piecing together a happy life, since they have no history."[47] There was a woman in Mauss's life. He confided to Hubert:

"I am allowing myself to be tyrannized by poor Marguerite, whom I love very much. In short, I'm still leading the life of a rather robust brute."[48]

Mauss's mother wanted only one thing for her son: a good marriage. "Let's talk seriously," she wrote him. "I'd like to see you married because you're at an age when you could do it under the best conditions, and if you put it off too much longer you'll marry foolishly or you'll remain single or rather an old bachelor."[49] Rosine's anxiety increased as her son aged, and her efforts to find him "a young lady who would please him and would have all the qualities he's looking for" appeared futile: "I'm not aware of any proposal. . . . I can't help worrying about it. Do you think you've become unmarriageable?"[50]

When she learned that a woman had been sharing her son's life for several years, Mauss's mother could not hide her anger or sadness. She felt powerless before Marcel, who was "responsible for his misfortune" and was "ruining his life." She could not stop "weeping and feeling exasperated."[51] Durkheim was no better equipped to prevent his nephew from "acting like a madman" and was also deeply shocked: "How can you call a matter that everyone who loves you sees is putting your dignity, your future, and your happiness in jeopardy 'a sexual matter that concerns only you'?"[52]

More than anything, the uncle feared "domestic anomie." In *Suicide*, he deplored the situation in which the single man found himself. This was the "infinity sickness" that anomie brought with it: "Since he can legitimately attach himself to whatever he likes, [the bachelor] longs for everything and is satisfied by nothing. . . . From the moment nothing stops you, you are unable to stop yourself. Beyond the pleasures you experience, you imagine others. If it so happens that you have experienced nearly the full range of the possible, you dream of the impossible: You are hungry for what does not exist." When hopes are once again dashed, weariness and disenchantment follow.[53]

Durkheim criticized his nephew for his "obliviousness to morality."[54] From the perspective of those around him, the nephew seemed to be resigned not to marry. But what other goal could he have in life? asked Durkheim. Obviously, there was politics. Mauss was more than ever involved in various militant activities: he managed La Boulangerie, created the newspaper *Humanité*, and traveled to Russia. Although he said he was "disgusted with politics," he had "boundless ambition," which led him "to spread himself too thin in all sorts of undertakings." This discouraged Durkheim: "You're at a critical moment. You need to decide if you're going to give up your legitimate scientific ambitions by putting them off year by year, while continuing to stumble onto tasks for which you need abilities and flaws that you don't have."[55]

Mauss was having difficulties with his work at the time. "My brain isn't working at all," he told Hubert. At most he managed to loaf about half-asleep: "The nephew is working lifelessly, loafing," he wrote, speaking of himself in the third person. "Very slowly he is doing a little study . . . on magic. . . . It's relatively interesting." For someone who felt that "everything's getting old, used up," it seemed there was "not much to hope for from any of us" except, he corrected himself, "academic and even military awards"![56] Everyone, and first of all his mother, wanted Marcel to "organize his life, his work, and his finances."[57]

7

JOURNALIST AT *HUMANITÉ*

THE FIRST ISSUE of *Humanité* appeared on April 18, 1904. It seems to have been Lucien Herr who found "the right name, the irreplaceable name that the communists adopted."[1] Jean Jaurès, by now a major parliamentary leader, was in charge of the new newspaper: he was both the editor in chief and the managing editor. His commitment to Dreyfus earned him the friendship of intellectuals and the sympathies of the Jewish community.[2] Lucien Lévy-Bruhl, Léon Blum, and Herr went about raising funds, more than 800,000 francs within a few months. Lévy-Bruhl's participation was particularly generous: he bought 1,000 shares for which he paid 100,000 francs.

Lucien Lévy-Bruhl (1857–1939), born to a relatively modest Jewish family in Metz, was a student at the École Normale Supérieure and an *agrégé* in philosophy (1879). He married well, combining his intellectual resources with the economic capital of a family much wealthier than his own. It was his wife's dowry that allowed him to become so deeply involved in the creation of *Humanité*.[3] Lévy-Bruhl enjoyed "a nearly miraculous immunity" in intellectual and academic circles. People spoke of him as of a "great professor," a "well-bred, courteous, distant grand bourgeois" who also worked toward "proletarian or working-class goals."[4]

Lévy-Bruhl, one of Jaurès's rare confidants and correspondents, had great admiration for his former classmate at the École Normale, a politician who not only had "a taste for day-to-day action," but who saw things from above as well "and wanted to anticipate future events so as to influence them instead of being surprised by them."[5] Lévy-Bruhl would always trust his friend Jaurès, a trust, Mauss would say, that "later grew into a spirit of devotion and sacrifice for Jaurès's cause, his party, and the proletariat."[6] Jaurès and Lévy-Bruhl were deeply republican and shared the same passion for justice and the same ideal, to "make humanity as a whole into an elite." But according to Mauss, Lévy-Bruhl "did not embrace the [Socialist] Party more fully" because he feared "the waste of time and pettiness in our rather insulated lives."[7] He nevertheless supported socialist fund-raising, cooperatives, journals, and schools "with all his might." Lévy-Bruhl was a comptroller alongside Blum at *Humanité*.

In his first article, "Our Goal," Jaurès justified the title of the newspaper by identifying socialism with the blossoming of humankind: "All societies strive toward the realization of humanity." The watchwords were exactitude, truth, loyalty, and freedom. The first issue was a success, with 140,000 copies printed. *Humanité* saw itself as a newspaper of ideas and of information. It got off to a good start, "much too good a start," Charles Andler would say.[8] With its seven Normalians and eight *agrégés,* the team attracted the lawyer Aristide Briand's sarcasm: "It's not *Humanité*! It's the humanities." There was a carefully respected political balance among various factions on the editorial staff, which was how Jaurès wanted it. On the "right" were Briand, Louis Fournières, and René Viviani; on the "left," the journalist Francis de Pressensé, the former professor Louis Révelin, and Jean Allemane. Allemane, a former convict in New Caledonia, now aged seventy, represented the old Communard tradition, which was both pro-worker and reformist, the same tradition that had appealed to Herr, Andler, and Mauss in their youth.

Several militants from the Groupe d'Unité Socialiste obtained key posts on the team: on foreign policy (Herr, Andler), on the syndicalist movement (Albert Thomas), on economic questions (Edgar Milhaud), and so on. Blum wrote for the literary pages. Mauss contributed financially to the newspaper, purchasing twenty shares, and he and Landrieu were jointly responsible for the "Cooperatives" section. Mauss's admiration for Jaurès and his loyalty were unreserved. Jaurès, he would later say, was a "unique man" whose two key qualities were authority—*imperium*—and a wise prudence. He concluded: "Jaurès was not only a hero but also a man of strength, a sage."[9]

Durkheim shared the same admiration for the popular socialist orator. Referring to Mauss's description of Jaurès in a letter written at the height of World War I, he congratulated him, adding a few nuances: "No, he was not a thinker; he was certainly a force of nature, as you say, altogether unselfconscious. . . . He went wherever his nature took him, without guiding it. The most original thing about his nature disappears when one tries to make him a thinker with a doctrine."[10]

The "Cooperatives" Section

Mauss participated in the paper's general meetings. He also went to the editing room on a regular basis, where he would meet Jaurès, completely focused on his work, putting the final touches on his articles despite the noise, the comings and goings, and the outbursts. Mauss was particularly proud that *Humanité* was "the first major newspaper, even within international socialism, to introduce a section on cooperatives." In his first article, he praised the cooperative organizations in Nord, which had provided help to workers during a strike.[11]

The section was addressed to socialists and union members, not all of whom did "their duty as consumers and militants in the cooperatives." Mauss's journalism both informed and educated. As we see in one of his early articles published in two columns on the front page, one of his first objectives was, "above all, to say why it is possible to speak of socialist cooperation and what must be understood by those words." His analysis reiterated the main elements of the reflections he had begun at *Mouvement Socialiste* on the political role of consumer cooperatives, but delved more deeply and added nuances.

To clear up misunderstandings and ambiguities, Mauss attacked both the "yellow" (antiunion) and the "red" (communist) cooperatives: the former because they were often administered by one of the "boss's creatures, a former driver or caretaker or shop minion," because they supported "bourgeois legality" and wanted "harmony and not a struggle against management"; the latter because they saw cooperation only as "a means useful to politics, a weapon in the service of an opinion." Mauss deplored the fact that in both cases individuals "used to their own advantage the various currents of the societies, fought for their favor and, thanks to these misunderstandings, sought to exploit them for their own personal interests." Although the Parti Socialiste was unified, Mauss did not believe the cooperatives should completely embrace the party: "The disadvantages of electoral politics, the clashes of opinion, the conflicts among people are such that there is every reason to keep them out of [cooperative] societies."[12]

In the case of *Mouvement Socialiste,* however, he thought that cooperation suffered less from meddling than from neglect. As was clear in rural cooperatives, the danger came from "bourgeois, conservative currents." "Through cooperation, the agrarians, the reactionaries, the priests . . . seize control of peasant organizations, collaborate energetically with them, and find in that means of emancipation a means of surveillance."[13]

According to Mauss, consumer cooperatives had to "act on their socialism," bring about "practical socialism," socialism here and now. It was not enough for them to be "sanctuaries for militants, unions, political groups" or to perform "a few socialist acts." They also had to "demonstrate experimentally what socialism preaches." Consumer cooperatives could be "true organizations where future laws are being drafted," as they were in England and Germany. There, collective labor contracts were negotiated with the unions and the principle of equal pay for equal work was respected. In addition, if it was the duty of cooperatives to offer various services (retirement pensions, for example), they were also obliged to assume a pedagogical function. They were "the ideal refuge for purely educational propaganda aimed at the proletariat." Mauss cited the example of the people's university supported by the cooperatives Ménagère and Bellevilloise. Finally and most important, cooperatives were an "economic force" and could become "powerful agents of transformation." "What makes a cooperative socialist is its constant aim to abolish wage labor through cooperation, among other means, and to act in ways that serve to emancipate the proletariat."[14]

Cooperation, though independent of political movements, remained closely tied to the "general trend in modern societies toward abolishing classes and wage labor." Mauss added a moral mission to that political aim: "As an agent of workers' moralization," the consumer cooperative was "the only means the worker has to escape the vices that poverty and social isolation engender." Mauss concluded enthusiastically: "The cooperative is the meat locker, the wine cellar, and the granary of the working class."[15]

Mauss was confident in the future, but refrained from "rushing things too much." "Let us act consistently and cautiously," he said repeatedly. This did not mean putting an end to propaganda; on the contrary, it was "becoming more and more necessary."[16] He was sorry that in France cooperative propaganda was in an "almost deplorable" state and that the effort expended was "almost worthless." "There is an enormous mass of possible cooperators in France who are not involved. They must get involved along with the others. To do that, activism is needed."[17]

The space in the column was devoted largely to polemics and doctrinaire debate—on "employment mutualism," for example—but it was also informative. It announced the publication of specialized works, the opening of cooperative restaurants, congresses held abroad.

Mauss was bored by the traveling he had to do: "I haven't decided anything about my trip to Budapest. I have no desire to go there as a journalist, none at all."[18] He found travel interesting only when he could connect journalism to his intellectual work. During his visit to England in the summer of 1905, he examined texts on the Eskimos that Beuchat had been unable to find in Paris. He worked "like an ox from ten o'clock in the morning till seven o'clock at night at the British [Museum] . . . and with consistent intensity."[19] Nevertheless, his participation at the congress of the English cooperative union in Paisley, where he represented the Bourses des Coopératives Socialistes, was not totally useless: "There are about fifteen of us [foreign delegates] studying. And we are working steadily."[20] Mauss confided to his friend Hubert: "By conferring with and studying the Wholesale, I've learned more in a week about the government of things and men, and about the English and Scottish peoples, . . . than in ten years of reading. Now what purpose will all that serve?"[21]

The congress of English cooperatives, with its many foreign delegates and its 1,700 representatives, impressed the special correspondent for *Humanité*. It was an "imposing and peaceful body, strong and calm, which gave . . . the impression that there was a power there, or rather, in the classic words of Mme Webb, a 'state within the state.'"[22] Mauss was surprised at the "exclusively working-class" aspect of the crowd and the presence of "bareheaded female citizens." But he deplored the "overly English," overly pragmatic nature of the debates. The question of creating a cooperative bank, for example, would have caused "an uproar" in France. Yet "here, no one is interested in anything abstract." Mauss himself questioned "many comrades," who all replied "bank" when he spoke of "principles."[23]

The burning question at the congress was political: must one require the cooperatives to join the workers' party that was then being formed? Mauss had a feeling that the proposal would be rejected because the party in question was poorly organized, but he allowed himself to dream: "What a defeat for neutral cooperation if English cooperation were to give up its famous neutrality! What a blow that gathering of talent and that sudden influx of power into the working world would be to international capitalism."[24]

An About-Face

The two reports Mauss wrote on the congress of English cooperatives were the last he published in *Humanité* in 1905. The newspaper experienced a grave crisis following a major drop in sales. Members of the editorial staff and administration were notified that "their services at the newspaper would be terminated on August 1."[25] Landrieu kept Mauss informed of the "vicissitudes of the fight": "At the newspaper . . . we are currently seeking arrangements. There is no longer money without strings attached. . . . In the offices of *Humanité,* there is intrigue in every nook and cranny. . . . Jaurès is distraught."[26]

For Jaurès's friends, these were indeed painful times. A few days later, Landrieu was even more alarmist: "*Humanité* is on its deathbed. . . . Jaurès sees no way out, he has lost faith, he's worn out."[27] But the next day, the situation reversed again, thanks to the influx of new funds—150,000 francs, according to Landrieu—and a reduction in the number of editors. The newspaper was saved, at least for a year. The new financial support came from workers' organizations, unionist and cooperative, but also from a generous citizen who made 50,000 francs available to Jaurès to fend off immediate difficulties.

Humanité retained only five editors besides Briand, Gustave Rouanet, Jaurès, and Viviani. Like Landrieu, Mauss was no longer part of the team. They were considered "devoted suckers who are owed nothing."[28] They were nonetheless free to refuse to continue contributing without compensation. Herr, Blum, and others distanced themselves from the newspaper and gradually stopped contributing. While remaining socialists, the intellectuals retreated and directed most of their activities to research or literature rather than participate in endless discussions and branch meetings. Friendships emerged intact from the turmoil, as did political loyalty.

When Mauss resolved to leave *Humanité,* Herr "altogether approved" of his friend's decision:

> You must now take up your work in earnest again, quickly finish your thesis, give the general public—I mean those who do not follow *Année* closely—an

exact sense of your scientific value and of your science. You must be ready for any eventuality. When you're at the Collège de France, you'll be able to return to the active life without sacrificing your life as a scientist. You know what I think of both; but you also know that, in the present society, eminent academic and scientific qualifications give practical action an authority and a value it would not necessarily have without them.[29]

Herr was not the only one to be pleased by Mauss's attitude. "Now you're rid of *Humanité*," Fauconnet wrote. "I'm delighted. I don't think that was your place and you were continuing the bad old ways of our generation, or rather, of our little group: the publishing house, La Boulangerie, and so on. One cannot be both an ethnographer and a journalist."

One thing was accomplished: after the congress held in April 1905 at Le Globe on boulevard de Strasbourg in Paris, the Parti Socialiste had reestablished its unity and had taken the name Section Française de l'Internationale Ouvrière, or SFIO (French branch of the workers' internationale). But was it true that the country was "gradually slipping toward socialism" and that, "after thirty years of being a republic in name only, we are beginning to bring about a true republic, to the great satisfaction of the people?"[30]

Landrieu, sorry that he had "wasted his energy," showed "a desire to work a great deal" by himself, but agreed to stand beside Jaurès.[31] He spent mornings at the laboratory of the Collège de France; in the afternoon, and sometimes until late into the night, he oversaw the administration of the socialist newspaper. Mauss too remained "respectfully and absolutely devoted" to Jaurès and joined the SFIO; he also agreed to be one of the party's ten representatives on the administration board of the new company responsible for publishing *Humanité*.

When he learned that his nephew had been lured back, Durkheim was furious, especially at not having been consulted: "By certain slight signs, which I have refrained from delving into, I've once again begun to fear that you're making serious commitments that everyone else knows of but that I haven't heard a word about. . . . You know the situation you're putting me in, yet you keep up that behavior. I seem to be the tiresome uncle nobody gives a damn about and who's told nothing."[32] Durkheim criticized his nephew for deliberately accepting a role that did not suit him: "You're totally lacking in modesty. You don't find any task daunting; you think you're fit for anything, even things for which you're totally unfit. At the same time, you speak contemptuously of what other people are doing. Think how much progress you would've made if you'd taken stock of your strengths just a bit!"[33]

Mauss had few illusions, however. He believed "the newspaper will never be more popular than it is once it's gone." In terms of political action, 1906 was a difficult and eventful year: La Boulangerie was liquidated, *Humanité* reorganized. In addition to these difficulties there was a personal disappointment for Mauss: his mission to Russia.

Mission to Russia

In July 1906 the minister of public education granted Mauss a "free mission to Russia and particularly to . . . Saint Petersburg and Moscow, for the purpose of pursuing ethnographic research there." Mauss also intended to go to Finland. Everything was arranged in a rush. He met with the minister and obtained a diplomatic passport at the last minute. Because Mauss did not know Russian and was unfamiliar with Saint Petersburg and the rest of Russia, contacts had to be set up for him. Colleagues and friends provided him with letters of recommendation. Sylvain Lévi wrote to one contact, Mme Mohilansky: "He's an anthropologist, an ethnographer, an Orientalist, a renaissance man, and above all a perfect gentleman. I recommend him to you as one of my treasures."[34]

The trip also had a political side, as Herr indicated in a letter of recommendation: "[Mauss] is going to Russia for *Humanité* . . . I know you'll do whatever's possible and even the impossible."[35] Mauss was also introduced as a "collaborator of Jaurès's" with the added comment that he could be spoken to "freely."[36] Mauss acknowledged this: "It was Jaurès who ordered me to go to Russia, somewhat against my will, since he knew how to demand of his friends even things they didn't want."[37] On "red Sunday" (January 22, 1905), Jaurès had begun a unified campaign in support of the Russian Revolution, in *Humanité* and through a series of meetings. Before he left, Mauss attended the socialist leader's discussions with several revolutionaries, liberals, and revolutionary socialists from the Russian community in Paris. It was thought at the time that Russian democracy would emerge victorious, but there was also a fear that the czar was planning a coup d'état. Mauss was to transmit Jaurès's "advice to be strong and cautious." "Don't be afraid," he repeated constantly. "Be strong. And have no fear, since you are revolutionaries, to make revolution. . . . Don't believe in your adversaries' sincerity or in their might. . . . Don't compromise, stand firm, and afterward you'll see."[38]

The second piece of advice, which "only a socialist who is also a historian and a statesman like Jaurès can give," concerned the "problem of land for the peasants." "It is both advice for caution and self-interest and advice for strength": "Above all, tell your friends to get to agricultural reform right away, any way they can. It is not necessary to finish everything at once but, above all, something must be accomplished. The Russian peasant is like the French peasant in 1789. He will understand a political revolution only if it is simultaneously an agrarian revolution. . . . A nation cannot always fight for an ideal, it must also win men over through self-interest."[39]

Mauss had a delicate mission. The czar, supported by French loans, was beginning to fight the Russian Duma. Jaurès was aware that "the interests of the Russian Revolution and of French socialism are connected." In July 1906 *Humanité* published a series of articles on the Russian Revolution: it was one of the only French newspapers at the time to "protest [against both] the French bourgeoisie and czarism."[40] When Mauss arrived in Saint Petersburg, the czar was dissolving the Duma. Hubert immediately sent him a telegram: "Come back." "Mauss's trip is becoming pointless," Herr would note. "In Russia even more than elsewhere, there are many inconsistent, fickle, and flighty men, and that is what prevents any kind of conjecture on the future progress of events in a country where a very small number of men are active and act like children or madmen."[41]

When he returned from his mission, Mauss, though disappointed, intended to publish an article in *Revue de Paris* on what was happening in Russia. Durkheim energetically advised against it: "You've just spent two weeks in Russia where you don't speak the language and you want to write an article on Russia! Doesn't the scientific method cry out that there is little seriousness in such a project?"[42]

The article would not appear. But from the trip he had just made with "his modest means," Mauss did gain a greater knowledge of Russian ethnographic museums. Traveling during the school vacation period, he was able to devote two weeks to "sustained studies": he met with a curator at the Museum of Russian Ethnography and of the Russian Empire and visited the Museum of Ethnography and the Academy of Sciences. The academy especially interested him because incomparable Eskimo collections located there allowed him to see that "the tribes of the American Pacific Northwest were once Russians."[43] On his way home, he stopped at the Polish Museum of Ethnography in Warsaw and the Museum of Ethnography in Berlin. In a letter he sent to the minister of public education, Mauss drew conclusions about his visits: "Allow me . . . to point out how seriously compromised the interests of French science are by the condition of the Trocadéro ethnographic museum [in Paris]; it is inadequately endowed and inadequately maintained compared with similar institutions abroad."[44]

The Fellow Traveler

Upon his return, the little leisure time afforded Mauss while teaching at the École Pratique des Hautes Études and publishing *Année Sociologique* was devoted to his thesis on prayer. But he did not turn his back on political activity. He agreed to teach courses on cooperation at the École Socialiste and to give lectures to the Groupe des Étudiants Collectivistes and at the people's universities. At the people's university in Sceaux, one of the lectures had to do with "the idea of religion." The invitation came from Charles Andler, one of his old friends, whose salon he attended on Sunday afternoons. At 17, rue des Imbergères in Sceaux there was a sort of "Sorbonne of the fields," a "place where the mind took flight," where socialists and men of letters mingled, including Lucien Herr, Gustave Lanson, Paul Desjardins, the historians G. Glotz and Charles Seignobos, the philosopher André Lalande, Albert Thomas, and the physician and art critic Élie Faure.[45]

Mauss, having apparently grown wiser, was busy with his "damned prayer" and avoided getting too involved in the undertakings of his friends and comrades. For example, he was not part of *Revue Syndicaliste,* created in May 1905 by Thomas with the financial support of Herr, Lévy-Bruhl, and Blum. The journal secured regular contributions from the sociologists Robert Hertz, Simiand, and Halbwachs. And when it stopped publishing in January 1910 and merged with *Revue Socialiste, Syndicaliste, et Coopérative,* whose director was Eugène Fournière, Mauss, unlike his friends Hertz and Halbwachs, did not publish articles in it. The journal's orientation was similar to his own, however. It sought to "revise and revive all the traditional concepts of socialism" since, the editorial staff claimed, socialism, "separated from syndicalism and cooperation," ran the risk of being "only a pointless dogmatism."

But Mauss could not remain indifferent to an initiative by Robert Hertz, who, driven by his "inclination for practice and accomplishment," in 1908 organized the Groupe d'Études Socialistes (Socialist Studies Group) on the model of the Fabian Society: "I don't need to tell you we'd be happy to have you with us and to benefit from the insight of your long experience and natural wisdom."[46]

Under Hertz's leadership, the Groupe d'Études Socialistes met regularly and critically examined the main theses of socialism, seeking to grasp their modes of application. The initiative received Jaurès's support. Members of the group had to be socialists, to accept joint municipal and legislative action, and to consider the Parti Socialiste the sole expression of socialism in France. To keep a "community of viewpoints and minds," participation was limited—there were about forty members in 1910—and recruiting selective. In addition to the members of the *Année Sociologique* clan (Marcel Granet, Halbwachs, Henri Lévy-Bruhl, Simiand), there was Edgar Milhaud, Ernest Poisson, Alfred Bonnet, Jacques Ferdinand-Dreyfus, and Albert Thomas. After the brilliant victory of the Parti Socialiste in the July 1914 elections, the group had two "representatives" in Parliament: André Lebey and Thomas.

In addition to a monthly dinner at a cooperative restaurant, the Groupe d'Études Socialistes held discussions with more or less regularly participating members. They spoke a great deal about socialism but also about cooperation, mutualism, strikes, alcoholism, industrial hygiene, workers' housing, cottage industries, and so on. When the articles that resulted seemed to offer "a useful contribution toward reforming policy," they were published in a series of pamphlets titled *Cahiers du Socialiste*.

These intellectuals were intent on performing their "new duties" and responding to the need for "exact knowledge and clear notions" felt by a large number of socialist militants. The objective was make available increasingly precise documentation, to work out concrete and practical solutions to the immediate problems, and, finally, to better adapt the doctrine to reality. It was, in other words, a way for Hertz to place Durkheim's sociology in the service of socialism: "At a time when our adversaries are attempting to defeat our party by mocking its sterile dogmatism and its inability to build anything, we must show more than ever that we are interested in bringing our doctrine into harmony with the present state of the social sciences and in demonstrating the realistic and organic character of socialism."[47]

Mauss was content to follow and to encourage the activities of his collaborator and friend Hertz. His participation was limited. He did take part in certain meetings, for example, when Bruckère presented a paper titled "Small Property Ownership, Social Danger and National Danger." Bruckère drew a "very dark" picture of the "broken-down, maleficent" class of small landowners. Though recognizing that this criticism was "in great part justified," Mauss was eager to add that "it has less to do with the character of an economic class than with our national temperament." He explained: "Let's not say anything bad about the French peasant: he's a tough producer and an excellent shopkeeper."[48]

Mauss was still a member of the administration board at *Humanité* and maintained close ties with its director. In 1910 "a second Dreyfus affair" erupted when Jules Durand, secretary of the strike committee for Le Havre dockworkers, received a death sentence for assaulting a "scab" foreman. Mauss responded to the appeal launched by Jaurès in the daily paper and joined other intellectuals—Andler, Herr, Anatole France, and others—in asking the president of the Republic for a pardon and a new trial. But his specifically journalistic contributions became less frequent, consisting only of a notice titled "La Maison du Peuple" in 1907 and two short texts signed simply "M." on the "Oudja affair" in 1911. Friends replaced him, including Halbwachs, who in 1908 agreed to supply articles on interest rates.

8

COLLECTIVE MADNESS

W HEN the French Republic became a reality in 1905 with the separation of church and state, Christianity lost its privileged status. The teaching of religious science itself was in jeopardy when faculties of Protestant theology were eliminated in 1906. For that sector of education and research, the problem became how to survive: how to preserve a place for the study of religion in public education while stripping it of its doctrinal character? It seemed imperative that the minister of public education fill an appreciable gap by creating courses in literature departments to replace the eliminated classes and by strengthening the section of religious science. Those in charge of the section at the École Pratique hoped to receive part of the money earmarked for teaching religious science in theology faculties and, feeling more useful than ever, dreamed of making their little section, which was marking its twentieth anniversary, into a true faculty.

Religion was at issue everywhere. Journals, newspapers, and salons discussed not only the future of religion and the "universal crisis in religion" but also themes as specialized as totemism and the rites and customs of Australian aborigines. The question of religion's origins, discussed in a proliferation of studies on so-called primitive peoples, elicited as much passion as had Darwin's discovery of the origin of species a few decades earlier.

Since the 1902 publication of Durkheim's important essay "On Totemism" in *Année Sociologique*, his adversaries at the Sorbonne had considered him a big shot who reduced everything to the totem. Durkheim was criticized for his lack of respect for religious beliefs. In 1906–1907, his public course was titled "Religion: Origins." The *Année* team, already broadly identified with the "return to the primitive" movement, still showed great interest in questions of religious sociology. In 1904 Hubert and Mauss published "Outline of a General Theory of Magic" in *Année*, and in 1908 their "Introduction to the Study of a Few Religious Phenomena" appeared in *Revue de l'Histoire des Religions*. In 1904 Mauss agreed to give a series of lectures under the title "Magic and Its Relationship to Religion" at the École Russe des Hautes Études Sociales. He also published a study called "The Origin of Magical Powers in Australian Societies" in *Revue de l'Histoire des Religions* and a short "Note on Totemism" in *Année*. Fauconnet presented a series of lectures in spring 1904 devoted to "contemporary theories on the origin of religion" at the École d'Anthropologie in Paris. The same year, Hubert and Isidore Lévy oversaw the translation of P. D. Chantepie de la Saussaye's *Manual of the History of Religion* and wrote its introduction.

Translating the manual meant siding with the scientific camp. Chantepie de la Saussaye, the eminent Dutch specialist in the history of religion, was more aware than anyone of the "persistent conflict between the facts of science and old notions of faith." At the congress of religious science in Stockholm in September 1897, he banished the old apologetic method from the field of science and reasserted "the need to replace it with a free and impartial search for the truth."

Mauss had no doubt that his friend Hubert's work was necessary. It was a difficult task and Hubert did not feel altogether up to it. He nevertheless wrote the substantial introduction to the French edition during a long trip to Asia in 1903 (he visited Hanoi, Canton, Macao, Tonkin, and other places).[1]

Hubert's introduction was some forty pages long and constituted a true "manifesto" for religious sociology, according to Mauss.[2] The history of religion presented by Hubert was no longer "the humble maidservant of theology" but a science. In that capacity, it had to "extirpate the unknowable from its field" in order "to explain as far as possible religious practices and beliefs as if they were gestures or human dreams." His object was religious facts, that is, both gestures (manual and oral rituals endowed with mystical efficacy) and representations (notions such as "god," "demon," "pure," and "impure," as well as myths and dogmas). The notion of the sacred, more than any other, dominated religious belief; it was the guiding idea of religion, Hubert explained, to such a point that religion could be said to be "the administration of the sacred."

The perspective was clearly Durkheimian, which is to say, sociological. Hubert was opposed to any individualist theory and considered religious facts social, recalling first and foremost the importance of the system of social relations in which individuals were inserted. "The individual becomes conscious of himself only in relation to his fellows. It is not the individual who projects his soul into society, it is society from which the individual receives his soul." The collective character of religious phenomena is manifest in the constraining authority of laws and beliefs, the singularity of mob psychology, the social organization (hierarchy) of religious societies. The school of sociology granted great importance to religion only because religious phenomena were "social phenomena par excellence" and necessarily entailed "social relationships."[3]

Mauss, who agreed with Hubert's viewpoint, was just as critical toward the "theological, even apologetic character" of studies devoted to religion: "There is not a thing, an essence, called Religion; there are only religious phenomena, more or less incorporated into systems called religions that have a definite historical existence in determinate human groups at determinate times." Mauss hoped there was a place between philosophy and history for "a strict inductive discipline." It was now possible, he believed, to "seek increasingly elementary religious phenomena." Sociology needed history and ethnography. Knowledge of the past could lead "to a better understanding of the present to help humanity become aware of its future."[4]

Mana

It is not easy to say, however, "what the order of religious phenomena is composed of." As Mauss explained, "Its borders are vague and vary depending on the age and the society." In that respect, magic occupies a "unique," "uncertain" place among religious phenomena, since it "resembles religion by its modes of action and notions."[5] Magic, a complex universe, includes magical rites in primitive societies, alchemy in the Middle Ages, and the still-vibrant superstitions of contemporary societies. And in every age, Mauss noted, "both in Palestine and among dispersed Jewry, there was a belief in the efficacy of magic."[6] It was possible to speak of "biblical religious magic." He wondered: "By what right can it be said that Hosea's healing, Moses' rod, the feast of waters are not magic just as curses are?"[7] Judaism, which Mauss knew well, had once included a number of superstitious beliefs and popular magic: people were wary of the evil eye and used incantations to ward off spells.

In considering magic, Hubert and Mauss wanted to show "the kinship that links magic to religion, even while leaving it in relative isolation."[8] For them, it was a way of broadening the field of sociology to study apparently individual and demonstrably irrational phenomena: "Since sociology encompasses everything, it must also include magic."[9] For Hubert and Mauss, magic provided "the opportunity to push [their] sociological analysis further." Acts of magic were "as far from public view as possible." To what extent, they wondered, and in what way were these facts social?[10]

In 1904 Mauss published a long article in the *Annuaire de l'École Pratique des Hautes Études* under the title "The Origin of Magical Powers in Australian Societies." As a colleague at the École noted, it was demonstrably the "product of a collaboration."[11] Neither Hubert nor Mauss concealed what they called their "intellectual brotherhood."[12]

Mauss's first text on magic was more limited in scope and provided the "substructure" for the subsequent "Outline of a General Theory of Magic," that is, the facts and observations collected by modern ethnography, all related to Australian societies. The method required patience and scientific rigor and attested to a "strict inductive discipline." Hertz, Mauss's student and friend, called it "a model of conscientious and reliable ethnographic investigation" and recommended it be read by "rigid souls who are still at the stage of professing a scornful skepticism about ethnography and comparative methodology."[13]

Once Mauss had established the vast scope of a magician's special power in the "extraordinarily backward" societies of Australia, he described the various ways one could become a magician. Magical power was rarely transmitted from father to son but was usually acquired by revelation in a dream or ecstatic state and by initiation. These two modes of entry into the magical profession were closely linked, since the new magician always had to learn the oral tradition of a certain number of necessary rites and formulas, then undergo the ordeals that conferred "an entirely new, entirely mythical quality, that is, the possession of special powers."[14] The magician, then, was integrated into a true guild whose power lay in creating a "state of collective belief" in the magician and his followers. The magician was a "being who believed himself and placed himself, just as others believed him and placed him, beyond the pale." His power, his "mysterious might"—his mana, said Mauss, borrowing a word from the Melanesian languages—had no "existence except through social consensus, public opinion."

Behind the scenes of this critical study of ethnographic documents, Mauss was once more calling into question James Frazer's theses. Frazer presented magic as a simple, quasi-technical application of the quasi-scientific laws of sympathy.[15] Mauss had already criticized him for providing an inadequate definition of religious phenomena in his otherwise "magnificent" *Golden Bough*.[16] His error was to establish a radical opposition between magic and religion and to consider magic prior to religion. Magic, according to Frazer, was the "first form of human thought," the "first stage in mental evolution," the other two stages being religion and science. This polemic was especially significant because it would lead a few years later to a debate on a question of precedence: was it Frazer or Hubert and Mauss who first spoke of taboo as "negative magic"?[17]

In "Outline of a General Theory of Magic," Hubert and Mauss returned to the question, with a close analysis of the studies of the English school of anthropology as a whole. Frazer was again attacked. In the second edition of *The Golden Bough*, he had reduced magical practice to the expression of the human mind's natural sophisms: association of ideas, analogical reasoning, false applications of the principle of causality. Part of "Outline" was devoted to discussing that theory, which was "more intellectualist" than its author intended and was constructed around the principle of sympathy and the laws of similarity and contiguity. According to the law of similarity, "like breeds like"; according to the law of contiguity, "things in contact are or remain united." According to Hubert and Mauss, all these "sympathetic formulas," like the notions of property and demons, were not enough in themselves "for the magician to justify his belief."

Hubert and Mauss repeated the approach they had taken in "Essay on the Nature and Function of Sacrifice." They made critical use of "very reliable documents"; studied magic comparatively in a limited number of societies; and juxtaposed magic in primitive and differentiated societies.

"Outline" had three parts: the definition of magic; the elements of magic; and an analysis and explanation of magic. The first task was to distinguish between two rites that resembled each other at more than one level: the magical rite and the religious rite. Hubert and Mauss used as their criteria the social conditions for performing the rite: the agents, the places, the degree of organization of the cult, and its public or private character. But in magic as in religion, there was a "pressing need for groups of individuals," since the state of the individual was "always conditioned by the state of society." "Behind Moses striking the rock is all of Israel, and, though Moses doubts, Israel does not. Behind the village dowser following his rod is the anxiety of a village searching for water."[18]

Magical rites and representations thus possessed the same collective characteristic as religion: they were "objects of belief." Hubert and Mauss did not hesitate to speak of "public credulity" and to assert that "universal consent can create realities." In this case, the laws of collective psychology violated the laws of individual psychology. Magic was a true profession, a matter of social qualifications—the magician's distinctive, even abnormal condition—and, especially, of public opinion. "It is public opinion that creates the magician and the influence he exerts." The magician was serious only because he was taken seriously, and he was taken seriously because he was needed. He was thus a "civil servant, often appointed by society, who never finds the source of his own power in himself."[19]

But what was the nature of belief in magic? Without going so far as to consider magic a scientific discipline or a primitive science, Hubert and Mauss established a "true kinship"—"knowledge is power"—between magic on the one hand and science and technology on the other, but also an interdependence. "Magic fed science and magicians became scientists." Nevertheless, the "treasure trove of ideas" that constituted magic was essentially an "art of doing," a "practical art," or rather, since magical rites and representations were inseparable, a "practical idea." Unlike science, which was "positive," "experimental," and in part "free," magic depended on faith in the first place. It was always a "system of a priori inductions" and left little or no room for "the creative or critical activity of individuals." It was possible to say that the mental operations characterized by magic included conscious arguments and true judgments but, far from being the work of individual minds, these were "the expression of social feelings." They were "value judgments."

In thus shifting the focus of their study to consider "the problem of reason," not only did Hubert and Mauss write a new chapter of religious sociology; they also provided a contribution to the study of collective representations. They sought to "find at the origin of magic the first form of collective representations, which have since become the foundations of individual understanding." In a certain number of societies, there was a central notion, "embodied elemental force" (force-milieu), which was a "peculiarly obscure representation altogether alien to our adult European understanding."[20]

To designate that notion, Hubert and Mauss again used the word mana. Mauss explained: "It is important never again to use primitive people's terms such as totem and taboo except when absolutely necessary. They have done enough harm to science. We will have to proceed differently only because of the inadequacy of the ancient languages from which we are entitled to borrow words."[21] The word mana was used only because of the absence of equivalents in Greek and Latin. The notion was also found in North America, among the Iroquois, for example, where it was called orenda, and among the Algonquins, who used the word manitou. Mana, the guiding idea behind magic, belonged "to the same order as the notion of the sacred." It was "force par excellence, the true efficacy of things." It was not simply "a force, a being," but also "an action, a quality, and a state." In other words, the word was "at once a noun, an adjective, and a verb."[22]

In short, as Claude Lévi-Strauss later said, half-seriously and half-ironically, mana was a "thingamajig, a whatchamacallit" with the idea of force or power, a mysterious force, a secret power.[23] Even though "Outline of a General Theory of Magic" stands as "the first clear statement of the role of orenda, or mana, in magic" and was thus what one reviewer called "the best analysis of magic we have,"[24] the use of the notion of mana spurred a long controversy. In the pages of Année Sociologique, Paul Huvelin opened the debate on the relationship between religion and magic. This was a frequent practice among the collaborators on Année, a practice that attested both to mutual respect and to a wish to pursue discussion.

No one questioned the existence of the notion of mana, but Hubert and Mauss were criticized for giving it a universal dimension.[25] Some, like Henri Berr at Revue de Synthèse Historique, were very harsh toward Hubert and Mauss, accusing them of "exceeding [their] rights" and "compromising the good name of sociology by unduly extending it to the far limits of dialectics."[26]

Their study extended beyond the framework of the history of religion. Hubert and Mauss offered valuable support to what was called the science of the mind. Hertz said they contributed to elaborating a "new theory of knowledge that is truly positive and experimental."[27] Durkheim and his collaborators asserted that concepts were "collective representations." In 1909 Durkheim also published an important text titled "Religious Sociology and the Theory of Knowledge" in Revue de Métaphysique et de Morale. A few years later, it would serve as an introduction to *The Elementary Forms of Religious Life* (1912).

It is important to note that Hubert and Mauss's *Mélanges d'histoire des religions* (Miscellany: The history of religion), published by Alcan in 1909, was dedicated—with a "respectful tribute" from the authors—to Théodule Ribot, their former philosophy professor at the Sorbonne, whose works (*Psychologie des sentiments, Essai sur les passions*; Psychology of the feelings, Essay on the passions) they found easy to cite in defense of the idea "that there are no religious feelings, only normal feelings of which religion . . . is a product and an object."[28] It is also not at all surprising that rationalist philosophers such as Gustave Belot reacted negatively to "Outline" and saw Hubert and Mauss's analysis as "the flip side and counterpart of the Kantian argument." "It is not an overstatement to say that, in their theory, collective madness plays the role with respect to individual experience that the other [theory] attributed to impersonal reason. It preexists that experience, imposes its forms on it, dictates its judgments to it: social constraint takes the place of transcendental necessity."[29] Belot, who was familiar with the studies by Durkheim and his collaborators, also made fun of the authors' "collective mind." Working collaboratively, they "undoubtedly made their argument less well than either of them would have done individually."

To counter rationalist philosophies, could the sociologist speak of "collective madness" when considering the mental operations of magic or religion? Did the logic of feelings stand in radical opposition to rational logic? For Hubert and Mauss, magical or religious judgments and chains of reasoning undoubtedly had a rational character: "There are limits to their absurdities. . . . The logic reigning in collective thought is more stringent than that governing the isolated man's thinking. It is easier to lie to oneself than to lie to one another."[30]

Hubert and Mauss took pleasure in rejecting all the various philosophical schools (empiricist, nominalist, rationalist) and in reaffirming the social foundation of knowledge. Categories, whether of the sacred, the soul, or time, were "ways of thinking in common" imposed on individuals by "social powers, tradition, language." They were "public rules of thought," "institutions." Aware that their argument was particularly fragile because "authentic examples" of a magical embodied elemental force were rare, Hubert and Mauss clung to their position. What they knew of the facts seemed "to justify the generality of [their] conclusions."

"Outline" was only one part of their work, though part two never appeared.[31] They were seeking "detailed research on a particular form of magic that would come along someday to verify its accuracy."[32] In an appendix to "Outline," they clearly established the limits and ambitions of their undertaking: "We want to understand magic before explaining its history. We leave aside for the moment, and reserve for a future essay, what this research ought to offer religious sociology in the way of new facts. We were tempted away from our usual concerns to contribute to the study of sociology in general, by showing how, in magic, the isolated individual is working with social phenomena."[33]

The "Dear Teacher"

According to Agathon (the pseudonym of Henri Massis and Alfred de Tarde), Durkheim was establishing his "intellectual despotism" over an entire generation of young teachers at the Sorbonne.[34] At the same time Mauss was pursuing his scholarly work with a small group of students at the École Pratique des Hautes Études.

The classroom was Mauss's laboratory. He "honed concepts" and trained students by placing them "in direct and extremely close contact with the facts."[35] He often asked them to give reports: Henri Beuchat on the Eskimos, Stefan Czarnowski on a book by Nasen called *Eskimoleben* (Eskimo life), Maxime David on sexual communism, Robert Hertz on sin, René Maunier on the relations between economic and religious phenomena, Jean Marx on the notion of soul. And just as Sylvain Lévi had done for him, he invited one of his students, Hertz, to replace him—for two trimesters, in 1908–1909—and to present his work on "rites for eliminating sin." The training Mauss intended to give was not only theoretical but also technical, leading to a mastery of intellectual work methods (including such details as the use of index cards).

The professor's relationship with his students, whose number varied between about fifteen and thirty, was close and friendly. From one year to the next, the same students returned. Hence, between 1902 and 1914, René Chaillié attended almost all of Mauss's classes. "He was one of the oldest and most faithful collaborators," Mauss would say. "Behind the appearance of an amateur who was difficult to persuade to work, he concealed a real devotion to our science, which he propagated with an extraordinary efficacy in the most various circles."[36] Mauss often followed his students' studies for several years running and maintained a regular correspondence with some of them: the Canadian Marius Barbeau, the Pole Stefan Czarnowski, Jules Bloch, Raymond Lenoir, René Maunier, Jean Przyluski, Henri Lévy-Bruhl, and others.[37] Some of his students joined the *Année Sociologique* team, first as proofreaders, then as authors of book reviews. They were, in order of their level of participation in volumes 8, 9, and 10 of the journal: Robert Hertz, Antoine Bianconi, Philippe de Felice, Jean Reynier, Henri Beuchat, Georges Gelly, and René Chaillié. Several of the new contributors had studied at the École Normale Supérieure, where they had taken the course Durkheim taught every year, beginning in 1904, on the history of secondary education in France. For the most part, they were *agrégés* in philosophy.

During their first exchanges, the students' attitudes toward their "dear teacher" was distant, respectful, even submissive. But the tone quickly changed, became friendly, sometimes affectionate. Mauss did not hesitate to help his students with advice, letters of recommendation, or even financial aid. The fact that he was a bachelor made him readily available. The social life that developed around him was especially strong when superimposed on political networks, as in the case of Hertz. Taken together, the social and political aspects formed "an environment of great mutual trust but also of severe criticism and—let us concede—perhaps of great demands."[38]

Henri Beuchat (1878–1914) was one of Mauss's oldest students and collaborators. In 1902–1903, Beuchat took Mauss's class on the elementary forms of prayer and, with Chaillié, Felice, and Lahy, actively participated in interpreting and discussing ethnographic texts on Melanesia. Beuchat had no university degree: he was self-taught.[39] After leaving school at age thirteen, he had worked at various occupations, first as a typesetter at a printing press, then as a bookkeeper in a pharmaceutical business. He devoted his leisure time to the history of printing and writing and to astronomy, chemistry, living languages, and the study of Central and South American tribes.

When his collaboration with Mauss began in 1903, Beuchat was secretary/treasurer of *Revue des Études Américaines* and was preparing an illustrated book on Mexican art with M. Le Souëf. Mauss noticed his student's technical skill and assigned him the task of preparing the tables and indexes for *Année Sociologique*. He also invited him to participate actively in the conferences he was teaching at the École Pratique, which at the time were devoted to the study of ethnographic documents on the relation between religion and the family in North America. Within the framework of the Monday conference, Beuchat gave four lectures on questions of pure ethnography, dealing with the Eskimos, their migrations, their social morphology, and their technology.[40] In 1904–1905, the conference again had to do with the Eskimos. It was a critical study of recently published documents and an analysis of totemism. Beuchat explicated Danish texts and prepared a study in collaboration with his professor on "the relations between the Eskimos' social, seasonal morphology and their religious and legal phenomena."[41]

The essay was published in *Année Sociologique* in 1906 under the title "On the Seasonal Variations of Eskimo Societies: Study of Social Morphology." According to the original outline, Mauss's participation was to be secondary. "I had thought merely of collaborating with Beuchat," he would write. But the relationship quickly shifted and the professor had to "take over the work completely."[42] Beuchat's collaboration became "partial," limited to preparing a part of the article and, thanks to his skills as a draftsman, to drawing the house plans and maps.

For Mauss, this was a way of pursuing, in a different field and at a different level, the study he had done with Durkheim on "Classifications." In that article, he had demonstrated that "the mentality of inferior tribes directly reflects their anatomical constitution." The issue at hand was methodological: to establish a correspondence between, on the one hand, "social life in all its forms—moral, religious, legal, and so on," and, on the other, its material substratum, that is, "the mass, density, form, and composition of human groups."[43] Mauss was adopting a hypothesis that Durkheim himself had sought to verify, first in *On the Division of Labor in Society* and then in *Suicide*. In the former case, the evolution of penal and civil law was a function of the morphological type of society; in the latter, individualist belief developed or weakened depending on the degree of a social group's integration.

Contrary to his usual practice, Mauss abandoned the comparative approach and confined himself to a single case. The study of Eskimo societies was presented as a "crucial experiment": "It is an error to believe that the credence a scientific proposal deserves closely depends on the number of cases believed able to verify it.... John Stuart Mill said somewhere that one well-conducted experiment suffices to demonstrate a law: Above all, it is infinitely more conclusive than many poorly conducted experiments."[44]

Mauss and Beuchat's intention was not to "collect the various peculiarities of the Eskimo peoples in a descriptive monograph," but to extract their unity. For these populations of hunters and fishermen who had neither a strict tribal organization nor a delimited territory, that unity lay in "settlement," the shared habitat of family groups. In this respect, the Eskimos offered a particularly privileged field of study, since their morphology was not the same at different times of the year. In summer there was a dispersion of the habitat and of families, who took shelter in tents; in winter, there was a "gathering in" around a longhouse, where several families lived. Travel and long migrations gave way to immobility in winter.

These seasonal variations were obviously an adaptation to environmental constraints. The Eskimos were obliged to disperse to hunt caribou and musk ox in summer, and they needed to join forces in winter to capture walruses. But this ecological determinism provided only an incomplete explanation, because it did not account for the intensification of collective life during the long winter months. The two seasons stood opposed as much at a religious and familial level as in the organization of goods and politics. One was symbolized by "reindeer skins," the other by "walrus skins." Summer was characterized by the minimal practice of a domestic cult, by the nuclear family, and by familial or individual appropriation of goods; winter by intense religious activity, many feast days, collective kinship, and communitarian distribution of food and goods. On one side, individualism (and egoism), on the other, collectivism. "A real community of ideas and interests in the dense agglomeration of winter and strong mental religious and moral unity contrast to an isolation, a crumbling of social life, an extreme moral and religious poverty, in the summer dispersal."[45] "Communism," both economic and sexual (with the exchange of women), was the object of fascination: it "shows the degree of moral unity the Eskimo community achieves [in winter]." It was the apogee of social life.

The "odd alternation" Mauss observed was not specific to the Eskimos but was also found among Pacific Coast Indians—for example, the Kwakiutl, whom Franz Boas had studied—and in pastoral populations in the mountains of Europe. Mauss even extended his comparative analysis to "our Western societies," where he observed the "same oscillations": in cities, periods of languor lasting from summer until the end of autumn, then an intensification of activities and relationships in winter; in the countryside, the reverse, dispersion and torpor in the wintertime, and feasts, serious work, and serious debauchery in summer.[46]

It was thus a general law. Social law "goes through successive and regular phases of increasing and decreasing intensity, rest and activity, expenditure and restoration." Because it did violence to consciousness, life in common was possible only if members of a group could "partly withdraw from it."

In addition to the overarching rhythm of the seasons, there were oscillations within each season, each month, each week, each day. The question of the rhythm of collective life had concerned Durkheim in *Suicide*; it also interested Hubert who, in his study of the idea of time in religion and magic, sought to explain how the calendar was formed.

For anyone aware of the difficulty in presenting synthetically the customs of far-ranging populations, "Essay on Seasonal Variations" may seem schematic. Although E. Sidney Hartland was impressed by Mauss and Beuchat's "well-developed" study, he persisted in believing that the life of collectivities was not as simple as that of birds. He criticized the authors for establishing "a difference of social organization between summer and winter that is greater than the facts allow." The English anthropologist, though very sympathetic toward *Année Sociologique*, did not believe it impossible that "the rhythm of dispersion and concentration, individual life and collective life, might correspond to a more general law." The whole question was whether "the variations are produced entirely by morphological changes."[47]

The English anthropologist R. R. Marett, an ardent defender of social psychology, praised the "brilliant contributors" to *Année Sociologique*, particularly Mauss—"the most able and thoroughgoing anthropological researcher"—then criticized them for going too far afield in "one-sided explanations of morphological derivation."[48] Mauss was eager to defend his point of view. In a letter to Marett he wrote, "I do not in the least attribute a preponderant importance to morphological factors. But I believed I had developed the physiological or [illegible] viewpoint so thoroughly in my earlier studies that I did not think it necessary to explain myself on that count. I don't need to tell you that, in society, I believe only in the existence of men affected by their place in time and space on the one hand, and by shared and social phenomena of consciousness on the other. . . . Like you, I define all phenomena that do not have to do with morphology, or with psychological reactions to morphology, in terms of consciousness, in terms of psychology."

Mauss also wanted to explain why he did not use "psychological language." It was for a "relatively accidental reason." "For the last twelve years, we have had to eliminate collective psychology in France; it was entirely mystical on the one hand, completely and intentionally confusing on the other." There had thus been something excessive in the effort he and his collaborators had made to explain "what is specific to social phenomena and to link them to their material substratum, namely, men gathered in a territory." Now that the field was cleared, he intended "to better limit the scope of his studies."[49]

Mauss had just published a long note in *Revue Philosophique* entitled "Art and Myth according to Wundt." His opposition to his colleague's *Völkerpsychologie* was clear. Mauss criticized collective psychology for detaching the facts it studied—language, myths, art, ethics—from their "natural ambience," that is, their social context. He concluded: "In fact, men have never entered into relations with one another except within defined and organized groups and, as a result, it is altogether high-handed to imagine a mental life independent of any organization. At the very least, the group they form always has a sense of itself and of its unity; and that sense, which varies depending on the nature, form, and composition of the group, necessarily affects all the representations that come into being within it."[50]

As he was writing "Essay on Seasonal Variations," Mauss broadened his Americanist field of interest in his classes and analyzed ethnographic texts dealing with societies of the American Northwest (the Kwakiutl, the Bella Coola, and so on), particularly books by Boas, whose interpretations he criticized. During the school year 1905–1906, Mauss did a comparative study of the potlatch, an institution that "affects and dominates all social phenomena in these tribes." One of his scholarship students, Marius Barbeau, a young Canadian with a law degree, was preparing a thesis at Oxford directed by Marett. It was entitled "The Totemic System of North Western Indian Tribes of North America" (1910). A few years later he became one of the first members of the ethnology team led by Edward Sapir, who in 1913–1914 would set up the first Canadian scientific expedition to the Arctic. Two anthropologists participated in that expedition, headed by N. U. Stefanson: Diamond Jenness from New Zealand and Henri Beuchat. For Beuchat, who was responsible for studying the language, manners, customs, and religious beliefs of the Arctic populations,[51] it would be "the greatest joy of his life." He would have the opportunity to become a professional anthropologist, to observe the Eskimos for four years, and to "know the peoples with whom he had long lived in his imagination."[52] In a long letter to Mauss in which he described the preparations, he concluded: "Everything augurs well for the success of the expedition."[53] But at the beginning of the expedition in January 1914, the trawler *Karluck* was shipwrecked and Beuchat died on Wrangell Island of hunger and exposure.[54]

When Robert Hertz, wanting to study religious and moral phenomena, enrolled at the École Pratique des Hautes Études, he already knew Mauss. In 1902 he had invited Mauss to give a lecture on "cooperative action," sponsored by *Prolétarienne*, at one of the people's universities.[55] Hertz was born in 1881 and graduated from the École Normale at a very young age, after a brilliant success at the *agrégation* (philosophy, 1904). He impressed people with his easy manner, the quality of his criticism, and his relentless work.[56] Durkheim did not hesitate to speak of the young Normalian's "warm-heartedness" and "thirst for justice."[57] Everything about Hertz—"his face, his mind, his manner"—corresponded to what Hubert called "the new way of thinking, the new faith." "Tall, well-built, clean-shaven with a high forehead, blond hair, and pale, soft, attentive, penetrating eyes, he seemed like a 'fellow' from England or America, one of those young university scientists who conducted scholarly research, did student teaching, played sports, and conducted social surveys all at once."[58]

Mauss and Hertz were about ten years apart. As someone who had witnessed Hertz's early career, Mauss was well aware of the wavering of his student, who, during his years at the École Normale Supérieure, could not choose between pure sociology on the one hand and ethics and politics on the other. Once he was an *agrégé*, Hertz opted for "questions where the ethical touches on the religious." Supported by a scholarship, he spent 1905 and 1906 in England.

In 1905 Mauss went to London to consult texts on the Eskimos at the British Museum. There he worked "like an ox from ten o'clock in the morning till seven o'clock at night . . . and with consistent intensity!" Next to him was the "worthy and excellent" Hertz, who was working like a "madman," quickly going through an enormous mass of books.[59] For Hertz, these were intoxicating days: he found new ideas, new facts, new avenues, new connections. Mauss had a great deal of sympathy for his student and his "sweet little wife." "They are very charming, childish, a little too serious but very nice."[60] Hertz's "beloved wife," as Durkheim called her, was Alice Sarah Bauer; she was four years Hertz's senior. During their time in London, Alice became interested in educational problems, studied pedagogy, taught school, and became involved in the Froebel Society, whose objective was to promote the idea of day care centers and kindergartens. She was so enthusiastic about them that, when she returned to Paris, she sought to introduce the new pedagogical methods into French schools and in 1909 opened the first day care centers in Paris.

Hertz joined the *Année Sociologique* team as it was preparing volume 8 (1903–1904), which appeared in 1905. Durkheim put him in charge of part of the section on religious sociology. The student and collaborator quickly became a friend. Durkheim said Hertz had a "rigorous and penetrating mind" and "an unusually noble character."[61]

In the field of religious sociology, Hertz advanced with confidence and control, distinguishing himself by the ingenuity and soundness of his mind, the scope of his erudition, the breadth and sharpness of his intelligence. Mauss later remembered him as already a master among masters, and his capacity for work was as great as the results he produced.[62] He was interested in the "dark and sinister sides of the human mind." What intrigued him was the mystery of forgiveness: How and why does a society erase sin and crime? How and why does it forget? In London, Hertz had long discussions with Mauss about funeral rites and collected a large quantity of facts he would use in his later studies. Under Durkheim's influence, but also "through soundness of mind, logic, and meditation," he organized his research program, which would include studies on the collective representation of death and on religious polarity, as well as an (unfinished) thesis on sin and expiation in primitive societies.[63]

When he returned from England, Hertz accepted a job as a *lycée* teacher in Douai, for ethical reasons, according to Durkheim. "Hertz believed that every citizen has a duty to perform a particular function in society."[64] These were "happy and fruitful" years, since Hertz liked to teach, though "the life of an academic is hardly auspicious . . . for one's own work."[65] In the second semester of 1906–1907, Hertz took Mauss's classes at the École Pratique. These courses dealt primarily with Africa, and in particular established "ethnographic instructions for observing the populations of French colonies in western Africa and the Congo" and for studying African religious systems. The same year, Hertz published an excellent essay in *Année Sociologique* on the notion of death. Two years later, Mauss was named assistant director and invited Hertz to replace him at the Tuesday conference. There Hertz presented the "rites for eliminating sin." He participated in the Tuesday conference for the next two years. In 1909–1910, he sought to establish the meaning of the words *maroi tapu*, *noa*, and *tamaoatia* as a way to determine the religious significance attributed to violating a taboo. In 1910–1911 he studied "the religious element of penal law" among the Polynesians, and particularly among the Maori of New Zealand. Among the students at the time were Henri Beuchat, Marius Barbeau, Stefan Czarnowski, René Chaillié, Georges Davy, Jean Marx, René Maunier, and a few others.

Hertz and Mauss had a close relationship. They both taught at the École Pratique, collaborated on *Année Sociologique*, and engaged in political activities. They had similar scientific interests: "I suppose you're in Épinal finishing the Prayer for good. . . . I'm up to my neck in penitence and don't find myself too badly off."[66] Hertz felt great admiration for his professor and friend. "Essay on the Nature and Function of Sacrifice" was an exemplary study in his view: "For the first time, a religious institution is studied in its integrity with the sole concern to constitute its type, to discover its mechanism and its function."[67]

Mélanges

As he was writing "Essay on Sacrifice," Hubert was toying with the idea for *Mélanges d'histoires des religions*, a collection of his and Mauss's articles.[68] The book was published by Alcan in 1909 and edited by Émile Durkheim. This was the second book in the series, after Bouglé's *Essays on the Caste System*.

The publication of the volume gave greater visibility to Hubert and Mauss's research as a whole, whose results had been scattered among scholarly journals. In Hartland's view, this was a "felicitous initiative," since it allowed "their studies to be more widely known and studied."[69] The articles were presented in the following order: "On a Few Results of Religious Sociology," "Essay on the Nature and Function of Sacrifice," "The Origin of Magical Powers in Australian Societies," and "The Representation of Time."[70]

The first article in *Mélanges*, initially published in *Revue de l'Histoire des Religions*, constituted a true "introduction to the analysis of a few religious phenomena." Hubert and Mauss took the opportunity to correct—in what was a "true retraction," said Alfred Loisy—some of their previous analyses and to respond to the criticism directed at them. They considered sacrifice, magic, and the problem of reason. Their attitude was defensive, but they did not hide their pride at having had a few victories. They had identified the notion of the sacred as a central religious phenomenon; had distinguished between positive and negative rites; and had studied the origins of understanding.

Since "Essay on Sacrifice," Hubert and Mauss's objective had been to understand institutions, that is, the public rules of action and thought, and to demonstrate that sacrifice and magic were social phenomena. The problem that concerned them was the relation between the individual and society: "What is the individual's attitude within the social phenomenon? What is society's share in the individual's consciousness?" The response was the same for magic, sacrifice, prayer, and myths: "The individual thinks and acts only as directed by tradition or impelled by a collective suggestion or, at the very least, by a suggestion of his own under pressure from the collectivity."[71]

Even though they granted little importance to labels, Hubert and Mauss reaffirmed that they were and remained sociologists. Their position was clear, as Hartland noted: "For the French authors the social influence is everything. Judgements, for them, are not dictated by the individual reason, but by social forces. We owe much to Prof. Durkheim and his disciples for calling attention to the social side of religion."[72] In terms of method, this meant that, unlike (English) anthropologists and (German) psychologists, who "proceed directly to similarities" and "everywhere seek only the human, the common—in a word, the banal," Hubert and Mauss paused to consider "the characteristic differences of special environments." It was through these environments that they hoped to "catch a glimpse of laws." The comparative approach Hubert and Mauss defended consisted of "studying, by society, the variations of analogous institutions or notions" and identifying "either what remains constant throughout these variations or the equivalent functions they all perform."[73] The objective was to discover the universal phenomena of social life, solidly grounding them in the study of particular institutions: sacrifices, magic, forms of classification. Hubert and Mauss, contrasting their studies of a few religious phenomena to theology-saturated speculations, placed themselves unambiguously on the side of fact and not faith.

Mélanges was a momentous event in the science of religion. Here was a sound inductive method, said Hertz, "standing at an equal distance from pure scholarship and from speculation," and leading to "nearly definitive results."[74] The book was analyzed from every angle, including form. The many neologisms the authors used, such as *heroization, communal, sacralization,* and *desacralization*, were denounced by some critics as "unwelcome strangers, true Barbarians."[75] The link to Durkheim was also a flaw according to some: "Unfortunately, the work as a whole is inspired by materialism. The mere name of Durkheim, which the authors invoke to protect themselves, announces the error."[76] The Reverend Father P. G. Schmidt's animosity toward Hubert and Mauss was keen. The director of the journal *Anthropos* had difficulty tolerating their "sarcastic irony" and, still opposed to their "incommensurately sociological" theory, he criticized them for "not grasping the primarily positive nature of the personality." In addition, he denied their "priority rights" to the theory of magic.[77]

There was an immediate reaction, and not just from sociologists,[78] anthropologists, and historians of religion—including some close to the authors, such as Salomon Reinach, who was mentioned in the preface—but also from theologians and philosophers. They found the "quiescence of [Hubert and Mauss's] usual assertions" upset by the "swaggering posture" the two authors sometimes adopted. Loisy, while thanking the authors for bringing attention to the social side of religious phenomena, criticized the overly ambitious nature of an approach that, "after presuming to dictate to history, encroaches on the field of philosophy." In his view, simply showing that categories of thought were social was not an adequate response to the questions philosophy raised "about the value of cognition and the reality of its object."[79]

9

A HEATED BATTLE AT THE

COLLÈGE DE FRANCE:

THE LOISY AFFAIR

FOR MAUSS, publishing *Mélanges* was a particularly felicitous idea because it made his "otherwise arid" studies accessible at a strategic moment in his career, when he was seeking to emerge from his "mouse-trap," as his mother called it, and had applied for a position at the Collège de France.

An old institution, founded by Francis I in 1530 to thwart the monopoly of the Université de Paris, the Collège was a refuge for disciplines or curricula that were not yet considered legitimate, but it also established the reputations of scholars who had distinguished themselves through original studies.[1] As an institution directly answerable to the Ministry of Public Education, it had particular characteristics. In its recruitment practices, it did not require a university degree; its teaching was public and did not prepare students for any exams; professors were free to choose the subject of their courses; and there were no permanent chairs. Nowhere else did scientific research enjoy such broad independence. That freedom was its raison d'être and had become its law.

Even though *Année Sociologique* had backing at the Collège, for example from Sylvain Lévi and the psychologist Pierre Janet (a classmate of Durkheim's at the École Normale), the institution remained out of reach for the journal's founder. In 1904, when Gabriel Tarde died and Henri Bergson obtained a chair in social philosophy, Durkheim had hopes that the chair in Greek and Latin philosophy that Bergson had held would be turned into a sociology chair. But historians and literature professors finally succeeded (on a vote of nineteen to eleven) in creating a chair of history and national treasures, which was awarded to Camille Jullian. With the master thrust aside, did his collaborators have any chance? Was there any hope for Mauss? Some, such as Lucien Herr, thought there was.

In early 1907 Albert Réville's death gave Mauss a first chance; he was thirty-five years old at the time. He could count on the support of his former teacher Sylvain Lévi but also on two contributors to *Année Sociologique*, Antoine Meillet and Charles Fossey, who had been appointed at the Collège the previous year. He was urged to apply. His qualifications,

as Sylvain Lévi said, permitted him "to legitimately aspire to the best position." Was he not the "acknowledged head of a school recruited from the
most hardworking and intelligent students, standing clearly apart from the
amateurs and the idle?"[2] Mauss decided to stay out of the limelight, however, not seeking to change the chair in the history of religion to a sociology chair or to be named to it. "Out of deference," he agreed to step aside
in favor of older scholars. In any case, despite what some "stupid, slan-
derous gossip" suggested, there was no question "of using the influence
of the press and a personal relationship with the minister to [get himself]
appointed in place of M. Jean Réville."[3] Mauss applied only as a candidate
en seconde ligne.[4]

The prime candidate to succeed Albert Réville, the man who had held
the chair previously and who was president of the section of religious
science at the École Pratique, was Réville's son, Jean (1854–1908). He
intended to pursue his father's work while maintaining "a generous tolerance, a disinterested passion for truth, and a scrupulous fidelity to scientificity" in his teaching.[5] A minister with a doctorate in theology (the title of
his thesis was "Religion in Rome during the Severian Age"), Jean Réville
was an extremely active pedagogue and university administrator. He had
a chair at the faculty of Protestant theology at the Université de Paris; was
a secretary and lecturer in the section of religious science at the École
Pratique; directed *Revue de l'Histoire des Religions*; and organized scientific
congresses. Like his father, he was an "ardent liberal" and a "free believer"
who rejected polemics. His teaching stood "halfway between science as it
is practiced and a rapidly spreading popularization."[6]

Réville's chief rival was Georges Foucart, a doctor in letters, Egyptologist,
and author of articles in specialized journals of archaeology and religious
history. He taught ancient Eastern history and religion in Aix-Marseilles. His
father, Paul Foucart, was a professor at the Collège de France and presented
his son's application, insisting that his candidacy was "purely scientific" and
"separate from any denominational concerns." He added that his son would
employ a "more rational method" than that used by scientists, who, in trying to "reconstitute humanity's primitive religion by collecting the beliefs of
savages on every side," arrived only at "results of dubious value."[7]

At the meeting of February 17, 1907, Jean Réville won in the second round,
securing votes that in the first round had gone to Marcel Mauss and Maurice
Vernes, both professors at the École des Hautes Études. Backed by Pierre
Janet, Camille Jullian, Antoine Meillet, and, of course, Sylvain Lévi, Mauss
presented himself *en seconde ligne*. He was competing with Georges Foucart,
Arnold Van Gennep, and Maurice Vernes. With little difficulty, he obtained
support from the majority of the thirty-six professors present: fifteen votes
in the first round, twenty-one in the second. His mother wrote: "I wonder
whether you've taken to heart, as you ought, the nominal success you're

seeking as a candidate *en seconde ligne*. If only all these events . . . inspired you to finish your book so as to be in a better position in the future."[8] Rosine wanted her son to "get [himself] in a position to apply with a respectable book of [his] own as quickly as possible." "There's no time to waste."[9]

That first campaign attested to Mauss's ambition and his desire to get out of the "mousetrap" that the École Pratique des Hautes Études had become for him, even though he had just earned the title of assistant director (with an increase in salary from 2,000 to 3,000 francs).

The year 1907 marked a turning point for sociology in France, with a consolidation of the place that contributors to *Année Sociologique* occupied within academia. Durkheim, named to a permanent chair a year before, was exerting a greater influence, particularly at the Sorbonne, where one of his collaborators, Célestin Bouglé, had succeeded Alfred Espinas to the chair in social economics. The same year, Lucien Lévy-Bruhl, closely associated with Durkheimian sociology, came to occupy the chair in modern philosophy. All three were orchestrating a campaign to support Fauconnet for the chair in social philosophy at Toulouse, left vacant by Bouglé. In his letter of support, Durkheim distinguished clearly between philosophers who "treat social matters intuitively" and those who "have acquired indispensable historical or statistical knowledge" and, "in a word, have given themselves a complete education."[10] Thanks to his "ten years of specialized studies," Fauconnet was finally named to the chair, even though he had not yet earned his doctorate.

The workload of the *Année Sociologique* team increased greatly. Its contributors were now being solicited from all sides, and they had trouble satisfying the demands of a journal that was taking a great deal of time from them all.[11] Durkheim, knowing he had reached "full maturity" and was "capable of doing something," complained about spending four months at *Année* "doing bibliography and reviews, etc." At forty-eight, he was aware that "what will not be done in the next ten years will never be done. One must therefore make a decision, looking at the situation like a man."[12]

Changing the format of *Année* became an urgent necessity. Durkheim believed that "if the group is to last, it must be in a different form." The solution envisioned was to publish annals of sociology that would include, "in addition to the published work, a bibliography without analysis." Mauss's "assistance" was still causing problems. His participation was "necessary" but his "unbelievable irregularities" caused his uncle "moral suffering" and "remov[ed] all reliability from a collaboration in need of it."[13] In 1907 the journal weathered a crisis that was particularly serious because it occurred at a time when relations between Durkheim and Mauss were deteriorating. Mauss was even thinking of "refusing to collaborate" on *Année*. His mother told him curtly that that would be much better for his future than "making a commitment and not keeping your word."[14] Faced with his nephew's "implausible behavior"—lack of candor, inconsistency, and so on—the uncle became angry and stopped speaking to him for a time.

Année Sociologique came out of the crisis only when it redefined its orientation. It now appeared only once every three years (1910 and 1913) and the essays were separated out, becoming material for a special series, the "Travaux de l'Année Sociologique" published by Alcan.[15] The first two books in the collection were Bouglé's *Essays on the Caste System* and Hubert and Mauss's *Mélanges d'histoire des religions*. Mauss continued to make significant contributions to *Année*. He wrote about forty reviews for each of the last two volumes in the first series; in addition, he played the role of recruiter for young researchers, including, of course, his own students (Jean-Paul Lafitte, Henri Jeanmaire, Georges Davy, Jean Marx, Maxime David).

When Jean Réville died in 1908, a second, more serious opportunity presented itself to Mauss. Fauconnet wrote him: "I hope Réville's death will encourage you to work. You really have an unexpected opportunity to give your life, your work, and your teaching the perfect environment. I'd like to be sure you have the ambition to carry it off."[16]

In his letter of application, Mauss presented a statement of not only his qualifications and main writings but also his research and teaching programs: the development of prayer, the relationship between magic and religion, the notion of the sacred and of ritual prohibitions, the dissolution of totemism, religious forms of the notion of substance, religious forms of the notion of value, and the general theory of myth. In addition to studies he called "general," Mauss wanted to consider more specialized or technical questions (for example, oath as ritual in the Bible and the Talmud; texts on the Brahmanic ritual; notions concerning food, fire, and the voice in the Vedas and Brahmanas; Origen's *De oratione*) and also to catalogue ritual prohibitions in the Talmud, in classical literature, in the epic and legal literature of India, in New Zealand and Madagascar, among the Eskimos, in the religions of Central America, in French and Germanic folklore, and so on.[17]

At the start of the campaign for the position at the Collège de France in June 1909, "the Mauss camp [was] strong and his appointment seem[ed] likely."[18] But as the number of candidates multiplied, the competition quickly grew keen. In addition to three candidates who applied with no real hope of success (Amélineau, Moret, and Révillout), there was Paul Foucart's son Georges, who had just published a new book titled *La méthode comparative dans l'histoire des religions* (Picard, 1909; The comparative method in the history of religion), and two professors from the École des Hautes Études, Maurice Vernes and Jules Toutain. The Protestants supported Vernes, whose interest in the Collège was known—he was a candidate *en seconde ligne* in 1893 for the chair in Hebraic languages and a temporary replacement in 1904 and 1905 for the chair in Hebraic, Chaldean, and Syriac languages and literatures. His allies wanted to use him to retain control of a chair that had been in their hands since the Collège was founded.

The situation became even more complicated when, in the fall, Alfred Loisy decided to enter the race and blurred the classic divisions by giving his candidacy a politico-religious dimension. Loisy, a priest and former Dreyfusard, was identified with the "modernist" current of the history of Christianity. In March 1908 he had been excommunicated by a decree from the Holy Office. His appointment, as Loisy acknowledged, ran the risk of looking like a "blow to the country and the Catholics, a response to the Pascendi encyclical."[19] Once again Loisy and Mauss found themselves going head to head: the theologian/historian against the sociologist/philosopher. Alfred Loisy, however, was not "one to condemn the application of the sociological method to the history of religion or to think that the history of religion has nothing to gain from that method."

In accordance with tradition, each of the candidates visited the faculty members at the Collège and presented his qualifications and writings. The bargaining was especially complex because it involved personalities outside the institution: the marquise Arconati-Visconti for Loisy,[20] Salomon Reinach for Mauss. Paul and Georges Foucart took pains to appeal for votes from members of the Académie des Sciences Morales and from Catholics who feared Loisy's appointment.

Mauss was assured of the support of his professors and friends Sylvain Lévi, Fossey, and Meillet. He could also count on votes from Émile Gley, a biologist born in Épinal; Georges Renard, former director of *Revue Socialiste* and a historian of labor; and Grégoire Wyrouboff, a Russian professor in the general history of science and a former Dreyfusard. Finally, Durkheim believed that Maurice Croiset, a reader of *Année Sociologique*, would be willing to say positive things about Mauss's last book. This was not enough. Sociology, and Durkheimian sociology in particular, was the object of keen opposition, especially from Jean Izoulet, who had taken an adamant position against the added requirement—which he considered a "national peril"— that Durkheimian sociology be taught in the two hundred French normal schools. Under such conditions, it was not easy for Mauss to broaden his base of support and become, as Salomon Reinach hoped, the "church's candidate against an excommunicant."

Because of the large number of candidates (eight), the discussion of qualifications on the afternoon of January 31 was long and lively. Thirty-six professors attended. The three main candidates—Georges Foucart, an Egyptologist; Alfred Loisy, restricted in spite of himself to the history of Christianity's origins; and Marcel Mauss, a specialist in "primitive religions"—were presented, respectively, by Professors Chuquet, Babelon, and Lévi. In his statement, Mauss's sponsor pointed to "his remarkable study on prayer." Meillet also took the floor to say that Mauss was the obvious candidate for a general curriculum on the history of religion. During the meeting, Maurice Croiset also spoke up, but only to add a few observations on the candidacy of Jules Toutain.[21]

In the first round, the race was close; it would take four more rounds to arrive at a decision on the leading candidate. Loisy won in the fifth round with a slight majority: nineteen against sixteen for Foucart. His victory was explained, first, by the extent of the initial support he had received, including that of Henri Bergson. In addition, the strategy of Mauss's supporters, who decided in the third round to block Georges Foucart, favored Alfred Loisy: they all gave him their vote, except one unyielding professor who agreed to "convert" only at the last minute, in the fifth round.

For the appointment *en seconde ligne* to Réville's chair, the race was also close and, against all expectations, Mauss was defeated by his colleague Jules Toutain, who won in the third round by a one-vote majority (seventeen to sixteen). That evening a large crowd gathered at Sylvain Lévi's home and there was an animated discussion of the results of the vote. People expressed consternation: they were especially disappointed that Mauss had been defeated as a candidate *en seconde ligne* because of the absence of any prior agreement between his supporters and those of Loisy.

Reactions to Loisy's appointment were keen and came primarily from Catholic circles on the right. According to the anti-Semitic writer Léon Daudet, the preference granted to a "champion of modernism . . . Salomon Reinach's protégé," whose writings were "dull" and whose person was "despicable," looked like "toadyism to the anticlerical forces in power."[22] The political figure Charles Maurras, also an anti-Semite and an extreme nationalist, felt the same indignation and was doubly scandalized by the affair: first, at a political level, because the Collège had rallied behind "the disgraceful anti-Catholic campaign" of the republican government; and second, at a religious level, because it had appointed a "heretic, a priest excommunicated for attacking the spiritual origins of Christianity."[23] The archbishop of Paris responded to the affront by prohibiting his congregation from communicating with the miscreant, and hence from attending his classes. The rumor spread that the highly conservative groups Camelots du Roi and Action Française would prevent the lectures from being held. As a result, on the morning of the first class there was a mob at the Collège. The police were present. But in the absence of "anti-Loisyists," the course could take place in peace. The new professor, wearing a redingote and a sad face, looking like a Protestant minister, read his lecture with great poise and, evoking Albert Réville, Jean Réville, and Ernest Renan, presented his method as critical, scientific, and historical.

For Paul Fauconnet, Loisy's appointment was an "error." He told Mauss: "You and you alone were the man for the chair. Scientifically, Loisy's appointment is an error. The Collège does not understand what the history of religion is." He added it was "an injustice toward you" and "a scandal, a real disgrace."[24] Like all Mauss's friends, Fauconnet was "deeply saddened." He was convinced that, in the words of Espinas, his former professor in Bordeaux, Marcel was "the right man in the right place" for the chair in the history of religion.[25] How to comfort Mauss other than by asserting: "The future is yours and you will have your revenge"?[26]

An Unfinished Prayer

After that ordeal, which ought to have earned him "something better than a cross,"[27] Mauss knew he would have to be patient and began to put the finishing touches on his doctoral thesis. Since the previous year, the study on prayer had been "drawing toward its amen," in the words of his student Claude Maître, who held a position at the École Française d'Extrême-Orient in Hanoi.[28]

The monograph on prayer was Mauss's masterwork. When he finally took it upon himself to finish writing his "poor thesis," work on his "vast subject"—with the accumulation of references, notes, and index cards on his readings—had already dragged on for nearly ten years.

The thesis was originally supposed to have had at least three parts. The first was devoted to the study of how prayer was formed in elementary religions (Australia); the second, to how the spiritual dimension of prayer developed (Vedic, Brahmanic, and Buddhist prayer in ancient India); and the last, to "the development of prayer as an increasingly individual rite," with the model provided by the Semitic religions in Syria and Palestine and by Christianity in its early centuries. A fourth part might be added to these three, to take into account the "regressions" that led to ritualism and fetishism. Such a plan would have allowed Mauss to completely survey his "garden," beginning with the first authors he had read (especially Bardaigne and Sylvain Lévi), then to analyze the evolution of prayer and religion as a whole. The perspective was to be clearly evolutionist, with the "progress" of prayer leading to greater spiritualization and individualization. For Mauss these two tendencies were so intimately connected that it could be said that the "'inner god' of the most advanced religions is also the god of individuals."[29]

Rather quickly, Mauss limited his ambitions "to the elementary forms of oral ritual," since, as he explained, "to understand the entire sequence of developments, one must first know the elementary forms."[30] In his first class of 1901–1902, though the objective was to "search for a definition of the religious rite in general and of prayer in particular," emphasis was placed on "the careful inventory of all the facts known about the oral rites of the Australians." The next year, having established the character of prayer in all Australian religions, Mauss went on to analyze the explanatory principle behind elementary forms of prayer and oral rites in general: "There are states of excitation and collective ecstasy where . . . a sort of hypnotic belief spreads to encompass an entire group of individuals."

For the most part, his time was taken up publishing essays and writing reviews for *Année Sociologique* (thirty-three in 1905, thirty in 1906, forty in 1907), but in 1908 and 1909 Mauss enjoyed a certain respite. *Année* now appeared only every three years, and that lull allowed him to write his long critical note titled "Art and Myth according to Wundt" (1908);[31] to publish a long essay, "Introduction to the Analysis of a Few Religious Phenomena" in collaboration with Hubert; and to put together and edit *Mélanges d'histoire des religions*.

Although he had read a great deal on prayer and had accumulated many notes, Mauss probably did not begin writing his thesis until 1907–1908, mostly in the summer. He took refuge in Épinal, "working calmly, except on days when [he] got lost in the woods," and later in Viroflay, where he rented a country house on rue Julien-Certain. His friends and colleagues hoped he was "completing Prayer for good," and knowing he was busy, were hesitant to "drag him away from [his] damned prayer."[32] Everyone encouraged him. Even though he considered it his "moral and professional duty" to respect his commitments, Mauss backed out of some of them, giving up the idea of presenting a paper, for example, at the International Congress on Religions to be held in Oxford in August 1908.

More than anyone else, Rosine Mauss was happy to see her son's work advancing: "May God allow you to keep working passionately and finally achieve a real success that will get you out of the mousetrap at the École des Hautes Études (the school of higher studies, not commercial ones)."[33] But because she was anxious and had no clear idea of how to help her son finish his book, she tirelessly repeated the same advice: "Don't let yourself idle away your time day after day"; "Get to bed early." She was especially afraid that her son's habit of getting up at ten in the morning, and his "usual dragging about" (eating breakfast, reading the paper, and so on), would make morning work "illusory."[34]

As Mauss was grappling with his *Prière*, Durkheim began work on *The Elementary Forms of Religious Life*. Maurice Leenhardt, Mauss's collaborator, would write that no one would ever know whether it was the uncle or the nephew who first thought of the "elementary forms of religion."[35] When Durkheim first raised the question of familial and religious relationships, which was rather difficult at the time, "Mauss built cubes for his uncle, placing a relative or ally on each face to indicate his or her relation to mother-right and thus illustrate exchanges and reciprocity between groups."[36]

The two men worked on the same data, particularly the discoveries of Baldwin Spencer and F.-J. Gillen (*The Native Tribes of Central Australia*, 1899; *The Northern Tribes of Central Australia*, 1904) and Carl Strehlow (*Die*

Aranda- und Loritja-Stamme in Zentral-Australia). Durkheim (in 1902) and Mauss (in 1905) had also published short articles on totemism in *Année Sociologique*, a subject both conceived as "the most frequently observed religious system in religions whose principle is social organization based on exogamic clans." Finally, both were fascinated by the Arunta, the best-known Australian tribe, which represented a "rare case, exceptionally rich in information and suggestiveness" and of "great scientific importance." "In the Arunta we find the most distant past perpetuating itself and the future in the offing," wrote Durkheim. "It is a mistake to see them as the backward representatives of humanity at its beginnings. It would be no less a mistake not to recognize everything that survives in them of the most primitive forms we have been privy to."[37] Mauss chose these Australian tribes as his field of research because they "bore signs of primitivism," but he declined to argue that they were primitive men, as several authors in a "sort of anthropological intoxication" had done. At most he felt justified in considering the facts he intended to study "provisionally primitive."[38]

As he was doing the final writing, Mauss encountered real difficulties: "I am advancing slowly, but headed toward the end of the book. In spite of a certain gusto, I feel there's something broken inside me."[39] Mauss circulated the manuscript of his essay to a few people, including, of course, Durkheim. On reading the first version of the preface, the uncle was disappointed, "chagrined": "The beginning especially seems utterly ludicrous."[40] Espinas was less harsh and would send him brief positive comments after reading a few pages.[41]

Two sections, about a fourth of the book, were typeset privately and provisionally in 1909 at the Félix Alcan printing press, but, on Sylvain Lévi's advice, Mauss withdrew them, since in the meantime he had become aware of new documents from Carl Strehlow (*Die Aranda- und Loritja-Stamme in Zentral-Australia*).

These data appeared particularly valuable because they allowed Mauss to produce a new and more extensive study. Mauss was quite familiar with the studies of Strehlow, a German missionary who had moved to Australia in 1892 and had begun to publish the first installments in what was to be a seven-part series. In his manuscript on prayer, Mauss quoted generously from the first two installments, published in 1907 and 1908, which he and Durkheim would review for *Année Sociologique*. When *The Elementary Forms of Religious Life* appeared, Durkheim would regret having been unable to take into account another of Strehlow's installments, which was published just as he was finishing his book, but he did use to advantage observations Strehlow had made in his first installments. The death of the book's publishers—Leonhardi in 1911, Hagen in 1919—and World War I would delay publication of the last installments. The seventh volume did not appear until 1920.

For Mauss, prayer was a "central phenomenon," a "point of convergence for a large number of religious phenomena," and belonged "both to the nature of the rite and to the nature of belief." At issue was the spoken word, but one whose efficacy was sui generis and required the intimate union of action and thought: "To speak is both to act and to think." Studying such an activity made it possible to reject both mythology and ritology: "Every rite necessarily corresponds to a more or less vague notion and every belief elicits movements, however weak they may be."[42]

Mauss's working definition of prayer was as follows: "Prayer is an oral religious rite bearing directly on sacred things."[43] That definition, in emphasizing the distinction between the sacred and the profane, allowed him to avoid the trap "of a nomenclature marked by theology." It was an invitation "not to see all things through Christian ideas" and not to take as one's starting point the modern notion of prayer, conceived as "a spiritual relationship between the man of faith and his god."

From a methodological perspective, prayer was also a privileged field. Although he believed "one must not perpetually debate questions of methodology," Mauss summarized the major steps in the scientific approach as he had presented them in "Sociology" (1901): definition (and rejection of prenotions); observation (and criticism of historical and ethnological documents); and finally, explanation. For that last phase, Mauss distinguished two equally permissible procedures, schematic explanation and genetic explanation. The first type, used in "Essay on Sacrifice," focused the analysis on a few phenomena, relatively large in number but carefully selected. The second type began with the most elementary forms of a fact, "moving gradually to increasingly developed forms." In La prière, Mauss adopted the genetic approach: the historical succession of forms became the important explanatory factor.

Pursuing his reflection, Mauss identified the first moment and the instrument of genetic explanation. The first moment was the genealogical classification of prayer types, that is, the constitution of types in order of their evolution. The method consisted of comparing various systems of prayer. Mauss was less concerned with concordances than with differences, which had to do with the specificity of the social environment: "There is a necessary connection between a given prayer and a given society and religion."[44]

As he had done in his study on sacrifice, Mauss could have drawn from the various ancient literatures he knew well. His introduction included many references to the Vedas, the Song of Songs, synagogal prayer, and so forth. But for La prière he chose to focus on "elementary oral rites" and, like Durkheim in The Elementary Forms of Religious Life, he confined himself to Australian societies, not only because they were "the best known of those conventionally called primitive" but also because they were "numerous enough, homogeneous enough, and at the same time heterogeneous enough to form a group eminently favorable for research on a ritual and all its variations." These societies formed "a sort of totality"; they had a "civilization."

That choice was also linked to the questions Mauss raised: Is prayer derived from magical incantation, as Müller, Marett, and Rivers thought? In the oral rites of the most "inferior" societies we know of, are there prayers in the strict sense? The documents collected allowed him to conclude that even in Australia there were "prayers and elements of prayer of a fairly evolved type." These were formulas of the totemic cult and of the initiation cult. His argument relied primarily on the study of formulas used during ceremonies—the Arunta intichiuma—whose "aim was to act on the totemic thing or specimen." These were melodic and rhythmic formulas, sometimes reduced to a monotonous and indefinitely repeated call that was chanted collectively, usually while dancing. Mauss's text ended with the meticulous description of an intichiuma ceremony by the caterpillar clan in Alice Springs, where the formulas had a "marked precative character." They appealed to the divine animal, the totem: "Just as erotic songs act on men's desires, formulas impel the beings (men, beasts, gods) reawakened by the rite, by the voice, to thrive and fulfill their destiny."[45]

A detailed description of all the intichiuma ceremonies among the Arunta can be found in *The Elementary Forms of Religious Life* (book 3, "Principal Ritual Conduct," a chapter devoted to positive worship). Durkheim's book also includes the intichiuma ceremonies of the Warraganga, which Mauss had set out to describe. Durkheim thus exploited the same ethnographic documents as Mauss, but in a somewhat different way. He wanted "to grasp, in the extreme diversity of practices, the most characteristic attitudes a primitive tribesman observes in the celebration of his cult; to classify the most general forms of his rites; to determine their origins and meaning." In a note, he indicated that he was leaving aside a certain form of ritual, "the oral ritual, which is to be studied completely in a special volume of the *Année Sociologique* collection."[46]

The book Durkheim was referring to was his nephew's, which was still unfinished in 1912. A closely argued critique of the various conflicting theses, a scrupulous discussion of all the documents, a conscientious search for contradicting facts, and a detailed description of ceremonies were characteristic of Mauss's approach, which could only be long and tedious. The nephew did not abandon his project, but his work was slowed by various obligations and health problems. Hubert advised his "poor old chum" not to rush things and to recover his health: "Don't start teaching again; go collect your thoughts, work at your own pace. And let's hope you'll soon be free to do as you please, while giving your loved ones the satisfaction of seeing your thesis done."[47]

During a trip to Frankfurt in 1912, Mauss attempted "to unearth Strehlow's documents and, to a lesser extent, to track down Strehlow himself."[48] Then, in the last volume of the first series of *Année Sociologique*, he published a review of two new installments of Strehlow's work. Devoted to the to-temic cult of the Arunta and the Loritja, they assembled a large quantity of documents. To study these rituals, Mauss could "rely on a solid philological foundation." Unfortunately, just as he was getting deep into his work, the war put an end to it.[49]

The End of an Era

Studies in the history of religion had their apogee in the first decade of the twentieth century. There were animated debates and numerous publi-cations. James Frazer prepared the third edition of his increasingly volu-minous *Golden Bough*. Salomon Reinach came out with a revised twelfth edition of his general history of religion, *Orpheus* (Picard, 1909). The debate turned on a few major questions: Are there peoples without religion? What is the relation between religion and magic? Is it possible to speak of a primi-tive monotheism? The study of religion among uncivilized peoples acquired a greater legitimacy in academic circles, as was obvious at the third inter-national congress on the history of religion. It was held in Oxford in 1908, overseen by the "imposing and venerable" Edward Burnett Tylor. It marked the "jubilee celebration of anthropology."

For the French school of sociology, and particularly for Durkheim, the 1910s also brought wider recognition. Jean Jaurès, now an influential mem-ber of the Chamber of Deputies, attended the tenth anniversary of *Année Sociologique* and "outshone all those doctor/professors, all those scien-tists, all those wits and select Normalians."[50] In 1913 Durkheim's friends at *Année* threw a party for his fifty-fifth birthday and presented him with a bust by the sculptor Landowski. Finally, new contributors wrote arti-cles and books on his work. Georges Davy published a long article titled "Mr. Durkheim's Sociology" in *Revue Philosophique* (1911) and a book, *Émile Durkheim* (Michaud, 1912); and Maurice Halbwachs produced an article called "Durkheim's Doctrine," also published in *Revue Philosophique* (1916). All this attention could not fail to delight Durkheim. He wrote to Davy: "Sympathies like yours make me oddly indifferent to the attacks of certain publicists."[51]

The Elementary Forms of Religious Life, published in 1912 with the sub-title "Totemism in Australia," was Durkheim's most important and most controversial work. It was a synthesis of the studies he and his collaborators had conducted for several years, and, as he himself said, provided "a few fragmentary contributions" to a new science that was complex and could "advance only slowly through collective work."[52] There were many refer-ences to studies by Hubert, Hertz, Meillet, and Mauss. He cited "On a Few

Primitive Forms of Classification," written in collaboration with Mauss, but also "Essay on Sacrifice," "General Theory of Magic," and "Essay on Seasonal Variations." Durkheim also adopted the notion of mana, which was central to Hubert and Mauss's theory: "That notion [of totemic principle] is not only of primordial importance because of the role it has played in the development of religious ideas; it also has a secular aspect that makes it of interest to the history of scientific thought. It is the first form taken by the notion of force."[53]

Elementary Forms was noteworthy for its methodology. In the first place, the study did not include all peoples in whom a more or less developed totemism could be observed: it focused on a limited group of Australian societies. Second, Durkheim gave a precise and clear definition of religion: "Religion is characterized by the distinction between the sacred and the profane." The importance of the analysis of totemism lay wholly in the fact that it contained the essential elements of any religion whatsoever. Totemism was not a disorganized pile of superstitions, as Frazer believed; it was a "religion in the strict sense." Finally, and this was the specific contribution to the sociological method, totemism as a religious system in the strict sense had an eminently social character. It was society that "made things sacred at will and, as a result, imprinted their religious character on them."

According to Durkheim and Mauss, the main conclusion to be drawn from the study of beliefs (the idea of the soul, personality, the idea of the great god) and of cults (for example, sacrifice) was as follows: "Finally, religion thus understood seems to consist primarily of a system of acts whose aim is to perpetually make and remake the soul of the collectivity and of individuals. Even though it has a speculative role to play, its principal function is dynamogenic. It gives the individual forces that allow him to transcend himself, to rise above his nature, and to dominate it. Yet the only moral forces that are higher than those available to the individual as such are those that individuals joined together unleash. Religious forces are and can only be collective forces."[54]

Durkheim's last book was part of a vast research project whose object—"human mentality"—went beyond the limits of religious sociology and touched on the theory of cognition. "Having started out from philosophy, I tend to return to it," Durkheim wrote: "Or rather, I am quite naturally led back to it by the nature of the questions I encountered on the way."[55] These questions, which had been raised by philosophers since Aristotle, had to do with the categories of the understanding, that is, "the essential notions that dominate our entire intellectual life . . .: notions of time, space, gender, number, cause, substance, personality, and so on."[56] In choosing to study primitive religious beliefs, Durkheim found along the way "the main categories in question," which were all "the product of religious thought."

The Elementary Forms of Religious Life was well received overall. In the English journal *Man* (1913), Hartland called it a brilliant work that opened a new chapter in the discussion of the origin of religion. Malinowski declared in *Folk-lore* (1913) that it was one of the most important contributions to science. In the United States, the *American Journal of Sociology* published two reviews, one by Hutton Webster in 1913 and the other by U. G. Weatherly a few years later. But there was also vigorous criticism. Philosophers reasserted "the autonomy of individuals in society"; specialists in anthropology called into question Durkheim's use of ethnographic data and his interpretation of totemism. In *American Anthropologist* (1915), Alexander Goldenweiser said he was unconvinced by the argument: Durkheim had poorly understood the primitive mentality, had chosen Australia arbitrarily, and so on. Even Alfred Radcliffe-Brown, the most Durkheimian of English anthropologists, denounced the ethnographic weaknesses of *Elementary Forms*.[57] In France, Arnold Van Gennep, author of a thesis titled "Taboo and Totemism in Madagascar" (1903) and founder of *Revue des Études Ethnographiques et Sociologiques* (1907), initiated the debate with a review of the book in *Mercure de France* (1912), then with a series of articles on totemism in *Revue de l'Histoire des Religions*.[58] In 1913, to defend "the philosophical implications of his research," Durkheim participated in a discussion of "the problem of religion and the duality of human nature" before members of the Société de Philosophie.

Mauss's contribution to the debate was limited to a review written in collaboration with Durkheim, in which he compared *Elementary Forms* with a recent book by Frazer, *Totemism and Exogamy* (1911). The nephew refrained from all critical comments even though, as he would later reveal, he was not completely in agreement with his uncle.

Like Stanley Arthur Cook's *Study of Religion*, published in England during World War I, *Elementary Forms* marked the end of an era. The opposition between science and religion was becoming less important. In addition, when the work appeared, totemism had already ceased to be the central concern of anthropology. In the field of religious history, the polemic lost some of its edge and the tone changed. As Paul Alphandéry remarked at the fourth international congress on the history of religion, held in Leiden in 1912, "There is a feeling that the time of manifestos has passed. There are neither accusers nor apologists."[59] Anthropologists distanced themselves from philosophical speculations, abandoned all literary pretensions, and turned resolutely to field research. They preferred analyzing social organization and the culture of so-called primitive societies to studying the origin of religion. In 1913 Malinowski published *The Family among the Australian Aborigenes*, and the next year W.H.R. Rivers published *Kinship and Social Organization*. In other words, there was less history of religion and more ethnography.

Durkheim's position within French academia remained strong. He taught at the Sorbonne, the École Normale Supérieure, and the École Pratique des Hautes Études. He was a member of the Conseil de l'Université (university council) and sat on many university and government committees. But the man called "the regent of the Sorbonne" became the target of all who resented the spirit of the new Sorbonne. In 1910, for example, Henri Massis and Alfred de Tarde published a collection of articles in *Opinion* under the pseudonym "Agathon." Similar in style to Péguy's criticism, their essays targeted primarily sociology and its "omnipotent master," who had established his "intellectual despotism" over an entire generation of professors, now "reduced to the role of humble civil servants."

Mauss, irritated by the tone of the articles, reacted immediately. He adopted his own pseudonym—"Criton"—to denounce the "new Agathons," whom he called "young bourgeois." And although he praised their audacity, he did so only to harshly criticize their method of investigation, which was "wholly tendentious, specious, deceitful." In conclusion, he adopted an ironic tone and invited his comrades to read the book *Les jeunes gens d'aujourd'hui*, where the Agathon articles were collected: "It will instruct you on the state of mind of today's young bourgeois: bloodthirsty, headstrong, pleasure-seeking, money-grubbing, philosophically utilitarian, cynical, practical (now called pragmatic), religious by tradition and not by faith."[60]

Between the time of his setback at the Collège de France and the start of World War I, Mauss was preoccupied with his research on prayer and did not begin any major new studies. He was still overwhelmed by the work involved in publishing *Année Sociologique*.[61] In Épinal the publication of each volume of *Année* was called a "sociological disease." Rosine Mauss, aware that publishing the journal represented "excessive work" for her son, "despaired of ever seeing his book finished."[62]

In his mother's view, Marcel was still in a "lousy situation." He had not changed his habits. His work was inconsistent; he had trouble "balancing his budget" and "living within his means."[63] She regularly had to advance him money. One of his mother's "two dearest wishes" was to see him "arrange a nice comfortable little life for himself, agreeable and modest."[64] The other was to see him "get back to a regular life by starting a family."[65]

But as Mauss indicated to his friend Hubert, his life was undoubtedly better organized than it had been. He worked regularly in the morning, did all his errands in the afternoon, and in the evening shared frugal dinners with friends.[66] But the old bachelor did not settle down. In the first place, he moved frequently: in 1906 to 3, rue de Cluny; in 1911 to 17, rue Malebranche; in 1912 to 39, rue de Saxe; and in July 1914 to 2, rue Bruller. Second, the breakup with Marguerite, greatly desired by his loved ones and often announced, was only partial. "The last ten days . . . have distanced me from Marguerite but my edginess has not abated. I'm thinking of her more stupidly than I did nearly a month ago. Yet I'm incapable of corresponding with her in a way that doesn't upset her."[67] Even when Mauss announced a "change in [his] life," his mother, not knowing if she ought to be happy about it, remained anxious.[68]

The relationship between Mauss and his best friend and collaborator, Henri Hubert, was still close. But the focus of their interests had diverged. Hubert had begun dividing his time between the École Pratique des Hautes Études and the Musée des Antiquités Nationales in Saint-Germain. Named assistant curator in 1910, he now worked as an archaeologist and muse-ologist. In August of the same year, he married Alma Schierenberg, a "very brilliant and cultivated" young woman from Wiesbaden whom he had met while at a health spa near Lucerne. He announced his marriage to his friend only belatedly.[69]

Everyone hoped that "good old" Hubert had done well for himself and would have a good marriage.[70] In 1913, when his first son was born (he was given the name Marcel), Hubert moved into a large house in Chatou with a view of the Seine.[71]

Even though they had grown apart, the two friends still worked as a team at the École Pratique, where they trained a new generation of researchers: Czarnowski, Davy, Jeanmaire, Lenoir, Maunier, Marx, Przyluski, and others. Mauss's students were still very attached to him. At a professional level, he strengthened his ties to English anthropologists, who had great respect for him. When Tylor retired, R. R. Marett tried to secure support for his French colleague. The Frazers were pleased to meet with Mauss in Paris or to entertain him in their home during his visits to England. Mauss had been to London in 1905. He returned there in early summer 1912 on a mission that also took him to Belgium and Germany. Its objective was twofold: to consult documentation on Australian tribes and to study the various institutions devoted to ethnography that were flourishing in those countries.[72]

Mauss stayed in England for over two months and visited his old colleague and friend Mabel Bode and his student Jean Marx. He worked at the British Museum every day; learned of the "Australian work" of Alfred Radcliffe-Brown, with whom he began a correspondence; and met with Rivers, an "all-round anthropologist" and a "moral example." He also met Haddon in Cambridge, Marett in Oxford, and Seligman in London. Haddon, Rivers, and Seligman all participated in the famous Cambridge Torres Strait Expedition, which, given its results, method, and the quality of the staff recruited, would be "one of those rare favorable events that occurs from time to time in the life of the sciences."[73]

Mauss's introduction to Charles S. Seligman (1873–1940), one of the young talents of the expedition, marked the beginning of a long and solid friendship. Seligman (who spelled his name "Seligmann" until 1914) was a brilliant physician who abandoned pathology in the 1890s in favor of physical anthropology. In 1898, at the last minute, he embarked with Haddon for the Torres Strait. The expedition changed his life. Thereafter, he devoted himself to anthropology and, with his wife, Brenda, did field research in New Guinea, the Sudan, and Ceylon. Seligman admired Frazer and discussed the results of his surveys with him.

Mauss greatly admired Charles and Brenda, considering them "shrewd and experienced observers." When he reviewed their *Veddas* (1911) for *Année Sociologique*, he pointed out the dual importance of the study, which presented an accurate description of Vedda society and provided an analysis of the relation between Shamanism and religion.

Mauss never completed his *Prière*. Perhaps, as Henri Lévy-Bruhl believed, it was because "his quick mind was loath to elaborate a 'doctrine'. . . . He was teeming with ideas, some ingenious, others profound, all new and original. He dispensed them freely in his classes, his lectures, his letters, his conversation."[74] Mauss was "the exact opposite of an author of manuals," said Lévy-Bruhl. In formulating hypotheses and outlining analyses, he preferred "to open new and productive avenues." In addition to "The Mother-in-Law Taboo" (1914), a paper he presented at the first international congress of ethnology and ethnography held in Neuchâtel, he published two short articles in the early 1910s, one on the notion of food in ancient Vedic literature, the other on the "origins of the notion of money." These works attested to Mauss's interest in the most varied questions, especially when they lay within the purview of cognition theory.

The first text, "Anna-Viraj," was an appendix to a much more extensive study. Because of its length, unintentional delays, and printing problems, the longer work could not be published in its entirety in *Mélanges d'indianisme offerts à Sylvain Lévi* (Miscellany on Indianism offered to Sylvain Lévi). Returning to his "early love," the Brahmanas, which he had studied with Lévi, Mauss analyzed the verse forms of Vedic prosody. He showed that the symbolic value of the *viraj*, a meter consisting of three ten-syllable feet, relied on the sacred character of the number 10 and that a series of equivalences could be established between the *viraj*, the number 10, and food. These associations, absurd to a European impervious to the joys of such symbolism, also characterized to some extent Western philosophy, which borrowed "words from every sort of vocabulary." Mauss wrote: "Who could say, for example, that in the theories of 'value' so plentiful today, notions borrowed from stock market speculation do not play a role?"[75]

Mauss himself returned to the question of value in a paper for the Institut Français d'Anthropologie, in which he presented "hypotheses, recommendations for further work, and provisional data" on the origin of the notion of money.[76] He explained that not only was the religious and magical character of money very prominent, but in several societies the notion of currency was expressly linked to that of magical power. In a general way, money was "a standard value but also a use value that is not fungible, that is permanent, transmissible, that can be the object of transactions and exchanges without deteriorating, but can be the means to procure for oneself other fungible or transitory values, enjoyments, services."[77] He took the example of the talisman, an object coveted by everyone and whose possession confers prestige and authority. Even today, faith in the value of gold was not very different, Mauss suggested. It might reside "in the confidence we have in its power," and more precisely "in the belief that, thanks to it, we will be able to obtain benefits—in kind or in services—that the state of the market will permit us to demand from our peers."[78]

Without abandoning the field of religious history, Mauss increasingly embraced ethnography, the "description of so-called primitive peoples." As a discipline, it was experiencing a "true eclipse" in France after the "major expeditions of the last century"; its development was much slower there than in English-speaking countries. Some of his students did fieldwork: Marius Barbeau in Canada, Claude Maître in Indonesia, René Maunier in Egypt.

Mauss did not engage in fieldwork, though he was invited to do so. At the very beginning of an Alaskan expedition, Beuchat told his professor of an opening: "I saw [Marius] Barbeau in Ottawa; he was charming. But there's nothing for you to do regarding the [illegible], since that's something he reserves for himself. Perhaps if you want to study the Montagnais (Algonkins) of Quebec province, you could be taken on temporarily at the anthropology division. Have a look, and if you like it, write Barbeau."[79] Mauss's interest in ethnography took more concrete forms when he began to consider ethnographic museology and when he agreed to develop questionnaires, such as the one requested by Claude Maître, now professor at the École Française d'Extrême-Orient in Hanoi.[80]

What Mauss prepared for his former student was not a questionnaire in the strict sense but "a sort of grid for observing facts." This consisted of "a certain number of very tricky rules that are difficult to apply" but that any sincere and serious observer ought to follow. For example: "Be precise"; "Always locate precisely the facts you are stating" (place, time, conditions); "Prove every assertion as far as possible"; "First and foremost, use all the material evidence available" (photos, sound recordings, and so on); "Learn the native language."

Mauss was also eager to convince his interlocutors of the practical and theoretical usefulness of sociology. In practical terms, sociological studies could be the best guides for administrators of the colonies. "Colonial policy may be the area in which the adage 'knowledge is power' is best confirmed. By respecting and using beliefs and customs, modifying the economic and technological system only with caution, not opposing anything directly, and using everything, [administrators] could arrive at humane, easy, and productive colonial practices." Otherwise, colonial policy became "pure empiricism"; it was a "perilous thing, of the moment; it [was] costly in time and money and sometimes [led] to disasters." Mauss also emphasized the theoretical interest for human history of studying a country such as Indochina in ethnographic terms. "It is moreover urgent that this study be done as quickly as possible. A certain number of facts will vanish. In a few years, there will be only a memory of them. Some of them have already become considerably rarer."[81]

Mauss again expressed that sense of urgency in 1913, in an article published in *Revue de Paris*. The article was written for a general audience and described the history of anthropology in Great Britain, the United States, Germany, the Netherlands, and France. Its objective was political: to point out the "stagnation" of ethnography in France, where there were "neither educational programs nor good museums nor bureaus for ethnographic research." Yet like the "other outdoor sciences"—zoology, botany, geology, and so on—ethnography, as a "science of observation," required three kinds of studies and three kinds of institutions. It needed, "first, field studies, second, museums and archives, and third, education."[82] In terms of research services, France cut "a scrawny and pale figure." In censuses and bibliographical references, French studies were poorly represented, as S. R. Steinmetz showed in his *Essai d'une bibliographie systématique de l'ethnologie jusqu'à l'année 1911* (Toward a systematic bibliography of ethnology up to 1911): only 14 percent of the titles were French, while 35 percent were German, 31 percent English, and 20 percent from other nationalities.[83]

The sacrifice Mauss demanded of his country was not, in his view, very great: "We ask that something be done about museums of ethnography, that something be done about a bureau of ethnography, and that something be done about research outside the colonies." This was a duty that had to be performed without delay, since "the very facts to be observed are vanishing every day" and it was becoming increasingly difficult to find "beautiful collection pieces" that were authentic. It was now or never: the task was especially urgent because France had "a cure of souls" and was "responsible to the human groups it was trying to govern without even knowing them."[84]

IO

NOT A VERY FUNNY WAR

ALTHOUGH he did not make peace an "exclusive goal," Mauss was a pacifist and an internationalist. He had declared a few years earlier: "For me, peace can only be an effect of the more or less slow constitution of an increasingly vast Internationale."[1] From his point of view, unless it was "the expression of a firm will on the part of the masses," pacifism was only a "Platonic protest."

Mauss thought it fortunate that the socialist Internationale, seeking to unite socialists across national borders, was being organized. It would, he said, "emancipate the workers, emancipate all peoples, bring about the brotherhood of man."[2] There was hope that someday there would be a "true human consciousness" and that men would stand together like citizens of a single nation.[3] But that day was still a long way off. Mauss had no illusions.

When France pursued its penetration policy in Morocco and French troops occupied Oujda in 1907, Jaurès and others feared that if the conflict continued, "nations will be surrounded like a squadron in a cyclone." Jaurès wrote: "The essence of capitalism is to make war." With the support of the Internationale, the French socialist leader hoped to undermine the "iron law of war." At the Stuttgart socialist congress in 1907, Jaurès headed the French delegation alongside Jules Guesde, Édouard Vaillant, and Gustave Hervé. The Belgian Émile Vandervelde, the Germans Karl Kautsky, August Bebel, Eduard Bernstein, and Rosa Luxemburg, and the Russian Lenin were all there as well. War and the role socialists could play in preventing it were at the heart of debates. The Internationale adopted the antimilitarist slogan "Wage War on War." Jaurès's position on peace was clear, but, unlike Édouard Vaillant, he did not go so far as to propose staging a general strike if troops were mobilized. During the 1911 conflict between Italy and Turkey, European socialist leaders had organized major demonstrations, and their vast size reinforced faith in the strength of the pacifist sentiment.

In Morocco the crisis continued. After the Fez insurrection in April 1912, the socialists denounced the "policy of pillage and adventuring" undertaken in Morocco by a "diplomacy of businessmen."[4] On the one hand, the army increased manifold its arbitrary requisitions for goods and men; on the other, with the complicity of the major companies, a huge wave of speculation put the country on the auction block. Some called the operation the Compagnie Générale du Maroc had carried out in Oujda "highway robbery."

The country was becoming a "powder keg." Jaurès pointed out the risks of a European conflict. Mauss, who had not published any articles in *Humanité* since 1907, took up his journalist's pen and devoted two short articles to the "Oujda affair." His knowledge of the situation in North African countries came largely from information collected by Edmond Doutté, one of the first contributors to *Année Sociologique* and "one of the best Arabic scholars in the world."[5]

Doutté, who was several years Mauss's senior, consulted him about his own work. He wrote him regularly, telling him how the North African situation was evolving and sending him various documents. Doutté did not conceal the anxiety he felt about French policy, especially the Fez expedition. He also did not agree with the SFIO's policy: "It cannot be expected that Morocco will evolve independently if it is abandoned by us. It will surely be taken over by a *tertius agens* and it is doubtful whether the latter will be a gentler protector than we are."[6]

Mauss, referring to the Oujda affair in a short article called "Pillage and Speculation," was outraged at the "sudden silence of the entire bourgeois press" and demanded that "debates be public."[7] An investigation made it possible to present "certain high crimes involving breach of trust, misappropriation of funds, pillage, arbitrariness, and extortion." "The moral is that we don't need metropolitan soldiers or diplomats in Morocco—since there is a Morocco now."

The socialists' position remained ambiguous: the SFIO did not ratify the protectorate the French imposed but it also did not adopt the principle of withdrawal. Among militants, antimilitarism took precedence over anticolonialism, and if the French policy in Morocco was denounced, it was done in the name of pacifism. That is why, with the end of the Moroccan crisis, the socialist critique of French imperialism in Morocco diminished in frequency and intensity.

The period immediately preceding the war was marked by a rise of antimilitarism in France. The socialists, facing a mobilization that extended military service to three years, began a campaign against the war in March 1912 and held demonstrations and political meetings. Young people in the student and syndicalist movements were particularly active, seeking to transform the fight "against the three years" into a battle against general mobilization.[8] Intellectuals—those associated with the Dreyfus Affair—again rallied behind Anatole France and Charles Seignobos.

Mauss was involved in the debate and in 1913 published an excerpt in *Humanité* taken from the deliberations of the general council in Vosges on the mobilization of reservists. At the invitation of Jean Texcier, he agreed in June to preside at a meeting held on the training grounds of the Panthéon on the theme: "The left united against nationalist reactionaries, against three years of military service." It was organized by the Fédération des Étudiants

Républicains de France (Federation of republican students of France), the Groupe des Étudiants Socialistes, and the Renaissance Républicaine. In addition, Mauss participated in drafting a petition "for national dignity, against military panic." The signatories did not declare themselves "systematically opposed to three years of military service if its real usefulness can be fairly and meticulously established." But they were anxious to present "the true scope of material, intellectual, and moral disorder" that the three-year policy risked bringing about. There would be "terrible repercussions": a significant drop in national production; upheaval in the practice of various professions and in apprenticeships and recruitment; a rise in depopulation through family impoverishment and delays in the ability of young men to marry; a likely drop in the level of public morality as a result of extending the period of army life; and a disastrous blow to French culture and to the nation's scientific, artistic, and technical activity. For all these reasons and for other, strictly military ones, the reform had to be examined "calmly and without haste." At stake was "not only material and moral power but the salvation of France and the future of the world."

Mauss also signed a petition in *Humanité* (March 13, 1913) that was a brief version of the same argument. In addition to Andler and Herr, a few members of the sociology clan signed as well: Bouglé, Durkheim, Lucien Lévy-Bruhl, Simiand. This group of "beloved professors" wanted to make themselves "the protectors of intellectual interests and the repository of French thought," to borrow Péguy's polemical expression.

Anxiety was running high. As Jaurès said, the choice was between war or peace, reaction or democracy, and the two pairs were inextricably linked. Mauss resumed his column in *Humanité*.[9] In late September and early October 1913, he observed the state of the "three-year army, the barracks army," first in Épinal and then in Nancy. It was a "fine mess," a "filthy hellhole." There was "not a moment to waste": patriotic duty required republicans "to overthrow that incompetent ministry and minister, those inept bureaus, that outdated, foolish, and demented general staff."[10]

In June 1913 Mauss published an article on the Franco-German conflict in the education journal *La Revue de l'Enseignement Primaire et Primaire Supérieur*.[11] It was the first in a series devoted to the "external situation." For Mauss, the danger of war had not been averted: "Europe is still in a militarist crisis, and it appears it has not yet sweated out its fever."[12] He added: "They are playing dangerous games and it's a battle between challenges in the press and diplomatic and military communiqués. The drums are beating in Austria, Russia, and Germany. What are we to do in this barracked-up Europe? What are we to do, if not speak of the dangers of war, the threat of invasion and of rivalries?" Mauss drew a comparison to certain primitive tribes where clans constantly challenged one another and hurled the worst insults. He described a curious practice among the Eskimos known as the "drum dance," where the loser was whoever allowed himself to be insulted the most during the beating of drums. He concluded: "Would to heaven that we have not reached that 'wise' barbarism!"[13]

Mauss acknowledged that relations between France and Germany were not simple but said that there were no real conflicts between them. The "race conflict" was "just some old rubbish in the philosophy of history." The "conflict of civilizations" to which the novelist and conservative politician Maurice Barrès referred was the invention of "politicking academics and caricaturists with more verve than drafting skill." Rather, France and Germany were "two civilizations of the same kind, rigorously complementary for more than a thousand years, first in their Catholicism, and then in Western capitalism."[14] It was therefore absurd to believe that the Germans and the French were "condemned to eternal conflict." It could all be summed up in a "painful and serious misunderstanding": "Bismarck's crime, committed against the rights of Alsatian-Lorranians, is the only thing—and it is a completely moral issue—separating these two countries, which everything ought to unite."[15]

"What hope is there? What is there to do?" wondered Mauss. And he replied: "Let us put all our hope in German democracy and in the defeat of the reactionary forces in France." In his view, peace and democracy were closely linked: "Peace can come only from the development of democracy; but democracy can advance only in peace." Was it a vicious circle? No, because "there are vicious circles only in logic. In practice, it is possible to work with both hands. We must do the impossible to rescue both peace and democracy, on both sides at once." Mauss was optimistic: "With patience, caution, and action, peace may be closer than we believe and the victory of democracy and of the working class is at hand."[16]

The democrats, especially the German democrats, had "only to do their duty." Mauss judged German social democracy harshly, saying he would like to see it "more republican, more antimilitarist, more antinationalist." Only Rosa Luxemburg, who had just been sentenced to a year in prison for a "very harmless speech compared with our antimilitarist literature," found favor in his eyes. "The seed will germinate, but it has only just begun to sprout, and it is a woman, a Jew, and a Pole who is the first to disseminate it."[17]

The "spark of life" was there; it would take only a "slight whiff of idealism and favorable external circumstances" for "democracy in Germany to regain the advantage." Mauss remained confident because the congress of the Internationale in Vienna "might send a jolt of humanity through the social democracy and the political Internationale." The congress was set for the beginning of August 1913 and was moved to Paris, where it was to be preceded by a major peace demonstration.

The situation nevertheless remained explosive. Whose fault was it? Mauss was highly critical of the French bourgeoisie, especially when he compared

it with the English middle class. He made many accusations. Secular education was "neither adequately endowed nor energetically defended"; public
works projects had been abandoned and the state's productive sector barely
safeguarded; agriculture was not sufficiently encouraged; the justice system
was in need of reform and was not keeping up with "the evolution of mores"; laws regarding public health and worker retirement pensions were not
enforced. By comparison, the English middle class was more enlightened
and was able to "bow to democratic pressure, obey popular appeals," with
the institution of old age pension programs, medical and disability insurance, a minimum wage for home workers, debt relief, and a social services
budget. These constituted a "major policy" elaborated by "statesmen, men
of great ability and often of great generosity." The best evidence of these
statesmen's "lofty vision" was their "inflexible will" in facing "England's age-
old injustice toward Ireland." "In a few years," Mauss believed, "the United
Kingdom may have become a federal state."[18]

The same was true at the diplomatic level. In foreign policy and in colonial issues, the radical French bourgeoisie was not up to the task. The
"underhanded conquest" of Morocco was a failure because it left the country "saddled with debt" to England and Spain and "the indentured servant"
of Europe as a whole. Such diplomatic action had "no plan, no sincerity,
no majesty." It was "entrusted to obscure bourgeois bureaucrats and career
aristocrats." In comparison, the results of English foreign policy were much
more positive: the definitive conquest of Egypt, "the healing of wounds" in
South Africa, prosperity in the Dominions (Canada, Australia, New Zealand,
India), a strong position in China and South America.

Mauss, convinced that "one arrives at higher things via narrow and difficult paths," addressed French pacifists, both radicals and socialists, and
suggested various forms of action: develop "a wise policy of esteem and
respect" between European countries; "found a popular and pacifist diplomacy toward foreign nations and chancelleries"; "work everywhere to federate the forces of democracy and peace." The best way to preserve the peace
in Europe was to end the diplomacy "of intrigue and adventuring" which, as
in Italy, was conducted by "true rogues with extreme roguery."[19] In addition,
an internationalism that was more than just superficial had to be developed
between socialist organizations. Mauss was disappointed that the second
Internationale, meeting in Stuttgart in 1911, "refused to envision general
strikes or any other revolutionary means against the war." He was again disappointed when the 1914 meeting held by the bureau of the Internationale
in Brussels ended with an "admission of powerlessness." He later observed:
"The attitude of the Germans and Austrians . . . was Jaurès's last great sorrow, his supreme disillusionment."[20]

Then came the Sarajevo attack on June 28, 1914: the heir to the throne
of Austria-Hungary, Archduke Francis Ferdinand, and his wife were killed

by Serbian nationalists. For Jaurès, who wrote his reaction the next day in *Humanité*, the double murder was "a stream added to the river of blood that has flowed in vain on the Balkan peninsula." European anxiety was calmed by the apparent restraint displayed by the old emperor Francis Joseph, who had been wary of his heir presumptive's liberal notions; these were also judged harshly by the military.

Mauss had no more inkling that war would follow than did other socialists. In an article devoted to that "stroke of fate," the portrait he drew of the "late heir" was not flattering: a "bungler," a "careerist," a "bit of an adventurer," one of those men "hungry for glory and power," a "fanatic and a brute." Francis Ferdinand was a "money-grubbing heir," a "danger for peace" and, in his "fight for a larger House of Austria," he had relied on the conservative forces of Catholicism, clericalism, and the Jesuits. His death did not represent a great loss for the imperial house of Austria: a "dangerous enemy of oppressed nations, free and peaceful smaller states, and liberal progress has vanished."[21]

With this "danger for peace" out of the way, Mauss was somewhat optimistic. He hoped the new heir, young Charles Francis Joseph, would not be "the prisoner of the great lords, bishops, and Jesuits," and that the peoples of Austria, Hungary, Bohemia, and Poland would have "time to educate themselves, regain control of themselves, federate themselves, become masters of their destiny." As he remarked, "in politics, especially in diplomacy, one must make plans and, at the same time, refrain from planning everything."[22]

That article appeared on July 12. Two weeks later, Austria launched an ultimatum and declared war on Serbia. There was only one hope left: that the conflict would remain localized. England proposed mediation by four parties—England, Italy, France, and Germany—but Germany, committed to supporting Austria, refused. Military machinations were already under way: a partial mobilization in Saint Petersburg, mobilization in Austria-Hungary, military measures in France. Mauss was visibly distressed by what was going on. "Humanity is a nasty race. But it is our race."[23]

French socialists exerted pressure on their government to restrain Saint Petersburg and Vienna. With fierce energy, Jaurès stepped up efforts to preserve peace: articles, political meetings, a session of the Bureau Socialiste International in Brussels. On the night of July 31, as he was dining in Paris with Pierre Renaudel and Philippe Landrieu, his collaborators at *Humanité*, the socialist leader was killed by a bullet to the head.[24]

The response was immediate and far-reaching. Three words, repeated mechanically, passed from mouth to mouth: "He is dead . . . He is dead . . ." In the telegram they sent Mauss, Renaudel and Landrieu wrote simply: "Jaurès murdered. Consternation." Like Jacques, the hero of the novelist Roger Martin du Gard's *Les Thibaut*, everyone repeated: "Jaurès dead . . . I can't believe it.. . . And especially, I can't pretend to measure, to imagine, the consequences." For Mauss, it was the loss of a friend and the death of a hero:

> If a scoundrel armed by the most sinister of conspirators had not robbed us of his power, the war, and especially the postwar, would have brought out his genius as a statesman. He might have been seen—dare I say it—as the equal of Caesar in power and in prudence. . . . He might have been considered worthy of Plutarch's great heroes. . . . Alas! We have not had, we no longer have, the man who might have saved his country and our ideals at the same time. . . . Jaurès was not only a hero but also a sage. We will never realize what we have lost, all of us, everyone, his friends.[25]

Lucien Lévy-Bruhl wrote of Jaurès: "A man necessary to France and to humanity, one of those incomparable spirits that are so scarce in nature! So powerful and so moderate! So inventive and so prudent! So much in possession of his ideas and so respectful of the facts!" He added: "How we miss Jaurès."[26]

The Soldier Interpreter

On August 1, "the irreparable" occurred. Berlin and Paris launched general mobilization orders. Germany declared war on Russia, then on France the next day. When the first bugle call sounded, the socialists abandoned their pacifist position: they responded to the appeal and went to war. Within a few hours, the socialist Internationale had collapsed. Disenchanted, some militants expressed outrage. Martin du Gard had one of his characters say: "It's over. There are no socialists left. There are only social-jingoists. . . . I see they've all agreed to go. . . . They think they're obeying their consciences by sacrificing their revolutionary ideals to the new myth of the threatened Fatherland. Those who were most relentlessly against the war are now the most eager to wage it."[27] On August 27, two socialists, Marcel Sembat and Jules Guesde, joined René Viviani's government.

In Belgium, the German armies were advancing west. They occupied Louvain on August 20 and Brussels on the 22nd. The extent of the French army's losses obliged it to retreat. The enemy was approaching Paris: Germany bombed the French capital three times in late August. At the military's request, the government moved to Bordeaux.

Mauss, who had recently been named *directeur-adjoint d'études*[28] at the École Pratique, was one of the people who wanted to join up. Deemed fit for armed service by the medical board of the Seine on August 17, 1914, he volunteered for the duration of the war on September 3. "I'm strong enough to make a good soldier," he wrote the minister.[29] His decision astonished his loved ones, particularly his mother. Upset, she wrote ironically: "I wonder why you challenged the medical discharge to get yourself into the army, you who've never carried a gun, and at forty-three! God willing it'll all end well, but it'll be one more torment, and not the least of them!"[30]

Although in August he had asked to serve as an interpreter, the new volunteer was assigned to the 144th infantry regiment, which irritated him somewhat. After all, he was still in the "ridiculous situation of an unarmed soldier." He did not know what his status would be: "Soldier? Noncommissioned officer? Officer? On horseback? On foot? In an automobile? On a general staff?"[31]

Billeted in Orléans for nearly a month, Mauss wrote his friend Hubert: "I don't know what they'll do with me but I confess I hardly care. I predict adventure but I don't pretend to judge."[32] He had no illusions: "They're imagining a short campaign, I think it'll be a long one. Germany is more determined than they believe and I'm afraid that country is as united as we are. . . . So there are millions of men to plow through, who will have to be plowed through, a horrible task that will take time. We'll all see action, my friend."[33]

A few days later, on December 15, Mauss was attached as an interpreter to a combat unit, the Twenty-seventh British Division, and sent to Le Havre. He was not unhappy with the situation: "I'm doing wonderfully. I just wasn't made for the intellectual life and I'm enjoying the life war is giving me."[34] He added: "I ride horses, I play soldier. A gentleman's life. I'm doing admirably well. I was made for this and not for sociology."[35] There was at least one good thing about a military career: "It keeps you from looking for something to do or even from thinking."[36] It also gave "that shoulder-to-shoulder feeling" and inculcated an "esprit de corps." Mauss, feeling well, drew the logical conclusion: "Moral: better war than *Année*."[37]

But war is war, and as a major battle unfolded in Flanders, his division soon had to go to the front, to Ieper and Armentières.[38] The battle of Ieper was particularly "furious and relentless." For three weeks, "repeated, hasty, and frenetic" assaults by the German army were all repelled. Mauss regretted the fact that he had little chance "to go one on one."[39]

Mauss stayed in contact with members of his family, primarily his mother and uncle, and with his friends and colleagues. He was sent money orders, cash, and packages (sometimes food, sometimes clothing, sometimes booklets and newspapers). In the many letters they sent him, friends and relatives gave news of the family and of one another; they also kept him informed of the military and political situation and discussed certain questions that concerned him, especially the financial situation of *L'Humanité* and activities at the École Pratique. As for Mauss, he sought to reassure his loved ones: "I'm feeling great," "I'm not in any danger," "we're pretty far from the front," "morale is still good." He also asked people to do him some "real services," to maintain his apartment or help a friend. Aware of his friend Marguerite's "total destitution," he had small sums of money sent to her through Hubert so that she wouldn't be left to starve.[40]

Mauss was made a corporal on March 1915 and in August of the same year was attached to the 112th infantry brigade of the Twenty-seventh British Division. This earned him teasing from his old professor Sylvain Lévi. "So you're a corporal now, on the way to becoming an officer, an emeritus interpreter and even an emeritus horseman! You seem to set great store in your horse."[41] Mauss was confident about the war: "So let's have hope. Let's hope victory will come to the French."[42] Nevertheless, he predicted that "the next months will be very hard."[43] But, as he told Hubert, they would be "the last. I know it."[44] "Let's have hope. Let's have hope. As for me, I'm sure of ultimate success and even of fairly imminent success."[45]

The important thing was victory, complete victory. Mauss was counting on the fact that the Allies would crush the "Boches" but was anxious to reassure his friend Hubert, whose wife was German: "Tell Alma I love her nonetheless, her and hers, my German friends, and the Germans."[46]

In early March 1915 Hubert was himself mobilized as an infantry sergeant. That worried his friend: "It upsets you, and, might I say, it's worn you down and you're doing your duty. I hope the war will finally be finished fairly soon, so you'll be spared going to the front, you'll be spared that tragedy, since you're already suffering quite enough."[47] Mauss's wish came true: Colonel Cordier of the Paris fire brigade named Hubert, who was too weak to serve at the front, to the second bureau of the artillery undersecretaryship shortly before it became the Ministry of Armaments. There Hubert found his old friends Simiand and Roques, now undersecretaries and close collaborators of Albert Thomas. What would be called the "Thomas network" was very active at the beginning of the conflict. Several socialist Normalians were there, ready to staunchly defend the nation and to promote the minister's program. In *Humanité* Milhaud denounced the exportation of French capital and championed "public initiative." In his column, Bourgin demonstrated how the war could become an unprecedented field for putting into practice the study of laws governing society. Emmanuel Lévy addressed the question of interest rates as a jurist.[48] The old Groupe d'Études Socialistes had come back to life.

Hubert, attached to the automobile transport service, worked relentlessly and developed his organizational skills, first speeding up the manufacture of motor vehicles and then secretly planning the production of tanks. When "good old" Thomas[49] went to England and later to Russia in April–June 1917, Hubert would accompany him as the mission's secretary and archivist.

The dream of a quick victory collapsed: "As for the end of the war, I don't see it yet."[50] For Mauss, however, the essential thing was that he was "in perfect health" and that things were going "painlessly." He was "getting along great" with everyone, he was on good (not friendly) terms with his general staff, and he was reading Homer in Greek and in translation.[51] Finally, during the "long periods of idleness and the hours of moral solitude," which he enjoyed after the "worst moments," the sociologist/soldier began to write a book he called "On Politics." As he explained in the introduction: "The book is of its time: it bears the marks and shortcomings of that era. It was written at the front. . . . As a result, the necessary scholarship and classicism will be lacking."[52] According to the outline Mauss composed, he intended to address the following themes: (1) civilization (the spread of commerce, technology, religion, language, and so on); (2) morphological phenomena (migrations, colonies, avenues of communications); and (3) social phenomena (wars, colonization, and so on). The book was never finished.

The war went on. In 1915 and 1916, the British division to which Mauss was attached was quartered in Armentières, Sailly-sur-Ly, Croix-du-Bac, Somme, Colincamp, Sailly-au-Bois, west and southeast of Arras, and Bienveilliers-aux-Bois. In June 1916 Mauss was transferred to the Fifth Australian Division. He held on to his "hopes and good spirits" but found that time dragged. Autumn and the four months of winter were particularly difficult. He was not spared illness. First, he was hospitalized in Amiens in October and November 1915 for "an extreme case of what is called trench jaundice"; then, during the winter, he suffered from pulmonary congestion after a difficult tour of duty in the Barnafay woods and had to be evacuated to Heily. After a serious relapse in February–March, he would be treated in Albert as bombs fell around him.

Great Sorrows

Until the Battle of Verdun in February 1916, the Allies' offensives had failed, incurring major losses. The counteroffensives conducted by the Germans had hardly more success. The death toll was in the hundreds of thousands. Close collaborators and friends of Mauss died at the front. "We're doing well but are very tired," wrote Lucien Herr. "Too many worries, too much bad news, too many losses, too much slaughter of our best men, of an entire generation that was supposed to replace us. Too much grief. Growing old."[53]

There was a great deal of bad news. Mauss's student and collaborator Maxime David was killed in 1914 at the head of an infantry platoon; Antoine Bianconi met the same fate in 1915; the same year, Jean Reynier was killed in the trenches by a missile. Bianconi and Reynier were both thirty-two. Then it was Robert Hertz's turn: he was first wounded slightly, then later killed during "the pointless attack of Marchéville on April 13, 1915, at age thirty-three, leading his platoon out of the trenches."[54] Mauss and Durkheim were deeply affected. "My nerves are on edge," Durkheim wrote. "I don't know why but, on learning the news, I felt that both you and André [Durkheim,

Émile's son] were more vulnerable than you had been. Up till now, death has struck only people who are rather peripherally associated with me, like Maxime David and Bianconi. This time it's someone close to my heart. And that's why I think about the others."[55]

The following December 18, 1915, André Durkheim died in a Bulgarian hospital from wounds received while commanding a far rearguard platoon during the retreat from Serbia. He had already been wounded once and evacuated to France two other times. His family would have to wait several months to learn the circumstances of his death. Mauss, hoping his cousin was a prisoner or "in a warm bed," wrote him "just in case": "My poor boy, you know I love you like a kid brother, and like a comrade, and also like a son. Let's hope you're still with us."[56] Durkheim, his "nerves failing" as a result of the anxious times he had endured, wrote his "dear Marcel." "I'm going to cause you great pain, but it's impossible to spare you. We can no longer hold on to our illusions. André was wounded and died of his wounds. He's buried in the little village of Davidovo. It hurts me to write these words. It will hurt you to read them."[57] Mauss was expecting the news but still replied: "It's a shock." He did not conceal his pain from his friend Hubert: "I don't need to tell you of my sorrow. André was the most charming boy, the epitome of tenderness and enthusiasm. For me he was a son and a brother and a pal. And I was his old chum! . . . I can hardly keep from crying in front of people. And it's even harder when I'm alone."[58]

Mauss advised his loved ones to "do something" and "not talk too much about misfortune." And he implored them to "stay as well, as firm, as confident as possible."[59] He tried to keep his own spirits up, to be "philosophical." "It's pointless to lament our losses and those of others," he wrote his mother. "The lucky ones will be those who escape safe and sound from this moral cataclysm, this material cataclysm, where every doctrine and every religion is foundering. The others will be carried off by this plague, whether it's called Providence and punishment or injustice and mere chance. What does it matter? Those who remain will have to live and to build again an inhabited, rich, and moral world, and it will take a long time before they've rebuilt it even to where it used to be. Let us soldier on, that's all."[60]

For the Durkheims and the Mausses, the sorrow was particularly great, since everyone knew Émile was stricken by his son's death: "The poor, poor man. . . . What grief," sighed Hubert.[61] The father had placed "his greatest and most noble hopes" in his son, one of his most brilliant students.[62] He had trained him and, in so doing, had made him "twice his son."[63] Émile repeated that he did not want "anyone to talk to him about the irreparable" and even asked his friends not to come see him. Mauss himself avoided mentioning it in his correspondence and advised Hubert "not to make a condolence visit." His loved ones felt Émile was fragile: "Durkheim is the kind of man who lets himself be consumed by grief without showing it."[64]

But the father agreed to "take on the cruel and sweet task of retracing [his son's] short life and physiognomy." He added: "That is the only way left by circumstances for me to pay him my last respects."[65]

All the nephew could hope for was that his uncle would "not let his feelings get the better of him."[66] He wrote his mother: "Let's hope Uncle will manage to get hold of himself. I urge him to steel himself; I fear the worst if he lets himself go. He has violent passions and quickly becomes exhausted when he lets them get the better of him."[67] Conversely, Marcel's mother admired her brother's courage but wondered "if less self-restraint wouldn't be better."[68] Sylvain Lévi was reassuring: "I was struck by how Durkheim has steeled himself with a sort of tense energy to perform his duties and satisfy demands over and above his personal suffering. That fierce attitude inspires respect and admiration but seems to command silence."[69] And a month later, he wrote: "I spent the evening with Durkheim. . . . His stoicism is admirable; grief is merely developing his will to make himself useful to the country and to the common good."[70]

The war continued, deadly as ever. Mauss had recently been named officer/interpreter third-class and was detached with the Fifth Australian Division (Australian Imperial Force), one of two new Australian infantry divisions formed in late February, which had received orders to go to the Western Front. The specialist on "primitive" Australian societies now found himself beside those who proudly called themselves "the Diggers." But "speculating on the sociology of the Australians" was out of the question, even though he had a few "authentic specimens" before him.[71]

On arriving at the front, the Fifth Australian Division infantry immediately came under fire. The major offensive of the Somme came in late June and early July. The Australian army suffered considerable losses after intense bombing that lasted several weeks. In a single day, the Fifth Division lost 5,530 of 17,800 men, more than 400 of whom were taken prisoner. In the fall, the rains turned the battlefield into a "vast slough of mud." And during the winter months, the soldiers, who were busy repairing the roads, had to fight the rain, the mud, and the cold. Living conditions were terrible.[72] The Australian soldiers had a considerable advantage over the French: "When we made a halt in mud or water, they could sit on their heels and rest while the 'waters,' as they called them, remained below their heels. I was forced to remain standing in my boots with my feet completely in the water."[73]

Nonetheless, he did not lose his "hopes and good spirits."[74] Facing "loneliness, discomfort, and cold," he hung on "by force and reason, by energy and a vague hope. But my early enthusiasm is gone." Even the "most hardened" men were struck down.[75] When the prospect of a leave surfaced, it truly delighted him: "At last, really home, with electricity and a hot bath every day."

From a distance, Mauss observed French domestic policy, especially that of his own party, "with an anxious eye." "There's cowardliness in the air, and on the other side there's bluster."[76] *Humanité* disgusted him, and the behavior of the socialists—who "seemed to have waded into the morass"—irritated him more than once: "Everyone is mean and maladroit."[77] His assessment of the politicians, particularly finance minister Joseph Caillaux, who expressed pacifist sentiments and in 1917 was arrested for allegedly contacting the Germans to discuss a negotiated peace, was harsh. Within the Parti Socialiste, only Albert Thomas and Renaudel occasionally found favor in his eyes. Most often, Mauss "did not seek to understand," since, "from a distance, it produces an even worse effect." Durkheim advised him "not to form theories about the events and to limit [himself] to living as quietly as possible."[78]

During the first years of war, Durkheim criticized the slogan "Workers of the world unite!"[79] and openly expressed his patriotism. He participated with Sylvain Lévi on a committee attached to the propaganda office (on the question of Russian Jews). In 1915 he organized and distributed studies and documents on the war and drafted satirical tracts (*Who Wanted War?*; *Deutschland über Alles*). And he collaborated with other academics—Ernest Lavisse, Charles Andler, Émile Boutroux, Henri Bergson, Gustave Lanson, Antoine Meillet, Charles Seignobos, and others—to publish *Lettres à tous les Français* (Letters to all French people). These letters were published as loose sheets and three million copies were distributed, with the objective of "giving a solid foundation to public opinion" and inviting the population to show "forbearance, effort, and confidence." Durkheim wrote: "We are all obliged to participate actively in the war, each in our own way, each in accordance with our means, and that active participation, in addition to being useful in itself, contributes toward reinforcing our resolution to stand firm. Indeed, faith is maintained only through action."[80]

We can therefore understand how hurt Durkheim was by M. Gaudin de Villaine's statement in the Senate identifying him "with a foreign tradition representing the German Kriegsministerium."[81] At the session of March 30, 1916, the minister of public education personally stepped forward to defend the "head of the French school of sociology." He pointed out "Durkheim's unflagging zeal in producing patriotic propaganda" and recalled that "his only son, one of the most brilliant students of our heroic École Normale Supérieure, shed his blood generously for the threatened nation." Mauss, informed by vague newspaper accounts that his uncle was, "in his absence, spinelessly insulted in the legislature at a time of sacred union," could not hide his indignation and immediately replied with rare virulence to defend his family's name: "It is I, therefore, who will naturally have the honor of slapping your face after the war."[82]

More than anything, his uncle's "health and strength" concerned Mauss. In December 1916 he wrote: "Very worried about Durkheim's health. He doesn't write me, I know he doesn't see anyone, and I know he's really demoralized. Very troubled by the turn of events."[83] A month later, after returning from a leave, Mauss wrote another of his friends: "My uncle is causing me a great deal of worry. My leave was busy, useful, and sad. My impressions are not very good."[84] Durkheim gave some information on his state of health and, when he was unable to hold a pen, dictated letters to his wife: "[Dr. Dupré] has demanded that I take a prolonged rest, which I'll do mostly in the countryside. . . . After that, he's advised me to retire and to work in moderation."[85] Although restricted to "personal work" and living "the life of a vegetable as much as possible," Durkheim continued to pursue a few intellectual projects. He wrote Mauss: "You've often said that war ought to provide new facts and new perspectives for the book I have in mind. So try to explain your ideas on that point: it will enrich our correspondence. . . . They intend to keep me in a state of complete rest, but I don't think I'll be forbidden to think about the subject a little, and as a result to talk with you."[86] That letter, like the previous one, written the evening of May 15, was dictated to Louise Durkheim by her husband and then signed by him.[87]

During the summer, Émile spent several weeks in Fontainebleau. When Marcel visited him in early July, he had a "better impression" of his uncle but observed that he still tired easily.[88] Durkheim's morale remained low: "It's not completely impossible for me to write, but it's better if I refrain. Fatigue comes quickly and it's wise to avoid it."[89] During a conversation with Davy, Durkheim confided: "I have the impression I speak to you of men and things with the detachment of someone who's already left this world."[90] The malaise he was suffering from had not totally disappeared by fall. He wrote his nephew that the illness seemed to be "nervous in origin" but claimed that no one knew "where that nervous trouble came from and why."[91] His sisters, Rosine and Céline, were very worried. Émile considered spending four or five months resting near Barbizon. "My condition . . . has not deteriorated. The insomnia and nervous spasms have even disappeared. It's my mental state that's not so good. It left much to be desired when you were here and it's only gotten worse."[92]

This was the last letter he wrote to his nephew. Five days later, he died at age fifty-nine. Mauss received a telegram from his cousin Marie, Durkheim's daughter: "Papa died peacefully this morning." And another from Hubert: "Durkheim died suddenly around noon." For the nephew, it was a "great sorrow": "Not only do I feel the void that being deprived of Durkheim's correspondence has created in my mind, but it leaves a void at the only times I could—albeit carefully—pour out my heart."[93] Friends and loved ones linked the father's death directly to his son's: "The poor father couldn't get over his grief."[94] *Dépêche de Toulouse* reported: "M. Émile Durkheim has just died. The death of his son, killed during the rugged retreat from Salonika, left him inconsolable."[95] Mauss also acknowledged this: "The loss [of André], experienced both as a father and as an intellectual, was the cause of Durkheim's death."[96]

Mauss was shaken but did not "let himself get beaten down" by his great sorrow. At the end of the hard year 1917, he wrote: "I still have my health, and hope."[97]

"It's Taking So Long!"

First came the battles of winter 1916 (the Combles woods, Morval, the Barnafay woods), then those of spring 1917: "Advance toward Bapaume, where [Mauss] was one of the first to enter, reconnaissance further on—Marchies, Havrincourt, Hindenburg Line. Return to Ieper October 1917 (third battle of Ieper, billeting, the fortifications of Lille)."[98] The third battle of Ieper—which the Australians would call the battle of Paschendaele, from the name of the place where they fought—was the "major battle of 1917." Eleven major attacks by the Allies decisively weakened the German forces. During five of them, the Australian divisions placed in the outposts once more suffered major losses.[99] Mauss was called a "very energetic" soldier who "speaks and writes English and German well" and "rides well"; he acquitted himself of his duties "promptly and intelligently."[100] The courage he showed was praised by his superiors: "On March 17, 1917, [officer/interpreter Mauss] entered Bapaume with the advanced guard of the division, doing the reconnaissance assigned him during violent bombing. Always among the best despite his age; his calm courage and sense of duty have created an exceptional situation between him and the British unit to which he is attached."[101]

When family and friends became anxious, Mauss tried to reassure them: "Don't worry. The place is not being bombed." "No point in telling anyone where I am. That would alarm them, which is utterly pointless, since it's unlikely I'll ever be permitted to go to the front ranks. I'll no doubt stay in the rear."[102] These were difficult months: "German aviation is gaining in strength. I was seriously bombed several times running in Amiens."[103] "For the first time, I'm living through turbulent times."[104] Mauss found a few reasons for hope: "Anything's possible. So let's hold on. I'm afraid it'll be hard to hold on this winter. But I'm sure we'll hold on"; "Advancing slowly"; "It's going well. The Boches are giving in." When the rumor circulated of a "demobilization of the old cohorts" in 1918, for a time Mauss considered "letting himself be demobilized," but abandoned the idea: "I won't accept. Unfortunately, I have no wife or children."[105]

In March and April 1918, there was a major German offensive, a last stand. For the Australian divisions, these months were particularly difficult. The attack on Australian troops in Villiers-Bretonneux in April 1918 was the hardest made against them during the war.[106] The German army dug out an enormous pocket surrounding Noyon, Catigny, Hangard-en-Santerre, Villiers-Bretonnneux, Albert, and Puiseux, but did not manage to break the Franco-British coalition or open the road to Paris. In Erich Ludendorff's words, these were "dark days" for Germany.

During these months, Mauss did not hide his suffering: "Constant change of sector, cold contracted during a long journey N[orth] to S[outh], fatigue and fear, not for myself but for my troops and my country."[107] Nevertheless, Mauss felt "happy to be at the front and in battle, or rather close to the battle," to "do [his] duty" and to "do some good." "An old woman here, a family there, a few properties saved, that's something, an effort to support the troops, another to preserve civilian life, all that serves a purpose. And it's honorable." The only way to hold on was not to think too much.[108] He did not lose his confidence: "I don't know which side time is on. I think it's on ours, given the circumstances. Let's hope. Let's have confidence."[109]

Amiens was saved. During the evacuation of Villiers-Bretonneux, Aubigny, and Corbie, Mauss distinguished himself: "Assigned to secure the rescue of civilian populations and of considerable wealth important for national defense, in a sector under constant and violent bombing, and sometimes under very perilous circumstances, he fulfilled his mission energetically and with an absolute disregard for danger."[110]

During the last months of war, the Allies conducted a continuous offensive: the order was to "attack, attack, and attack again." The air force leapt into action and increased the bombings. In October the German army retreated all along the Western Front: "It's definitely going well. The Boches are taking off in a hurry."[111] Mauss was still outraged by the attitude of his party and of *Humanité*: "Stupidity and cowardliness," he exclaimed.[112] His "antipathy toward all leaders" remained extreme.[113]

He was in excellent physical and moral shape. The last months had gone fairly well, were it not for the fact that he was homesick for the first time. When bells tolled to mark the Armistice, it put him somewhat on edge, since they reminded him too much of the death of his loved ones.[114] In Épinal, there was "delirious joy, a time of celebration for everyone," but, as his mother pointed out, there too "it [was] mingled with tears at the thought of our dearly departed."[115] A euphoric president of the fourth section of the École Pratique made the following declaration at the faculty meeting of November 17, 1918: "Let us give free rein today to the joy inspired by the victorious outcome of the struggle and the incomparable glory France has achieved. . . . France is once more taking its place in the vanguard of all nations; a new age is dawning in the history of modern peoples."[116]

On December 1, 1918, Mauss was assigned to the Commission de Navigation du Rhin (Rhine navigation commission). A year later, he was loudly complaining about still being kept in Cologne. One of his most cherished plans was to "settle down" but everything seemed up in the air. His mother observed: "I don't know anyone I would wish on him."[117]

At the very start of the war, Sylvain and Danielle Lévi had wished their "dear soldier whom we love so much, to whom we owe everything," "victory first and happiness second, the inexpressible happiness of coming home."[118] Four years later, the "dear old boy" did come home, tired but crowned with glory and sporting many medals: the Croix de Guerre (two bronze stars), two citations (order of the Brigade), the Croix de la Victoire, the interallied medal (for the first six months of war), the Croix du Combattant, the Croix du Combattant Engagé Volontaire, the Médaille de la Victoire, the Medal for Distinguished Conduct on the Field, and the Military Cross.

It is not easy to visualize the postwar period. Mauss wrote his friend Hubert: "The D[urkheims] are gone and I have only you."[119] Fortunately there was the prospect of collaborative work. Both men had given it some thought during the war. "If I come back from the war," Mauss had written one day, "we'll have to make arrangements to work, unless the Soviets don't allow it."[120] "Of course we must work after the war," Hubert had replied. "Sociology's time has not yet passed."[121] Mauss took his walks with the latest volume of Spencer under his arm, but did not manage to read it. In the autumn of 1918, the question arose in a more serious way. Mauss wrote: "We must consider working. . . . We must also organize our material and moral lives in such a way that I can work and work with you. All that will be difficult. But I will sincerely try."[122] More than anyone else, Hubert was impatient to have his "old chum" back and to know he had "buckled down again to the common task."[123] When Mauss learned he was finally demobilized in January 1919, he wrote his friend with his itinerary: "Leave Cologne January 12. I'll be in Nancy, my demobilization center, on January 15. Return to Paris around 15–20. And for good. And forever. We'll talk. . . . Europe's future looks very weak, very dark to me. But anyway, we'll work."[124]

PART III

THE HEIR

THE WAR was a terrible ordeal. Some eight million men were mobilized. Countless died. Three million were wounded, and a quarter of those were permanently disabled. The cry went out: "Never again."[1] Mauss did not forget the long years he had spent in uniform. Physically and morally, he carried his violent experiences within him. They expressed themselves as a fear of death, or as anxiety at the prospect of waiting.[2] He had felt old even before the war; now he was forty-six. His "uncle" Sylvain Lévi gently teased him: "Don't talk about your age anymore, you'll make me think about mine."[3]

The war forced Émile Durkheim's nephew to grow up. Hubert Bourgin observed: "You feel your heart beating faster and stronger and you see that your intelligence has quietly lowered some artificial barriers."[4] Henri Hubert also felt that his friend "had gained a lot by the war" and hoped his party and his country would benefit.[5] Maurice Leenhardt would say that a man of Mauss's value could not have spent time in the army "without learning a great deal from what he had seen."[6]

When Mauss returned to Paris after the war, he moved back into his apartment at 2, rue Bruller. And thanks to the law of November 22, 1918, he reclaimed his place in the section of religious science at the École Pratique. Demobilized in January 1919, he delayed resuming his classes until the start of the 1919–1920 school year, taking time to put his life back in order. Fauconnet had already drawn up a "program" for him: "Enjoy the victory immensely and rest in comfort—then get Hautes Études to call you back to cut short the delay in getting yourself discharged—get married—go back to work."[7]

The country was in a state of confusion. No one knew what was happening in Germany. The Left felt the absence of Jaurès more intensely than ever. "Poor great Jaurès!" wrote Mauss's colleague Paul Rivet. "So many things were done that he might have prevented."[8]

In March 1919 Mauss was called as a witness at the assize court of the Seine in the trial of Raoul Villain, who was accused of assassinating Jaurès.[9] On March 29, by a vote of eleven to one, the jury acquitted Villain. Everyone was outraged. On the first Sunday of April, a crowd of more than 150,000 marched from Place Victor-Hugo to Square Lamartine, where a bust of Jaurès stood. It was the first demonstration by the Left since the start of the war and served as Jaurès's real funeral.

The political landscape was changing. In 1919 the Bloc National, which the Radicals had joined, won the election with the slogan: "United, as we were at the front." The Parti Socialiste's representation in the legislature fell from 103 to 68 deputies; Jean Longuet and Pierre Renaudel were defeated, but Léon Blum was elected. Former socialists such as Alexandre Millerand and Aristide Briand came to power. Others left the stage.

Former minister of armaments Albert Thomas had been the Parti Socialiste's best hope on the eve of war. During the war he assumed the stature of a statesman and became the symbol for Normalian socialists and intellectuals advocating a realistic socialism. Thomas, however, was more interested in concrete economic problems and practical solutions than in ideological debates. He became head of the Bureau International du Travail (International labor office) in Geneva, under the auspices of the League of Nations. He surrounded himself with "skilled technicians." His counterpart in Paris was Mario Roques. Among the heads of technical departments in the new international organization were Georges Fauquet (cooperatives) and Edgar Milhaud (production). These were people whom Mauss knew well and who on occasion would request his services.

Thomas was motivated by a simple "faith in reason." He believed that "science and the clearly defined and rapid development of technology can help us find solutions to the alarming problem human reason now faces."[10] Although Mauss had once despaired of humanity, believing that, "after civilization, we were returning to a kind of Middle Ages," he now shared his friend's hope. Of course, the idea of "absolute progress" still seemed unacceptable to him, since every advance could be assessed only in relation to a given society; but he thought it possible to speak of a "certain general progress" of humanity. "There is more good sense, clarity, morality, knowledge, and feeling in human consciousness than there was in the past. There is a general movement toward an enhanced sense of being and toward something stronger and finer. I do not say toward greater well-being."[11]

The World War I veteran reestablished contact with his friends in the Parti Socialiste, especially Pierre Renaudel. He also met "new figures," "latecomers" with little understanding and a devotion of "fresh date."[12] He did not participate in his comrades' initiatives at the end of the war—a plan to publish an activist newspaper, *France Libre*, in the summer of 1918; the organization of a new socialist club in the autumn of 1919; and the founding of the Parti Socialiste Français in March 1920. He was somewhat out of his element and initially avoided getting directly involved in the debates dividing the Left. Fauconnet was amazed at his friend's "wisdom": "I'm not unhappy to see you resuming your life as an 'old scholar' and reading the Greek physicians. But I'm still opposed to your life as an 'old bachelor.' A passable marriage would be better than remaining single."[13]

Mauss's abstention from politics would be short-lived. The "old militant" could not remain indifferent to "social and political action," problems relating to peace, Bolshevism, cooperatives, and the economic crisis.

II

(THE SOCIALIST) LIFE GOES ON

THE POSTWAR years were particularly rich not only in ideas, precise observations, and new research but also in "proposals, tactics, and modern organizations." According to Mauss, they "would be considered by our descendants one of the great eras of sociological and political thought."[1]

With Durkheim now dead, Mauss became the trustee of his mode of thought and methods. Yet he did not simply embrace "pure science" as his uncle had done. When Durkheim founded *Année Sociologique*, he left his history of socialism unfinished—something Mauss noted that Durkheim "would always regret"—but social questions remained "at the root of his concerns." The nephew was anxious to remind people of this and published the course his uncle had taught in Bordeaux between November 1895 and May 1896. A significant part of it was devoted to Saint-Simon, the "first socialist messiah," who had become fashionable again after the war. Mauss wrote in the introduction, "Socialism, as the force of the workers and as a political force, is indispensable therein."[2]

Could sociology and socialism be reconciled? When Mauss made comments at a discussion of the foundations of socialism before members of the Société Française de Philosophie, he did not hesitate to move from one register to the other: "It is as a sociologist on the one hand and as a socialist on the other that I will venture to reply to you."[3] Somewhat like his friend François Simiand, the impetus he wanted to give to his career was that "of a socialist fully devoted to the study of society."[4]

The projects Mauss developed in the early 1920s were inseparably intellectual and political. He thought of doing a major study on the nation, and in 1920 presented its first elements in Oxford, in a paper titled "The Problem of Nationality." He also planned to write a book on Bolshevism and made an outline for it after publishing "Observations on Violence." What concerned him most during that troubled period was politics, nationalism on the one hand and socialism on the other. His friend Fauconnet advised him, "Better to write your 'Politics' than to write letters. . . . Get to work!"[5] To focus on that work was a major challenge, since Mauss specialized in the religious history of so-called primitive peoples and not in the pressing problems of the day.

War and Peace among Nations

The relations between France and Germany were a foremost concern of the French government. Passions were running high and the parties were mobilizing. Everyone wanted peace, but everyone was divided on the way to preserve it. According to some, peace depended on stronger defense and good alliances; others felt it necessary to promote a Franco-German rapprochement and to set in place arbitrating institutions such as the League of Nations. On one side were the patriots who embraced President Raymond Poincaré; on the other were the pacifists and internationalists who looked to Briand as their leader. Public opinion oscillated between one position and the other, wanting both reparations and Franco-German reconciliation, alliances and international organizations. The Treaty of Versailles, signed on July 28, 1919, illustrated the difficulty of achieving a "peace settlement" that would respond to both sides' demands. In France there was a general sense of a "marred victory" and a fear of the enemy's desire for revenge.

It was as a combat veteran that Mauss addressed the question of peace. "Never again," he exclaimed, along with everyone else who had experienced the worst atrocities for months and years. For him, one fact was unavoidable: the peoples of various nations no longer wanted to make war. They wanted peace and they preferred disarmament to an armed peace—"rightly or wrongly," he said.

Skepticism, he believed, ought not to lead people to forget that the "most renowned moral and political act of peace, however shaky it may be, is the recognition of the principle of arbitration established by the League of Nations pact."[6] Mauss was one of those in the socialist movement who displayed a great deal of sympathy for the Genevan institution and optimism about its future. "Peaceful patriotism," to use Antoine Prost's expression, was combined with a true internationalism. There should be security and disarmament, of course, but also and above all arbitration.

At a time when the nationality principle prevailed, everything converged to make the "life of nations" an object of reflection not only for militants but also for specialists in the human sciences.[7] People wondered whether peace among nations, international solidarity, was possible. In 1918 Mauss's longtime friend, the linguist Antoine Meillet, published *Les langues de l'Europe nouvelle* (The languages of the new Europe). He observed: "The world is not yet ready for a true international unity based on the elements shared by civilized Europe and implemented in practical relations among all nations of the world."[8] Arnold Van Gennep was preparing his vast *Traité comparatif des nations* (Comparative treatise on nations), whose first (and only) volume would be published in 1922 under the title *Les éléments extérieurs de la nationalité* (The external elements of nationality).

Probably in late 1919 or early 1920, shortly after the peace treaty was signed, Mauss began composing the first chapters of a major study on the nation, part of which was to deal with "socialism and its nationalization."[9] It was both a study of the problem of nationality and a reflection on socialism. These were the two aspects of a "written foray into the realm of the normative," which would lead Mauss to write "Elements of a Modern Politics," an article that was interrupted and resumed many times.

His approach was to be theoretical and his aim to treat jointly the two major movements prevalent in contemporary societies: nationalism and socialism. Mauss explained: "Our work is primarily political and consists of describing the current situation of nations, and of deducing from it a few precepts about rather unusual practices." This was an especially difficult task because "the necessary hindsight is not yet available." It was also an ambitious project: The fragments that survive (several hundred pages in all) suggest that the work would have been "monumental."[10]

In the autumn of 1920 Mauss presented "The Problem of Nationality" at a philosophy colloquium held at Oxford. This gave him the opportunity to see friends and colleagues—Mabel Bode, the Frazers—and to work at the British Museum. In addition, it provided him with a forum to defend French thought, the "Durkheimian" tradition, and his own ideas, as Élie Halévy had invited him to do.[11]

Mauss's first discussion of nationality indicated the method he intended to follow. With an audience composed of philosophers, he did not want to approach the question abstractly. What interested him as a sociologist were the "realities," and, more precisely, the "altogether concrete question of nations, of their place in human history, of their current ethical role, of their relations."[12] His relatively short paper was composed of two parts: a definition of the nation and an analysis of internationalism (which he distinguished from cosmopolitanism).

For Mauss, a "group of men living together in a determinate, independent territory, and adhering to a determinate constitution" formed a society, but not necessarily a nation. What was a nation? The word itself had only been used for a short time and was often confused with the term "state." To clarify the question, he indulged in a bit of comparative philology, a little "history of ideas," then sketched out a general history of how societies organized themselves politically. To that end, one of the distinctions Durkheim had introduced in his courses on the family proved valuable: on the one hand, there were "polysegmental," or tribal, societies based on clans; on the other, "nonsegmental," or integrated, societies. Although he adopted this classification, Mauss also introduced another distinction within nonsegmental societies that took into account the type of central power each had and made it possible to distinguish nations from states (or empires). The nephew was fine-tuning the uncle's thesis. In Mauss's view, the criteria for being a nation were: the possession of a stable central power and a legislative and administrative system; and a codification of citizens' and of the nation's rights and duties.[13]

According to Mauss, the term "nation" applied "only to a small number of societies known to history; in some cases, it has only been recently applied." He added: "Not all human societies currently in existence are of the same nature and at the same place in their development. Far from it. To consider them equal is an injustice toward those in which civilization and the notion of rights are more fully developed."[14] Nations, especially great ones, were "the beautiful, but still rare and fragile, flowers of civilization and human progress."[15] Mauss established a hierarchy among contemporary societies: He considered Great Britain, France, and Germany "the highest ones"; Switzerland and Norway were models of small nations. But as yet, none of these collectivities was "perfect or in an equal state of perfection in every area."

In his most developed definition of the nation, Mauss applied the same criteria and, like Renan, granted a great deal of importance to the spiritual and cultural dimension: "By nation we understand a materially and morally integrated society with a stable and permanent central power, with determinate borders, and with relative moral, mental, and cultural unity among the inhabitants, who consciously adhere to the state and its laws." In addition to political, legal, and economic unity, there had to be a "general, conscious, constant will." "A nation worthy of the name has its own aesthetic, moral, and material civilization, and almost always its own language. It has its mentality, its sensibility, its morality, its will, and its form of progress, and all the citizens composing it participate in the Idea guiding it."[16]

As a militant socialist, Mauss was wary of nationalism, which often "generates ills in the national consciousness." But one fact was key: in modern times many individualized nations had been constituted. These nations believed in their race, their language, and their civilization and were endowed with a "collective spirit" or what could be called a "collective character." That spirit was often the "unconscious handiwork of generations and circumstances," but at present was the result of a "conscious formation of national character."

An Ideal: Internationalism

To a certain extent, what was true of individuals was also true of entire peoples: "individuation in the formation of nations" was the condition and expression of a new solidarity founded on increased trade and a more extensive division of labor. Hence it was progress. Instead of contrasting the development of national individuality and internationalism, Mauss showed

that these two movements were closely linked: "Organic, conscious solidarity among nations and the division of labor among them based on soil,
climate, and population will lead to the creation of an atmosphere of peace
where they will be able to live their lives fully. These factors will thus have
the effect on collective individualities that they have on personalities within
the nations: They will secure their freedom, their dignity, their uniqueness,
their greatness."[17]

Mauss was clearly inspired by Durkheim. The conclusions of *The Division
of Labor in Society* were being applied to the relations among societies themselves. Just as there were no isolated individuals, there were no "closed,
self-sufficient societies."[18]

There had always been and there continued to be frequent contact between
societies. Societies borrowed a great deal from one another, whether at an
economic, technical, aesthetic, religious, linguistic, or legal level. There was
communication and interdependence. In "The Problem of Nationality," Mauss
briefly described the principal facts of interdependence in modern societies:
(1) an absolute economic interdependence (a world market, a division of
labor between possessors of raw materials and manufacturing societies); (2)
an increasing moral interdependence; (3) a desire on the part of different
peoples to no longer wage war; (4) a limitation on national sovereignty.

This interpenetration called for the new ideal of internationalism. Mauss
was among those who were optimistic after the peace treaty was signed and
who believed that relations among nations would gradually lead to agreement. He also placed a great deal of hope in the newly created League of
Nations, the Bureau International du Travail, and the Cour Permanente
d'Arbitrage et de Justice (Permanent arbitration and justice court). Mauss's
interest in these international organizations was especially great because his
friends Edgar Milhaud and Albert Thomas were associated with the Bureau
International du Travail in Geneva.[19] He hoped there would be "an entire
movement of social forces tending toward the practical and moral regulation of societies' relations with one another" and even perhaps toward the
possibility of peace.

The combat veteran was thus far from insensitive to the "hymns to peace
and the imprecations against war." He paid homage to the various pacifist
movements "of goodwill," which kept up a "useful agitation." An internationalist at heart, Mauss adopted the famous slogan: "Workers of the world,
unite." But just as he did not embrace the policy of man-as-citizen-of-the-
world, he could not imagine an ethics that would transcend the realities of
social life. That would be naïve cosmopolitanism, utopianism. Any human
ethics, he thought, had to be based in national and international reality.[20]

Ought one to despair of nations? A worried Mauss did not believe in the
immediate realization of universal peace. "Just as it is impossible to create
a universal language and get it adopted before there is a universal society,

so too is it impossible to create a universal peace before there is a universal society." One must advance "by degrees, creating larger and larger societies or, since the current trend is toward small nations as well as large, increasingly vast federations and confederations."[21] In fact, "the spirit of peace is, above all, a spirit of federation; it is possible only through federation, which one must create to have peace, and not, conversely, create peace to build the United States of Europe or of the World. It is when there is a United States of Europe that there will be peace in Europe, when there is a United States of the World that there will be peace in the world. Not before; let us take upon ourselves the boldness, the risk, and the absurdity of that prophecy."[22]

From that standpoint, to think about "human civilization" as some writers did was to indulge in ideology, to dream. According to Mauss, if there was anything new about their lives, it lay in the constitution "of a growing capital of international realities and international ideas." Hence intellectuals, and philosophers in particular, had a responsibility to "serve as the vanguard in that march" and find "wise and necessary formulations."[23]

There was no point in hiding the fact that troubles lay in the future: there would again be "national violence" and "national arrogance." But for Mauss one thing was certain: the "common ground" was increasing in scope and quality, the "capital of humanity" was growing. His optimism led him to think that "therein lies civilization,"[24] and that there was a certain overall progress.[25] Nevertheless, just as progress did not mean greater well-being, civilization thus understood did not necessarily bring happiness.

Reflections on Violence

The book on the nation remained in the planning stages. No one had forgotten the war, and there were other reasons for anxiety that held people's attention. Living conditions remained difficult and the unemployment rate was high. The 1920 railway workers' strike set in motion a true social crisis. In addition, the question of whether to join the Third Internationale was of great concern to socialist and syndicalist militants. Ever since the dawning of "the bright glimmer from the east," as the writer Jules Romains described it, socialist militants had regarded the new Soviet regime with sympathy and had judged allied military intervention against it unacceptable. But they were still divided: did Bolshevism as a (worldwide) revolutionary strategy suit France?

Greatly influenced by "Jaurésian synthesis," French socialism considered itself democratic and parliamentary as well as anticapitalist. At its February 1920 congress in Strasbourg, the SFIO rejected the idea of simply joining the communist Internationale, but adopted a motion affirming "its will to work toward the reconstitution of socialism's worldwide unity." Armed with that mandate, Ludovic Oscar Frossard, general secretary of the SFIO, and Marcel Cachin, director of *Humanité*, went to Moscow in June of the same year. When they returned, the two socialist delegates maintained that the "reconstruction" of the Internationale could be brought about within the framework of the communist movement. A broad debate opened in the communist press. Léon Blum founded the Comité de Résistance Socialiste à l'Adhésion (Socialist committee to resist joining). That committee, composed of two distinct groups, made up what was called the party's right wing. One group was run by Blum, Alexandre Bracke, and Paoli, secretary of the fourteenth arrondissement branch, the other by Pierre Renaudel, who headed a new political weekly, *Vie Socialiste*.

After Mauss resumed his activities as a journalist in summer 1920, he regularly published in *Vie Socialiste*, writing articles devoted to the cooperative movement as well as to his memories, reflections on the "new forms of socialism," and short analyses of the international political situation (in Poland, Great Britain, and Italy). He did not overlook the pressing question of whether to join the Third Internationale. The Cachin-Frossard dispatch caused "something of a commotion," and *Vie Socialiste* immediately organized a counterattack, composing a protest letter and gathering support.

Memories of Jaurès were omnipresent at *Vie Socialiste*. The weekly published excerpts of his books and lectures, quoted him in epigraphs ("Preparing for the disarmament of Europe is the loftiest and most pressing task incumbent upon the proletariat"). Renaudel, an assistant editor, was a Jaurès devotee. Everyone called Renaudel "the Big Guy," for his experience, good nature, rectitude, inflexible honesty, and political courage.[26] Surrounded by young people on the editorial board—Marcel Déat, Gustave Rouanet, and Jean Texcier—Renaudel wanted to make the journal a "coalition . . . faithful to Jaurès's inspiration and heir to the wartime majority spirit, vigorously antibolshevist and courageously reformist."[27] "*Vie Socialiste* is not Bolshevist because it is socialist," he explained. There was sharp opposition to the new majority's newspaper, *Humanité*. Marcel Déat said: "In *Vie Socialiste* one finds what *Humanité* doesn't publish."

Mauss shared these views. Aware "that the future of [his] party and of French socialism was at stake," he quickly became involved in the debate. In Épinal for his vacation the summer of 1920, he began to campaign alongside Deputy Aimé Piton to urge the members of the Vosges socialist federation to vote against an alliance with Moscow. His assessment of the survey Cachin and Frossard had conducted in Russia was harsh: the information was "rather willy-nilly"; there was no criticism of "official documents and statements"; there was no "sense of history or skepticism"; there were no interviews with non-Bolshevists or "prominent opponents." Nothing in it was very serious: it was "Cachin in a nutshell." He was hiding his eyes to see better, said Mauss ironically. "He's confusing duty with truth."[28]

Having known Cachin for twenty-five years, Mauss was expecting to be insulted, to be called "traitor, lost soul, counterrevolutionary." He was unperturbed. One must know and tell the truth, even in the face of insults. Indeed, like the ancient orator, one would say of those who hurl insults: "It's because you're lame that you ride such big horses."

Vie Socialiste, with Renaudel at its head, participated in the Comité de Résistance Socialiste à l'Adhésion and supported the Blum-Paoli motion "for international unity." The inevitable rift came in December at the Socialist congress in Tours and led to the creation of the Parti Communiste Français. Immediately after the congress, that party had twice as many members as the SFIO: in 1921, 120,000 versus 50,000. What were the chief motivations of first-generation communists? What led them to accept the twenty-one conditions set by the Third Internationale? Of course, the denunciation of war and the revolt against the "betrayal" by socialist leaders such as Jules Guesde and Marcel Sembat played a role.[29] But also and especially, as Mauss observed of his comrades in the Vosges federation, it was confidence in the Russian Revolution and a certain revolutionary romanticism: "The comrades who have wanted to join with Moscow go there as if on a pilgrimage. They are moved by an act of faith. For them, it's like the star rising in the east. They are guided by the star. Christ is born. Socialism has become a reality in Russia: Bethlehem is Moscow."[30]

Mauss did not share his comrades' delirious enthusiasm. Yes, the Russian Revolution could be seen as a "practical experiment in socialism," a "great thing," but it was foolish to obey the orders of the "Moscow sectarians." He reminded those who were turning to the new "Muscovite popes" that one ought to have "neither God nor master." He was in the minority camp, Blum in the camp of "socialism and democracy." In fact, it was "with indifference," "in a perfectly cold manner," that he learned in December 1920 that he "was not a communist and was no longer on the administration board of *Humanité*." And it was "without emotion" that he left the "old house" he had played a role in founding and separated from his "old comrade" Cachin and from all "those Johnny-come-latelies."[31]

Immediately after the congress in Tours, the SFIO seemed to be in a state of complete decomposition. Of its 68 deputies elected in 1919, a dozen had joined the Communist Party. The SFIO lost control of *Humanité*. A rift occurred in the syndicalist movement in 1921–1922, and there were many internal divisions. Rather than "go on a wild goose chase," Blum preferred to stay and "preserve the very life of socialism." He again found himself at the head of the party, with Paul Faure as general secretary, and he took charge of *Populaire*, the SFIO's new organ. Blum's intellectual and moral authority within the party was indisputable. For Blum, an intellectual from a bourgeois background whom some described as a "fin-de-siècle aesthete," socialism was "as much an ethics and a quasi-religion as a doctrine." His conception of social revolution was spelled out in a short brochure titled "Pour être socialiste" (To be a socialist), published by the SFIO in 1919. It put him at odds with the champions of historical materialism and the Leninist conception of a dictatorship of the proletariat. His communist adversaries criticized him for serving as cabinet chief to Marcel Déat, socialist minister of the Sacred Union government during the war, and accused him of being a "social-chauvinist."

From Épinal, Mauss observed his party's "state of disorganization." It was a movement "without order, divided, split into factions." Lucien Lévy-Bruhl, Jaurès's former confidant and now an intimate of Renaudel and Blum, was worried as well. He believed that it would "take time to reabsorb the majority of the extremists" and that a "fairly large contingent of holdouts" would always remain.[32]

Mauss remained optimistic. The unity of workers and peasants would come about, he believed, and would impose unity on the divided militants.[33] It was all a question of time, education, and intellectual action. Mauss, who had lived through the adventure of *Mouvement Socialiste* and the founding of *Humanité* and *Cahiers du Socialiste*, believed it was indispensable to "transform, adjust, and at the very least propagate, in a new and relevant form, the old doctrine and the old tactics." The way to succeed was to "reconstitute intellectual centers within the party and in the circles sympathetic to it." Why not a socialist school? Mauss concluded: "It is a necessity, vital for our ideas, because doctrines and dogmas do not age well. And to update them is to remain faithful to the life and example of Jaurès, Vaillant, and Sembat."[34]

Fidelity was an essential value for Mauss. Although, having reached a certain age, he wanted "to refrain from living too much in the past, from remembering too much, from conversing too much with the dead," he willingly agreed to share his memories. These included the advice Jaurès had given him before his trip to Russia in 1906,[35] the last conversations he had with him in July 1914, and his last exchange with his friend Marcel Sembat in July 1922. Sembat's death had affected him deeply.

He certainly wanted to be faithful, but he was also anxious to see a revival of socialism. Unlike Cachin and Frossard, Mauss did not think that "the light comes from the north." The former student revolutionary had had enough of the "old formulas dating to the *Communist Manifesto* and Proudhon," all those "old theories of revolution with full orchestra, of the eradication of class through class struggle." His admiration for Lenin and Trotsky was relative: "I admit I'm not impressed by the theoretical value of Lenin's writings and even less so by that of Trotsky's." He had read them conscientiously but found them simplistic. Among the characteristics of those "naysayers, those nihilists convinced that only the destruction of the bourgeois state will suffice to make peoples happy," he admired only one thing: their political skill.[36]

Mauss was one of the rare French socialist militants who was an Anglophile, preferring "the intensity of the movement of ideas in England" to Lenin's "creative genius."[37] During a trip to England in the autumn of 1920, he was amazed at the "specifically English" organization of the cooperative and syndicalist movement. "It is cautious, energetic, inspired by the need for action and by a concern for the facts."

The finest examples of the new English reformist thinking were without a doubt Beatrice and Sidney Webb, two English theorists well known in France. Their program included the creation of two parliaments (political and economic), decentralization, municipalization, nationalization, the establishment of a "republic of consumers," the organization of property, and moral education. According to Mauss, it was more than a program: "It is a new society in the planning stages." And, he added, it would be possible to build it "without violence and without chaos." Impartiality, the need for "wise and immediate action," and a concern for the facts were the lessons he drew from the movement of ideas in England.

More than anything, the peevishness and whining of his French comrades irritated him. What was there to say about the behavior of militants who had remained faithful to the old party and mobilized around "the idea of autonomy and unity with the communists!"[38] For Mauss, the "old unified party" had to impose discipline within its ranks; otherwise, "the house divided against itself will not stand." When the Parti Communiste bowed to the orders of the "Sacred Congregation of Rites"—that is, the Internationale—and adopted the tactic of a "single proletarian front," Mauss reacted sharply: "No to the single front, yes to unity." His position was clear: there could be no question of forming a single front "under Moscow's watchful eye."[39]

Populaire, founded by Jean Longuet four years earlier, made inroads as the socialists' central organ. Longuet, author of a motion to "join with reservations," was the party's favorite child, whom the right-wing press called "Quarter-Boche." He had gone over to Blum's side during the congress in Tours. The two took charge of the newspaper at a time when its circulation was low: in late 1922, there were 22,000 regular readers, 7,000 subscribers, and a deficit estimated at about 20,000 francs a month.[40] In 1930 *Populaire's* circulation would reach 63,000, with 40,000 subscribers. This was still small compared to *Humanité's* circulation, which was close to 150,000 at the time.

When the newspaper became a morning daily, Mauss agreed to be a member of its administration and management boards. Though a modest newspaper, it was proud of its intelligence, integrity, independence, and honesty.[41]

Between 1921 and 1925 Mauss published many articles in *Populaire*. The first was more cultural than political and dealt with a book titled *Les hommes fossiles* (Fossil men) published by M. Boule, a paleontologist at the museum of natural history. From that book, which described the "primitive forms of humanity," Mauss drew a political conclusion about the relativity of things: "What a lesson for those who believe that modern man and present-day societies are the perfect outcome of evolution. What a lesson as well for all those who are in too much of a hurry and who imagine that their violence will give birth to a perfect society and to a race with no need to advance further."[42] These words were clearly addressed to the communists.

Bolshevism worried Mauss, who shared Léon Blum's "socialist ideal": "More than any other party, socialism abhors violence and blood."

In 1923 Mauss published a series of five long articles in *Vie Socialiste* called "Observations on Violence." Why had Russia been swept away by a "sort of mass hysteria"? Mauss sought to understand the Russian people, who had been "fiercely boycotted by almost the entire world," and who were now "isolated, starving, bankrupt, deserted by most of their best elements."[43] The (historical and sociological) explanation was simple: here was a country that, like Italy, was "backward, poor, and unlucky." According to Mauss, the tyranny developing there was proof of the "political incompetence of this people." Bolshevism and Fascism attested to the "regression" of modern societies;[44] they were "political episodes in the life of politically uneducated peoples." Because there was no public opinion, civic education, or, in a word, citizens in those countries,[45] the political realm was left to "activist minorities." It was therefore not surprising that the "Kremlin brutes" with their "adventuristic practices" had prevailed.

Mauss's series of articles, subtitled "Fascism and Bolshevism," was presented as a response to Georges Sorel's *Reflections on Violence*, which had been published in 1908. Mauss was not unhappy to engage in a polemic with his old comrade, whom he had met in 1895 and whom he presented as "an embittered old man with no concern for the consequences of his acts, with no mandate, with no scientific scruples."[46] Sorel had become the apostle of violence and "direct action," announcing the "victory of minorities over majorities." For Mauss, it was particularly important to criticize that "ideology of so-called realists," because he considered Sorel to be Lenin's and Mussolini's "sponsor." But beyond polemics, what Mauss wanted was to better understand the Bolshevik Revolution, certain aspects of which he had already harshly criticized in *Populaire*. His diagnosis was merciless. Of course, "certain claims to glory" and "a few benefits" of the Bolshevik Revolution could be identified: it had destroyed the bureaucracy and the Russian aristocracy, had ushered in federalism, had emancipated "a few tyrannized populations," and had returned lands to the peasants after "a few years of aberration." But, on the whole, the liabilities were "awful."

For Mauss, Bolshevism would be known for "the poverty of its ideas and of its legal and administrative accomplishments."[47] What was his criticism of the Russian communists? First, they believed "that it is possible to establish laws and rights by decree, by violence, that it is possible to oversee

various interests without the consent and confidence of the interested parties."[48] Second, they had "destroyed everything" in the economy, had abol-
ished all private commerce, had eliminated all markets, all stock exchanges,
all speculation. Third, and even worse, they had "dried up the very source of
any social life: confidence and good faith."[49] Finally, they had waged social
revolution "against the most active classes in the country, against the institutions most dear to it and those that would be most essential to its success."[50]
For Mauss, this was a historical paradox: "In Moscow, the dictatorship of
the proletariat has become a dictatorship of the Communist Party over the
proletariat."[51]

A defender of the doctrine of "activist majorities," Mauss condemned violence. In Russia and in Italy, it was "pointless and mad." From his standpoint, the best administration was the one that was least intrusive. "In our
nations, the more mighty a regime, the less it needs to use its might."[52]

Mauss held on to the hope that the proletarians could draw the lesson
from those "last two adventures of activist minorities" and be cured "of the
myth of violence and faith in social miracles." But slipping into an "unlim-
ited legalism" was out of the question. Wanting to be neither a "worshipper
of our laws" nor a "perpetually plotting insurgent," Mauss sought to reject
"legalism, fetishism, and bourgeois legality" on the one hand and "revolu-
tionarism and communism" on the other.

It was a tricky position. Bernard Lavergne of *Revue des Études Coopératives*
warned Mauss: "You're going to bring all the thunderbolts of the socialist
school down on you, and you run the risk of being manhandled by them
one of these days."[53] Sociology taught Mauss "that there is no society without discipline, without constraints, without sanctions" and that "the law,
even when enacted by the majority, is always to some degree tyrannical."
His political experience had led him to lose his naïveté: Socialism was not
a "doctrine of bleating lambs," and "the establishment of socialism, even
gradual, even partial," was not possible without "clashes and harm to some
interests."[54]

Did not the great Jaurès, whom Mauss presented as a democrat and a revolutionary, continually "call on the masses to exert their force?" What had to
be condemned was "a force imposed against the law or without law." Mauss
criticized the way some had used force but claimed its use was sometimes
necessary. He thus did not express an "absolute repugnance" for the word
"dictatorship," provided it meant "dictatorship of the majority" and that
such a mode of government would be temporary, "exercised in the forms
stipulated by law." "A state, a national economy, can be made to function
only through the citizens' goodwill." Therefore the myth of direct action by
minorities had to end and the "doctrine of effective majorities" had to be
embraced. Mauss drew "a great lesson of democracy, but also of caution and
force": "Let us be ourselves. Strong and cautious so long as we are not the

majority, wise and vigilant when we are, always on the alert for demagogu-ery and reactionary attitudes."[55]

After this series of articles was published, Mauss toyed with the idea of writing a book "in a rather accessible form," whose title would be "Sociological Appreciation of Bolshevism." Because his knowledge of the Russian language was weak, he could not write an original and scholarly work. His more modest intention was to "give an account of Bolshevism in the simplest and most accurate way . . . possible" and to respond calmly and impersonally to a serious question of general political theory: "To what extent does the Bolshevik experiment prove or disprove socialism?"[56]

At issue was to judge the Bolshevik experiment or, to use an older formu-lation, to "appreciate" that phase in the history of Russia and contemporary history. Mauss wanted "to situate a moment in history, in its quasi necessity, within history as a whole," somewhat like Marx in his famous tracts on class struggle in France and on the Paris Commune.

Durkheim's heir was "won over and excited" by the new form of organi-zation represented by the soviets. It was "the first attempt at a national and professional organization of both property and the state." He was motivated to write the book on Bolshevism because he noticed a kinship, between Durkheimian theory and the practice of the soviets. "The idea and reality of the soviet may correspond—if I am not mistaken—to the two rare moral, political, and economic outcomes Durkheim always recommended and that his death prevented him from seeing realized." Had not Durkheim reached the conclusion that only the professional group was an "organ of power and control" strong enough to discipline individuals, and that, as Mauss put it so succinctly, only that form of intermediate-level organization could be a "regulator of the individual but also of the state"? This observation did not fail to cause "powerful anxiety" in Durkheim's nephew. "Were our most cherished, our most hard-won, our most ardently recommended ideas going to emerge invalidated or confirmed?"[57] His motivation was twofold: "The ardor of the scientist mingled with that of the politician and grew stronger within me."[58]

The Presses Universitaires de France, newly created in 1921 and orga-nized as a cooperative, was more than willing to publish Mauss's book, given that he was one of its founding members. The book was to have five chap-ters, plus an introduction and a conclusion. The chapters would address the following issues: (1) To what extent was Bolshevism an experiment? How did Bolshevism take over the Russian Revolution?; (2) to what extent was Bolshevism socialism? Bolshevism and communism; (3) economic and moral failure; (4) political success; (5) the new political economy.

Mauss published only parts of the book, which would never be fin-ished. "A Sociological Appreciation of Bolshevism" appeared in 1924 and "Socialism and Bolshevism" the next year. The criticism of Bolshevism was

not new. Albert Thomas, a fierce defender of reformism, had already published a booklet in 1919 entitled *Bolshevism or Socialism*, in which he refused to recognize the revolutionary and socialist character of Bolshevism.
The new director of the Bureau International du Travail in Geneva remained
skeptical.[59] Blum, wanting to mark his distance from communism, also
analyzed Bolshevism. In an article published in April 1922, entitled "Rosa
Luxemburg," he denounced "the utopian character of Bolshevism" from a
Marxist point of view. A few years later, the socialist leader collected his
analyses in a brochure titled *Bolshevism and Socialism* (1927). True to the
theses he had defended in 1920, he sought to distinguish Bolshevism from
socialism. In his view, there had been no revolution in Russia. "Bolshevik
communism is not true socialism," Blum would declare in Tours in the early
1930s, "but rather its deformation and parody."

Mauss's views were more nuanced. He wanted neither "to hold up the
Russian Revolution as an example nor to hang it out like a scarecrow."[60] As
Revue Slave noted, his study displayed "a rigorous method and a great effort
at impartiality."

Mauss acknowledged that the great social movement that had shaken
Russia combined the two true characteristics of a revolution, namely, "contempt for earned rights and the adoption of a different way of life, both
political and social."[61] But what was missing in Russia was will: Bolshevism
was not "the product of a clear will, of an act by a strong nation ripe for
socialism."[62] Far from being a methodically conducted sociological "experiment," it was only a huge instance of adventurism.[63]

The Russian Revolution looked like a sort of "natural inevitability": it
was born "of war, poverty, and the fall of a regime." As a social revolution, it
faced the worst conditions possible: "it inherited from a bankrupt society."[64]
From a sociological standpoint, no social movement was "exclusively the
work of those who say they are its authors": "determinism is even more true
of societies than of men."[65]

As Mauss defined it, the analyst's task also consisted of giving an "appreciation," that is, of "diagnosing, as in medicine, whether a particular
event is good or bad." A few years later, in the conclusion to another article,
"Divisions and Proportions of Divisions in Sociology," Mauss reminded sociologists that their duty was to provide a constant appreciation of present
things, not only "to tell societies in general, or each in particular, what they
are doing, where they are going, but also to tell them frankly if they are
right, practically and ideally, to continue in one direction or another."[66]

In his "Sociological Appreciation of Bolshevism," which he published in
Revue de Métaphysique et de Morale, he drew a series of "practical conclusions" and formulated various "precepts, combined with theoretical observations of more or less universal importance." These "recommendations
for a descriptive sociology and a positive politics" identified a number of

errors committed during the "gigantic social convulsion" of the Bolshevik Revolution. The new system, far from being the work of the citizens' "general will," was imposed by a minority; "tacit international pacts" were broken when foreign debt was declared void and properties of foreign nationals were confiscated without compensation. "Consumer communism," absurd in itself, led to the "destruction of what constitutes the economy, namely, the market." The installation of a "military economy," contrary to man's bartering nature, destroyed the industrial and commercial freedom indispensable to any modern economy. When the "intermediate collectivities"—for example, the professional group and the cooperative—were weakened, "essential work in the transition toward a socialist government" was undermined.

Mauss's conclusions, both scientific and practical, were clear: all nations wanting to reform themselves had to preserve both the market and their currency. They also had to "develop all collective institutions possible" and avoid "establishing an incompatibility between free associations and collectivism, or between the right to free association, including the majority's right, and individualism."

For Mauss, the terms "freedom" and "collective control" were not contradictory, and socialism did not consist "of suppressing all forms of property but one." No one should harbor illusions: "There are no exclusively capitalist societies and there will probably be no purely socialist ones."[67] In other words, the only possibility was a mixed economy, that is, "a mixture of capitalism, statism, administrative socialism, free collectivities, and individualism."

The events in Russia did not excessively undermine Mauss's confidence in socialism, since they "neither confirmed nor contradicted" it. He had even less reason to despair of socialism, since the failure of the Russian Revolution proved only one thing in his view: the political incompetence of a people. None of the great nations of Europe and America would have launched "the risky adventure of bankrupting the commonwealth so as to rebuild it again." If socialism were someday to take root in one society or another, it would be "neither by violence nor during a catastrophe" but through "the clear, conscious actions of citizens." The chances of socialism's success were thus greater in old industrial democracies such as England, which Mauss knew well, and where the Labour Party, "a legal party stemming from a large, organized, educated democracy," could "put its program into practice."

Mauss reminded the "builders of future societies," whose "minds were filled with revolutionary hallucinations and who thought they could recast all of human society," that "the law does not create, it sanctions." In addition, "the law must not precede mores—and a fortiori the economy and technology—but must follow them." Like "naïve sociologists," communists forgot "that a new social order can be installed only in an orderly manner and with enthusiasm." They also made the mistake of "believing that the sovereign order or the law can create from nothing, ex nihilo, like the word of God." Mauss called this "political fetishism" and considered it one of the causes of the "Bolsheviks' defeat." The other cause was violence. The author of "Observations on Violence" repeated his conclusions "on general policy" and, at the risk of "sounding old-fashioned and like a spouter of clichés," returned to the old Greek and Latin concepts of charity, friendship, and community, which he considered "the delicate essence of the commonwealth."[68] His ethics was composed "of gentleness and legalism."

Mauss was aware that "he was preaching gentleness, peace, and foresight too generally and too generously." Was not his model of the man of action Socrates, the "wise, thrifty, virtuous citizen, guardian of the law, wise and cautious above all else"? But if caution often counseled "to play for time, to wait," it could also command "to move quickly, leap over hurdles, break down resistance." The important thing was to be a realist and to have a "precise awareness of the facts." As a defender of a "socialism without doctrines," Mauss wanted politics to abandon as far as possible words ending in "-ism"—"capitalism, liberalism, and all the others, all that hair-splitting substantialism"—and become a "rational art."[69]

Mauss was criticized for getting carried away by the "dream of a sociological government."[70] Yet from his perspective, the role of the intellectual was not to lead but "to accustom others to think modestly and practically without a system, without prejudice, without emotion" and "to educate peoples to use their common sense, which, in the case in point, in politics, is also a sense of the social, in other words, of the just."[71] Just as it was not a panacea, sociology was not a means to make human beings happy. At most it was a good way to educate society. Mauss concluded: "The only effect of science and art is to make man stronger and more in control of himself."[72] In adopting that position toward Bolshevism and, more broadly, toward politics, Mauss wanted to remain faithful both to Jaurès's political notions and to the scientific method Durkheim had founded. That dual loyalty—political and intellectual—protected him from the temptation to follow his communist comrades and to march with them in the "direction of history."

Cooperation, More than Ever

For Mauss the militant, political ideas were valid only to the extent that they were "realized ideas," "ideas of the masses." And what filled him with wonder was the often "groping, blind, empirical" actions of groups of individuals or small organizations, and all the "treasures of devotion" that collective effort entailed.

Mauss devoted a long chapter in his book on the nation to what he called "economic movement from below," distinguishing three manifestations of it: syndicalism, cooperation, and mutual insurance. Democracy had to limit itself to the political sphere: a "workers' democracy," a "consumer democracy," and a "mutual democracy" ("insurance for all by all, of each by all") had to be established.[73]

As a specialist in the history of religion, Mauss took the liberty of comparing these movements of fundamental democracy to the grandiose or modest beginnings of the major religions or of the major sectarian movements within religions, which were characterized by the spirit of sacrifice, the search for ideas and formulas, and the violence of passions. The difference was that the self-sacrifice in this case was not for a divine power but in the interest of others: it was a sort of religion of man for man, as Saint-Simon, Comte, and Enfantin had imagined it.

Immediately after the war, Mauss returned to his chosen field of action, the cooperatives. He still believed that the consumer cooperative could be a way of reforming the system governing consumption, production, and property. He saw the success of the Rochdale Pioneers in England as proof. Their principles—a true "table of cooperative law"—were revolutionary: a democratic administration (members were elected to the committees, all members had equal rights) and a quest not for profit but for the lowest prices. The power of the cooperative system lay in the fact that, even as it respected the normal conditions of commerce, it situated itself in a "place of honesty and morality."

One of the first articles Mauss wrote after the war had to do with cooperatives in Russia.[74] The data he collected, though incomplete, gave an idea of the "tremendous development of Russian cooperatives, absolutely unique in the economic history of the world." In the widespread collapse of all higher forms of economic life in Russia, only "the vessel of cooperation did not founder."

The cooperative movement had thus survived the storm in Russia: it was a "strong, independent, extremely vast" movement. For Mauss, who wanted to draw a lesson for France, such a miracle could be explained by the "keen concern for independence" from governments and public opinion that Russian cooperatives had always expressed. "Their policy was to move away from politics. And this was the condition for their survival." The warning was addressed to French communist comrades and to all who wanted "to make our movement serve ends other than its own."[75] Mauss suggested that such people had to be removed from the cooperatives if the movement was to retain its force, authority, and purity.

In France, the cooperative movement developed rapidly after the war. Between 1914 and 1921, the number of consumer cooperatives rose from 3,261 to 4,790, and the number of members from 864,922 to nearly 2.5 million. The consumer cooperative movement achieved its unity through its autonomy and independence from the political parties, then equipped itself with wide-ranging economic institutions: first, the Magasin de Gros des Coopératives de France; then, during the 1922 congress in Marseilles, the Banque des Coopératives de France (Bank of French cooperatives). Cooperation gained institutional legitimatcy in 1920 when the Collège de France, responding to a request by the Fédération Nationale des Coopératives de Consommation (National federation of consumer cooperatives), estab-lished a ten-year chair for teaching cooperation and appointed Charles Gide to fill it. Mauss was delighted: "There is no doubt that M. Gide's authority and that of the institution where he will teach will greatly serve the prestige of our movement in France and even in the world, since the Collège de France is universally known."[76]

The French cooperative movement remained fragile, however, because of the cooperators' "lack of education" and the lack of information avail-able to the general public. In January 1920 Mauss agreed to contribute ar-ticles regularly to *Action Coopérative*. Education was one of his principal concerns: "It is a matter both of forming frameworks and of educating the masses."[77] The cooperative movement, inextricably economic and moral, could realize its ideal—"to replace the competitive regime with the coop-erative regime"—only by sharing it with the vast majority of citizens. As in England, Germany, and Belgium, the necessary financial resources had to be devoted to propaganda—advertising, publications, lectures, courses—and the needed measures taken.

Mauss kept informed of everything happening abroad (particularly in England) and attentively read what was written on the cooperative move-ment, especially the works of Beatrice Webb and Sidney Webb, to whom he liked to refer. When the two theorists of consumer democracy came to Paris in May 1921, Mauss devoted an article to them in *Populaire*.[78]

The longtime cooperator was an active propagandist. In Paris, and in Épinal during his vacations, he had no hesitation in becoming involved in organizing cooperatives and in educating their members. *Action Coopérative* published more than twenty of his articles between January 1920 and August 1921. Hence Mauss's involvement in the cooperative movement did not end with World War I.[79] His political interest in cooperation was inseparable from his theoretical positions. His opposition to a purely economic interpre-tation of social relations led him to try to constitute what could be called "a complete science of cooperative relations between different ages and differ-ent peoples as well as between individuals and families."[80]

Proud of his "old experiment" and his "rather extensive direct knowledge of the needs of the movement and of its possibilities,"[81] Mauss always con-sidered himself "one of the leaders of the cooperative movement in France." Until 1925 he remained a member of the technical office of the Fédération Nationale des Coopératives de Consommation and in 1922 agreed to par-ticipate in a new teaching committee set up by the federation to "gather all useful documentation on the best methods for teaching cooperation and for moving into public education."[82]

When militants and specialists in cooperation launched the plan for *Revue des Études Coopératives*, a "scientific organ wholly devoted to the study of the problems of cooperation," Mauss agreed to join its editorial board and, along with each of the other founders, to pay the sum of 500 francs. The secretary of the board was Bernard Lavergne, professor at the Nancy law school, and board members included both academics and militants: Charles Gide, Ernest Poisson, Paul Ramadier.

The journal's editors, convinced of the truth of the "cooperative idea" and aware of the importance of consumption, intended "to examine and propose what reforms, both immediate or over the long term, seem possible, viewed from the objective and scientific standpoint." These intellectuals sought to replace the "a priori and too often childish idealism" of many of their contemporaries with an "enlightened idealism, corrected by daily observation of the facts and objective study of the difficulties." They wanted to combine "the internal spark" with "a much more solid sense of the experimental method and of scientific analysis."[83]

The "cooperative manifesto" appeared in the journal's first issue. Among the signatories were several of Mauss's friends and some of Durkheim's former collaborators: Charles Andler, Maurice Halbwachs, Lucien Herr, Sylvain Lévi, Lucien Lévy-Bruhl, Antoine Meillet, Dominique Parodi, Abel Rey, Gaston Richard, François Simiand, Xavier Léon. This group of friends expressed the same democratic inclinations and scientific habits they had shared before the war. They believed it was possible for an undertaking to live and prosper in the absence of conditions the political economy posited as ineluctable, namely, the profit motive and the pressure of competition. Their objective was not to elaborate a "program with rigid frameworks" but to draw a few lessons from the history of the movement and to identify directives that might allow cooperatives, true "laboratories for social experimentation" in Jaurès's expression, to contribute to a project of "social reconstitution."[84]

The only article Mauss published in *Revue des Études Coopératives* was "The Need for a Statistical Department at the Fédération Nationale des Coopératives de Consommation." The argument was simple: the dearth of statistic-collecting bureaus devoted to cooperatives in France had to be remedied, and "contempt for anything written, skepticism about anything numerical"—a very French failing—had to be corrected as well. "All those superstitions against science, writing, and competence belong to another age. Let us banish them."[85]

And, Mauss might have added, let us follow the example of other countries such as England, Germany, and Switzerland. The movement needed to know where it was going and, to that end, how to use science. Mauss wrote: "To deprive oneself of [science] is to resign oneself to ignorance and impotence." Everyone would gain, including the movement's administrators and theorists. For the former, statistics provided a guide, a sort of pressure gauge; for the latter, they supplied reliable data for their studies.

One major question had always divided the militants: did cooperation have to be subordinated to politics? The French cooperative movement was cautious, always maintaining it ought not to take part in political struggles and particularly in elections, but ought to work with all the parties and all the candidates to satisfy consumers' demands. Convinced that "this view has only grown stronger over the course of events," Mauss published a short report in *Action Coopérative* on "cooperation in England and the cooperative party."

The English cooperative movement was paving the way. Rejecting both partisanship and apoliticism, the English militants had adopted an "intermediate approach." They had decided to form their own political party, a cooperative party with no platform other than that of the Rochdale Pioneers. Although the results the new party saw in the November 1922 elections were quite satisfactory, Mauss did not broach the delicate question of the relationship between politics and cooperation. His mission was primarily journalistic: to inform militants of events occurring abroad.[86]

When the "proletarian" point of view made advances on the political scene with the creation of the Parti Communiste, the Fédération Nationale des Coopératives de Consommation increasingly became the target of attacks. It was criticized for its "class collaborationist attitude" and was accused, notably at the 1922 federation congress in Marseilles, "of not coordinating its actions with those of working-class advocacy organizations." At the congress held the next year in Bordeaux, a "turbulent and eccentric" minority managed to poison the atmosphere of the general assembly by trying to impose their "formula for revolutionary cooperation and class struggle" on a majority expressing a broad-minded tolerance. The majority of delegates reasserted the autonomy of the cooperative movement and asked the political parties to "allow the movement its full independence" in its effort to "construct a society of economic and social justice based on the elimination of capitalist profit."[87]

Mauss, co-chair with Bourgin of the special conference devoted to the Boulangerie cooperatives, was at the Bordeaux congress and followed the debates. His point of view was well known: the French cooperative movement could not remain strictly neutral, but it had to establish relations solely "with organizations that were pursuing the same goal." The relationship could be full or partial: full in the case of trade unions, mutual insurance groups, and workers' parties, where the goal was pursued persistently; partial for noncooperative organizations (the teaching league, the human rights league, temperance societies, and so on).[88]

Several militants imagined a "cooperative Republic," the title of a book by Ernest Poisson that appeared in the early 1920s. They were seeking a third way between individualism and state or revolutionary socialism. It was believed that such a regime could solve social problems without appealing to the dangerous and ruinous expedient of revolution. They reminded socialist theorists who considered society solely from the viewpoint of producers that production was not an end in itself and that society had to be reorganized in the first place as a function of consumers' interests. Far from opposing the idea of a single consumer cooperative per country, Mauss shared the ideal of a "consumer democracy." But for practical reasons (the immature state of individuals and institutions), he opposed expanding the large consumer cooperatives, a move he judged premature. Caution was required.

Although Mauss rejected the idea of a cooperative republic and refused to see the cooperative movement as a "complete economic system," he did not reduce consumer cooperation to its technical dimension alone. Cooperatives had to have "social goals," had to develop "charitable works, community centers." Mauss believed this was the only way to "cement not only the interests but also the collective soul of cooperators." Not everything was commerce or business: there was also the "moral world." The watchword for the immediate future was therefore: "More internal effort, more moral effort, more productive effort. . . . With that as our aim, cooperation will prevail." Hence Mauss, "unrepentant, perhaps in error," always presented himself as a "socialist and pro-worker cooperator."

The Exchange Rate Crisis

In December 1922, during a major international conference in Brussels, Mauss began to publish a series of seven articles on the "exchange rate crisis" in *Populaire*. His interest in a narrowly economic question may seem surprising, though Mauss owned a few shares of stock, had administrative experience at *Humanité*, *Populaire*, and the Boulangerie cooperative, and regularly discussed these questions with François Simiand. Mauss's friend held a chair in social economics at the Conservatoire National des Arts et Métiers (National conservatory of arts and crafts), contributed to the *Revue d'Économie Politique*, and was about to publish *La formation et les fluctuations des prix du charbon en France (1887–1912)* (The establishment and fluctuation of coal prices in France, 1887–1912).[89] He invited Mauss to work "without imposing conclusions in advance and with a concern and desire for information, for reflection, and for open and broad-ranging discussion."[90]

The financial situation looked critical. Successive administrations in France could not balance the country's budget and were even less successful in stabilizing the franc. There was a monetary crisis: as Marcel Déat would recall, the financial situation was at the center of political passions. Exchange rates were anxiously consulted every day. Since the stability of the franc was considered the sign and gauge of French greatness, any depreciation was interpreted as a national disaster. If the franc dropped, the political world was seized with panic. Monetary battles were granted almost as much importance as military successes: parallels between World War I battles and operations on the exchange came naturally to politicians' lips and appeared in journalists' articles. The Left believed in a conspiracy of a "wall of money" and launched accusations at the "two hundred families."

The tone of Mauss's first articles was alarmist: "The plague is spreading. The fate we are facing may be irrevocable." Europe was going bankrupt. And what was there to say about the situation of wage earners, civil service workers, and people on fixed incomes, retired people, or those living on their investments? If there was another drop in the franc, and if it led to another rise in prices, there would be poverty and unhappiness. A single solution presented itself: stabilize the exchange rate by securing international credit.[91]

The Internationale Syndicale had proposed that solution, but no one had listened. Mauss was furious and railed against former president Georges Clemenceau, calling him "that lightweight, slow-witted, arrogant old man." He placed the blame on Poincaré's ministry of foreign affairs. France had become "the greatest power of resistance to good sense and goodness" and its inaction might lead the country and Europe to ruin.[92] Mauss's intention was not to "ward off what may be an implacable fate" but to understand and inform. In good socialist fashion, he was doing so because "every socialist is obliged to have a few notions about political economy, or economic sociology as we now say."[93]

It was a complex problem. "Nothing is more difficult than to define an exchange rate policy." Mauss, relying on the example of other countries, both nineteenth-century England and contemporary Latin American states, proposed immediate measures: devalue the franc and urge the devaluation of other European currencies; establish an inheritance tax and a value-added tax; stop all borrowing and balance the budget by imposing "new sacrifices" (new taxes, spending cuts). Everything had to be done at once "without leaving out anything, within a reasonable space of time."[94] National interest was of primary importance. The first objective was to "safeguard national capital." Although he was a socialist, Mauss did not hesitate to say that "bourgeois France" had to be allowed "to save itself through a series of sacrifices."

In late December 1923, Mauss stopped writing his column. A year later, he resumed it, quite satisfied with the articles he had written earlier and especially proud of the predictions he had made, which, he said, had been confirmed.[95] The exchange rate crisis still preoccupied the Parti Socialiste, which, in its tracts, denounced the Bloc National's policy: ruinous borrowing, taxes burdening the common man, a weakening bond market, the fall of the franc. Mauss believed such a policy could lead to bankruptcy and war. The SFIO claimed it was the only political force capable of "restoring the franc by establishing peace and making the ones who ought to pay do so."[96]

Mauss was more sure of himself and went ahead courageously, predicting: "The dollar will float between 20 and 25 francs but will not go much higher than that." He acknowledged this was a "bold assertion, which militants and scientists must venture only very scrupulously." In fact, far from improving, the situation worsened and the franc lost another third of its value. The dollar, worth 11 francs in 1921, now surpassed 24. Mauss carefully studied the price curves, the exchange rates, and the banknotes issued between 1918 and 1920 and observed "an exact parallelism among them, with a very short time lag, as if the quantitative theory of currency were mathematically true in every respect."[97] Nevertheless, practicing "advanced economics" was out of the question. Rather than seek to establish how these three phenomena influenced one another, Mauss confined himself to identifying causes, denouncing the guilty parties, and proposing solutions, just as he had done in the first series of articles. A few months before the elections, his objective was to prove that the Bloc National was responsible for a "concealed bankruptcy" and to explain to militants the causes of the French people's suffering.[98]

Mauss, continuing his analysis, studied fiduciary inflation month by month, from November 1923 to March 1924, then day by day, from March 6 to March 20, 1924. He concluded that the decisive factor was not inflation but "the panic in the markets and in prices, which cause inflation and a drop in the franc."[99] There were many causes for that panic: persistent errors on the public's part, the errors of successive governments, recent errors by the Department of the Treasury, the accumulated mistakes of French capitalists and banks.[100] In the Chamber of Deputies, the socialists attracted attention to various political and administrative issues: exorbitant military expenses, the absence of any effort to restrict civilian and military budgets, lack of control over spending, and so on.

What solution could Mauss offer? He still held the same views; he advised calm and repeated: "Stabilize! Stabilize!" But he was aware it was not so easy, since storms were brewing "from every direction." "These are human phenomena at work: collective psychology, imponderables, beliefs, credulity, confidence, all swirling about."[101]

One of Mauss's favorite targets was Lucien Klotz, "an incompetent Jew" and "insignificant personality," whom Clemenceau had placed in the Department of Finance, "perhaps out of Satanism." He wanted that "bad shepherd" to be sent back to the desert.[102] Mauss was a good deal less harsh toward Poincaré, who had been reelected to the Senate in 1920 and reappointed premier in January 1922 with the foreign affairs portfolio. Mauss even praised Poincaré's courage when the head of government changed course in April 1924. Mauss thought he was an "energetic, obstinate" man "pursuing his aims with the rigor of a Lorrainian." Such praise of Poincaré might seem surprising: Mauss was quick to explain that it attested to "the sense of truth, impartiality, and justice" at *Populaire*. It is true that his financial policy—higher taxes, prosecution for tax evasion, a balanced budget—appeared "as honest as possible" and corresponded to the policy Léon Blum and his party had defended since 1920.[103]

It was April 1924, a month before the elections. Mauss had gotten involved in the campaign, agreeing to preside over debates at the federal congress of the socialist federation of the Vosges, which had been held in December 1923 at the Maison du Peuple in Épinal. At the time, he considered the Cartel des Gauches—which brought together the radical Left, the socialist republicans, and the socialists (SFIO)—an "extraordinary tactic for extraordinary times" and believed it ought to be used "exclusively in the interest of peace, the republic, and socialism."

Mauss was convinced that the Cartel would win, but feared the bourgeoisie's reaction: "Will it display patriotism . . . when it means supporting . . . a nation governed by the leftist parties?"[104] Mauss ended his long series of articles on the exchange rate with a "word of warning, of emphasis, and of hope."

In an article he never published, Mauss attempted to draw a general conclusion from his study of exchange rates. His main idea, borrowed from his friend Simiand, was that the great economic revolutions were "monetary in nature." The manipulation of currencies and credit could be a "method of social revolution," a "method without pain or suffering." Mauss thus wanted to give an "economic content" to juridical socialism. He claimed that, alongside Emmanuel Lévy, he was one of the defenders of juridical socialism, but in his view it remained "much too political, legislative, formal." He wrote: "In the first place, it suffices to create new monetary methods within the firmest, the narrowest, bounds of prudence. It will then suffice to manage them with the most cautious rules of economics to make them bear fruit among the new entitled beneficiaries. And that is revolution." According to Mauss, the importance of that discovery was especially great because it allowed the common people of different nations to know "how they can have control over themselves—without the use of words, formulas, or myths."[105]

On the Left

In the elections of May 11, 1924, the Right again won the majority of the votes, despite its divisions. But because of the way the voting took place, the Cartel des Gauches won a broad majority in the Chamber, with 328 of the 582 deputies. These results delighted what Mauss called the "socialist democrats," those who, emulating Jaurès, had never separated democracy from socialism. With its some hundred deputies, the SFIO, the old party of Sembat, Guesde, Vaillant, and Jaurès, became the largest party on the left. For socialist militants, it was a time of euphoria. In his article "Socialist Democracy," Mauss was extremely optimistic: "Socialist democracy is on its way! . . . The future is ours. . . . We are living in a great time."[106]

He was enthusiastic, to be sure, but he was also tired. In June 1924, just after the SFIO had won a major electoral victory, the directors of *Populaire* had to suspend publication because of financial problems. From then until 1927, *Populaire* would be only a bimonthly bulletin for militants. Mauss, the "old grunt from the merchant regiment," could not keep from "grumbling a little," seeing the death of the socialist daily as a "bitter failure." After the victory, the party in effect lost "a powerful medium for propaganda, defense, attack, and action." Just as serious in Mauss's view was the failure of both socialist journals, *Avenir* and *Vie Socialiste*, since the party needed organs "to galvanize it somewhat and allow it to truly play its leading role in pro-worker and republican action."[107] Deprived of its media, the SFIO would have trouble being "the action group and pressure group for the working class and for laborers in general." Mauss deeply regretted the absence of these publications.

After the 1924 election, he was afraid that the Cartel des Gauches, which was supposed to be "a one-hour cartel," would become "a permanent cartel." "The real danger is that, having won the victory, we will not know how to use it."[108] For the SFIO, the victory opened a huge debate about participation in the government. At the congress in Marseilles, Blum proposed the solution of a "limited cartel," a "one-minute cartel." Would he accept the invitation to play a governmental role extended by Édouard Herriot, the Parti Radical leader called on to form the government? Blum said no, but the socialist leader came out in favor of "the government of reform." He had the same attitude toward Poincaré when he succeeded Herriot the next year. Support, it was thought, did not rule out "safeguarding absolute independence." But the problem of participation, far from being settled, arose again at every congress, with participationists and antiparticipationists facing off. On one side were Joseph Paul-Boncour, Vincent Auriol, and Renaudel; on the other, Blum, Alexandre Bracke, and Paul Faure. The Parti Socialiste was divided within itself and wedged between a Parti Radical that regularly invited it to exercise power and a Parti Communiste that was proposing a single front. It seemed to be in complete disarray. Its leader, Léon Blum, was at the time "the most insulted man in France."[109] Charles Maurras declared: "There's a man who ought to be shot, but in the back."

Mauss did not deny the importance of a "broad-ranging discussion of the doctrine and practice" of participation. But on the eve of the special national congress of the Parti Socialiste in early June 1924, he was intent on attracting attention to "more modest questions," for example, the adoption of a new rule in the Chamber and Senate to keep the work of the legislature from being blocked. Such a measure would allow those in the Radical and Socialist parties to "expedite the maximum number of reforms in the minimum period of time": to place the country's finances "on a practical, sound, and just foundation"; and to reform the army, the navy, and a certain number of large government services where only "necessary budget cuts" could be made.

In raising these questions, Mauss was aware that he was being somewhat niggling. According to him, however, that was the only way to advance matters and to attach the party's name to results. He concluded: "If we abstain from exercising power, we must demonstrate by clear acts that we are worthy of one day holding it entirely in our own hands."[110]

12

A BURDENSOME INHERITANCE

AFTER THE WAR ended, Hubert warned his friend Mauss that he might be disenchanted. He advised him "not to be exclusively political." "You must also [think] about science, teaching, about the country's intellectual and moral value, and there will not be many of us, and there will be a lot of poseurs."[1] Fauconnet, who was delighted to see Mauss "resuming [his] life as an 'old scholar,'" had the same advice.[2]

It was a burdensome inheritance. As Mauss pointed out, few groups of researchers had "suffered so dreadfully" during the war as the Durkheimians. "We have been deprived of an entire generation, of our best and most vigorous collaborators. Hundreds of problems might have been treated that we can only glimpse at."[3] The situation was catastrophic because the number of researchers had dropped just as the field of studies was broadening. Mauss observed in 1920: "We have no museum of ethnography in France worthy of the name; we have no laboratories dedicated specifically to the study of indigenous peoples; sociology does not exist here. The general public knows nothing of our research." Everything remained to be (re)done: "We must therefore recruit new students, build laboratories, make an appeal to the government. . . . Scientists must do publicity, since a science can become popular only through vulgarization."[5]

Durkheim's many unpublished writings also represented an "enormous burden" for Mauss, who felt "a duty toward [his] uncle" to defend his writing and to "use it to benefit the public as much as possible." He believed this was the only way to "fully disseminate a mode of thought . . . whose influence and eminence are growing and will continue to grow for a long time yet."[5] In September 1918 Lucien Lévy-Bruhl reminded him that he was expecting an introduction to his uncle's ethics and some of his unpublished letters for *Revue Philosophique*. At the time, he thought it would be good to "publish them this winter."[6]

Durkheim's "Introduction to Ethics" appeared in 1920 with a short introduction and many explanatory notes written by Mauss. The following year, *Revue Philosophique* published one of Durkheim's courses called "The Conjugal Family." *Revue de Métaphysique et de Morale* did its "pious duty," publishing Durkheim's "Rousseau's *Social Contract*" (1918) and "Rousseau's Pedagogy" (1919). Then came various articles drawn from his courses on socialism: "The Definition of Socialism" (1921), "The History of Socialism: Socialism in the Eighteenth Century" (1923), and "A Critique of Saint-Simon and Saint-Simonism" (1926). Another of Durkheim's unpublished fragments, "Saint-Simon, Founder of Positivism and Sociology," appeared in *Revue Philosophique* in 1925 to mark the centennial of the death of the "illustrious founder of sociology."[7] These articles prepared the way for the 1928 publication of Durkheim's *Socialisme*, with an introduction by Mauss.[8]

Durkheim's legacy was secure. Three of the four university chairs recognized as "sociological" were held by Durkheimians: Maurice Halbwachs at Strasbourg and Paul Fauconnet and Célestin Bouglé at the Sorbonne.[9] And, thanks to Paul Lapie, a former contributor to *Année* and now director of primary education in France, sociology was part of the curriculum for the *licence* in philosophy. This controversial initiative was attentively followed by the Durkheimians: they held informational weeks at the Sorbonne for school principals and developed the curriculum.[10]

Like Mauss, Durkheim's other collaborators and disciples were also involved in defending his work. Davy published a long study titled "Durkheim, the Man and the Work" in *Revue de Métaphysique et de Morale* (1919 and 1920). Fauconnet devoted his inaugural lecture at the Sorbonne to "Durkheim's Pedagogical Work."[11] Bouglé, who had recently published *Guide de l'étudiant en sociologie* (1921; Guide for the student in sociology), published "Émile Durkheim's Spiritualism" in *Revue Bleue* (1924). He was still ambivalent about certain Durkheimian theses, as is clear from his *Evolution of Values: Studies in Sociology* (1922), but he nevertheless prepared six of Durkheim's articles for publication under the title *Sociology and Philosophy* (1924).

A contributor to the first series of *Année Sociologique* and the author of the first book published in the "Travaux de L'Année Sociologique" series, Bouglé had played a major role in making Durkheimian ideas well known before the war.[12] An indefatigable propagandist, he managed ably to defend sociology in every situation and to maintain ties between the Durkheimians and other groups or journals, for example, the *Revue de Métaphysique et de Morale*. His incomparable qualities—clear and rapid debating skills, talent as an orator, conviction, the ability to adapt to any audience, quick repartee—predisposed that "sparkling conversationalist" to academic diplomacy.[13]

Maurice Halbwachs (1877–1945) was intimately familiar with Durkheim's doctrine and had presented it to readers of *Revue de Philosophie* shortly before the war. He took on the project of summarizing *The Elementary Forms of Religious Life* in a small book, *Les origines du sentiment religieux d'après Durkheim* (1925; The origins of religious sentiment according to Durkheim). Halbwachs, an Alsatian and the son of a German professor, was part of a dynamic new team of professors—with Charles Blondel, Marc Bloch, Lucien Febvre, and Georges Lefebvre—who in 1919 agreed to set up a "new Sorbonne" in Strasbourg, which they sought to make a center for "the spirit of synthesis," in Henri Berr's expression.[14] A philosopher by training and the author of a book on Leibniz, Halbwachs turned to sociology and began to contribute to *Année Sociologique* in 1905. His socialist convictions led him to tackle pressing questions of the day—for example, in his *Les expropriations et le prix des terrains à Paris, 1860–1900* (1909; Expropriation and the price of property in Paris, 1860–1900)—to familiarize himself with the works of Karl Marx and Max Weber, and to study social class, particularly the working class. His fields of interest also included statistics and demography, or what was called "social morphologies" at the time.

In France and abroad, Durkheim's authority remained strong.[15] It was even recognized by his rivals, who increasingly defined themselves in relation to him.[16] He was called "the Galileo or Lavoisier of sociology."[17] Philosophers regretted "the current abuse of the terms *sociology* and *sociological*, often applied to anything having to do with relations of human beings among themselves." But it was no use: they could no longer ignore the fact that "societies are a reality sui generis."[18] *Revue Philosophique*, directed by Lucien Lévy-Bruhl, generously opened its pages to contributors to *Année Sociologique*: Marcel Granet published "Language and Chinese Thought"; Georges Davy, "The Idealism of Law"; Charles Lalo, "The Social Functions of Fashion"; and Maurice Halbwachs, "Matter and Society" and "Statistical Experimentation and Probabilities." *Revue de Métaphysique et de Morale* also did not hesitate to take on social themes, publishing titles as diverse as "Consumption," "The Rhythms of Economic Life," "Trade Unions," "Property, a Natural Force of the Economy," and "Savings."

Vocabulaire technique et critique de la philosophie (Critical and technical vocabulary of philosophy), published in *Bulletin de la Société Française de Philosophie* between July 1902 and July 1923 and reissued by Alcan with corrections and a supplement in 1926, introduced a large number of sociological concepts: anomie, civilization, clan, collective (and *conscience collective*), magic, myth, primitive, religion, sacred, sacrifice, social, society, sociocentrism, solidarity, taboo, totem, and so on. The editor, André Lalande, granted a central place to Durkheim's works and those of his collaborators and often consulted Durkheim's followers when he needed explanations: Davy on the term "civil," Fauconnet on "collective."[19]

Sociology's adversaries, philosophers for the most part, did not relent, several times attacking the course taught in the normal schools beginning in 1920. Sociology, they thought, could not serve as a foundation for ethics; it could only have a "harmful effect" on poorly prepared young minds. Mauss reacted forcefully to these attacks, when, for example, sociology was criticized for being riddled with axioms and question-begging. "The only axiom [our research] has is the following: never forget that man thinks in common with others in society. It has only one aim: to determine the share of the social in thought."[20] It was an eminently Durkheimian response. After the war, the nephew was also not reluctant to draw attention to his uncle's work: "Let us recall the stunning, century-long verification of the main laws of statistics, and in particular the accuracy of the discoveries about suicide made by Durkheim and others."[21]

Yet Mauss remained cautious when faced with the adversaries of the French school of sociology and was even willing to recognize the "weaknesses of the Durkheim school." He usually sought to play for time, to add nuances. There was predetermination, of course, but there was a "certain sort of freedom" everywhere, a possibility of choice; there was constraint, obligation, and authority, but there was also cooperation and reciprocity. For Mauss, the most important thing was to be wary of "excessive enthusiasm" and to avoid looking like charlatans offering the anxious mob the solutions it clamored for in ethics, politics, economics, and life itself. He would confess: "We know very little."[22] Hence he continued to call his writings "essays" and to present his explanations as "recommendations," mere hypotheses, sometimes apologizing for their brevity, generality, and incompleteness.

Returning to the École

At the École Pratique, situated on the fringe of the *grandes écoles* and of academic disciplines, Mauss's teaching reached only a small number of students, but that number was growing: about fifteen in 1920–1921, some forty in 1937–1938. Returning to his chair in the religions of uncivilized peoples in the winter of 1920, Mauss addressed the same subject he had tackled in 1913–1914: the relation between legal and religious organization. But now he based himself on newly available ethnographic documents. Both in his courses and in his writings, he pursued the three issues he had dealt with before the war: prayer (and, more generally, oral rites), the archaic mentality and categories of thought, and contractual law and the service system (*système de prestation*). Each of these fields of study was an opportunity to elaborate on "previous results," his own and those of his close collaborators, while at the same time making corrections and pursuing them further. According to him, that was the work of a "true scientist."[23]

It is clear from the series of three lectures Mauss gave in May 1920 to the Institut des Hautes Études in Belgium that he was still working on the history of religion and remained interested in the "origins of prayer." His name and Hubert's were still associated with *Revue de l'Histoire des Religions*. In November 1919, a number of professors and friends of "French high culture" created the Ernest Renan Society in the hope of developing "a taste for studies in the history of religion" in France and of securing a larger place for that discipline in general education. Mauss and Hubert joined along with their friends, including Sylvain Lévi and Antoine Meillet, both professors at the Collège de France, and colleagues from the École Pratique.[24]

There was an uneasy feeling among specialists in the history of religion. Religious studies, once a rising star, now appeared to be on the decline. The curriculum at the university level was sketchy and there was little interest from the general public. If these researchers wanted to have any influence at all, they had to respond at all cost. One way was to hold various gatherings (lectures, congresses, and so forth). In 1922 the Ernest Renan Society invited James Frazer to give a public lecture titled "Tribute to Renan by a Student of Comparative Religion"; it also arranged for the Université de Paris to award an honorary doctorate to the "illustrious Cambridge professor." The next year, at the society's initiative, a congress on the history of religion was held in Paris. Mauss was on the organizing committee for the congress; its secretary was Paul Alphandéry, one of his colleagues at the École.

It was no longer necessary to fight for a place for ethnology within the history of religion: the idea of the "continuity and homogeneity of human history" had entered people's consciousness, and the study of non-Christian religions, particularly "elementary" religions, now appeared indispensable.[25] But religious sociology, especially in its Durkheimian form, was still the object of keen opposition from certain intellectual and Catholic quarters. In a virulent article entitled "The Dogmatic Atheism of Religious Sociology," Gaston Richard, one of Durkheim's former collaborators, criticized the Durkheimians for wanting not only to "monopolize the teaching of sociology in France to the exclusion of any other kind of sociology" but also and especially to "disseminate a sociology of religion incompatible with the Christian faith."[26]

Stuck at the École Pratique, Mauss sought less to defend himself against the attacks than to continue an intellectual tradition and pursue the research he had begun before the war. One of his courses (the Monday conference) dealt with oral ritual (moral ritual and negative ritual, musical drama, poetry, magical art, linguistic taboos). This was also the theme of one of the first scientific papers written in the early 1920s: "The Compulsory Expression of Feelings" concerned the oral ritual of Australian funerary cults and argued for the collective character of apparently spontaneous and individual emotions.[27] Mauss summarized in a few details the argument the late Robert Hertz and Émile Durkheim had already made; he also drew on the documents Strehlow had collected on the Loritja and the Arunta, which he also intended to use in his thesis on prayer. The privileged geographical area was still Australia, with a few incursions into Africa, America, and later, northeast Asia. The division of labor established between Mauss and Hubert—the study of rites for one, of myths for the other—was becoming blurred. Although Mauss was more interested in the "ritual" dimension of social life, he was inclined to broaden his analysis to study the relations between rites and myths. The documents he was studying established a correspondence between them. Everything went together: "The word is an act . . . but, conversely, the rite is a word."[28]

In 1920 Mauss began to consider the question of potlatches in his courses at the École Pratique. These were systems of usurious religious and legal services, which W.H.R. Rivers had described in his *History of Melanasian Society* (the subject of Mauss's courses in 1921–1922 and in 1922–1923) and Malinowski in his studies on the tribes of the Trobriand Islands (Mauss's 1923–1924 course). Mauss knew Malinowski well and, though he was critical of him, later invited him to one of his lectures in the late 1930s. Born in Crakow in 1884, Malinowski was at the time the dominant figure in the English school of social anthropology. At the London School of Economics, he exerted a strong influence on the generation of students that would constitute that famous school for the next thirty years.

Courses Offered by Marcel Mauss at the École Pratique des Hautes Études, Section of Religious Science, 1920–1940

1920
  Analysis of Documents (Sir Baldwin Spencer, Stuhler)
  Analysis of Thurnwald's Documents on the Buiss Tribe
1920–1921
  Origin of the Belief in the Efficacy of Formulas (Australia)
  Political and Religious Organization in Melanesia
1921–1922 (resumed in April)
  Text Explication of August Comte on Fetishism, with C. Akamatsu
1922–1923
  Australian Oral Ritual
  Secret Societies and Men's Societies in Melanesia
1923–1924
  Australian Dramatic Poetry: The Corroboree
  Analysis of Malinowski's Documents on the Tribes of the Trobriand Islands
1924–1925
  Australian Oral Rites
  Analysis of Documents concerning Nigritian Religions
1925–1926
  Same as 1924–1925
1926–1927
  Australian Oral Rituals; Moral Ritual and Negative Ritual
  French Sudan
1927–1928
  Linguistic Taboos in Australia
  Analysis of Wirz's Documents on the Marind-Anim (New Guinea)
1928–1929
  Negative Oral Rites in Australia
  Explication of Documents concerning Ritual and Mythology (New Guinea)

1929–1930
   Elementary Forms of Oral Ritual in Australia.
   The Relation between Myth and Rite in Papua New Guinea
1930–1931
   Oral Ritual in Australia
   The Relation between Mythology and Ritual in Papua New Guinea
1931–1932
   The Relation between Myth and Rite in Australian Religions
   The Relation between Religion and Art in Ashanti
1932–1933
   The Religions and Civilizations of Eastern and Northern Siberian Peoples
   Characteristics of the Maori Religion (Polynesia)
1933–1934
   Explication of Documents concerning the Religions of Northeast Asia
   Study of Documents concerning the Polynesian Religions
1934–1935
   The Cosmological Notions of the Peoples of Northeast Asia
   Maori Documents concerning Cosmology
1935–1936
   Study of Documents concerning the Cosmologies and Nature Cults among
      the Populations of Northeast Asia
   Study of the Book *Hawaiian Antiquities*
1936–1937
   Shamanism and Cosmology in the Societies of Northeast Asia
   Study of a Major Ritual in Hawaii: The Erection of the War Temple
1937–1938
   Study of Malinowski's *Coral Gardens*
   Study of Documents on Hawaiian Cosmology
1938–1939
   Games and Cosmogonies in Polynesia and North America
   Ball Games and the Notions of Cosmology and Cosmogony in America

In the winter of 1920 Mauss found a few of his former students among his audience, including the unwavering René Chaillié, one of "his oldest and most faithful collaborators," who concealed a "real devotion" to sociology under the appearance of an amateur.[29] Also attending were Raymond Lenoir, Alexandre Koyré, Edmond Mestre, Alfred Métraux, André Varagnac, Georges Dumézil, Marcel Griaule, Charles Le Coeur, Georges-Henri Rivière, Jeanne Cuisinier, and Madeleine Francès, as well as many foreign students.[30] Finally, some of his colleagues, including Ignace Meyerson of the Institut de Psychologie and the American F. H. Hankins, attended some classes. Mauss also directed theses on diverse topics: "The Moral Character of African Cults" (Le Coeur), "A Few Results of a Comparison between

Modern Chinese Characters and Suo-Chuan" (Mestre), "The Religion of the Tupinamba" (Métraux), "The Yao Tribes of Southern China" (Ling), "Burlesque in Slavonic Folklore" (Reich).

A Serious Illness

In the autumn of 1921 Mauss went to England to participate in a congress and to work at the British Museum: "I was able to get through all the necessary work in five days at the British. Which did me in. . . ."[31] He was seriously ill when he returned and could not teach his courses the following winter. He asked for a three-month leave to recuperate in the Midi.

He was suffering from pulmonary congestion, which ultimately forced him to take a long sick leave from December 1921 to May 1922. "Weak lungs" was the diagnosis of family members when referring to Mauss's health. His friends were surprised and advised complete rest. But, as Bouglé lamented, "still in the planning stages is the state, the nation, and all the rest!"[32]

Mauss went to Bandol, in the south of France, to convalesce. It was hoped that while there he would be able to "get back on his feet quickly."[33] It was only a month later that he visibly recovered "his color, muscular strength, stamina, and weight." He was gradually able to engage in his favorite activity, long hikes, up to sixteen or eighteen kilometers in the course of a day. The convalescence still lasted longer than planned.

In the autumn of 1922 Mauss went back to writing short articles. But he had to avoid working too hard. Hence he could not resume his book on the nation, as he confided to Sir James and Lady Frazer in a letter written in English: "Unhappily my great work on 'La nation' is rather backwards not through my fault. But if my health keeps strong enough I hope to be able to finish it next year and return after that to my former studies."[34] He resumed teaching at the École Pratique and began publishing the new series of Année Sociologique. He confided to Hubert in August 1923: "It's obvious that I have to drop everything to be able to finish La nation and do Année."[35]

"The Limits Must Be Respected"

The heroic age was at an end, the old battles over. When Durkheim had established his work plan, it had been possible to believe that sociology was seeking to reduce psychology to subsistence wages. In his 1924 lecture "The Relation between Psychology and Sociology," Mauss would make a point of recalling that his uncle had known how to "defend sociology against Tarde's individualist oversimplification, Spencer's brutal oversimplification, and against the metaphysicians of ethics and religion."[36] But now that the misunderstandings had been cleared up, the new head of the school of sociology no longer had to lock swords with everyone. The open war against psychology and the psychologists was over. Rather than display an imperialist attitude, sociology now had a duty to "respect limits." As Mauss acknowledged: "Whatever the collectivity's power of suggestion, it always leaves the individual a sanctuary, his consciousness, which belongs to you [psychologists]." He added: "We know there are two specialized realms: the realm of consciousness on the one hand, and the realm of the *conscience collective* and collectivity on the other. We know these two realms are in the world and in life, that they are in nature. And that is something."[37]

Never before had Durkheim's nephew followed so attentively the work of psychologists; never had he been so open to "accepting the progress of psychology," which had been considerable in the previous decades. Although he said he was "relatively incompetent in psychology" and presented himself as an "amateur" in that science, he played an active role in the Société de Psychologie and in 1923 agreed to be its president. As he declared in his inaugural address, he hoped as a sociologist to help "show the full importance of the mental fact and all the benefits of studying [psychology]."[38] The next year Mauss stood before the members of the same society and addressed the delicate question of the practical relationship between sociology and psychology. He ventured to discuss four points: mental or nervous health or debility; psychosis; the notion of symbol; and the notion of instinct. In 1926 Mauss returned to speak with the psychologists, discussing "thanatomania," a phenomenon consisting of "a violent negation of the life instinct by the social instinct."[39] There was no doubt in his mind that sociology needed psychology "for the important share of its work whose object is collective representations." "Call this subject collective psychology if you like; it would be better to say sociology plain and simple."[40]

Mauss considered the psychologists Charles Blondel and Georges Dumas friends. Other friends included Ignace Meyerson, assistant editor of *Journal de Psychologie Normale et Pathologique*. Meyerson, a Jew born in Warsaw in 1888 and the nephew of Émile Meyerson, a historian and philosopher whom he joined in Paris in 1906, had done studies in medicine and philosophy before studying muscle and nerve physiology. He later specialized in psychology. After the war, when he agreed to relaunch *Journal de Psychologie* in collaboration with Pierre Janet, Meyerson proved to be very open-minded, accepting contributions from historians, sociologists, and linguists. In addition, his interest in psychoanalysis led him to translate Freud's *Interpretation of Dreams* into French (under the title *La science des rêves*), which was published by Alcan in 1926.

Mauss also carefully followed the work of his friend the English anthropologist Charles Seligman, who, along with Rivers, was one of the best field anthropologists of his generation in Great Britain. He specialized in applying psychology and psychoanalysis to the field of anthropology.[41] In 1923 he gave a lecture before the Royal Anthropological Institute (he had just been elected its president) on the relationship between psychology and anthropology. One of the questions that concerned him was the meaning of dreams in non-European populations. His wife and collaborator, Brenda Z. Seligman, was also interested in "the unconscious share of the social inheritance." When Mauss saw his friend Seligman daring to speak of the psychoanalysis of races and societies, he lamented that he was "pushing Freudianism or Jungianism too far."[42]

In the 1920s writers were excited about psychoanalysis, which was becoming fashionable in literary salons. In 1926 twelve pioneers, including Marie Bonaparte, founded the Société Psychanalytique in Paris. Resistance remained strong in academic and medical circles, however. Salomon Reinach, after reading an article by a "pseudo-scientist" seeking to prove that art is derived from sexual feelings, exclaimed: "That's Freudianism, they say; there's Freudianism everywhere today, and I suspect [the Freudians] of being Cubists and free-versifiers as well. They all walk hand in hand on the wide way leading to [the insane asylum] Charenton."[43]

In *Essays Presented to C. G. Seligman*, published in the mid-1930s, several texts referred to psychoanalysis, including Marie Bonaparte's "Psychoanalysis and Ethnography."[44] She wrote: "I know that psychoanalysis is far from enjoying favor among most ethnographers." Her response to ethnologists, who were often ignorant about the field and who found the new discipline at times superfluous, at other times too hypothetical, was as follows: "One has to have undergone analysis oneself to be able to judge the value of psychoanalysis."[45]

Psychoanalysis faced certain difficulties in becoming established in France. Freud believed the hurdle was "essentially national in nature."[46] Théodule Ribot, who introduced a "French-style science of the soul," condemned "Freudian dogmatism." He rejected the theory of the libido and the primacy of the unconscious over the conscious mind, and questioned the symbolism of dreams. The psychologist Alfred Binet, though he published articles by Jung in his journal *Année Psychologique*, was just as critical of psychoanalysis, considering it a police interrogation technique. He directed his efforts toward studying the mechanisms of intelligence and developed tests that would be widely used in the United States. His rival, Ribot's disciple Pierre Janet, was also not sparing in his criticism of Freudianism. And Janet's friend Dr. Georges Dumas made a sport of ridiculing psychoanalysis in the classes he taught at Sainte-Anne Hospital.

Ribot, Janet, and Dumas all represented links between Mauss and psychology. When he discussed psychosis, hysteria, or instinct, Mauss aligned himself with the school of psychiatry and French neurology, with Joseph Babinski and Pierre Janet, two of the neurologist Jean Charcot's students.

And although he did not deny the importance of the "new theories" of the dream, he was anxious to keep his distance from psychoanalysis. He asserted: "Of course, we will not indulge in the excesses of psychoanalysis. . . . But though we fear the exaggerations, we believe these ideas have an enormous capacity to advance and endure."[47]

Mental confusion, inhibitions, delirium, and hallucinations were all phenomena that keenly interested Mauss. But unlike the psychologists, he did not view them as pathological manifestations. In the tradition of Durkheim and Espinas, Mauss's major concern continued to be the "relation between the individual and the social." He analyzed "the physical effect on the individual of the idea of death suggested by the collectivity" in several groups of societies—Australia, New Zealand, and Polynesia—drawing on documentation collected by Hertz, but his objective was to further the "nuanced and profound" study Durkheim had done on suicide. That study gave him the opportunity to use documentation he had collected as part of his research on the origin of the belief in the efficacy of words in Australia. It also allowed him to turn to advantage his collaboration with Durkheim as he was writing *The Elementary Forms of Religious Life* and to detail cases where death was caused by the idea that it was the necessary consequence of a sin, a crime against the totem, for example. His argument allowed him to present evidence of how the moral acts on the physical, how the social influences the physical. There were even situations, though they were rare, in which the individual believed he was "in a state close to death" "solely as a result of the collectivity." Mauss concluded that these facts "confirm and extend the theory of anomic suicide, which Durkheim set out in a fine example of sociological argument."[48]

Année Sociologique, Part 2

Année Sociologique was more than a publication, more than a collective enterprise. As Mauss recalled: "We formed a group around it, in the strongest sense of the word *group*." After the war, there were only a handful of contributors left. Mauss explained: "Our group looks like those little woods in devastated regions where a few old splintered trees attempt for a few years to grow green again." But he urged them to "take heart" and "work again for a few years."[49]

When the war ended, Hubert wondered if *Année* had to be "redone." The answer was yes, as he wrote to Mauss, "if we don't kill ourselves doing it. No, if we are to spend those years doing nothing but criticism and no positive work. It's a work of collaboration and organization. In any case, I don't believe we can keep to fixed deadlines."[50] All the former collaborators still had a "keen sense of [*Année's*] necessity" and wanted to pursue "the obscure and anonymous bibliography and book review work," which, by organizing ideas and facts, made it possible to construct a "constantly updated sociology manual."[51]

In early 1921 some effort was made to relaunch *Année Sociologique*. But no one had the material means or the energy necessary.[52] In addition, Mauss's severe illness intervened to put a stop to the project.[53] In the winter of 1922, shortly after he had resumed teaching, which was "up to a certain point successful," and had begun to write short articles again, Mauss remained circumspect: "I don't know if we'll start up *Année Sociologique* again; we're getting older, there are fewer of us, and things are harder for our young people than they were for us."[54]

Bouglé became insistent: "When I was abroad, I was able to observe how impatiently people are waiting for *Année* to reappear. Let's hope we can be successful."[55] Organizers would have to make sure the contributors would do their part, that the necessary financial resources could be raised, and that a publishing house would agree to publish it. The future editors, all former contributors to *Année Sociologique*, were Bouglé, Simiand, Fauconnet, and Hubert. Like Mauss, they thought it would be "a serious mistake not to seek to reestablish it." Paul Huvelin, working in Lyons, was of the same opinion: "It's a duty we owe to Durkheim's memory; it's a duty to ourselves and to French science."[56]

But although there was a great deal of goodwill for the project, there was little urgency: no one wanted to get involved in an undertaking that would clearly be as heavy a burden as it had been for Durkheim. Friends also recommended that Mauss save his strength and not kill himself for *Année*.[57]

No *Année* editor or contributor was as readily available after the war as before it. The members of the editorial board acknowledged that they were much in demand. Some had heavy professional responsibilities, others had family obligations, and still others, political commitments. Whether they were researchers—Mauss, Hubert, and Simiand—or university teachers—Bouglé and Fauconnet—the people who were spearheading the new initiative were all busy. Hubert, retained by the military authorities in 1919 to reorganize museums in some of the French cities affected by enemy bombs, resumed his many activities but "with diminished strength." In addition to teaching national archaeology at the École Pratique and at the École du Louvre, he was assistant curator at the Museé des Antiquités Nationales in Saint-Germain, where he was responsible for setting up a whole series of new rooms. It was a great deal of work: "I sacrificed myself. . . . My health did not and does not allow for such a tiring task. . . . You know, old friend, that at our age, managing work is a question of life or death."[58]

Until 1920 Simiand, in a "spirit of extreme abnegation" according to Max Lazard, held the post of director of labor, workers' legislation, and social assistance in Strasbourg. After that date, he obtained two teaching posts, at the Conservatoire National des Arts et Métiers and at the École Pratique des Hautes Études.[59]

Bouglé, a professor of social economics at the Sorbonne beginning in 1919, was and remained active in the ranks of the Parti Radical and the Parti Radical-Socialiste. He was a regular contributor to *Dépêche* (Toulouse), a four-time candidate for a deputy's seat (in 1902, 1906, 1914, and 1924), and vice president of the Ligue des Droits de l'Homme. He also directed the Centre de Documentation Sociale (Center of social documentation), which had been associated with the École Normale Supérieure since its creation in 1920. The center was financed by the banker Albert Kahn, and its objective was to promote the documentation of political and social life. Of the four new young collaborators for the second series of *Année Sociologique*, three were Normalians and *agrégés* of philosophy recruited by Bouglé. One of them, Marcel Déat, was the archivist for the Centre de Documentation Sociale between 1920 and 1923.

Fauconnet, who had been a *chargé de cours* in pedagogical science and sociology at the Sorbonne since 1921, was still interested in health and financial problems. He agreed to contribute but without great enthusiasm and with certain conditions: he would have to be compensated and new collaborators would need to be recruited.

There were many difficulties in such an undertaking, and as Mauss explained, they could be overcome only if everyone was "sure of the desire of all the former collaborators and of the few Durkheim disciples who have contributed the most to our work since the war." "Purely scientific differences" between certain collaborators could not be allowed to turn into "personal antagonisms." Mauss himself was embroiled in a conflict with Davy and wanted to calm things down. "We need one another right now. We are so few in number, so poor, and so powerless."[60]

When Davy defended his thesis, "The Swearing of Faith," in April 1922, Mauss was supposed to be on the committee along with Lucien Lévy-Bruhl, Bouglé, Fauconnet, Lalande, and Dumas. The candidate wanted the discussion to be sanctioned by Mauss's authority. But at the last minute, an "unfortunate accident" scuttled the plan: Mauss scalded his foot and had to be replaced by Marcel Granet. Granet, *directeur d'études* at the École Pratique des Hautes Études, was a specialist in the history of China and had spent two years (1911–1913) in that country. He had just published *The Religion of the Chinese People* (1922). Everyone, and especially Lévy-Bruhl, regretted Mauss's absence: "You were the man who should have discussed and fleshed out Davy's thesis, particularly on the potlatch, whose importance you were the first to discover and point out."[61] Mauss was not overly upset to miss the meeting, because he had "serious objections," which he preferred to make privately rather than in public.[62]

The quarrel grew more acrimonious when Granet published a harsh critique of the thesis in *Journal de Psychologie Normale et Pathologique* (December 1922). Davy was hurt when he read the review, which he found to be a "systematic distortion." Contrary to what Granet seemed to be insinuating, Davy claimed he had "never concealed and had even sometimes publicly acknowledged what [he] owed to sociology and to [Mauss] in particular."[63]

Mauss did not consider chastising his student for encroaching on his own field by using Mauss's documentation on the potlatch. And though he criticized him harshly on a few points—Mauss thought Davy's analysis superficial and confused, his information insufficient—he did so only after congratulating him and reaffirming his friendship: "It never crossed any of our minds to do you a disservice. On the contrary. We're no longer so numerous that we're obliged to let some get ahead of the others. We can all march in the front ranks." As Mauss told him, he was counting on Davy "to eventually take over *Année*."[64]

Once the incident was settled, Davy said he was naturally available to offer his services to *Année* if Mauss succeeded in "resuscitating" it. Various questions worried the future collaborators. In the first place, the journal's financial situation obliged them to modify the original plan. Halbwachs wondered: "Couldn't we streamline the format, abandon the idea of being complete, and hold on to the group above all?" The other question had to do with the contributors. It was hoped that their number would be reduced to the essential "for the sake of brevity and homogeneity," and in the interest of *Année*'s prestige, which "had only grown since 1914."[65]

At the preliminary meeting of March 1, 1923, held on rue de Poitiers, a dozen people attended: Bouglé, Bourgin, Philippe de Felice, Fauconnet, Granet, Hubert, Henri Jeanmaire, Raymond Lenoir, Henri Lévy-Bruhl, Lucien Lévy-Bruhl, Claude Maître, Mauss, and Jean Marx. Some agreed to participate but could not come to the meeting, either because they were detained or because they were too far away.[66] That was the case for Halbwachs, who was working in Strasbourg. But he gave his approval and supported in advance whatever Mauss would decide. For the most part, the collaborators were *agrégés* who taught either in the national university system (in faculties of letters, theology, or law) or at the École Pratique. The group also included a few public officials from the Ministry of Public Education and the Archives Nationales, and a professor from the Collège de France.

At the March 1 meeting, the discussion focused on founding a scholarly sociology society independent of *Année Sociologique*. There was quickly unanimous agreement. They were thinking of the Société Biologique or the Institut d'Anthropologie, that is, of "a closed society composed of a limited number of active members who recruit others and increase their numbers by automatically giving old members honorary status and replacing them with younger members."[67] According to its bylaws, the aim of the Institut Français de Sociologie (IFS) would be to "bring together specialists in the various sciences that, considered together, constitute the science of man living in society." In practical terms, however, the society was formed to aid in the publication of *Année Sociologique*. When the IFS was founded in June 1923, its executive members were chiefly responsible for the journal: Marcel Mauss, president, François Simiand, vice president, Paul Fauconnet, secretary, and Henri Hubert, treasurer. But it was clear that "being a member of the IFS does not necessarily carry with it a duty or a right to contribute to *Année Sociologique*."[68]

To finance the journal, Mauss hoped to get a grant of at least 8,000 francs from the Confédération Générale des Sociétés Savantes (General confederation of scholarly societies). But for the 1923 volume (to be published in 1924), the publication costs, including printing costs and miscellaneous expenses, were more than 20,000 francs. That budget included compensation for the secretary (4,000 francs) and honoraria for the authors. In a letter written in English, Mauss explained: "We cannot inflict on younger generations the same weight as Durkheim and we took on our shoulders."[69]

The objective was to accumulate liquid capital of at least 18,000 francs. Mauss, convinced that the new series of *Année* "could have the same success" as the first, committed himself to raising the money. The steps he took made it possible to build a fund within a few months "that promises to rise to more than thirty-five thousand francs."[70] There was no longer any doubt that *Année* would be revived, though production costs were higher than predicted.[71] Hubert and Mauss pledged a large part of a Le Fèvre–Daumier Award, worth 15,000 francs, granted them by the Académie des Sciences Morales et Politiques in July. Friends and everyone who had "already shown great interest in the work of Durkheim and his collaborators" were also called on to contribute. Mauss wrote his English, American, Belgian, and Canadian friends and correspondents: Marius Barbeau, Franz Boas, James Frazer, L. Hostelet, Bronislaw Malinowski, Alfred Radcliffe-Brown, Charles G. Seligman, James T. Shotwell, Beatrice and Sidney Webb. With the aid of "devoted friends," he was able to raise funds and "establish *Année* on a solid foundation for some time, for a greater or lesser length of time."

Since the financial situation looked "fairly good in the short term," in June 1924 the editors signed a contract with the publishing house Félix Alcan, the terms of which had been approved the previous January by members of the IFS. They planned to print 1,500 copies of the journal; the subscription price was set at 40 francs inside France. Mauss, who would receive royalties—12.5 percent for the first thousand copies and 15 percent thereafter—was also assigned by the same publisher to edit the series "Travaux de *L'Année Sociologique*" and immediately arranged to publish Durkheim's *Moral Education*, Halbwachs's *Les conditions sociologiques de la mémoire* (The sociological conditions of memory), and Granet's *Festivals and Legends of Ancient China.*

The publishing deadlines were very tight. All the collaborators set to work purchasing books, dealing with other scholarly societies and journals, sending out circulars. It was truly a "cooperative enterprise with the work divided among us all."[72] The journal was organized into roughly the same sections as in the first series:

1. General sociology, Bouglé, editor, with the cooperation of Fauconnet, Lenoir, Mauss, and others.

2. Religious sociology, Mauss, editor, with Hubert, Jeanmaire, Granet, Maître, Jean Marx, Doutté, Gernet, Davy, Roussel, and Czarnowski assisting.

3. Legal sociology, Fauconnet, editor, with Henri Lévy-Bruhl, Jeanmaire, Bourgin, Granet, Mauss, Doutté, E. Lévy, Huvelin, Gernet, Roussel, Aubin, Hourticq, Davy, Ray, and Czarnowski assisting.

4. Economic sociology, Simiand, editor, assisted by Bourgin, Bouglé, Maunier, Mauss, and Halbwachs.

5. Miscellaneous, Mauss, editor, with the cooperation of Halbwachs, Maunier, and Demangeon (social morphology); A. Meillet (linguistics), who usually brought a completed manuscript; R. Lenoir, H. Hubert, and J. Marx (aesthetics); Lenoir and Hubert (technology).

For the first volume, the bibliographical labor was reorganized somewhat, if only because criminal sociology and moral statistics and social morphology merited separate sections. The number of contributors grew to more than thirty-some researchers and academics. In addition to friends and former collaborators—Lucien Lévy-Bruhl, Georges and Hubert Bourgin, Charles Lalo, Claude Maître, Jean Marx, Antoine Meillet, Dominique Parodi—there were now a few colleagues: Charles Blondel and André Piganiol from the Université de Strasbourg, Albert Bayet and Alexandre Moret from the École Pratique. A few students also contributed: Max Bonnafous, Marcel Déat, Françoise Henry, and others. The majority of contributors had a background in philosophy. According to one of the contributors, eighteen of them knew how "to give up the abstract systems Condillac spoke of."[73] Of the others, there were six historians, two geographers, two linguists, three jurists, and three ethnographers. With respect to disciplinary diversity as well, then, *Année* was true to tradition. But the age distribution of contributors to the new series was the opposite of what it had been in the first: very few were under thirty and there were many "old men" of at least forty. This was logical, since there were few newcomers, and the older contributors generally belonged to the same generation as Mauss and Hubert.[74] Mauss would say that the postwar period did not favor "young recruits": "The French student's and scholar's life was more painful than any other until 1928. It was shattered, fragmented more than others, even more than that of German students and scholars. And yet we continued our science."[75]

Just as before, the members of the French school of sociology did not constitute, in the words of Mauss's student René Maunier, "a sort of cult or a kind of secret society involving an initiation and some sort of dogma." In comparing two years (1896 and 1926), Maunier explained that the only thing all the contributors had in common was "the inclination and need for positive research emancipated from all prejudice and delivered from all bias; the constant and formal intention to found the study of social man on observation. Each of us has his opinions and beliefs, of course; but he must forget them when he crosses the threshold of our Academy. . . . We are seeking science together; and art belongs to the personal realm."[76]

Those who were newcomers were not to "replace the old-timers" but rather to seek "as best [they] can to do what they would have done." Some contributors wanted to bridge the gap between the old *Année* and the new by reviewing the contributions made to sociology between 1913 and 1923, when Année did not appear.[77] Such an undertaking, which would be extensive and costly, could not be seriously considered.

When he was again publishing the journal, Mauss informed and mobilized his foreign friends and colleagues. He wrote in English to A. W. Small of *American Journal of Sociology*: "We will be very proud if the American Sociological Society will consider us as a sort of sister society. I would be very glad if . . . you put ourselves on your exchange lists."[78] The support he received from the Americans was encouraging: "We look at France as the homeland of Sociology and we expect you still lead us in our endeavors to promote the development of science."[79] The journal *Social Forces* agreed to announce the imminent publication of *Année* and invited its readers to "subscribe in advance."[80]

From October 11 to November 1, 1924, Mauss went to England to "reestablish the necessary relations between a number of scientific societies, public institutions, and private businesses concerned with sociological problems and *Année Sociologique*, the major French periodical we have been able to revive."[81] The visit also allowed him to meet with "his people," the Balfours, Marett, Seligman, and Malinowski.[82] After Mauss returned, he invited Radcliffe-Brown, who held the chair in social anthropology at the University of Capetown in South Africa, to join the Institut Français de Sociologie, "a closed society with fifty members," and asked him to send a few very brief notices on the important things he might have to say.

The task was huge, Mauss explained, because "sociology has become something very vast." There were "infinite" publications, which were "infinitely more plentiful, interesting, and varied than a quarter century ago." They therefore had to make choices, hoping to "improve [their] work every year" and to make it "the indispensable work tool for sociologists in every country for many years to come."[83]

The first volume in the new series of *Année* was no more compact than before. It had some thousand pages, more than eight hundred of them devoted to the critical bibliography. The largest sections, apart from the section on general sociology (treatises, manuals, social philosophy, psychology and sociology, questions of methodology, civilization, race), were those on economic sociology (182 pages), moral and legal sociology (166 pages), and religious sociology (165 pages).[84]

Mauss's contributions were the most significant. Not only did he provide two original essays—"In Memoriam: The Unpublished Works of Durkheim and His Collaborators" and "The Gift"—but he was in charge of several sections and signed some hundred reviews and critical notes on works and articles published in 1923 and 1924. More than half these books and articles were in the field of religious sociology, particularly the study of religious systems of so-called inferior societies.[85] The superficial curiosity and weak organization of some authors—for example, the German anthropologist Leo Frobenius—annoyed Mauss as much as they ever had. The ethnological theology of others—P. W. Schmidt and company—exasperated him more than ever. He said he preferred the "honest, simple, and philological documentation of in-depth ethnography" to such a "wide-ranging and hasty" study. What interested him was not "systematizing philosophies" but rather facts, those collected by Boas, Malinowski, E. C. Parsons, P. Radin, R. S. Rattray, the Seligmans, and others.

Mauss and his collaborators wanted to defend the comparative method and research procedures Durkheim had perfected, whose value no one really denied any longer. They also wanted to pursue the directions Durkheim had suggested (for example, logic and the theory of cognition) and to develop their own studies. Fauconnet warned his friends: "I would tone down anything suggesting the idea of a coterie, a group devoted to the cult of personality. 'The Master' Dk [Durkheim] didn't like that."[86] The first volume of the new series was presented as a tribute to the founder, with a photograph of him and many references. In "In Memoriam," which he dedicated to Durkheim and his students, Mauss wrote: "Let's try to do something that honors their memory and is not too unworthy of what our master inaugurated. Perhaps the sap will rise again. Another seed will drop and germinate."[87]

The publication of the new series was hailed in scientific circles as a "consolation and an example." As Alphandéry said, thanks to Mauss, the driving force of the operation, "the sociological school is remaining coherent and active, is becoming complete again, is being renewed with energy and with youthful and diverse temperaments."[88]

THE INSTITUT D'ETHNOLOGIE

PARIS, 1925. Two shows were all the rage: the Revue Nègre with Josephine Baker at the music hall on the Champs-Élysées; and the Fisk Jubilee Singers concerts at the Maison Gaveau.[1] The same year, at a banquet given at La Closerie des Lilas in honor of Saint-Paul Roux (1861–1940), a poet André Breton considered his precursor, the Surrealists caused a scandal by publicly opposing the war in Morocco. For Michel Leiris, who supposedly uttered "deliberately seditious cries" at the demonstration, it was truly a "rebellion against so-called Western rationalism."[2]

Parisian intellectual and artistic circles had been in turmoil since the early 1920s. There was the birth of cinema, radio, and the phonograph; the invasion of "Negro art"; a "new departure" for music with Francis Poulenc, Georges Auric, Darius Milhaud, and Maurice Ravel; and the birth of African-American music, with King Oliver, Louis Armstrong, Duke Ellington, and Fletcher Henderson. Everyone was excited about jazz, an "elementary art" astonishing for the freedom of its sound and its accelerated rhythm.[3] Leiris wrote: "For me it was the exoticism of American civilization. Jazz was part of that industrial civilization and part of Africa."[4]

The new exoticism attracted a new audience to ethnology, not just missionaries and administrators of colonies but also writers and artists. Vlaminck, the Cubists, Gris, and Picasso were fascinated by the statuettes from Dahomey and the Ivory Coast. Africa was also making inroads in the decorative arts. Pierre Lerain produced furniture—a chair made of lacquered palm wood, for example—directly influenced by sub-Saharan Africa. The arts of Oceania, especially Easter Island, also played a major role in the artistic revival. The Surrealists drew inspiration from them: for André Breton, Easter Island was a kind of "modern Athens of Oceania"; Max Ernst collected birdman sculptures.

An Institute of Ethnology at the University

A problem of terminology arose: Was the discipline anthropology, ethnography, or ethnology? The term *anthropology* was vague until the late nineteenth century, then spread rapidly with the planning of courses, the profusion of publications, and the creation of societies and museums. In its broadest sense, anthropology encompassed ethnology and ethnography.

In France, however, the three terms referred to different disciplines and specific theoretical and institutional fields. Anthropology is the comparative study of beliefs and institutions, understood as the foundation of social structures. Ethnography entails the description of ethnic groups, while ethnology studies these same groups in terms of the unity of their linguistic, economic, and social structure and in terms of their evolution. Mauss played somewhat on these distinctions, embracing both sociology and anthropology or ethnology. He would never allow himself to be confined to one category.

Shortly before World War I, Mauss had submitted a plan to the minister of public education to create a "bureau, institute, or department of ethnology, whatever you want to call it," to bring together specialists from different parts of the world (Africa, America, Oceania, and Asia). He wanted the institute to have a "strictly scientific character." "Like any science, ethnography can be practiced only with a concern for absolute impartiality."[5] According to Mauss, the best way to proceed was to attach that institute not directly to a ministry, as in certain countries (Canada, for example), but rather to the university system, giving it an autonomous organization and a scientific staff.

Mauss was categorical: the future institute "must not have a teaching function in the beginning." It was not a matter of teaching ethnography but of practicing it. He also suggested that explorations of Oceania, Asia, and Africa be immediately organized and that the entire staff take the "colonial tour." This was "absolutely urgent."[6]

The idea resurfaced in 1924 under pressure from "public opinion, which is obscurely aware of its necessity."[7] That year Mauss confided his "secret" to his English colleague Radcliffe-Brown: "Keep this to yourself . . . but it's possible we will soon have a bureau of ethnology in France."[8] He was still thinking of a center that would devote its efforts to "organizing ethnographic study in the colonies and to publishing."[9]

In Paris at the time, teaching and research in anthropology occurred at different institutions: the École d'Anthropologie, the Muséum d'Histoire Naturelle with its anthropology chairs, the École Pratique des Hautes Études for the religions of uncivilized peoples, the Collège de France for prehistory, the Institut de Paléontologie Humaine—supported by the prince of Monaco—the Musée d'Ethnographie du Trocadéro, the École Coloniale, and the École des Langues Orientales Vivantes. Lucien Lévy-Bruhl believed it necessary to coordinate the various existing curricula while adding "a small number of lectures of a technical nature given by specialized scientists and designed to train future ethnologists."[10]

As Mauss noted, at the time the word *ethnology* designated "the descriptive form of the study of human groups and primarily of populations wrongly called primitive." In France as in the United States, the word was applied "exclusively to the knowledge of peoples with an inferior civilization and to the set of phenomena they display, from biological to sociological and linguistic characteristics."[11] The new institute's name, Institut d'Ethnologie, was thus strategic and allowed the institution to differentiate itself from organizations and groups already identified with anthropology and ethnography. For Louis Marin, a key figure in the Société d'Ethnographie, there was no doubt that Lucien Lévy-Bruhl, Mauss, and Rivet, in opting for the term *ethnology,* were unambiguously expressing their desire to undertake and promote studies of an explanatory and theoretical nature.[12]

The Institut d'Ethnologie was created in December 1925 with the help of Édouard Daladier, minister of colonies, and the colonial governors general, including Alexandre Varenne, who was serving in Indochina at the time. According to some, the institute was only a "foundation" of the Ministry of Colonies, which was skillful at turning Lucien Lévy-Bruhl's notoriety and connections to its own advantage. Daladier, a representative of the Radical-Socialist Party who belonged to the Cartel des Gauches, was also a state minister in the Herriot government. And although the socialists refused on principle to be part of a "bourgeois cabinet," the new government's policy satisfied voters on the left. The remains of Jean Jaurès were transferred to the Panthéon; amnesty was granted to the railway workers dismissed after the 1920 strikes; civil service workers were granted the right to unionize; and a national economic council was created. With the victory of the Cartel des Gauches in May 1924, conditions were in place to create an institute of ethnology headed by academics identified with the SFIO.

The Institut d'Ethnologie, housed at 191, rue Saint-Jacques, in the building of the Institut de Géographie, opened its doors in early 1926. The leadership, composed of Mauss, Lévy-Bruhl, and Paul Rivet, was a true reflection of the three "currents" of ethnology, which allowed it to maintain relations with three institutions: the École Pratique des Hautes Études, the Sorbonne, and the Muséum d'Histoire Naturelle. The management board also included Antoine Meillet, professor at the Collège de France; Maurice Delafosse, colonial governor and professor at the École des Langues Orientales Vivantes; and Louis Finot, professor at the Collège de France and director of the École Française d'Extrême-Orient.

Lucien Lévy-Bruhl (1857–1939), a professor of history and modern philosophy at the faculty of letters at the Université de Paris and director of *Revue Philosophique* since 1920, was the oldest and best known of the three. His *Primitive Mentality* (1922) had been quite a success.

Like Durkheim, Mauss "often and openly" resisted Lévy-Bruhl's views. He did not conceal his irritation at the idea that there was a prelogical mode of thought impervious to contradiction, and when Lévy-Bruhl was invited to give a paper on "primitive mentality," Mauss took advantage of the occasion to present all his criticisms: the weakness in Lévy-Bruhl's historical perspective, his methodological problems, and the absence of explanation and analysis regarding the relation between collective representations, social institutions, and the social environment. Mauss's was a Durkheimian perspective: "Reason has the same voluntary and collective origin in the most ancient societies as in the most preeminent forms of philosophy and science."[13]

Mauss would always be critical of Lévy-Bruhl's "philosophical-style" theories but would nevertheless respect and admire him: "It is beautiful and clear scholarship. . . . A fine French model with a hint of English wit." Lévy-Bruhl was sixty-eight years old and about to retire; in his teaching and his many administrative activities, he felt the "satisfaction of having accomplished his task." As Mauss later noted, he also continued to lead a civic and public life that was active and estimable.[14] Henri, one of his sons, a former student of Mauss's and his friend, was a dedicated socialist and a law professor. He sent contributions to the new series of *Année Sociologique* on everything related to legal sociology.

Paul Rivet was an assistant in the anthropology laboratory at the Muséum d'Histoire Naturelle. Born in 1876 in Wasigny in the Ardennes, as a young military doctor he joined the French scientific expedition of 1901–1906, which was assigned to measure an arc of the meridian in the Andes. There, it was said, Rivet discovered his scientific vocation; he amassed a wealth of documents on the populations of Ecuador and prepared a book, *L'ethnographie ancienne de l'Équateur* (The ancient ethnography of Ecuador), which he published in 1912. The war forced him to interrupt his research. Mobilized as a doctor from August 2, 1914, to July 25, 1919, he became head of epidemiology and hygiene for the allied armies. In 1919 he resumed his duties at the museum and continued his study of the autochthonous languages of the American continent. He also became general secretary for the Société des Américanistes and the Institut Français d'Anthropologie, and also, from 1921 to 1925, for the council of the Association Française pour l'Avancement des Sciences (French association for the advancement of science). He was an organizer and leader of considerable energy and always had ten projects in his head. As Mauss's student Jacques Soustelle would recall, Rivet was also "passionate, combative . . . a leader with innate authority."[15] Friends and collaborators admired his keen intelligence, his decisiveness, his sense of responsibility and composure. But it was better to agree with him than to oppose him. For several young researchers, Rivet would be a "great motivator" and in difficult times an unwavering supporter.

Rivet and Mauss were the pillars of the new institute. Their personalities were very different, but neither was easy to get along with. Mauss "often retreated behind a wall of gloom, though he could be disarmingly good-natured, while Rivet combined a wide-ranging and clear intellect with an inconsistent and passionate character."[16] But Mauss's encyclopedic mind and

Rivet's methodical science and pragmatic organization skills complemented each other, especially since the two shared the same political convictions.

The aim of the new institute, despite what adversaries such as Louis Marin thought, was not theoretical. Rather, it sought to attract attention through its publications to "facts recently discovered and new methods" and to "send ethnographic expeditions into the field." The time was now past when "the honor of major ethnological studies in the French colonies" was left to foreigners. The work was especially urgent because objects were "in danger of imminent disappearance."[17] It was an "absolute duty," Mauss would say.[18]

There were also practical concerns, however. The institute intended to train professional ethnologists but also to give instructions to everyone— administrators, doctors, missionaries—who lived or were planning to live in the colonies and who were often in a position to make good ethnographic observations. For a society such as France, which possessed colonies and had to administer populations of "civilizations inferior to or very different" from its own, good ethnologists seemed just as important as engineers, forest rangers, or doctors. Since the most important natural resource was the indigenous population, there was "a key interest in studying it methodically as well, in having an exact and thorough knowledge of its languages, its religions, and its social frameworks, which it is so unwise to thoughtlessly destroy."[19] As Mauss noted, the Institut d'Ethnologie was therefore "at the disposal of colonial governments and protectorates for any information concerning expeditions (French or foreign), the study of the indigenous races, the conservation and study of monuments and collections, or the study of social facts."[20]

The vocation of the institute, which presented itself as a "purely scientific institution," was thus twofold: "to work for the progress of ethnological science" and "to place the results of that science in the hands of our native policy whenever we are asked."[21]

At first there was "a little hesitancy," restraint in taking too great a risk. The leaders were cautious and wanted to adapt their efforts to the resources available. Hence there was no initial fieldwork or major ethnological journeys, with the exception of one expedition assigned to one of the students, M. Gromand, who was studying the Berber settlement in Morocco. Those at the institute undertook only what it was possible to complete, namely, the drafting of instructions or questionnaires, the publication of the first in the series "Travaux et mémoires"(Studies and essays) and the establishment of teaching programs.[22]

According to the institute's bylaws, the following were to be taught: "Research methods and ethnological description and the institutions of indigenous peoples, particularly their languages, religions, customs, technologies, anthropological characteristics, history, and archaeology." In the institute's first year, in addition to the courses offered by various institutions of higher learning in Paris (the Collège de France, the Muséum d'Histoire Naturelle, and so on), which appeared in its advertising, it offered its twenty or so enrolled students the following courses: instructions in descriptive ethnography, taught by Mauss (22 lectures); instructions in descriptive linguistics, taught by Marcel Cohen (5 lectures); African linguistics and ethnography, taught by Maurice Delafosse (5 lectures); and the linguistics and ethnography of east Asia and Oceania, taught by Jean Przyluski (5 lectures). There was also a series of four lectures open to the public, two by Arnold Van Gennep on the geographical method of folklore and two by René Maunier on industrial guilds in North Africa.[23]

The teaching program was quickly expanded, first, with Paul Rivet's courses on physical anthropology (6 lectures) and abbé Henri Breuil's on exotic prehistory (6 lectures), then with Étienne Rabaud's courses in zoological and biological anthropology (10 lectures), Léonce Joleaud's on the geology of the Quaternary Period and human paleontology (10 lectures), and Paul Guillaume's on the psychophysiology of humans and anthropoids (4 lectures). The course in African linguistics and ethnography was divided into two parts: the first (linguistics) was assigned to Mlle L. Homberger, and the second (ethnography) to Henri Labouret. Mauss remained the most active participant for some time.

A year after the institute opened, Mauss was feeling extremely satisfied.[24] The creation of a certificate in ethnology at the faculty of letters in 1927 and at the faculty of sciences in 1928 led to a considerable increase in the number of students: 67 in 1927–1928, 89 in 1928–1929. Such success obliged the institute to provide better accommodations: practical studies in anthropology, geology, and human paleontology were created; new rooms were set up (a library, a lecture hall, and a room for practical studies); excursions and museum visits were organized; students were evaluated by exam; and theses were directed.

"The Gift"

Mauss had long been conducting research on the archaic forms of the contract, particularly on a practice typical in the American Northwest known as the potlatch. The gift was not a new concern: in "Essay on the Nature and Function of Sacrifice," Mauss had analyzed the gifts men made to the gods. In addition, he had read studies and taken courses by Théodule Ribot, author of *Psychologie des sentiments*. For Ribot, the fundamental conditions for any society were reciprocity and solidarity. Mauss also knew that solidarity had been analyzed from the point of view of trade, in 1909, for example, at the congress of the Institut International de Sociologie.

One of Mauss's students, René Maunier, had written a summary of the congress in which he recognized that solidarity was "in some sense the constant and specific character of the social fact."[25] Inspired by a paper by Charles Gide, a theorist of the cooperative movement, he had given the following definition: "Solidarity is any exchange of a present good, individual or collective, for a future and necessarily collective good."[26] There was no doubt in Maunier's mind or in that of other participants that the discussion had a political dimension. They had observed "the existence of a tendency, contemporary with development, toward institutions of solidarity." The examples most often cited were producer and consumer cooperatives.

Shortly before the war, Mauss had written a review of a book by the English anthropologist Charles Seligman for *Année Sociologique*. In discussing *The Melanesians of British New Guinea*, he had noted that there was an institution, the potlatch, in all these Melanesian tribes and also in America, which Seligman had not acknowledged but that was "extremely clear." "It is a form of primitive contract whose frequency will be increasingly observed as we study systems of exchange in inferior societies. It is a contract that brings whole groups together in communal feasts, weddings, and so on."[27]

After the war, the first papers Mauss delivered to the Institut Français d'Anthropologie (a scholarly society) dealt with "the expansion of the potlatch in Melanesia" and with "a few facts concerning the archaic forms of the contract among the Thracians."[28] That form of collective exchange was known through Boas's "admirable studies" on the Kwakiutl, particularly in British Columbia, and constituted a "system of total services." Its chief characteristic was the transaction, which began with complimentary gifts, involved a host of services of every kind, and was sumptuary in nature. It then assumed an agonistic dimension with constant rivalry, sometimes leading to a battle to the death. Mauss had no doubt that these total services existed nearly everywhere, especially among Africans and Polynesians. But what about the Indo-European world? In reading the Greek texts of antiquity, particularly Xenophon and Thucydides, Mauss discovered "forms of treaties, marriage, exchange, and religious/aesthetic services very much like those in Melanesia and North America." He did not rule out the possibility that the same was true among the Germanics and the Celts.

In 1923 Mauss presented another paper to the institute on "the obligation to return presents." The system of gift exchange he analyzed in New Zealand presupposed, first, the obligation to give, second, the obligation to receive, and third, the obligation to return. Relying on studies by his late friend Robert Hertz, he pointed out the spiritual character of these exchanges. The gifts, because they were endowed with *hau*, or spirits, could not be kept but had to be returned.[29] In the course he taught at the École Pratique des Hautes Études in 1923–1924, he dealt with Malinowski's studies and the potlatch in particular. He also discussed the notions of gift, disinterest, and pledge.

In a short text titled "Gift, Gift," which he presented in 1924 as part of a tribute to Charles Andler by his friends and students, Mauss continued his analysis of the system of total services: "The thing received as a gift, the thing received in general, connects the donor magically, religiously, morally, and legally to the recipient. Coming from one person, manufactured or appropriated by him, belonging to him, it confers power on him over the one who accepts it."[30] As the two senses of the word *gift* in the different Germanic languages indicate, the "present" is also a "poison." It is therefore not surprising that it produces both pleasure and displeasure in those who receive it. All the facts and all the themes of "The Gift" were rapidly sketched out in this short text.

At the invitation of the Société de Psychologie, Mauss agreed the same year to analyze the "real and practical relationship between psychology and sociology." He repeated his declaration of the previous year—"Sociology, psychology, and physiology: everything must be combined"[31]—seeking less to erect walls than to build bridges between the disciplines and show what they could offer one another. He also identified urgent tasks to be shared, including "the study of the complete, concrete human being." Mauss used the expressions "phenomena of totality" and "total human beings": "Fundamentally, everything mingles here, body, soul, and society.... That is what I propose to call phenomena of totality, in which not only the group participates but also, through it, all the personalities, all the individuals in their moral, social, mental, and above all corporeal and material integrity."[32]

The "complete" or "total human being" is also "the ordinary human being," the same one sociologists generally study: "The average human being of our time . . . is a 'totality' . . . The study of that 'totality' is key."[33]

To define the facts as "collective suggestion," Mauss turned to the notion of "total facts" in his "Idea of Death Suggested by the Collectivity," since these facts displayed a characteristic (totality) proper to what were wrongly called primitive peoples. Mauss would conclude that this only added grist to the mill of the Durkheimian thesis of "homo duplex," man's inseparably psycho-organic and social nature.[34]

"The Gift," published in 1925 in volume 1 of the new series of *Année Sociologique,* granted a central place to the notion of "total phenomenon." As Henri Lévy-Bruhl would say, Mauss used "all the resources of his great erudition"—more than five hundred footnotes and hundreds of references—to solve the problem of the form and nature of the primitive economy.[35] The study also used to advantage the expertise of former students and collaborators: Marius Barbeau, Maurice Cahen, Davy, Granet, Hertz, Hubert, Huvelin, Leenhardt, Raymond Lenoir, Henri Lévy-Bruhl, Maunier, Meillet,

Mestre, and Simiand. The study of the potlatch was more than a shared concern: it was a true research program, and "The Gift" was only a fragment of it. Volume 2 of the new *Année Sociologique* would include a long essay by Maunier on the same practice in and around the Mediterranean basin. For the time being, Mauss formulated the following questions: "What is the code of law and of self-interest that dictates that the present received in backward or archaic societies must be returned? What force is there in the thing given that makes the donor return it?"[36]

His method was comparative. He wanted to establish "the enormous scope" of total services through examples taken from determinate areas (Polynesia, Melanesia, the American Northwest, Germania, India). Observations were "borrowed from all sorts of legal systems, magical practices, religions, and economies in all sorts of societies, from Melanesia, Polynesia, and North America to our own ethical system."[37] "The Gift" is the best known of Mauss's writings, his "key work";[38] his "masterpiece,"[39] some would say. For the first time in the history of ethnology, an effort was being made to "transcend empirical observation and reach deeper realities,"[40] or, in Mauss's words, to touch "one of the human bedrocks on which our societies are built."

Among what are called primitive peoples, there is nothing resembling a natural economy, the barter of material objects between individuals. On the contrary, we find exchanges between entire collectivities, which occur in the guise of ordered and sanctioned ritual gifts. One of the most developed forms of exchange, which puts into circulation not only goods and wealth but also many other things (courtesies, feasts, rites, military service, women, children, and so on), is the potlatch. As Mauss had already indicated, it is a system of total services of the agonistic type that has been observed in the American Northwest, in Melanesia, and in Papua New Guinea. Certain intermediate forms of it are found elsewhere, even in the Indo-European world. Mauss initially focused on the case of Polynesia, Samoa in particular, where such a system of contractual gifts can be found, despite what some people had long believed. He also showed that in Melanesia the kula, which Malinowski describes in his *Argonauts of the Western Pacific* (1922), was "only a moment, the most solemn moment, in a vast system of services and counter-services" and that this system of intertribal exchange constituted a sort of large potlatch with an obligation on both sides to receive and to give. The same institutions were also found in a "more radical and more prominent" form in the tribes of the American Northwest, from Alaska to British Columbia. The potlatch characteristic of these tribes illustrates the obligation of a chief and his clan to give, even to "expend" without limits and to destroy wealth. It is all a question of prestige and honor, and of the risk of "losing face." There is thus an obligation to give, but there is also an obligation to receive and to return.

These phenomena are difficult for the modern mind to grasp. The jurist Henri Lévy-Bruhl commented: "Our legal and economic categories are not pertinent here."[41] Mauss wondered why it was in "the nature of the gift to oblige within time limits." But instead of considering the structure of exchange as the foundation of that obligation, he turned to another type of explanation, as he had done while expounding his theory of magic using the notion of mana. He emphasized the "spiritual power" of things given as gifts. There is a "force of things," a "virtue that forces gifts to circulate, to be given and returned." In Polynesia that force is the *hau*, the spirit of the thing given: "To present something to someone is to present something of oneself. . . . One understands clearly and logically within that system of ideas that it is necessary to return to the other what is in reality part and parcel of his nature and substance, for to accept something from someone is to accept something of his spiritual essence, his soul."[42] The essay considered the notion of *hau* as a starting point, not an endpoint. This was fortunate, Lévi-Strauss later commented, since he feared that the ethnologist had allowed himself to "be fooled by the native."[43]

Mauss might have remained within the field of ethnography. But convinced that the facts presented had a "general sociological value," he pursued his investigation diachronically, searching for traces ("relics") of the principles he had just analyzed. He studied the law of the Roman *familia*, the status of the gift in Hindu law, and the specific vocabulary of old Germanic law and Chinese law.[44] As a member of the Société d'Histoire du Droit (Society for the history of law), Mauss had long been interested in the law, and as Henri Lévy-Bruhl noted, he contributed "unexpectedly and with extreme effectiveness" to its history and even prehistory.

By way of conclusion, Mauss extended his observations to our own societies: Invitations must be reciprocated; one must play the "lord of the manor" at celebrations, weddings, and communions; things that are sold have a "soul," as could be seen in the Vosges. In short, not everything is a commodity relationship, a utilitarian calculation. "A considerable part of our ethics and lives still unfolds in the same atmosphere of gift, obligation, and freedom." There is still "pure and irrational expenditure."

For Mauss, the importance of his discovery was so great that observing the fact was not enough. One also had to draw ethical conclusions from it. Let us return to "the archaic," he exclaimed. Let us reinvent mores of "noble expenditure" and recover "the joy of giving in public, the pleasure of generous artistic expenditure, of hospitality, of the private and public feast." Rejecting "the egoism of our contemporaries . . . the individualism of our laws," and "the excesses of generosity and communism," he defended a "new ethics" founded on mutual respect and reciprocal generosity that would ensure the redistribution of amassed wealth. This, he thought, was the necessary condition for the happiness of individuals and of peoples. As

Durkheim had recommended, respect for the principles of honor, disinterest, and solidarity was possible and desirable at the level of professional groups. It was also possible to conceive what a society would be where such principles would prevail. Legislatures would adopt social insurance laws (against unemployment, illness, old age); businesses would create a social assistance fund; measures would be taken to limit the profits of speculation and usury; corporate solidarity would develop. Ethnography and politics intersected. Mauss, who was very active in the cooperative and socialist movement, had completed his long series of articles on "exchange rates" and had just published his important "Sociological Appreciation of Bolshevism." He did not despair of contributing to the definition of a policy that would consciously organize life in common on the basis of all these studies.

As Maunier emphasized in his review of "The Gift," Mauss's merit lay in the fact that he had demonstrated two things: first, "the life of 'primitives' is more complex, more active, more mobile than generally believed: it must not be represented as 'static'"; and second, economic life is profoundly related to morality and religiosity. Everything is in everything else.[45] Mauss, by introducing the notion of "total social fact" and trying to describe "totalities," whole social systems, succeeded in "providing insights to solve old problems."

> There is a heuristic principle in this way of treating a problem that I would like to draw out. The facts we have studied are all total social facts so to speak, or, if you like—but I am less fond of this expression—general social facts. That is, in certain cases they set in motion the whole of society and its institutions (potlatch, clashing clans, tribes visiting one another). . . .
>
> All these phenomena are at once legal, economic, religious, and even aesthetic and morphological.[46]

The concept of total social fact made it possible to consider several different areas: the structure of social life, history, mental representations, and so on. As Mauss noted, such a method had a dual advantage: not only did the researcher deal with "facts that have some chance of being more universal," he also managed to "see social things themselves in the concrete, as they are." The sociologist's task was not to produce abstractions but "to observe what is given," and the given "is Rome, Athens, the average Frenchman, the Melanesian on one island or another." This formulation sums up an idea Mauss had developed a few years earlier while speaking to the Société de Psychologie: "Now, we sociologists . . . are dealing . . . with the total human being composed of a body, an individual consciousness, and of that part of consciousness that comes from the *conscience collective* or, if you like, that corresponds to the existence of the collectivity. What we find is a human being who lives in flesh and spirit at a determinate point in time and space, in a determinate society."[47]

Reiterating the comparison he had made between psychology and sociology, Mauss now concluded: "Having by necessity divided and abstracted too much, sociologists must endeavor to reconstitute the totality. . . . The study of the concrete, which is a totality, is possible and more captivating and even more explanatory in sociology."[48]

Hubert, on vacation in the region of Var, read and reread the article, and wrote his friend: "I don't yet understand very well the expression *total services*. . . . There's a long stream of words in discussing the facts that cannot take the place of formal generalization or more precise definitions."[49] Hubert did not find the article easy to read: "It's often rather vague." And he criticized his friend for combining his analysis with "considerations of policy and practical ethics." "Are you really sure that the development of social insurance can be attached to your 'human bedrock,' as you say? In that paragraph, you were thinking more about your book on the nation than about the subject at hand."[50]

For the most part, the reaction of foreign colleagues to the published form of "The Gift" was positive. According to Boas, it was an "interesting investigation."[51] Malinowski read Mauss's "admirable article" with "great interest": "Remarkably enough I have come to very similar conclusions in working on the problem of law (now in print)."[52] Mauss was becoming one of the "leading students of primitive economics."[53] But the interpretation he gave of Maori facts, and particularly of *hau*, was quickly disputed by Raymond Firth in *Primitive Economics of the New Zealand Maori* (1929). It was the beginning of a long controversy.[54]

Once "The Gift" had been published, Mauss addressed the question of the potlatch only sporadically in his courses at the École. Other themes, always diverse, held his attention: totemism, taboo, religion and art, cosmology. And though Mauss still privileged Australia in discussing oral rites, he was interested in other geographical areas when he studied different themes, and especially in Africa (Gold Coast, French Sudan, Upper Volta) and northeast Asia.

"The Gift" was only "a fragment of a more extensive study," said Henri Lévy-Bruhl.[55] Mauss continued his study of "systems of total services" in a brief paper presented to the Institut Français d'Anthropologie in 1926. Borrowing P. Radin's expression, it dealt with "joking relationships." These were fascinating phenomena that had certain similarities to the potlatch, since, as Mauss recalled, "rivalries of generosity" were the occasion for insults but also for hospitality. Between relatives and allies there were exchanges of obligations but also of jokes. Taboos and etiquette did not rule out irreverence. These jokes performed obvious functions—the need to relax, moral oversight—but it was clear that "joking relationships correspond to reciprocal rights and that when these rights are unequal they correspond to a religious inequality."[56]

The idea of reciprocity, insufficiently developed by Durkheim,[57] now assumed its rightful place and led to a formulation of the problem of "social cohesion" in fairly new terms. When he discussed that problem before his colleagues at the Institut de Sociologie, Mauss was eager to summarize his little study on joking relationships. He wanted to counter the (Durkheimian) image of a society functioning as a "homogeneous mass" with the image of a more complex collectivity, groups and subgroups that overlap, intersect, and fuse together.[58] There were certainly communities, but there was also a system of reciprocity between them.

14

SOCIOLOGY, A LOST CAUSE?

WITH the relaunching of *Année* and the creation of the Institut d'Ethnologie, Mauss had never before accumulated so many administrative and scientific responsibilities. In addition, he was a contact person for the Laura Spelman Rockefeller Foundation.

A Trip to the United States

The Laura Spelman Rockefeller Foundation, a philanthropic entity, created in 1918 by the American businessman John D. Rockefeller in memory of his wife, was dedicated to aiding women and children.[1] It moved into the field of social sciences when a young academic, Beardsley Ruml, took over in the mid-1920s. One of the foundation's new objectives was to promote the development of the social sciences from a humanitarian perspective and to favor the establishment of solid and effective research institutions throughout the world. In the United States, the Social Science Research Council, founded in 1923, was one of its creations. Other academic centers in Chicago, at Harvard, and at Columbia benefited from its financial aid.

In 1924 the foundation created a scholarship program for young foreign researchers and broadened its policy to subsidize European research centers in the social sciences. It offered financial support to the London School of Economics and the Deutsche Hochschule für Politik in Berlin. By making it easier for students in the social and political sciences to spend time in the United States and Europe, it hoped to inspire a "spirit of audacious liberalism," a "passion for truth," and a "desire to pursue the facts" among the "future shapers of public opinion." Young researchers were advised: "Place yourselves before the facts like a child, abandon any preconceived idea."[2]

When an office of the foundation opened in Paris in 1917, the capital of France became the hub of its European expeditions and operations. But it did not take on a concrete role until the mid-1920s, when it set up a scholarship program. Along with Mauss, the chief contact in France was Charles Rist, a professor of law in Paris, a member of the editorial board for *Revue d'Économie Politique*, and assistant director of the Banque de France. In 1925 Rist prepared a report for the foundation in which he proposed to create an institute of social and economic sciences independent of the university system. But because of difficult economic circumstances, he suggested putting off the plan. The same year, Ruml, the foundation's director, invited Mauss to the United States.[3] The objective was to "visit certain major institutions, universities, and research institutes" and to "hold some seminars."[4]

Mauss accepted the invitation of one of the largest and wealthiest scientific foundations in the world, and in May 1926 began his journey to the United States. It would allow him to meet American academics who had shown an interest in *Année Sociologique*. Hubert put him in touch with the Potter family, who lived on Long Island and whom Hubert knew well.

The trip got off to a bad start. Mauss fell ill—he was probably suffering from dysentery—and was hospitalized.[5] The doctor prescribed complete rest and forbade him to work. Mauss would later recount: "I was flat on my back. I wasn't allowed to do anything and I was bored."[6] When he got out of the hospital, Mauss spent a few days resting at the Potters' house. He also took the opportunity to pay a visit to the family of his old classmate and friend Joe Stickney.

There was also bad news. Two close friends died: Maurice Cahen, who had recently been appointed to the École Pratique des Hautes Études and with whom Mauss was "planning to write a commentary on the Havamal, the Younger Edda"; and Lucien Herr, "who we knew was dying of cancer." "I really loved [Herr] a lot," Hubert wrote Mauss. "I think of him only with the deepest sorrow."[7] Mauss was very moved. "Since the death of P.L. [Philippe Landrieu], it's been one horror after another; and this year reminds me of the saddest [years] of the war."[8]

Mauss's itinerary in the United States took in six cities: New York, Boston, New Haven, Chicago, Washington, and Philadelphia. It was a heavy schedule: seven seminars at Harvard and the University of Chicago on the topic "The Unity of the Human Sciences and Their Mutual Relationship: Anthropology, Psychology, Social Science";[9] a visit to major American universities and to several anthropology museums; a study of how research institutes were organized;[10] contact with a few scholarly societies; and meetings with many researchers and academics, including Franz Boas, Bronislaw Malinowski,[11] Edward Sapir, the sociologists Franklin Henry Giddings, E. Burgess, Robert Faris, and Robert Park, the philosopher John Dewey, the psychologist Elton Mayo, the political scientist Charles Edward Merriam, and the economist L. C. Marshall.[12] Mauss discovered a "charming country," new landscapes, and new populations."[13] He took walks through various city neighborhoods, including the black section of Philadelphia.[14] In addition, he made observations—for example, on the gait of American nurses and the incomparable running ability of a Hopi chief—which he would later use in his analysis of "bodily techniques."[15]

He was particularly impressed by the scope of research in the United States. The Social Research Institute in Chicago had demonstrated that, by scientifically recording the facts, sociology could affect policy and could acquire prestige and authority. What further impressed him was the "conscious" and "rational" way that, for the first time in history, the United States was succeeding in "treating the noble problem of a nation's formation":

> This entails forming both a lineage and a society with its traditional morals and its capacity for development—moral, technological, and intellectual—composed of an optimum number of sound and handsome people. . . . We know that Americanization is a problem of "civics." That is how it ought to be posited. Material, anthropological recruitment and moral, economic, technological, and educational recruitment must entail not only learning but also choice. That is how a great people places its entire social system, its entire demographic composition, as well as its destiny and its full individuality under the jurisdiction of a practical reason finally enlightened by science and, in any case, rationally managed by scientists and by the people themselves.[16]

Mission accomplished? Mauss was very satisfied with the welcome he had received. And he had learned a great deal. But the trip produced no immediate results.[17] Charles Rist remained the privileged correspondent of the Rockefeller Foundation in France.

The Failure of *Année Sociologique*

Reviving *Année Sociologique* was "particularly difficult." Hubert believed it was a task that "probably surpasses our strength."[18] For Mauss, it was an obsession. He wrote to Ignace Meyerson: "I'm going to emerge from the nightmare of *Année I* only to enter the nightmare of *Année II*. I can't go on."[19] Immediately after the first volume's publication, Paul Fauconnet, the journal's editor, decided to "resign from his position immediately."[20] It was not easy to recruit new collaborators. Marc Bloch, who was slow in composing book reviews, did not dare "promise to be a very active contributor to *Année*."[21]

The second volume, which was to analyze the output of the years 1924–1925, was published in 1927 after a one-year delay and included only the first half of the original essays. In addition to a few short biographical notices compiled by Mauss, there was an essay by Maunier on "ritual exchange in North Africa" and part of a long discussion by Mauss titled "Divisions and Proportions of Divisions in Sociology."

There was clearly too little time, and it was not easy to survey and properly classify the literature as a whole. Mauss admitted it openly: "We are far from the ideal." He hoped for an *Année Sociologique* whose space was "better allocated, better proportioned: that is the first definite goal we are pursuing. May the new effort we are all making earn the favor of young workers; may they, in collaborating with us, find and note the gaps in our knowledge, extend their own, and tailor a better costume of abstraction to the body of social phenomena."[22]

There were many gaps. Social morphology, especially in the field of demography, was not allotted all the space it deserved. The differentiation among several topics made social phenomena look like "things that had been fragmented, shattered into institutions, notions, and so on, separated, divided, specialized." The section dealing with politics or the theory of the state was underdeveloped and did not take into account "one of the major discoveries of modern times," namely, that "an important part of our social and political life is not a political reality but a technological and economic one." The section devoted to the science of religion focused too much on the "primitive" and not enough on the major religions. Mauss felt no sense of accomplishment. On the contrary. According to him, the scientist's first obligation was to confess his ignorance. "We don't have the final word, or even perhaps the last chronologically. . . . Let us therefore learn how to criticize ourselves."[23]

The real work remained to be done. Judging that one of the distinctive characteristics of the social fact was that it be quantified, Mauss did not hesitate to recommend the systematic use of quantitative methods so long as they were handled with caution and intelligence: "Fundamentally, every social problem is a statistical problem. . . . Statistical procedures are not only the way to measure but also the way to analyze any social fact."[24] He added: "Everything is measurable and ought to be quantified."[25] That point of view was largely shared by the contributors to *Année* and in particular by Halbwachs, who used statistical data in most of his writings. His interest in statistics led him to develop his mathematical expertise and to publish a book for a general audience with Maurice Fréchet: *Le calcul des probabilités à la portée de tous* (1924; The calculation of probabilities accessible to all).

In the United States, Mauss encountered sociologists better equipped to carry out vast studies. French sociologists, instead of concerning themselves exclusively with what was "easy, amusing, odd, bizarre, or passé because it belonged to societies that were dead or remote from their own," needed to conduct conclusive studies of present-day life, to be on the lookout for new social movements, to orient themselves more toward "modern things" in turmoil, and to observe emerging institutions. In short, they needed to direct their attention to the "witch's cauldron" in which society was concocted.[26]

As a defender of "both a general and a concrete sociology," Mauss also identified a whole series of general questions of growing importance that could no longer be neglected. For example, it was indispensable to begin studying phenomena rather misleadingly grouped under the term *civilization*: societies as social systems, forms of thought, and especially, the categories of number and space, politics, theories of the state, and other modern problems (social insurance, immigration). In addition to these, there was the delicate question of the relation between sociology and other disciplines, including psychology and biology. Mauss coined the slogan: "Let us establish connections." Three fields could benefit from interdisciplinarity: language and symbolic studies, research on "mentality," and studies of civilization and collective ethology (collective characteristics).

If one wanted to explain a social fact, one could not limit oneself to studying a single order of facts. One had to apprehend social facts as a whole, describe the "social whole integrating individuals who are themselves totalities," succeed in "reconnecting with the complete individual," observe "man as a whole." Mauss reformulated the idea of "totality": "A whole in itself [a human society] is only a relationship. . . . Everything in society, even the most specialized things, is, and is above all, a function and an operation. Nothing can be understood except in relation to the whole, to the collectivity as a whole and not in relation to separate parts. There is no social phenomenon that is not an integral part of the social whole."[27] The advantage of such a view was that it allowed one to demonstrate the unity of social phenomena and thereby justify that of sociology: "We are intent on recalling that this is the most productive principle of Durkheim's method. There are not social sciences but only a science of societies. Naturally, it is necessary to isolate each social phenomenon to study it. . . . But sociology exists to keep us from forgetting any of the connections."[28]

In "Divisions and Proportions of Divisions in Sociology," Mauss rose to "the ethereal heights of sociology" and not without a certain pride. He confided to Sylvain Lévi: "No one will be able to say that I am unproductive vis-à-vis dogma."[29] The "remixing" of the divisions he proposed surprised and amazed friends and collaborators. Halbwachs wrote: "Many of these pages seemed first-rate to me and as a whole really shook me up, since my mind is rather too much oriented toward abstractions . . . and you are truly doing me a service in reminding me that there are concrete wholes."[30]

In the second volume of *Année*, Mauss also published his "Methodological Note on the Scope of Sociology," in which he reasserted that the word *sociology* is "a synonym for social science, the sciences of societies, the totality of the social sciences, we would say. All social phenomena form a single realm, the object of a single science. The name matters little; the principle is primordial."[31] It was with some anxiety that he observed the development of sociology in various countries. Sociology, isolated from the other social sciences, was becoming "philosophical" once again, a sort of "lazy philosophy," and was hardly distinguishable from political and moral sermonizing. Given the excessive enthusiasm and the easy successes the young science produced, it was better to "firmly discourage naïveté and premature propaganda." The sociologist's first duty was to teach the public to have no illusions and above all to accustom it to having the "critical sense" required. The sociologist had "simply to preach patience and caution to those who place too much hope in sociology from the practical—or, as it's called, the 'social'—point of view."[32] There were no miracles.

As an engagé intellectual, Mauss was very familiar with politics, though he said he did not practice it. And though he insisted on the necessary separation between sociology and politics, he showed he was very concerned with applying science: "Even the common people expect a less purist, a less disinterested attitude from us."[33] What could sociology offer? First, sociologists could take politics as an object of study and show to what degree "political problems are social problems." The model Mauss had in mind was the United States, where sociologists helped politicians and bureaucrats by doing "impartial surveys, simply recording the facts."

Mauss believed in a "positivist politics," and he believed it would some day be possible to form diagnoses and propose remedies with a certain reliability. "On that day, the cause of sociology will be won. The usefulness of sociology will be self-evident."[34] Nevertheless, sociology was the very opposite of a panacea. It was only "the principal means for educating society. It is not the means to make human beings happy. Even social art and politics are incapable of that, though they pursue that illusory goal. Durkheim has shown this very well. The only effect science and art have is to make human beings stronger and give them more self-control."[35]

The second volume of *Année Sociologique* was clearly unfinished. Mauss's methodological note on the scope of sociology, which served as an introduction to the second part of the analyses and reviews, ended with the words "As if we . . ." A very enigmatic "as if"! For some unknown reason, the last pages of the text were not typeset even though they had been written.

In the unpublished part of that note, Mauss tried to respond to those who accused Durkheim and his disciples of a "certain exclusivity, a certain intolerance," even an "urge to monopolize."[36] Mauss, far from wanting to "block all avenues" and isolate himself, launched an appeal to specialists, hoping that sociology could attract "true men of science" and lead them to collaborate with one another. Durkheim's little group of disciples had no intention of establishing a tyranny.

The founding period was over. Sociology existed, it had its method. It was time to move on to the next stage and "contribute to the organization of our sciences." This was merely a "scientific strategy" that consisted of gathering researchers and, "once they were united, of directing them, or rather allowing them to direct themselves, toward the sites where they will best use their strengths." What were these sites? Where was there a lack of knowledge? Mauss did not believe that "the problems in vogue—race crime and emigration, for example—[are] best addressed when they lead to imitation by everyone wanting to write the book of the moment. New and better things could be done by looking elsewhere, looking farther." He concluded: "Everyone's goal should be to create strengths that can be directed toward unknowns. It is the unknown that needs to be revealed."[37]

There would be nothing further. The second volume would be the last in the new series of *Année*. The suspension of publication was a surprise, since Mauss had been optimistic about the future. "*Année II* is under way. *Année III* is getting rolling. Onward to *Année V* . . . I'll have had my fill. Finally, it's a success."[38] He had already prepared a long methodological note on the notion of civilization for the third volume. He would use it for a lecture, "Civilization: Elements and Forms," presented a few years later at the first "Synthesis Week" held by Henri Berr.

Halbwachs, still working in Strasbourg, was concerned about the journal's future and wrote earnestly: "I realize you're often snowed under. But this is obviously a fairly critical time for *Année* and I'd really like to know what's been done, what's under way."[39]

Other Ordeals, Other Obligations

Everyone, and Mauss most of all, wanted to see more studies and hoped that the blueprint provided by *Année Sociologique* would allow "workers" to "make the best choice in their work." But who would these workers be? Mauss had trained few students himself and they specialized either in the history of religion or in ethnology. Under such conditions, it was not easy to preserve the Durkheimian legacy and keep a real team assembled around *Année Sociologique.* The last major project Mauss and Hubert planned was a history of religion in three volumes, aided by collaborators (Philippe de Felice, Marcel Granet, Jean Marx, Raymond Lantier, Jean Przyluski) and colleagues (Marcel Cahen, Alexandre Moret, Gabriel Millet, Isidore Lévy, Paul Rivet). The project was never completed.

The *Année* team's unity was particularly fragile because no one was really available and everyone tended to withdraw into his own area or specialty: archaeology for Hubert, economics for Simiand, demography and statistics for Halbwachs. In addition, the team, already small, was further handicapped by deaths and ordeals. Hubert, who had been sickly for many years, "required a great deal of care." He was increasingly "prone to physical fatigue."[40] Salomon Reinach described him as someone who "worked a great deal, taught a great deal, suffered a great deal."[41] In May 1924, the death of his wife, Emma, following the birth of their second son, was a terrible ordeal. Hubert displayed courage and self-restraint, bearing his misfortune "like a man who wants to go on living."[42] The next year his heart troubles worsened, forcing him to take a long winter vacation in the Midi and to take several courses of treatment in Néris.

Two years later, his health was no better.[43] Hubert died on May 25, 1927, in his villa in Chatou. The previous day, he had put the finishing touches on a note for *Année Sociologique*. He was fifty-five at the time and left two young children, Marcel and Gérard. "Another loss!" exclaimed Danielle Lévi. "What a cemetery our memories have become."[44] All Hubert's friends, colleagues, and students had the greatest respect and the most sincere admiration for him. One of his students, Alfred Métraux, pointed out: "He embodied French science: a profound erudition combined with an elegance and a clarity of expression."[45] The English journal *Man* wrote that it was a great loss for anthropology and history.[46] And, Mauss would add, obviously for French sociology as well.[47]

Mauss did not conceal his distress. "I'm recovering slowly from Hubert's death," he wrote Sylvain Lévi."[48] It was a horrible shock. A few months later, he confided to Radcliffe-Brown: "I don't know what I did at the time. The scientific and moral burdens that have fallen to me are overwhelming. If only my health were as strong as my will."[49] Everyone knew it was a cruel blow for Mauss and "the definitive end of something that occupied a large place in [his] life."[50]

His friend and collaborator was irreplaceable. It was the end of "renowned constructions," the result of a collaboration between Hubert's and Mauss's "contrasting merits." *Mélanges* was the best example of that, displaying extensive knowledge, audacious and solid thinking, perfect composition.[51] Acting as literary executor, Mauss had to organize his friend's papers, do an inventory of his library, and prepare his manuscripts for publication, a considerable task.

Mauss was willing to endure that "waste of time." But he realized, once he had begun to inventory the texts, that the scientific chore was even more back-breaking than he had believed. Fortunately, he could count on the devotion of two former students at the École: Jean Marx and Raymond Lantier. Marx was Hubert's successor at the École Pratique and Lantier his successor at the museum in Saint-Germain. Mauss optimistically believed he would be able to give Henri Berr Hubert's book on the Celts before the end of August 1927 and would finish the job on Hubert's study of the Germanics the following year.[52] He also hoped to find the second part of the essay on magic he wrote with Hubert and to publish it "as is, without notes."[53]

Mauss, the "trustee" of Hubert's thought after thirty years of "fraternal collaboration," knew the secrets of his style well enough to be "the scrupulous editor of the unpublished part of his work."[54] But it was not always easy. He had to summarize lectures, condense material, and compose a conclusion on the basis of various drafts. In the autumn of 1927, when Mauss returned to work after a three-week vacation in Lamalou-les-Bains, he faced many academic obligations: "It looks like there will be brilliant students, theses, chores, an invitation to the University of London." He made up a simple plan: "Publish *Année [Sociologique]* ... write the last chapters of Hubert's 'Celts' with Marx and Lantier; after that, I'll edit the 'Germanics' with Jansé."[55] It was an ambitious undertaking. *The Celts* would not be published until 1932.

Mauss had little time to complete his own work. He devoted himself to biographical notices: in 1927 he wrote them for Claude E. Maître, Maurice Cahen, Edmond Doutté, Paul Lapie, Louise Durkheim, and Lucien Herr.[56] The following year, he published "Frazer's Sociological and Anthropological Work"[57] in the journal *Europe* and brought out Durkheim's courses under the title *Le socialisme* (translated as *Socialism and Saint-Simon*) through the Alcan publishing house. He was also involved in publishing the writings of Robert Hertz, his former student and close collaborator who had been killed in the war. The collection appeared in 1928 with a foreword by Mauss, under the title *Mélanges de sociologie religieuse et de folklore* (Miscellany: Religious sociology and folklore).[58] That was only part of the "enormous labor" done by the young Hertz. There were still huge file cabinets filled with fragments and drafts. Mauss, anxious not to keep that "treasure" to himself, began to rewrite and complete the book "in an approximate and abridged form."[59] He also hoped to publish Hertz's thesis on Greek and comparative mythology, "The Myth of Athena," even though Durkheim, Hubert, and Mauss himself had expressed "very strong reservations" about it before the war.[60] But no trace remains of the thesis. For several years, Mauss used that documentation in his courses and in preparing a few publications, especially "The Physical Effect on the Individual of the Idea of Death Suggested by the Collectivity." He apologized: "I allowed myself to draw on that documentation," but immediately added: "All the details of that argument will be found in Hertz's book and we will not dismember it any further."[61] In November 1927, when Mauss learned of the death of Alice Hertz, Robert's wife, he exclaimed: "Another piece of my life disappearing."[62]

An Ambitious Project: A Sixth Section

At the École Pratique des Hautes Études, things were going fairly well. Although Mauss said he "did not have time for intrigues and did not see anyone outside [his] neighborhood," he actively followed what was going on at the École, especially when new appointments were made. He also intervened on questions of general policy. He believed the number of chairs devoted to Christianity was excessive, and claimed the section had to keep doing five exegeses (biblical, evangelic, Talmudic, Koranic, and Buddhist). In his classes, Mauss resumed and deepened his study of negative oral rituals and of prohibitions concerning speech and language in Australia: the silent treatment of one person or another, taboos on words, and so on. The objective was to demonstrate the symbolic efficacy of words and the religious value of breath and the voice. Prayer was still at the center of his concerns. After accepting the invitation of the London School of Economics in June 1928, he presented a series of three lectures titled "Theory of the Elementary Forms of Prayer (Australia)."

The number of students increased at the Institut d'Ethnologie; in 1929–1930 there were more than 110 enrolled. Similarly, the specifically scientific work of the institute took shape, with an annual budget of about 180,000 francs, most of it provided in subsidies from the colonies. New books in the "Travaux et mémoires" collection were published and lectures held. Many linguistic questionnaires were distributed abroad, and above all, archaeological expeditions and excavations were financed. The Institut d'Ethnologie established close ties with other institutions, especially the anthropology laboratory at the Muséum d'Histoire Naturelle and its annex, the Musée d'Ethnographie du Trocadéro. In 1928 the secretary of the institute, Paul Rivet, succeeded René Verneau at the Trocadéro; he began to rebuild the museum and to entirely rethink its organization and enrich its collections.

Rivet, assisted by Georges-Henri Rivière, wanted to take advantage of his skill as an organizer and his political savvy to give France a museum worthy of its colonial power and scientific renown. After presenting a series of lectures in Mexico, he brought back a large archaeological collection as well as rare books that had been published there. Several students at the institute earned money by classifying objects, preparing museum exhibits, and organizing missions, within a structure that left them time to finish their theses. As a result, as Mauss noted, the necessary conditions were present to train a first generation of ethnologists who could devote themselves to research.

Mauss was always concerned with how to set up research. He had maintained ties with the Rockefeller Foundation since his trip to the United States. After conversations with C. E. Merriam in 1929, he agreed to compile a report for the foundation dealing with research in the social and human sciences in Paris.[63] Such research encompassed a large field: anthropology in all its forms (somatology, prehistory, biometrics), psychology (human and comparative, pure and applied), the pure social sciences (comparative religion, law, economics, linguistics), and the applied social sciences (political science, international law). Faced with problems resulting from dispersion and a lack of resources, Mauss sought a solution that privileged university institutes over private foundations or institutes. Doing so would allow each of the sectors to cluster various research institutions at the Université de Paris and "increase the number of workers and research projects."

Constructing a new building for the human sciences as a whole would be ideal, but Mauss said it would also be possible to exert a "preponderant and organizing" influence on the various establishments and institutes "by subsidizing their work and the staff assigned to it and by improving their equipment and subsidizing their publications." For each group of disciplines, Mauss proposed to reorganize research by locating it in institutes at the Université de Paris: for psychology, the Institut de Psychologie; for anthropology and ethnology, the Institut d'Ethnologie. In addition, there would be a new research institute in the social sciences.

This last project was the most ambitious, especially if, as Mauss wished, one was committed to placing the new institute in a desirable location and to creating a sixth section—of economic and social sciences—at the École Pratique des Hautes Études. "The unity of the social sciences will be demonstrated only when all teachers and all students, whatever their area of specialization in that vast field, are obliged to meet, and do meet, in a place where the material means for work and contact have been expanded."[64]

A goal of this sort might seem utopian. Mauss thought that such an institute could begin operations and research immediately, even without any buildings. He proposed that a survey of the city of Paris, similar to the one the Laura Spelman Foundation had funded in Chicago, be set in motion right away. Such an initiative, if done quickly, "would be a monument of sociological science and would immediately make the future institute renowned in Paris and France as a whole."

The Rockefeller Foundation was under the influence of Charles Rist, who considered Mauss "essentially a politician who produces nothing on his own."[65] The foundation deemed Mauss's report unusable, though it contained some useful information. Criticisms multiplied. The project was too far-reaching; it did not define its program or its methods precisely; and it was not explicitly aimed at better social control. In the end, Rist prevailed. His plan for an institute based on a quantitative and empirical research program devoted to contemporary economic and social life corresponded more precisely to the foundation's expectations. In 1931 that plan was awarded a $350,000 grant for a period not to exceed seven years.

The Strict Duty of the Militant

When *Populaire* began to appear again in 1927, Mauss agreed to do his "strict duty." He subscribed and continued to participate on the administrative and management board. He was dreaming of a "major newspaper" for the party, a newspaper with a large circulation that could compete with *Humanité*. "Let us appeal to the spirit of enterprise and at the same time to the spirit of sacrifice," he wrote to the newspaper's director. "Let us spur enthusiasm. Major efforts—long, hard, and relentless—are the only ones worthy of the working and peasant classes and of our party. A dreary duty is performed half-heartedly."[66]

At *Populaire*, Mauss renewed contact with Adéodat Compère-Morel, its administrative director whom he had known a long time. The two were the same age, and both were longtime socialist militants and ardent defenders of the cooperative movement. But the twists and turns of Compère-Morel's political career did not always make relations easy. He had begun as a Guesdist and was a specialist in agrarian questions and an active propagandist. During the war he joined the right wing of the SFIO, only to ally himself later on with its left wing. In addition, Compère-Morel's antipathy toward Léon Blum, the newspaper's political editor, made for a tense atmosphere at the paper. Mauss quickly became discouraged. He was not alone, Blum too was "extremely pessimistic."[67]

Although Mauss agreed to "continue the meager sacrifice of time and money [he] was still capable of," he did so only "from a sense of duty and while waiting to see what would happen."[68] In spite of everything, he still had "faith, a belief in his ideas and in his people." He was still "attracted to action and even to politics." He participated regularly at meetings of the SFIO's fifth branch. That branch, rebuilt by Déat after 1920, had about a hundred members at the time, for the most part intellectuals, teachers, students, and wage laborers.[69] Those close to Mauss could not avoid asking him: "Why don't you run for office? Why don't you try to get elected to Parliament?" His attitude toward politics was still that of a "belated romantic," as he himself said. "We socialists don't need careers. You don't know the joy of militant action. As union members, cooperators, and members of our party, we can act within our organizations, create things ourselves and lead others to create them, without being in the spotlight."[70]

The model Mauss embraced was less that of a politician or a party man than that of the engagé intellectual. Lucien Herr, a longtime friend Mauss saw often and was very fond of, embodied that model. Mauss admired Herr's "intense passions," "his violent reaction to evil and especially to error, his boundless devotion to truth, to the good, and to friendship." He saw him as a sort of saint, as he wrote to Halévy: "Herr believed in life within a group, work in common, rational self-sacrifice. But he criticized everything, reacted at every instant. He believed that the wise man must also hold back, withdraw from the mob, live a separate life—an aristocratic life if you like. His chief aim was to be a model for us all. He succeeded. He was an active intellectual worker, but a good worker enthralled with the individual masterpiece."[71]

In Mauss's view, the SFIO, which struck compromises with the bourgeoisie, seemed "too ingenuous, too purely intellectual," when compared to the communists, who, once their party had become Bolshevized, had sought to root themselves deeper in the working world.[72] When the Parti Communiste adopted a sectarian, "class warfare" tactic, it took a harder line against the Parti Socialiste: supporting Socialist candidates in the second round of voting, if communist candidates had been eliminated, was now out of the question.

"Oh, if only Jaurès were here," thought Mauss, still confident, but more critical than ever of his party, reproaching it for committing "major errors, particularly against Herriot with regard to the Rhône federation"[73] and for not having a "strong workers' policy." "It's a long way from the working class of 1920," he lamented. The "old militant" got angry at Blum during the 1928 electoral campaign when Blum, breaking with an old "tradition," supported the attorney Maurice Delphine in Puteaux against the laborer Jacotot, mayor of that city.

In the 1928 elections, the socialists consolidated their position, however, with more than 1,700,000 votes in the first round. But the communists' tactic cost the Left votes and allowed the right wing to win back the majority of seats. Blum was defeated in the Charonne–Père Lachaise district by Jacques Duclos, a communist militant. Duclos's recent conviction "for anarchist acts" had made him a regular Robin Hood. The following year, Édouard Daladier, head of the radical Left, offered the SFIO participation in the government on the basis of a true leftist platform. Blum, reelected in a by-election, opposed the plan but was outvoted by his own parliamentary group. Nevertheless, he managed narrowly to win the support of his party's national committee.

The socialists' participation in the government did not bother Mauss. All in all, it was a secondary question that had to be analyzed in terms of the historical circumstances. Some of his friends, classmates, and students were members of other parties. He preferred open and frank discussion to confrontation: "One of the charms of life in Paris and of French urbanity is that they allow people of every party to converse freely and—except for the communists, let us say—even frankly. People clash, challenge one another, examine one another with the utmost courtesy, and often even with respect."[74]

In August 1929 Mauss resigned from the administrative and management board of *Populaire*, where he had served as a member "of the party newspaper since 1904, six months after *Humanité* was founded." The minority current, with Renaudel and Déat in the lead, were demanding proportionate representation on the administrative board of *Populaire* and in party management. Even as he reaffirmed his devotion to the newspaper, to which he pledged 500 francs, Mauss declared he "would joyfully return to his post as soon as the friends he was following at that moment also reclaimed their places."[75] As he would later say, the circles he frequented at *Populaire*, in the fifth section of the École, and at the federation of the Vosges, had become "not suffocating, but uninteresting."[76]

PART
IV

RECOGNITION

T HE YEARS surrounding 1930 were a turning point in France, marked by the demise of several political figures: Georges Clemenceau and Ferdinand Foch in 1929, Joseph Joffre in 1931, Aristide Briand in 1932. A new generation took charge of the French government, as the second-largest colonial empire continued to enjoy great intellectual and political prestige. The Colonial Exposition took place in 1931; the Nobel Prize was awarded to the philosopher Henri Bergson in 1928 and to Louis de Broglie, father of wave mechanics, the following year. Paris was an international capital of arts and letters and welcomed many foreigners: Picasso, Henry Miller, Hemingway, Fitzgerald.

Although the country was not yet in the grips of a depression, the future was ominous, with the stock market crash, the dominance of machines, the decline of liberal and humanist values. It was the end of an era. Should it be called a crisis of civilization? The expression was on everyone's lips. In May 1929 the theme for the First International Synthesis Week held by Henri Berr was "Civilization: The Word and the Idea." The discussions were scientific, of course, but, as Mauss noted, they also addressed the political problems intellectuals had been debating since World War I.

In his lecture "Civilizations: Elements and Forms," Mauss criticized various ethnological theories, proposed definitions, and captivated his audience by speaking of necktie knots, collars, the angle at which a neck is held, gait, fashion, the use of English spades.[1] His perspective was clearly relativistic: "Every social phenomenon has one essential attribute:. . . it is arbitrary. All social phenomena are to some degree the work of the collective will, and to speak of human will is to invoke a choice between different possibilities. . . . The realm of the social is the realm of modality."[2]

Hence there are civilizations. So long as humanity does not form a single society, there will be cultural diversity. The civilization philosophers and politicians speak of is only a dream, if not a myth. Mauss concluded that such bric-a-brac stems from ideology, ethnocentrism: "Naturally, that civilization is always Western," he added. "It is elevated to the level of a shared ideal and seen as the rational foundation for human progress; and, with a little optimism added, it is made the condition of happiness."[3]

Once he had clarified these matters, Mauss allowed himself to use the word *civilization* in its ordinary sense and to speak of progress or, more precisely, of "novelty": "It seems to me that it is now in the facts and not in ideology that something like civilization comes about. First, although nations are not disappearing, though they are not even all formed yet, a growing capital of international realities and ideas is being constituted. The international nature of the facts of civilization is intensifying."[4] Mauss was particularly impressed by progress in the sciences and the new forms of communication—film, the phonograph, wireless telephony. And this was only the beginning: "Humanity's capital is growing in any case. . . . Nothing prevents us from saying that that is what civilization is. Unquestionably, all nations and civilizations are currently moving toward something more, something stronger, more universal, and more rational."[5] He did not say, however, that such a common foundation could be constituted without violence—national violence, national arrogance—or that it necessarily led to happiness.

What did the future hold? The spirit of the 1930s would be marked by refusal: a revolt against the nature of things, a search for a third way between capitalism and communism, a glorification of the community. Mauss would feel the weariness of an old militant; he would have some personal success and would earn "a little glory," but he would also lose his last illusions about love and about politics.

15

A PLACE AT THE COLLÈGE DE FRANCE

I N SPITE OF the 1909 setback, Mauss had not lost all hope of teaching at the Collège de France. Fifteen years later, he still aspired to find his place in that "refuge of freedom, independence, and pure science." And it is true that no chair conferred more authority.[1]

Mauss could boast of new accomplishments: he had relaunched *Année Sociologique*, had published "The Gift," had founded the Institut d'Ethnologie. His renown was international: he had given a lecture, "The Notion of Primitive Civilization," in Oslo in December 1925; had been elected Honorary Fellow of the Royal Anthropological Institute;[2] had delivered university lectures in Davos, Switzerland ("New Methods of Ethnography," "Results of Ethnographic Methods," "New Problems in Ethnography"), where he had met Albert Einstein; and had been invited to give three lectures in English at the London School of Economics in June 1928, on the theory of the elementary forms of prayer in Australia.

But with regard to the Collège, he had to wait until circumstances were favorable. In 1925 two different proposals for a chair in ethnography were made; but because the proposals came from Alfred Loisy, they received no support. It seemed to be an open question as to who would succeed the numismatist Théodore Reinach (1862–1928), whose position became available in November 1928. Some, including Lucien Lévy-Bruhl, thought that ethnography or ethnology ought to have its chair and that Mauss ought to be designated to fill it. Antoine Meillet, who had been a professor of comparative grammar at the Collège since 1906, believed likewise.[3] It would be a delicate maneuver. After considering it, Mauss preferred to wait until Jean Izoulet or Alfred Loisy retired: "My fundamental impression is that, unless you disagree, it's better if you sit this round out without doing anything but speak of me. . . . I'd probably be wasting my time with a risky candidacy, whereas a little patience might put me in a good position to apply for one of the chairs that will ultimately become vacant."[4]

In the end, it was abbé Henri Breuil (1877–1961), professor of prehistoric ethnography at the Institut de Paléontologie Humaine, who succeeded Reinach. He was supported by Édouard Le Roy and prevailed in the sixth round of voting. Studies in prehistory became part of the Collège before ethnology.

Izoulet's Successor

When Jean Izoulet, who occupied the chair in social philosophy, died a few months later, people naturally looked to Mauss. No one had forgotten that the chair of social philosophy should have gone to Émile Durkheim in 1897. The father of French sociology had not been appointed. Some thirty years later, the nephew was well placed to save the honor of the French school of sociology. Nothing was predetermined, however, though Mauss benefited from solid support. In addition to Meillet, there was Sylvain Lévi (Sanskrit language and literature), who had backed Mauss's candidacy against Loisy in 1909. There were also other former professors and colleagues: for example, Louis Finot (Indochinese history and philology), Alexandre Moret (Egyptology), and Gabriel Millet (aesthetics and art history). Mauss could also count on the friends of friends and on "co-religionists"—Jacques Hadamard, professor of mechanical engineering; André Mayer, professor of natural history—not to mention the professors Mauss had associated with in political circles. In particular, there was Charles Andler (German language and literature) and Paul Langevin, professor of general and experimental physics, who had allied himself with the socialists in 1913 against the three-year military service law. There were also two "newcomers," Charles Gide, who held the teaching chair in co-operation, and Georges Renard, who occupied the chair in the history of labor. But was it enough? Mauss was fifty-eight years old: this was his last chance.[5]

There was a little of everything at the Collège de France: scientists and literary types, priests and atheists, people on the right and on the left, sons of distinguished leaders and sons of peasants. Four tracks converged: scholarship (École Pratique des Hautes Études, Bibliothèque Nationale, museums, French schools abroad), scientific research (laboratories at the École and at the Collège, engineering schools), universities, and the politico-administrative network (a few chairs were established by fiat).

Ordinarily, a vacancy at the Collège unleashed a flood of competition not only in Paris but in the provinces as well.[6] The campaign involved two stages: first the discipline the chair would fall under was defined and then the appointment in the strict sense was made. But everything was played out in the first phase. The second was usually a mere formality.

Mauss quickly received the expected support. Andler wrote him: "I believe this is an excellent opportunity for you and you must seize it."[7] His former adversary, Alfred Loisy, had "no objection" to his applying for a chair in sociology to replace Izoulet: "It's completely natural."[8] Finally, Finot, who was on an expedition abroad, was "sorry to be too far away to cast his vote," but he hoped Mauss would replace Izoulet.

Some professors, however, were reluctant to support Mauss's candidacy. Charles Fossey, for example, had lost out to Hubert by a few votes at the

École Pratique des Hautes Études and hence was not inclined to support Mauss now. He explained to Mauss that since his decision was made, there "was nothing more for him to do than to wish [Mauss] good luck, regretting he couldn't help [him]."[9] It was therefore necessary to redouble efforts, multiply contacts, establish a real plan of action.

Friends outside the Collège intervened, including, of course, Lucien Lévy-Bruhl, the only one in a position to persuade Pierre Janet, who had already committed himself to backing a different candidate. Salomon Reinach, a member of the Institut de France, also promised to "support Mauss's candidacy by every means."[10] Everyone gave Mauss a great deal of advice: to visit one professor or another at the Collège, to make sure that still another would be at the meeting. From Châteaumeillant in Cher, Meillet was "absolutely only for Mauss," and closely followed the campaign as it unfolded, suggesting the course to be followed.[11]

In the autumn of 1929, "the situation seemed to be favorable, even very favorable, as rumor had it."[12] Mauss was optimistic when he returned to Paris after a rough vacation in Épinal—a young cousin had died; his mother's state of health was "worrisome"; Hubert's *Celts* was published only with difficulty. Once he had nearly finished his visits to the faculty members at the Collège, he began calmly to compose his statement of qualifications.[13]

In presenting his qualifications and writings, each candidate was supposed to take into account his strengths and weaknesses and adapt his statement to the intellectual context of the debate (the name of the chair and the qualifications of the various candidates). What to emphasize was an especially delicate matter since the candidate was addressing an audience that was heterogeneous in its intellectual and political formation and orientation. Mauss followed the advice Sylvain Lévi and Meillet had given him, opting to be brief and to confine himself to the essential: the titles of his publications, a presentation of his "critical work" at *Année*, a few titles of courses he had taught, and a few titles of works by other people where his collaboration had been "major and useful." He subsequently wrote in *Revue de Paris* that he had given no information on his political articles, "not even those on Bolshevism or the cooperative movement."[14]

After his statement of qualifications and writings was printed up, Mauss added a note about his "four years and five months of war service, including twenty days short of four years in combat units." The presentation of his writings was divided into two major parts, original studies and critical studies, with the second part including both book reviews and the lengthy methodological notes published in *Année Sociologique*. In terms both of his teaching and of his publications, Mauss directed the Collège faculty's attention to his three fields of interest: the history of religion, descriptive ethnology, and sociology.

But he was not the only one in the race. There was also Georges Blondel. Since he had been Izoulet's temporary replacement for several years, there was a danger he would look like Izoulet's legitimate successor. And there was Étienne Gilson, a specialist in medieval philosophy associated with the revival of Thomism. After making their intentions known, all other candidates withdrew or were persuaded to withdraw. This was the case for the historian Albert Mathiez: Charles Andler persuaded him to withdraw, even though he was aware of his "great value." For a time, Lucien Febvre, professor of history at the Université de Strasbourg, was also tempted to apply.[15] He explained his position to "dear Mauss": He certainly was not eager to "jump back into a very dubious campaign" or to "undermine" Mauss or "complicate the task" before him. But he worried about the initiative of other colleagues and was afraid "of being led to take a position in spite of [him]self." He added it would be done not out of some "muddleheaded (and no doubt tactless) ambition but out of a legitimate desire" to hold on to his chances for the future.[16] When he learned two days later that Mathiez was not in the competition, Febvre withdrew and wished Mauss good luck. He told Mauss his application would do more than draw a majority of the votes: it would be "close to unanimous."

The first question, the designation of the chair, was less simple to settle than some might have believed. Social philosophy, sociology, or ethnology? For abbé Breuil, the new professor of prehistory, sociology was out of the question, since "there are already a number of chairs so designated." In particular, there was a chair in Muslim sociology, first occupied by Alfred Le Chatelier from 1919 to 1924 and, beginning in 1926, by Louis Massignon. From Breuil's point of view, Mauss did "ethnic sociology or social ethnology."[17] Meillet also identified Mauss with ethnology, and believed that ethnology was better than sociology and that the designation "Methods and Sociology" would be disastrous.[18] Mauss believed "nothing [was] better than sociology" but acknowledged the objections.

Although he was very aware "that ethnology is the best designation for getting the appointment," Mauss was inclined to use it "only in the event of danger." "If I still have some time left to live, I am resolved to take a step back from primitive tribes and it's a moral torment to be limited to them at this point."[19]

Neither the "sociology" nor the "ethnology" designation would be proposed. Mauss's sponsor, Sylvain Lévi, spoke in favor of maintaining the chair of social philosophy.[20] Paradoxically, Georges Blondel, Jean Izoulet's temporary replacement, wanted to change the chair. "Questions of social philosophy and sociology have already been examined thoroughly and have led to the publication of a large number of books," he explained. "The creation of a chair devoted to the study of Europe's political and economic organization seems useful to me."[21] This was precisely the theme of the classes he had taught at the Collège for two years. In 1927–1928 he had analyzed changes in Europe since the war; in 1928–1929, changes in mentality and the consequences of demographic growth in Poland, Czechoslovakia, and Yugoslavia.

At the meeting of November 6, 1929, the Collège faculty were supposed to discuss three proposals for the name of the chair: the political and economic organization of Europe, the history of medieval philosophy, and social philosophy. This meant that at least three candidates had presented their "writings and qualifications" and had managed to convince others of the value of their candidacies. In addition to Georges Blondel and Mauss, there was Étienne Gilson, as Lucien Febvre had predicted. Gilson was born in 1884; he was an *agrégé* in philosophy (1907, ranked sixth) and a doctor in letters (1913). Since 1921 he had been a lecturer in the history of medieval philosophy at the faculty of letters in Paris and the *directeur d'études* for medieval theology and philosophy in the fifth section at the École Pratique des Hautes Études. He was a Catholic philosopher well known for his books on Saint Thomas Aquinas and Saint Augustine.

In the first round, the political and economic organization of Europe (Blondel) received only two votes. The vote was very close for the other two chairs: twenty for the history of medieval philosophy (Gilson) and twenty-two for social philosophy (Mauss). In the second round, the two votes for Europe's political and economic organization went to the history of philosophy and placed Gilson and Mauss in a tie, with twenty-two votes apiece. The next ballot was postponed. The following day, Andler analyzed the situation: "The Collège faculty has sensitivities I don't yet understand."[22]

This lack of victory can be explained by the absence of certain professors— Louis Finot, William Marçais, Alexandre Moret, and Henri Maspero—who might have supported Mauss and by the strong support that had been mobilized on behalf of his competitors. Paul Hazard, for example, was staying in England, but made an enormous effort to come vote for Gilson. The failure could also be explained, said Mauss's friends, by "certain lies." Although they had "underestimated the strength of their adversaries," Mauss's allies were ultimately glad they had "gathered enough votes to reach a stalemate."[23]

The campaign had to begin again. Bouglé wrote: "I learned about the 22–22 vote . . . at the goddamn Collège. Let's hope the flu and the junkets will work in your favor at the next one. Nonetheless, the opposing clan is strong. All the more reason to redouble our energies."[24] Mauss was perplexed: "I don't hate battle . . . I like only honorable defeats. . . . I don't like pointless battles. I was never optimistic about this business. Even now I'd have no hope if I didn't interpret the voting in a completely different way from you. . . . You can be sure that I'll willingly sacrifice the minimal ambition to teach at the Collège for the sake of my work and tranquility."[25] He also did not rule out "giving up on this business." But then Gilson decided to withdraw his candidacy.[26]

Nothing had been accomplished, however. Mauss could still count on the group of professors who supported him and whose "loyalty is of such long standing that it is unshakable." But what about the opposing camp, which was in fact very heterogeneous? William Marçais wondered whether it "would allow itself to dissolve," and decided: "It's possible." In any case, it was clear it would all come down to just a few votes.[27] At the faculty meeting of January 12, 1930, there were only two proposals, but the designations had changed: on the one hand, a chair in the history of social philosophy, defended by Édouard Le Roy; on the other, a chair of sociology, defended by Sylvain Lévi and receiving the explicit support of Jacques Hadamard and Meillet. Almost the entire faculty was present. In the first round, there was a tie, twenty to twenty, with three abstentions. Same result in the second round. The decision again had to be postponed.

Why had this happened, just when everyone thought the withdrawal of Gilson's candidacy would result in an agreement between some of his supporters and those of Mauss? As Halbwachs remarked, there was obviously a scheme "that did not fail completely but did not entirely succeed. A provocation of that sort would turn against its authors if there were any order to the world."[28]

Meillet further explained that Mauss's friends had run up against several "prejudices"—"one conservative (Le Roy), another antisociological (Hazard, etc.), a third personal against [Mauss] perhaps."[29] When joined together, they formed a bloc that was difficult to budge. Le Roy's opposition was the most dangerous, because the faithful and militant Catholic, an *agrégé* in mathematics and Bergson's successor, was "the most powerful force at the Collège."

Mauss was the first to be "outraged and exasperated." All his friends had the same reaction. Halbwachs wrote him: "I'm outraged and painfully distressed as well, not only for your sake, but because one is outraged and distressed every time one discovers men are more fanatical and mediocre than one believed."[30] Henri Lévy-Bruhl was also "disgusted, outraged at what has happened." "I didn't think the 'churchies' were so strong at the Collège, but they must be blinded by passion to give you and Chevalier the same weight."[31] It wasn't funny, added Abel Rey, another supporter. It was quite simply scandalous.[32]

Was trying to enter a "house" that was a regular "hovel," and where "the usher at Saint-Sulpice has every chance of success if he condescends to apply," even worth the trouble?[33] For the honor of French sociology, which Mauss represented "brilliantly," his friends hoped he would not give up. As Halbwachs insisted: "One must nevertheless press on forever."[34] Mauss did not for a moment consider sitting out his turn once again.

Since the Collège faculty was not set to meet again until June, both camps had five months to prepare for battle.

An Interlude in Morocco

In late March 1930, while his future at the Collège de France hung in the balance, Mauss left for Morocco. He had several personal reasons for the trip, which he hoped would be "beneficial for [him], a poor traveler who needs a little rest."[35] He also had professional reasons: the Institut d'Ethnologie had received a 10,000-franc grant from the French protectorate of Morocco. The trip's objective was twofold: "to visit the Institut des Hautes Études in Rabat and hold a class there" and "to advise the representative general of Morocco regarding ethnographic services in Morocco."

Mauss was somewhat familiar with the country, having read some of the late Edmond Doutté's works, which had become classics (*En Tribu, Marrakech*; In the tribe; Marrakech),[36] as well as books by Robert Montagne and his students.[37] One of them, Charles Le Coeur, had recently been named *maître de conférence* of ethnography at the Institut des Hautes Études in Rabat. He was completing an essay titled "The Moral Character of West African Cults."[38] Mauss consulted Le Coeur when organizing his trip: "I don't like sightseeing and I'm not particularly fond of pontificating in official circles or strolling around luxury hotels in a dinner jacket."[39] He thus did not intend to be "just a tourist": he wanted "to make inquiries before giving advice."[40] And in Marrakech he wanted at all cost to see the Haoussa dancers of Bori.

The schedule Mauss finally agreed to included a lecture in Rabat, plus three days in Fez, one day in Meknes, and a few excursions around Marrakech. His lecture in Rabat was on organizing ethnographic collections and allowed him to give "some unofficial advice" and to suggest that an ethnographic museum be created in Morocco. "We must hurry," he said. "In a few years, the most unusual techniques, the most singular utensils and products will have completely vanished." Mauss was able to observe on his own "the admirable labor" of the Mtougalla potters and was amazed at the "infinitely beautiful products" woven almost completely by hand by Glaoui women.

Mauss made no claim to competence: "I know too little to speak at length." In the account he gave to the Institut Français d'Anthropologie on his return, he confined himself to presenting "a few remarks for [his] personal edification."[41] First, he expressed the view that "Morocco is not and has never been an Arab country": "Five-sixths of the population is Berber, with the rest composed of six hundred thousand Arabs or Arabized people, approximately one hundred thousand Jews, and one hundred thousand Europeans. It's true that all the Berbers are Islamized, that many speak Arabic, and that even more read the Koran. But they are not Arabs from the somatological point of view, or from the linguistic point of view, or from the standpoint of civilization and social organization."[42]

Contact with Arab and Berber civilizations inspired Mauss to make a more general, theoretical remark: "A civilization must be defined more by its deficiencies, its shortcomings, its refusal to borrow, than from what it has borrowed, the points it shares with others . . . its identical industries."[43] In Morocco, whether in joinery, weaving, or haberdashery, there was a "curious mix of skill and ignorance."

For Mauss, the most important thing was that he had achieved his "personal goal" of visiting one of the Negro brotherhoods of Bori. He met with a "good old" sheikh in Marrakech, spoke with him for hours, and received his blessing. It was an "instructive sociological experience." Aware that his contribution to the ethnographic study of Morocco was inadequate, Mauss would formulate just one wish: "We must observe these societies. . . . There is no doubt that we will thereby immediately collect key documents both for sociology and for human history, and perhaps even for the history of African peoples in general."[44] Apart from these "few words," he said, he would not publish anything else on his "fieldwork" in Morocco.

Victory at Last

In the weeks preceding the faculty meeting at the Collège de France, Mauss's allies again mobilized. At the last minute, they had to make sure that all his supporters would be there. Loisy, for example, was taking a break in Champagne,[45] and Georges Renard had to be brought to Paris by car from eighty kilometers away. Since everyone knew that "things would hang on a very few votes," no one wanted to undermine Mauss's candidacy by being absent. Confidence grew, since Mauss could now count on his friends whose absence had been felt during the earlier votes: Moret, Marçais, Finot, and Maspero would all be there.[46]

At the June 15 meeting, it was agreed that Andler, and not Sylvain Lévi, would be Mauss's advocate. But since it would be a true "counteroffensive," he wanted backup: "Meillet must come across forcefully. I would stress the philosophical aspect of your work, about which little has been said. . . . It would be unfortunate if Meillet did not speak up. I hardly think I can succeed on my own, when Meillet and Sylvain Lévi did not. But I'll fight with the intention of winning."[47] Andler and Meillet would thus defend the proposal to create a chair in sociology. Pierre Janet would also speak to the matter. The two other proposed chairs, in the history of French philosophy and in the history of medieval philosophy, were supported by Édouard Le Roy and Louis Massignon, respectively.

Andler proved to be a "capable advocate" and gave a "perfect presentation."[48] Since the philosophy section at the Collège was small, in the first part of his presentation he attempted to show the "philosophical interest" in teaching sociology as Mauss could do. He believed he was justified in proceeding in that way, especially since he sensed a "bias against Durkheimian sociology in general" among some of his colleagues. He confided: "I once shared that bias, which was as profound and complete as you can imagine. To free my conscience, I'd like to tell you how I got over it." Before speaking of the nephew, then, he had to settle matters with the uncle.

Andler explained that he had once disliked the idea of a "single consciousness," had not believed it possible to analyze the "social soul," the "social psyche," unless, like Boas, one had "direct ethnographic experience," had spent "long periods of time among primitive people," and had acquired a "very refined knowledge of the nuances of their language." In short, before "moving on to synthesis," one had to "do pure ethnography for fifty years." But he changed his mind when he became aware of how complex the demands of science were: "Science demands synthesis even before the analyses of the facts collected are complete, so as to focus these analyses." According to Andler, Durkheim's "analytical genius" was that he had "succeeded in seeing things more clearly than the worker on site but unskilled in his methods." His *Elementary Forms of Religious Life* was a "fine specimen of what the power of analysis can be."[49]

Such were the "foundations" of an edifice "under construction." Everything was "subject to reflection," as attested by Lucien Lévy-Bruhl's studies on the prelogical mentality, which "expanded Durkheim's sociology," and by studies of Durkheim's writings, especially by Hubert and Mauss, which were "suffused" with Pierre Janet's scientific psychology and still in touch with Bergson's philosophy.

Once Durkheim and his school had been introduced, Andler proceeded to the second part of his presentation: praise for the man who represented a discipline that had been "expanded, [that was] not yet constructed but under construction." This was Marcel Mauss, of course, "the acknowledged leader of the surviving group of Durkheim's students." His chief intellectual qualities were such that Andler ventured to say he was "better equipped" than Durkheim, with whom he had "always collaborated." Mauss had an "extraordinary capacity for work, a rare abnegation, a mind of vast scope," a knowledge of several ancient languages, complete training as an ethnographer, competence as a museographer, and a commitment to "constantly revise the very rules of method." He had the capacity to "admit mistakes, which are inseparable from creativity," and "the art of correcting them." In short, he had everything needed to produce significant work.

Andler cited most of Mauss's writings. It was, he said, "an imposing body of work, made more significant by what it promises. At stake is a science and a new form of speculation whose object had to be created along with its method." Mauss had to be given the "means to fully realize his potential" while "his capacity for work is still intact."

Choosing Mauss, then, would not only secure him a "lofty reputation," it would also make it possible for him to "complete a body of work" and "train a new group driven by the same passion and sense of fraternity that, in Durkheim's old workshop, [allowed for] the constant exchange of ideas, mutual supervision, harsh criticism in the reconstruction of the facts and, beyond their reconstruction, in the art of interpreting them." Finally—this was a barely veiled threat—for the Collège de France it was the last opportunity not to overlook "one of the most original segments of science and French philosophy, disciplines that bring the greatest honor to the country" and "not to close itself off forever to what in other countries is admiringly called the French school of sociology."[50]

However eloquent Andler's argument may have been, it did not convince everyone. Far from it. "Lady Sociology," as Finot noted ironically, made her entrance at the Collège only after three rounds of voting and with a small majority: twenty-one for sociology in the first round, twenty-three in the second, and twenty-four in the third. Finot's and Maspero's presence was the determining factor. They were, wrote Mauss, "the architects of my definitive success at the Collège. I owe my victory to the EFEO [École Française d'Extrême-Orient]."[51] It was, to be sure, a "hard-won" victory "with a half-vote majority," but what joy and above all, what a relief.[52] For the Durkheimians, it was a "decisive event, all the more decisive because the resistance was stiff."[53]

Once the chair in sociology was created, tensions eased. Mauss said: "It seems to me that the situation will be uncomplicated and that my friends will not have to do as much as they have in the past."[54] But they had to co-ordinate their actions to get a candidate from the group named *en seconde ligne*. It appeared that Georges Davy had friends at the Collège and sought to step forward. Maurice Halbwachs, annoyed by Davy's gambit, was reluctant to "get involved in a tilting match with and against Davy,"[55] since he had to go off to the United States. For Mauss, the question was rapidly resolved: in the end, the candidate *en seconde ligne* would be Halbwachs, professor at the Institut de Philosophie attached to the Université de Strasbourg. This friend and close collaborator on the new series of *Année Sociologique* would have preferred "to remain on the sidelines," but he was willing to "do a service" for Mauss, who "more naturally thought of [him] than of Davy."[56]

The final vote to fill the chair in sociology would be held at the faculty meeting of November 29, 1930. The day before, Mauss's mother died in her home on rue Sadi-Carnot in Épinal; she was eighty-two. Thus she never knew the result of the deliberations. In addition to her son, there were two candidates: André Joussain, professor of philosophy at the Périgueux *lycée*,[57] and Dr. Papillault, professor of anthropology at the École Pratique des Hautes Études. As predicted, Halbwachs, with Andler as his sponsor, applied only *en seconde ligne*. This time Mauss was defended by Meillet and it was Janet who presented the qualifications and writings of the other two candidates. Mauss won in the first round with twenty-four votes, versus ten for Papillault and two for Joussain. It took two rounds to arrive at a candidate *en seconde ligne*: Halbwachs received eighteen votes in the first and twenty-two in the second.

The battle for the Collège de France was "long and tough," but ended well. On February 3, 1931, the president of the Republic, on the recommendation of the minister of public education and the fine arts, appointed Mauss to the chair of sociology to replace Jean Izoulet. As Edgard Milhaud pointed out, his friend Mauss owed his access to the fortress to his "enormous labor, guided by a revolutionary scientific vision." He could now hope "for many years there to train the younger generations in the methods of the science to which [he] has given [his] life."[58]

The Guru

Mauss delivered his opening lecture to the Collège on February 23, 1931. The hall was packed, as his student Jacques Soustelle reported, and Mauss sought to mark the event by paying tribute to "his ancestors from the rabbinical schools of Alsace and Lorraine."[59] It was "a dazzling lecture"[60] and at the same time, commented Finot, an "extremely private celebration" for those who had worked on Mauss's behalf.[61] Finot, living in Var, could not conceal his admiration for the "activism" of the new professor at the Collège: "Six or seven classes a week! Wow!"

In addition to teaching at the École Pratique and the Institut d'Ethnologie, Mauss began a series of seventeen conferences at the Collège. Preferring the seminar to the lecture format, he refused to speak in a lecture hall, insisting on a room equipped with a large table. As at the École des Hautes Études, his method consisted of commenting on the book of a missionary or explorer. Soustelle recounted: "We were few in number (a half-dozen usually), grouped around him there. . . . It was a marvel to contemplate that vigorous and supremely free thought, agile and powerful, in its nascent state so to speak, sometimes like a torrent leaping from rock to rock, sometimes like a wide peaceful river."[62]

Mauss's first course was "The Observation of General Phenomena in the Collective Life of Societies of the Archaic Type," a continuation and expansion of the course he was teaching at the Institut d'Ethnologie. He identified his objects of study: the phenomena of national life (social cohesion, education, and tradition), international phenomena (war and peace, phenomena of civilization), and collective psychology (mentality and collective relations). He was deeply absorbed in preparing the course. "I did it on one of the most difficult and newest questions available to me, and I didn't begin to breathe easy until May."[63] Mauss would get an essay from that effort and would publish it in *Annales Sociologiques* under the title "Fragment of an Outline for a Descriptive General Sociology."

The next year Mauss used the forum provided him by the Collège to pay tribute to Durkheim. He expounded ideas on "civic and professional ethics" that his uncle had developed, first in Bordeaux and then at the Sorbonne shortly before his death. At the time Mauss intended to begin publishing that part of Durkheim's work but, for lack of time and strength, he would publish only three of his uncle's lectures devoted to the subject (and not until 1937) in *Revue de Métaphysique et de Morale*, accompanied by a brief introduction.[64] In the following years Mauss presented the writings of his deceased colleagues and friends, in particular Hertz's "Sin and Expiation in Inferior Societies" and Hubert's "Germanic Civilization and Peoples." He also began to study the relation between certain games (kite flying, greased-pole climbing) and the cosmological myths that accompanied them in archaic societies (Polynesia, North America). He addressed these themes in some of his seminars at the École Pratique des Hautes Études.

Marcel Mauss's Courses at the Collège de France, 1931–1940

Winter 1931
   Observation of General Phenomena of Collective Life in Societies of the
      Archaic Type
1931–1932
   Exposition of Durkheim's Doctrine on Civic and Professional Ethics
   The Use of the Notion of the Primitive in Sociology and in the General
      History of Civilization
1932–1933
   Restatement and Updating of Robert Hertz's Unpublished Research on Sin
      and Expiation in Inferior Societies
1933–1934
   Sin and Expiation in Inferior Societies
1934–1935
   Sin and Expiation in Inferior Societies
   Henri Hubert's Work on Civilization and the Germanic Peoples
1935–1936
   Sin and Expiation in Inferior Societies
   The Formation of Germanic Peoples: Research on Law
1936–1937
   Sin and Expiation in Inferior Societies: The Formation of Germanic
      Civilizations
1937–1938
   The Relations between Certain Games and Cosmology

The Germanics (*continued*): Research on Germanic law and religion
1938–1939
  Indian Games
  The Germanics
1939–1940
  Cosmology and Games
  The Germanics

At a professional level, joining the faculty at the Collège de France offered undeniable advantages. Mauss's salary increased from 45,900 francs in 1930 (at the École Pratique), to 72,000 francs in 1934.[65] In addition there was the stipend he received as *directeur d'études* at the École Pratique (12,000 francs) and for his teaching at the Institut d'Ethnologie (thirty lectures at 300 francs apiece). Mauss kept his modest apartment, however, four rooms in a seven-floor walkup on rue Bruller.

His integration into the Collège was made easier by the presence of several of his friends: Sylvain Lévi, Meillet, Andler. The new professor complained of only one thing regarding the prestigious institution: its organization. "It's all poorly conceived, needs a reappraisal, especially for the social sciences."[66] The new appointee participated in turn in the appointment of others. He was consulted, courted. André Siegfried, Étienne Gilson, Jean Baruzi, Lucien Febvre, Marc Bloch, Georges Dumézil, and Paul Mantoux all wrote him and requested interviews. Former friends and politicians, including Jean Longuet, also wrote Mauss, hoping to influence his decisions.[67]

Between 1930 and 1935, about fifteen new professors joined the Collège de France. Jean Przyluski, *directeur d'études* at the École Pratique and temporary replacement at the Collège, became professor of Indochinese history and philology. In 1932 Gilson and Febvre were appointed, the first to the chair of medieval history and philosophy, the second to the chair in the history of modern civilization. In 1933 it was Isidore Lévy's turn (ancient history of the Semitic East). The same year, Jean Baruzi succeeded Alfred Loisy (history of religion); Paul Léon was named to a chair in the history of monumental art; and André Siegfried brought economic and political geography to the Collège for the first time.[68] Mauss personally knew several of his new colleagues: Lévy's sister-in-law was the wife of Mauss's brother Henri; Léon had studied at the *lycée* in Épinal; and Przyluski had been a *chargé de cours* at the Institut d'Ethnologie.

Mauss was inside the fortress, and that opened the way to recruiting new contributors to *Année Sociologique*. The appointment of Simiand in November 1931 to fill the chair in the history of labor, where he succeeded an old friend, Georges Renard, was applauded by all Durkheimians. "So Simiand is at the Collège," exclaimed Halbwachs. "Now both of our group are shining bright, and I for one am glowing about it."[69]

16

WHERE PROFESSORS DEVOUR

ONE ANOTHER

MAUSS'S APPOINTMENT to the Collège de France established his reputation, broadening his prestige and authority. He was often invited to speak: to the technical committee of the human sciences at the Caisse Nationale des Sciences (National science fund), at the Société Préhistorique Française (French prehistoric society), at the Institut d'Histoire des Sciences et des Techniques (Institute for the history of science and technology), at the Société de Biotypologie (Biotypology society), to the honor committee celebrating the fiftieth anniversary of the death of French diplomat and man of letters Joseph Gobineau, and so on.[1]

The new professor at the Collège did not intend to confine himself to studying so-called primitive peoples. He wanted to pursue comparative studies while remaining on the fringes of several sciences—sociology, anthropology, psychology, philosophy—the place where professors "devour one another," in Goethe's apt expression, which Mauss liked to quote. But through his teaching and through his writing, Mauss was still identified with the history of the religions of so-called primitive peoples and, more broadly, with ethnology.

A Revival of Interest in Ethnology

Ethnology, a science constituted as an independent discipline only belatedly, according to Paul Rivet, was experiencing considerable growth at the time. His colleague Georges-Henri Rivière would call it a "great wave."[2] In 1928 the Musée d'Ethnographie du Trocadéro was attached to the Muséum National d'Histoire Naturelle, and in particular to its chair of anthropology. Rivet and Mauss were members of the consulting board set up by Jacques Chevalier, the director of higher education. At that time, the anthropology chair became the chair of "the ethnology of present-day men and fossil men." The plan of Paul Rivet, who held the chair, was to "reconstitute the team of workers that the war had destroyed."[3]

With the collaboration of Rivière, Rivet began to reorganize the Musée d'Ethnographie, setting up new rooms, organizing the collections and the library, carefully labeling and indexing objects, publishing a bulletin. The two men wanted to make the museum, which had looked like a second-hand shop, a truly modern museological institution with a fourfold mission: to promote science, popular education, art, and the nation (through colonial and cultural propaganda).[4] Rivet's dream was that his museum would be a "marvelous instrument of popular education," and would have an influence not only on specialists and future specialists but also on a broader public, through temporary exhibits and lectures.[5] As Soustelle would say several years later, the slogan was "Let's open the doors of culture."[6]

Mauss was more convinced than ever that it was urgent to "record and preserve the facts, at least for the populations administered by France." "In that respect we are responsible to future science and to our country and the peoples themselves."[7]

A host of collaborators had to be assembled. At the Institut d'Ethnologie, now attended by well over a hundred enrolled students, Mauss delivered more than thirty lectures in descriptive ethnography each year.[8] His objective was to give instructions for fieldwork. Each lecture began with the litany: "Who? What? When? Where? How? With whom? For whom? Why?" The course originally comprised six main parts: (1) methodology (scientific techniques: photography, film, music, and so on); (2) human geography/social morphology; (3) technology (materials, their manufacture and use); (4) aesthetics (tattooing and music); (5) economics: individual and collective property; (6) general phenomena: (a) languages; (b) national phenomena; (c) psychological-sociological phenomena; (d) the phenomena of mentality; (e) biosociological phenomena.[9] Each year Mauss focused more particularly on one theme or aspect of his teaching (technology, aesthetics, and so forth) and modified his syllabus, abandoning "general phenomena," for example, to give more room to legal, moral, and religious phenomena. The outline was largely inspired by one he had established for the study of society in his essay "Divisions and Proportions of Divisions in Sociology," published in *Année Sociologique*.

As always, Mauss emphasized the facts more than the theories. Addressing not only young students from the faculty of letters or the faculty of science, but also travelers, missionaries, and administrators of the French colonies, he wanted to provide them with "the instructions necessary to constitute scientifically the archives of these more or less archaic societies."[10] All the knowledge he had acquired through theoretical reflection, readings, or personal observations, he used to his advantage. True to his nature, the professor told anecdotes, showed flashes of wit, assumed the guise of storyteller, and summoned memories (of his childhood, his family, World War I). He also spoke of his "field experience" in Morocco and presented everyday observations, boasting that he could recognize an Englishman by his gait.[11] Secondary objects took on great importance: "A tin can characterizes our societies better than the most sumptuous jewel or the rarest stamp."[12]

The objective of the course was not to learn to interpret facts but to "learn to observe and classify social phenomena."[13] Since the purpose of ethnology was to observe societies, the first courses were devoted entirely to "questions of method" relating to observation. Mauss declared in 1929–1930: "Observation requires that one be clear, complete, objective; it must approximate the so-called exact sciences." Every means to that end were legitimate: "material observations" of course (cartography, statistics, genealogy, collections of objects, photography, film, sound recordings) but also "literary-philological observations."[14] And Mauss would add the "sociological method" of observation, which consisted "above all of social history."

Mauss was not in a position to introduce future ethnographers to every one of these methods. Even though he was familiar with the techniques used by English and American anthropologists, he did not emphasize participant observation. And though he gave priority to the "intensive method," that is, the thorough observation of a single population (tribe), he proposed "makeshift instructions" that would make it possible to carry out "intermediate work between an extensive study and an intensive one." His approach was rather "documentary," consisting of the collection of objects, biographical accounts, stories, and so on.

He gave a great deal of practical advice: "Don't be credulous, don't be surprised, don't lose your temper"; select witnesses carefully; keep a "field journal"; draw up an inventory and index cards in duplicate for every object collected; develop film as quickly as possible; "go out in small groups." This advice sometimes took the form of rules of sociological or ethnological method: "It is essential to never deduce a priori. . . . In the first place, we must learn to be suspicious of common sense." "Never forget the moral aspect in studying material phenomena, and vice versa." "Every object must be studied: (1) in itself; (2) in relation to the people who use it; (3) in relation to the entire system observed." "The study of relations between the individual and the collective will hold the observer's attention for a long time." "Let us remember that representations and rites must not be studied separately."

Mauss's instructions for descriptive ethnography were inspired by *Notes and Queries*, compiled by the Royal Anthropological Institute of London and designed for people with no professional training. They were a guide to observation and provided a catalog (or rather, a classification) of the social phenomena that needed to be observed, from "material phenomena" (morphology, technology, economics) to laws to "ideal phenomena" (ethics, religions).

Mauss explained: "The fundamental error of 'mentalistic' sociology is to forget that there are things, material facts, in collective life."[15] Never had Mauss granted so much importance to material phenomena, and in particular to technology. He spoke easily of various types of weapons (heavy weapons, projectiles, defensive weapons, parrying weapons, firearms), different methods for preparing food (raw, smoked, dried, boiled, roasted, fried), and varieties of fabrics (simple, twilled, braided, combed, serged). Finally, a whole section of the course was devoted to aesthetic phenomena, which were almost indistinguishable from technical phenomena: games, the plastic arts, dance, and so on.

Everything that had once interested or that still interested Mauss can be found in his instructions: sacrifice, prayer, and totemism, of course, but also money, the potlatch and total services, contracts, secret societies, joking relationships, bodily techniques, games (pole climbing and so on). Although he often referred to studies by Durkheim and some of his collaborators (Hubert, Fauconnet, Hertz) and students (Granet, Griaule, Maunier, Montagne, Soustelle), he did not present the "thinking" of a school. Finally, though Mauss defended some of his analyses—the universalist dimension of the notion of mana, for example—he did not do so with the intention of discussing anthropological or sociological theory. What he drew from studies by Boas, Frazer, Malinowski, and Rivers was above all problems to be solved. There were concrete examples, some of which could not fail to fire his students' imaginations: cannibalism among certain tribes, deformations of the sexual organs, prostitution by priestesses. Every year Mauss took his students on excursions to the Saint-Germain museum or the Musée d'Ethnographie du Trocadéro. The professor was not so much seeking to define a research program as to "interest his listeners and make them recognize their callings." "His courses were essentially a questionnaire designed to give his audience food for thought," his student André-Georges Haudricourt later explained.[16] As Pierre Métais noted, these were "the ideas that spiritually nourished an entire generation" or, to be more precise, more than a generation.[17]

In addition to the first students Mauss had trained before the war, several of whom were recruited to be collaborators on Année Sociologique, there were now new students, including several who went on to careers in ethnography or ethnology.[18] During his courses, Mauss would stand with his hands in his pockets, a few notes in front of him, and improvise. The fascination exerted by the professor did not diminish. With his white-haired head held high and his curly beard, whose unruly, overzealous bristles seemed to poke out of his ears and nostrils in tufts,[19] Mauss cut an impressive figure: "A big beard was something unusual at the time." His memory was "inexhaustible, fed by vast reading." And the stories he told were gripping.

He was seductive, "an extraordinary man . . . almost magically informed of everything, possessed of great flashes of insight."[20] His students had great admiration for their professor: "I loved Mauss, I loved his teaching," his student Germaine Tillion confided.[21] Denise Paulme added that Mauss was "a man without preconceptions. There was no dogmatism in him. He showed me a way of looking at things. Freedom and respect for others typified him."[22]

But as Soustelle acknowledged, Mauss was by no means an easy professor. Beginning students were "dumbstruck when they heard his cavernous voice gushing from a mouth concealed under a thick beard, enumerating unfamiliar writings and authors." Mauss helpfully warned them that "unless they knew the languages of classical antiquity—Sanskrit, Hebrew, Chinese—not to mention German, English, and Dutch, it was pointless to tackle ethnology." Some students were discouraged and gave up, but for others, once they overcame their initial confusion, what had looked chaotic took on an orderly appearance, and they were dazzled. They found unexpected connections, had incisive intuitions, watched the facts march by in close formation.[23] To them, Mauss looked like a "patriarch, a nonconformist, facetious at times, but someone who had never abandoned Messianism and was unquestionably gifted with a sort of second sight."

At the Collège, the Institut, and the École, people listened to Mauss as if he were Scheherazade. He loved to astonish and provoke his listeners, even deigning on occasion to display a dandyism in his dress that was not widespread among his colleagues. He would wear a lightweight tweed with large black and light-gray checks, a striped pearl-gray shirt with a long pointed collar, a lemon-yellow bow tie. One day, when he was speaking of the distinctive characteristics of the different races, he lifted his trouser leg without a second thought, showing off his calf and exclaiming: "So you see, I'm one of the hairiest men in the world!"

Mauss's appointment at the Collège de France in no way changed the nature of his relations with his students. Because he was a bachelor, he was always very available. One of his female students acknowledged: "Simply because he wasn't married, Mauss was unlike the other professors. He was an old student, he liked to spend his time at restaurants in the Latin Quarter, he liked to be around people younger than he. We were a little club."[24] Mauss had a habit of meeting his students after his classes. Some he invited to accompany him from rue Saint-Jacques to Parc Montsouris, a long walk he adored. Once a year, he had all his students over to his apartment, and frequently invited those he had made friends with to have breakfast with him. When they wanted to indicate that they shared their professor's political opinions, they came over with *Populaire* under one arm.

For future ethnologists, the road was fairly difficult. While lavishing them with his "affectionate and far-sighted thinking," Mauss also helped them with "flattering encouragement" and "moral support."[25] He also backed their grant applications to the Rockefeller Foundation or the Caisse Nationale des Sciences (the National science fund, whose technical committee in the human sciences, social science section, Mauss had been a member of since 1931). For all men and women interested in ethnology, Mauss thus became an indispensable reference. Even people who were not his students asked to see him and solicited his advice: Roger Bastide, Jacques Berque. Claude Lévi-Strauss, who had taken a keen interest in ethnology, wrote Mauss immediately after earning his *agrégation* in philosophy.[26]

In the late 1920s and early 1930s several of Mauss's students began field research. Marcel Griaule, charged with a government mission to Abyssinia (Ethiopia) in 1927–1928, took over the Dakar-Djibouti expedition in 1931–1933. Georges-Henri Rivière accepted the position of assistant director of the Musée d'Ethnographie du Trocadéro in 1928. Alfred Métraux (born in Lausanne, Switzerland, in 1902) went to Argentina, where he served as director of the Institute of Ethnology at South Tucumán University from 1928 to 1934. In 1930, after a short stint studying in England, Charles Le Coeur began a survey of rites and tools in Morocco. Jacques Soustelle was a scholarship student for two years (1930–1932) at the École Française in Mexico City, where he conducted studies on the Otomi. In 1932 Jeanne Cuisinier spent eighteen months in the Malay States, where she collected data on magic. The same year, Georges Devereux took up residence with the Moï Sedang tribe. Paul-Émile Victor, sent on an expedition to Greenland, conducted research on the Eskimos. In December 1934 Thérèse Rivière, accompanied by Germaine Tillion, moved to the Aurès in Algeria for a one-year expedition. The next year Denise Paulme spent nine months among the Dogon society in French Sudan (now Mali). These were the best years of the Institut d'Ethnologie: Mauss offered courses, Rivet traveled, and students did their first fieldwork and prepared their theses.

The most important ethnographic and linguistic expedition originating from the Institut d'Ethnologie was the Dakar-Djibouti mission, which was financed by the French government (law of March 31, 1931, unanimously passed by Parliament) and by the Rockefeller Foundation. Griaule, the young Africanist, was named to lead it. He had served as an assistant in the ethnology laboratory at the École Pratique des Hautes Études in addition to conducting the expedition to Abyssinia in 1928.[27] Mauss did everything he could to secure him financial and political support. Shortly before the Dakar-Djibouti expedition was to depart, Rivière held a major fund-raising event at the Cirque d'Hiver. This was a boxing match featuring the "African" boxer Al Brown, and it attracted all of Paris high society. Legend has it that Mauss exchanged a few blows with the champion that night.[28] In any case, in Bordeaux on May 19, the members of the mission boarded the *Saint-Firmin*.

The expedition, armed with *Instructions sommaires pour les collecteurs d'objets ethnographiques* (A short list of instructions for collectors of ethnographic objects),[29] would cover twenty thousand kilometers in two years and would criss-cross French West Africa, Nigeria, Cameroon, French Equatorial Africa, the Belgian Congo, Anglo-Egyptian Sudan, Abyssinia, Eritrea, and French Somaliland. The objectives were "to study certain black populations and their various activities" and to constitute a collection designed to "fill the gaps in the Musée d'Ethnographie."[30] It was an impressive yield: 3,500 objects; an inventory of thirty language or dialects, most of them previously unknown; a large collection of ancient and modern Abyssinian paintings and more than three hundred Ethiopian manuscripts and amulets; a zoological collection for the Muséum de l'Histoire Naturelle that included several live animals; six thousand photographs; six hundred sound recordings; and so on. The expedition also provided the scientific world with "the certainty that, with the exception of technical expertise, black African societies possess a civilization that is very evolved in many respects."[31]

The ethnological expedition involved real teamwork, just what Mauss wanted on every such mission. Griaule recruited eight dedicated young collaborators who applied the methods taught at the Institut d'Ethnologie: Marcel Larget, Michel Leiris, Eric Lutten, Jean Mouchet, André Schaeffner, Deborah Lifszyc, Abel Faivre, and Gaston-Louis Roux. Because they had to be continually on the move, the researchers could use the intensive method only during short stopovers. Usually they had to give preference to the extensive method. Yet that method had been disparaged because, as Mauss remarked, it only grazed the surface: "It is necessary to do extensive ethnology; [but] don't think it is sufficient."[32] Griaule did not disagree, but justified his choice by the need for a "quick and reliable" method that would ensure a "scientific yield of good quality acquired in the minimum amount of time and at minimum cost."

Leiris, the archivist for the mission and a researcher in charge of religious sociology, wrote a "travel log" or "travel narrative" that quickly became an "intimate journal," with personal impressions, dreams, and so on. He was openly critical of the way work was conducted. The expedition, he said, at times resembled tourism (in search of the picturesque or the exotic), at other times a circus (always on the move with the same show at every stop), at still others colonial plunder. The researchers had to overcome incredible difficulties: securing transportation (boat, railroad, automobile, caravan), going through customs, training staff, and so on.[33]

Leiris does not seem to have taken to colonial adventure or to have had any devotion to science. At one particular moment, in a state of dejection, he wondered: "What's the point of ethnographic study?"[34] His published travel journal was not very well received in academic and political circles. "An unfortunate book," they muttered. Griaule was furious. Even Mauss gave Leiris a talking-to, but "in a paternalistic, easy-going way."[35] Mauss was afraid the book would "undermine ethnographers in the eyes of colonials." His impression of his student was not very positive. Leiris, he said repeatedly, was a "literary type" and not "very serious."[36] Leiris would acknowledge that ethnography bored him and that all he wanted was to have "as little as possible to do at the Trocadéro."[37]

Of his relationship with Mauss, Leiris would simply say: "It was the relationship of a student to his teacher. I was a student with respect for the teacher." But he owed him a great deal: "Thanks to you, the young writer I was when you met me acquired a taste for science and learned to appreciate the admirable nobility of something that is simple only in appearance: the integrity of the true scientist."[38]

The head of the expedition hoped that its accomplishments could stand as "a valuable object of emulation" and constitute "a key element in the development of ethnological science." There was no doubt that such an expedition would be likely to elicit great interest in the general public. There would be exhibits and a new Africa room at the Musée d'Ethnographie. For the researchers who participated, the Dakar-Djibouti expedition provided an excellent opportunity to "learn ethnographic research in the field" and to go on to do surveys.[39]

It seems an odd paradox that Mauss, who never did fieldwork, exerted such a profound influence on an entire new generation of researchers. The "last and best of the armchair anthropologists" sent his students to every corner of the world, arming them with rules and advice that would be "the most valuable of provisions." His students expressed their gratitude without any prompting: "In all sincerity, you prepare your students for close contact with the facts observed."[40] A few years later Métraux explored Easter Island to "compose the map of all relics from the past" and was also eager to thank his former professor: "Your predictions were correct, once again you got it right. . . . I must say my memory of your courses has served as a valuable guide to me. Once again your teaching will have borne fruit in the field."[41]

Art and Ethnology: The Journal *Documents*

Artists, writers, and the general public were learning about ethnology, "taking a great liking to it and showing great interest."[42] That movement culminated in the large-scale Colonial Exposition of 1931. Several ethnologists, including Maurice Leenhardt, made its many pavilions, its reconstruction of Angkor Wat, and its zoo in Vincennes a great fair that attracted millions of visitors. The spectacle was challenged by Surrealists and anticolonialists, among others, but it was "the best attended in the history of France."[43] The Musée d'Ethnographie du Trocadéro simultaneously presented various exhibits that proved to be a success. One of these was devoted to the material from the Dakar-Djibouti expedition, another to the French colonies. Publishing houses followed suit and introduced series in anthropology and ethnology. Translations of relevant English and American books multiplied.[44]

A few decades earlier, such an interest in ethnology would have been inconceivable: "Almost all native art was unknown," observed Mauss. Those of his generation saw them as "curiosities," "junk," "trinkets," "fetishes," "grotesques." Even at *Année Sociologique*, both the old series and the new, aesthetics occupied a secondary place, covering a large, poorly delimited area, from primitive art and archaeology to games to literature and music.[45] Aware of the "vast dimensions of the aesthetic phenomenon," Mauss hoped aesthetics would become a branch of sociology.[46]

Sensibilities evolved: a beautiful mask from an African country no longer prompted laughter; a bronze from Benin or a jewel from Dahomey made a strong impression. Native arts now appeared to be "arts as worthy as many of our own," wrote Mauss. "Contact with them breathes new life into our own; they suggest new forms, new styles, even when tradition makes them as stylized and sophisticated as our own." For the old professor it was a joy—"a pure, undiluted joy"—to see the younger generation "face life with that broad-mindedness and proclaim by their actions that they heartily agree with everything beautiful humanity has produced."[47] Mauss collaborated on an issue of *Lyon Universitaire* devoted entirely to the "native arts," which included Jacques Soustelle's "A Few Primitive Poems," Maurice Leenhardt's "Neo-Caledonian Art," and Stephen Chauvet's "Introduction to the Study of Negro Art."

Mauss, and especially his students, participated in the encounter between art and ethnology. Griaule, Leiris, Métraux, Rivière, and André Schaeffner frequented the "exclusive milieu" of the literary and artistic avant-garde. They regularly met on the terrace of the Le Flore restaurant, where the "Prévert gang" (Jacques and Pierre, the poet and his brother) held court; and they went to the Bal-Nègre, the famous revue with Josephine Baker, on rue Bonnet on Saturday nights.[48]

Rivière had initially wanted to be a pianist and composer. He was a jazz aficionado. Leiris was a poet and knew several artists personally: André Masson, Pablo Picasso, Marcel Duchamp. Schaeffner, head of the department of musical ethnology at the Musée de l'Homme beginning in 1929 and author of a study on the music of the Dogons, was himself a musician, a jazz lover, and a fan of contemporary music (Rameau, Janequin, Debussy, Ravel, Satie, Poulenc).[49]

The "valorous, mysterious, tormented" Métraux was one of the writer Georges Bataille's oldest friends; they had met when Bataille was studying at the École des Chartes in 1921–1922.[50] Their "obscure sense that there was a certain physical resemblance between them" and the same love of travel drew them together.[51] Bataille shared his literary tastes with his young friend and had him read Gide and Nietzsche; Métraux introduced Bataille to anthropology and, during long walks along rue de Rennes, spoke to him of Mauss and his studies on the potlatch. In 1928 both contributed to the special issue of *Cahiers de la République des Lettres, des Sciences et des Arts* on the ancient civilizations of America, published in conjunction with the first major exhibition of pre-Columbian art. "Vanished America" was one of Bataille's first texts. A nonconformist at heart, he was fascinated by the facts ethnologists were collecting and the theories they produced.

When Bataille left the Surrealist movement, he took charge of *Documents*. The new journal, published in 1929 with financial aid from Georges Wildenstein, a dealer in old paintings who also published the *Gazette des Beaux-Arts*, was subtitled "Archaeology, Fine Arts, Ethnography, Variety Shows." The juxtaposition of such diverse disciplines was in itself a criticism of the taxonomies and hierarchies in art, literature, and the human sciences. As its title indicated, *Documents* granted a great importance to the facts, the data. Not just any facts, however, but "the most exasperating works of art," "odd creations, heretofore neglected," "the most troubling facts, those whose consequences have not yet been spelled out." In Schaeffner's words, it was a sort of "ethnographic museum," bringing together texts, images, and various objects. Each issue was presented as a collage and might casually juxtapose a Picasso, a Giacometti, an African mask, and an advertisement (for an American film or a music-hall show). Truly a "Janus publication," according to Leiris, *Documents* had one face turned "toward the lofty spheres of culture . . . the other toward a wilderness where one ventured with no map or passport of any kind."[52]

When the journal paid homage to Picasso, Mauss was asked to take part. He agreed to write a short article, although he claimed that "others more competent than he" might be more suitable. He wondered about the request: "Am I to say that, in the early years of this century, I was one of the young people seduced by your paintings and drawings, and who even managed to convince a few art lovers? Or rather, do the people in charge of publishing this anthology, knowing my modest expertise in so-called primitive, Negro, or other art (which is merely art as such), simply want me to say how your paintings and drawings bring us closer to the purest sources of impression and expression?"[53]

For some, the mixing of disciplines in *Documents* and the publication of texts by Mauss and his students in that journal appeared to be evidence "of a remarkable affinity between avant-garde art and the Durkheimian school."[54] This was probably jumping the gun. Mauss very much liked Picasso's canvases, but he had come to know the painter only through a few of his students. His tastes were more "classical" (Flaubert, Stendhal, and Dostoyevsky in literature, Richard Wagner in music) than those of his friend Meillet, who was a great lover of contemporary music (Debussy, Ravel). Nevertheless, Mauss was "intensely curious about all that adds sumptuousness to life: poetry, art, great passion."[55] He considered himself "broad-minded," regularly listened to jazz and marveled at both contemporary and "native" art. And he defended without hesitation a largely unknown Abyssinian art produced by the young boys of Godjam: "We are convinced that an ethnographic knowledge of the native arts has already served to advance our own arts."[56]

The *Documents* adventure lasted only two years. Leiris's inventory of the weaknesses of that "far-fetched" enterprise was titled "From Bataille the Impossible to the Impossible *Documents.*" He found the journal poorly organized, splintered into trends, and unable to ensure high production standards in its issues. A few years later, another journal closely associated with the Surrealist movement would appear: *Minotaure.* It expressed the desire to "rediscover, bring together, and summarize elements that have constituted the spirit of the modern movement and to extend their influence." That new publishing venture made a place not only for writers, poets, and artists but also for the scientists most representative of their generation in the history of religion, psychoanalysis, and ethnography. In the first issue, alongside texts by André Breton and Paul Éluard and drawings by Picasso and André Masson were articles by Jacques Lacan ("The Problem of Style and Paranoid Forms of Experience") and Leiris ("Dogon Funeral Dances"). The second issue of *Minotaure* was devoted entirely to the Dakar-Djibouti expedition: "Of the disciplines that exist today, ethnography is indisputably one of the most important," declared the journal's editors. "In vogue with the general public thanks to the recent craze for what is conventionally called 'Negro art,' it provides essential material for two major instruments of human knowledge, sociology and psychology, and is simultaneously one of the most active catalysts for modern aesthetics!"[57]

After that special issue was published, *Minotaure* paid less attention to ethnography and became a review of art and literature. Artists returned to their studios, ethnographers to their museums or fieldwork. Schaeffner devoted his time to setting up a department of ethnomusicology at the Musée d'Ethnographie. Métraux became deeply involved in first-hand research and, inspired by the techniques of American-style participant observation, became "the fieldworker's fieldworker," to use Sidney Mintz's expression.[58] Leiris explained: "As ethnographers, we had to defend ourselves against the accusation of being literary; unfortunately, ethnography has become laden with jargon, because by using jargon people assert their scientificity."[59] This gradual change became obvious with the renovations at the Musée d'Ethnographie du Trocadéro. For example, wooden display cases were replaced by metal ones "to look more sober, more rigorous, more rigid, shall we say."[60] Thanks to the generosity of Georges Wildenstein, who had financed *Documents*, a bulletin was published with an intentionally austere appearance: technical articles, narrowly expository iconography, dry scholarship, succinct reports. "Everything had been a fetish, everything became a totem," comments scholar Jean Jamin.[61]

The differentiation between fields, professionalization, and autonomy characterized the evolution ethnology was experiencing at the time. But those who had personally lived through the encounter between art and ethnology, whether at *Minotaure* or at *Documents*, remained profoundly marked by that experience. Leiris became a professional ethnologist and used that avenue to pursue his interests as a writer. He published articles in *Critique Sociale, Nouvelle Revue Française*, and other journals. He and Bataille would cross paths again a few years later, at the Collège de Sociologie.

Old Problems, New Avenues of Research

With heavy teaching duties and the long labor involved in editing Hubert's *Rise of the Celts*,[62] Mauss had little time to complete his own research. His writings remained dispersed and were often fragmentary. Mauss recognized this and, in fact, granted little importance to publishing: between 1930 and 1940, he rarely published more than one article a year on average.[63] From his perspective, a relative indifference toward publishing was a character- istic, not to say a strength, of the French university system, where some professors published little or not at all. Mauss believed the important thing was to have academics who "love scientific work and do research for its own sake ... who think, who are knowledgeable."[64] He spoke to the American anthropologist Earle Edward Eubank about his own way of working:

> I'm not interested in developing systematic theories. . . . I simply work on my materials and if a valid generalization emerges here or there, I record it and go on to something else. My main concern is not to elaborate some grand, univer- sal theoretical scheme covering the entire field—that's an impossible task—but only to show a few of the dimensions of the field, which we have touched on only at the margins. We know something here and there—that's all. Because that is the way I work, my theories are dispersed and nonsystematic, and nobody could ever aspire to summarize them. . . . There are so many things to do that seem more important than to dig up the old stuff again. When I'm completely finished with an essay, I forget it, I set it aside, and I go on to something else.[65]

Mauss was fond of making informal oral comments (either at meetings of the Institut Français de Sociologie or during the International Synthesis weeks), since this allowed him to discuss studies by his colleagues— Fauconnet, Maunier, Bloch, Granet, Ray, Simiand, Henri Lévy-Bruhl—and by foreign researchers, for example, the American philosopher John Dewey and the Swiss psychologist Jean Piaget. Mauss knew them both: he had met Dewey in the United States in 1926, Piaget in Davos in 1928. Although he liked discussions, Mauss avoided getting dragged into long philosophico- theoretical debates. He was wary of them and did not tolerate them from his students or friends.[66]

Mauss discussed diverse themes in the early 1930s, including the teach- ing of sociology, the League of Nations, the political Right and Left, and money. His main scientific contributions took the form of papers, which often repeated elements from his courses: "Social Cohesion in Polysegmental Societies" (1931, Institut Français de Sociologie), "Bodily Techniques" (1934, Société de Psychologie). In addition to these two papers, in 1934 Mauss published "Fragment for an Outline of Descriptive Sociology" in the first issue of *Annales Sociologiques.* That essay was taken from conclusions he had drawn in his course "Ethnological Instructions," which he taught at the Institut d'Ethnologie and continued at the Collège de France in the winter of 1931.

Mauss did not altogether give up the (Durkheimian) dream of social harmony. He was still preoccupied with the problem of the "solidity and perpetuity of the whole." In his course at the Collège de France, he analyzed a few "general phenomena of collective life in societies of the archaic type," taking an interest specifically in social cohesion, authority, tradition, and education. Pursuing his reflections before his colleagues at the Institut de Sociologie, he asked: "What is the source of cohesion?"

For Mauss, the cohesion of a society lay less in the presence of an authority—the state in contemporary societies, for example—than in the formation of a whole series of overlapping groups: clans, divisions by sex, age cohort, generation. Even the archaic society was far from a "homogeneous mass" but was composed of various groups and subgroups that "overlapped, intersected, melded together."[67] Direct and indirect reciprocity was thus at the heart of social life, as the contemporary family made clear. Mauss reiterated: "It is what your father did for you that you must do for your son."[68] His clearly structural analysis had to do with systems of exchange: "Hence all groups overlap one another, are organized in relation to one another by reciprocal services, by the confusion of generations, of sexes, by tangles of clans and stratified age groups."[69] Mauss emphasized not the functions that one or another institution could perform but the structure of relationships between units or social groups.[70]

Finally, Mauss attempted to bring to the fore a question that had disappeared from the sociological horizon: peace. Convinced that the study of archaic societies could be useful in understanding our own societies, the ethnologist ventured a generalization: "This view of the necessity of overlapping subgroups applies to our own societies."[71] As Mauss reminded his readers, Durkheim, in his attempt to find a solution to the problem of individualism and socialism, had established an intermediate force, the professional group, between individualist anarchy and the overwhelming power of the state. Mauss pursued the idea: "[In our modern societies] it is necessary to create a number of subgroups and constantly reinforce others, professional groups in particular, that either do not exist or do not exist to a sufficient degree. It is necessary to let them fit together naturally, if possible under the authority of the state when required, and to its knowledge and under its control in any case."[72]

Mauss continued the discussion with his uncle when he sent *Annales Sociologiques* an essay subtitled "Classification of and Method for Observing the General Phenomena of Social Life in Societies of the Archaic Type (Specific Phenomena of the Inner Life of Society)." The elaboration of an "outline" for sociology, with divisions and subdivisions, always obsessed the Durkheimians, Durkheim included. In 1927 Mauss developed a long argument titled "Divisions of Sociology" for the new series of *Année Sociologique*. But he did not intend to resume that discussion in *Annales Sociologiques*. Maintaining the old distinction between morphological phenomena and physiological phenomena was no longer at issue: "Let us therefore abandon [that] division," he declared from the outset. Resistant to any "fragmentary and fragmented" sociological study, he preferred to speak in terms of the "total social fact," "totality," or the "social system."

The outline for a general descriptive sociology proposed by Mauss applied only to the study of archaic societies in the French colonies. Taking certain well-known matters for granted—methods of investigation, the analysis of demographic and linguistic phenomena, and so on—he limited his reflection to the general phenomena of intrasocial life and, more specifically, to anything regarding the "solidity and perpetuity of the whole": social cohesion, authority, tradition, and education.

These were all Durkheimian themes, and Mauss had already addressed them in his paper on social cohesion in polysegmental societies. When he returned to them, he was intent on warning against any form of ethnocentrism that consisted of speaking of "our European ideas," of the *conscience collective* proper to us. "Nothing is more dangerous than to transfer our names for things, especially social things."[73] "One must begin with the way [forms of social life] are represented in the *conscience collective* of the type we are studying."[74]

But what is an archaic society? Mauss wanted to correct his uncle, who, in *The Division of Labor in Society*, called the solidarity of these societies "mechanical." The nephew said that was "a bit hasty." There was also organic solidarity in archaic societies, but of a different nature from that found in modern Western societies. That organic solidarity linked not only individuals but also subgroups. It was the result not of contracts but of exchanges, influences, and services. Far from being in a state of anarchy, as people too often believed, archaic societies displayed a complex mode of social organization, with many politico-domestic subgroups (clans, phratries), a multitude of divisions (by sex, age, generation, social class, caste), and finally, a complex system of alliances (matrimonial and otherwise).

The same year, Mauss made comments after a paper titled "Money, a Social Reality" was delivered by Simiand to the Institut Français de Sociologie, and again insisted on the phenomena of exchange and reciprocity, but this time focused on the notion of expectation or anticipation of the future, as "one of the forms of collective thought." He added: "We are with one another in society in order to expect some result from one another; that is the essential form of community. We may have used the expressions *constraint, force,* and *authority* in the past, and they have their value. But that notion of collective expectation is in my view one of the fundamental notions we need to work on. I know of no other notion that generates law and economics: 'I expect' is the very definition of any act of a collective nature. It is the origin of theology: God will hear—I don't say answer, but hear—my prayer."[75]

In a superb intuition, Mauss saw that "expectation" has no value as a concept. He did not go any further. Also in 1934, reiterating elements from his course in descriptive ethnology at the Institut d'Ethnologie, he presented a paper titled "Bodily Techniques" to the Société de Psychologie. The field of research was still new, falling under the rubric "Miscellaneous" in journals. "An ugly rubric," commented Mauss: "I had to teach while carrying with me the disgrace and opprobrium of that 'miscellaneous' at a time when the rubric 'Miscellaneous' was truly an odd assortment in ethnography."[76]

Mauss was a keen observer. He recounted anecdotes and gave several examples, as he usually did in his courses. Some were drawn from his experiences as a soldier (the handling of spades and the gait of English and French soldiers, movements in close formation, the way Australian soldiers during the war squatted), others from sports (techniques in swimming, footraces, and mountain climbing), still others from daily life (table manners, hygiene, the way nurses in an American hospital walked). Ethnology was a valuable source of information and provided many other examples: the swaying hips of Maori women (New Zealand), hunting and racing rituals in Australia.

Such examples could be multiplied ad infinitum: ways of making a fist, of sitting down. They were habitus, ways of acting. As the work of "collective and individual practical reason," they varied by age and sex and from one society to another.

Everything was open to observation: sleep, dance, care of the body, shows of force, sexual positions, and so on. The everyday was a source of astonishment, from the Kabyles in their babouches to Western women in high heels. The simple enumeration of facts produced a sort of dazzlement. The techniques in question varied so much from one society to another and from one age to the next that the variations could be used to understand humanity: there were cradle people and cradleless people, braid people and braidless people, bench people and benchless people, pillow people and pillowless people, table people and tableless people.

On the basis of his various observations, Mauss formulated a general claim: "We find ourselves dealing with physio-psycho-sociological assemblages of series of acts."[77] Remembering how he had learned mountain climbing, the ethnologist was eager to demonstrate the role of education in vision, in walking, in keeping one's composure. "It is thanks to society that consciousness intervenes. It is not thanks to the unconscious that society intervenes. It is thanks to society that there is a sureness of movements ready at hand, a domination by the conscious mind of emotion and the unconscious."[78] That analysis is valid not only for swimming or walking, but also for an activity such as prayer, which, Mauss emphasized, is also a bodily technique. "A socio-psychobiological study of mysticism needs to be done. I think there is necessarily a biological method for entering into communication with God."[79]

All this was "fallow land." "This is what needs to be plumbed. We are certain that truths are to be found there: first, because we know we do not know, and second, because we have a keen sense of the large number of facts."[80] "All this can and must be observed in the field," Mauss said repeatedly. "There are hundreds of these things yet to be known."[81] It was an "enormous task," Lévi-Strauss would note fifteen years later, expressing the hope that an international organization such as UNESCO would make a commitment to carry out such a research program.[82]

Annales Sociologiques

The idea of sociology gained ground and the Durkheimians consolidated their position in the university system. Mauss and Simiand were at the Collège de France; Halbwachs was about to join Bouglé (recently named director of the École Normale Supérieure) and Fauconnet at the Sorbonne; Gurvitch, who was teaching a course at the École Pratique, would replace Halbwachs in Strasbourg. But there was a palpable uneasiness caused by a limited number of chairs in the faculties, an absence of consensus on the definition of the discipline, and a lack of interest in sociological theory.[83]

The criticism coming from "old rival forces" was still harsh. Then there were the violent reactions elicited by the pedagogical successes of sociology: "What distress that wretched program was going to elicit! And what anger! Once again, political passions and pedagogical trends combined to cause outbursts. People shouted that it was socialism, irreligion. . . . Don't think those fires are completely extinguished."[84] In *Watchdogs*, Paul Nizan virulently attacked Durkheim's sociology: "The introduction of sociology into the normal schools has secured the victory of that official ethics. Years ago Durkheim built his body of work and spread his teaching with great obstinacy, with a great authoritarian force, by giving that work the venerable appearance of science. In the name of that appearance, in the name of that science, teachers taught children to respect the French Nation, to justify collaboration between social classes, to accept everything, to receive Holy Communion in the cult of the Flag and of Bourgeois Democracy."[85]

A communist intellectual, Nizan presented the old team at *Année Sociologique* as "bourgeois thinkers," a "sort of resistance battalion . . . deliberately constituted to bar the way to true socialism."[86] Bouglé, who was attacked by name, would reply: "The only thing I can say is that I do not recognize myself in the account of the education trends in which I participated."[87]

Sociology was going through a difficult time. In his overview "Sociology since 1914," Mauss claimed that "on precise points . . . we have made progress," but his overall evaluation was harsh: "On the whole, sociological work has ceased to be systematic and oriented toward generalization."[88] Of course more young people were taking sociology courses, but, Mauss lamented, they were not doing so out of love for the work or scientific interest. They were motivated either by the prospect of respectable remuneration or by political interests.

When an American colleague asked him, "Who are the most promising young researchers in the field of sociology?" Mauss was at first reluctant to respond, then gave three names: Georges Davy, Marcel Granet, and Max Bonnafous. Yet in effect, Davy and Bonnafous were disqualified—Davy, rector at the Université de Rennes, was not considered a "real sociologist" by Mauss, and Bonnafous had recently defected from the university to take a government job. There was only one hope left: Mauss's friend and colleague Granet.[89] Hence there was a problem replacing the old guard. A whole generation had been decimated by the war, and the young were too interested in politics. As Raymond Aron pointed out, if young people were to choose the path of sociology research, they needed "courage and a firm scientific calling."[90]

The general situation, marked by economic crisis, called for a reorientation. Sociology had to abandon "the field of ideas for that of facts." Mauss believed it had to develop the "purely descriptive side" of the social sciences: "We must now set down the fundamental traits of the societies we live in, using all the resources of our sciences."[91]

The completion of that vast program was hindered by the inadequate number of collaborators. "A finite number of workers cannot do an infinite amount of work," remarked Mauss, who had been aware since his trip to the United States that the problem was resources and organization. Still worried about the future of research in the social sciences, he made a second proposal to create a section within the École Pratique that would give students specializing in economics, sociology, law, and social history training in research.

Mauss remained a contact person for the Rockefeller Foundation in France, agreeing to visit with American academics recommended to him and to support the grant applications of French students and researchers. But the foundation mistrusted him, probably for political reasons, and rather than negotiate directly with an isolated researcher, they now preferred to turn to the rector of the Université de Paris, Sébastien Charlety, an *agrégé* in history who had been won over to the cause of the social sciences. After a survey conducted by T. B. Kittredge among the French faculties, schools, and institutes concluded that research was too dispersed and poorly coordinated, the Rockefeller Foundation temporarily abandoned its general plan and adopted a strategy to be implemented in phases. It began by supporting isolated institutions destined to play an important role in the development of the social sciences. The objective was still to "familiarize the younger elements at the university with the methods of observation and the work necessary to solve economic, sociological, and political problems." Sociology was enlisted to develop "true methods for social control" and to elaborate an "experimental politics," that is, a "serious political program relying on a complete and precise analysis of the environment on which one intends to act."

For the school year 1932–1933, the modest $3,000 grants were divided between the Institut de Droit Comparé at the law school in Paris, the Institut d'Ethnologie, and the Centre de Documentation Sociale. These grants were renewed the following year. The grants awarded to the Institut d'Ethnologie were earmarked for research in Mauss's cultural anthropology and looked like a sort of consolation prize.

Bouglé, who was also in contact with the Americans, took a trip to the United States in December 1929 at the foundation's invitation. The grant received by the Centre de Documentation Sociale, which Bouglé directed, made it possible to hire assistants and, in keeping with the foundation's wishes, to encourage research in "inductive sociology": for example, Georges Friedmann's work on mechanization and Philippe Schwob's on industrial organization in France. As Bouglé wrote ironically, there was a desire "to marry the tradition of the Le Play school to that of the Durkheim school."[92] The center, which had been founded in 1920 and financed by the banker Albert Kahn until the 1929 crisis, had as its objective to collect documentation on the pressing political and social questions of the day. Its first archivist was Marcel Déat, who served from 1920 to 1923.

When the Rockefeller Foundation changed its policy in 1935 and decided to finance not institutes but research programs, it allotted a grant of $25,000 a year for five years to the Conseil Universitaire de la Recherche Sociale (University council of social research), a new coordination and orientation group set up to distribute the funds provided by the foundation. The Durkheimians received a large share of the grants. Between 1935 and 1940, 350,000 francs went to Bouglé and his team and more than 400,000 francs to Henri Lévy-Bruhl, Rivet, and their collaborators at the Institut d'Ethnologie (Griaule, Leroi-Gourhan, Lévi-Strauss, Curt Sachs, Soustelle, Germaine Tillion). Mauss received nothing for his own work. Everything went to his friends, collaborators, and former students. Some said that the chief concern of the Rockefeller Foundation was not to study the customs and languages of various peoples, but to make people happy.[93]

The project closest to the hearts of Durkheim's former collaborators was to "perpetuate his work," despite the failure of the new series of *Année Sociologique*. They continued to identify strongly with the master. Davy wrote: "One school is undoubtedly gaining ascendancy both by the rigor of its scientific method and by the volume of its output and its indisputable influence in the field of sociology and outside it. That is the Durkheim school."[94] Mauss still greatly admired his uncle, whom he considered "the greatest sociologist France has ever had," and for many reasons: his vast learning, subtlety, and meticulous attention to his work, the thoroughness of his materials, the originality and freshness of his thought, his capacity to mobilize and train the researchers around him.

Halbwachs, "more Durkheimian than Durkheim himself," continued the master's study of suicide, taking a particular interest in the "relationship between economic crises, bankruptcies, movements [illegible] and intentional deaths." The book was longer than expected and was provisionally called "New Research on Suicide." Halbwachs wanted it to appear simultaneously with the reissue of Durkheim's *Suicide*.[95] Two years later, in 1930, Alcan published the new edition of *Suicide* and Halbwachs's *Causes of Suicide* with a foreword by Mauss.

Everything was done to lend credence to the idea that a tradition of research was being perpetuated.[96] The Durkheimians did not represent all of French sociology or even everything that mattered in French sociology. But, though Durkheim was still the object of lively criticism,[97] they were convinced that "theirs was the true sociology of France."[98] In addition, the Durkheimians were still the representatives of French sociology abroad. Mauss had considerable prestige in the United States and his work was "known and appreciated" there.[99] He was "one of the most important contemporary French sociologists," said Eubank. There was a desire "to see his articles collected and published." And Métraux, one of Mauss's former students working in Hawaii, observed with pride and joy his influence on American and English ethnography. "Might not your role have been greater in this country than in France?"[100] As Métraux observed during a stay in Chicago, Mauss's influence was particularly obvious in the social sciences department of the University of Chicago: "Lloyd Warner . . . was a pure Durkheimian. . . . Do you know no one can get a degree without being familiar with *The Elementary Forms* and without reading at least one of your articles? Not just graduate students, but the entire student body."[101]

Robert Lowie, a professor of anthropology at the University of California, devoted a chapter of his *History of Ethnological Theory* (1937) to "French sociology," that is, to Durkheim, Mauss, and Lévy-Bruhl.[102] Radcliffe-Brown was the most convincing example, so much so that Lowie classified him as one of the "French sociologists." And why not? retorted Mauss: "Radcliffe-Brown says he is truly a French sociologist. And we take him to be one."[103]

Alfred Radcliffe-Brown (1881–1955), trained by Rivers at Cambridge, had solid field experience in Australia and had just published a vast overview of his research, *The Social Organization of Australian Tribes* (1931). As a Durkheimian, he was considered closer to Mauss than to Durkheim himself.[104] He gladly agreed when asked by a former student of Mauss's "whether he of all the foreign scientists was the one whose thinking and ideas are closest to Mauss's."[105] Mauss did not conceal his respect for Radcliffe-Brown, whom he had long known through Haddon and Rivers: "As a scholar, as a professor, as a researcher, as a fieldworker, as chair of the sciences, Alfred Radcliffe-Brown seems to be one of the best now living." He also did not hesitate to support his candidacy for the chair of social anthropology at Oxford University.[106]

Mauss was an Anglophile who purchased his clothes at the Old England shop. As he claimed, he was without a doubt "one of the French sociologists and anthropologists in closest contact with the English school of anthropology."[107] Solid ties of friendship linked him to Charles Seligman and his wife, Brenda. The Frazers, whenever they came to Paris, were entertained by Mauss and even made suggestions about what foods to prepare.[108] When Malinowski presented three lectures at the Institut d'Ethnologie, he hoped Mauss would be able to attend at least one of them: "They are written—as much of my work on kinship—very largely for you as the main representative of the French Socio. School."[109] Although he criticized his English colleague's "theoretical weakness and total lack of erudition," Mauss admired his capacity to gather and present the facts.[110]

American anthropologists and sociologists also knew Mauss well. Some wrote to him,[111] others came to see him in Paris: Herbert Blumer, W. Lloyd Warner, and Emory Stephen Bogardus in 1932, Howard Becker and Earle Edward Eubank in 1934.[112] Edwin R. R. Seligman, professor of political economics at Columbia, requested Mauss's participation when he began work on the *Encyclopedia of the Social Sciences*. Unfortunately, Mauss did not have the time to quickly compose "substantial articles." "[A] few of the subjects upon which I would like to express my ideas beyond the letter L: Method, Society, Sociology, Magic, Religion, Primitive, Ritual. The only one I see for the time being is: Gift."[113] But Mauss accepted the position of editorial consultant and published a (single) short notice on Henri Hubert.[114] His contribution was much less significant than those of his friends and collaborators: Simiand and Charles Rist were the advisory editors for France; Georges Bourguin, Bouglé, and Halbwachs wrote several pieces, including a notice on Durkheim; and, for the first volume, Henri Lévy-Bruhl composed the introductory text on sociology in France, Belgium, and Switzerland. In that short historical note on the social sciences, written for English-speaking researchers, Lévy-Bruhl presented Durkheim's work as "the most vigorous and coherent effort ever made in France to study human societies." He added: "The designation 'French school of sociology' can be legitimately attributed to all who work in that spirit."[115]

The chief meeting place for the Durkheimians was the Institut Français de Sociologie. There were discussions of the scientific studies under way and of certain pressing questions, such as the place of sociology teaching in the normal schools. That question particularly impassioned members of the institute, several of whom were part of the ministerial commission created in 1933: Bouglé, Fauconnet, Lévy-Bruhl, Mauss, and Simiand. The commission's mandate was "to study the results obtained teaching sociology in the normal schools and propose any modifications to the programs or their application suggested by the experiment." Bouglé, who favored retaining the course of study, conducted a survey among directors of normal schools on the practice and on the results. The study revealed strong opposition to any change. Mauss did not hide his dissatisfaction but avoided taking a public position for or against eliminating the course.

Mauss regularly attended the institute's meetings but rarely spoke there. At most he commented on his colleagues' papers.[116] Until *Annales Sociologiques* began appearing in 1934, his comments were published in *Bulletin de l'Institut Français de Sociologie*.

Bouglé, one of the most active defenders of Durkheimian sociology, launched a plan for the new journal in March 1930. He wrote Mauss: "Don't you think it's time for us to take steps to organize work on the *Année Sociologique* after next?"[117] It seems that several people set to work again, since Schneider of the Alcan publishing house set a final deadline of June 30 for Mauss to "complete the current *Année*."[118] Halbwachs, who was traveling in the United States, was worried: "Can *Année* still be saved? I think that depends on you. It would be good to show our American friends that we exist. Sociology is truly a reality for them."[119] Even though the deadline was extended, it was never met, to Fauconnet's great despair: "Old friend, you must finish *Année* and before January 4, vacation or no vacation. I won't repeat the disadvantages of sinking into powerlessness and absurdity—of failing—nor will I repeat our obligation to finish the task, if we are to finish honorably."[120]

Fauconnet refused to "kill the publication." But a year later, nothing had budged. Everything had to be begun again from scratch. Bouglé invited his friends to a meeting at his home to decide together whether they wanted to start up the journal again.[121] These became serious discussions by the summer of 1933. Hence a few benchmarks were set in place for the future *Annales Sociologiques*. That new initiative benefited from 60,000 francs in grants between 1935 and 1940, which the Rockefeller Foundation awarded to Halbwachs and Fauconnet to publish studies by the Institut Français de Sociologie. In terms of thematic and methodological orientations, the foundation's influence was clear in the first installment of *Annales*, published in 1934. There was a section on the "experimental method" in sociology and an article by André Philip on a major survey titled "Recent Social Trends" carried out in the United States.[122]

The title of the new journal was closer to that of other periodicals in the human sciences: *Annales de Géographie, Annales d'Histoire Économique et Sociale*. The objective of *Annales d'Histoire*, created by Lucien Febvre and Marc Bloch in 1929 and bringing together historians, economists, geographers, and sociologists, was to link history to the social sciences and reduce the compartmentalization of history into various specialized fields. It was believed that these were the conditions for developing a social and economic history. The editors of the journal, both professors in Strasbourg, were in their own way part of the Durkheimian tradition. They even solicited contributions from Halbwachs, Simiand, and Mauss.[123]

Only Halbwachs, also a professor in Strasbourg, agreed to be on the editorial board of *Annales d'Histoire Économique et Sociale*. That commitment did not prevent him from playing an active role in relaunching *Année Sociologique* in its new format. He was assisted in his work as secretary of the editorial board by Jean Ray and Georges Lutfalla and even became the linchpin of the undertaking, especially after 1935, when he was appointed at the Sorbonne. The editorial board of *Annales Sociologiques* was composed of Durkheimians: in addition to Halbwachs, there was Bouglé, Fauconnet, Mauss, and Simiand. Among the collaborators were "old-timers": the jurists Emmanuel Lévi and Henri Lévy-Bruhl, the linguist Marcel Cohen, the economist Georges Bourgin, the sociologist of art Charles Lalo, and others.

For the most part, however, the collaborators were newcomers: twenty-seven of the forty-six had not participated in either the first or the second series of *Année Sociologique*. Among these "willing workers,"[124] several were the students of members of the editorial board or were associated with the Centre de Documentation Sociale at the École Normale Supérieure headed by Bouglé: Raymond Aron, André Kaan, Henri Mougin, Raymond Polin, Jean Stoetzel. The center's small team was largely responsible for publishing the general sociology installments of *Annales Sociologiques*. Raymond Aron, Mauss's cousin, quickly came to be a "serious collaborator."[125]

The cousins were on friendly terms. Mauss regularly had dinner at Aron's house and drew the young Raymond into the socialist camp, introducing him around at the fifth branch of the SFIO. When Aron married Suzanne Gauchon in 1933, Mauss immediately wanted to "get to know the new cousin" and welcomed her with a ringing, "Do you know how to cook rice?"[126] Aron, associated with the Durkheimians' work, nonetheless remained critical of Durkheim's sociology: "The formulation 'God or society' offended and shocked me. Explaining suicides by statistical correlation left me unsatisfied."[127]

Memories of Durkheim were still fresh. *Annales Sociologiques*, published by the Félix Alcan publishing house, appeared in the "Travaux de *L'Année Sociologique*" collection, which Durkheim had founded. There was a desire to maintain "the spirit of synthesis" characteristic of *Année*: "We persist in thinking that to advance the science of social life, it is incumbent upon us to link the various disciplines that study one or another of its aspects, to standardize their methods, to coordinate their results, and to bring them into line with one another." But for "practical reasons," the old format of a single volume was abandoned in favor of the freer and more flexible format of separate installments, with each installment to unite essays, general surveys, analyses, bibliographical notes, and minutes of sessions at the Institut Français de Sociologie. This was believed to be the best means for "closely following the sociological movement."[128]

The five installments planned reflected the branches of the sociological network: (a) general sociology (directed by Bouglé); (b) religious sociology (directed by Mauss); (c) legal sociology (directed by Ray); (d) economic sociology (directed by Simiand); (e) social morphology, technology, and aesthetics (directed by Halbwachs). That division was also the result of a splintering of the old Durkheimian group. It was unusual for a contributor to write in more than one series. Only Halbwachs contributed to four of them. As Mauss would remark, sociological work was no longer "systematic and oriented primarily toward generalization." "Without losing contact with one another, we were walking in a rather dispersed formation. The fields to be covered proved so vast, finding them so difficult, that we all felt we had to give up premature systematization. We therefore more or less staked out our areas; we worked one vein or another of the social facts; we focused our efforts on certain points."[129] Although Alcan wanted to publish *Annales Sociologiques* as "a single annual volume devoted to the five sections,"[130] the installment format was maintained.

If we exclude the material in general sociology, the areas emphasized by the *Annales* team were economic sociology, social morphology, and legal and moral sociology. Simiand, Halbwachs, and Bouglé were responsible for these fields and were in charge of publishing the first installments in 1934 and 1935.[131] Halbwachs, the assistant editor, was relatively satisfied with the first installment of the journal, though several changes were required: bibliographies would be reduced in size, reviews of philosophy books cut, and so forth.

For the first installment, Mauss provided a short obituary of his friend and colleague Antoine Meillet, who died in 1936,[132] and his "Fragment for an Outline of a Descriptive General Sociology," which inaugurated series A, general sociology. Mauss's blueprint opened many avenues to readers of *Annales Sociologiques*. He wanted to "replace the vague and various rubrics with a logical blueprint for research and observation." But a universal sociological theory or a synthesis of all knowledge was not at issue. Mauss could have "philosophized" about general sociology, but he decided it was pointless, especially "when there is so much to know and learn, and so much to do subsequently to understand." Hence Mauss proposed to observe and to take things in small doses. He identified a multitude of objects, including the different modes for transmitting social cohesion: tradition in all its forms (oral and other), general education and specialized education (teaching bodily techniques, manual techniques, techno-scientific traditions, aesthetic education, and so on).

There were two other, more schematic parts to "Fragment of an Outline for a General Descriptive Sociology," one dealing with international phenomena (peace, war, civilization), the other identifying facts of collective psychology and anthropo-sociology (biometrics, somatological anthropology). These facts were imaginary intellectual elements (dreams, trances), affective elements (courage, the sensation of happiness), inventions, creations, mob psychology, and so on. For Mauss, societies in every stage of development had to be studied from a threefold perspective: sociological, psychosociological, and sociobiological.

The journal's assistant editor was delighted that Mauss had made a contribution. Halbwachs wrote: "It was good that from the outset we were back in the strong, invigorating atmosphere of the old *Année*—thanks to you. . . . All the same, it's taking a rather long time."[133] Mauss's participation was limited to the first installments of *Annales Sociologiques* and did not include any book reviews, though Halbwachs requested them several times, especially for the "Technology," "Linguistics," and "Aesthetics" sections.

Friends and colleagues were well aware that Mauss had little time to devote to his own work. Yet the assistant editor at *Annales Sociologiques* tried to get the essay Mauss had promised: "Have you thought about it? I'm more convinced than ever that publishing an issue on religious sociology, even if it's very short and incomplete, fragmentary, would immediately give the impression we are forging on."[134]

These appeals came to nothing: Mauss was busy with other things. At the Sorbonne[135] and at the Collège de France, the Durkheimians controlled the field of sociology, and with *Annales Sociologiques* they had the means to keep the Durkheimian tradition alive. But they had to meet a considerable challenge—to give their discipline a more clearly empiricist orientation for dealing with social problems and to professionalize it, as the United States had done. And Mauss had to give priority to that task.

"Life Is Not Very Cheery"

With so many obligations, Mauss was confined to "the provisional, the preliminary." A second book by Hubert that he was editing, *Les Germains* (The

Germanics), was dragging on. Bothered by health problems, he complained that his teaching was hard, that his teaching and administration load was heavy, and that, unlike his colleagues in American universities, he did not have the services of an "army of secretaries and assistants" to help him in his work.[136] His administrative tasks were especially burdensome because he had to do many things for his students at a financial, professional, and personal level: support "dear Gurvitch"; encourage Lévi-Strauss (and his wife), of whom he had only good things to say and whom he considered, along with Soustelle, the "hope" of French Americanism; speak to his American colleagues on behalf of Robert Marjolin and also on behalf of Alfred Métraux,[137] one of "his most brilliant students," about a position at the Bernice P. Bishop Museum in Honolulu. Mauss paid just as much attention to the research of other students not working directly in the fields of sociology and ethnology.[138] Having "good students" was his chief gratification.

The professor at the Collège de France was very much in demand. Shortly after being elected, Léon Blum asked his friend Mauss to support the candidacy of a "very close" friend of his "comrades from Toulouse." Requests of every sort were made to him: to support people seeking to become naturalized citizens, to confer a chair at the Collège de France on Albert Einstein, to write prefaces, grant applications, obituaries. Colleagues invited him to present lectures or to read manuscripts. Foreign researchers applying for jobs asked him to intervene in their favor: Hoccart, Radcliffe-Brown,[139] Evans-Pritchard, R. F. Fortune, R. Firth. Young researchers solicited his advice on their works in progress: Georges Friedman, Jacques Berque, Roger Bastide, Gabriel Le Bras.

Even former colleagues turned to Mauss. Arnold Van Gennep, for example, had for several years been seeking "something stable for [his] old age" and had already sought Mauss's support in creating a chair in French and comparative folklore at the Collège de France. He was persistent, trying either to get a grant or to be appointed *directeur d'études* in religion or popular customs at the École Pratique.[140] Mauss was still willing to lend a hand and, when friends or students ran into difficulties, to personally provide them with financial aid.

In addition to these many professional obligations, there were now conjugal responsibilities. Relatives and friends had wanted to marry off Mauss for a long time. Sylvain Lévi's wife, Danielle, had written him in 1917: "If I love you now, dear Marcel, I'd love you even more—is that possible?—if you became responsible and finally got married. Responsible, a responsible Marcel Mauss, would we lose anything thereby? That would depend on her obviously."[141]

After Hubert became a family man, he regularly badgered his friend, even when Mauss was gravely ill: "Come on, old friend, you'll have to get married and settle down."[142] Only his mother had lost her illusions. In 1919 she had written Hubert: "I'm constantly waiting for Marcel. . . . As for his marriage

ıs, I, like you, think he'd like to settle down but everything seems to be
in the air and I don't know anyone I'd wish on him."[143]
Jntil Rosine's death in 1930, Mauss spent most of his vacation time in
ınal, returning there as often as possible to care for his mother and to
ıoy the company of his nephews and nieces, who found him "very funny."
regularly went mountain climbing or hiking in Switzerland. In appear-
ce, he led the life of a confirmed bachelor.

But there had been a woman in Mauss's life since the early 1920s. Her
ıme was Marthe Rose Dupret, and she too lived on rue Bruller. Mauss
ıd her type his manuscripts: she was the only one who could decipher his
ındwriting. Their relationship was not purely professional, however, as
:tested by the love letters she wrote during Marcel's brief stay in England
ı autumn 1924: "No one matters to me anymore except you. . . . I realize it
ıore and more. . . . My regards, my darling, and a big kiss. How happy I'll
ıe to see you again."[144]

Mauss did not marry Marthe Dupret until 1934, that is, four years after
his mother's death and more than ten years after he first met Marthe. Mauss's
wife was fourteen years his junior. She was born in Lamalou-les-Bains
(Hérault) and received a Catholic education; she was also reputed to be an
excellent musician. Her father was Hippolyte Dupret, who worked in sales.
She had been married once before, to Louis Chamboredon; the couple had
divorced. The American researcher Eubank met Mauss's new wife "briefly"
in the summer of 1934 when he consulted Mauss. He noted: "She seemed
much younger than her husband, who is sixty-one."[145]

The marriage was a great surprise to friends and family, since Mauss
informed them only after the fact. "What news!" exclaimed Lucien Lévy-
Bruhl, who considered Mauss one of his dearest friends and one of those
he was most proud of. He was quite willing to consider Mme Mauss "our
friend already."[146] His friends said they were happy for the "good news."
They congratulated and teased him: "Best wishes to M.D., or M.M.D., or
M.M.M.D. It will make a charming little name," wrote Fauconnet.[147] Some
learned of the marriage only several months later: "I can't believe what I've
heard! You're married. That's your right, your duty even, but you didn't even
tell us!"[148] The first reaction from his students was jealousy. Jeanne Cuisinier
wrote him, "You know one instinctively feels a vague mistrust when anything comes about to change the life of those one loves."[149]

Mauss decided to leave his little apartment on rue Bruller, and, using to advantage his stature as a professor, moved into a new Ville de Paris building at
95, boulevard Jourdan, where he settled comfortably into a large eight-room
apartment. No more noise and pollution from rue Bruller! The apartment
was located on the eighth floor and looked out on a large terrace. Mauss, who
had dreamed of buying a house in Sceaux with a garden, planted greenery
and a few fruit trees. "I'm the gardener of my terrace," he said.

The following September 27, on returning from a trip to the mountains, Mauss found his wife at home, "poisoned by a gas leak." "Anywhere but Paris, she would have been dead," he said. "Fortunately, we saved her and I'm sure she'll recover completely. . . . I'm afraid it will be a long time yet."[150] Was it an unfortunate accident or a suicide attempt? No one knew. The poisoning was serious and required intensive care. Mauss had to travel long distances to spend every night at the hospital in Chatenay, south of Paris. His wife was still hospitalized a year later. It was not until late 1935 that she could come home "without it being a shock"; Mauss hoped to care for her better there than in Chatenay. At the time he was living "a rather secluded life."[151] When he could get away, in the summer for example, he went for short vacations in Contrexéville, where he treated his "very painful neuritis" or his sciatica. Months went by and nothing changed.

"Life is not very cheery."[152] The 1930s, though marked by personal success—for example, he was awarded the title of officer in the Legion of Honor in 1937—were difficult years for Mauss. There were health problems, his own and his wife's, and there was more loneliness following the death of close friends and colleagues: Simiand, Sylvain Lévi, Meillet.

Simiand died suddenly in April 1935, while taking some time off in Saint-Raphaël. After a bad flu and a first warning, he had been forced to cancel his courses at the Collège. Everyone knew "the deep and solid affection" Mauss and Simiand had had for each other.[153] In *Populaire* Mauss praised his friend, whom some considered the greatest French economist.[154] He was also "one of the most eminent, the most influential, the most active, and the best known" people in the socialist movement, alongside Lucien Herr and Jaurès, and in the sociological movement next to Durkheim. Mauss wrote: "He died serving the cause as a scientist."[155]

When Mauss lost his "second uncle," Sylvain Lévi, the same year, he could not conceal his pain: "Our sorrow and our memories will always remain fresh." Lévi died "mid-action, on his feet, very quickly" at the start of a meeting of the central committee of the Alliance Israélite Universelle, which Mauss was attending. It was truly a sacrifice: "He wanted to die suddenly, on the job," said Mauss. "He got his wish. There is always something of the martyr in a saint's death and it attests to his faith."[156]

The next year Meillet passed away. Mauss "had not left [him] for an instant since 1895, not even during the war, at least in his thoughts." Mauss was honored that Meillet had confided in him. As he had done for Simiand and Lévi, he was intent on composing the traditional "In memoriam" to show what Meillet had done for sociology and "as witness to a personal friendship."[157] Every new death increased his feeling of emptiness. "Nothing but death and serious illness around me," he complained. "Let us be careful, let us be very careful."[158]

17

ENOUGH TO MAKE YOU

DESPAIR OF POLITICS

THE 1930s marked something of an apogee in Mauss's life. On the one hand, he was appointed to the Collège de France; on the other, the Left returned to power in 1932 and Léon Blum's Front Populaire took over the government. Very quickly, however, fissures appeared: a heavy pedagogical and administrative workload, health problems, divisions within the SFIO, and, in the background, the rise of fascism.

The Return of the Left

France had been through three political experiments since the war: the Bloc National in 1919, the Cartel des Gauches from 1924 to 1926, and the Union Nationale from 1926 to 1932. The country was facing an economic crisis amid the government's ultraconservatism; in the 1932 elections, the desire for change was obvious. The socialists had a chance. Preoccupied with personal problems, Mauss had little time to devote to political action. Yet although the new professor at the Collège de France was "weary of being a party militant," he could not remain indifferent to politics or cut himself off completely.

Mauss was not very concerned with the socialists' participation in the government. At the time of the elections, he made the following wager: "The Left will certainly win the chamber, and within the leftist majority there will be a Radical majority, followed closely by the Socialists." He analyzed the situation this way: "One of the waves that is carrying the country to the left comes from a great tide that cannot be stopped. The terrible world crisis is shaking the world as a whole and it is altogether inaccurate to say that this country is less shaken than the rest."[1]

His predictions came true. The Right was defeated and the Left was victorious, with a large share of the vote going to the Radicals. The SFIO made advances, with the number of its deputies rising from 113 to 130, but Léon Blum once again refused to participate in the government. The Radicals decided to govern without aligning with the socialists and to conduct a financial policy very distant from what the latter had expected. It was a precarious situation. The Radical Party leader Édouard Herriot lost the premiership in December 1932. When subsequent Radical premier Édouard Daladier again offered the socialists a significant role—the Ministry of Finances to Auriol, Agriculture to Compère-Morel, Commerce to Renaudel, Aviation to Déat—the antiparticipationists within the party prevailed. The government had reached an impasse and, against the background of politico-financial scandals that the rightists used against the leftists, a new political crisis loomed.

The Neos

Within the SFIO, tensions were high and a rift seemed inevitable. The Parti Socialiste continued to lay claim to orthodox Marxism (criticizing capitalism and promoting class struggle and the socialization of the means of production), but in practice the measures its leaders defended were reformist and their methods of action lawful. There was no effort to seize power through violence: Léon Blum preferred the exercise of power to the ultimate objective, the acquisition of power. The party was divided between a leftist minority—Alexandre Bracke, Jean Zyromski, Jean-Baptiste Lebas—which made many revolutionary proclamations, and the right—Pierre Renaudel, Vincent Auriol, and Joseph Paul-Boncour—which considered the party a reformist organization that had to accept the responsibilities of power.

The possibility for doctrinal innovation was limited. Several intellectuals thought that new avenues had to be found to deal with the new social and economic realities. Their leader, Marcel Déat, often presented as Blum's heir apparent, had just "avenged the honor" of the socialists by defeating Jacques Duclos in the twentieth arrondissement. He was not yet forty years old. He was a brilliant intellectual trained at the École Normale, an *agrégé* in philosophy; he was also a combat veteran who had gone to war at the age of twenty. Lucien Herr was his protector and adviser. Célestin Bouglé, one of his professors, took note of him and, after getting him interested in sociology, assigned the "Docu" (the Centre de Documentation Sociale at the École Normale Supérieure) on rue d'Ulm to him. Déat was thus associated with the "efforts by Durkheim's faithful disciples" to revive *Année Sociologique*.[2] Along with Bouglé, he composed a brief guide for the sociology student and in 1924 published *Notions de sociologie* (Sociology notions) with Alcan.

Déat was an active socialist militant who respected his leader, Léon Blum, but who was annoyed by Blum's "emotional, emotive, and a tiny bit whining style." The break occurred shortly after the publication of his *Perspectives socialistes* (1930; Socialist perspectives), in which, as he confided to Mauss, "Durkheim and Marx stand side by side."[3] Déat became aware of the distance that separated him from Blum, whom the irreverent young socialists nicknamed the "Dalai Lama." Déat saw himself as a "revisionist" and claimed that a pragmatic socialism had to be developed, one that was more concerned with effectiveness and the "command of forces" than with collective appropriation. Then the base of political action had to be broadened by drawing in all the exploited classes, including the middle classes. Déat later explained: "Socialism absolutely had to be able to assemble all its forces under the sign of anticapitalism. And I invented three mottos that summed up that policy: don't cut yourself off from the middle classes; don't cut yourself off from democracy; don't cut yourself off from the nation."[4]

At the special congress of the SFIO in July 1933, Blum listened attentively to Déat, André Marquet, and the other "neosocialists," then let slip: "I'm frightened to death." The neos—twenty-eight deputies and seven senators—left the party to form the Parti Socialiste de France. Among the dissidents who rallied around *Vie Socialiste* were Mauss's friends; foremost among them was Pierre Renaudel. For the socialist militants, it was not easy to choose between loyalty to friends and allegiance to ideas. Several wavered between Blum and the "neosocialists" for some time. More than 20,000 members left the SFIO as a result of the rift.

During the 1932 election Mauss personally supported Déat, contributing financially to his campaign. The two combat veterans felt a solidarity of long standing. But everything that was happening within the party irritated Mauss, who saw it as merely "the result of horribly Byzantine discussions." He exclaimed indignantly that these were "phenomena of sheer obliviousness." Neither camp had "a sense of proportion."[5]

The "idiotic situation" in which the party found itself put Mauss in a bind. At the time of the rift, the socialist friends who were standing with Renaudel and Déat asked him to come to a meeting where a new fifth arrondissement group would be formed. Renaudel urged him to "get involved in the new party."[6] What to do? It was a heart-wrenching decision. Mauss would later confide to Blum that he felt like "a body without a soul."[7]

Mauss was obviously with Renaudel "in heart and mind." He would even have been a neo, if his friends had not "confused their Jacobinism" (of which he approved) with "new forms of socialism that do not exist." But out of "discipline" he remained with the party he had "twice contributed toward founding and whose central organs [he] had tried to save three times and had succeeded at twice." From his point of view, it was better to be excluded than to leave the "old house" voluntarily.[8]

Although he agreed to provide aid—300 francs in March 1934—to the Parti Socialiste de France, Mauss kept his distance and, after reflection, left the administrative board of *Vie Socialiste*. This decision deeply hurt Renaudel, who was resting at the time in Porto de la Cruze, trying to treat a case of tuberculosis that was taking its toll on him. But Renaudel did not insist and was content to cite the proverb: "There's no accounting for taste."[9]

Renaudel's death in 1935 saddened Mauss, who lost "one of his oldest and most faithful friends." He confided to Déat: "His loss, irreparable for the socialist Republic, for peace, and for the country, is even more irreparable for me."[10] More than ever convinced that he was right not to follow his old friend Renaudel, Mauss intended to remain true to his ideas. His faith remained intact, but his enthusiasm had cooled.[11] That "relative coolness" can be explained as much by the bind he found himself in than by the serious difficulties he was facing. When he sent the Déat group a "modest contribution," he reminded them that he "had never run from a fight" and was eager to explain his attitude: "My dear Déat, believe in the personal feelings I have for you in any case. I hold on to the hope that some day unity, which was as dear to Pierre Renaudel and to Jaurès as it is to me, will return again." The tradition he defended, his own and Jaurès's, claimed that "if socialism is to transcend the class perspective, it is only the working class as such that is capable of doing it."[12]

"Let Us Nationalize, Therein Lies the Future"

The neo movement partook of the spirit of the 1930s: rebellion against the existing order, critique of liberalism, search for a third way between capitalism and communism, proposal for an organized, united, or planned economy, extolling of the community. This was the generation of refusal, which would anticipate the post-1945 innovations. New journals appeared: *Revue Marxiste* (1929), *Critique Sociale* (1931), *Plans* (1931), and *Esprit* (1932). Robert Aron and Arnaud Dandieu's *La révolution nécessaire* (1933; The necessary revolution) and Emmanuel Mounier's *Manifeste au service du personnalisme* (1936; Manifesto in the service of personalism) were standard bearers. Marxism moved from propaganda to exegesis: Marx's selected works were published in French, then Hegel's selected works and Lenin's notebooks on Hegel's logic. Finally, though it had little influence, the collection called *Révolution constructive* (1932; Constructive revolution) attested to a need for innovation in political thought and a desire to regenerate socialism through values said to be new, simpler, or more sound.

In the face of economic crisis, original solutions were sought that would break away from the doctrines of the past and make it possible to escape liberal anarchy. Central planning became an appealing idea. In the United States, the "spirit of engineering" triumphed. In Belgium, the socialist Henri de Man became an advocate of central planning and proposed a plan to his party that would open a third way between capitalism and Marxist socialism. That blueprint for a planned economy keenly interested Déat and the neosocialists and also appealed to trade unionists, both those in the Confédération Générale du Travail and those in the Confédération Française Démocratique du Travail (French democratic labor confederation), who saw it as a possible solution to the crisis. Intellectuals of diverse political leanings united around Jules Romains and Albert Fabre-Luce and developed the plan of July 9, 1934. The idea was to promote reform of the state in an authoritarian direction and, at the social level, to establish state corporatism.[13]

In a time of crisis, it is difficult to ignore issues of the day. The Centre de Documentation Sociale, awarded a grant from the Rockefeller Foundation, undertook "new research" in keeping with the foundation's new objectives. That work, headed by Bouglé and conducted by research teams, studied the social psychology of entire peoples: opinion trends and ideological transformations, standards of living, the middle classes, worker psychology and mechanization, advertising, and so on. The results of this research were published in three anthologies under the general title *Inventaires* (Surveys), edited by Bouglé: *Crise sociale et idéologies nationales, Économique et politique*, and *Classes moyennes* (Social crisis and national ideologies; Economics and politics; The middle classes). Societal demand contributed to the birth of an inductive sociology founded on field research and, as Raymond Aron noted, made it possible for young laborers to come into contact with social reality.[14]

Annales Sociologiques, subsidized by the Rockefeller Foundation, did not intend to disappoint its "American friends."[15] The first installment of series A (general sociology) included a text by André Philip, "An Overall View of the Evolution of a Contemporary Society" (1934). Like Déat, Philip was interested at the time in Henri de Man's ideas, which he played a role in diffusing throughout France. The other installments published by *Annales Sociologiques* in 1934 and 1935 were on economic sociology and included studies by Simiand titled "Currency" and "The Social Psychology of Short-term Crises and Economic Fluctuations." Halbwachs, the journal's secretary, pursued his work on social demography, shifting the orientation of his research toward an analysis of the evolution of the working class's needs.[16] In 1940 he would also publish a long reflection on Keynes's General Theory in *Annales Sociologiques*.

Robert Marjolin (1911–1986), one of the young contributors to *Annales*, in 1932 played a part in founding Révolution Constructive, a club headed by Georges Lefranc and consisting of about a dozen people, including Lévi-Strauss. Thanks to the support of Mauss and Bouglé, Marjolin received a grant from the Rockefeller Foundation and spent a year in the United States studying the evolution of trade unionism.[17] On his return, he resumed his law studies, collaborated on research at the Centre de Documentation Sociale, and branched out into economics. His thesis, which he wrote while maintaining his economics column at *Populaire* (under the name Marc Joubert), was called "Essay on Long-term Economic Movements" and dealt with "prices, currency, and production."[18]

Connections between the Étudiants Socialistes, the École Normale—especially the Centre de Documentation—and the Durkheimians at *Annales* were
increasingly close. With Lucien Herr gone, Mauss and Simiand epitomized
the politically committed intellectual: "Simiand and [Mauss], you are our two
elder brothers," acknowledged Halbwachs. At the time of his friend's death in
1935, Mauss paid him the following tribute: "The spirit of his career, of all
his action, was that of a socialist who devoted himself entirely to the study
of society and, in society, to the study of what mattered to the proletariat,
wage laborers. He wanted to share the development of his thought with the
working masses, make them benefit from his action at every moment."[19]

Mauss advised his students "not to run, despite all the risks, from objects
of study that pit different camps against each other and inflame passions."[20]
During his rare moments of leisure, probably until the mid-1930s, he continued to write his book on the nation, which was to include a chapter on
the principle of nationalization.

His plan was to analyze contemporary economic and political reality as
a whole, that is, all at once: (1) economic facts proper (state industries, the
national organization of capitalists, trusts, cartels, and so on); (2) "political
and economic movement from above" (legislation to reduce capitalist anarchy, control of trusts, protection of laborers); and (3) "political-economic
movement from below, from the mass of citizens" (cooperatives, unions,
mutual insurance companies, mass parties, public pressure).[21]

Mauss hoped that the book, which would deal with countries such as
the United States, Great Britain, Germany, and France, would make it possible to complete the portrait of modern capitalism—before and after the
war—and to analyze the dual movement of "growing socialization and decreasing individualization" that was already impelling capitalist interests to
move "from blind and anarchical competition to a system of increasingly
complete, conscious, well-ordered collectivization." Mauss again came out
in support of nationalization. This "new" idea, which he had discovered in
Britain, excited him because it followed from an observation of the facts,
namely, that "the best administration of things is done by the interested
parties." But from his point of view, nationalization presupposed replacing
the notion of sovereign–irresponsible–poor administrator state with the idea
that "the nation is a natural group of users, interested parties, a vast consumer cooperative that entrusts its interests to responsible administrators
and not to political bodies, which are generally recruited on the basis of
public opinion, and are in short incompetent."[22]

That view was very remote from the "directed revolution" or "central
planning" elaborated, for example, by Déat in *Perspectives socialistes*. Déat
was opposed to nationalization and favored "effective control" by the state.

The "principle of nationalization" held a central place in Mauss's work
because it was inseparable from the socialist project of the same period.

Nationalization appeared to be "the most recent form of socialism and probably the one with the best future." Mauss felt adequately informed to give a brief history of socialism. He would later confide to Charles Le Coeur, "I know a little of the history of socialism. Not only did I edit Durkheim's *Saint-Simon* but I also had enough contacts with Proudhon's and Marx's successors, their direct successors, to know and feel things you do not feel. I lived the struggle against Marxism even more than you did."[23] Nevertheless, unlike his uncle,[24] Mauss granted great importance to the facts and demonstrated the national dimension of socialism: "Socialism is nothing other than the set of ideas, forms, and collective institutions whose function it is to regulate—through society, socially—the collective economic interests of nations."[25] According to Mauss, a society cannot transform itself into a social republic before it has been formed into a nation. It is impossible to skip steps: the transition to socialism has a greater chance of being realized in a society at an advanced stage of democratic life (having proclaimed the rights of man and of the citizen) and economic development (capitalism). In other words, only modern nations can participate in the movement leading them to an awareness of their economic life and to the desire to govern it conscientiously.

The "very sketchy" history Mauss gave of socialism was divided into three periods: the "critical and rhetorical" period of Saint-Simon, "true founder of socialism"; the "pamphleteering" period of Proudhon and Marx; and the period when socialist political parties were founded and the first workers' organizations played a role. His theories were set out in a few pages and contained a scathing critique of the doctrinaire theorists who held capitalism "responsible for all the evils of society" or who dreamed of an "El Dorado" to which a "simple political revolution" would provide access. Mauss, the opponent of all Marxist and revolutionary phraseology, reiterated his criticism of the Russian Revolution and especially of Bolshevism, which, he said, brought nothing new in the way of doctrine, "absolutely nothing." It was "out-and-out Marxism," a "revolutionary state socialism limiting itself to the socialization of capital."[26]

He did not conceal his preferences. Socialism interested him only when it began to be "constructive and positive" (as in Brousse's, Allemane's, and Fournière's possibilism) and when, in giving priority to immediate reforms, it led "the struggle in the field of facts and sought the possible, all that is possible."[27] Mauss also liked the Fabians for their "British spirit": their rejection of idealistic, utopian conceptions contrary to experience, their instinctive fear of all theory, their desire for action, but "constant and gradual action," the "step by step" and the "blow by blow."

Mauss said little about ideas. He did not linger on doctrines. What held his attention was the "economic movement from below," whose principal manifestations were syndicalism, cooperation, and mutual insurance. He believed these were spontaneous and nonobligatory forms of democracy. Just as there is a political democracy, there can be a "workers' democracy," a "democracy of consumers," and even a "mutual insurance democracy" ("insurance for all by all, for each by all").

Mauss had already spoken of cooperation. Despite certain failures, including the 1934 bankruptcy of the Banque des Coopératives (which affected him directly),[28] he was still amazed by the actions of groups of individuals and small organizations—often "groping along blindly, empirically"—and by all the "gifts of self-sacrifice" they entailed. He exclaimed: "Nothing gives a greater sense of the limitless possibilities involved in collective effort and of the freedom allowed within that effort, since these initiatives elicit countless inventions and countless actions."[29]

Mauss did not hesitate to compare these profoundly democratic movements to the grandiose or modest beginnings of the major religions: the spirit of sacrifice, the search for ideas and formulas, the violence of passions. The difference was that people were no longer sacrificing themselves for a divine power but rather for the interests of others. It was therefore a sort of "religion of man for man," as Saint-Simon, Comte, and Enfantin had dreamed it.

Mauss shared certain ideas with the English socialists and, in his study on "economic movement from below," would have preferred to deal with "industrial democracy" as a whole, the totality of corporate bodies. He confined himself to the "political problem of the time," namely, the "workers' democracy," and drew a rough historical sketch of syndicalism in Europe, from the heroic founding period with its "moral, sacrificial side" to legal recognition. According to him, the worker or trade union movement of his own time had the following characteristics. It was legal; it performed a collective function, signing contracts that linked it not to individuals but to collectivities; it was becoming a national organization; and it formed a "general class organization" for the working class.[30] The power the movement had acquired gave its actions a political dimension and sometimes, as in the case of the general strike, a revolutionary character.

All these tendencies had been reinforced since the war. There had been a "considerable expansion" in the number of union members; a transition from professional federations to industry federations; a diffusion of the idea of "worker control" or of a role in managing the industry. For Mauss, who observed the development of a stronger, more unified trade unionism, one conclusion was unavoidable: "The workers' democracy is being transformed into a true industrial democracy and is coming to understand how the citizen as producer can oversee the totality of at least certain production processes." In other words, everything was in place for a takeover of property by large "natural" employee organizations, and hence for nationalization.[31]

This was a long way from the corporatist ideology of Mussolini's Italy and elsewhere with which some sought to identify Durkheimian sociology. The themes of nation, peace, democracy, Europe, and socialism at the heart of Mauss's analysis are found again among those who wanted to reinvigorate socialist doctrine and who, like Déat, then sought to reconcile nationalism, socialism, and pacifism. Nevertheless, though Mauss paid attention to the measures taken by the leader of the new Parti Socialiste de France, he did not follow him. Just as he was unconvinced by the thesis of the "rise of the middle classes," the "old militant" rejected the formula "order, authority, nation" dear to the neos.

What might have become of Mauss, had it not been for his ethnicity and his loyalty to Jaurès? The splintering of the Parti Socialiste and the failure of the Déat venture demoralized him and alienated him from partisan politics. His book on the nation remained unfinished.

Peace, Bread, Freedom

There was a grave threat of war. In 1933 Mauss wondered: "What will we do when Hitler has his army, eight months from now at the latest? I think about that constantly."[32] Two years later, the external situation was even more serious. Mauss fretted: "Anything is possible there. They may even keep quiet out of cowardice."[33]

His fear was well founded. France was witnessing the development of Far Right organizations—Action Française, Jeunesses Patriotes, Croix-de-Feu—and major antiparliamentary demonstrations. Were these signs of the rise of fascism? On February 6, 1934, one of these demonstrations turned into a bloody riot, leaving 15 dead and more than 1,400 wounded. On the morning of the 7th, *Populaire* ran the headline: "The Fascist Coup Has Failed." Although the reality was more complex, February 6 played an essential role in the formation of the Rassemblement Populaire (Popular assembly, later renamed the Front Populaire). In the face of the fascist threat, communists and socialists moved closer together and promoted a broad alliance.

Mauss participated in the major joint demonstration of February 12. It was organized by the Confédération Générale du Travail to protest the riot and was joined by the Comité de Vigilance des Intellectuels Antifascistes, two of whose leaders were Mauss's colleagues: Paul Langevin, professor at the Collège de France, and Paul Rivet of the Institut d'Ethnologie de Paris. The third leader was Alain, a philosophy professor at the *lycée* Henri-IV. The objective of the movement formed on March 4, 1934, was to "save from a fascist dictatorship the public rights and freedoms won by the people" and to "sacrifice all to prevent France from submitting to a regime of bellicose oppression and destitution."[34] It was also a pacifist movement resolutely determined to take "persistent action against war."[35] The first important move taken by the Comité de Vigilance was to elaborate and distribute its

manifesto "To the Workers," which in less than a month obtained the support of more than two thousand people. Mauss was part of the first wave of
signatories, alongside Julien Benda, André Breton, Félicien Challaye, Léon-
Paul Fargue, André Gide, Lucien Febvre, Lucien Lévy-Bruhl, Paul Mantoux,
Romain Rolland, and others.[36]

In the 1936 election, the Comité de Vigilance des Intellectuels Antifascistes,
facing a looming fascist threat, turned to "a few eminent men" to obtain their
support "for the electoral success of the Rassemblement Populaire." The
committee's president, Paul Rivet, personally wrote to Mauss to get a brief
declaration from him. In his reply, Mauss paid tribute to the Confédération
Générale du Travail for being unlike "the proletarian parties engaged in
quarrels with enemy brothers." He also took up the defense of intellectuals
who had leapt into the melee, "but in their proper place, and their place was
with the workers."[37]

The unity of the Left could only delight Mauss. But he found the Front
Populaire's platform ("bread, peace, freedom") and proposals, both political
(the defense of liberties, of union rights, and of secular education) and economic (public works projects, the creation of an unemployment insurance
fund, retirement pensions for aging workers, a reduction of work hours with
no drop in salary, and so on), too moderate. Nevertheless, he maintained
that intellectuals did not "have the right, or even the capacity, even less the
might, to leave the ranks."

Mauss stood with Blum. When the socialist leader was wounded on
February 16, 1936, on boulevard Saint-Germain, Mauss lost no time in expressing his sympathy. "Thank you for your letter, my dear and old friend,"
Blum replied. "Thank you for your call, which brings me a little comfort in
my affliction. But I have not yet recovered my courage."[38]

After a lively campaign, the May 3 election gave the majority to the
Rassemblement Populaire: 376 seats, versus 236 on the right. Two days
later, Mauss wrote his dear friend Blum to congratulate him on the "success
of our camp."[39] Blum accepted the responsibilities of power and formed a
new government. Mauss then felt it his duty to take up his old place in the
party, where he believed he could be useful. But he did not consider becoming an editor or administrator at *Populaire* or being part of an "American-
style brain trust."

Mauss could have easily played the role of éminence grise. But he refused:
he did not want to be the one who "gave copious advice" and attempted to
gain access to the prime minister. At most he ventured to attract his friend's
attention to "a few points": the need to reorganize the party newspaper,
Populaire, and to restaff the ministries and especially the embassies.

Mauss was naturally very happy about the Front Populaire's success, but
displayed some anxiety: "It is not enough to cut, one must also mend."[40]
Several of his "comrades" again found themselves in power, including seven

members of the old *Cahiers du Socialiste* group: Blum, Auriol, R. Jardillier, Monnet, Paul Ramadier, Sellier, and Spinasse. Auriol was minister of finance; Monnet, minister of agriculture; Sellier, minister of public health; and Spinasse, economics minister. Mauss was willing to help out and was consulted by his minister comrades, especially Auriol and Monnet, but he felt he was being cast aside. "Even poor old men like you and me can still be useful," he confided to his friend Emmanuel Lévy.[41]

Somewhat annoyed, the "old journalist" decided to devote himself to reflection and study. Assured that he had the Parti Socialiste's "active sympathy," he suggested transforming *Cahiers du Socialiste*, at that time merely a collection of brochures, into a real monthly journal. Mauss announced it would be "centered on traditional socialism but free of dogmatism, faithful, in a word, to the spirit of Robert Hertz, its original founder, a publication for the free discussion of ideas and objective documentation."[42]

Once again, funds had to be raised. Those in charge of the project, with Mauss in the lead, went in search of some thirty underwriters who could provide a thousand francs each. A few months later, finding it impossible to collect that amount, the members of the *Cahiers* group were obliged to postpone their plan and to ponder their future.

For the first issue of *Cahiers*, Mauss wanted to compose a text about ten pages long on "the parties and conspiracies of modern political history."[43] The ethnologist was well aware of the "significant role" of "men's organizations" in societies of the archaic type: "Secret brotherhoods very effectively ensure social stability," he wrote. He was preoccupied at the time with the question of "secrecy and plotting" in politics. Following a paper delivered by Élie Halévy on "the age of tyrannies" before members of the Société Française de Philosophie, he returned to it: "I stress the fundamental fact of secrecy and plotting more than you do. . . . Even sociologically, it may be a necessary form of action, but it is a backward form. That is no reason for it not to be fashionable. It satisfies the need for secrecy, influence, action, youth, and often tradition."[44]

For many, the thesis of a "conspiracy" was more present than ever. On the right, people feared a communist plot, the communist revolution advancing behind the Front Populaire. On the left, they worried that people such as Eugène Deloncle, former member of Action Française, wanted to overthrow the regime. The anticommunism of one camp came up against the antifascism of the other.

When the Blum government first came to power, it elicited great hopes for reforming the Banque de France, nationalizing the war industries, and providing paid vacations. People thought it was the beginning of a new era, which would lead not only to the improvement of living conditions but also to cultural enrichment: the creation of a state agency to organize leisure activities and sports, the adoption of measures favoring the development of popular culture. In 1937 the opening of the Musée de l'Homme and of the Musée des Arts et Traditions Populaires was part of that vast movement, whose motto, in Jacques Soustelle's words, would be: "Let's open the doors of culture."

But the golden days of summer 1936 quickly passed. The Front Populaire experiment, violently criticized, was short-lived. After the Parti Radical's defection, Blum submitted his resignation on June 22, 1937. Far Left militants called it a "failed revolution," reproaching the government for decreeing a "short break" in social progress and for its nonintervention policy in Spain's civil war.

A powerless witness, Mauss observed the general trend of European society toward Bolshevism and fascism. It was a "return to the primitive," he said, which could end only in tragedy.

THE TIME OF MYTHS

"1936: A crucial year? A year of war?" So wrote Michel Leiris in his journal.[1] Once Hitler had come to power, Germany was a threat to peace. Anxiety was growing. Ignace Meyerson wrote to Mauss: "Painfully we gain a day at a time, telling ourselves each evening: There was no catastrophe today, but what about tomorrow?"[2] In a long letter addressed to Mauss, A. S. Szczupac, a professor at Jerusalem University, analyzed the Palestinian question and the international situation. He concluded: "I have the impression that war is at hand in Europe. I only hope I'm a false prophet."[3]

The Rise of Fascism

Like some other combat veterans—he was still a dues-paying member of the Amicale des Anciens Poilus du XIVe (Association of veterans of the Great War from the fourteenth arrondissement)—Mauss wanted to avoid a new outbreak of war. He even saw pacifism as a "sign of strength."[4]

After World War I, combat veterans such as Félicien Challaye (b. 1875) had become "veterans for peace" and had made pacifism their way of life. Challaye, whom Mauss had known at the Librairie Bellaye, was active in the Ligue Internationale des Combattants de la Paix (International league of veterans for peace) and in 1932 published a pamphlet whose title was unambiguous: "For Peace without Reservations." The position defended by Challaye, a philosophy teacher at the Condorcet *lycée*, was "utter pacifism": "For an absolute evil, an absolute remedy: utter pacifism, peace without reservations."[5]

With the rise of fascism in Europe, pacifism took two different forms among combat veterans. On the one side, there were those who, favoring a rapprochement between Germany and France, did not hide their sympathy for Hitler's regime; and, on the other, there were those who were involved in the antifascist struggle. Mauss immediately joined the antifascist movement, taking many measures to aid "victims of Hitler's reign of terror" such as Jules Lips, director of the Museum of Ethnography in Cologne. And, like his new colleague Henri Wallon, he gave his support to the Comité de Vigilance des Intellectuels Antifascistes.[6] When the Comité Mondial contre la Guerre et le Fascisme (Worldwide committee against war and fascism) was created, Mauss also agreed to participate in some of its activities.

That committee, founded by Henri Barbusse with Romain Rolland as its sponsor, brought together European and North American intellectuals. France was represented by Paul Langevin, Jean Longuet, and André Malraux. In 1937 and 1938, when "one of the most tragic episodes in fascism's battle against democracy" unfolded in Spain, an effort was made to obtain declarations from personalities in different countries, "people of goodwill who command some authority with public opinion." Mauss was among them.

In July 1938 his colleague Paul Langevin asked him to reply to two questions, the first on the duties of democratic governments toward the legitimate government of Republican Spain, the second on the duties the major organizations fighting for peace and freedom had to the Spanish people.[7] In his reply, Mauss immediately recognized that "naturally, the duties of democratic governments toward the legitimate government of Republican Spain are absolutely those one has toward any legitimate government." He was sorry that the major democracies had accepted the overthrow of the Republicans as a fait accompli and, because of their "horror of risk and disgust at effort," had not sought to save a democracy, even at the risk of going to war.[8] Under such conditions, those who were true to their principles were obliged to "trust only [their] own actions." According to Mauss, the first duty of the major organizations for peace and freedom, but also of all "democratic camps," was "to try to offer relief to the families of the dead, the wounded, and the victims of war."

When Mauss was asked by Halbwachs's wife, Yvonne, to help Spanish refugee children, he did not hesitate to make cash gifts. In addition, he agreed to encourage and support a group of "republican students." They belonged to several antifascist clubs, which in February 1938 created an association with the motto: "Freedom!" The goal of Action Universitaire pour la Liberté (University action for freedom) was to "defend the great tradition of free research and free discussion in French universities against the theorists and practitioners of violence."[9]

Everything happening in Europe was disturbing. The "Boches," as Mauss still called them, were dangerous.[10] There was a risk that the situation would turn tragic. Mauss confided to his old friend Edgar Milhaud that none of it "had anything to do with our ideals, or with victory, or with common sense, or with justice."[11] Mauss was especially troubled when he saw that certain fundamental tenets of sociological theory, of the French school of sociology, were also being called into question. Hence, when corporatist ideology was propagated, some were tempted to establish a kinship between that ideology and the Durkheimian theory of professional groups.

Déat said he had been "enriched by the philosophical thinking of masters such as Durkheim, Lévy-Bruhl, Brunschvicg, Marcel Mauss."[12] His political philosophy was founded on the idea of (national) solidarity: "What is socialism in the last analysis," he wondered, "if not the gradual and complete reintegration of the individual into a society where, in a sense, one breathes the same air as in the family community? With, let us say, something of the heartfelt intensity that sociologists discover in the primitive clan."[13] Nostalgic for the old camaraderie of wartime, Déat defended the community spirit in the name of romanticism: "We are about to discover life in common. . . . Heroism is not only bravery on the battlefield, it is also devotion to the common interest, it is the feeling that individuals are not complete unless they are integrated into a group, the sense that individuals are nothing unless they are capable of devoting themselves to the collectivity and sacrificing themselves for it."[14] Referring to the "rise in the social temperature" that Europe was experiencing, he added: "I will not hesitate to say that it is something religious in the most profound, the most noble sense of the term. True religion may be the feeling of communal warmth."[15]

Mauss was intent on correcting such errors. He was, for example, "in a rush" to publish three lectures in *Revue de Métaphysique et de Morale* excerpted from one of Durkheim's classes ("Civic and Professional Ethics"). "I know where the sore spot is in all those goddamned modern forms of corporatism. The vast difference between Durkheim's ideas, my own, and even Briand's, is that what is at stake is the organization of corporate property."[16] In his introduction, Mauss recounted the history of the text—it consisted of lectures he had heard in 1890–1892—and gave a few pointers on how to read it. According to him, Durkheim's merit was to have developed the principles of a professional ethics, though in an "obviously provisional and schematic form," and to have, "by clear intuition, proposed the right, the practical solution: moral, legal, and economic." Mauss believed it necessary to make Durkheim's thinking better known, especially at that time, which was "the time of soviets, of corporate groups of every kind, of every form of corporatism."[17]

While claiming to agree with Élie Halévy, whose 1938 book was titled *L'ère des tyrannies*, Mauss linked "the age of tyrannies" to the doctrine of active minorities, violence, and corporatism as elaborated by Sorel. Under his very eyes, he added, it had spread from Sorel to Lenin and Mussolini. For Sorel, that corporatism corresponded to "a reactionary view of our societies' past."[18]

The Durkheimians felt that the sociology they defended was well suited for developing a concern with objectivity, a sense of relativism, and also a feeling of solidarity.[19] And as Bouglé was inclined to recall, the feeling of solidarity necessarily entailed membership in groups, especially, in modern societies, professional groups.

Durkheim's disciples were forced to correct the false interpretations. Referring to the role sometimes played by "rousing meetings where collective enthusiasm is forged," Bouglé recognized that in *The Elementary Forms of Religious Life*, Durkheim had suggested that such enthusiasm was not outdated, that it would still have a role to play whenever societies felt the need to take on some major project of reorganization. But he was eager to explain: "Obviously, [Durkheim] was thinking at the time of socialism and regenerative faith."[20]

A worried Svend Ranulf, Mauss's former student, asked the question directly: Was the emergence of fascism an event Durkheim would have welcomed as a salvation from individualism? Ranulf replied that logically, there was no doubt about it. But he added that some aspects of fascism probably would have been unacceptable to Durkheim. The new solidarity, when it materialized, seemed even worse than the evils it wanted to remedy.[21]

Mauss provided the following explanation to his Danish correspondent: "I believe that Durkheim and those of us who follow him originated the theory of the authority of collective representations." But neither he nor they could have predicted that "great modern societies, having more or less emerged from the Middle Ages, could be as suggestible as Australians are to their dances, could be set spinning like children playing Ring around the Rosey." And Mauss added: "That return to the primitive was not the subject of our reflections. We confined ourselves to a few allusions to mob psychology, though that is a very different thing."[22]

For Mauss, "one of the sorrows of his life" was to witness, in the late 1930s, "the worst crimes and the regression—or even, in a few cases, the disappearance—of whole societies in the name of the state's preeminence."[23] Everything that was happening, he reminded Ranulf, was "too strong a verification of things we had pointed out and proof that we ought to have expected such verification to come about through evil rather than through good."[24]

President of the Section of Religious Science

In February 1938, Marcel Mauss became president of the section of religious science at the École (he received fifteen votes, with one abstention), that "place of erudition, of coolness and impartiality."[25] He succeeded his colleague Alexandre Moret, who had died suddenly, while "still vigorous, still active." Mauss wrote: "I am losing a friend of more than forty years: one of the joys of my life has disappeared."[26] The tradition continued: the president of the section of religious science was a professor at the Collège de France.

The sciatica from which Mauss was suffering did not make his task easy. He could devote "only a minimum amount of time to [his] most absolute obligations."[27] Every year, he spent a few weeks in Contrexéville, a spa in Vosges, but feared a "relapse of [his] major illness."[28] The new president of the section could not engage in "unflagging intellectual labor," as an American correspondent hoped he would.[29] His wife's state of health had not changed. Mauss had to perform "not only the duties of nurse but also those of housekeeper morning and evening."[30] He confided to Charles Le Coeur, "I am the servant of my servants and of my unfortunate wife, and my life is not my own."[31]

Mauss was sixty-six. As he was wont to say, he belonged to the generation of "bearded gentlemen in hats." At the École Pratique, he was one of the "old men," along with Charles Fossey, Gabriel Millet, and Paul Masson-Oursel. The old faculty had made way for the new: Jean Marx had succeeded Henri Hubert; Georges Dumézil and Marcel Granet had become *directeurs d'étude*; Alexandre Koyré had left the École to teach at the University of Cairo; Roger Caillois had been assigned to teach a course. Nearly four hundred students from every background were enrolled in the section. About forty of them regularly took Mauss's courses. These included his faithful and unwavering supporters, who also went to listen to their teacher at the Institut d'Ethnologie and the Collège de France.

Mauss was probably not yet thinking of his successor, but he asked Leenhardt, who had been his student at the École Pratique in 1932 and who was assigned to teach a course the next year, to replace him during the second semester of 1936–1937. Leenhardt felt enormous gratitude toward his professor: "Through all the difficulties I have encountered, you and M. Lucien Lévy-Bruhl have unflaggingly supported me and respected my dignity."[32] Mauss found a kindred spirit in Leenhardt, a Protestant missionary six years his junior. Leenhardt was a charming storyteller who had at his fingertips a stock of stories drawn from his field experiences in Africa and New Caledonia. The two looked alike—large beard, imposing stature—and neither seemed cut out for purely intellectual work.[33] They also had common interests—the question of religion and rites, of course, but also the notion of "person." Although their lives and political convictions were different, the professor and the student became friends and took to meeting for breakfast every Thursday to discuss ethnology, teaching, and their personal problems. What Mauss found fascinating about Leenhardt was his extensive familiarity with fieldwork. From 1903 to 1926, he had lived in New Caledonia, "a choice field for observation," according to Mauss, and had acquired an excellent mastery of the Houallou language.[34] After becoming an ethnologist, the missionary published a book that attracted a great deal of attention, *Gens de la Grande-Terre: Nouvelle-Calédonie* (Gallimard, 1937; People of the great earth: New Caledonia).

The late 1930s were a favorable time for French ethnology: the Musée de l'Homme and the Musée des Arts et Traditions Populaires opened; the Trans-Greenland, Sahara-Cameroon, and Aurès Mountains expeditions were sent out; Lévi-Strauss went to Brazil, André Leroi-Gourhan to Japan, Cuisinier-Delmas to Indochina; many exhibits were held; lectures were given by foreign researchers, including one by Malinowski at the École

Pratique; documentary films were shown publicly. With the new Musée de l'Homme, which had been designed in keeping with the most modern museology data, ethnologists had a true research laboratory: scientific collections, a library, a photo library, sound archives, classrooms, and lecture halls. Mere access to the various departments of the museum made it possible to initiate students "in a practical way, better than any number of readings would have done."[35] The Institut d'Ethnologie, installed in the Palais de Chaillot on Place du Trocadéro and assured of financial support, pursued its work more actively than ever, training "future professional ethnologists" and colonial administrators. It had 144 students in 1936–1937, 165 in 1937–1938. The institute's series "Travaux et Mémoires" published about fifteen titles between 1935 and 1940, in several cases written by Mauss's students or collaborators.[36]

The "charms of the life of the mind" gained by training young researchers was Mauss's "greatest reward."[37] He still carefully followed the work of the new generation of ethnologists: Jeanne Cuisinier, Germaine Dierterlen, Louis Dumont, Marcel Griaule, Michel Leiris, Nina Lévi-Strauss and Claude Lévi-Strauss, Alfred Métraux, Denise Paulme, Georges-Henri Rivière, Thérèse Rivière, Jacques Soustelle, André Schaeffner, Germaine Tillion, André Varagnac, Paul-Émile Victor.

In August 1938, when Mauss went to the congress of anthropological and ethnological sciences in Copenhagen, he was surrounded by a delegation that included eight of his students.[38] For these young scientists, Mauss was the "faithful protector of all ethnological research in France."[39]

When he was asked to take charge of the section of religious science, Mauss agreed, but without enthusiasm. He regretted that this duty, along with his other chores, took a great deal of his time.[40] He had to manage the section's inadequate budget, arrange for the appointment of new *directeurs d'études*, and solve a thousand and one little problems: set up commissions, publish essays, purchase materials, do repair work and library research. In his administrative work, which put him in direct contact with the minister of education, he was aided by the section secretary, Henri-Charles Puech, *directeur d'études* for Gnosticism and Manichaeanism at the École since 1929.

The first years Mauss was in charge of the section passed with no major problems, with one exception: the Péguin affair. In November 1938, Paul Péguin, one of Jean Marx's students, had a dispute with the professors of the section. The affair erupted when the professors, after reading a report by Georges Dumézil and Henri-Charles Puech on the student's thesis, formulated various criticisms (it was unoriginal work; the bibliography was incomplete; there were grammatical mistakes) and refused to grant Péguin his degree. Furious, Péguin sent out a number of insulting letters and published an abusive article about the section in *Pilori*.[41]

The incident was not resolved until several years later: the student agreed to apologize to Dumézil and to redo his thesis on "what are known as pagan fires." But the little affair did not escape the notice of the novelist Louis-Ferdinand Céline who, in an anti-Semitic pamphlet titled *L'école des cadavres* (School of cadavers), attacked the section of religious science and its professors. He accused it of being a "subghetto," a "synagogue of excessive pressure" where degrees were awarded among co-religionists and official titles distributed like manna from heaven. The text identified a few of the "skullcapped, unlikely professors," including Mauss, and ended with the words: "Jews! . . . Jews . . . And counter-Jews![42]

In addition to his tasks at the École Pratique, Mauss took on various administrative and scientific chores. There was the Collège de France, whose faculty was changing rapidly, the Commission Nationale des Arts et Traditions Populaires, where he served as vice president, the Commission des Voyages et Missions Scientifiques et Littéraires (Commission on scientific and literary journeys and expeditions), the commission responsible for studying the question of excavations (the Caisse Nationale de la Recherche Scientifique), and the Comité du Jubilé de la Psychologie Française (Jubilee committee of French psychology), of which he was a member. In short, it was "a great deal of work,"[43] especially since research in France was in a distressing state. Mauss complained about it continually. Any comparison with England and the United States put France in an unfavorable light. Not only did these other countries devote more money to science, making it possible to conduct research that was unimaginable in France,[44] but researchers' working conditions were also better (they were released from professional obligations and had laboratories and secretarial staffs).

Mauss wanted only one thing, "the extension and development of research." For the social sciences alone, he recommended "certain emergency measures": establish a section of social sciences at the École des Hautes Études; create "chairs devoted exclusively to the social sciences in faculties of letters and law (to be distinguished from chairs in normative policy, ethics, and practical law)"; create two chairs in statistics (one in the sciences and the other in the social sciences) at most universities; add positions at the École Pratique. Only such efforts would make it possible to do major surveys like "Social Trends" in the United States and to "advance sociological knowledge of the French empire, statistical knowledge of the metropolis, ethnographic knowledge of both the metropolis and the French empire, not to mention knowledge of the rest of the world."

Mauss was in favor of creating a "research corps" (the Caisse Nationale de la Recherche Scientifique, or CNRS, was established in 1939) that would ensure young researchers a "regular future and regular employment," but only on the condition that teaching and research not be totally separate. From his point of view, researchers were "obliged not only to account for their research but also to enter into contact with future scientists, whose research they would be able to oversee and whose technique they would be able to perfect."[45]

For Mauss, research and teaching remained inseparable. His immediate plans were to pursue his work on Germanic law and religion, topics to which he had for several years devoted one of his courses at the Collège. Various work remained in the planning stages, including the research undertaken in the 1930s on kites, greased poles, and myths of conquering the sky, on which he said he had been working for a long time. In 1934, during the International Congress of Anthropological and Ethnological Sciences in London, Mauss presented a few observations on the relationship between rites and myths among the Maori. One of these had to do with an institution, or rather a game, the "greased pole," and another with ritual objects, precious tikis, beautiful jade sculptures shaped like fetuses.[46] The course Mauss had given in 1933–1934 at the École Pratique was also devoted to "the study of religious documents concerning the Polynesian religions," those collected by John White in his *Ancient History of the Maori*. Mauss had already studied them with Robert Hertz at the British Museum and now rediscovered them thirty years later.[47]

That year, obliged to stand in for an ailing Father Teilhard de Chardin, Mauss gave an impromptu lecture to members of the Institut Français d'Anthropologie on the "macrocosm and the microcosm." Reiterating his previous observations on the god Tiki, he again analyzed the documents collected by White.[48] The subject of one of the courses Mauss gave in 1937–1938 at the Collège de France was the "relationship between certain games and cosmology" and was based on the same documents.

Also in 1937, Mauss made comments following a paper given by his student and colleague Paul Mus titled "Primitive Mythology and Thought in India," and announced the forthcoming publication of his work in the installment of *Annales Sociologiques* devoted to religion, which, he added, "was very late": "[This work] bears a rather wide-ranging title: 'Macrocosm and microcosm,' and is subtitled 'Tiki.'"[49] This time, the object of study belonged to (religious) history, sociology, and ("if you like," added Mauss), philosophy. It was about the so-called primitive mentality and categories of thought. "There is no reason at all to speak of Polynesians as primitives. . . . We are dealing with a great civilization."[50]

Leenhardt, on an expedition to New Caledonia, learned of the forthcoming publication of Mauss's study on Polynesian mythology and could not conceal his eagerness to read it.[51] Mauss was making no progress on the book. The many books he read enriched his various courses, but the transition from oral to written was more difficult than ever. "His thinking was too detailed, too teeming with ideas, and, at the same time, at odds with the complacency of the time. It became less and less accommodating of the rhetorical practices and courtesy of written exposition."[52]

Mauss did not forget the other commitments he had made, usually out of friendship: to write a short, fifteen-page chapter on collective psychology for a treatise by George Dumas; to prepare a "short study on a detail of psychosociology and a few memories of Ribot's courses" for the jubilee of French psychology;[53] and finally, to publish Hertz's admirable study on the notion of expiation. Mauss was still entertaining the idea of publishing a first installment of series B, religious sociology, for *Annales Sociologiques*, to the great despair of its secretary, Maurice Halbwachs, who could hardly count on Mauss's punctuality. That first installment would appear only in 1939 and would include a voluminous study by Marcel Granet titled "Matrimonial Categories and Relations of Proximity in Ancient China." The next year, another, more modest-sized (117-page) installment of series B would appear. In addition to Stefan Czarnowski's essay "The Argonauts in the Baltic," a number of reviews appeared in it, written by Mauss's students—Paul Leiris, Anatole Lewitzky, Jacques Soustelle—and dealing with research conducted at the Institut d'Ethnologie de Paris.

The *Annales* team, already small, lost another contributor in December 1938. Paul Fauconnet was a friend Mauss had known for more than forty years: the two had long "drawn the same plow under the same yoke." Mauss admired this man of conviction for his "civic virtues and devotion to so many causes." He added: "His public activities were always marked by his devotion, his firmness, his generous spirit." Fauconnet, a sociologist whose authority was acknowledged abroad, performed great service in his teachings, but poor health prevented him from "making an impact through a large mass [of writings]."[54]

For Mauss, but also for *Annales Sociologiques*, that "sudden parting" left a void, as Leenhardt emphasized: "Your heart takes the measure of your loneliness. . . . Since Hubert's death, you walk alone, you continue to bring to fruition what your collaborators began, they who were cut down too early."[55]

Mauss's last major contributions before the war were papers he delivered, one in London and the other in Copenhagen. Before an audience at the Huxley Memorial Lecture, Mauss discussed the history of the idea of "person," the idea of the "self." "That subject is still part of the current program of the French school of sociology devoted to the social history of categories of the human mind."[56] As Mauss himself concurred, the topic was "immense." His study was presented as merely an unassuming rough sketch. He was not going to say everything. He would not consider linguistics or psychology but would merely present a piece of research in law and ethics. Nor would he reconstitute a general history from prehistoric times to the present. He limited himself to the study of a few forms of the notion of "self."

About ten years earlier, following comments by Lucien Lévy-Bruhl on the "primitive soul" before members of the Société Française de Philosophie, Mauss had indicated his intention to do a study on the notion of personality.

He wanted to present the results at the Congress in the History of Religion in Lund: "Let us go back in time: Persona equals mask. That is the original sense of the word. It was the Romans who transformed the notion of mask, mythic personality, into the notion of moral person. I will explain why and how elsewhere. It was a new and major event."[57]

Mauss took the same approach ten years later. His comparative method obliged him to "walk through the world and through time at an excessively rapid pace" and to visit "the museum of facts as it were . . . those that ethnography presents to us."[58] He considered, first, the Zuni Indians of New Mexico, then the Kwakiutl of the American Northwest, and finally, the Arunta and the Loritja of Australia. A first conclusion was unavoidable: "An entire set of societies arrived at the notion of persona, of a role to be filled by the individual in sacred dramas, in the same way that he plays a role in family life. The function created the formula, which has endured from very primitive societies down to our own."[59]

Beginning with the notion of persona, Mauss arrived at that of person (*persona* in Latin), whose original sense, he said, was (ritual or ancestral) mask. Other civilizations, including Brahmanic and Buddhist India and ancient China, developed ideas of the same kind, only to "dissolve them almost definitively." With the Romans, history continued on its way: the "person" was not only a matter of organization or the right to be a persona. As a "synonym for the true nature of the individual," it also became a "fundamental legal right," at least for free men, since only they had the right to a persona.

But this was a long way from the category of the self. It did not come about until the work of the Greek and Latin philosophers, particularly the Stoics with their psychological reflection on consciousness. There was also and above all the influence of Christianity, which would make the moral person a "metaphysical entity," that is, a "rational individual substance." The edifice was finally completed through the "long labor" of modern philosophers, especially Descartes, Spinoza, Hume, Kant, and Fichte. The notion of person was then identified with self-knowledge, psychological consciousness.

"The revolution of mentalities is complete," concluded Mauss. "Each of us has our own self."[60] The long trek could be summed up in a few words: "From a simple masquerade to a mask, from a persona to a person, a name, an individual, and from that to a being of metaphysical and moral value, from moral consciousness to sacred being, and from sacred being to a fundamental form of thought and action."[61] At no time did Mauss refer explicitly to the spiritualist current—personalism—that was developing at the journal *Esprit* and which asserted the primacy of man in opposition to any form of collective materialism. The prospectus for the journal claimed: "A person . . . is a cog wheel of freedom, of creation, of love." But Mauss was targeting that current when he criticized the idea of the person that "everyone finds natural, sharp and clear deep within his consciousness, fully equipped to be the basis of ethics, which is deduced from it." That current represented a naïve view of history. Mauss suggested that a "more precise view" had to be presented.[62]

During the summer of 1938 Mauss was invited to attend, as its vice president, the International Congress of Anthropological and Ethnological Sciences held in Copenhagen. That trip allowed him to reestablish contact with his few former Scandinavian students. He was very active at the congress, where he represented France: he participated in a debate on "the relations between the religious and sociological aspects of ritual" and presented a paper titled "Social Fact and Character Formation." His friends gently teased him: "You must have basked in your glory a little, without seeking it out."[63]

The social fact was the "fact of civilization," that is, the set of collective representations and practices that formed a society's mentality. The problem that still concerned Mauss was the relation between the individual and society: "When and how did that collective mentality assert itself and take root in the individual?" he wondered. "How can [the individual] act on society and how can the latter act on the individual?"[64] Finding a response to these questions required that psychology and sociology not be set up as opposites. Mauss declared at the outset: "Perhaps you know that for me, as for Durkheim, my teacher and uncle, the field of sociology in which I work . . . does not rule out all psychological consideration of the same facts in the individual and in his social environment."[65]

For Mauss, as for Durkheim, society's impact on the individual could best be seen in the area of child rearing. Both recognized the importance of a sociology of childhood, of relations between generations, a "fundamental phenomenon we have not adequately taken into account."[66] And child rearing involves training—in the sense that an animal is trained—of one generation by another, of the child by the adult: "Man is an animal that rears and trains his children." Mauss gave concrete examples drawn from everyday life in our societies: table manners, the way one responds to a child's cries, how one takes him in one's arms. On that point as well, he referred to so-called primitive societies and their initiation rites.

At the end of his lecture, Mauss recalled the conclusions of his study on the notion of person: "Man was a persona long before being a person."[67] A consciousness of oneself and of others, he said, was thus a trait of civilization in our societies: "The individual has finally become the subject and the object, the agent responsible for social life. What he was unconsciously, a prisoner of his social rank and his habits, he became consciously. He is aware of his own power." Mauss went further: "It is now the individual who is the impetus of social change. He always was, but he didn't know it."

On his way to Copenhagen, Mauss crossed Germany by train. Soustelle recounted: "The train was constantly being shunted off onto a sidetrack. There were soldiers everywhere. It was clear Germany was preparing for war . . . that everything was about to lead us to catastrophe."[68] More than ever, it seemed obvious that the sacred character of the person, as Mauss reminded his audience, was a fragile acquisition: "We have great benefits to defend. The idea [of person] may disappear with us. Let us not moralize."[69]

The Collège de Sociologie

The "return to the primitive" was the return to the community, but also the return to the sacred, and even, perhaps, the return of the gods. The sacred, rites, secret societies, and myths were no longer merely objects of study: they were active forces—"dark forces," Roger Caillois would say—which had to be liberated if the West was to be saved. At this point, the history and sociology of religion intersected the critique of the modern world and provided the foundations for a new utopia, a world founded on the power of the irrational. People dreamed of an "elective community" conceived on a religious model: the secret society.

The Collège de Sociologie, created in 1937, attracted ethnologists (Michel Leiris, Caillois, Lewitzky)[70] to the central figure of Georges Bataille. All had studied under Mauss. Bataille himself raised "problems that were hardly distinguishable from those ethnologists were trying to solve."[71] Thanks to Alfred Métraux, he discovered Mauss's studies on the potlatch, developed the "notion of expenditure" in an article in *Critique Sociale*, and, inspired by one of Mauss's aphorisms ("taboos are made to be violated"), began to analyze transgression, which would lead him to a systematic exposition of his vision of the world in *The Accursed Share*, written after the war. There was a thematic affinity between Mauss's teachings and the conferences given at the Collège de Sociologie: the sacred, power, shamanism, and secret societies were all at issue. The object of the college's activities was itself sacred sociology, that is, "the study of social existence in all manifestations where the active presence of the sacred appears."[72] Bataille called it a "unique undertaking, difficult to reduce to the usual forms of activity."

It was natural that Mauss's name should be associated with the college, especially since one of its founders and most active members was Roger Caillois. Born in 1913, Caillois had taken Mauss's courses at the École Pratique between 1933 and 1935, while a student at the École Normale Supérieure. In 1936, the same year he passed his *agrégation* (in grammar), he earned a degree from the section of religious science at the École. He later published his thesis, "Noontime Demons." A recipient of a grant from the Caisse Nationale de la Recherche Scientifique, Caillois continued to be interested in the history of religion, as attested by the book reviews and articles he published in *Cahiers du Sud*, *Nouvelle Revue Française*, and *Revue de l'Histoire des Religions*.

For several years, Caillois lived within the Surrealist movement's sphere of influence. Recruited by André Breton in April 1932, he left the movement two years later following an acrimonious discussion about Mexican jumping beans. He was the "young wolf among the Luperci." In June 1936 he published the first and only issue of *Inquisitions*, a journal he founded with Jules-Marcel Monnerot, Gaston Bachelard, Louis Aragon, and Tristan Tzara; he also contributed to *Acéphale*, Georges Bataille's review.[73] In 1937, the themes Caillois addressed in his reports at the Collège de Sociologie were "sacred sociology and the relation between society, the organism, and being"; in 1938, "power," "brotherhoods, fraternal orders, secret societies, churches," and, in collaboration with Bataille, "sacred sociology of the contemporary world"; in 1939, "sociology of the torturer" and "the fête." Caillois was still involved in the courses Mauss was teaching. During the school year 1938–1939, Mauss invited him to speak at the École on the relationship between ball games and notions of cosmology and cosmogony.

In many respects, the curriculum at the Collège de Sociologie looked dangerous. In "Winter Wind," Caillois denounced the "broken-down, senile, quasi-crumbling society" and campaigned for a resacralization of the social. In 1938, at the time of the Munich crisis, he presented the college as a "source of energy" and invited people to fight against the "de-virilization of man." Finally, in *Le mythe et l'homme* (Myth and man), he championed a revalorization of charismatic power.

Mauss never hesitated to support Caillois and Leiris intellectually, morally, and financially (through grant applications), but he did not participate in any of the public demonstrations at the college. He did not take seriously the way they spoke of ethnology and sociology, and was wary of false prophets who sought to find succor in them. What he hated more than anything, as Caillois knew, was the search "for remote and absolute causes such as sex or the economy, by which it is only too easy to explain everything without distinction, and the frivolous conjectures it is always easy to put forward and almost impossible to verify."[74] When he received the manuscript of *Le mythe et l'homme* from Caillois (published by Gallimard in 1938), Mauss was appalled:

> What I believe is a general derailment—of which you yourself are a victim—is the sort of absolute irrationalism with which you conclude in the name of a modern myth: the labyrinth and Paris. But I believe that, right now, all of you are probably under the influence of Heidegger, a Bergsonian held back by Hitlerism, legitimating a Hitlerism infatuated with irrationalism. And above all, it's the political philosophy of sorts that you try to draw from it, in the name

of poetry and a vague sentimentality. As persuaded as I am that poets and men of great eloquence can sometimes establish the rhythms of social life, so too am I skeptical of the capacities of a philosophy of any kind, and especially of a philosophy of Paris, to establish the rhythms of anything at all.[75]

This letter, addressed to "my dear Caillois" and ending with a word of encouragement ("all the best") and a "strong handshake," allows us to measure the distance that separated the professor from his student and shows what he thought of the influence Heidegger was exerting on the young. It also makes a clear connection between the German philosopher and Hitlerism. It was written in 1938.

Michel Leiris was the first to distance himself from the college, refusing to participate in the group's activities because of his doubts: "If we embrace sociological science as men such as Durkheim, Mauss, and Robert Hertz constituted it, it is indispensable that we conform to its methods. Otherwise, to clear up any misunderstanding, we must stop calling ourselves 'sociologists.'"[76] Leiris criticized Bataille for mixing literature with politics and for constituting a "sacred sociology" contrary "to the acquisitions of modern sociology, and especially, to the Maussian notion of total phenomenon." He also feared that the group would degenerate into "the worst kind of literary coterie."

In the weeks after his lecture on the fête, Caillois accepted an invitation from Victoria Ocampo, founder of the review *Sur*, and left for Argentina, where *Le mythe et l'homme* had just been translated into Spanish. He arrived in Buenos Aires in July 1939 and remained there throughout the war. For this man who had loudly asserted his taste for violence and had maintained a kind of political neutrality for as long as possible—to such a point that some believed him "open to fascism"[77]— it was time for self-criticism and an "about-face." "The house was on fire and we were reorganizing the closet. We should have fanned the fire. We did not dare."[78] In October 1939, Caillois published "The Nature of Hitlerism" in a special issue of *Sur* devoted to the war.

The Myth of the Germanics

Mythic Germany was also the country of Germanic myths. The subject was particularly delicate in that Indo-European studies were dominated by a race prejudice at the time: preference was given to blonds over brunets and Aryans were considered superior. Hubert had vehemently opposed such slogans: "[The Germanics] are not the direct representatives of the pure race," he had exclaimed. "The expression Indo-Germanic is to be rejected."[79] With his study on the Celts, Hubert had become involved in the "controversy of the two races,"[80] defending the idea that French identity was of Celtic origin and thereby bore civilization within it: "The historic role of the Celts was not a political role, since their political organizations were null and void. But it was a civilizing role."[81]

After *The Celts*, Hubert had taken on *Les Germains* (The Germanics). His plan was to "seek out what ethnic elements and what influences could have given birth to Germanism."[82] One of his hypotheses, which he borrowed from Meillet, was that "the Germanics are a people of Europe, Indo-Europeanized, or who adopted an Indo-European language."[83]

One of the courses Mauss taught at the Collège de France beginning in the mid-1930s was on Germanic peoples. To prepare it, Mauss relied on his friend's unpublished studies, of which, he said, he was the "trustee." As he was preparing the edition of *Les Germains* (with Olaf Jansé, Hubert's former student and collaborator), Mauss went in search of *Homo nordicus*, in a field where he knew he was less qualified than Hubert or his colleague Émile Benveniste, whose doctoral thesis had been on the origins of Indo-European name formation (1935).[84]

At the first conference on historical synthesis in 1938, Mauss presented a brief paper titled "Differences between the Migrations of the Germanics and of the Celts," which was published the following year in *Revue de Synthèse*. Mauss defended the thesis of "composite societies." Yes, there were languages particular to the Germanics, "moral traditions proper to each of their root stocks," but one ought to be careful not to form an idea of these ancient societies "based on our modern concept of modern nations rooted in a determinate territory." The argument was clear: "One must take into account the absolute permeability of ancient societies. . . . One must therefore not imagine vast circles of isolated cultures at that time, but rather countless interpenetrations."[85] There were differences, of course, between the Celts, the Germanics, the Indo-Iranians, and so on, but there were also many important resemblances. Hubert spoke of the "intimate relations" that had long existed between the Celts and the Germanics. To be convinced, one had only to observe linguistic kinships. "The word *Reich*," observed Mauss, "is similar to the Celtic word for king, *rix*, which is the same word as the Latin *rex*."[86]

In June of the following year, 1939, Georges Dumézil, Hubert's and Mauss's former student and Caillois's friend, published *Mythes et dieux des Germains* (Myths and gods of the Germanics), a book that owed a great deal to what Mauss and Marcel Granet had taught him, as Dumézil confirmed. Mauss at first judged his student's "early work" harshly: "Dumézil's thesis is a dirty joke, but it will make a good impression."[87] But Mauss's later review of *Festin d'immortalité* (Banquet of immortality) for *Année Sociologique* was more nuanced: Dumézil's comparison with the Semitic world was brief, the analysis of Hindu documents flawed, but the conclusion was correct.[88]

The student's political choices were very different from the master's: Dumézil was close to Maurras and *Action Française*, contributed to the Far Right newspaper *Jour*, and expressed his sympathies for Fascist Italy. Although Dumézil was pro-fascist (but resolutely anti-Nazi),[89] Mauss was willing to help him. He later claimed that Dumézil was "one of the most brilliant teachers in the section of religious science."[90] This praise may be surprising for anyone who knows that Dumézil was long criticized for writing that he hoped to see Hitler "remythologize" Germany.[91] In fact, however, the argument Dumézil presented in this book was a historical analysis and not a political judgment, and was received as such at the time.

Mauss was now preoccupied with myth. He absolutely wanted to finish the study he had begun a few years earlier and "to soon publish a portrait of Maori mythology, including the entire cosmogony, the entire cosmology, and a classification of spaces and times."[92] In late May 1939, at the invitation of Henri Berr, he agreed to deliver the opening lecture at the eleventh synthesis colloquium, a conference devoted to "the notion of matter," where professors and researchers from various disciplines (history, ethnology, philosophy, biology, physics, astronomy) had gathered. Mauss briefly outlined the results of his ongoing research on the notion of substance and Maori mythology.

Addressing the philosophers, he first reminded them that "philosophy leads to everything, provided it begins with everything." He declared from the start: "Philosophies and sciences are languages." And he added: "But though our way of thinking is derived at every moment from everything that constitutes social life, the scientific mentality is intimately connected to the total mentality as a whole and cannot be separated from it."[93] The study of the notion of matter is thus necessarily sociohistorical: everything, even in science, is "both continuous and discontinuous, contingent and difficult to predict." Never before had Durkheim's nephew, who shared a positivistic view of science with his colleagues at *Annales Sociologiques*, acknowledged with such lucidity the possibility of a sociological analysis of scientific developments.[94]

After presenting the hypothesis that it was with Spinoza that the opposition between "thought" and "extension" first appeared, Mauss quickly left the field of philosophy and the history of science to "borrow facts from the primitives, as they are so erroneously called." That was an excellent way to "remove ourselves from our usual surroundings" and to learn to "think otherwise than as *Homo sorbonnus* or *Homo oxonimus*."[95]

The facts Mauss presented came both from studies done by his former friends and collaborators, Hubert and Hertz, and from his research on the notion of food: "I have been preoccupied with the notion of food for a long time. . . . Hence food connotes subsistence (a word that is used as a synonym for food), and substance or matter."[96] And drawing on the studies of

Spencer, Gillen, and other anthropologists of the same period, he did not hesitate to generalize his theory regarding the kinship between the notion of matter and that of food.

The presentation might seem anecdotal, but, as Berr exclaimed, "what a feast!"[97] Mauss took the opportunity to again defend the originality of the French school of sociology and to show the importance of studying the various categories of the mind. As he explained during the discussion period, every system of thought was organized around series of binary oppositions: masculine/feminine, high/low, left/right, uterine descendancy/nonuterine descendancy, and so on.

At the end of his lecture, Mauss was careful to warn against the error of studying myths one by one, separating them from what had come before: "[Myths] form a whole in relation to their collectivities. A myth is a nodal point in a web and not a dictionary entry. One must see and interpret the whole."[98] The lesson was clear: one must not believe in myths, one must analyze them.

In those troubled times, divisions were becoming blurred and political trajectories unpredictable. Shifts in allegiance were common, both in political parties, primarily the SFIO and the PCF, and among intellectuals. The Munich Pact of September 30, 1938, when Western democracies abandoned Czechoslovakia to Hitler's demands, produced rifts. Most Jewish intellectuals were opposed to a policy of appeasement. Marcel Cohen, Jacques Salomon, Georges Politzer, Georges Friedmann, Marc Bloch, René Cassin, Benjamin Crémieux, and others were all anti-Munich. Others, though fewer in number—Emmanuel Berl, Lucien Lévy-Bruhl, André Weil, Simone Weil, Marcel Mauss—were still marked by the suffering of World War I and thought that the preservation of peace had to prevail over any other consideration. Mauss signed the petition "We Do Not Want War" circulated by André Delmas, secretary of the Syndicat National des Instituteurs (National teachers union) and by Ginoux, secretary of the Syndicat des PTT (Postal workers union), and supported by the Comité de Vigilance des Intellectuels Antifascistes and the Centre Syndical d'Action contre la Guerre (Center for unionist action against the war). Blum himself was torn: "War has probably been avoided, but the conditions are such that I, who have never ceased to fight for peace, can no longer feel any joy about it and feel divided between slight relief and shame."[99] Later the socialist leader would do battle with the pro-Munich forces and would oppose Paul Faure, general secretary of the SFIO, and those who favored further concessions.

The increasingly sharp political differences did not prevent scientific discussion or end friendships. Although Mauss rarely saw Déat, who was "pressed on all sides by his many commitments,"[100] and though he would not follow him in his "deviation" (which led from central planning to collaboration with the Nazis), he maintained his friendship with him, at least until the spring of 1939. In April, when Déat managed to sneak his way between the SFIO, Communist, and Radical candidates and was elected deputy of Angoulême, Mauss renewed his subscription to *Tribune de France* and even sent him a word of congratulation: "You are one of the rare men who want and are able to do something. I have seen very few articles by you lately that I would not have approved of."[101]

Déat, the chief political contributor to the "modest weekly" *Tribune de France*, would not definitively commit to fascism until May 1940.[102] A year earlier, the image of the pacifist dominated: he was among those who, for the time being, intended to "wage the last battle for peace one step at a time." It was in *Tribune*, he later wrote, "that one would have to go looking for the best articles the peace team published in those feverish times."[103] He sometimes caused a stir: his famous "To Die for Gdańsk?" published in *Oeuvre* in May 1939, set off a firestorm.

What would happen? "I am totally incapable of predicting what is going to occur,"[104] wrote Mauss. "As far as work goes, the president of the section of religious science still has an awful lot to do, a mass of administrative work," not to mention all the refugees he had to deal with. "There are too few of us for too many things," he lamented, "and moreover, everything's sort of falling apart right now, and necessarily so."

EPILOGUE

THE WAR AND POSTWAR YEARS

THE MONTH of September 1939, wrote Halbwachs, "weighed heavy on our shoulders."[1] France and Great Britain declared war on Germany—nothing very tragic as yet, but "one feels oppressed." "Let us hold on to our hope," suggested Leenhardt from distant New Caledonia, and added: "If human folly begins to weaken, will there not be a brief moment of salvation?"[2] The younger researchers were mobilized: Georges Gurvitch (discharged as unfit for service after three weeks), Michel Leiris, Robert Montagne, and others. From Algeria, where the fortunes of war had taken him, Leiris wrote to "Dear Mr. Mauss": "I wish I could take the opportunity to do a little ethnography. But military life does not always allow you to do as you please."[3]

That autumn, Mauss chose to retire as professor from the École Pratique des Hautes Études, even though he was asked to stay on. "My duty," he explained, "is to stand aside for the young." He wanted a "kind of temporary replacement position" to again be offered to Leenhardt, who had returned from New Caledonia: "He has everything required to replace me in every capacity."[4] Mauss remained president of the section of religious science, at the École Pratique, however, solely "out of a sense of order and duty." "I don't have a very good idea of what will happen with everything we're doing—all I know is that I have the duty to do it."[5] His administrative activities were limited to the "relatively provisional." He did what was possible to "fill the gaps" in the schedule, to award a few degrees, provide training to a few students.

When the École Pratique reopened its doors in the fall, about sixty students were enrolled in the section of religious science. After a "short month of vacation" in Épinal and Contrexéville, Mauss had returned to his post as president. It was no "bed of roses," he confided. For some time he had been "the only staff member present" and had to go around picking up cigarette butts himself. He had to take care of everything: "I'm the president, the secretary, the bookkeeper, and occasionally the mace bearer and office boy of the École."[6]

Mauss's isolation only worsened. In March 1939, there was the death of Lucien Lévy-Bruhl, a friend to Durkheim, Hubert, Simiand, and Mauss himself.[7] Mauss recalled that Lévy-Bruhl liked "to be of service, of use. . . . He took joy in accomplishing a task. In short, he had a noble civic, public, and moral life."[8]

Mauss intended to publish Lévy-Bruhl's *Carnets*, a journal of sorts he had kept from January 1938 to February 1939.[9] In early 1940 he learned of Abel Rey's death, then that of Célestin Bouglé, "that proud Archer, that brilliant

Sagittarius," whose death was not unexpected.[10] Mauss's few remaining friends were getting old: "At my age and with my heart, I am quite useless," Charles Seligman confided to him.[11]

Mauss led a "very mediocre, rather boring" life. His sciatica was slow to heal. He had "a mass of administrative work." His wife, still ill, had "memory lapses" and was "not at all worried about the war or what could happen to her!" During alerts, both remained "calmly in their beds," but they were aware that "these perpetual alerts . . . try the nerves and health of even the heartiest people."[12] For a time, Marcel considered moving to the Midi, perhaps even to Lamalou or the Toulon region, where his wife had family. But he changed his mind: "All I know is that I'll leave only under orders. My poor wife wants to move even less than I do."[13]

Mauss remained calm, refusing to "make predictions," satisfied with the "presence of mind and caution with which [the war] was being conducted." He displayed a certain optimism: "The result is not in doubt. But what an implausible story."[14] No one had any illusions left: "Hitler will not leave us be."[15] Mauss therefore did not join with the appeal for "immediate peace" launched by the pacifists Louis Lecoin, Ludovic Zoretti, and Léon Émery in September 1939. The combat veteran now toyed with the idea of "returning to join up with [his] Australians when they come back."[16] Only the decrees rejecting "people of [his] age" prevented him. He was obliged to continue practicing his profession, that is, teaching at the Institut d'Ethnologie and the Collège de France, where his course was "rather well attended."

Winter semester 1940 was "harsh," "very tiring," with fifty conferences at the Institut d'Ethnologie and thirty-two at the Collège de France. As in the previous year, the Wednesday conferences Mauss taught at the Collège dealt with "cosmology and games" and the Friday conferences with Hubert's works as a whole on "the origin of the Germanics," which he still hoped to edit for publication. His subject was the "Germanic barbarians." The appearance of *Homo nordicus* in Germania was, he noted, "of late date."

Everything went on "middling well." Neither the publications of the Institut d'Ethnologie nor those of *Annales Sociologiques* were suspended; three installments of the latter appeared in 1940, with texts by Jean Stoetzel ("Social Psychology and the Theory of Attitudes"), Henri Lévy-Bruhl ("The Collective Personality"), Jean Ray ("The International Community"), Henry Laufenberger ("The Notion and Operation of Markets in Germany"), and Maurice Halbwachs ("Keynes's General Theory"). But Mauss had little time to do his own work on the notion of "microcosm" among the Maori and on the god Tiki. The study on Tiki encountered serious difficulties when three essential volumes, which Mauss had filled with notes, were stolen from him. "It made me disgusted with everything," he confided to a friend.[17]

Mauss intended to remain in Paris "as long as that makes sense." "In fact," he added, "I'm obliged by my administrative position to be here. . . . I will have to keep watch, or rather stand guard."[18] There was little news of the war: "Almost nothing is happening on the front. The country's morale is superb, the troops' even better."[19] He was also happy that Winston Churchill was at the helm in Great Britain. He had met Churchill at the front and knew he had guts.[20] An optimist, Mauss believed that "the situation is getting better and better . . . every day. By virtue of intelligence and patience, we will have the Boches again like we once had them."[21] But how long would it take?

Even in such an unstable situation, Mauss refused to make personal plans: "We will always have time to sort things out at the last minute."[22] He had no choice, he said, but to "remain in charge of [his] school, in charge of the Institut d'Ethnologie, and of all sorts of other idiotic things!"[23] These "idiotic things" were all the "individual questions" he had to settle, the friends and colleagues he had to help. In the absence of his secretary, Henri-Charles Puech, and because several professors were mobilized, it became increasingly problematic to schedule teaching at the section of religious science.

"Almost everyone is at the front," observed Mauss. But he added, somewhat relieved, that "up to now no one around me has been hurt. My young relatives, my friends, my students are all in one piece."[24] They all had to hold on, he proclaimed. Mauss took many personal measures, exerting pressure on the Rockefeller Foundation to save the libraries of Bouglé, Fauconnet, and Abel Rey and to preserve the Centre de Documentation Sociale. He requested authorization to bring two Jewish scientists to France, Oskar Goldberg and Adolf Caspary.[25] He bailed out Patrick Waldberg, backed the Sinologist H. Stein's request for naturalization, and organized lectures in the history of Semitic law for Herman Weil at the École Pratique.[26] He wrote letters to the American anthropologist Robert Lowie and the director of the Smithsonian on behalf of his cousin Hubert Schwab, a "brilliant scholar." And finally, he defended the records of brothers Jacques and Jean-Pierre Vernant, two of "his most brilliant and worthy students," who, for political reasons, were refused promotions in the army.[27] He complained to Raymond Aron, "I have a lot to do, all sorts of things, not including my work, a pile of individual and administrative business."[28] He also agreed to make gifts— 200 francs a month—to the town hall of the fourteenth arrondissement to "provide relief to those citizens whose situation is especially desperate because of the war."[29] But he did not frequent official circles: "I have enough to do with my own little administrations."[30]

Vichy

Up to that time, life was close to normal in Paris. But there was a clear sense that the coming weeks would be terrible. The defeat of the French armies and the occupation of Paris in June 1940 by German troops created great confusion: exodus of the population, a general disruption of services. Marshal Henri Philippe Pétain was named premier and set up his government in Vichy. Preoccupied with reestablishing order and ensuring the "country's recovery," he quickly took various "purification" measures: the law of July 17, 1940, on public service; the law of July 30 (called the "Frenchification of public service"), which targeted foreign-born civil service workers; the law of August 13, dissolving "secret societies" and targeting the Freemasons.

Repression was beginning and fear took hold. What would tomorrow bring? "Will there be courses held in Paris, in occupied Paris, hence under the control of the Germans?" wondered Lucien Febvre.[31] Mauss maintained that the École Pratique des Hautes Études ought to close. Life became especially difficult in Paris when ration cards were issued that summer. In August, each person was allotted 500 grams of sugar, 250 grams of pasta, 100 grams of rice, 125 grams of soap, 300 grams of margarine. These rations did not satisfy minimum daily requirements and brought severe hardship.[32] People lined up outside food shops. The writer Marcel Aymé titled one of his short stories En attendant (Waiting). There were signs the winter would be harsh and there was a shortage of coal. Mauss complained of not having enough heat for his large library.[33]

In the autumn, Mauss asked for authorization to resign his position as president of the fifth section of the École Pratique. "In the action I have taken, there is no trace of fatigue or of a desire to run from responsibilities. . . . But I was able to persuade my colleagues that it was in the interest of the École that I leave my post. In the current situation, it is pointless for me to be a target through whom the École could easily be attacked. Though I fear nothing for myself, it is my duty to endanger only myself."[34]

Hence, as he reiterated to his colleagues during the September 29 faculty meeting, he had resigned only to "safeguard the interests of the École," that is, to keep the presence of a Jew at the head of the section from causing "disadvantages that the École as a whole would have to suffer."[35] On the following November 18, Marcel Granet was named president in his place, and Maurice Leenhardt, back from New Caledonia, was appointed directeur d'études. A month later, Granet died suddenly. For Mauss, the loss of a man he considered "one of [his] best and most beloved friends," was another great sorrow.[36] "He was taken away from us in a few minutes," Mauss recounted. "He was in perfect health. He left an enormous unfinished body of work, much greater even than what he'd published."[37] Gabriel Le Bras, directeur d'études in the history of canonical law, succeeded Granet as president of the section.

In October, well before Germany had exerted even the slightest pressure,[38] the Vichy government instituted an exclusionary quota system and adopted a law on the status of the Jews: "A person is regarded as Jewish if three grandparents are of the Jewish race or if two grandparents are of said race if the spouse is also Jewish." Access to elected office, to high government positions, to the magistrature, and to the army were forbidden to Jews. And in no case could they occupy positions of responsibility in the press, in film, or in radio broadcasting. The law of October 4 authorized prefects to intern foreign Jews in special camps or to keep them under house arrest.

This anti-Semitic legislation, however, did not apply as rigorously to combat veterans and families long established in France. According to Pétain, being a World War I veteran or being decorated with the Legion of Honor or Médaille Militaire mitigated the impact of the law. In a note Mauss composed for the director of the Collège de France, he stressed his family's profound Frenchness and patriotism, but without concealing his Jewish origins: "All my grandparents' relations were born of French parents"; "my father served for seven years."[39]

Although a nonobservant Jew and a member of the Union Rationaliste,[40] Mauss never denied his place within Judaism. He liked to tell his students of his "rabbinical family" and openly acknowledged "how profound the influence of the religious atmosphere" of his home had been.[41] His mastery of Hebrew and his knowledge of biblical texts proved very useful, not to say indispensable, as is clear in several articles and book reviews. In about thirty of the many reviews he authored, he touched on various aspects of Judaism: the ritual prohibitions relating to menstrual blood, the periodic breaks from everyday life (the Sabbath), the feast of Purim, the synagogue as a prayer society.

Mauss never adhered to traditional religious interpretation. In the only article he published in *Revue d'Études Juives*, he showed, using circumcision as an example, that Judaism was a sense of belonging, a culture: "For us, circumcision is essentially a form of tattooing. It is a tribal or even national sign."[42] Similarly, from a sociological point of view, prohibitions stemmed from a social group's desire to "gather itself together, to separate itself from others." Israel, in abominating anyone who cooked the kid in the milk of its mother, wanted "to distinguish itself from worshippers of gods other than its own and pastors of less illustrious and less pure stock."[43]

Moreover, though he had never engaged in debates about Zionism, in the mid-1930s Mauss agreed to become a member of the central committee of the Alliance Israélite Universelle, at the invitation of his former professor and friend Sylvain Lévi, its president since 1920. "I followed him, partly out of sympathy for a very fine charitable organization, as I saw it at work in Morocco, but especially for him, to help him, support him, stand in for him a little, above all to hold him back a little, force him to take care of himself."[44] Even after Lévi died in 1935, Mauss maintained his ties with the Alliance Israélite, participating in some of its meetings. He also collaborated with the Groupement Israélite de Coordination, d'Aide et de Protection (Israelite group of coordination, aid, and protection) to bring foreign researchers to France. One of them, interned in a camp in Carmaux, wrote his "dear protector" as follows: "You are our only hope of being liberated."[45] And as already noted, when his cousin Hubert Schwab needed help to leave France, Mauss immediately took steps to obtain a grant for him from the Rockefeller Foundation and to get him admitted to an American university.[46]

Anti-Semitism "was growing every day" and was now being expressed openly.[47] The publisher Denoël launched what it called a "national interest" series at Nouvelles Éditions Françaises titled "The Jews and France." Dr. George Montandon, an academic and ethnologist, became the "theorist" of racism and published a book titled *Comment reconnaître le juif?* (How to recognize the Jew). A specialist in "French ethnicity," he had used portraits of Sylvain Lévi and Léon Blum a few years earlier to describe the supposed principal physical "characteristics" of the Jews.[48] At Éditions Denoël, Dr. Querrioux published *La médicine et les juifs* (Medicine and the Jews) and Lucien Pemjean *La presse et les juifs depuis la Révolution française* (The press and the Jews since the French Revolution). Others denounced "the Jewish invasion" in film and theater. Jewish publishers looked on as their companies were "bought out." In early August 1940 Otto Abetz, a former drawing professor, was named ambassador to the Reich in Paris. His task was to influence French personalities through subsidies to newspapers and to get them to collaborate.

Life became difficult for some of Mauss's friends and family. His brother, Henri, and his wife had to leave the region of the Vosges, which had fallen into the hands of the Germans in June 1940 and was now in the "forbidden zone." Épinal, after being heavily bombed, had surrendered to the enemy. It was the beginning of a long occupation marked by rationing, arrests, and deportations. Pierre and Marie Mauss, Marcel's nephew and niece, lost their jobs in elementary school administration. Henri Durkheim lost his job as public prosecutor in Caen. Several colleagues and friends were dismissed: Raymond Aron, André Mayer, Marc Bloch, Paul Léon, Henri Lévy-Bruhl, Isidore Lévy. As Georges Friedmann later wrote, it was "a blow to the head, to the heart," for everyone involved.[49]

On October 13, 1940, in conformity with instructions from the Ministry of National Education concerning "the cessation of services by the Jews in universities," Mauss, still a professor at the Collège de France, submitted his resignation, and a month later turned in a "complete dossier" to the administration. Although he did not know what was going to happen to him, he tried to keep his spirits up. "That's the essential thing," he said.[50] Agnès Humbert notes that those around him noticed a strange smile on his face, "like that of a Buddha, at once ironic, calm, and confident. That of a great serene spirit floating above everything and foreseeing everything."[51]

There were not many choices for those who wanted to survive. Staying in Paris was a risk for any Jew, but a few academics agreed to take it: Dr. Debré, Louis Halphen (for a short time), Isidore Lévy. Lévy, one of Mauss's allies and a professor of ancient history at the Collège de France, continued to go to the Sorbonne and the Paris libraries to do his research on the Book of Esther. His sisters, Jeanne and Irma, would be deported to Auschwitz in 1944.

Mauss's loved ones and former students took refuge in the free zone or left the country. Meyerson moved to Toulouse, where a core of intellectuals resisting the regime had formed around Jean Cassou: Clara Malraux, Edgar Morin, Jean-Pierre Vernant, Léo Hamon, Georges Friedmann, Jules Moch, Vladimir Jankélévitch. While running an underground newspaper, *Armée Secrète du Sud-Ouest* (Secret southwest army), Meyerson pursued his research in psychology and created the Société Toulousaine de Psychologie Comparative (Toulouse society of comparative psychology). He corresponded regularly with his friend Mauss throughout the war. Meyerson, optimistic at the start of the conflict, remained so to the end, both about events and about human beings.[52]

Henri Lévy-Bruhl was away from Paris and remained in contact with Mauss. A member of the Consistoire Central, the main Jewish religious assembly, he was one of the many people who believed that the anti-Jewish measures had been imposed by the occupying authorities. He believed it was "like a ransom demanded by external powers, like a sacrifice that would benefit the French community as a whole."[53] In Lyons, where he had once been a professor, Lévy-Bruhl regularly participated in meetings of the consistory. He was also in charge of the Comité d'Assistance aux Intellectuels Juifs (Assistance committee for Jewish intellectuals) and worked at the employment office helping dismissed civil service workers.

At the time of the debacle, Raymond Aron was mobilized and assigned to work as a meteorologist near the Belgian border. After many relocations, he found himself back in Toulouse, where he had been a *maître de conférence* before the war. His opposition to Vichy led him to leave France in June and to join General Charles de Gaulle in England, where he wrote and translated articles for *France Libre*.[54]

For anyone who needed to seek safe haven, the safest destination was North America, as Aron recognized. Visas were usually obtained and other arrangements worked out through the Emergency Rescue Committee, set up with the support of the Rockefeller Foundation and the New School for Social Research in New York, which was headed by Alvin Johnson. The American Jewish Joint Distribution Committee also helped Jewish intellectuals get to the United States. André Mayer, a Collège de France professor specializing in the natural history of organizations, was officially "on a mission" to Harvard. Gurvitch, Koyré, and Lévi-Strauss took refuge in New

York, where their studious, calm, and monotonous lives allowed them to teach a few courses—notably at the École Libre des Hautes Études—and to work. It was a way to be useful and to prepare for the rebirth of thought and science in France.[55]

Marc Bloch was also planning to go to the United States at the invitation of the Rockefeller Foundation. Because of administrative delays and the difficulty in obtaining visas for his two adult sons, however, he put off leaving and finally canceled his trip in 1941. Fired and then rehired through the intervention of Jérôme Carcopino, a former student and protégé of his father, Bloch obtained a position in Montpellier. But because he could not imagine a fate outside France for him or for his children, he turned his "refuge" into a "combat post" and joined the Resistance. In late 1942 he went underground.[56]

Mauss avoided "making demands with respect to his own career" but still wanted "to be held only to the obligations of a free citizen."[57] In late March 1941 he wrote the minister to learn whether "his retirement application was complete."[58] This was a particularly urgent matter since Mauss had received no salary for three months. A few months later, drawing on his "personal relationship," he again wrote to Minister Jérôme Carcopino and asked for his "administrative situation" to be clarified.[59] "I have no reason to want to be kept on until I've reached the obligatory retirement age, on May 10, 1942, but my wife's disability and lack of protection impose a duty on me to leave her in the clearest situation possible if something should happen to me."[60]

On June 27, 1941, an order signed by Carcopino confirmed Mauss's retirement and his right to a pension beginning on December 21, 1940.[61] The same measure was applied to Isidore Lévy on the following December 9. As the *Annuaire de la Collège de France* indicates, neither was teaching when the 1941–1942 school year began. Nor were their Jewish colleagues Émile Benveniste, Jules Bloch, and Paul Léon. The other faculty members at the Collège taught their courses as usual.[62] Only in March 1943 did the faculty meeting at the Collège de France discuss the use of funds previously earmarked for the chair of sociology. It proposed the creation of a chair in collective psychology, which would be assigned nearly a year later to Halbwachs, Mauss's friend and close collaborator. This was a way of maintaining the tradition of teaching social science at the Collège. When he joined the faculty, the new professor would have to present a genealogical tree of his and his wife's families and declare he was not Jewish.[63]

Ethnology and Racism

It was impossible for anthropology to remain above the fray. One of its privileged fields of study was race, or, in George Montandon's expression, "raciology." Montandon was a physician who held the chair in ethnology at the Muséum d'Histoire Naturelle in Paris. In 1936 he became curator of the Broca Museum. At a scientific level, he had initially identified himself as a follower of Mauss, later focusing only on the somatic dimension of the study of races.[64] He was an authority on the subject, publishing *La race, les races: Mise au point d'ethnologie somatique* (1933; Race, races: A restatement of somatic ethnology) and translating *Races of Africa* by the English anthropologist Charles Seligman.

Montandon, who became director of the journal *Ethnie Française* in 1941, was a former sympathizer with the Bolshevik cause and did not consider himself a racist—he preferred to speak of "ethnicity"—but was known for his anti-Semitism. He became the German occupation authorities' expert on the Jewish race and, in December 1941, was attached to the General Office on Jewish Questions in his capacity as an ethnologist. His job, apparently very lucrative, was to deliver, in exchange for cash, certificates attesting that the bearee did not belong to the Jewish race.[65] His 1940 book *Comment reconnaître le juif?* had caused a stir. Like *Ethnie Française*, it included portraits of Jews. In 1943 Montandon, a disciple of the anthropologist Georges Vacher de la Lapouge, who had written on the "Aryans," did a French translation of the *Manual of Human Eugenics and Heredity* by the Nazi geneticist Othmar von Verschuer, head of the Anthropology Institute in Berlin. The entire École d'Anthropologie de Paris, including its director, Louis Marin, espoused the ethnic theses of the Vichy regime and granted that regime academic legitimacy.[66]

The National Revolution, Pétain's collaborationist program, also called on ethnologists to promote "the real man" and the revival of folklore.[67] That work seems to have been less compromising, however. Georges-Henri Rivière, director of the Musée des Arts et Traditions Populaires, commissioned four "intellectual worksites": "Traditional Furniture," "The Leisure Activities of Workers," "Regional Architecture," and "Traditional Artisanal Workshops."

"What is to be done?" wondered Marcel Maget. "Either we must resign ourselves to doing folklore at home and to grinding out theory in the shadow of libraries at half-staff; or we must accept, with the minimal reverence due any power in place, ways to contribute to a partial completion of the emergency program."[68] The director of the Musée des Arts et Traditions Populaires and his collaborators opted for the second solution and assumed the associated risks. Maget took charge of the Peasant Folklore Department of the agricultural guild. André Varagnac became director of the bureau of regionalist propaganda for the Toulouse region. Marcel Griaule sat on the Empire Commission of the Comité National de Folklore. In 1943 he would also accept the chair in ethnology newly created at the Sorbonne. These researchers, most of them Mauss's former students and considered leftists, seized on the major theme of a "return to the earth" to develop the field of rural studies.

Other ethnologists, also Mauss's former students, sided squarely with the opposition and joined the Resistance.[69] After being demobilized, Anatole Lewitzky, a researcher at the Musée de l'Homme, refused to accept the German victory. In late summer 1940, convinced that it was "better to die in battle than to survive in defeat," he organized "the first and the most solid Resistance network in Paris."[70] His code name was "Chazelle." Along with his fiancée, the fiery Yvonne Oddon, a librarian at the museum, his colleague Boris Vildé, also, like himself, from Russia, and a few others— Claude Aveline, Jean Cassou, Marcel Abraham, Jean Paulhan, and Agnès Humbert—he printed and distributed the bulletin *Résistance*, whose first issue appeared on December 15, 1940. "No, France is not defeated," he wrote in one of his editorials. Everyone considered de Gaulle "the man who is right" or rather, "the man who is of the same opinion as we are."[71] Rivet, the museum director, had similar ideas and lent his support, authorizing use of the duplicating machine he had purchased in 1934 while on the Comité de Vigilance des Intellectuels Antifascistes.

A few months later there was what Michel Leiris called the "Trafalgar strike at the Trocadéro."[72] On the night of February 14, 1941, Lewitzky and Oddon were arrested. Also picked up was Mme Merouchkowsky, a "woman of a certain age" who lived in the same building. "Perfectly harmless," she earned a difficult living repairing and conserving the museum's textiles.[73] Neither Vildé nor Rivet was harassed, since they were in the free zone at the time, Vildé for a month and Rivet for less than three days. In fact, the museum director had just left Paris, intending to go to Colombia at the invitation of an ethnographic institution. Vildé, who felt "it was his calling to take charge of everything having to do with the Resistance"—to help fugitives, get people over into the free zone, collect and transmit information—decided to return to Paris to help Lewitzky. The following March 26, he too was arrested on place Pigalle.

Mauss knew Lewitzky well, calling him the "man from the cold." He had directed Lewitzky's thesis on Siberian shamanism, and Lewitzky had been his student at the Institut d'Ethnologie and at the École Pratique. He distinguished himself the first year (1934–1935) with three "excellent lectures" on shamanism, and the following year with an "excellent and significant study" on the religion and civilization of the Goldes. When he got a job at the Musée de l'Homme and a grant in 1938, Lewitzky was able to pursue his ethnological research and publish a few articles, including a detailed study, "The Religious Life of the Peoples of Central and North Asia," in *L'histoire générale des religions*. The war interrupted a promising career and impelled a frail and self-effacing man, someone hardly predisposed for a life of adventure, to take action.

When Lewitzky and his friend were arrested, Mauss initially sought information, since no one had "news of where Lewitzky could be" or knew "what acts Mlle Oddon was accused of." According to loved ones who saw Mauss go out one morning carefully dressed, he approached his former student Marcel Déat and members of the government, probably Jérôme Carcopino, to secure their liberation.[74] He wrote: "Keeping them [under arrest], if it continues, could be gravely detrimental to the museum and all its equipment, not to mention the personal situation of a certain number of interesting young people."[75] It was more difficult to defend Lewitzky, who was a foreigner and whose brother and father had also been arrested. Mauss explained that his presence was "indispensable for the museum's operation," since he was in charge of recording and numbering all the objects in the collections and of keeping the registries and doing the inventories. He also provided some personal information: "Belongs to the Russian gentry. Nothing Jewish about him . . . fought this war honorably . . . became a French citizen several years ago."[76] The information was important, since the patronymic "Lewitzky" could be thought to be Jewish. The Musée de l'Homme was later taken to task and called "Judeo-Masonic."[77]

These measures were without effect. Even the efforts of Carcopino, a colleague and friend of Vildé's father-in-law, Ferdinand Lot, were useless. "I was staggered by my powerlessness," he would confide.[78] Lewitzky and his companions stayed in prison. A year later, on January 8, 1942, their trial got under way, and the following February 23 Lewitzky was shot on Mont Valérien, along with Boris Vildé and five other companions from the Musée de l'Homme network. When he learned of Lewitzky's death, Mauss wrote his friend's sister, Oleg: "I am in mourning for your brother."[79]

The Vise Tightens

Life in Paris was difficult for Mauss, but not impossible.[80] His wife was still bedridden but without too much discomfort. When he could, Mauss sent money to friends or relatives having problems and responded to the "appeals to all Jews" from the Comité de Coordination des Oeuvres de Bienfaisance Israélites (Coordination committee for Israelite charitable works) in Paris. He also defended dismissed colleagues. Dumézil, for instance, lost his position at the École Pratique because he belonged to a Masonic lodge. Mauss wrote the minister: "I am frightened for his family and for his loved ones' health and fate."[81]

Mauss saw a few friends—Halbwachs, Georges Bourgin, Maunier, Pierre Métais, Leenhardt, and others—and talked with old militants in his neighborhood about the state of the cooperative movement, to which he had been so devoted since the end of the previous century.[82] He still corresponded regularly with his friends and students. His scientific and administrative activities were limited. He attended a few lectures, including Jean Piaget's in April 1942; read some colleagues' manuscripts, for example, Leroy's on Sainte-Beuve or Masson-Oursel's on the metaphysical fact; requested grants for students and researchers. The Institut d'Ethnologie published only a few studies between 1940 and 1944: Déborah Lifszyc's *Textes éthiopiens magico-religieux* (1940; Magical-religious Ethiopian texts), Solange de Ganay's *Les devises des Dogons* (1941; Dogon mottos), Bernard Maupoil's *La géomancie à l'ancienne Côte des esclaves* (1943; Geomancy on the old Slave Coast).

Mauss did little writing. "I'm not working on anything, not even for myself," he wrote Meyerson.[83] When Meyerson invited him to prepare a paper on "techniques and technologies" for a conference to be held in Toulouse on the psychology and history of labor and techniques, Mauss's first impulse was to refuse: "I hate publishing in these times (for a thousand reasons)."[84] Lucien Febvre and Georges Friedmann agreed to participate. Mauss then promised an article, which the organizer awaited impatiently: "Where is your study on the general theory of technologies? You know how it is anticipated, how it will be appreciated, how it will be read. Don't delay in finishing it."[85] It was a subject that interested Mauss. Ever since he had founded the technology section in *Année Sociologique* with Hubert, he had never forgotten what the "technical mentality" was. He was also one of the few French professors to have given a course on systematic technology.[86] A few years earlier, during a debate with Robert Marjolin, he had stressed the importance of the progress of science (applied and basic) and of technological innovations: radio, the automobile, aviation, steel, biochemistry, vitamins, and so on. And he had then criticized the economists for not taking into account "the power of technical facts." "When they enter the economy, they change it. But especially, in wartime and in peacetime, they also directly change the destinies of men. These new powers are unleashed and drive society toward unpredictable ends, toward good and evil, toward law and arbitrariness, toward other scales of values."[87]

If obliged to provide a definition of man, Mauss would probably have adopted the one proposed by his friend Halbwachs: "Man is an animal who thinks with his fingers."[88] In his paper, which would be published only after the war, he returned to a method dear to him. He defined technique ("a group of motions or acts, generally and primarily manual, organized, and traditional, coming together to obtain a goal known to be physical or chemical or organic"). Then he classified the various technology sectors and identified avenues for research and reflection. The sociologist had already set forth a few ideas on bodily techniques. He referred to them (briefly) only to remind his audience that "techniques, while human by nature, are distinctive for each social ranking."[89] Mauss wrote Meyerson: "I enjoyed summarizing all sorts of old stories I know, including the story of central planning."[90]

His attention focused especially on the important question of the relation between technique and science: "Even science is becoming increasingly technical, and technique is having an increasing effect on it. . . . The circle of relations between science and technique is increasingly vast, but at the same time increasingly closed."[91] The results were impressive: "The praise of nineteenth-century science and of the trades is more justified than ever in the twentieth century. . . . That's what we're experiencing. And it's not over." According to Mauss, when faced with the "demon unleashed," people ought not to be afraid or appeal to morality. They also ought not leave things to chance. It was a time for study bureaus, plans of action, and even central planning. It was more than a trend, exclaimed Mauss, it was a necessity.[92]

Planning, in his mind, was less a government project than "the activity of a people, a nation, a civilization." Mauss added: "More than ever, to speak of a plan is to speak . . . of morality, truth, efficiency, utility, the good. . . . It is pointless to contrast mind and matter, ideal and industry. In our times, the power of the instrument is the power of the mind and its use implies ethics and intelligence."[93]

The vise was tightening its grip on the Jews. An Office on Jewish Questions was established (law of March 29, 1941), headed by Xavier Vallat; a census of the Jews was taken (law of June 2, 1941); the police on Jewish Questions was organized (order of October 19, 1941). And beginning in 1942, repression hit hard; arrests and deportations multiplied. Fame did not always provide enough protection from the Nazis.[94] In the autumn of 1942, Jews residing in the occupied zone were required to wear the yellow star. Mauss bowed to the requirement and sewed his own star onto his coat.

In August 1942, Mauss and his wife were evicted from their large apartment on boulevard Jourdan, which was requisitioned for a German general. A few students enthusiastically helped Mauss put his books—"so many sacred things"—in boxes and store them at the Musée de l'Homme. Misfortune serves some purpose: "Everything from my past was saved," said Mauss. "This is also a great relief. I feel free and liberated from too burdensome a past, scientific and otherwise, which frequent memory losses are aggravating (symptoms from the Durkheim side, my grandmother, my mother)."[95]

The Mausses moved into a tiny ground-floor apartment at 2, rue Porto-Riche in the fourteenth arrondissement. It was an "appalling slum" that quickly became "impracticable" because it was "so cold, dark, and dirty."[96] His friends worried. The winter was harsh and "took its toll on [his] body." "The winter I've just been through was hard on me. I had accidents. My diabetes worries me a little."[97] Suffering "rather gravely," Mauss asked to be classified as ill. He recovered—a "resurrection," according to his doctor—owing to "the excellent reserves [his] system possessed."[98]

The situation became "nearly kaleidoscopic": everything was constantly changing. The plan to move, which Mauss was considering, still seemed "impossible from every angle." "Let's not think about it," he wrote. "I would not handle travel well."[99] He tried to keep up his spirits, but it was no time for rejoicing: "Life is painful and expensive," he complained.[100] "What makes me particularly gloomy is that I'm having rather too much bad luck."[101] "What a nasty gift life is!" Charles Fossey exclaimed.[102] Mauss's former colleague had retired and moved to Monte Carlo. He urged Mauss: "As far as possible, finish your technology [book] and get it published. And as soon as you're done, start something else. One must die with one's boots on."[103]

The only complete piece of work Mauss had, which he hoped to publish if authorized to do so, was his course "Instructions for Descriptive Sociology" ("exotic" ethnology). "I'm in the process of cleaning up Mme Schaeffner's [Denise Paulme's] typing. It's better if it goes out under my name rather than Griaule's."[104] Deprived of a library, Mauss was barely able to work on his planned book on technology. He composed only a few pages of a text that was to have three parts: "I have no stenographer, otherwise I'd make an effort to dictate. . . . It's my thumbs that don't want to work."[105]

As Mauss wrote Meyerson, from time to time he amused himself "trying to understand the huge social crisis" Europe was going through.[106] He wrote a few short notes, a page long at most, based on observations he had made in the street or at the market. One such note had to do with the "origins of the bourgeoisie," another with "social crises." His observations led him to reevaluate the concept of anomie, which he did not like: "To my uncle's great irritation, I found it too philosophical, too juridical, too moralistic, insufficiently concrete."[107]

Since the Occupation, Mauss remarked, Parisians had lived in a "state of selfishness, absolute individualism." The population was "completely outside the law and, in fact, beyond any rules except those imposed on it." But how to describe simply that isolation of the individual? It was in seeing one butcher girl pass meat jelly to another that Mauss had an "illumination": "Crisis . . . is the moment when 'things don't stick together anymore' or when everyone comes unstuck from everyone else."[108]

At least that image was concrete. For Mauss—and in this respect he remained a Durkheimian—a society was an "organism composed of units that are disparate, distinct, but that ultimately communicate with one another, forming a whole." In other words, "it is something that holds together." Among the different groups that compose it, "there is, there must be, a minimal cohesion, ethics, order, confidence and foresight, and predictability." Minimal cohesion and ethics had long ago deserted France, and it was practically only in his neighborhood that Mauss observed a "sort of fraternity and egalitarian social life."[109]

When his friends worried about his situation and health, Mauss reassured them: "Morally, I'm not suffering. I'm standing firm against the troubles that assail me."[110] The life he led varied little. He cared for his wife, did his

errands, and saw a few intimate friends; he went only rarely to the École
Pratique des Hautes Études, the Musée de l'Homme, and the Collège de
France. His friends, both the "faithful" and the more casual, came to visit
him in what he called his "slum."

According to information from the Red Cross, in early 1944 Mauss was
in good health and still in Paris.[111] One of his former students said he had
escaped "miraculously" from his "enemies' dull-witted ferocity."[112] Despite
the threats around him, he did not want to leave the capital and stood ready
to face any eventuality: "I still have my revolver," he confided to his visitors.
"If [the Germans] come, I'll know what to do." His niece Marie was working
at the Musée des Arts et Traditions Populaires under the name Mlle Maurin,
and he must have learned that his nephew François had joined the first division of the French Free Forces.

It is possible that Mauss was protected at the time by his relationships
or his fame. German scientists held him in great esteem; a few collaborators, including the influential George Montandon, knew him personally.
Montandon, already known for his anti-Jewish attitudes, was named in
1943 to head the Institut d'Études des Questions Juives et Ethno-Raciales
(Institute for the study of Jewish and ethno-racial questions). There were
also his old friends (almost all of them on the left) or colleagues in administrative or political positions: Jérôme Carcopino, secretary of national
education; Max Bonnafous, former cabinet chief to Ludovic Oscar Frossard
(1938) and André Marquet (1940), then a prefect, then a state secretary
from 1942 to 1944; Hubert Lagardelle, named minister of labor in March
1942; and Marcel Déat, named minister of labor two years later.

Déat, the founder of the Rassemblement Populaire, openly collaborated
with Vichy. Full of Durkheimian ideas about "community" and the "total
man," he did not hesitate to cite them to develop his own doctrine. Déat
persisted in justifying the anti-Semitic policy of the first Vichy laws by distinguishing between "the undesirable Jews who have inundated the West
in recent years, and the old, long-assimilated French Jews."[113] He also said
he favored the creation of a Jewish state, seeing no solution to the "grave"
Jewish question.[114] In his memoirs, he would refuse to recognize his share of
responsibility and would try to defend his position in the following terms:
"Unfortunately, German propaganda joined forces with Vichy operations
and fairly odious abuses and true catastrophes quickly occurred. At least I
never displayed complacency toward that loosed pack of hounds or howled
with the wolves. And every time I could, I and my friends helped the perse-
cuted Israelites." Déat would complain that he had had "to comment on and
apply Vichy's decisions on the Jews."[115]

Déborah Lifszyc was deported and killed at Auschwitz; Bernard Maupoil
died at Dachau; Marc Bloch was executed on June 16, 1944; Henri Maspero,
arrested in July 1944, was deported to Germany; Halbwachs, who had

recently been appointed a professor at the Collège de France, was also arrested and imprisoned. Worn down by illness, Halbwachs and Maspero both died, the first in March and the second in August 1945, at the Buchenwald concentration camp.[116]

Oblivion

Paris was liberated in late August 1944. Mauss told Michel Leiris, who came to visit with Patrick Waldberg, an American art critic and former student at the Institut d'Ethnologie, that on the morning of August 26 his wife was almost killed by a sniper. Leiris recounted: "A bullet passed through the window of their ground-floor apartment and lodged in the wall, slightly above the wooden bed in which Mme Mauss was lying."[117]

The victory brought an end to anguish and despair. Then came the settling of accounts: Montandon was killed by the Resistance in Clamart; Carcopino was arrested; Bernard Fay, a professor of American civilization at the Collège de France and general director of the Bibliothèque Nationale, was suspended from the Collège, then fired and sentenced to a life of hard labor; Georges-Henri Rivière, accused of collaboration, was suspended from his duties as museum curator at the Musée des Arts et Traditions Populaires.

Rivière, when he learned of the decision against him, appealed to Mauss, whom he had always venerated and from whom he sought consolation.[118] Mauss agreed without hesitation to defend him. "I attest that the zeal, distinction, and impartiality of G.-H. Rivière are beyond suspicion and that I trust him completely and have feelings of true friendship for him." He added that Rivière was a man recognized for his "broad-mindedness, his hard work, and his sense of organization." Other friends—Michel Leiris, Denise Paulme, André Schaeffner—also lent their support and wrote letters on his behalf, recalling that Rivière had made desperate attempts to save Lewitzky and Vildé and that on many occasions he had helped Jews escape persecution.[119]

Mauss sought to reclaim his apartment on boulevard Jourdan and, though his library was dispersed, to return to work. Requests arrived immediately: an invitation to attend meetings of the Institut Français de Sociologie; to read papers; to finish editing Hubert's *Les Germains*. Former students such as Germaine Tillion reaffirmed their "very old, very faithful, and very deep affection,"[120] and wanted to see him and ask for advice.[121] "I saw him again after the war, in 1945," Soustelle recalled. "The war had been an ordeal and he was sick. He was working on the civilizations of Oceania."[122]

Everything returned to normal, or almost. An order dated November 21, 1944, restored Mauss to his position at the Collège de France for the period between December 20, 1940, and May 10, 1942, and allowed him to draw a retirement pension dating from May 10, 1942.[123] In the early part of the following year, Edmond Faral, director of the Collège de France, wrote his colleague to inform him that, beginning on February 23, 1945, Mauss was a "professor emeritus."

But the old professor no longer responded to the requests of his friends or former students seeking to reestablish contact: "No news for a long time";[124] "days, weeks, and months go by and I have no news of you."[125]

Mauss withdrew into silence, as Jean Poirier has written. In his apartment at the Cité Universitaire, his retirement was disturbed only by visits from his nephews and nieces, Pierre, François, Jacqueline, and Marie, and from friends and former students. People were eager to associate his name with the three initiatives following the war that marked the "revival of sociology": in 1946, the creation of the Centre d'Études Sociologiques[126] and of *Cahiers Internationaux de Sociologie;*[127] and, in 1949, the "resurrection"[128] of *Année Sociologique.* One of the first colloquia organized by the new center was conceived as a tribute to Marcel Mauss: "Mauss and the Social Sciences."[129] For those who still had great affection for their "dear teacher," it was a tremendous disappointment to find him "diminished," unable to remember their names. "He did not recognize me," lamented Lévi-Strauss. "He mistook me for Soustelle." "Mauss had lost his memory," confirmed Louis Dumont. "It was sad. He thought I was Leiris."[130] These memory lapses made his loved ones fear he would get lost when he went out walking or would buy the same item several times. His brother, Henri Mauss, a recent widower who was not working, moved into the apartment on 95, boulevard Jourdan to take care of him. This was not always an easy situation, especially when Mauss resisted with his fists the rules imposed on him. Ill and still bedridden, his wife, Marthe, died on August 1, 1947.

The war, the Occupation, and all his torments thus prevailed over Mauss, and the vigor and liveliness of his mind were affected. Debilitated by bronchitis, he "gently passed away" at home on February 11, 1950, at the age of seventy-seven, surrounded by his brother and his nephews and nieces.[131] As he turned to look at a photograph of Hubert placed on a bureau near the radio, he is reported to have evoked his old friend and music: "Friendship and beauty are the two most beautiful things in life."

"There were only a few of us at his funeral," recounted Denise Paulme. "It was a civil funeral, very intimate, at the Bagneux cemetery."[132] A few months later, Maurice Leenhardt, to break "the silence that has surrounded Marcel Mauss for so many years," invited friends and former students to "pay the public tribute to him that could not be paid at the time of his death."[133] They praised him: "A good, sensitive, and refined man,"[134] "a warm-hearted and thoughtful man,"[135] "a faithful friend,"[136] "a leader of men,"[137] "after Durkheim, the greatest and most original French sociologist,"[138] "the undisputed master of the French school of ethnology."[139]

Some, such as Henri Lévy-Bruhl, eventually formulated a plan to produce a volume in grateful tribute to that "great disseminator of ideas." As everyone was aware, Mauss deserved "some kind of big potlatch," that is, the return of the "inestimable present" he had offered his collaborators and students.[140]

Who would take up the torch? So wondered Lucien Febvre at the end of his tribute to the man who had taught "something new, profound, and unprecedented about man."[141] A few names came immediately to mind: Maurice Leenhardt in the history of the religions of uncivilized peoples, Denise Paulme and Germaine Dieterlen in ethnology, Henri Lévy-Bruhl and Georges Gurvitch in sociology, Claude Lévi-Strauss in anthropology. The "high priest" side of Durkheim, who had wanted to establish a secular ethics inspired by the scientific spirit, still troubled some. In comparison, the nephew, with his "sorcerer" side, who believed in "the spirit of things" and the power of words, had everything required to please. We may draw two lessons from his life and his work: first, faithfulness is not in itself an obstacle to creativity; and second, critical distance is the condition for maintaining a tradition.

NOTES

INTRODUCTION

1. Georges Condominas, "Marcel Mauss, père de l'ethnographie française": part 1, "À l'ombre de Durkheim," *Critique* 28, no. 297 (February 1972): 118–39; part 2, "Naissance de l'ethnologie religieuse," *Critique* 28, no. 301 (June 1972): 487–504.

2. Claude Lévi-Strauss, "Introduction à l'oeuvre de Marcel Mauss" (1950), in Marcel Mauss, *Sociologie et anthropologie*, 3rd ed. (Paris: PUF, 1966), xxiv.

3. Georges Gurvitch, "Avertissement" (1950), in Mauss, *Sociologie et anthropologie*, viii. Gurvitch adds: "Unquestionably, the publication of Mauss's complete works is an imperative." Georges Gurvitch, "Nécrologie: Marcel Mauss," *Revue de Métaphysique et de Morale* 2 (April–June 1950): 2.

4. Jean Cazeneuve, *Mauss* (Paris: PUF, 1968).

5. Marcel Mauss, *Oeuvres*, vol. 1 (Paris: Éditions de Minuit, 1968), vols. 2 and 3 (1969). In 1971 a selection of texts published in the three volumes under the title *Essais de sociologie* appeared in a paperback edition (Paris: "Points," Éditions du Seuil, 1971).

6. Denis Hollier, "Ethnologie et sociologie. Sociologie et socialisme," *Arc* 48 (1972): 1 (issue on Marcel Mauss).

7. Henri Lévy-Bruhl, "Nécrologie: Marcel Mauss," *Journal de Psychologie Normale et Pathologique* 43 (1950): 318.

8. Henri Lévy-Bruhl, "In Memoriam: Marcel Mauss," *Année Sociologique*, 3rd ser. (1948–1949; Paris: PUF, 1951), 1.

9. Ibid., 2.

10. Steven Lukes published a short biographical notice ("Marcel Mauss") in the *International Encyclopedia of the Social Sciences*, vol. 10 (New York: Macmillan/Free Press, 1968), 78–82. Victor Karady's excellent "Présentation de l'édition" (in Mauss, *Oeuvres*, 1:i–liii) includes a great deal of biographical information.

11. As Mauss indicated in his paper "Fait social et formation du caractère," delivered at the International Congress of Anthropological and Ethnological Sciences in Copenhagen in 1938 (manuscript, Hubert-Mauss collection, Archives of the Collège de France, 3).

12. "I do not have the impression that Marcel Mauss would have wanted people to study his writings independent of the time and circumstances in which he was led to write them; in that sense, he can be said to be a structuralist. As a good philologist . . . he studied every word in its context." André-Georges Haudricourt, "Souvenirs personnels," *Arc* 48 (1972): 89.

13. Marcel Mauss, "L'oeuvre sociologique et anthropologique de Frazer," *Europe* 17 (1928), repr. in Mauss, *Oeuvres*, 3:532.

14. Some readers, such as Jacques Le Goff in the preface to the new edition of Marc Bloch's *Rois thaumaturges* (Paris: Gallimard, 1983) and Pierre Birnbaum in his short article "Du socialisme au don" (*Arc* 48 [1972]: 41), mistakenly call Mauss "Durkheim's disciple and son-in-law." Such an error may be explained by the fact

that the heir in intellectual families is often the son-in-law: did not Georges Davy, one of the contributors to *Année Sociologique*, want to marry Durkheim's daughter?

15. Marcel Mauss, "L'oeuvre de Mauss par lui-même" (1930), *Revue Française de Sociologie* 20, no. 1 (January–March 1979): 209.

16. Mauss's personal archives at the Collège de France include a large number of letters, more than five hundred of them written by Durkheim to his nephew. See Émile Durkheim, *Lettres à Marcel Mauss*, ed. Marcel Fournier and Philippe Besnard (Paris: PUF, 1998).

17. Condominas, "Marcel Mauss, père de l'ethnographie française."

18. Karady, "Présentation de l'édition," v.

19. "Marcel Mauss Transcript," interview with Marcel Mauss by Earle Edward Eubank (1934), in Dirk Kaesler, *Sociological Adventures: Earle Edward Eubank's Visits with European Sociologists* (New Brunswick, N.J.:Transaction Publishers, 1991), 145.

20. Karady, "Présentation de l'édition," xvi.

21. Maurice Leenhardt, "Marcel Mauss (1872–1950)," *Annuaire de l'École Pratique des Hautes Études, Section des Sciences Religieuses* (1950): 23.

22. Cazeneuve, *Mauss*, ii.

23. In the words of Henri Lévy-Bruhl, "Nécrologie: Marcel Mauss," 320.

24. Durkheim, *Lettres à Marcel Mauss*.

25. Marcel Mauss, *Écrits politiques*, ed. Marcel Fournier (Paris: Fayard, 1998).

CHAPTER 1
ÉPINAL, BORDEAUX, PARIS

1. Henri Lévy-Bruhl, "In Memoriam: Marcel Mauss," *Année Sociologique*, 3rd ser. (1948–1949; PUF, 1951), 1.

2. Archives of the Collège de France, C-XV Marcel Mauss, 27A.

3. Letter from Rosine Mauss to Marcel Mauss, December 4, 1894.

4. Letter from Rosine Mauss to Marcel Mauss, Épinal, November 10, 1897.

5. Marcel Mauss, "La mutualité patronale," *Humanité*, May 16, 1905, 1.

6. Letter from Émile Durkheim to Louis Liard, Bordeaux, December 5, 1893, repr. in *Revue Française de Sociologie* 20, no. 1 (January–March 1979): 114.

7. Marcel Mauss, "Les techniques du corps" (1935), in Mauss, *Sociologie et anthropologie*, 3rd ed. (Paris: PUF, 1966), 368.

8. Émile Durkheim, "Contribution à l'Enquête sur la guerre et le militarisme" (1899), in Durkheim, *Textes*, 3 vols. (Paris: Éditions de Minuit, 1975), 2:160–61.

9. Lévy-Bruhl, "In Memoriam: Marcel Mauss," 1.

10. Michael Graetz, *Les Juifs en France au XIXe siècle* (Paris: Éditions du Seuil, 1989), 64.

11. J.-J. Weiss, *Au pays du Rhin* (Paris: Charpentier, 1886).

12. Freddy Raphaël and Robert Weyl, *Juifs en Alsace* (Toulouse: Privat, 1977), 408–9.

13. Reybell, "Le socialisme et la question d'Alsace-Lorraine," *Revue Socialiste* 229 (January 1904): 88.

14. Émile Durkheim, "Contribution à H. Dogan, Enquête sur l'antisémitisme" (1899), in Durkheim, *Textes*, 2:252–53.

15. Graetz, *Les Juifs en France*, 432.

16. Émile Durkheim, *Le suicide, étude de sociologie* (1897; Paris: PUF, 1975), 159–60.

17. Ibid., 159.

18. Jean-Claude Filloux, *Durkheim et le socialisme* (Geneva: Droz, 1977), 8.

19. Georges Davy, "Durkheim, voie nouvelle ouverte à la science de l'homme" (1960), repr. in Davy, *L'homme, le fait social, et le fait politique* (Paris: Mouton, 1973), 18. See also Georges Davy, "Émile Durkheim," *Annuaire de l'Association Amicale des Anciens Élèves de l'École Normale Supérieure* (1919): 65.

20. Célestin Bouglé, "Émile Durkheim," *Encyclopedia of the Social Sciences*, vol. 5, ed. E.R.A. Seligman (New York: Macmillan, 1930), 28.

21. Filloux, *Durkheim et le socialisme*, 8.

22. Dominick LaCapra, *Émile Durkheim, Sociologist and Philosopher* (Ithaca: Cornell University Press, 1972), 28.

23. Étienne Halphen, "Préface," in *Durkheim, Cent ans de Sociologie en France* (Bordeaux, 1987), 6.

24. Critical note by M. Guyau, in Émile Durkheim, *L'irreligion de l'avenir* (1887), in Durkheim, *Textes*, 2:160.

25. Bernard Lacroix, *Durkheim et le politique* (Paris: Presses de la Fondation nationale des sciences politiques, 1981).

26. Hubert Bourgin, *De Jaurès à Léon Blum, l'École normale et la politique* (Paris: Librairie Arthème Fayard, 1938), 217.

27. Célestin Bouglé, "L'oeuvre sociologique d'Émile Durkheim," *Europe* 23 (1930): 291.

28. Xavier Léon, "Durkheim," *Revue de Métaphysique et de Morale* 26, no. 6 (1917): 749.

29. Bourgin, *De Jaurès à Léon Blum*, 217.

30. Letter from Sylvain Lévi to Marcel Mauss, February 17, 1917.

31. Davy, "Durkheim, voie nouvelle à la science de l'homme," 17.

32. Interview with Marie Mauss, Paris, March 1, 1989.

33. Letter from Gerson Mauss to Marcel Mauss, Épinal, November 8, 1894.

34. Letter from Marcel Mauss to Maxime Leroy, March 4, 1941.

35. Marcel Mauss, "Critique interne de la légende d'Abraham" (1926), in Mauss, *Oeuvres*, vol. 1 (Paris: Éditions de Minuit, 1968), vols. 2 and 3 (1969), 2:532n13.

36. Steven Lukes, "Marcel Mauss," *International Encyclopedia of the Social Sciences*, vol. 10 (New York: Macmillan/Free Press, 1968), 78–82.

37. Victor Karady, "Présentation de l'édition," in Mauss, *Oeuvres*, 1:xix.

38. Letter from Émile Durkheim to Marcel Mauss, undated [1899].

39. Letter from Rosine Mauss to Marcel Mauss, March 2, 1904.

40. Letter from Marcel Mauss to Henri Hubert, undated.

41. Letter from Rosine Mauss to Marcel Mauss, Épinal, March 3, 1899.

42. Letter from Rosine Mauss to Marcel Mauss, Épinal, April 6, 1898.

43. Letter from Marcel Mauss to Henri Hubert, undated [1902].

44. Durkheim, *Le suicide*, 169–70.

45. Marcelle Hertzog-Cachin, *Regards sur la vie de Marcel Cachin* (Paris: Éditions sociales, 1980), 26.

46. Marcel Mauss, "Théodule Ribot et les sociologues" (1939), in Mauss, *Oeuvres*, 3:566.

47. Marcel Mauss, introduction to Émile Durkheim, *Le socialisme* (1928), repr. in Mauss, *Oeuvres*, 3:506.

48. [The *agrégation* is a competitive exam taken by French college students to qualify them to teach in *lycées* and in some fields at the university level. A student who has passed the *agrégation* is called an *agrégé.*—Trans.]

49. Émile Durkheim, "La science positive de la morale en Allemagne" (1887), in Durkheim, *Textes*, 1:342–43.

50. [Roughly, assistant professor.—Trans.]

51. Christophe Charle, "Le beau mariage d'Émile Durkheim," *Actes de la Recherche en Sciences Sociales* 55 (1974): 44–49.

52. Marcel Mauss, "Notices nécrologiques" (1927), in Mauss, *Oeuvres* 3:523–24.

53. Davy, "Émile Durkheim," 65.

54. Marcel Mauss, "In Memoriam: L'oeuvre inédite de Durkheim et de ses collaborateurs," *Année Sociologique*, n.s. (1925), in Mauss, *Oeuvres*, 3:473–99.

55. Filloux, *Durkheim et le socialisme*, 34.

56. Mauss, "L'oeuvre inédite de Durkheim," 483–84.

57. [The Durkheimian concept of *conscience collective* encompasses both senses of the French term *conscience*, "consciousness" and "conscience." Hence "the 'beliefs and sentiments' comprising the *conscience collective* are, on the one hand, moral and religious, and, on the other, cognitive" (Steven Lukes, *Émile Durkheim: His Life and Work* [New York: Harper & Row, 1972], 4).—Trans.]

58. Émile Durkheim, "Préface à la première édition," in Durkheim, *De la division du travail social* (1893; Paris: PUF, 1960), xxxiv.

59. Durkheim, *De la division du travail social*, 406. In the preface to the second edition (1902), Durkheim would argue for a reform of economic life through reliance on professional groups.

60. Lucien Muhlfeld's commentary, published in *Revue Philosophique* (1893), is quoted in the introduction to *Division du travail et lien social*, ed. Philippe Besnard, Massino Borlandi, and Paul Vogt (Paris: PUF, 1993), 2.

61. Léon Brunschvicg and Élie Halévy, "L'année philosophique 1893," *Revue de Métaphysique et de Morale* (1896): 565–66.

62. Charles Andler, "Sociologie et philosophie," *Revue de Métaphysique et de Morale* (1896): 245. The response to Andler's critique of sociology would come from Célestin Bouglé, who would borrow the main lines of Durkheim's argument on the nature of social facts. Célestin Bouglé, "Sociologie, psychologie et histoire," *Revue de Métaphysique et de Morale* (1896): 362.

63. Marcel Mauss, "L'oeuvre de Mauss par lui-même"(1930), *Revue Française de Sociologie* 20, no.1 (January–March 1979): 210.

64. Letter from Émile Durkheim to Marcel Mauss, Bordeaux, n.d. [1897].

65. On Durkheim and his critics, see Lukes, *Durkheim: His Life and Work*, 497ff.

66. Mauss, introduction to *Le socialisme*, 28–29.

67. Marcel Mauss, "Sylvain Lévi" (1935), in Mauss, *Oeuvres*, 3:344.

68. Letter from Émile Durkheim to Marcel Mauss, n.d. [1899].

69. Lacapra, *Durkheim, Sociologist and Philosopher*, 1.

70. "Constatation de services" [Statement of service], Ministry of War, October 12, 1931 (Service historique de l'armée de terre, 1414437/N num. 15/26). Mauss belonged to the cohort of 1892 (no. 864).

71. G. Delprat, "L'enseignement sociologique à l'université de Bordeaux," *Revue Philomatique de Bordeaux et du Sud-Ouest* (August 1900): 357.

72. Mauss, "In Memoriam: L'oeuvre inédite de Durkheim," in Mauss, *Oeuvres*, 3:497.

73. Ibid., 484–85.

74. Ibid., 486.

75. Letter from Émile Durkheim to Marcel Mauss, Sunday, n.d. [1898].

76. Marcel Mauss, introduction to Émile Durkheim, "Morale civique et professionelle" (1937), repr. in Mauss, *Oeuvres*, 3:502.

77. Ibid., 503.

78. Mauss, "L'oeuvre de Mauss par lui-même," 210.

79. Georges Davy, "L'oeuvre d'Espinas," *Revue Philosophique* 96 (1923): 264.

80. Daniel Essetier, *Philosophes et savants français au XXe siècle*, vol. 5, *La sociologie* (Paris: Librairie Félix Alcan, 1930), 4.

81. Alfred Espinas, "Être ou ne pas être ou du postulat de la sociologie," *Revue Philosophique* 2 (1901): 449.

82. Alfred Espinas, "Les études sociologiques en France," *Revue Philosophique* 14 (1882): 366.

83. Davy, "L'oeuvre d'Espinas," 265.

84. Letter from Émile Durkheim to Marcel Mauss, Bordeaux, n.d.

85. Letter from Alfred Espinas to Marcel Mauss, June 6, 1898.

86. Émile Durkheim, "Nécrologie d'Octave Hamelin," *Temps*, September 18, 1907, repr. in Durkheim, *Textes*, 1:428.

87. Émile Durkheim, preface to Octave Hamelin, *Le système de Descartes* (1911), repr. in Durkheim, *Textes*, 1:433.

88. Dominique Parodi, "La philosophie d'Octave Hamelin," *Revue de Métaphysique et de Morale*, year 29, no. 2 (1922): 178. See also Dominique Parodi, *La philosophie contemporaine en France: Essai de classification des doctrines* (Paris: Alcan, 1917).

89. Parodi, "La philosophie d'Octave Hamelin," 182.

90. Letter from Marcel Mauss to Henri Hubert, n.d. [September 1907].

91. See Jean-Marie Mayeur, *Les débuts de la IIIe République, 1871–1898* (Paris: Éditions du Seuil, 1973).

92. Mauss, introduction to *Le socialisme*, 29.

93. Émile Durkheim, "Notes sur la définition du socialisme," *Revue Philosophique* (August 1893), repr. in Durkheim, *La science sociale et l'action* (Paris: PUF, 1970), 233.

94. Letter from Émile Durkheim to Marcel Mauss, n.d. [1903].

95. Mauss, introduction to *Le socialisme*, 507–8.

96. Émile Durkheim, "L'individualisme et les intellectuels," *Revue Bleue* (1898), repr. in Durkheim, *La science sociale et l'action*, 270.

97. Émile Durkheim, "L'élite intellectuelle et la démocratie," *Revue Bleue* (1904), repr. in Durkheim, *Textes*, 1:280.

98. Mauss, introduction to *Le socialisme*, 29.

99. Hertzog-Cachin, *Regards sur la vie de Marcel Cachin*, 38.

100. G. Bourgeois and Jean Maitron, "Marcel Cachin," in *Dictionnaire biographique du movement ouvrier français*, ed. Jean Maitron (Paris: Éditions ouvrières, 1984), 21.

101. Letter from F. de [Monsi] to Marcel Mauss, October 19, 1893.

102. Marcel Mauss, "Conceptions qui ont précédé la notion de matière," *Centre International de Synthèse*, XIe Semaine Internationale de Synthèse (1939), in Mauss, *Oeuvres*, 3:164.

103. In a note titled "Marcel Mauss—Services civils," which Mauss sent to the administration of the Collège de France, he mentions his *licence* scholarship (1891–1892) and his *agrégation* scholarship (1893–1894) (Archives of the Collège de France, C-XII, Marcel Mauss, 27D). He also received a doctoral scholarship (1895–1896).

104. Letter from Émile Durkheim to Marcel Mauss, n.d.

105. *Bulletin Administratif de l'Instruction Publique*, no. 1627, September 15, 1894.

106. Karady, "Présentation de l'édition," xx.

107. Jean-François Sirinelli, *Génération intellectuelle: Kâgneux et Normaliens dans l'entre-deux-guerres* (Paris: Fayard, 1988), 141–42.

108. Émile Durkheim, "L'enseignement de la philosophie de l'agrégation de philosophie" (1895), in Durkheim, *Textes*, 3:421.

109. "Enseignement" (signed NDLD), *Revue de Métaphysique et de Morale*, year 3 (1895): 232.

110. Mauss, "In Memoriam: L'oeuvre inédite de Durkheim," 482.

111. Letter from Émile Durkheim to Marcel Mauss, Bordeaux, June 18, 1894.

112. Marcel Mauss, "Paul Fauconnet" (obituary), n.d. [1938], 3 (Hubert-Mauss collection, Archives of the Collège de France).

113. [*Maître de conférences* corresponds roughly to "associate professor"; *directeur de conférences* is a full professor with certain administrative responsibilities.— Trans.]

114. Letter from Edgar Milhaud to Marcel Mauss, Geneva, June 24, 1932.

115. Letter from Rosine Mauss to Marcel Mauss, Épinal, n.d. [May 1895].

116. Letter from Rosine Mauss to Marcel Mauss, n.d. [May 1895].

117. Letter from Émile Durkheim to Marcel Mauss, n.d. [May 1895].

118. Mauss concluded: "We are probabilists, or, to use the modern term, we are [illegible] relativists. That said, we in no way claim to be skeptics." Hubert-Mauss collection, Archives of the Collège de France.

119. Individual evaluation of Marcel Mauss, *agrégations* and certificates of qualifications, Ministry of Education, Archives Nationales, F^{17} 7662.

120. Letter from Octave Hamelin to Marcel Mauss, August 26, 1895.

121. Letter from Marcel Mauss to Octave Hamelin, January 6, 1896 (Bibliothèque Victor-Cousin).

122. Mauss, "L'oeuvre de Mauss par lui-même," 214.

123. Letter from Rosine Mauss to Marcel Mauss, Épinal, January 23, 1896.

124. Letter from Edgar Milhaud to Marcel Mauss, Geneva, June 24, 1932.

125. Richard D. Sonn, *Anarchism and Cultural Politics in Fin de Siècle France* (Lincoln: University of Nebraska Press, 1989).

126. Christophe Charle, *Naissance des "intellectuels," 1880–1900* (Paris: Éditions de Minuit, 1990), 105–6.

127. See Yolande Cohen, "Avoir vingt ans en 1900: A la recherche d'un mouvement socialiste," *Mouvement Social* 120 (July–September 1982): 11–31; Georges Weisz, "Associations et manifestations: Les étudiants français à la Belle Époque," *Mouvement Social* 120 (July–September 1982): 31–45.

128. Géraldi Leroy, *Péguy: Entre l'ordre et la révolution* (Paris: Presses de la Fondation nationale des sciences politiques, 1981), 54.

129. Letter from Émile Durkheim to Marcel Mauss, Bordeaux, February 19, 1894.

130. Letter from A.S. to Marcel Mauss, n.d. [1900].

131. Mauss, introduction to *Le socialisme*, 506.

132. Georges Sorel, "Les théories de M. Durkheim," *Devenir Social*, year 1, 2 (May 1895): 179–80.

133. In addition to these book reviews, there is a short critical note of a book titled *L'idée spiritualiste* (Paris: Alcan, 1896), which Mauss wrote under the pseudonym Roisel (*Devenir Social*, year 3, no. 4 [1897]: 382–83).

134. Marcel Mauss, review of G. de Greef, *L'évolution des croyances et des doctrines politiques*, *Devenir Social*, year 2, no. 4 (April 1896): 373.

135. W. Paul Vogt, "Un durkheimien ambivalent: Célestin Bouglé, 1870–1940," *Revue Française de Sociologie* 20, no. 1 (January–March 1979): 123.

136. Ibid., 127.

137. Marcel Mauss, review of Célestin Bouglé, *Les sciences sociales en Allemagne*, *Devenir Social*, year 3, no. 4 (April 1897): 373.

138. Letter from Émile Durkheim to Célestin Bouglé, Bordeaux, December 14, 1895, in *Revue Française de Sociologie* 17, no. 2 (April–June 1976): 166.

139. Letter from Émile Durkheim to Marcel Mauss, n.d. [1897].

140. Letter from Marcel Mauss to Henri Hubert, n.d. [1898].

141. Marcel Mauss, "L'action socialiste," lecture of Friday, March 15, 1899, Cercle des Étudiants Collectivistes, 2 (Hubert-Mauss collection, Archives of the Collège de France).

CHAPTER 2
STUDENT AT THE ÉCOLE PRATIQUE DES HAUTES ÉTUDES

1. Marcel, Mauss, "L'oeuvre de Mauss par lui-même"(1930), *Revue Française de Sociologie* 20, no.1(January–March 1979): 214.

2. Émile Durkheim, "Les études de sciences sociales" (1886), in Durkheim, *La science sociale et l'action* (Paris: PUF, 1970), 184–214.

3. Émile Durkheim, review of M. Guyau, *L'irreligion de l'avenir* (1887), in Durkheim, *Textes* (Paris: Éditions de Minuit, 1975), 2:160.

4. Émile Durkheim, "Lettre au directeur" (1907), in Durkheim, *Textes*, 1:404.

5. Letter from Émile Durkheim to H. Uzener, May 6, 1898.

6. Letter from Émile Durkheim to Marcel Mauss, n.d. [1898].

7. Jan De Vries, *Perspectives in the History of Religions* (Berkeley: University of California Press, 1977), 79.

8. Alfred Loisy, *Mémoires pour servir à l'histoire religieuse de notre temps* (Paris: Émile Noury, 1932), 2:96.

9. Jean Réville, "La situation de l'enseignement de l'histoire des religions," *Revue de l'Histoire des Religions* 43 (1901): 63.

10. Ibid., 62.

11. Less than a year later, the Société d'Études Juives had more than 450 subscribing members.

12. Michel Abitbol, *Les deux terres promises: Les Juifs en France et le sionisme, 1897–1945* (Paris: Olivier Orban, 1989), 19.

13. Sylvain Lévi, "Une renaissance juive en Judée," *Temps*, July 30, 1918, quoted in ibid., 255n4.

14. Charles Péguy, *Cahiers de la Quinzaine*, July 17, 1910, repr. in Péguy, *Notre jeunesse* (Paris: Gallimard, 1933), 76.

15. Louis Liard (1846–1917), named director of higher education in 1884, had just begun a major reform of the system. A former student at the École Normale Supérieure and an *agrégé*, Liard was professor of philosophy at the Université de Bordeaux. He was also the author of *Histoire de l'éducation en France au XIXe siècle* (History of education in nineteenth-century France). We have already seen the role he played in Durkheim's appointment to *chargé de cours* in Bordeaux in 1887. On Louis Liard, see Ernest Lavisse, "Louis Liard," *Revue Internationale de l'Enseignement* 72 (1918): 81–89.

16. Jean-Pierre Vernant, "Les sciences religieuses entre la sociologie, le comparatisme et l'anthropologie," in Vernant, *Cent ans de sciences religieuses en France* (Paris: Éditions du Cerf, 1987), 80.

17. Sylvain Lévi, "Discours prononcé aux obsèques de Paul Alphandéry," *Revue de l'Histoire des Religions* 105 (1932): 143.

18. Jean Réville, "La leçon d'ouverture du cours d'histoire des religions au collège de France," *Revue de l'Histoire des Religions* 55 (1907): 190.

19. Anathon Hall, "Le congrès des sciences religieuses de Stockholm," *Revue de l'Histoire des Religions* 36 (1897): 265.

20. Minutes of the committee meeting, section of religious science, École Pratique des Hautes Études, notebook 1, session of December 2, 1900.

21. Auguste Sabatier, review of Albert Réville, *Jésus de Nazareth*, *Revue de l'Histoire des Religions* 36 (1897): 162.

22. Ibid.

23. Ivan Strenski, "L'apport des élèves de Durkheim," *Cahiers de Recherche en Sciences de la Religion* 10 (1991): 117–20.

24. Lévi, "Discours prononcé aux obsèques de Paul Alphandéry," 143.

25. Marcel Mauss, "Sylvain Lévi" (1935), in Mauss, *Oeuvres*, vol. 1 (Paris: Éditions de Minuit, 1968), vols. 2 and 3 (1969), 3:535.

26. Alfred Foucher, "Sylvain Lévi," *Annuaire de l'École Pratique des Hautes Études, Section des Sciences Religieuses* (1936): 17–23.

27. The book in question is probably not Berdaigne's doctoral thesis, *Les dieux souverains et la religion védique* (1877) but rather the two volumes of *La religion védique d'après les hymnes du Rig Véda* (1877–1883), which Mauss quotes in his "Essai sur le sacrifice." Berdaigne, born in 1838, died following a mountain-climbing accident in 1888. A linguist, he was a tutor in Sanskrit at the École Pratique des Hautes Études (1868–1869), then *maître de conférence* (1877), and finally professor of Sanskrit language and literature at the faculty of letters in Paris (1885).

28. Mauss, "Sylvain Lévi," 535.

29. Ibid., 536.

30. "L'homme au foulard blanc," *Temps*, Sunday, September 27, 1936, 1.

31. Marcel Mauss, "In Memoriam: Antoine Meillet (1866–1936)" (1936), in Mauss, *Oeuvres* 3:548. The Avesta and the Zenda are the sacred texts of the Zoroastrian religion.

32. *Annuaire de l'École Pratique des Hautes Études, Section des Sciences Historiques et Philologiques* (1902): 85.

33. Léon Marillier, "Le folk-lore et la science des religions," *Revue de l'Histoire des Religions* 41 (1901): 181.

34. Marcel Mauss, "L'enseignement de l'histoire des religions des peuples non civilisés à l'École des hautes études," *Revue de l'Histoire des Religions* 45 (1902), repr. in Mauss, *Oeuvres*, 3:462–64.

35. Marcel Mauss, review of Léon Marillier, "La place du totémisme dans l'évolution religieuse," *Revue de l'Histoire des Religions* (1899), repr. in Mauss, *Oeuvres*, 1:175.

36. Marcel Mauss, review of Léon Marillier, "Religion," *Année Sociologique* 5 (1902), repr. in Mauss, *Oeuvres*, 1:128.

37. Maurice Liber, "Israël Lévi," *Annuaire de l'École Pratique des Hautes Études, Section des Sciences Religieuses* (1939): 43.

38. Marcel Mauss, "Israël Lévi: Quelques souvenirs personnels," *Annuaire de l'École Pratique des Hautes Études, Section des Sciences Religieuses* (1939): 44.

39. Mauss, "Sylvain Lévi," 538.

40. *Annuaire de l'École Pratique des Hautes Études, Section des Sciences Historiques et Philologiques* (1897): 78.

41. Paul Masson-Oursel, "Nécrologie de Sylvain Lévi," *Revue de l'Histoire des Religions* 112 (1935): 112.

42. Foucher, "Sylvain Lévi," 543.

43. Mauss, "Sylvain Lévi," 538.

44. Letter from Sylvain Lévi to Marcel Mauss, July 26, 1896.

45. Letter from Sylvain Lévi to Marcel Mauss, October 2, 1897.

46. Mauss, "Sylvain Lévi," 539.

47. Letter from Sylvain Lévi to Marcel Mauss, Katmandu, February 19, 1898.

48. Mauss, "Sylvain Lévi," 542.

49. Isidore Lévy, "Sylvain Lévi (1863–1935)," *Revue d'Études Juives* 6, no. 2 (July–December 1935): 2.

50. Abitbol, *Les deux terres promises*, 77.

51. Marcel Drouin, "Henri Hubert," *Annuaire: Association de Secours des Anciens Élèves de l'École Normale Supérieure* (1929): 46.

52. Letter from Marcel Mauss to Henri Hubert, n.d. [1898].

53. Hubert Bourgin, *De Jaurès à Léon Blum, l'École normale et la politique* (Paris: Librairie Arthème Fayard,1938), 107.

54. Ivan Strenski, "Henri Hubert, Racial Science and Political Myth," *Journal of the History of Behavioral Sciences* 21, nos. 2–3 (1987): 354.

55. Letter from Henri Hubert to Marcel Mauss, n.d. [1897].

56. Henri Hubert, "Texte autobiographique" (1915), in *Revue Française de Sociologie* 20, no. 1 (January–March 1979): 205.

57. François A. Isambert, "Henri Hubert et la sociologie du temps," *Revue Française de Sociologie* 20, no. 1 (January–March 1979): 184.

58. Drouin, "Henri Hubert," 48.

59. Salomon Reinach, "Henri Hubert," *Revue Archéologique* 26 (July–September 1927): 178.

60. Bourgin, *De Jaurès à Léon Blum*, 381.

61. Letter from Marcel Mauss to Henri Hubert, Leiden, n.d. [1897].

62. Mauss, "L'oeuvre de Mauss par lui-même," 216.

63. Marcel Mauss, "Henri Hubert," manuscript, Hubert-Mauss collection, Archives of the Collège de France. See Marcel Mauss, "Henri Hubert, 1872–1927," *Encyclopedia of the Social Sciences*, vols. 7–8 (1932): 527.

64. Letter from Émile Durkheim to Marcel Mauss, n.d. [1898].

65. Letter from Henri Hubert to Marcel Mauss, n.d. [1897].

66. Letter from Marcel Mauss to Henri Hubert, n.d. [1898].

67. Letter from Sylvain Lévi to Marcel Mauss, February 19, 1898.

68. Daniel Halévy, *Pays parisiens* (Paris: Grasset, 1932), 170.

69. Letter from Marcel Mauss to Henri Hubert, Leiden, n.d. [1897].

70. Letter from Paul Fauconnet to Marcel Mauss, January 13, 1898.

71. Letter from Marcel Mauss to Henri Hubert, Oxford, n.d. [1898].

72. Letter from Marcel Mauss to Henri Hubert, n.d. [1897].

73. Letter from Marcel Mauss to Henri Hubert, n.d.

74. Letter from Émile Durkheim to Marcel Mauss, n.d. [1898].

75. Mauss, "L'oeuvre de Mauss par lui-même," 214.

76. Ibid., 210. Mauss may have also played a role in mapping out suicides in France for the International Exposition held in Bordeaux in 1895. R. Lacroze, "Émile Durkheim à Bordeaux," *Actes de l'Académie Nationale des Sciences, Belles-Lettres et Arts à Bordeaux* (1960), cited in Lukes, *Émile Durkheim: His Life and Work* (New York: Harper & Row, 1972), 191.

77. Philippe Besnard, *L'anomie, ses usages et ses fonctions dans les disciplines sociologiques depuis Durkheim* (Paris: PUF, 1987), 77.

78. Letter from Émile Durkheim to Marcel Mauss, n.d. [1897].

79. Conjugal anomie also produces victims: Durkheim observed that throughout Europe the suicide rate rises in direct proportion to the number of divorces.

80. This analytical model constructed around two axes allowed Durkheim to identify not two but four types of suicide: there is also altruistic suicide, which results from too great an integration, and fatalistic suicide, resulting from an "excess" of regulation. These two types of suicide are not common in modern societies. For an introduction to Durkheim's analytical model, see Besnard, *L'anomie*.

81. Émile Durkheim, *Le suicide, étude de sociologie* (1897; Paris: PUF, 1975), 324.

82. Gustave Belot, review of *Année Sociologique*, vol. 1, *Revue Philosophique* 45 (June 1898): 653.

83. Paul Fauconnet, review of Émile Durkheim, *Le suicide*, *Revue Philosophique* 45 (April 1898): 428.

84. Paul Fauconnet and Marcel Mauss, "La sociologie" (1901), in Mauss, *Oeuvres*, 3:168.

85. Ibid.

CHAPTER 3
RITES OF INSTITUTION

1. Marcel Mauss, review of A. Bastian, *Mythologie und Psychologie*, *Revue de l'Histoire des Religions*, year 17, 33 (1896): 209–12.

2. Marcel Mauss, "L'oeuvre de Mauss par lui-même" (1930), *Revue Française de Sociologie* 20, no.1 (January–March 1979): 214.

3. Marcel Mauss, "La religion et les origines du droit pénal d'après un livre récent" (1896), in Mauss, *Oeuvres*, vol. 1 (Paris: Éditions de Minuit, 1968), vols. 2 and 3 (1969), 2:652.

4. Émile Durkheim, *De la division du travail social* (1893; Paris: PUF, 1960), 59.

5. Visiting card from Gabriel Tarde to Marcel Mauss, n.d.

6. Letter from S. R. Steinmetz to Marcel Mauss, The Hague, April 9, 1897.

7. Letter from Émile Durkheim to Marcel Mauss, Bordeaux, n.d. [June 1897].

8. Letter from Émile Durkheim to Marcel Mauss, Bordeaux, December 22, 1897.

9. Émile Durkheim, review of Marcel Mauss, "La religion et les origines du droit pénal" (1898), in Durkheim, *Journal sociologique* (Paris: PUF, 1969), 129.

10. Letter from Rosine Mauss to Marcel Mauss, Épinal, March 21, 1897.

11. Letter from Émile Durkheim to Marcel Mauss, n.d. [1897].

12. Letter from Émile Durkheim to Marcel Mauss, Bordeaux, n.d. [1897].

13. These are the same words Durkheim used in the outline of a letter (n.d.) that he suggested his nephew send to the director when he applied for his scholarship.

14. Letter from Marcel Mauss to Paul Lapie, March 1898.

15. Maurice Olender, *Les langues du paradis* (Paris: Gallimard/Éditions du Seuil, 1989), 20.

16. Max Müller, *Nouvelles leçons sur la science du langage* (Paris: A. Durand and Pedore Lauriel, 1868).

17. Marcel Mauss, review of Max Müller, *Nouvelles études de mythologie* (1899), in Mauss, *Oeuvres*, 2:273–76.

18. Letter from Rosine Mauss to Marcel Mauss, Épinal, December 23, 1897.

19. Marcel Mauss, review of Willem Caland, *Die altindischen Toten- und Bestattungsgebrauche* (1898), in Mauss, *Oeuvres*, 1:325–29.

20. Letter from Marcel Mauss to Henri Hubert, Leiden, n.d. [1898].

21. Letter from Willem Caland to Marcel Mauss, Breda, January 12, 1898.

22. Letter from Marcel Mauss to Henri Hubert, Leiden, n.d. [1897].

23. Letter from Marcel Mauss to Henri Hubert, Leiden, n.d. [1897].

24. Letter from Marcel Mauss to Henri Hubert, Leiden, n.d. [1898].

25. Letter from Marcel Mauss to Henri Hubert, Leiden, n.d. [1898].

26. Letter from James Frazer to Marcel Mauss, July 14, 1899.

27. Marcel Mauss, "L'enseignement de l'histoire des religions des peuples non civilisés à l'École des hautes études," *Revue de l'Histoire des Religions* 45 (1902), in Mauss, *Oeuvres*, 3:460.

28. E. Sidney Hartland, "Presidential Address," *Folk-lore* 11, no. 1 (March 1900): 57.

29. Ibid., 58.

30. R. A. Downie, *Frazer and the Golden Bough* (London: Gollancz, 1970).

31. Hartland, "Presidential Address," 80.

32. Letter from Marcel Mauss to Henri Hubert, Leiden, n.d. [1898]

33. Letter from Marcel Mauss to Henri Hubert, Leiden, n.d. [1898].

34. Letter from Louis Finot to Marcel Mauss, March 24, 1897.

35. Letter from Rosine Mauss to Marcel Mauss, Épinal, May 1, 1898.

36. Letter from Émile Durkheim to Marcel Mauss, Bordeaux, May 3, 1898.

37. Letter from Marcel Mauss to Henri Hubert, Oxford, n.d. [1898].

38. Letter from Marcel Mauss to Henri Hubert, Oxford, n.d. [1898].

39. Letter from Marcel Mauss to Henri Hubert, Oxford, n.d. [1898].

40. Letter from Marcel Mauss to Émile Durkheim, n.d.

41. Marcel Mauss, "Notices biographiques" (1927), in Mauss, *Oeuvres*, 3:524.

42. Marcel Mauss, review of J. G. Frazer, *The Golden Bough*, *Notes Critiques*, July 21, 1901, 223.

43. Mauss, "L'oeuvre sociologique et anthropologique de Frazer," *Europe* 17 (1928), in Mauss, *Oeuvres*, 3:525.

44. Robert Ackerman, *Frazer, His Life and Work* (Cambridge: Cambridge University Press, 1987), 124.

45. Letter from James Frazer to Marcel Mauss, July 14, 1899.

46. Letter from Marcel Mauss to Henri Hubert, Oxford, n.d. [May 1898].

47. Letter from Émile Durkheim to Marcel Mauss, n.d. [January 1898].

48. Célestin Bouglé, "Métaphysique et morale en France: L'oeuvre de Xavier Léon," *Revue de Paris*, May 1, 1936, 203.

49. Dominique Merllié, "Les rapports entre la *Revue de métaphysique* et la *Revue philosophique*," *Revue de Métaphysique et de Morale* 1–2 (January–June 1993): 59–109.

50. Letter from Émile Durkheim to Célestin Bouglé, Bordeaux, May 16, 1896, in Durkheim, *Textes* (Paris: Éditions de Minuit, 1975), 2:392.

51. Letter from Émile Durkheim to Célestin Bouglé, Bordeaux [December 1896], in Durkheim, *Textes*, 2:393.

52. Mauss, "L'oeuvre de Mauss par lui-même," 210.

53. Albert Milhaud contributed only to the first volume of *Année Sociologique*. While preparing that volume, Durkheim expressed certain misgivings about him. Letter from Émile Durkheim to Marcel Mauss, Bordeaux, n.d. [June 1897].

54. Paul Fauconnet, review of Émile Durkheim, *Le suicide*, *Revue Philosophique* 45 (April 1898): 430–31.

55. François Simiand, "L'Année sociologique française 1897," *Revue de Métaphysique et de Morale* 6 (1898): 608–53.

56. Of the first twelve contributors to *Année*, only Emmanuel Lévy (doctor of law) was not an *agrégé*. There were eight *agrégés* in philosophy, two in history, and one in grammar. When the first volume appeared in 1898, the average age of the contributors was 29.3 years. The oldest was Émile Durkheim (40) and the youngest Paul Fauconnet (24).

57. Also joining the team for the first *Année Sociologique* were Gaston Richard and Emmanuel Lévy. Richard (b. 1860) was slightly younger than Durkheim and had been his classmate at the École Normale Supérieure. An *agrégé* in philosophy (1885), he was still a *lycée* teacher despite having earned his doctorate in letters (1892). Emmanuel Lévy (b. 1871) had earned a doctorate in law (1896) and was a *chargé de cours* at the law school in Lyons.

58. Philippe Besnard, "Présentation des lettres d'Émile Durkheim à Henri Hubert," *Revue Française de Sociologie* 28, no. 1 (1987): 485.

59. Letter from Marcel Mauss to Henri Hubert, December 15, 1912.

60. Letter from Émile Durkheim to Marcel Mauss [1899].

61. Letter from Marcel Mauss to Henri Hubert, n.d. The expression "dogmatic publications" appears often in the correspondence. It refers to studies with theoretical aspirations.

62. Mauss, "L'oeuvre de Mauss par lui-même," 210.

63. Émile Durkheim, "Préface," *Année Sociologique* (1898), repr. in Durkheim, *Journal sociologique*, 30.

64. Letter from Émile Durkheim to Marcel Mauss, n.d. [1897].

65. Letter from Émile Durkheim to Marcel Mauss, Bordeaux, July 3, 1897.

66. Mauss, "L'oeuvre de Mauss par lui-même," 213.

67. Letter from Émile Durkheim to Marcel Mauss, n.d. [July 1897].

68. Letter from Émile Durkheim to Marcel Mauss, July 15, 1897.

69. Letter from Émile Durkheim to Marcel Mauss, Friday, n.d.

70. Marcel Mauss, "L'Année sociologique," *Internationales Archiv für Ethnographie* 11 (1898): 232.

71. Letter from Henri Hubert to Marcel Mauss, n.d.

72. Victor Karady, "Présentation de l'édition," in Mauss, *Oeuvres*, 1:xxv.

73. Terry N. Clark, "The Structure and Functions of a Research Institute: The *Année sociologique*," *Archives Européennes de Sociologie* 9, no. 1 (1968).

74. Durkheim, "Préface," *Année Sociologique* (1898), repr. in Durkheim, *Journal sociologique*, 36.

75. Mauss, "L'oeuvre de Mauss par lui-même," 210.

76. Marcel Mauss, "Paul Fauconnet" (biographical notice), n.d., 4 (Hubert-Mauss collection, Archives of the Collège de France).

77. Mauss, "L'oeuvre de Mauss par lui-même," 210.

78. Letter from Émile Durkheim to Marcel Mauss, n.d. [July 1897].

79. Mauss, "L'oeuvre de Mauss par lui-même" (1930), 210.

80. Davy, "Émile Durkheim," 65.

81. Philippe Besnard, "The *Année sociologique* Team," in *The Sociological Domain: The Durkheimians and the Founding of French Sociology*, ed. Philippe Besnard (Cambridge: Cambridge University Press, 1993), 26–28.

82. Mauss, "L'oeuvre de Mauss par lui-même," 260.

83. Letter from Émile Durkheim to Xavier Léon, August 19, 1897, in Durkheim, *Textes*, 2:463.

84. Letter from Émile Durkheim to Célestin Bouglé, Bordeaux, July 6, 1897, in Durkheim, *Textes*, 2:400.

85. Gustave Belot, review of *Année Sociologique* 1, *Revue Philosophique* 45 (June 1898): 650.

86. Ibid.

87. Letter from Émile Durkheim to Célestin Bouglé, Bordeaux, May 25 [1897].

88. Mauss, "L'oeuvre de Mauss par lui-même," 212.

89. Henri Lévy-Bruhl, "In Memoriam: Marcel Mauss," *Année Sociologique,* 3rd ser. (1948–1949; Paris: PUF, 1951), 9.

90. Besnard, "The *Année sociologique* Team," 32–33. See also U. Nandam, *The Durkheimian School: A Systematic and Comprehensive Bibliography* (Westport, Conn.: Greenwood Press, 1977).

91. Victor Karady, "Stratégies de réussite et modes de faire-valoir de la sociologie chez les durkheimiens," *Revue Française de Sociologie* 20, no. 1 (January–March 1979): 75.

92. Émile Durkheim, "Préface," *Année Sociologique* (1898), repr. in Durkheim, *Journal sociologique*, 136.

93. Letter from Émile Durkheim to Marcel Mauss, n.d. [June 1897].

94. Letter from Émile Durkheim to Henri Hubert, n.d. [1901], in *Revue Française de Sociologie* 28, no. 1 (1987): 531.

95. Letter from Émile Durkheim to Henri Hubert, Bordeaux, December 10, 1897, in *Revue Française de Sociologie* 28, no. 1 (1987): 486.

96. Letter from Émile Durkheim to Rosine Durkheim-Mauss, October 18, 1907.

97. Letter from Émile Durkheim to Marcel Mauss, n.d. [1898].

98. Letter from Émile Durkheim to Henri Hubert, n.d. [1898], in *Revue Française de Sociologie* 28, no. 1 (1987): 498.

99. Ibid., 499.

100. Letter from Émile Durkheim to Marcel Mauss, n.d. [1898].

101. Letter from Émile Durkheim to Henri Hubert, n.d. [1901], in *Revue Française de Sociologie* 28, no. 1 (1987): 520.

102. Georges Renard, "Carnets de guerre," November 20, 1917, B.H.V.P., Archives Renard.

103. Letter from Marcel Mauss to Rosine Mauss, n.d. [1914].

104. Letter from Émile Durkheim to Marcel Mauss, n.d. [January 1898].

105. Mauss, "Sylvain Lévi," 538.

106. Marcel Mauss, review of Sylvain Lévi, *La doctrine du sacrifice dans les Brahmanas*, *Année Sociologique* (1900), repr. in Mauss, *Oeuvres*, 1:352.

107. Father Marie-Joseph Lagrange, *Études des religions sémitiques* (Paris: Librairie Victor Lecoffre, 1905), 274.

108. Ernest Renan, *Histoire du peuple d'Israël* (Paris, 1887), 1:52, repr. in Ernest Renan, *Oeuvres complètes* (Paris: Calmann-Lévy, 1953), 6:61.

109. Letter from Henri Hubert to Marcel Mauss, n.d. [1898].

110. Henri Hubert, "Introduction," in P. D. Chantepie de la Saussaye, *Manuel d'histoire des religions* (Paris: Alcan, 1904), xviii.

111. Henri Hubert and Marcel Mauss, "Essai sur la nature et la fonction du sacrifice," *Année Sociologique* 2 (1899), repr. in Mauss, *Oeuvres*, 1:305.

112. Émile Durkheim, "Préface," *Année Sociologique* 2 (1899), repr. in Durkheim, *Journal sociologique*, 139. Durkheim adds: "Of course, the importance [they] thereby attribute to [religious] sociology does not in any way imply that religion in present-day societies ought to play the same role it did in the past. In a sense, the opposite conclusion would be more justified."

113. Émile Durkheim, "De la définition des phénomènes religieux," *Année Sociologique* 2 (1899), in Durkheim, *Journal sociologique*, 165.

114. Letter from Émile Durkheim to Marcel Mauss, Sunday, n.d. [1898].

115. W. Robertson Smith, *Lectures on the Religion of the Semites* (1889; London: Adam and Charles Black, 1914), 392. See also his article "Sacrifice," *Encyclopedia Britannica*, 9th ed. (Edinburgh, 1876), 21:132–33.

116. Henri Hubert and Marcel Mauss, "Introduction à l'analyse de quelques phénomènes religieux," *Revue de l'Histoire des Religions* (1906), repr. in Mauss, *Oeuvres*, 1:5.

117. Letter from James Frazer to Marcel Mauss, Cambridge, July 14, 1899.

118. Ibid.

119. James Frazer, *The Golden Bough: A Study in Comparative Religion*, 2nd ed. (London: Macmillan, 1900), 3.

120. Mauss, "L'oeuvre de Mauss par lui-même," 217.

121. Henri Hubert, "Texte autobiographique" (1915), in *Revue Française de Sociologie* 20, no. 1 (January–March 1979): 206.

122. Letter from Marcel Mauss to Henri Hubert, Oxford, n.d. [1898].

123. Letter from Émile Durkheim to Marcel Mauss, n.d. [1898].

124. Letter from Marcel Mauss to Henri Hubert, Oxford [?], May 1898.

125. Letter from Émile Durkheim to Marcel Mauss, n.d. [January 1898].

126. Letter from Henri Hubert to Marcel Mauss, n.d. [1898].

127. Letter from Marcel Mauss to Henri Hubert, n.d. [June 1898].

128. Letter from Henri Hubert to Émile Durkheim, n.d. [1898].

129. Letter from Marcel Mauss to Henri Hubert, Oxford, n.d. [1898].

130. Letter from Henri Hubert to Marcel Mauss, n.d. [1898].

131. Letter from Sylvain Lévi to Marcel Mauss, Katmandu, February 19, 1898.

132. Letter from Henri Hubert to Marcel Mauss, n.d. [1898].

133. E. Sidney Hartland, review of *Année Sociologique* 2 (1899), *Folk-lore* 12, no. 1 (1900): 95.

134. Alfred Loisy, review of Henri Hubert and Marcel Mauss, *Mélanges d'histoire des religions*, *Revue Critique d'Histoire et de Littérature* (May 1909): 403.

135. Hubert and Mauss, "Essai sur le sacrifice," 1:199.

136. Letter from Marcel Mauss to Henri Hubert, Oxford, n.d. [1898].

137. Letter from Émile Durkheim to Marcel Mauss, Bordeaux, June 15, 1898.

138. Hubert and Mauss, "Essai sur le sacrifice," 205.

139. Letter from Marcel Mauss to Émile Durkheim, Oxford, n.d. [1898].

140. Hubert and Mauss, "Essai sur le sacrifice," 302.

141. Marcel Mauss, review of Arnold Van Gennep, *Les rites de passage*, *Année Sociologique* (1910), repr. in Mauss, *Oeuvres*, 1:554.

142. Hubert and Mauss, "Introduction à l'analyse de quelques phénomènes religieux," 16–17.

143. Ibid.

144. Mauss, "L'oeuvre de Mauss par lui-même," 218.

145. Letter from Marcel Mauss to Émile Durkheim, n.d. [1898]. In that long letter, Mauss sets out an outline for the work he was beginning with Hubert. He also indicates that Hubert would deal more particularly with the question of the murder of God.

146. Letter from Émile Durkheim to Marcel Mauss, Bordeaux, June 15, 1898.

147. E. E. Evans-Pritchard, *Theories of Primitive Religion* (Oxford: Clarendon, 1965), 85.

148. Marcel Mauss, review of P. Tiele, *Elements of the Science of Religion*, *Année Sociologique* 2 (1899), repr. in Mauss, *Oeuvres*, 1:544–45.

149. Hubert and Mauss, "Essai sur le sacrifice," 307.

150. Gustave Belot, review of *Année Sociologique* (1904), in *Revue Philosophique* 54 (April 1905): 423.

151. Letter from Alfred Espinas to Marcel Mauss, December 24, 1898.

152. Letter from Octave Hamelin to Marcel Mauss, Bordeaux, January 5, 1900.

153. *Folk-lore* 9, no. 3 (September 1898): 254.

154. Hartland, review of *Année Sociologique* 2, 96.

155. Ibid.

156. Léon Blum, *Souvenirs sur l'Affaire* (1935; Paris: Gallimard, 1982), 42.

157. Letter from Rosine Mauss to Marcel Mauss, Épinal, January 30, 1898.

158. Letter from Rosine Mauss to Marcel Mauss, Épinal, February 20, 1898.

159. Letter from Rosine Mauss to Marcel Mauss, Épinal, January 23, 1898.

160. Émile Durkheim, "Contribution à H. Dogan, Enquête sur l'antisémitisme" (1899), in Durkheim, *Textes*, 2:252–53.

161. Letter from Émile Durkheim to Marcel Mauss, Sunday, n.d. [January–February 1898].

162. Letter from Émile Durkheim to Marcel Mauss, n.d. [February 1898].

163. Letter from Émile Durkheim to Célestin Bouglé, Bordeaux, March 18, 1898, in Durkheim, *Textes*, 2:417.

164. Letter from Émile Durkheim to Célestin Bouglé, Bordeaux, March 22, 1898, in Durkheim, *Textes*, 2:423.

165. Émile Durkheim, "L'individualisme et les intellectuels" (1898), in Durkheim, *La science sociale et l'action* (Paris: PUF, 1970), 278.

166. Gabriel Deville, "L'affaire Dreyfus et le socialisme," *Devenir Social*, year 4, (November 1889): 803.

167. Charles Rappoport, *Une vie révolutionnaire, 1883–1940* (Paris: Éditions de la Maison des Sciences de l'Homme, 1991), 166.

168. Daniel Halévy, *Pays parisiens* (Paris: Grasset, 1932), 170.

169. Letter from Marcel Mauss to Henri Hubert, n.d. [1898].

170. Letter from Marcel Mauss to Henri Hubert, n.d. [1898].

171. Marcel Mauss, "La guerre du Transvaal," *Mouvement Socialiste*, June 1, 1900, 644–45, repr. in Mauss, *Écrits politiques*, ed. Marcel Fournier (Paris: Fayard, 1998), 87–90.

172. Ibid., 645.

PART II
THE TOTEM AND TABOO CLAN

1. Marcel Mauss, "Paul Fauconnet," n.d. [1938], 2 (Hubert-Mauss collection, Archives of the Collège de France).

2. Letter from Marcel Mauss to Henri Hubert, Leiden, n.d. [1898].

3. Letter from Émile Durkheim to Marcel Mauss, March 19 [1898].

4. Letter from Émile Durkheim to Marcel Mauss, March 19 [1898].

5. Letter from Rosine Mauss to Marcel Mauss, Épinal, February 1, 1897.

6. Letter from Rosine Mauss to Marcel Mauss, Épinal, May 24, 1898.

7. Letter from Rosine Mauss to Marcel Mauss, Épinal, June 20, 1898.

8. Letter from Marcel Mauss to Henri Hubert, Oxford, n.d. [1898].

9. Letter from Marcel Mauss to Henri Hubert, Oxford, n.d. [1898].

10. Paul Bernard, "Introduction," in Max Jacob and Salomon Reinach, *Lettres de Liane de Pougy* (Paris: Plon, 1980), 60.

11. Letter from Henri Hubert to Marcel Mauss, n.d. [1898].

12. Letter from Marcel Mauss to Henri Hubert, n.d. [1899]. Mauss, aware that he and his friend had several journals available to them in addition to *Année* (*Anthropologie, Revue de l'Histoire des Religions, Revue Philosophique, Notes Critiques,* and others), adopted the strategy of "penetrating already-formed, almost always lamentable, and already influential organizations, where we will be sure to be heard."

CHAPTER 4
IN THE CENACLE

1. Letter from Émile Durkheim to Marcel Mauss, January 24, 1900.

2. Letter from Marcel Mauss to Émile Durkheim, n.d. [1900].

3. The others were Religion of Uncivilized Peoples (L. Marillier), Far Eastern Religion (L. de Rosny), Religions of Ancient Mexico (G. Renaud), Religions of Egypt (M. Amélineau), Religions of Israel and the Eastern Semites (M. Vernes), Talmudic and Rabbinical Judaism (Israel Lévi), Christian Islamism (A. Sabatier and E. de Faye), History of Dogmas (A. Réville and F. Picavet), History of the Christian Church (J. Réville), Byzantine Christianity (G. Millet), and History of Canonical Law (M. Esmein).

4. Letter from Willem Caland to Marcel Mauss, June 17, 1901.

5. Letter from Émile Durkheim to Marcel Mauss, n.d. [1901].

6. Letter from Marcel Mauss to Henri Hubert, n.d. [1901].

7. Marcel Mauss, "Yoga," in *La Grande Encylopédie* (Paris: Société anonyme de la Grande Encyclopédie, 1901), 3:1276.

8. Léon Marillier, "Nécrologie A. Sabatier," *Revue de l'Histoire des Religions* 41 (1901): 245.

9. Marcel Mauss, review of Auguste Sabatier, *Esquisse d'une philosophie de la religion d'après la psychologie et l'histoire, Année Sociologique* 1 (1898), in Mauss, *Oeuvres,* vol. 1 (Paris: Éditions de Minuit, 1968), vols. 2 and 3 (1969), 1:536.

10. Letter from Henri Hubert to Marcel Mauss, Saturday evening [1901].

11. Letter from Marcel Mauss to Henri Hubert, n.d. [1901].

12. Letter from Marcel Mauss to Henri Hubert, n.d. [1901].

13. Copy of a letter from Émile Durkheim to "Mon cher ami" [My dear friend], n.d. [1901].

14. Alfred Loisy, *Mémoires pour servir à l'histoire religieuse de notre temps* (Paris: Émile Noury, 1932), 2:29–30.

15. Letter from Jean Réville to Henri Hubert, July 12, 1901.

16. Minutes of the committee meeting of June 9, 1901, section of religious science, École Pratique des Hautes Études, 259.

17. Minutes of the committee meeting of June 18, 1901, section of religious science, École Pratique des Hautes Études, 264.

18. The results of the three rounds of voting were as follows. Round 1, with fourteen voting: Hubert (7), Fossey (5), Monceau (2). Round 2, with thirteen voting: Hubert (7), Fossey (5), Monceaux (1). Round 3, with fourteen voting: Hubert (7), Fossey (5), abstentions (2).

19. Letter from Émile Durkheim to Henri Hubert [June 1901], in *Revue Française de Sociologie* 28, no. 1 (1987): 519.

20. Jean Réville, "Léon Marillier, 1863–1901," *Revue de l'Histoire des Religions* 44 (1901): 131.

21. Léon Marillier, "Chronique" (review of *Année Sociologique* 1 [1898]), *Revue de l'Histoire des Religions* 27 (1889): 287.

22. Letter from C. P. Tiele to Marcel Mauss, Leiden, November 8, 1901.

23. Letter from Émile Durkheim to Marcel Mauss, n.d. [1901].

24. Although he divulged his preferences, Réville remained cautious: "All the same, I'm inclined to think that [the course on the religions of uncivilized peoples] will be retained, but I cannot make any claims in advance. If it is retained, you are certainly a front-runner among those applying to teach it. But once again I can only express a personal opinion and you'll understand why in my position I abstain from any prior declaration that would amount to a commitment" (letter from Albert Réville to Marcel Mauss, November 4, 1901).

25. Loisy, *Mémoires pour servir à l'histoire religieuse*, 2:32.

26. Jean Réville, "Chronique," *Revue de l'Histoire des Religions* 44 (1901): 173.

27. Letter from Émile Durkheim to Marcel Mauss, n.d. [1901].

28. Letter from Émile Durkheim to Marcel Mauss, Friday [1901].

29. Marcel Mauss, "Sylvain Lévi" (1935) in Mauss, *Oeuvres*, 3:539.

30. Letter from Alfred Espinas to Marcel Mauss, December 2, 1901.

31. Marcel Mauss, "L'enseignement de l'histoire des religions des peuples non civilisés, à l'École des hautes études," *Revue de l'Histoire des Religions* 45 (1902), in Mauss, *Oeuvres*, 2:229–30.

32. Marcel Mauss, review of Henri Mager, *Le monde polynésien*, *Notes Critiques* 3 (November 1902): 259.

33. Mauss, "L'enseignement de l'histoire des religions des peuples non civilisés," 2:367.

34. Ibid., 370–71.

35. Georges Condominas, "Marcel Mauss, père de l'ethnologie française," part 2, "Naissance de l'ethnologie religieuse," *Critique* 28, no. 301 (June 1972): 494.

36. Jean Réville, "Chronique," *Revue de l'Histoire des Religions* 44 (1901): 473.

37. Marcel Mauss, "L'oeuvre de Mauss par lui-même" (1930), *Revue Française de Sociologie* 20, no. 1 (January–March 1979): 211.

38. Henri Lévy-Bruhl, "Nécrologie: Marcel Mauss," *Journal de Psychologie Normale et Pathologique* 43 (1950): 318.

39. "Marcel Mauss (1872–1950)," faculty meeting, Collège de France, 1950, 2.

40. Letter from Marcel Mauss to Henri Hubert, December 3, 1902.

41. *Annuaire de l'École Pratique des Hautes Études, Section des Sciences Religieuses*, (1902): 29.

42. Lévy-Bruhl, "Nécrologie: Marcel Mauss," 368.

43. Mauss, "L'oeuvre de Mauss par lui-même," 209.

44. *Annuaire de l'École Pratique des Hautes Études, Section des Sciences Religieuses* (1907): 36. For Mauss, "a knowledge of peoples, of their language, religion, mores, and economic and technical resources, along with a geographical knowledge of their habitat, are the necessary conditions for good administration." Letter from Marcel Mauss to the minister, n.d. (1907). In that respect, France was to follow the example of other countries, particularly the United States and its Board of American Ethnology.

45. Mauss, "L'oeuvre de Mauss par lui-même," 211–17.

46. Letter from Rosine Mauss to Marcel Mauss, Épinal, January 29, 1903.

CHAPTER 5
CITIZEN MAUSS

1. Hubert Bourgin, *De Jaurès à Léon Blum, l'École normale et la politique* (Paris: Librairie Arthème Fayard, 1938), 255–57.

2. Jean-Denis Bredin, *L'Affaire* (Paris: Julliard, 1983), 263.

3. Daniel Lindenberg and Pierre-André Meyer, *Lucien Herr, le socialisme et le destin* (Paris: Calmann-Lévy, 1977), 160.

4. Bourgin, *De Jaurès à Léon Blum*, 131.

5. Marcel Mauss, "Herr et D.[urkheim]," n.d., 1–2, in Mauss, *Écrits politiques*, ed. Marcel Fournier (Paris: Fayard, 1998), 741.

6. Ibid., 740.

7. Letter from Jeanne L. Herr to Marcel Mauss, February 8, 1926.

8. Marcel Mauss, "Notices biographiques" (1927), in Mauss, *Oeuvres*, vol. 1 (Paris: Éditions de Minuit, 1968), vols. 2 and 3 (1969), 3:524.

9. Marcel Mauss, "Herr et H.H. (Hubert)," 1. This is one of seven short notes made available to me by the Mauss family.

10. Charles Péguy, *Marcel, premier dialogue de la société harmonieuse* (Paris: Librairie G. Bellais, 1898).

11. Letter from Marcel Mauss to Henri Hubert, n.d.

12. Letter from Marcel Mauss to Henri Hubert, n.d.

13. Daniel Halévy, *Pays parisiens* (Paris: Grasset, 1932), 208.

14. Géraldi Leroy, *Péguy: Entre l'ordre et la révolution* (Paris: Presses de la Fondation nationale des sciences politiques, 1981), 114.

15. Marcel Mauss, "Herr et Péguy," in Mauss, *Écrits politiques*, 9.

16. Charles Péguy, "Marie Victor, comte Hugo," *Cahiers de la Quinzaine*, October 23, 1910, in Charles Péguy, *Oeuvres en prose, 1909–1914* (Paris: Gallimard, Bibliothèque de la Pléiade, 1957), 669.

17. Marcel Mauss, "François Simiand," *Populaire*, April 18, 1935, 2.

18. Letter from François Simiand to Georges Renard, n.d., in Christophe Prochasson, *Les intellectuels, le socialisme, et la guerre, 1900–1938* (Paris: Éditions du Seuil, 1993), 125.

19. In addition to Marcel Mauss and François Simiand, these were Léon Blum, Hubert Bourgin, Paul Fauconnet, Hubert Lagardelle, Philippe Landrieu, Jean Longuet, Edgar Milhaud, Eugène Petit, Abel Rey, and two older men, Charles Andler and Lucien Herr, that is, eight *agrégés* out of thirteen.

20. The Editors, "Déclaration," *Mouvement Socialiste*, year 1, 1 (January–July 1899): 1.

21. Police report of May 30, 1899.

22. Marcel Mauss, "L'action socialiste," *Mouvement Socialiste*, October 15, 1899, 455.

23. Ibid., 459–60.

24. Ibid., 451–52.

25. Ibid., 458.

26. Ibid., 461–62.

27. Charles Andler, *Vie de Lucien Herr, 1864–1926* (Paris: Rieder, 1932), 162.

28. Marcel Mauss, "Le congrès. Ses travaux: L'union et la question ministérielle," *Mouvement Socialiste*, December 1, 1899, 641.

29. Ibid., 642–43.

30. Leroy, *Péguy: Entre l'ordre et la révolution*, 113.

31. Marcel Mauss, "Le jugement de la Haute Cour et la propagande socialiste," *Mouvement Socialiste*, February 1, 1900, 130.

32. Ibid., 130–31.

33. Letter from Émile Durkheim to Marcel Mauss, n.d. [1899].

34. Letter from Jean Longuet to Marcel Mauss, July 15, 1899.

35. Letter from Hubert Lagardelle to Marcel Mauss, May 13, 1900.

36. Letter from Suzanne Carruette to Marcel Mauss, July 13, 1899.

37. Letter from Marcel Mauss to Henri Hubert, n.d. [1901].

38. Draft of a letter from Marcel Mauss to Hubert Lagardelle, December 10, 1901.

39. Marcel Mauss, "À propos de la guerre du Transvaal," *Mouvement Socialiste*, February 15, 1902, 293.

40. Draft of a letter from Marcel Mauss to Hubert Lagardelle, n.d. [1904].

41. Letter from François Simiand to Marcel Mauss, January 2, 1899.

42. Bourgin, *De Jaurès à Léon Blum*, 350.

43. Max Lazard, "François Simiand, 1873–1935," excerpted from "Documents de travail," *Bulletin de l'Association Française pour le Progrès Social* 218–19 (1939): 68.

44. Mauss, "François Simiand," 2.

45. Letter from Paul Lapie to Célestin Bouglé, February 18, 1900, in *Revue Française de Sociologie* 20, no. 1 (January–March 1979): 41.

46. Letter from Émile Durkheim to Marcel Mauss, n.d. [1900]. In a letter to Bouglé, Lapie refers to the "crisis" *Année Sociologique* was going through at the time: "It's clear that [the journal] is consuming Durkheim."

47. Paul Fauconnet, review of *Année Sociologique* (1898–1899), in *Mouvement Socialiste*, Year 2 (August 1, 1900): 189–90.

48. Marcel Mauss, review of *The Cooperative Wholesale Societies Limited Annual*, *Notes Critiques* 2 (March 1901): 83.

49. Letter from Marcel Mauss to "Monsieur" (not identified), Paris, October, 20, 1904.

50. Henri Desroche, "Marcel Mauss, citoyen et camarade," *Revue Française de Sociologie* 20, no. 1 (January–March 1979): 223.

51. Jean Jaurès, "Économie sociale," *Petite République Socialiste*, February 24, 1903.

52. Marcel Mauss, "Les coopératives et les socialistes," *Mouvement Socialiste*, February 1, 1901, 138.

53. Hubert Lagardelle, review of D. D. Bancel, *La coopération devant les écoles sociales*, *Devenir Social*, year 3, 8–9 (August–September 1897): 755–58.

54. Marcel Mauss, "Le Congrès international des coopératives socialistes," *Mouvement Socialiste*, year 2 (October 15, 1900): 499–501.

55. *Premier Congrès national et international de la coopération socialiste*, held in Paris on July 7, 8, 9, and 10, 1900 (Paris: Société Nouvelle de Librairie et d'Édition, 1900), 121.

56. Ibid., 163–64.

57. Ibid., 153.

58. Undated summary of comments made by Mauss, written on the back of a list of awards for the Fédération Coopérative de la Région Parisienne, whose offices were then at 84, rue Barrault. Hubert-Mauss collection, Archives of the Collège de France.

59. Mauss, "Le Congrès international des coopératives socialistes," 502.

60. Ibid., 138.

61. Letter from Marcel Mauss to Henri Hubert, n.d. [1900].

62. Letter from Philippe Landrieu to Marcel Mauss, October 18, 1901.

63. Contract between Arthur Lainey, director of Grands Moulins de Corbeil, and Dr. V. Kasimir and M. Mauss, June 10, 1902.

64. Letter from J. Dodier to Marcel Mauss, July 26, 1902.

65. Draft of a letter from Marcel Mauss to Émile Durkheim, n.d. [1902].

66. Letter from Émile Durkheim to Marcel Mauss, n.d. [1902].

67. Letter from Émile Durkheim to Marcel Mauss, n.d. [1902].

68. Draft of a letter from Marcel Mauss to Rosine Mauss, n.d. [1902].

69. Letter from Philippe Landrieu to Marcel Mauss, July 2, 1905.

70. Letter from Philippe Landrieu to Marcel Mauss, July 25, 1905.

71. Letter from the cooperative's assistant director to Marcel Mauss, February 22, 1906.

CHAPTER 6
RUE SAINT-JACQUES

1. Letter from Émile Durkheim to Marcel Mauss, n.d. [1901].

2. Letter from Émile Durkheim to Henri Hubert, January 9, 1901, in *Revue Française de Sociologie* 28, no. 1 (1987): 512.

3. Letter from Émile Durkheim to Xavier Léon, August 19, 1897, cited in Steven Lukes, *Émile Durkheim: His Life and Work* (New York: Harper & Row, 1972), 301.

4. Letter from Émile Durkheim to Marcel Mauss, n.d. [1898].

5. Letter from Henri Hubert to Marcel Mauss, n.d. [1898].

6. Letter from Émile Durkheim to Marcel Mauss, Bordeaux, May 15, 1894.

7. Letter from Émile Durkheim to Marcel Mauss, Bordeaux, n.d. [1897].

8. Letter from Henry Michel to Célestin Bouglé, July 1897, in *Revue Française de Sociologie* 20, no. 1 (January–March 1979): 103.

9. Émile Durkheim, "La sociologie et les sciences sociales," *Revue Internationale de Sociologie* 12 (1904): 83–84, followed by discussion, 86–87.

10. Letter from Émile Durkheim to Marcel Mauss, November 7, 1899.

11. Letter from Émile Durkheim to Marcel Mauss, n.d. [1897].

12. Émile Durkheim, "La sociologie," in *La science française* (Paris: Larousse, 1933), repr. in Durkheim, *Textes* (Paris: Éditions de Minuit, 1975), 1:109–18.

13. Marcel Mauss, "La sociologie en France depuis 1914," in *La science française*, repr. in Mauss, *Oeuvres*, vol. 1 (Paris: Éditions de Minuit, 1968), vols. 2 and 3 (1969), 3:436.

14. Letter from Émile Durkheim to Marcel Mauss, Tuesday, n.d. [1901].

15. Paul Fauconnet and Marcel Mauss, "Sociologie," *La Grande Encyclopédie* (1901), repr. in Mauss, *Oeuvres*, 3:150.

16. Ibid., 159.

17. Ibid., 152.

18. Marcel Mauss, "Philosophie religieuse, conceptions générales," *Année Sociologique* 7 (1904), repr. in Mauss, *Oeuvres*, 1:93.

19. Fauconnet and Mauss, "Sociologie," 163.

20. Ibid., 160.

21. Hubert, "Introduction," in P. D. Chantepie de la Saussaye, *Manuel d'histoire des religions* (Paris: Alcan, 1904), xiii.

22. Mauss, review of P. Tiele, *Elements of the Science of Religion*, *Année Sociologique* 2 (1899), in Mauss, *Oeuvres*, 1:544–45.

23. Letter from Rosine Mauss to Marcel Mauss, Épinal, June 29, 1902.

24. Letter from Émile Durkheim to Octave Hamelin, October 21, 1902, in Lukes, *Émile Durkheim*, 366.

25. Ibid.

26. Letter from Émile Durkheim to Octave Hamelin, May 13, 1903, in Bernard Lacroix, *Durkheim et le politique* (Paris: Presses de la Fondation nationale des sciences politiques, 1981), 38.

27. Letter from Émile Durkheim to Henri Hubert, March 8, 1902, in *Revue Française de Sociologie* 28, no. 1 (1987): 524.

28. Letter from Émile Durkheim to Henri Hubert, March 14, 1902, in *Revue Française de Sociologie* 28, no. 1 (1987): 525.

29. Letter from Émile Durkheim to Marcel Mauss, n.d. [1902].

30. Letter from Émile Durkheim to Marcel Mauss, n.d. [1902].

31. Letter from Émile Durkheim to Marcel Mauss, Bordeaux, July 10, 1899.

32. Émile Durkheim, "Sur le totémisme," *Année Sociologique* (1902), in Durkheim, *Journal sociologique* (Paris: PUF, 1969), 315.

33. Marcel Mauss, "L'oeuvre de Mauss par lui-même" (1930), *Revue Française de Sociologie* 20, no. 1 (January–March 1979): 210.

34. Émile Durkheim and Marcel Mauss, "De quelques formes primitives de classification, contribution à l'étude des représentations collectives," *Année Sociologique* 6 (1903), repr. in Mauss, *Oeuvres*, 2:14.

35. Ibid., 83.

36. Ibid., 82.

37. Ibid., 15.

38. Salomon Reinach, review of Émile Durkheim and Marcel Mauss, "De quelques formes primitives de classification," *Anthropologie* 14 (1903): 601. See also Henri Berr, "Les progrès de la sociologie religieuse," *Revue de Synthèse*

Historique 12, no. 34 (1906): 16–43. Criticism of the 1903 article was harsh, focusing on its excessive systematization based on inconsistent sources; its logical error in the suggestion that all societies must have the same classifications in identical social organizations; its lack of proof for the temporal succession of types of classification; and its confusion between collective representations and cognitive operations. Rodney Needham, "Introduction," in Émile Durkheim and Marcel Mauss, *Primitive Classifications* (Chicago: University of Chicago Press, 1967), vii–xlviii.

39. E. Sidney Hartland, review of *Année Sociologique* (1903), *Folk-lore* 27, no. 4 (December 1903): 434.

40. Mauss, "L'oeuvre de Mauss par lui-même," 218.

41. Hubert Bourgin, *De Jaurès à Léon Blum, l'École normale et la politique* (Paris: Librairie Arthème Fayard, 1938), 222.

42. Charles Péguy, "De la situation faite à l'histoire et à la sociologie dans les temps modernes," *Cahiers de la Quinzaine* (1906), in Péguy, *Oeuvres en prose, 1909–1914* (Paris: Gallimard, Bibliothèque de la pléiade, 1957).

43. Letter from Célestin Bouglé to Daniel Halévy, n.d., in Philippe Besnard, "The *Année Sociologique* Team," in Philippe Besnard, ed., *The Sociological Domain: The Durkheimians and the Founding of French Sociology* (Cambridge: Cambridge University Press, 1993), 24.

44. Letter from Marcel Mauss to Henri Hubert, n.d. [1903].

45. Letter from Marcel Mauss to Henri Hubert, n.d. [1904].

46. Letter from Marcel Mauss to Henri Hubert, n.d. [1903].

47. Letter from Marcel Mauss to Henri Hubert, Paris, December 19, 1904.

48. Letter from Marcel Mauss to Henri Hubert, n.d.

49. Letter from Rosine Mauss to Marcel Mauss, Épinal, May 19, 1903.

50. Letter from Rosine Mauss to Marcel Mauss, June 21, 1904.

51. Letter from Rosine Mauss to Marcel Mauss, Épinal, March 8, 1905.

52. Letter from Émile Durkheim to Marcel Mauss, n.d. [1905].

53. Émile Durkheim, *Le suicide, étude de sociologie* (1897; Paris: PUF, 1975), 304–5.

54. Letter from Émile Durkheim to Marcel Mauss, n.d. [1905].

55. Letter from Émile Durkheim to Marcel Mauss, n.d. [1904].

56. Letter from Marcel Mauss to Henri Hubert, n.d.

57. Letter from Rosine Mauss, Épinal, January 22, 1907.

CHAPTER 7
JOURNALIST AT *HUMANITÉ*

1. Charles Andler, *Vie de Lucien Herr, 1864–1926* (Paris: Rieder, 1932), 170.

2. Alexandre Zévaès, *Jean Jaurès* (Paris: Édition de la Clé d'or, 1951), 178.

3. Dominique Merllé, "Présentation: Le cas Lévy-Bruhl," *Revue Philosophique* no. 4 (October–December 1989): 495.

4. Hubert Bourgin, *De Jaurès à Léon Blum, l'École normale et la politique* (Paris: Librairie Arthème Fayard, 1938), 228.

5. Lucien Lévy-Bruhl, *Quelques pages sur Jean Jaurès* (Paris: Éditions de L'Humanité, 1916), 67.

6. Marcel Mauss, "Lucien Lévy-Bruhl," *Populaire*, March 16, 1939, 4.

7. Ibid.

8. Andler, *Vie de Lucien Herr*, 170.

9. Marcel Mauss, "Souvenirs: Conseils de Jean Jaurès pour une Révolution russe," *Vie Socialiste*, July 30, 1921, 2.

10. Letter from Émile Durkheim to Marcel Mauss, Paris, May 20, 1916.

11. Marcel Mauss, "Les coopératives rouges," *Humanité*, June 16, 1904, 4.

12. Marcel Mauss, "La coopération socialiste," *Humanité*, August 3, 1904, 1.

13. Marcel Mauss, "Mouvement coopératif," *Humanité*, October 4, 1904, 3.

14. Mauss, "La coopération socialiste," 1.

15. Marcel Mauss, "Mouvement coopératif," *Humanité*, May 8, 1905, 4.

16. Marcel Mauss, "Une exposition," *Humanité*, December 23, 1904, 1.

17. Marcel Mauss, "Mouvement coopératif: Propagande coopérative," *Humanité*, January 3, 1905, 4.

18. Letter from Marcel Mauss to Henri Hubert, Épinal, n.d. [1904].

19. Letter from Marcel Mauss to Henri Hubert, n.d. [1905].

20. Marcel Mauss, "Le Congrès des coopératives anglaises," *Humanité*, June 16, 1905, 3.

21. Letter from Marcel Mauss to Henri Hubert, n.d. [1905].

22. Marcel Mauss, "Le Congrès des coopératives anglaises," *Humanité*, June 15, 1905, 1.

23. Mauss, "Le Congrès des coopératives anglaises," *Humanité*, June 16, 1905, 3.

24. Marcel Mauss, "Le Congrès des coopératives anglaises," *Humanité*, June 25, 1905, 1.

25. Letter from the administrative representative at *Humanité* to Marcel Mauss, July 7, 1905.

26. Letter from Philippe Landrieu to Marcel Mauss, July 25, 1905.

27. Letter from Philippe Landrieu to Marcel Mauss, July 28, 1905.

28. Letter from Philippe Landrieu to Marcel Mauss, July 29, 1905.

29. Letter from Lucien Herr to Marcel Mauss, September 8, 1906.

30. As A. Hamon and D. Hamon, professors at the Collège Libre des Sciences Sociales de Paris and the Université Nouvelle de Bruxelles, claimed in "The Political Situation in France," *American Journal of Sociology* 11, no. 1 (July 1905): 128.

31. Letter from Philippe Landrieu to Marcel Mauss, October 14, 1905.

32. Letter from Émile Durkheim to Marcel Mauss, n.d. [1906].

33. Letter from Émile Durkheim to Marcel Mauss, n.d. [1906].

34. Letter from Sylvain Lévi to Mme Mohilansky, July 21, 1906.

35. Letter from Lucien Herr to Jean Poirot [Finland], July 20, 1906.

36. Letter from Yaul Boyer to Dr. Ignatov and G. Vessilovki, July 20, 1906.

37. Mauss, "Souvenirs: Conseils de Jean Jaurès," 2.

38. Ibid.

39. Ibid.

40. Ibid.

41. Letter from Lucien Herr to Marcel Mauss, September 8, 1906.

42. Letter from Émile Durkheim to Marcel Mauss, n.d. [1906].

43. Letter from Marcel Mauss to "Monsieur le Ministre" [minister of public education], n.d. [1906].

44. Ibid.

45. Jean Raymond, "Charles Andler," in *Dictionnaire biographique du mouvement ouvrier français*, ed. Jean Maitron (Paris: Éditions ouvrières, 1984), 142.

46. Letter from Robert Hertz to Marcel Mauss, February 11, 1908.

47. Groupe d'Études Socialistes, report on *Année* (1910, 1911), 1 (Hubert-Mauss collection, Archives of the Collège de France).

48. Marcel Mauss, comments after a paper by Bruckère, "La petite propriété, danger social et danger national," in the minutes of the April 8, 1913, meeting of the Groupe d'Études Socialistes (Hubert-Mauss collection, Archives of the Collège de France).

CHAPTER 8
COLLECTIVE MADNESS

1. Letter from Henri Hubert to Marcel Mauss, n.d. [1903].

2. Marcel Mauss, review of Chantepie de la Saussaye, *Manuel d'histoire des religions*, *Notes Critiques*, June 5, 1904, 177.

3. Henri Hubert, "Introduction," in P. D. Chantepie de la Saussaye, *Manuel d'histoire des religions* (Paris: Alcan,1904), xlvii–xxxviii.

4. Marcel Mauss, "Philosophie religieuse, conceptions générales," *Année Sociologique* 7 (1904), in Mauss, *Oeuvres*, vol. 1 (Paris: Éditions de Minuit, 1968), vols. 2 and 3 (1969), 1:94.

5. Marcel Mauss, "Introduction à la sociologie religieuse," *Année Sociologique* 5 (1902), repr. in Mauss, *Oeuvres*, 1:90.

6. Marcel Mauss, review of Ludwig Blau, *Das altjudische Zauberwesen*, *Année Sociologique* 3 (1900), repr. in Mauss, *Oeuvres*, 2:381.

7. Marcel Mauss, review of T. Witton Davies, *Magic Divination and Demonology*, *Année Sociologique* 3 (1900), repr. in Mauss, *Oeuvres*, 2:380.

8. Mauss, "Introduction à la sociologie religieuse," 1:90.

9. D.J., review of Henri Hubert and Marcel Mauss, *Mélanges d'histoire des religions*, *Revue Historique du Droit Français* (1909): 585–86.

10. Henri Hubert and Marcel Mauss, "Introduction à l'analyse de quelques phénomènes religieux," *Revue de l'Histoire des Religions* (1906), in Mauss, *Oeuvres*, 1:25.

11. Jean Réville, "Chronique," *Revue de l'Histoire des Religions* 44 (1901): 325.

12. Letter from Henri Hubert to Marcel Mauss, August 15, 1904.

13. Robert Hertz, review of Henri Hubert and Marcel Mauss, *Mélanges d'histoire des religions*, *Revue de l'Histoire des Religions* 60 (1909): 219.

14. Marcel Mauss, "L'origine des pouvoirs magiques dans les société australiennes," *Annuaire de l'École Pratique des Hautes Études* (1904), repr. in Mauss, *Oeuvres*, 2:364.

15. Ibid., 320.

16. Marcel Mauss, review of J. G. Frazer, *The Golden Bough*, *Année Sociologique* 5 (1902), repr. in Mauss, *Oeuvres*, 1:137.

17. Henri Hubert and Marcel Mauss, "Esquisse d'une théorie générale de la magie," *Année Sociologique* 7 (1904), repr. in Mauss, *Sociologie et anthropologie*, 3rd ed. (Paris: PUF, 1966), 32.

18. Ibid., 124.

19. Ibid., 119.

20. Ibid., 100.

21. Marcel Mauss, "Notes sur la nomenclature des phénomènes religieux," *Année Sociologique* 9 (1906), repr. in Mauss, *Oeuvres*, 1:41.

22. Hubert and Mauss, "Esquisse d'une théorie générale," 101.

23. Claude Lévi-Strauss, "Introduction à l'oeuvre de Marcel Mauss" (1950), in Mauss, *Sociologie et anthropologie*, xli.

24. J. T. Shotwell, "The Role of Magic," *American Journal of Sociology* 15, no. 6 (May 1910): 790.

25. J. B. Jevons, "The Definition of Magic," *Sociological Review* 2 (April 1908): 105–7.

26. Henri Berr, "Les progrès de la sociologie religieuse," *Revue de Synthese Historique* 12, no. 34 (1906): 16–43.

27. Hertz, review of Henri Hubert and Marcel Mauss, *Mélanges d'histoire des religions*, 219.

28. Hubert and Mauss, "Introduction à l'analyse de quelques phénomènes religieux," 39.

29. Gustave Belot, review of *Année Sociologique*, *Revue Philosophique* 59 (April 1905): 424.

30. Hubert and Mauss, "Introduction à l'analyse de quelques phénomènes religieux," 27.

31. After Hubert's death in 1927, Mauss took on the responsibility of inventorying his friend's unpublished writings; he would search in vain for the second part of "Outline."

32. Hubert and Mauss, "Esquisse d'une théorie générale," 130.

33. Ibid., 140.

34. Henri Massis and Alfred de Tarde used the pseudonym "Agathon" when they attacked the Sorbonne in a series of articles appearing in *Opinion*. In 1910 they published the collected articles under the title *Les jeunes gens d'aujourd'hui* (The young people of today). See chapter 9, under heading "The End of an Era."

35. Marcel Mauss, "L'oeuvre de Mauss par lui-même" (1930), *Revue Française de Sociologie* 20, no. 1 (January–March 1979): 220.

36. Marcel Mauss, "In Memoriam: L'oeuvre inédite de Durkheim et de ses collaborateurs," *Année Sociologique*, n.s. (1925), repr. in Mauss, *Oeuvres*, 3:497.

37. It is to be noted that ten women also came to hear Mauss in the years between 1902 and 1914: Mme Weise, Mlle Schmieder, Mlle Klavé, Mme Albertini, Mme Gorastchenko, Mlle des Portes, Mme Moukhine, Mlle Spengler, Mlle Brizard, et Mlle Sourine (*Annuaire de l'École Pratique des Hautes Études, Section des Sciences Religieuses* [1902–1914]).

   As is clear from Mauss's conferences, the section of religious science welcomed students of various nationalities. To take only one example, during the school year 1904–1905, among the 593 students in the section, more than twenty nationalities were represented: 447 were French, 42 Russian, 18 German, 13 Swiss, 12 American, 10 Romanian, 9 British, 8 Austrian, 8 Greek, 8 Belgian, 3 Armenian, 2 Persian, 2 Dutch, 2 Norwegian, 2 Serb, 1 Brazilian, 1 Italian, 1 Danish, 1 Swedish, 1 Bulgarian, 1 Luxembourgeois, and 1 Turkish.

38. Mauss, "In Memoriam: L'oeuvre inédite de Durkheim," 495.

39. Marius Barbeau, "Henri Beuchat," *American Anthropologist* 18 (1916): 105.

40. *Annuaire de l'École Pratique des Hautes Études, Section des Sciences Religieuses* (1904): 59.

41. *Annuaire de l'École Pratique des Hautes Études, Section des Sciences Religieuses* (1905): 43.

42. Mauss, "L'oeuvre de Mauss par lui-même," 211.

43. Marcel Mauss (in collaboration with Henri Beuchat), "Essai sur les variations saisonnières des sociétés Eskimos," *Année Sociologique* 9 (1906), repr. in Mauss, *Sociologie et anthropologie*, 475.

44. Ibid., 391.

45. Ibid., 470.

46. Ibid., 473.

47. E. Sidney Hartland, review of *Année Sociologique* 9 (1906), *Folk-lore* 27 (March 1907): 100.

48. R. R. Marett, "A Sociological View of Comparative Religion," *Sociological Review* 1 (1908): 52.

49. Letter from Marcel Mauss to "Cher Monsieur" [R. R. Marett], Paris, February 18, 1908.

50. Marcel Mauss, "L'art et le mythe d'après Wundt," *Revue Philosophique* 66 (July–December 1908), repr. in Mauss, *Oeuvres*, 2:225.

51. Diamond Jenness, *The Life of the Cooper Eskimos: A Report of the Canadian Arctic Expedition, 1913–1918* (Ottawa: F. A. Acland, 1923), 12:9.

52. Barbeau, "Henri Beuchat," 109.

53. Letter from Henri Beuchat to Marcel Mauss, Victoria, June 16, 1913.

54. Mauss, "In Memoriam: L'oeuvre inédite de Durkheim," 3:489.

55. Letter from Robert Hertz to Marcel Mauss, May 31, 1902.

56. Paul Alphandéry, "In Memoriam, 1914–1918," *Revue de l'Histoire des Religions* 79 (1919): 336.

57. Émile Durkheim, "Hertz (Robert), né à Saint-Cloud le 22 juin 1881, tombé au champ d'honneur à Marchéville (Meuse) le 13 avril 1915" (1916), repr. in Durkheim, *Textes*, 3 vols. (Paris: Éditions de Minuit, 1975), 1:439.

58. Hubert Bourgin, *De Jaurès à Léon Blum, l'École normale et la politique* (Paris: Librairie Arthème Fayard, 1938), 481.

59. Letter from Marcel Mauss to Henri Hubert, n.d. [1905].

60. Letter from Marcel Mauss to Henri Hubert, n.d. [1905].

61. Durkheim, "Hertz," 439.

62. Marcel Mauss, "Introduction et conclusion à Robert Hertz," *Revue de l'Histoire des Religions* (1922), repr. in Mauss, *Oeuvres*, 3:511.

63. Mauss, "In Memoriam: L'oeuvre inédite de Durkheim," 493.

64. Durkheim, "Hertz," 440–41.

65. Letter from Robert Hertz to Marcel Mauss, November 10, 1905.

66. Letter from Robert Hertz to Marcel Mauss, September 29, 1907.

67. Hertz, review of Hubert and Mauss, *Mélange d'histoire des religions*, 219.

68. "I'm beginning seriously to consider the need to collect our little studies into a sort of miscellany of religious history. . . . It would be heartbreaking to see our studies, which are linked in significant ways, scattered haphazardly in all the journals." Letter from Henri Hubert to Marcel Mauss, n.d. (1898).

69. E. Sidney Hartland, review of Henri Hubert and Marcel Mauss, *Mélanges d'histoire des religions*, *Folk-lore* 21, no. 4 (December 4, 1910): 524.

70. This last text was written by Hubert and was published in 1905 in *Annuaire de l'École Pratique des Hautes Études, Section des Sciences Religieuses*.

71. Hubert and Mauss, "Introduction à l'analyse de quelques phénomènes religieux," 25.

72. Hartland, review of Hubert and Mauss, *Mélanges d'histoire des religions*, 525.

73. Hubert and Mauss, "Introduction à l'analyse de quelques phénomènes religieux," 38.

74. Hertz, review of Hubert and Mauss, *Mélanges de l'histoire des religions*, 219.

75. Salomon Reinach, review of Henri Hubert and Marcel Mauss, *Mélanges d'histoire des religions*, *Revue Archéologique* (1909): 191–92.

76. O. Relle, review of Henri Hubert and Marcel Mauss, *Mélanges d'histoire des religions*, *Mois Littéraire et Pittoresque* (June 1910).

77. Reverend Father P. G. Schmidt, review of Henri Hubert and Marcel Mauss, *Mélanges d'histoire des religions*, *Anthropos* 3 (March–June 1910): 578.

78. *American Journal of Sociology*, which was very interested in the studies produced by the French school of sociology, published a short review of *Mélanges* by A. Loos (17 [May 1911]: 406).

79. Alfred Loisy, review of Henri Hubert and Marcel Mauss, *Mélanges d'histoire des religions*, *Revue Critique d'Histoire et de Littérature Religieuse* (May 1909): 406.

CHAPTER 9
A HEATED BATTLE AT THE COLLÈGE DE FRANCE

1. When the Collège was founded, it had only five royal lectors—two for Greek, two for Hebrew, and one for mathematics. Subsequently, it developed a great deal, especially in the nineteenth century, and introduced new courses of study: Orientalism (Sanskrit, Egyptology, Assyrian archaeology, comparative grammar, and so on), classical antiquity (Latin philology), French language and literatures, foreign languages and literatures (Slavic, Celtic, Germanic), history (art, religion, science), geography, philosophy, economics and political science, chemistry and natural history, physics, medicine, and so on. Major names were associated with the history of the institution: Georges Cuvier, Victor Cousin, Claude-Louis Berthelot, René Laënnec, and Claude Bernard in the sciences; Jules Michelet, Joseph-Ernest Renan, Théodule Ribot, Gabriel Tarde, and Henri Bergson in the human sciences.

2. Sylvain Lévi, "Présentation des titres de Marcel Mauss," faculty meeting of the Collège de France, February 17, 1907 (Archives of the Collège de France, C-XII, Mauss-2).

3. Letter from Marcel Mauss to "Monsieur le Président," n.d. [1907].

4. [Candidacies *en seconde ligne* are specific to the Collège de France. Largely symbolic, they allow scholars to declare their future ambition to seek a Collège chair but do not entail obtaining a teaching position at the Collège.—Trans.]

5. Jean Réville, "Leçon d'ouverture du cours d'histoire des religions au Collège de France," *Revue de l'Histoire des Religions* 55 (1907): 189–207.

6. Paul Alphandéry, "Jean Réville," *Revue de l'Histoire des Religions* 57 (1908): 273.

7. Paul Foucart, "Présentation des titres et travaux de Georges Foucart," faculty meeting of the Collège de France, February 17, 1907 (Archives of the Collège de France, G-IV-g. 32 L).

8. Letter from Rosine Mauss to Marcel Mauss, Friday [February 1907].

9. Letter from Rosine Mauss to Marcel Mauss, Sunday [March 1907].

10. Letter from Émile Durkheim to "M. le Directeur" (Charles Bayet), December 4, 1907, in *Revue Française de Sociologie* 20, no. 1 (January–March 1979): 116.

11. Letter from Paul Fauconnet to Célestin Bouglé, Cherbourg, February 26, 1907, in *Revue Française de Sociologie* 20, no. 1 (January–March 1979): 44.

12. Letter from Émile Durkheim to Henri Hubert, n.d. [May–June 1906], in Philippe Besnard, "Lettre d'Émile Durkheim à Marcel Hubert," *Revue Française de Sociologie* 28, no. 1 (1987): 530.

13. Ibid., 531.

14. Letter from Rosine Mauss to Marcel Mauss, Épinal, March 6, 1907.

15. Émile Durkheim, "Préface," *Année Sociologique* 11 (1910), in Durkheim, *Journal sociologique* (Paris: PUF, 1969), 626.

16. Letter from Paul Fauconnet to Marcel Mauss, n.d. [1908].

17. Draft of a letter from Marcel Mauss to "Monsieur l'administrateur" (M. Levasseur of the Collège de France), n.d. [1909].

18. Letter from M. Houtin to Alfred Loisy, June 17, 1909, in Loisy, *Mémoires pour servir l'histoire religieuse de notre temps* (Paris: Émile Noury, 1932), 2:39.

19. Loisy, *Mémoires pour servir à l'histoire religieuse*, 2:83.

20. Thanks to a financial contribution in 1906 from the marquise Arconati-Visconti, née Peyrat, the Collège de France had created a complementary course in general history and historical method. The course was offered until 1911.

21. Croiset's comments were a surprise, since he was thought to support Mauss. According to Durkheim, who knew Croiset, he was "a reader of *Année* and [would] say good things about your book" (letter from Émile Durkheim to Marcel Mauss, January 22, 1909).

22. Léon Daudet, "Les maîtres d'erreurs," *Courrier de l'Aude*, February 8, 1909.

23. Charles Maurras, "Chez Loisy" (1909) (Archives of the Collège de France, C-XII, Loisy, IIB).

24. Letter from Paul Fauconnet to Marcel Mauss, n.d. [1909].

25. Letter from Alfred Espinas to Marcel Mauss, February 27, 1909.

26. Letter from Abel Rey to Marcel Mauss, February 3, 1909.

27. Letter from Robert Hertz to Marcel Mauss, January 16, 1909.

28. Letter from Claude Maître to Marcel Mauss, February 12, 1908.

29. Marcel Mauss, *La prière*, vol. 1, *Les origines* (1909), repr. in Mauss, *Oeuvres*, vol. 1 (Paris: Éditions de Minuit, 1968), vols. 2 and 3 (1969), 1:362.

30. Ibid., 366.

31. Marcel Mauss, "L'art et le mythe d'après M. Wundt," *Revue Philosophique* 66 (July–December 1908), repr. in Mauss, *Oeuvres*, 1:3–39.

32. Letter from Robert Hertz to Marcel Mauss, February 11, 1908.

33. Letter from Rosine Mauss to Marcel Mauss, February 3, 1908.

34. Letter from Rosine Mauss to Marcel Mauss, March 29, 1908.

35. Maurice Leenhardt, "Marcel Mauss (1872–1950)," *Annuaire de l'École Pratique des Hautes Études, Section des Sciences Religieuses* (1950): 20.

36. Ibid.

37. Émile Durkheim, "Sur le totémisme," *Année Sociologique* (1902), repr. in Durkheim, *Journal sociologique*, 351–52.

38. Mauss, *La prière*, 427.

39. Letter from Marcel Mauss to Henri Hubert, August 16, 1908.

40. Letter from Émile Durkheim to Marcel Mauss, November 10, 1908.

41. Letter from Alfred Espinas to Marcel Mauss, February 27, 1909.

42. Mauss, *La prière*, 358–60.

43. Ibid., 358–60.

44. Ibid., 397.

45. Ibid., 477.

46. Émile Durkheim, *Les formes élémentaires de la vie religieuse: Le système totémique en Australie* (1912), 427.

47. Letter from Henri Hubert to Marcel Mauss, April 14, 1919.

48. Letter from Marcel Mauss to Henri Hubert, September 9, 1912.

49. The printed text of *La prière* is 176 pages. Victor Karady published the unfinished first part of Mauss's thesis, which consisted of two books, in Mauss's *Oeuvres* (vol. 1). Book 1 was an introduction, which seemed to be "in its final form"; book 2 was titled "The Nature of Elementary Oral Rites" and was a "series of observations in support of later arguments." As the editor indicates, "the rest of the text remains unknown. We do not even know if it was ever written."

50. Bourgin, *De Jaurès à Léon Blum*, 192.

51. Letter from Émile Durkheim to Georges Davy, July 14, 1911, in Davy, *L'homme, le fait social, et le fait politique* (Paris: Mouton, 1973), 300.

52. Durkheim, *Les formes élémentaires de la vie religieuse*, 28.

53. Ibid., 290.

54. Émile Durkheim and Marcel Mauss, review of J. G. Frazer, *Totemism and Exogamy* and Émile Durkheim, *Les formes élémentaires de la vie religieuse, Année Sociologique* 12 (1913), repr. in Mauss, *Oeuvres*, 1:189.

55. Letter from Émile Durkheim to Georges Davy, September 13, 1911, in Davy, *L'homme, le fait social, et le fait politique*, 301.

56. Durkheim, *Les formes élémentaires de la vie religieuse*, 12–13.

57. See Adam Kuper, *The Invention of Primitive Society: Transformation of an Illusion* (London: Routledge, 1988), 177.

58. These articles were later collected under the title *L'état actuel du problème totémique* (Paris: Leroux, 1920).

59. Paul Alphandéry, *Revue de l'Histoire des Religions*, year 33, 65 (1912): 230.

60. Marcel Mauss, "Les jeunes gens d'aujourd'hui et Agathon," handwritten text signed "Criton," n.d. [1910], 6.

61. Letter from Marcel Mauss to Henri Hubert, October 15, 1912.

62. Letter from Rosine Mauss to Marcel Mauss, Épinal, January 12, 1913.

63. This is a recurrent theme in the correspondence between Rosine Mauss and her son. Mme Mauss regularly helped Marcel financially so he could pay his debts or deal with unexpected expenses.

64. Letter from Rosine Mauss to Marcel Mauss, Épinal, December 15, 1913.

65. Letter from Rosine Mauss to Marcel Mauss, Épinal, Sunday [December 1912].

66. Letter from Marcel Mauss to Henri Hubert, n.d. [1912].

67. Letter from Marcel Mauss to Henri Hubert, Épinal, July 23, 1912.

68. Letter from Rosine Mauss to Marcel Mauss, Épinal, October 15, 1915.

69. Letter from Henri Hubert to Marcel Mauss, n.d. [May 1910].

70. Letter from Rosine Mauss to Marcel Mauss, Épinal, May 27, 1910.

71. "Your nephew will be called Marcel François Charles Philippe . . ." (letter from Henri Hubert to Marcel Mauss, n.d. [1913]).

72. Letter from Marcel Mauss to the minister, n.d. [1912].

73. Marcel Mauss, "W.H.R. Rivers," *La Grande Encyclopédie*, repr. in Mauss, *Oeuvres* 3:466.

74. Henri Lévi-Bruhl, "Nécrologie: Marcel Mauss," *Journal de Psychologie Normale et Pathologique* 43 (1950): 319.

75. Marcel Mauss, "Anna-Virāj," in *Mélanges d'indianisme offerts par ses élèves à Sylvain Lévi* (1911), repr. in Mauss, *Oeuvres*, 2:600.

76. On the institute, see René Verneau, "L'Institut français d'anthropologie," *Anthropologie* 22 (1911): 110.

77. Marcel Mauss, "Les origines de la notion de monnaie" (1914), repr. in Mauss, *Oeuvres*, 2:110–12.

78. Ibid., 112.

79. Letter from Henri Beuchat to Marcel Mauss, Victoria, June 16, 1913.

80. It appears that as early as 1907 Mauss indicated an interest in the position of director of the Trocadéro museum. A few years later, he wrote directly to M. Bayet, director of higher education, "about the importance of ethnography and anthropology." The vacant post at the Trocadéro, he was told, had just been filled (letter from M. Bayet to Marcel Mauss, October 17, 1910). The new director was René Verneau, professor of anthropology at the Muséum d'Histoire des Religions and editor in chief of the journal *Anthropologie*. "A competent scientist, but absorbed by other duties," Mauss would say (Marcel Mauss, "L'ethnographie en France et à l'étranger," *Revue de Paris* [1913], repr. in Mauss, *Oeuvres*, 3:426).

81. Marcel Mauss, "Le questionnaire a à la fois un but théorique et un but pratique. De l'utilité des recherches de sociologie descriptive dans l'Indochine française," n.d. (Hubert-Mauss collection, Archives of the Collège de France).

82. Mauss, "L'ethnographie en France et à l'étranger," 420.

83. Victor Karady, "Les phénomènes de la légitimité dans l'organisation historique de l'ethnographie française," *Revue Française de Sociologie* 22, no. 1 (1982): 30.

84. Mauss, "L'ethnographie en France et à l'étranger," 432.

CHAPTER 10
NOT A VERY FUNNY WAR

1. Letter from Marcel Mauss to "Monsieur" [not identified], Paris, October 20, 1904.

2. Marcel Mauss, "La guerre du Transvaal," *Mouvement Socialiste*, June 1, 1900, 645, repr. in Mauss, *Écrits politiques*, ed. Marcel Fournier (Paris: Fayard, 1998).

3. Mauss, "À propos de la guerre du Transvaal," *Mouvement Socialiste*, February 15, 1902, 293.

4. Daniel Rivet, *Lyautey et l'institution du protectorat français au Maroc, 1912–1925* (Paris: L'Harmattan, 1988), 1:114.

5. Marcel Mauss, "Notices biographiques" (1927), in Mauss, *Oeuvres*, vol. 1 (Paris: Éditions de Minuit, 1968), vols. 2 and 3 (1969), 3:520–21.

6. Letter from Edmond Doutté to Marcel Mauss, March 17, 1911.

7. M. [Marcel Mauss], "L'affaire d'Oudjda. Pillages et spéculations," *Humanité*, October 28, 1911, 1.

8. Yolande Cohen, *Les jeunes, le socialisme, et la guerre* (Paris: L'Harmattan, 1989), 220.

9. Marcel Mauss, "Un coup dirigé contre les coopératives," *Humanité*, March 8, 1913, 6; Marcel Mauss, "Les commerçants prétendent interdire aux fonctionnaires d'entrer dans les coopératives," *Humanité*, April 1, 1914, 6.

10. M. [Marcel Mauss], "Gâchis militaire: Notre armée de l'Est est dans le désordre le plus complet," *Humanité*, October 4, 1913, 2.

11. Marcel Mauss, "Le conflit franco-allemand," *Revue de l'Enseignement Primaire et Primaire Supérieur* 35 (June 1913): 284–85.

12. Marcel Mauss, "La situation extérieure. Roulements de tambours," *Revue de l'Enseignement Primaire et Primaire Supérieur* 27 (March 1914): 215.

13. Ibid., 216.

14. Mauss, "Le conflit franco-allemand," 283.

15. Ibid.

16. Mauss, "Le conflit franco-allemand," handwritten text, 8.

17. Marcel Mauss, "La situation extérieure: Échec momentané," *Revue de l'Enseignement Primaire et Primaire Supérieur* 24 (March 1914): 192.

18. Ibid.

19. Marcel Mauss, "La situation extérieure. Chose d'Italie," *Revue de l'Enseignement Primaire et Primaire Supérieur* 17 (January 1914): 136.

20. Marcel Mauss, "Souvenirs: Conseils de Jean Jaurès pour une Révolution russe," *Vie Socialiste*, July 30, 1921, 2.

21. Marcel Mauss, "La situation extérieure: La Maison d'Autriche," *Revue de l'Enseignement Primaire et Primaire Supérieur* 42 (July 1914): 337.

22. Ibid.

23. Letter from Marcel Mauss to Henri Hubert, n.d. [1913].

24. Letter from Marcel Mauss to Lord Listowell, June 17, 1935. Mauss was replying to Lord Listowell, who had asked for information on Jaurès's death.

25. Mauss, "Souvenirs: Conseils de Jean Jaurès," 2.

26. Lucien Lévy-Bruhl, *Quelques pages sur Jean Jaurès* (Paris: Éditions de L'Humanité, 1916), 84.

27. Roger Martin du Gard, *Les Thibault,* vol. 4, *L'été 1914* (1936; Paris: Gallimard, 1964), 302.

28. [Roughly, assistant to the chair.—Trans.]

29. Copy of a letter to "Monsieur le Ministre," n.d. [August 1914]. In this letter, Mauss asked to be an interpreter: "I know German and English at both a practical and a theoretical level. I am familiar with Germany and England and have fairly extensive contacts in both countries."

30. Letter from Rosine Mauss to Marcel Mauss, Épinal, August, 19, 1914.

31. Letter from Marcel Mauss to Rosine Mauss, n.d. [1914].

32. Letter from Marcel Mauss to Henri Hubert, December 1, 1914.

33. Letter from Marcel Mauss to Henri Hubert, n.d. [December 1914].

34. Letter from Marcel Mauss to Rosine Mauss, n.d. [1914].

35. Letter from Marcel Mauss to Rosine Mauss, January 1, 1915.

36. Letter from Marcel Mauss to Rosine Mauss, n.d. [1914].

37. Letter from Marcel Mauss to Rosine Mauss, December 9, 1916.

38. Marcel Mauss, "Services militaires," n.d. (Hubert-Mauss collection, Archives of the Collège de France).

39. Letter from Marcel Mauss to Henri Hubert, December 29, 1914.

40. Letter from Marcel Mauss to Henri Hubert, March 25, 1915.

41. Letter from Sylvain Lévi to Marcel Mauss, March 25, 1915.

42. Letter from Marcel Mauss to Henri Hubert, Pas-de-Calais, May 18, 1915.

43. Letter from Marcel Mauss to Rosine Mauss, May 6, 1915.

44. Letter from Marcel Mauss to Henri Hubert, June 12, 1915.

45. Letter from Marcel Mauss to Henri Hubert, September 3, 1915.

46. Letter from Marcel Mauss to Henri Hubert, n.d. [1915].

47. Letter from Marcel Mauss to Henri Hubert, September 3, 1915.

48. Christophe Prochasson, *Les intellectuels, le socialisme, et la guerre, 1900–1938* (Paris: Éditions du Seuil, 1993), 128.

49. Letter from Henri Hubert to Marcel Mauss, December 6 [1915].

50. Letter from Marcel Mauss to Rosine Mauss, November 23, 1915.

51. Letter from Marcel Mauss to Rosine Mauss, October 4, 1915.

52. Marcel Mauss, "De la politique," n.d., 1 (Hubert-Mauss collection, Archives of the Collège de France).

53. Letter from Lucien Herr to Marcel Mauss, July 15, 1915.

54. Marcel Mauss: "In Memoriam: L'oeuvre inédite de Durkheim et de ses collaborateurs," *Année Sociologique*, n.s. (1925), repr. in Mauss, *Oeuvres*, 3:493. See *Un ethnologue dans les tranchées août 1914–1915: Lettres de Robert Hertz à sa femme Alice* (Paris: CNRS Éditions, 2002).

55. Letter from Émile Durkheim to Marcel Mauss, April 23, 1915.

56. Letter from Marcel Mauss to André Durkheim, n.d. [1916].

57. Letter from Émile Durkheim to Marcel Mauss, February 29, 1916.

58. Letter from Marcel Mauss to Henri Hubert, February 1916.

59. Letter from Marcel Mauss to Rosine Mauss, February 29, 1916.

60. Letter from Marcel Mauss to Rosine Mauss, March 21, 1916.

61. Letter from Henri Hubert to Marcel Mauss, February 28 [1916].

62. Mauss, "In Memoriam: L'oeuvre inédite de Durkheim," 498.

63. René Maunier, review of *Année sociologique*, *Revue Philosophique* 4, nos. 9–10 (July–December 1927): 306.

64. Letter from Paul Fauconnet to Marcel Mauss, February 29, 1916.

65. Émile Durkheim, "Durkheim (André)" (1917), in Durkheim, *Textes*, 3 vols. (Paris: Éditions de Minuit, 1975), 1:446.

66. Letter from Marcel Mauss to Henri Hubert, February 1916.

67. Letter from Marcel Mauss to Rosine Mauss, March 7, 1916.

68. Letter from Rosine Mauss to Marcel Mauss, Épinal, January 29, 1916.

69. Letter from Sylvain Lévi to Marcel Mauss, March 8, 1916.

70. Letter from Sylvain Lévi to Marcel Mauss, April 4, 1916.

71. Letter from Marcel Mauss to Rosine Mauss, September 6, 1916.

72. C.E.W. Bean, *Anzac to Amiens: A Shorter History of the Australian Fighting Services in the First World War* (Canberra: Australian War Memorial, 1946), 266. See also C.E.W. Bean, *The Imperial Forces in France*, vols. 3 and 4 (Sidney: Angus and Robertson, 1979).

73. Marcel Mauss, "Les techniques du corps" (1935), in Mauss, *Sociologie et anthropologie*, 3rd ed. (Paris: PUF, 1966), 374.

74. Letter from Marcel Mauss to Henri Hubert, November 2, 1916.

75. Letter from Marcel Mauss to Henri Hubert, December 8, 1916.

76. Letter from Marcel Mauss to Henri Hubert, December 27, 1916.

77. Letter from Marcel Mauss to Henri Hubert, October 1, 1917.

78. Letter from Louise Durkheim to Marcel Mauss, November 26, 1916.

79. Letter from Émile Durkheim to Marcel Mauss, April 5, 1915.

80. Émile Durkheim and Ernest Lavisse, *Lettres à tous les Français* (1916; Paris: Armand Colin, 1992), 27.

81. Letter from Sylvain Lévi to Marcel Mauss, December 24–25, 1916.

82. Letter from Marcel Mauss to "Monsieur" [Gaudin de Villaine], April 1, 1916.

83. Letter from Marcel Mauss to Henri Hubert, December 8, 1916.

84. Letter from Marcel Mauss to Constantin, January 12, 1917.

85. Letter from Émile Durkheim to Marcel Mauss, Tuesday, [May] 15, [1917].

86. Letter from Émile Durkheim to Marcel Mauss, May 17, 1917.

87. In a letter she sent to Mauss in November 1916, Louise Durkheim explained the situation: "Your uncle was particularly busy all week and has been very tired since. It's better if for a while he writes and reads as little as possible. So I read to him and I hold the pen for whatever he has to write" (letter from Louise Durkheim to Marcel Mauss, November 28, 1916).

88. Letter from Marcel Mauss to Rosine Mauss, July 17, 1917.

89. Letter from Émile Durkheim to Marcel Mauss [August 25,] 1917.

90. Georges Davy, *L'homme, le fait social, et le fait politique* (Paris: Mouton, 1973), 23.

91. Letter from Émile Durkheim to Marcel Mauss, November 4, 1917.

92. Letter from Émile Durkheim to Marcel Mauss, November 10, 1917.

93. Letter from Marcel Mauss to Henri Hubert, December 11, 1917.

94. Letter from Raoul Bloch to Marcel Mauss, November 19, 1917.

95. Gabriel Séailles, "Émile Durkheim," *Dépêche de Toulouse*, Monday, November 15, 1917.

96. Mauss, "In Memoriam: L'oeuvre inédite de Durkheim," 498.

97. Letter from Marcel Mauss to Henri Hubert, December 30, 1917.

98. Mauss, "Services militaires," 1.

99. Bean, *Anzac to Amiens*, 376.

100. Notes written on a sheet describing the campaign and signed by the head of the general staff of Courcel, January 15, 1917 (SHAT 141437/N. no. 15/26).

101. Taken from general order no. 210, signed by Colonel de Bellaigue de Buchas, head of the military mission attached to the British Army, July 28, 1917 (SHAT 141437/N. no. 15/26).

102. Letter from Marcel Mauss to Henri Hubert, October 22, 1917.

103. Letter from Marcel Mauss to Henri Hubert, February 19, 1917.

104. Letter from Marcel Mauss to Henri Hubert, March 26, 1917.

105. Letter from Marcel Mauss to Rosine Mauss, October 11, 1917.

106. Bean, *Anzac to Amiens*, 426.

107. Letter from Marcel Mauss to Henri Hubert, May 27, 1918.

108. Letter from Marcel Mauss to Henri Hubert, April 13, 1918.

109. Letter from Marcel Mauss to Henri Hubert, May 10, 1918.

110. Taken from general order no. 423, signed by General de Laguiche, November 26, 1918 (SHAT 141437/N. no. 15/26).

111. Letter from Marcel Mauss to Rosine Mauss, August 5, 1918.

112. Letter from Marcel Mauss to Henri Hubert, November 11, 1918.

113. Letter from Marcel Mauss to Henri Hubert, n.d. [November 1918].

114. Letter from Marcel Mauss to Rosine Mauss, September 2, 1918.

115. Letter from Rosine Mauss to Marcel Mauss, Épinal, November 17, 1918.

116. Minutes of the governing committee of the section of religious science, École Pratique des Hautes Études, session of November 17, 1918, notebook 2, p. 623.

117. Letter from Rosine Mauss to Henri Hubert, January 12, 1919.

118. Letter from Sylvain Lévi and Danielle Lévi, December 31, 1914.

119. Letter from Marcel Mauss to Henri Hubert, April 20, 1918.

120. Letter from Marcel Mauss to Henri Hubert, December 11, 1917.

121. Letter from Henri Hubert to Marcel Mauss, December 21, [1917].

122. Letter from Marcel Mauss to Henri Hubert, October 12, 1918.

123. Letter from Henri Hubert to Marcel Mauss, January 1, 1919.

124. Letter from Marcel Mauss to Henri Hubert, December 5, 1919.

PART III
THE HEIR

1. "Plus jamais" (Never again) was the title of a book by Edgar Milhaud published in 1919.

2. Marcel Mauss, "Rapports réels et pratiques de la psychologie et de la sociologie," *Journal de Psychologie Normale et Pathologique* (1924), repr. in Mauss, *Sociologie et anthropologie*, 3rd ed. (Paris: PUF, 1966), 281–310.

3. Letter from Sylvain Lévi to Marcel Mauss, August 23, 1921.

4. Letter from Hubert Bourgin to Marcel Mauss, December 12, 1925.

5. Letter from Henri Hubert to Marcel Mauss, December 20 [1919].

6. Maurice Leenhardt, "Marcel Mauss (1872–1950)," *Annuaire de l'École Pratique des Hautes Études, Section des Sciences Religieuses* (1950): 21.

7. Letter from Paul Fauconnet to Marcel Mauss, November 23, 1918.

8. Letter from Paul Rivet to Marcel Mauss, November 18, 1919.

9. Subpoena, March 20, 1919. In the end, Mauss did not testify because he was not in Paris in August 1914

10. Letter from Albert Thomas to Marcel Mauss, April 22, 1921.

11. Marcel Mauss, comments following a paper by Joseph Vendryès, "Le progrès de la langue," *Bulletin de la Société Française de Philosophie* (1922), repr. in Mauss, *Oeuvres*, vol. 1 (Paris: Éditions de Minuit, 1968), vols. 2 and 3 (1969), 2:483.

12. Marcel Mauss, "Lettre de province: Effet de la scission," *Vie Socialiste*, January 23, 1921, 2.

13. Letter from Paul Fauconnet to Marcel Mauss, May 12, 1919.

CHAPTER 11
(THE SOCIALIST) LIFE GOES ON

1. Marcel Mauss, "Lettre de l'étranger: Un livre de Webb," *Action Coopérative*, October 30, 1920.

2. Marcel Mauss, introduction to Émile Durkheim, *Le socialisme* (1928), 30, in Mauss, *Oeuvres*, vol. 1 (Paris: Éditions de Minuit, 1968), vols. 2 and 3 (1969), vol. 3.

3. Marcel Mauss, comments following a paper by A. Aftalion, "Les fondements du socialisme," *Bulletin de la Société Française de Philosophie* (1924), in Mauss, *Oeuvres*, 3:634.

4. Marcel Mauss, "François Simiand," *Populaire*, April 18, 1935, 4.

5. Letter from Paul Fauconnet to Marcel Mauss, Toulouse, June 4, 1920.

6. Marcel Mauss, "The Problem of Nationality," *Proceedings of the Aristotelian Society* (1920), repr. in Mauss, *Oeuvres*, 3:632.

7. Eric Hobsbawm, *Nations and Nationalism since 1780* (New York: Cambridge University Press, 1990).

8. Antoine Meillet, *Les langues dans l'Europe nouvelle* (Paris: Payot, 1918), 332.

9. Henri Lévy-Bruhl, "Avertissement" (1956), repr. in Mauss, *Oeuvres*, 3:571.

10. Ibid., 572.

11. Letter from Élie Halévy to Marcel Mauss, February 29, 1920.

12. Mauss, "The Problem of Nationality," 3:626.

13. Ibid.

14. Marcel Mauss, "La nation" (1920), repr. in Mauss, *Oeuvres*, 3:584.

15. Mauss, "The Problem of Nationality," 627.

16. Mauss, "La nation," 591.

17. Ibid., 633.

18. Ibid., 608.

19. Edgar Milhaud, born in Nîmes in 1873, first taught philosophy at Beffont *lycée*. He pursued his career at the Université de Genève, where he was a professor of political economics. In 1908 he founded the international monthly *Annales de la Régie Directe* and became an advocate of "municipal socialism."

20. Mauss, "The Problem of Nationality," 632–34.

21. Marcel Mauss, "Phénomènes morphologiques," (unpublished manuscript, Hubert-Mauss collection, Archives of the Collège de France). 49–50.

22. Ibid., 49.

23. Mauss, "The Problem of Nationality," 633–34.

24. Marcel Mauss, "Les civilisations: Éléments et formes" (1929), repr. in Mauss, *Oeuvres*, 2:478.

25. Marcel Mauss, comments following a paper by Joseph Vendryès, "Le progrès de la langue," *Bulletin de la Société Française de Philosophie* (1922), repr. in Mauss, *Oeuvres*, 2:483.

26. Marcel Déat, *Mémoires politiques* (Paris: Denoël, 1989), 137.

27. Ibid.

28. Marcel Mauss, "Impression sur l'enquête en Russie," *Vie Socialiste*, September 25, 1920, 1.

29. See Annie Kriegel, *Aux origines du communisme français* (1914–1920), 2 vols. (Paris: Mouton, 1964).

30. Marcel Mauss, "Pour Moscou," *Vie Socialiste*, January 15, 1921, 1.

31. Marcel Mauss, "Effet de la scission," *Vie Socialiste*, January 8, 1921, 2.

32. Letter from Lucien Lévy-Bruhl to Marcel Mauss, December 21, 1921.

33. Marcel Mauss, "Le socialisme en province," *Vie Socialiste*, April 23, 1921, 1.

34. Marcel Mauss, "Marcel Sembat. Souvenirs," *Vie Socialiste*, October 14, 1922, 1.

35. Marcel Mauss: "Souvenirs: Conseils de Jean Jaurès pour une Révolution russe," *Vie Socialiste*, July 30, 1921, 2.

36. Marcel Mauss, "Théories, formes nouvelles du socialisme," *Vie Socialiste*, October 23, 1920, 2.

37. Marcel Mauss, "Lettre de l'étranger: Formes nouvelles du socialisme, I," *Vie Socialiste*, November 6, 1920, 2.

38. Marcel Mauss, "Il faut choisir," *Vosges Socialistes*, Saturday, September 30, 1922, 1.

39. Marcel Mauss, "Front unique? Non. Unité? Oui," n.d. [1921], 1 (incomplete typewritten text, Hubert-Mauss collection, Archives of the Collège de France).

40. Jean Lacouture, *Léon Blum* (Paris: Éditions du Seuil, 1977), 183.

41. Marcel Mauss, "Les changes: Du calme," *Populaire*, January 18, 1924, 1.

42. Marcel Mauss, "L'homme fossile," *Populaire*, April 11, 1921, 2.

43. Marcel Mauss, "II. La violence bolchevik. Sa nature. Ses excuses," *Vie Socialiste*, Saturday, February 10, 1923, 2.

44. Marcel Mauss, "III. La violence bolchevik. Bilan de la Terreur. Son échec," *Vie Socialiste,* Saturday, February 17, 1923, 2.

45. Marcel Mauss, "Réflexions sur la violence: Fascisme et bolchevisme," *Vie Socialiste,* Saturday, February 3, 1923, 1.

46. Ibid.

47. Mauss, "III. La violence bolchevik. Bilan de la Terreur," 1.

48. Mauss, "II. La violence bolchevik. Sa nature," 2.

49. Mauss, "III. La violence bolchevik. Bilan de la Terreur," 1.

50. Marcel Mauss, "IV. La violence bolchevik. La lutte contre les classes actives," *Vie Socialiste*, Saturday, February 24, 1923, 1.

51. Ibid.

52. Mauss, "II. La violence bolchevik. Sa nature," 2.

53. Letter from Bernard Lavergne to Marcel Mauss, May 6, 1922.

54. Marcel Mauss, "Contre la violence. Pour la force," *Vie Socialiste*, Saturday, March 5, 1923, 2; Marcel Mauss, *Vosges Socialistes*, Saturday, April 14, 1923, 1.

55. Mauss, "Contre la violence. Pour la force," 2; Mauss, *Vosges Socialistes*, Saturday, April 14, 1923, 2.

56. Marcel Mauss, "Socialisme et bolchevisme," *Monde Slave*, 2nd series, year 2, no. 2 (February 1925): 201.

57. Marcel Mauss, "Appréciation sociologique du bolchevisme," *Revue de Métaphysique et de Morale*, year 31, no. 1 (1924). See also B. Brewster, translator's notes to M. Mauss, "A Sociological Appreciation of Bolshevism," *Economy and Society* 13, no. 1 (1984): 378.

58. Mauss, "Socialisme et bolchevisme," 210.

59. Albert Thomas, "L'organisation internationale du travail. Origine. Développement. Avenir," *Revue Internationale du Travail* 1, no. 1 (January 1920): 21.

60. Mauss, "Appréciation sociologique du bolchevisme," 128.

61. Mauss, "Socialisme et bolchevisme," 213.

62. Ibid., 221–22.

63. Ibid., 211–12.

64. Mauss, "Appréciation sociologique du bolchevisme," 105.

65. Mauss, "Socialisme et bolchevisme," 211.

66. Marcel Mauss, "Divisions et proportions des divisions de la sociologie," *Année Sociologique*, n.s., 2 (1927), repr. in Mauss, *Oeuvres* 3:243–44.

67. Mauss, "Appréciation sociologique du bolchevisme," 130.

68. Ibid., 116.

69. Ibid., 131.

70. Letter from Paul Huvelin to Marcel Mauss, April 23, 1924.

71. Mauss, "Appréciation sociologique du bolchevisme," 132.

72. Mauss, "Division et proportions des divisions de la sociologie," 245.

73. Marcel Mauss, "Les faits: Le mouvement économique d'en bas," typewritten text, n.d. [1920], 72–76 (Hubert-Mauss collection, Archives of the Collège de France). This text is about fifty pages long (numbered 51 to 112) and constitutes a part of Mauss's manuscript on the nation.

74. Marcel Mauss, "Les coopératives russes," *Revue de Paris*, year 27, vol. 2 (March–April 1920): 96–121.

75. Ibid., 111.

76. Marcel Mauss, "La chaire de la coopération au Collège de France," *Action Coopérative*, December 11, 1920, 1.

77. Marcel Mauss, "L'éducation coopérative en Allemagne," *Action Coopérative*, August 14, 1920, 2.

78. Marcel Mauss, "Les Webb sont à Paris," *Populaire*, May 4, 1921, 1.

79. Henri Desroche, "Marcel Mauss, 'citoyen' et 'camarade,'" *Revue Française de Sociologie* 20, no. 1 (January–March 1979): 231.

80. In the words of Gaston Richard in "La crise de la science économique," *Revue Philosophique*, year 46 (March–April 1922): 301.

81. Marcel Mauss, "Nécessité d'un département statistique à la Fédération Nationale des coopératives de consommation," *Revue des Études Coopératives*, year 1, no. 4 (October 1921): 413.

82. E. Bugnon, "L'enseignement de la coopération," *Revue des Études Coopératives*, year 3, no. 6 (1923): 189–91.

83. Editorial board, "Lettres à nos lecteurs," *Revue des Études Coopératives*, year 1, no. 1 (October–December 1921): 4.

84. "Manifeste coopératif des intellectuels et universitaires français," *Revue des Études Coopératives*, year 1, no. 1 (October–December 1921): 15–29.

85. Mauss, "Nécessité d'un département statistique," 414.

86. Marcel Mauss, "Un parti coopératif," *Action Coopérative*, December 30, 1922, 3.

87. Jean Gaumont, "Le Congrès national de la coopération française," *Revue des Études Coopératives*, no. 7 (1923): 331.

88. Marcel Mauss, "Note préliminaire sur le mouvement coopératif et spéciale-ment le mouvement coopératif de consommation, plus spécialement sur le mouve-ment coopératif français," n.d., 7 (Hubert-Mauss collection, Archives of the Collège de France).

89. François Simiand, *La formation et les fluctuations des prix du charbon en France (1887–1912)* (Paris: Rivière, 1925). This book marked an important turning point in the research Simiand had conducted for several years on the fluctuation of prices and wages. He published a synthesis of his findings in three volumes a few years later: *Le salaire, l'évolution sociale et la monnaie* (Paris: Félix Alcan, 1932).

90. François Simiand, "La semaine de la monnaie," *Revue d'Économie Politique* 37 (1923): 569.

91. Marcel Mauss, "Les changes: Dangers des mesures arbitraires," *Populaire*, December 9, 1922, 2.

92. Marcel Mauss, "Les changes: Une politique; un exemple sinistre, l'Autriche," *Populaire*, December 5, 1922, 1.

93. Marcel Mauss, "Les changes: L'inflation des francs," *Populaire*, February 27, 1924, 1.

94. Marcel Mauss, "Les changes: Conclusion," *Populaire*, December 21, 1922, 3.

95. Marcel Mauss, "Les changes: Du calme," *Populaire*, January 18, 1924, 1.

96. From a tract of the Parti Socialiste (SFIO) titled "Le Bloc national a ruiné la France," 2 pp.

97. Marcel Mauss, "Les changes. L'inflation: Qui a inflationné le franc?" *Populaire*, March 1, 1924, 2.

98. Marcel Mauss, "Les changes. L'inflation fiduciaire: Comment le Bloc national maintint puis fit crouler le franc. L'accalmie de 1921," *Populaire*, March 10, 1924, 1.

99. Mauss, "Les changes. L'inflation: Qui a inflationné le franc?" 1.

100. Marcel Mauss, "Les changes. Deux fautes à éviter," *Populaire*, February 23, 1924, 2.

101. Marcel Mauss, "Les changes. L'inflation: La dépréciation intérieure," *Populaire*, February 29, 1924, 1.

102. Marcel Mauss, "Les changes. L'inflation fiduciaire: La responsabilité person-nelle de M. Klotz," *Populaire*, March 3, 1924, 1, 2.

103. Marcel Mauss, "Les changes. L'inflation fiduciaire: En quelle mesure le gouvernement Poincaré défendit-il et laissa-t-il faiblir le franc," *Populaire*, March 11, 1924, 2.

104. Marcel Mauss, "Les changes. La crise de la trésorerie de 1923–1924," *Populaire*, April 17, 1924, 2.

105. Marcel Mauss, "Deuxième conclusion générale. Un moyen de refonte sociale: La manipulation des monnaies," n.d., 9 (Hubert-Mauss collection, Archives of the Collège de France).

106. Marcel Mauss, "Démocratie socialiste," *Populaire*, May 6, 1924, 2.

107. Marcel Mauss, untitled handwritten text published in *Populaire*, bimonthly bulletin [1924], 4 (Hubert-Mauss collection, Archives of the Collège de France).

108. Ibid., 2.

109. Lacouture, *Léon Blum*, 212.

110. Marcel Mauss, "Questions pratiques: Actes nécessaires," *Populaire*, May 29, 1924, 1.

CHAPTER 12
A BURDENSOME INHERITANCE

1. Letter from Henri Hubert to Marcel Mauss, December 20 [1919].

2. Letter from Paul Fauconnet to Marcel Mauss, May 12, 1919.

3. Marcel Mauss, "La sociologie en France depuis 1914," in *La science française*, in Mauss, *Oeuvres*, vol. 1 (Paris: Éditions de Minuit, 1968), vols. 2 and 3 (1969), 3:437–38.

4. Marcel Mauss, "L'état actuel des sciences anthropologiques en France," *Anthropologie* (1920), repr. in Mauss, *Oeuvres* 3:434–35.

5. Marcel Mauss: "In Memoriam: L'oeuvre inédite de Durkheim et de ses collaborateurs," *Année Sociologique*, n.s. (1925), repr. in Mauss, *Oeuvres*, 3:488.

6. Letter from Lucien Lévy-Bruhl to Marcel Mauss, September 10, 1918.

7. These were the words of Maxime Leroy ("Le centenaire d'Henri de Saint-Simon," *Revue d'Économie Politique* 39 [1925]: 749). A committee called "Les Amis de Saint-Simon" (The friends of Saint-Simon) was created to plan the commemoration. Members included Lucien Lévy-Bruhl and Bouglé. The commemoration took place at the Sorbonne on May 13, 1925, with Thomas presiding and an audience of more than 3,500. Mauss also participated: he published "Saint-Simon et la sociologie," in an issue of *Revue de l'Enseignement Primaire* (May 1925) and took part in a session of the Société de Philosophie (March 1925) devoted to Saint-Simon's thought.

8. The manuscript produced from Durkheim's notes for the courses he taught in Bordeaux between November 1895 and May 1896 was written out almost entirely by his wife, Louise Durkheim. Mauss confined himself to helping her with the difficult passages, verifying quotations, and making a few changes in chapter titles and in the division of the text into lessons.

9. The fourth chair was in Bordeaux, occupied by Gaston Richard, a former Durkheimian.

10. Roger Geiger, "La sociologie dans les écoles normales primaires," *Revue Française de Sociologie* 20, no. 1 (January–March 1979): 257–68.

11. Paul Fauconnet's article was published in *Revue Philosophique* (1922) under the title "L'oeuvre pédagogique d'Émile Durkheim." It was translated into English as "The Pedagogical Work of Émile Durkheim" and published in the *American Journal of Sociology*, no. 5 (March 1923): 529–53.

12. Célestin Bouglé, *Qu'est-ce que la sociologie?* (Paris: Alcan, 1907). Bouglé, the son of a Breton officer, was born in 1870 and had a very typical career trajectory: École Normale Supérieure, *agrégation* in philosophy (1893, ranked first), study abroad in Germany, doctorate in letters (1899) with a thesis titled *Egalitarian Ideas*, *lycée* teacher in Saint-Brieuc, university professor in Montpellier and Toulouse.

13. Maurice Halbwachs, "Célestin Bouglé sociologue," *Revue de Métaphysique et de Morale*, year 48, no. 1 (January 1941): 47.

14. John E. Craig, "Maurice Halbwachs à Strasbourg," *Revue Française de Sociologie* 20, no. 1 (January–March 1979): 276.

15. The anthropologist Alfred Radcliffe-Browne, working in Pretoria, South Africa, learned of Durkheim's death only in 1921: "It is only recently that I learned with great regret of Professor Durkheim's death. . . . As you know, I have great admiration for Durkheim's work and for yours as well. They were a source of inspiration for me" (letter from Alfred Radcliffe-Browne to Marcel Mauss, Pretoria, May 24, 1921).

16. See Roger Lacombe, *La méthode sociologique de Durkheim: Étude critique* (Paris: Félix Alcan, 1926).

17. J. Benrubi, *Les sources et les courants de la philosophie contemporaine en France* (Paris: Félix Alcan, 1933), 159.

18. André Lalande, *Vocabulaire technique et critique de la philosophie* (1926; 7th ed., Paris: PUF, 1956), 1004.

19. As he was preparing the fourth edition in 1932, Lalande consulted Mauss on the notion of civilization (letter from André Lalande to Marcel Mauss, April 4, 1931).

20. Marcel Mauss, comments following a paper by Louis Weber, "Liberté et langage," *Bulletin de la Société Française de Philosophie* (1921), repr. in Mauss, *Oeuvres*, 2:122.

21. Ibid., 2:124.

22. Marcel Mauss, "Note de méthode sur l'extension de la sociologie" (1927), in Mauss, *Oeuvres*, 3:294.

23. Marcel Mauss, comments following a paper by Marcel Granet, "La droite et la gauche en Chine," *Bulletin de l'Institut Français de Sociologie* (1933), repr. in Mauss, *Oeuvres*, 2:147.

24. The first meeting of the Renan Society was held on December 18, 1919, on the campus of the Collège de France.

25. Gustave Belot, "Quelle place est-il possible de faire à l'histoire des religions dans l'enseignement secondaire?" *Revue de l'Histoire des Religions* 81 (1921): 390.

26. Gaston Richard, "L'athéisme dogmatique en sociologie religieuse," *Revue d'Histoire et de Philosophie Religieuse* (1923): 125–37.

27. Marcel Mauss, "L'expression obligatoire des sentiments (rituels oraux funéraires australiens)," *Journal de Psychologie* (1921), repr. in Mauss, *Oeuvres*, 3:269–79.

28. Marcel Mauss, comments following Weber's "Liberté et langage," 2:121.

29. Mauss, "In Memoriam: L'oeuvre inédite de Durkheim," 497.

30. Akamatsu and Matsumoto (Japan), Ling (China), MacSweeney (Ireland), Moë (Norway), Ranulf (Denmark), and others.

31. Letter from Marcel Mauss to Henri Hubert, October 4, 1921.

32. Letter from Célestin Bouglé to Marcel Mauss, December 16, 1921.

33. Letter from Lucien Lévy-Bruhl to Marcel Mauss, December 21, 1921.

34. Letter from Marcel Mauss to Sir James Frazer, December 1922.

35. Letter from Marcel Mauss to Henri Hubert, August 9, 1923.

36. Marcel Mauss, "Rapports réels et pratiques de la psychologie et de la sociologie," *Journal de Psychologie Normale et Pathologique* (1924), repr. in Mauss, *Sociologie et anthropologie*, 3rd ed. (Paris: PUF, 1966), 284.

37. Ibid.

38. Marcel Mauss, address to the Société de Psychologie, *Journal de Psychologie* (1923), in Mauss, *Oeuvres*, 3:282.

39. Marcel Mauss, "Effet physique chez l'individu de l'idée de mort suggérée par la collectivité," *Journal de Psychologie Normale et Pathologique* (1926), in Mauss, *Sociologie et anthropologie*, 311–30.

40. Mauss, "Rapports réels et pratiques," 288–89.

41. Meyer Fortes, "Obituary: C. G. Seligman," *Man* 41 (1941): 4. See also Bertrand Pulman, "Aux origines du débat anthropologie et psychanalyse: Seligman (1873–1940)," *Gradhiva*, no. 6 (1989): 35–50.

42. Marcel Mauss, "Divisions et proportions de divisions de la sociologie," *Année sociologique*, n.s., 2 (1927), repr. in Mauss, *Oeuvres*, 3:231.

43. Letter from Salomon Reinach to Liane de Pougy, August 23, 1923, in Max Jacob and Salomon Reinach, *Lettres de Liane de Pougy* (Paris: Plon, 1980), 200.

44. Like other friends of the deceased—James Frazer and G. Elliot Smith, for example—Mauss was not in a position to respond to the invitation of Evans-Pritchard, one of the editors of the tribute to Seligman.

45. Marie Bonaparte, "Psychanalyse et ethnographie," *Essays Presented to C. G. Seligman*, ed. E. E. Evans-Pritchard, R. Firth, B. Malinowski, and I. Schapera (London: Kegan Paul, Trench, Trubener & Co., 1934), 25.

46. Élisabeth Roudinesco, *Histoire de la psychanalyse en France*, vol. 1, *1885–1939* (Paris: Éditions du Seuil, 1986), 224.

47. Mauss, "Rapports réels et pratiques," 293.

48. Marcel Mauss, "Effet physique chez l'individu de l'idée de mort," 330.

49. Mauss, "In Memoriam: L'oeuvre inédite de Durkheim," 28.

50. Letter from Henri Hubert to Marcel Mauss, September 27, 1919.

51. Subscription bulletin for *Année Sociologique* (reprint of all 12 volumes), 1927.

52. Editorial board, "Avant-propos," *Année Sociologique*, n.s., 1 (1925): 1.

53. Letter from Marcel Mauss to Charles Gabriel Seligman, June 30, 1923.

54. Letter from Marcel Mauss to Sir and Lady James Frazer, Paris, December 5, 1922.

55. Letter from Célestin Bouglé to Marcel Mauss, April 23, 1923 (Célestin Bouglé collection, Bibliothèque Nationale).

56. Letter from Paul Huvelin to Marcel Mauss, Lyons, February 21, 1923.

57. Letter from Paul Mantoux to Marcel Mauss, Geneva, March 3, 1923.

58. Letter from Henri Hubert to Marcel Mauss, June 21, 1924.

59. Max Lazard, "François Simiand, 1873–1935," excerpt of work documents (Paris, 1935), 7.

60. Letter from Marcel Mauss to Georges Davy, February 26, 1923.

61. Letter from Lucien Lévy-Bruhl to Marcel Mauss, March 30, 1922.

62. Letter from Marcel Mauss to Georges Davy, March 23, 1922, in *Revue Française de Sociologie* 26, no. 2 (April–June 1985): 248.

63. Letter from Georges Davy to Marcel Mauss, Dijon, February 25, 1923.

64. Letter from Marcel Mauss to Georges Davy, February 26, 1923.

65. Letter from Maurice Halbwachs to Marcel Mauss, Strasbourg, February 21, 1923.

66. Missing were Paul Lapie, Hubert Bourgin, François Simiand, Albert Demangeon, Antoine Meillet, Edmond Doutté, and Dominique Parodi, all from Paris; Emmanuel Lévy and Paul Huvelin (Lyons); Pierre Roussel, Maurice Halbwachs, Abel Aubin, and Robert Hourticq (Strasbourg), Georges Davy (Dijon); René Maunier and Louis Gernet (Algiers); and Jean Ray (Japan).

67. Institut Français de Sociologie, minutes of the meeting of March 1, 1923, 4. On this institute, see Johan Heilbron, "Note sur l'Institut français de sociologie," *Études Durkheimiennes* 9 (1983): 9–14.

68. Institut Français de Sociologie, minutes of the meeting of March 5, 1924, 2.

69. Letter from Marcel Mauss to Charles Gabriel Seligman, June 30, 1923.

70. "Deuxième compte rendu d'activités," n.d. [1923], 1 (Hubert-Mauss collection, Archives of the Collège de France).

71. Marcel Mauss, "Mémoire complémentaire concernant *L'Année sociologique*," n.d. [1923], 2 pp. (Hubert-Mauss collection, Archives of the Collège de France).

72. René Maunier, review of *Année Sociologique*, *Revue Philosophique* 4, nos. 9–10 (July–December 1927): 305.

73. Ibid.

74. Johan Heilbron, "Les métamorphoses du durkheimisme, 1920–1940," *Revue Française de Sociologie* 26, no. 2 (March–April 1985): 224.

75. Mauss, "La sociologie en France depuis 1914," 3:438.

76. Maunier, review of *Année Sociologique*, 305.

77. Letter from Paul Huvelin to Marcel Mauss, Lyons, February 21, 1923.

78. Letter from M. Mauss to A. W. Small, October 11, 1924. *American Journal of Sociology* agreed to publish a short version of Mauss's letter under the title "A Durkheim Revival." The previous year, the journal had translated Paul Fauconnet's inaugural lecture, "The Pedagogical Work of Émile Durkheim," *American Journal of Sociology* 28, no. 5 (March 1923): 529–53.

79. Letter from Charles A. Ellwood to M. Mauss, November 4, 1924. Ellwood was president of the American Sociological Association.

80. F. H. Hankins, "Announcement of the Renewal of *L'Année sociologique*," *Social Forces* 2, no. 5 (September 1924): 736.

81. Marcel Mauss, "Rapport sur l'exécution d'une mission en Angleterre" (1924), 1 (Hubert-Mauss collection, Archives of the Collège de France).

82. Letter from Marcel Mauss to Alfred Radcliffe-Brown, December 6, 1924, in *Études Durkheimiennes*, no. 10 (October 1984): 2–3.

83. Ibid., 3.

84. René Maunier, "Note sur l'étude sociologique du socialisme," *Année Sociologique*, n.s., 1 (1925): 891.

85. Mauss used the term "inferior" only reluctantly. He found no better term to "give a sense of how long and wide-ranging all evolutions are."

86. Letter from Paul Fauconnet to Marcel Mauss, January 16, 1925.

87. Mauss, "In Memoriam: L'oeuvre inédite de Durkheim," 28–29.

88. Paul Alphandéry, "Publications récentes," *Revue de l'Histoire des Religions* 93 (1927): 177.

CHAPTER 13
THE INSTITUT D'ETHNOLOGIE

1. See James Clifford, *The Predicament of Culture: Twentieth-Century Ethnography, Literature, and Art* (Cambridge, Mass.: Harvard University Press, 1988), 122.

2. Sally Price and Jean Jamin, "Entretien avec Michel Leiris," *Gradhiva* 4 (1988): 30.

3. André Schaeffner, *Le Jazz* (1926; Paris: Jean-Michel Place, 1988), 160.

4. Price and Jamin, "Entretien avec Michel Leiris," 32.

5. Marcel Mauss, plan for an institute of ethnology, November 1913, 1–2 (Hubert-Mauss collection, Archives of the Collège de France).

6. Ibid., 5.

7. Lucien Lévy-Bruhl, "L'institut d'ethnologie de l'université de Paris," *Annales de l'Université de Paris*, May 1926, 207. See also Walter Hough, "Discussion and Correspondence, University of Paris," *American Anthropologist*, n.s., 28 (1926): 451–52.

8. Letter from Marcel Mauss to Alfred Radcliffe-Brown, December 6, 1924.

9. Letter from Lucien Lévy-Bruhl to Marcel Mauss, November 14, 1924.

10. L. Lévy-Bruhl, "L'institut d'ethnologie de l'université de Paris," 207.

11. Marcel Mauss, "Remarques à la suite de l'article de Paul Descamps 'Ethnographie et ethnologie,'" *Revue de Synthèse Historique* (April–June 1931): 202.

12. See Herman Lebovics, "Le conservatisme en anthropologie et la fin de la Troisième République," *Gradhiva* 4 (Summer 1988): 3–16.

13. Marcel Mauss, comments following a paper by Lucien Lévy-Bruhl, "La mentalité primitive," *Bulletin de la Société Française de Philosophie* (1923), repr. in Mauss, *Oeuvres*, vol. 1 (Paris: Éditions de Minuit, 1968), vols. 2 and 3 (1969), 2:131.

14. Marcel Mauss, "Lucien Lévy-Bruhl (1857–1939)," *Annales de l'Université de Paris*, 14 (1939): 408–11, repr. in Mauss, *Oeuvres*, 3:565.

15. Jacques Soustelle, *Les quatre soleils: Souvenirs et réflexions d'un ethnologue au Mexique* (Paris: Plon, 1967), 25.

16. Ibid., 26.

17. L. Lévy-Bruhl, "L'institut d'ethnologie de l'université de Paris," 208.

18. Marcel Mauss, "La sociologie en France depuis 1914," in *La science française*, repr. in Mauss, *Oeuvres*, 3:446.

19. Ibid., 206.

20. Letter from Marcel Mauss to the resident general of the French Republic in Morocco, December 30, 1925, 2.

21. L. Lévy-Bruhl, "L'institut d'ethnologie de l'université de Paris," 206. See also Lucien Lévy-Bruhl, "L'institut d'ethnologie pendant l'année scolaire 1925–1926," *Annales de l'Université de Paris*, January 1927, 94.

22. L. Lévy-Bruhl, "L'institut d'ethnologie pendant l'année scolaire 1925–1926," 90–91.

23. Most of the students were from the École Normale Supérieure, the École Pratique des Hautes Études, and the École des Langues Orientales. Others were colonial civil servants on leave and foreign students in France. At the end of the first year, Lévy-Bruhl said he was disappointed that, as a result of "circumstances beyond his control," no students from the École Coloniale had attended the institute.

24. Letter from Marcel Mauss to Sylvain Lévi, June 20, 1927.

25. René Maunier, "Sociologues et solidarités," *Revue d'Économie Politique* 23 (1909): 704.

26. Ibid., 710.

27. Marcel Mauss, review of Charles G. Seligman, *The Melanesians of British New Guinea* (Cambridge, 1910), in *Année Sociologique* 12 (1913): 371–74, repr. in Mauss, *Oeuvres*, 3:34.

28. Mauss was an active participant in the Institut Français d'Anthropologie. In 1927 he became its treasurer, replacing Hubert.

29. Marcel Mauss, "L'obligation à rendre les présents," *Anthropologie* 33 (1923): 193–94, repr. in Mauss, *Oeuvres*, 3:44–45.

30. Marcel Mauss, "Gift, gift," in *Mélanges offerts à Charles Andler par ses amis et ses élèves* (Strasbourg: Istra, 1924), 243–47, in Mauss, *Oeuvres*, 3:46–51.

31. Marcel Mauss, address to the Société de Psychologie (1923), in Mauss, *Oeuvres*, 3:281.

32. Marcel Mauss, "Rapports réels et pratiques de la psychologie et de la sociologie," *Journal de Psychologie Normale et Pathologique* (1924), repr. in Mauss, *Sociologie et anthropologie*, 3rd ed. (Paris: PUF, 1966), 303.

33. Ibid., 306.

34. Marcel Mauss, "Effet physique chez l'individu de l'idée de mort suggérée par la collectivité," *Journal de Psychologie Normale et Pathologique* (1926), repr. in Mauss, *Sociologie et anthropologie*, 329.

35. Henri Lévy-Bruhl, review of Marcel Mauss, "Essai sur le don," *Revue Historique du Droit Français et Étranger*, 4th ser., year 6 (1927): 123.

36. Marcel Mauss, "Essai sur le don: Forme et raison de l'échange dans les sociétés archaïques," *Année Sociologique*, n.s., 1 (1925), repr. in Mauss, *Sociologie et anthropologie*, 148.

37. Ibid., 50.

38. Maurice Leenhardt, "Marcel Mauss (1872–1950)," *Annuaire de l'École Pratique des Hautes Études, Section des Sciences Religieuses* (1950): 23.

39. Claude Lévi-Strauss, "Introduction à l'oeuvre de Marcel Mauss" (1950), repr. in Mauss, *Sociologie et anthropologie*, xxiv.

40. Ibid., xxxiii.

41. H. Lévy-Bruhl, review of "Essai sur le don," 124.

42. Mauss, "Essai sur le don," 161.

43. Lévi-Strauss, "Introduction à l'oeuvre de Marcel Mauss," xxxviii.

44. The same year, Mauss published a short analysis in *Revue Celtique* titled "Un texte de Posidonius: Le suicide contre-prestation suprême" (A text by Posidonius: Suicide as supreme counterservice), in Mauss, *Oeuvres* 3:52–57. The potlatch is clearly at issue.

45. René Maunier, review of *Année Sociologique*, *Revue Philosophique* 4, nos. 9–10 (July–December 1927): 307–8.

46. Mauss, "Essai sur le don," 274.

47. Marcel Mauss, address to the Société de Psychologie, *Journal de Psychologie* (1923), repr. in Mauss, *Oeuvres*, 3: 280–81.

48. Mauss, "Essai sur le don," 276.

49. Letter from Henri Hubert to Marcel Mauss, Les Lecques, December 21, 1925.

50. Ibid.

51. Letter from Franz Boas to Marcel Mauss, December 1925.

52. Letter from Bronislaw Malinowski to Marcel Mauss, London, November 12, 1925.

53. Robert H. Lowie, *The History of Ethnological Theory* (New York: Farrar & Rinehart, 1937), 216.

54. "Essai sur le don" was not translated into English until 1954, as *The Gift*, trans. I. Cunniso (London: Cohen and West). E. E. Evans-Pritchard composed a laudatory introduction for the 1967 edition (New York: Norton).

55. H. Lévy-Bruhl, review of "Essai sur le don," 124.

56. Marcel Mauss, "Parentés à plaisanterie," *Annuaire de l'École Pratique des Hautes Études, Section des Sciences Religieuses* (1926), repr. in Mauss, *Oeuvres*, 3:122.

57. Malinowski made this remark to Mauss (see Mauss, "Parentés à plaisanterie," 110).

58. Marcel Mauss, "La cohésion sociale dans les sociétés polysegmentaires," paper presented to the Institut Français de Sociologie, *Bulletin de l'Institut Français de Sociologie* (1931), repr. in Mauss, *Oeuvres*, 3:20.

CHAPTER 14
SOCIOLOGY, A LOST CAUSE?

1. In 1929 the Laura Spelman Rockefeller Foundation became part of the Rockefeller Foundation itself and continued its work within the new division of the social sciences. On this subject, see Brigitte Mazon, "La fondation Rockefeller et les sciences sociales en France, 1925–1940," *Revue Française de Sociologie* 26, no. 2 (April–June 1985): 311–43.

2. These were the terms used by Raymond Fosdick, one of the directors of the Laura Spelman Rockefeller Foundation. See Charles Rist, "Nouvelles et notices," *Revue d'Économie Politique* 39 (1925): 1120.

3. Travel expenses and lodging were entirely paid by the Rockefeller Foundation. In addition, a payment of a thousand dollars was made to Mauss to cover his "unusual expenses" (letter from Beardsley Ruml to Marcel Mauss, New York, December 23, 1925).

4. Letter from Marcel Mauss to "Monsieur le Ministre," August 2, 1926. Mauss was reporting on the mission the ministry had assigned to him "free of charge."

5. Letter from Henri Hubert to Marcel Mauss, May 26 [1926]. See also the letter from Paul Fauconnet to Marcel Mauss, May 15, 1926.

6. As reported by Ignace Meyerson. See Riccardo Di Donato, *Per una anthropologica storica del mondo antico* (Florence: La Nuova Italia, FSC, 1992), 204.

7. Letter from Henri Hubert to Marcel Mauss, May 11, 1926.

8. Letter from Marcel Mauss to Ignace Meyerson, New York, May 31, 1926, Ignace Meyerson collection.

9. According to Jean Poirier, "Marcel Mauss et l'élaboration de la science ethnologique," *Journal de la Société des Océanistes* 4, no. 6 (December 1950): 216.

10. The research institutes Mauss visited were: in Boston, the Business School and the International Research Foundation at Harvard and the Pollack Foundation; in Chicago and Philadelphia, the Social Research Department and the Social Research Institute; in Washington, D.C., the National Research Council, the Economic Institute, the Census Bureau, the Department of Labor, and the Smithsonian Institution.

11. "I've seen Malinowski, who is quite ill-informed." Letter from Marcel Mauss to Henri Hubert, May 3, 1926.

12. The list of people Mauss met included more than twenty academics: at Harvard, R. Dixon, Tozzer, and Hooten (anthropology); at Yale, Yerkes, Dodge, and Bingham (psychology), I. Fisher and C. Day (economics and economic history), and Keller (anthropology); at the University of Chicago, Fay-Cooper Cole (anthropology) and Edith Abbott (social work); and in Washington, D.C., W. Hamilton of the Brookings Graduate School of Political Economy.

13. Postcard (East Rock, New Haven) from Marcel Mauss to Henri Hubert, June 21, 1926 (Bibliothèque du Musée de l'Homme).

14. In a letter to a "dear friend," Mauss would recall that visit almost ten years later: "As for the Negroes in the United States, many speak of them, and speak very ill. My personal impressions are completely foreign to what is said about them. Two days in the black section of Philadelphia absolutely convinced me that our information is worthless" (letter from Marcel Mauss to "Mon Cher Ami," December 11, 1936).

15. Mauss would remember his observations during his brief visit to the United States and later recorded them in "Techniques du corps." In the first place, he had a "sort of revelation": "I was in the hospital. I was wondering where I'd seen young ladies walking like my nurses. I had time to reflect. It finally occurred to me that it was at the movies. When I returned to France, I noted how common that gait was, especially in Paris; these young women were French and they too walked that way. Thanks to the movies, the American way of walking was beginning to come here." Then, in Washington, Mauss saw the chief of the confederation of the Hopi, who had come with four of his men "to protest the prohibition on using certain types of alcohol for their ceremonies." "He was certainly the best runner in the world. He had run 250 miles straight. All the Pueblos were used to extreme physical feats of all sorts. . . . That same Indian was a dancer without peer." Mauss, "Les techniques du corps" (1935), in Mauss, Sociology et anthropologie, 3rd ed. (Paris: PUF, 1966), 380.

16. Mauss, "Divisions et proportions des divisions de la sociologie," Année Sociologique, n.s., 2 (1927), repr. in Mauss, Oeuvres, vol. 1 (Paris: Éditions de Minuit, 1968), vols. 2 and 3 (1969), 3:188.

17. Mauss was aware of this from the beginning of his trip: "I believe my trip will not be useful immediately, except for us personally and for our work and methods" (letter from Marcel Mauss to Ignace Meyerson, New York, May 31, 1926, Ignace Meyerson collection).

18. Letter from Henri Hubert to Marcel Mauss, April 3, 1925.

19. Letter from Marcel Mauss to Ignace Meyerson, August 20, 1925, Ignace Meyerson collection.

20. Letter from Paul Fauconnet to Marcel Mauss, December 13, 1925.

21. Letter from Marc Bloch to Marcel Mauss, Strasbourg, April 22, 1926.

22. Mauss, "Divisions et proportions des divisions," 3:200.

23. Ibid., 179.

24. Ibid., 226.

25. Ibid.

26. Ibid.

27. Ibid., 214.

28. Ibid., 215.

29. Letter from Marcel Mauss to Sylvain Lévi, June 12, 1927.

30. Letter from Maurice Halbwachs to Marcel Mauss, Strasbourg, February 27, 1927.

31. Marcel Mauss, "Note de méthode: Sur l'extension de la sociologie," *Année Sociologique*, n.s., 2 (1927), repr. in Mauss, *Oeuvres*, 3:289.

32. Ibid., 296.

33. Mauss, "Division et proportions des divisions," 3:168.

34. Ibid., 171.

35. Ibid., 173.

36. Marcel Mauss, "Appel aux spécialistes," handwritten text, n.d. [1927] (Hubert-Mauss collection, Archives of the Collège de France).

37. Ibid., 23–24.

38. Letter from Marcel Mauss to Sylvain and Danielle Lévi, April 8, 1927.

39. Letter from Maurice Halbwachs to Marcel Mauss, Strasbourg, November 18, 1928.

40. Salomon Reinach, "Henri Hubert," *Revue Archéologique* 26 (July–September 1927): 176.

41. Ibid., 178.

42. Marcel Drouin, "Hubert (Henri)," *Annuaire. Association des Secours des Anciens Élèves de l'ENS* (1929), 50.

43. Letter from Marcel Mauss to Sylvain Lévi, April 9, 1927.

44. Letter from Danielle Lévi to Marcel Mauss, Tokyo, June 25, 1927.

45. Letter from Alfred Métraux to Marcel Mauss, May 29, 1927.

46. Charles G. Seligman, "Henri Hubert," *Man* 27, no. 110 (September 1927): 162.

47. Marcel Mauss, "Henri Hubert, 1872–1927," *Encyclopedia of the Social Sciences*, vols. 7–8 (1932): 527.

48. Letter from Marcel Mauss to Sylvain Lévi, July 4, 1927.

49. Letter from Marcel Mauss to Alfred Radcliffe-Brown, January 7, 1928, in *Études Durkheimiennes*, no. 10 [October 1984]: 4. Radcliffe-Brown replied: "I was distressed to hear [of] the death of Hubert" (letter from Alfred Radcliffe-Brown to Marcel Mauss, Sidney, March 27, 1928).

50. Letter from Mme Lucien Herr to Marcel Mauss, Tuesday [May 1927].

51. Roger Caillois, *Rencontres* (Paris: PUF, 1978), 27.

52. Henri Berr was born in Lunéville in 1863. After passing the *agrégation* in letters (1884) and earning his doctorate in letters (1899), he pursued a career in secondary education, teaching at *lycées* in Tours, Douai, and Buffon and at the *lycée* Henri-IV in Paris. In 1900 he founded *Revue de Synthèse Historique*, which in 1930 became *Revue de Synthèse*. In 1920 he became editor of the series "L'évolution de l'humanité," and, four years later, he and his friend Paul Doumer created the Centre International de Synthèse, a science foundation, for which he served as director. See Giuliana Gemeli, "Communauté intellectuelle et stratégies intellectuelles: Henri Berr et la fondation

du Centre international de synthèse," *Revue de Synthèse* 4, no. 2 (April–June 1987): 225–59.

53. Letter from Marcel Mauss to Sylvain Lévi, June 20, 1927.

54. Marcel Mauss, "Avertissement," in Henri Hubert, *Les Celtes et l'expansion celtique jusqu'à l'époque de La Tène* (1932; Paris: Albin Michel, 1974), 10.

55. Letter from Marcel Mauss to Sylvain Lévi, November 20, 1927.

56. Marcel Mauss, "Notices biographiques" (1927), in Mauss, *Oeuvres*, 3:517–24. Mauss also had to "make the necessary arrangements" regarding the work of the linguist Maurice Cahen, another contributor to *Année*.

57. Marcel Mauss, "L'oeuvre sociologique et anthropologique de Frazer," *Europe* 17 (1928), in Mauss, *Oeuvres*, 3:527–34. To pay tribute to Sir James Frazer, Mauss happily agreed to organize the "ballyhoo" around Mme Sembat's portrait of his distinguished English colleague (letter from Marcel Mauss to Sylvain Lévi, April 9, 1927).

58. Marcel Mauss, "Avant-propos et notice biographique sur Alice Hertz," in Robert Hertz, *Mélanges de sociologie religieuse et de folklore* (Paris: Félix Alcan, 1928), vii, xv–xvi.

59. Summary of 1932–1933 course, *Annuaire du Collège de France* (1933), in Mauss, *Oeuvres*, 3:513.

60. Letter from Marcel Mauss to Alfred Radcliffe-Brown, December 6, 1924.

61. Marcel Mauss, "Effet physique chez l'individu de l'idée de mort suggérée par la collectivité," *Journal de Psychologie Normale et Pathologique* (1926), repr. in Mauss, *Sociologie et anthropologie*, 317. See also "Le péché et l'expiation dans les sociétés inférieures. Mise au point des recherches de Robert Hertz. Un cours inédit de Marcel Mauss," *Gradhiva* 2 (1987): 42–53.

62. Letter from Marcel Mauss to Sylvain Lévi, November 20, 1927.

63. Excerpts of the notes were published under the title "Les sciences sociales à Paris vues par Marcel Mauss," *Revue Française de Sociologie* 26, no. 2 (March–April 1985): 343–52.

64. Marcel Mauss, "Projet d'un Institut de recherches des sciences sociales de l'université de Paris," report to the Rockefeller Foundation (1929), 15; excerpts published under the title "Les Sciences sociales à Paris vues par Marcel Mauss," *Revue Française de Sociologie* 26, no. 2 (March–April 1985): 343–52.

65. *Gunn's Diary* of May 20, 1930, in Mazon, "La fondation Rockefeller et les sciences sociales en France," 325n57.

66. Letter from Marcel Mauss to Adéodat Compère-Morel, September 7, 1927.

67. Letter from Léon Blum to Marcel Mauss, September 24, 1927.

68. Letter from Marcel Mauss to Paul Faure, October 31, 1927.

69. Jean-François Sirinelli, *Génération intellectuelle: Khâgneux et normaliens dans l'entre-deux-guerres* (Paris: Fayard, 1988), 380.

70. Marcel Mauss, "Prédictions pour une prochaine législature: Chez les autres," *Vie Socialiste*, April 28, 1928, 8.

71. Letter from Marcel Mauss to "Mon cher Ami" [Élie Halévy], December 16, 1932.

72. Mauss, "Prédictions pour une prochaine législature," 8.

73. In July 1926, when President Doumergue asked Herriot to form a new government, the deputies responded with a vote of no confidence. That was the end of the Cartel des Gauches.

74. Mauss, "Prédictions pour une prochaine législature," 7.

75. Marcel Mauss, "Une lettre de Mauss," *Populaire*, August 11, 1929, 2. Compère-Morel, the administrative director of *Populaire*, was hurt by the "determination" of his comrade and friend and hoped to see him "at his side" again soon.

76. Letter from Marcel Mauss to "Mon cher Ami," November 6, 1933.

PART IV
RECOGNITION

1. Mauss's definition of *civilization*: "A set of facts with a set of characteristics composed of these facts corresponding to a set of societies—in a word, a sort of hypersocial system of social systems." Marcel Mauss, "Les civilizations: Éléments et forme" (1929), in Mauss, *Oeuvres*, vol. 1 (Paris: Éditions de Minuit, 1968), vols. 2 and 3 (1969), 2:463.

2. Ibid., 470.

3. Ibid., 476.

4. Ibid., 477.

5. Ibid., 478.

CHAPTER 15
A PLACE AT THE COLLÈGE DE FRANCE

1. Marcel Mauss, "La chaire de la coopération au Collège de France," *Action Coopérative*, December 11, 1920, 1.

2. Letter from Bronislaw Malinowski to Marcel Mauss, London, December 16, 1925. This was a brief word of congratulations.

3. Letter from Antoine Meillet to Marcel Mauss, Châteaumeillant, November 1, 1928.

4. Letter from Marcel Mauss to "Mon Cher Maître" [Meillet], November 2, 1928.

5. The average age of the professors appointed between 1900 and 1930 was 51.6 years old, that is, nearly the same age as professors holding chairs at the Sorbonne. This was slightly higher than it had been previously. This slowing in the pace of careers was linked to the longer training period and the scarcity of new chairs being created. The Collège de France thus saw its role in establishing reputations increase at the expense of its research function. Christophe Charle and Eva Telkès, *Les professeurs du Collège de France, Dictionnaire biographique, 1901–1939* (Paris: Éditions du CNRS, 1988); see also Christophe Charle, "Le Collège de France," in *Les lieux de mémoire: La nation*, ed. P. Nora (Paris: Gallimard, 1986), 3:388–424.

6. With the announcement of Izoulet's death, Halbwachs, a professor in Strasbourg, expressed his intention to apply, though he was warned that Mauss would apply and would have "every chance of being appointed."

7. Letter from Charles Andler to Marcel Mauss, Bourg-la-Reine, May 30, 1929.

8. Letter from Alfred Loisy to Marcel Mauss, June 4, 1929.

9. Letter from Charles Fossey to Marcel Mauss, June 5, 1929.

10. Reinach was asked for his help by the uncle of Mauss's friend Ignace Meyerson (letter from Ignace Meyerson to Marcel Mauss, June 4, 1929).

11. Letter from Antoine Meillet to Marcel Mauss, Châteaumeillant, June 2, 1929.

12. Letter from Marcel Mauss to "Mon cher Ami," July 22, 1929.

13. Letter from Marcel Mauss to "Mon cher Maître," July 22, 1929.

14. Letter from Marcel Mauss to "Mon cher Maître" [Meillet], October 7, 1929.

15. Reinach had died the previous year, and at that time Lucien Febvre expressed his intention to apply for a chair in sixteenth-century history (the Reformation and Renaissance). His colleague Marc Bloch did the same for a chair in comparative history. Febvre was born in 1878 and became an *agrégé* in history in 1902 (ranked fourth) and a doctor of letters in 1911. Since 1919 he had been a professor of modern history in the faculty of letters at the University of Strasbourg. When Alfred Loisy retired in 1932, he applied again (for a chair in the history of modern civilization), and, thanks to the support of Alexandre Moret, won with a very narrow margin in the third round. His chief adversary at the time was Jean Baruzi, who had been Loisy's replacement, in which capacity he had taught the history of religion since 1926.

16. Letter from Lucien Febvre to M. Mauss, Strasbourg, July 14, 1929.

17. Letter from Henri Breuil to Marcel Mauss, June 17, 1929.

18. Letter from Antoine Meillet to Marcel Mauss, October 8 [1929].

19. Letter from Marcel Mauss to "Mon cher Maître" [Meillet], October 10, 1929.

20. Letter from Sylvain Lévi to "Monsieur l'administrateur," October 7, 1929.

21. Letter from Georges Blondel to "Monsieur l'administrateur," October 14, 1929.

22. Letter from Charles Andler to Marcel Mauss, Bourg-la-Reine, November 7, 1929.

23. Letter from Maurice Halbwachs to Marcel Mauss, November 21, 1929.

24. Letter from Célestin Bouglé to Marcel Mauss, November 15, 1929.

25. This was a draft of a letter written in late 1929 or early 1930, probably addressed to Antoine Meillet (Hubert-Mauss collection, Archives of the Collège de France).

26. Perhaps as a result of pressure from Lucien Lévy-Bruhl, who had directed his *diplôme des études supérieures* in philosophy in 1906. Étienne Gilson would be hired at the Collège in 1932 as professor in the history of medieval philosophy.

27. Letter from William Marçais to Marcel Mauss, January 10, 1930.

28. Letter from Maurice Halbwachs to Marcel Mauss, Strasbourg, January 17, 1930.

29. "And if sociology had been voted on, I'm not sure you'd be here," added Meillet (second letter from Antoine Meillet to Marcel Mauss, March 6, 1930).

30. Letter from Maurice Halbwachs to Marcel Mauss, January 17, 1930.

31. Letter from Henri Lévi-Bruhl to Marcel Mauss, January 13, 1930.

32. Letter from Abel Rey to Marcel Mauss, January 18, 1930.

33. Letter from Henri Delacroix to Marcel Mauss, January 15, 1930.

34. Letter from Maurice Halbwachs to Marcel Mauss, January 17, 1930.

35. Letter from Marcel Mauss to Fernand Benoît, December 28, 1929.

36. Marcel Mauss, "Notices biographiques" (1927), in Mauss, *Oeuvres*, vol. 1 (Paris: Éditions de Minuit, 1968), vols. 2 and 3 (1969), 3:521.

37. In 1930 Robert Montagne published *Les Berbères et le Makhzen dans le Sud-Marocain: Essai sur la transformation politique des Berbères sédentaires* in the series "Travaux de *L'Année Sociologique*" (Alcan). It had been his doctoral thesis. Born in 1893, Montagne studied at the École Navale and then pursued a military career. While posted in Morocco, he learned Arabic and Berber and did his first sociological surveys. He then traded his uniform for academic robes, taught sociology at the University of Algiers (1932–1934) and then returned to France, where in 1936 he founded the Centre des Hautes Études d'Administration Musulmane (Center for higher studies in Muslim administration). He would be named a professor at the Collège de France in 1949 and held the chair in the history of Western expansion.

38. An *agrégé* in history and geography, Charles Le Coeur later wrote a "serious study" of rites and tools. After completing his military service in the region of Souss, in the far southern part of Morocco, he took Mauss's courses at the École Pratique in 1924–1925 (as an auditor) and in 1925–1926 (as an enrolled student), before being assigned to the Collège Musulman in Rabat at his request.

39. Letter from Marcel Mauss to Charles Le Coeur, February 17, 1930.

40. Letter from Marcel Mauss to "Cher Monsieur" [F. Benoît], [January] 1930.

41. Marcel Mauss, "Voyage au Maroc," *Anthropologie* 40 (1930), repr. in Mauss, *Oeuvres*, 2:562–63.

42. Ibid., 563.

43. Ibid., 564.

44. Ibid., 567.

45. During the previous meeting, Loisy had voted "without the slightest hesitation" to create a chair in sociology; he now supported Mauss's candidacy. "Mauss has shortcomings, and I would not venture to loudly defend his ideas. But he is a powerful mind, very sincere, someone who has done major research, who knows how to think and to write, who represents a new science and is perfecting its method" (letter from Alfred Loisy to "Monsieur l'administrateur" [Joseph Bédier], June 11, 1930).

46. Letter from Marcel Mauss to Georges Renard, June 6, 1930.

47. Letter from Charles Andler to Marcel Mauss, Bourg-la-Reine, May 29, 1930.

48. Letter from Charles Fossey to Marcel Mauss, n.d. [June 1930].

49. Charles Andler, "Proposition en vue de la création d'une chaire de sociologie au Collège de France," statement made on June 15, 1930, faculty meeting minutes, 1925–1934, Archives of the Collège de France, G 11-13, p. 176.

50. Ibid., 180.

51. Letter from Marcel Mauss to M. Coadès, June 24, 1930.

52. Letter from Maurice Halbwachs to Marcel Mauss, Strasbourg, June 17, 1930.

53. Letter from Maurice Halbwachs to Marcel Mauss, Chicago, November 24, 1930. Halbwachs was on a tour of the United States at the time. He met several American colleagues (Edward Sapir, Ernest Burgess, Robert Park) and gave a few lectures, including one at the University of Chicago titled "The Current State of Sociological Research in France." By way of introduction, Halbwachs mentioned the history of Mauss's candidacy.

54. Letter from Marcel Mauss to "Mon cher Ami," September 19, 1930.

55. Letter from Maurice Halbwachs, Saint-George-de-Didonne, August 29, 1930.

56. Letter from Maurice Halbwachs to Marcel Mauss, September 4, 1930.

57. André Joussain was born in 1880 and became an *agrégé* in philosophy and a doctor of letters (1920). He was the author of several books: *Fondement psychologique de la morale* (1909), *Romantisme et religion* (1910), *L'Allemagne contre la France* (1923), *Romantisme et politique* (1924), and *Les sentiments et l'intelligence: Leur rôle dans la vie des peuples* (1930). When he applied for the position, he announced the forthcoming publication of his two-volume *Manuel de sociologie*.

58. Letter from Edgar Milhaud to Marcel Mauss, Geneva, June 24, 1932.

59. Interview with Jacques Soustelle, Paris, November 6, 1989.

60. Letter from Henri Berr to Marcel Mauss, n.d.

61. Letter from Louis Finot to Marcel Mauss, Toulon, March 1, 1931.

62. Jacques Soustelle, *Les quatre soleils: Souvenirs et réflexions d'un ethnologue au Mexique* (Paris: Plon, 1967), 16.

63. Letter from Marcel Mauss to Olaf Jansé, July 11, 1931.

64. Marcel Mauss, "Introduction à la 'Morale professionnelle' d'Émile Durkheim" (1937), in Mauss, *Oeuvres*, 3:500–507.

65. According to his 1930 tax return, Mauss earned about 57,700 francs in 1929. In addition to his salary at the École and his stipend from the institute, there was some income from securities and stocks (3,900 francs) and "professional perquisites" (journal editing: 750 francs). In addition, Marcel declared a "loss resulting from an operating deficit" on the order of 17,350 francs, which included professional expenses (book purchases, entertainment expenses for foreign scholars, transportation costs, correspondence, typing, and so on).

66. Letter from Marcel Mauss to "Mon cher Ami" [Marc Bloch, February 20, 1936].

67. Letter from Jean Longuet to Marcel Mauss, June 15, 1932.

68. Charle and Telkès, *Les professeurs du Collège de France*.

69. Letter from Maurice Halbwachs to Marcel Mauss, December 7, 1923. Simiand presented his inaugural lecture on "the history of labor at the Collège de France" on December 2, 1932.

CHAPTER 16
WHERE PROFESSORS DEVOUR ONE ANOTHER

1. It might seem surprising to find Mauss's name on the list of members of the honor committee headed by Édouard Herriot, minister of foreign affairs. The committee included politicians (De Monzie, Léon Bérard, Joseph Caillaux), men of letters (Robert Dreyfus, Romain Rolland), and academics (Sébastien Charenty, Dr. Verneau, Henri Lichtenberger).

2. Georges-Henri Rivière, "Témoignages," in *Ethnologiques: Hommages à Marcel Griaule*, ed. Solange de Ganay (Paris: Hermann, 1987), xi.

3. Paul Rivet, "Programme d'avenir," in *Titres et travaux scientifiques de Paul Rivet* (Paris, 1927), 29.

4. According to a typewritten note dated December 14, 1931, in Jean Jamin, "Tout était fétiche, tout devint totem," *Bulletin du Musée d'ethnographie du Trocadéro* (Paris: Éditions Jean-Michel Place, 1988), xvii.

5. Rivet, "Programme d'avenir," 31.

6. Jacques Soustelle, "Musées vivants," *Vendredi*, June 26, 1936.

7. Marcel Mauss, "La sociologie en France de 1914 à 1933," *La Science française* (1933), in Mauss, *Oeuvres*, vol. 1 (Paris: Éditions de Minuit, 1968), vols. 2 and 3 (1969), 3: 445–46.

8. During the school year 1932–1933, the number of enrolled students rose to 145 from 129 the previous year.

9. Course notes taken by Yvonne Oddon and Thérèse Rivière in Mauss's course (1929–1930) at the Institut d'Ethnologie, revised by B. P. Feuilloley, typewritten text, 61 pp. (Hubert-Mauss collection, Collège de France).

10. In 1932–1933, the student body at the institute was composed primarily of students from the faculties of letters (39) and science (22), and from the École Orientale (28). There were also colonial troop doctors (2), colonial administrators (3), and missionaries or future missionaries (12).

11. André-Georges Haudricourt and Pascal Dibie, *Les pieds sur terre* (Paris: Éditions Métaillé, 1987).

12. A line attributed to Mauss in Jamin, "Tout était fétiche, tout devint totem," xviii.

13. Interview with Denise Paulme, February 17, 1989.

14. Class notes taken by Oddon and T. Rivière.

15. Marcel Mauss, *Manuel d'ethnographie* (course taught at the Institut d'Ethnologie, Université de Paris), ed. Denise Paulme (Paris: Payot, 1947; 2nd ed. 1967), 203.

16. Haudricourt and Dibie, *Les pieds sur terre*, 25.

17. Pierre Métais, review of Marcel Mauss, *Manuel d'ethnographie*, *Année Sociologique* (1940–1948), 3rd ser. (1950): 305.

18. In the 1920s, they included Jeanne Cuisinier, Georges Dumézil, Madeleine Francès, Marcel Griaule, Charles Haganauer, Alexandre Koyré, Raymond Lenoir, Edmond Mestre, Alfred Métraux, Georges-Henri Rivière, and André Vargnac; in the 1930s, Roger Caillois, Germaine Dieterlen, Louis Dumont, André-Georges Haudricourt, Maurice Leenhardt, Michel Leiris, André Leroi-Gourhan, Anatole Lewitzky, Deborah Lifszyc, Jean Margot-Duclot, René Maunier, Bernard Maupoil, Pierre Métais, Yvonne Oddon, Denise Paulme, Maxime Rodinson, Thérèse Rivière, André Schaeffner, Jacques Soustelle, Germaine Tillion, Jean-Pierre Vernant, and Paul-Émile Victor. This group of students was heterogeneous in age, nationality, training, and professional orientation. There were a relatively large number of young women. In 1933–1934, the African statesman and poet Léopold Sédar Senghor, then a student at the Sorbonne, took courses from Mauss, Rivet, and Marcel Cohen at the Institut d'Ethnologie: "Each of them [was] one of the founders of his discipline, which was transformed into a human, but modern, science" (Léopold Sédar Senghor, "Préface," in Ganay, ed., *Ethnologiques: Hommages à Marcel Griaule*, 3).

19. Patrick Waldberg, "Au fil du souvenir," in *Échanges et communications: Mélanges offerts à Claude Lévi-Strauss à l'occasion de son 60e anniversaire*, ed. Jean Pouillon and Pierre Maranda (Paris: Mouton, 1970), 2:587.

20. Interview with Jacques Soustelle, November 6, 1989.

21. Interview with Germaine Tillion, December 26, 1989.

22. Interview with Denise Paulme, February 19, 1989.

23. Jacques Soustelle, *Les quatre soleils: Souvenirs et réflexions d'un ethnologue au Mexique* (Paris: Plon, 1967), 16.

24. Interview with Denise Paulme, February 19, 1989.

25. Letter from André Schaeffner to Marcel Mauss, June 22, 1934.

26. Letter from Claude Lévi-Strauss to Marcel Mauss, n.d.

27. After finishing his studies at the *lycée* Louis-le-Grand, Marcel Griaule (1898–1956) intended to go to the École Polytechnique. In 1917 he joined the army, leaving only in 1924 with the rank of air force second lieutenant. He then resumed his studies, receiving a degree in Abyssinian in 1927 from the École Nationale des Langues Orientales Vivantes. Griaule decided on his choice of career after meeting an Abyssinian (Jean-Paul Lebeuf, "Marcel Griaule," in Ganay, ed., *Ethnologiques: Hommages à Marcel Griaule*, xxi).

28. According to Georges-Henri Rivière, speaking to James Clifford; see Clifford's *The Predicament of Culture: Twentieth-Century Ethnography, Literature, and Art* (Cambridge, Mass.: Harvard University Press, 1988), 136. That evening, boxing's world champion, Al Brown, defeated a man by the name of Simendé in a third-round knockout. The gate took in more than 100,000 francs. Rivière, "Témoignage," in Ganay, ed., *Ethnologiques: Hommages à Marcel Griaule*, xi.

29. Paris, Musée d'Ethnographie, May 1931, 32 pp. These instructions were formulated by Griaule himself with the collaboration of Michel Leiris, probably under Mauss's supervision.

30. Marcel Griaule, "Introduction méthodologique," *Minotaure* 2 (June 1933): 7.

31. Germaine Dieterlen, "Les résultats des missions Griaule au Soudan français (1931–1956)," *Archives de Sociologie des Religions*, year 2, no. 3 (January–June 1957): 138.

32. Mauss, *Manuel d'ethnographie*, 13.

33. Michel Leiris, *L'Afrique fantôme* (Paris: Gallimard, 1934).

34. Ibid., 210.

35. Sally Price and Jean Jamin, "Entretien avec Michel Leiris," *Gradhiva* 4 (1988): 51. See also Élisabeth Roudinesco, *Histoire de la psychanalyse en France*, vol. 1, *1885–1939* (Paris: Éditions du Seuil, 1986), 1:331.

36. Michel Leiris, *Journal, 1922–1989*, edited and annotated by Jean Jamin (Paris: Gallimard, 1992), 302–3. See also Jean Jamin, "Michel Leiris," *Gradhiva* 9 (1991): 3–4.

37. Leiris, *Journal*, 418.

38. Letter from Michel Leiris to Marcel Mauss, January 3, 1941.

39. Leiris, "Titres et travaux," unpublished text edited by Jean Jamin, *Gradhiva* 9 (1991): 7. Parallel to his ongoing work (putting together the collection of objects), Leiris conducted two surveys: one on *sigi so*, the initiatory language of the Dogon society of Sanga (French Sudan, now Mali); the other on the *zâr* genie cult among the Christians of Gonder (Ethiopia). He earned various certificates and diplomas. At the École Pratique, his thesis, presented in 1938, dealt with "the secret language of the Dogons of Sanga."

40. Letter from Boris Vildé to Marcel Mauss, August 31, 1938. See also Georges Devereux's testimonial: "You taught me much more than the facts. You taught me the art of drawing something from the facts. And you were very good to me. . . . I earned my spurs under your excellent leadership." Letter from Georges Devereux to Marcel Mauss, Berkeley, November 7, 1938.

41. Letter from Alfred Métraux to Marcel Mauss, Easter Island, September 11, 1934.

42. Paul Rivet and Georges-Henri Rivière, "La réorganisation du musée d'Ethnographie du Trocadéro," *Bulletin du Musée d'Ethnographie du Trocadéro* 1 (January 1931): 9–10.

43. Erik Orsenna, *L'Exposition coloniale* (Paris: Éditions du Seuil, 1988), 335.

44. For example, Charles G. Seligman, *Les races de l'Afrique*; A. M. Hoccart, *Le progrès de l'homme*; Robert Lowie, *Traité de sociologie primitive*; and E. Westermack, *L'origine et le développement des idées morales*.

45. At *Année Sociologique*, Charles Lalo was the contributor most closely identified with aesthetics. An *agrégé* in philosophy and a doctor of law, he wrote *Esquisse d'une esthétique musicale* (Alcan, 1908; Outline for an aesthetics of music). He was appointed professor at the Sorbonne in 1933 (Marcel Fournier, "Durkheim, *L'Année sociologique*, et l'art," *Études Durkheimiennes* 12 [January 1987]: 1–11).

46. Marcel Mauss, "Divisions et proportions des divisions de la sociologie," *Année Sociologique*, n.s., 2 (1927), repr. in Mauss, *Oeuvres*, 3:193.

47. Marcel Mauss, "Les arts indigènes," *Lyon Universitaire* 14 (1931): 1–2.

48. Pierre Verger, "Trente ans d'amitié avec Alfred Métraux, mon presque jumeau," *Acéphale: Les Amis de Georges Bataille* 2 (1992): 176.

49. See Jean Jamin, introduction to André Schaeffner, "Musique savante, musique populaire, musique nationale," *Gradhiva* 6 (1989): 68–75. Schaeffner published a study on Les Kissi, a black society, and its musical instruments (1951). A few months before his death in 1980, he published a collection of texts under the title *Essais de musicologie et autres fantaisies* (Essays on musicology and other fantasias) (Paris: Le Sycomore, 1980). He did pioneering work. While continuing his studies on scholarly music and contemporary forms of music, including jazz, he introduced a new field of research: ethno-musicology.

50. Rivière, "Témoignage," ix.

51. Alfred Métraux, "Rencontre avec les ethnologues," *Critique* 19, no. 195 (September 1963): 676.

52. Michel Leiris, "De Bataille l'impossible à l'impossible *Documents*," *Critique* 19, no. 195 (September 1963): 688.

53. Marcel Mauss, "Hommage à Picasso," *Documents* year 2, 3 (1930): 117.

54. Edward A. Tiryakian, "L'école durkheimienne à la recherche de la société perdue: La sociologie naissante et son milieu culturel," *Cahiers Internationaux de Sociologie* 66 (1979): 97–114.

55. Waldberg, "Au fil du souvenir," 585.

56. Marcel Mauss and Marcel Griaule, "Introduction," in Marcel Griaule, *Silhouettes et graffitis abyssins* (Paris: Larose, 1933), 5.

57. *Minotaure* 2 (June 1933): 6.

58. Sidney Mintz, "Introduction to the Second English Translation," in Alfred Métraux, *Voodoo in Haiti* (New York: Schocken Books, 1972).

59. Price and Jamin, "Entretien avec Michel Leiris," 40.

60. Ibid.

61. Jamin, "Tout était fétiche, tout devint totem," ix–xxii.

62. Henri Hubert, *Les Celtes et l'expansion celtique jusqu'à l'époque de La Tène* (1932; Paris: Albin Michel, 1974). Mauss wrote a foreword for this book (repr. in Mauss, *Oeuvres*, 3:455–59).

63. In addition to these short texts were a few prefaces, work Mauss usually refused: an introduction to Marcel Griaule's *Silhouettes et graffitis abyssins* (1933), a preface to Khateb Chatila's *Le mariage chez les musulmans en Syrie* (1934).

64. "Marcel Mauss Transcript," interview with Marcel Mauss by Earle Edward Eubank (1934), in Dirk Kaesler, *Sociological Adventures: Earle Edward Eubank's Visits with European Sociologists* (New Brunswick, N.J.: Transaction Publishers, 1991), 146.

65. Ibid., 145.

66. Georges Gurvitch submitted the introduction to one of his books to Mauss, who replied: "That whole introduction, which involves discussing ad infinitum—jumping from one opinion to the next—people of such different value who are treated as equals for the occasion, Durkheim on one hand, Max Weber and every Scheller who's ever lived on the other, is of interest only on a purely dialectical level."

67. Marcel Mauss, "La cohésion sociale dans les sociétés polysegmentaires," paper presented to the Institut Français de Sociologie, *Bulletin de l'Institut Français de Sociologie* (1931), repr. In Mauss, *Oeuvres*, 3:20. In the case of division by sex, Mauss regretted that "our sociology is very inferior to what it ought to be. . . . We have done only the sociology of men and not the sociology of women, or of both sexes" (ibid., 15).

68. Ibid., 19.

69. Ibid., 20.

70. The anthropologist Alfred R. Radcliffe-Brown at the University of Chicago was directly inspired by Durkheim's work. Although he made use of the notion of function to explain social cohesion, he refused to consider himself a "functionalist," except when such a perspective "leads to a study of all aspects of social life in relation to one another." From his standpoint, the notion of function implied the notion of structure, with structure defined as "a set of relations amongst unit entities" (Alfred R. Radcliffe-Brown, "On the Concept of Function in Social Sciences," *American Anthropologist*, n.s., 37 [1935]: 394). During the same period, Durkheim's *On the Division of Labor in Society* was translated into English by George Simpson and published by Macmillan. W. Lloyd Warner was sorry to see that it was a poor translation. He believed that the "great French theorist" was in danger of being "misunderstood by English and American anthropologists" (W. Lloyd Warner, review of Émile Durkheim, *The Division of Labor in Society*, *American Anthropologist*, n.s., 37 [1935]: 355).

71. Mauss, "La cohésion sociale dans les sociétés polysegmentaires," 26.

72. Ibid.

73. Marcel Mauss, "Fragment d'un plan de sociologie générale descriptive," *Annales Sociologiques*, ser. A, installment 1 (1934), repr. in Mauss, *Oeuvres*, 3:339.

74. Ibid., 318.

75. Marcel Mauss, comments following a paper by François Simiand, "La monnaie, réalité sociale," *Annales Sociologiques*, ser. D, installment 1 (1934): 61, repr. in Mauss, *Oeuvres*, 2:117.

76. Marcel Mauss, "Les techniques du corps" (1935), *Sociologie et anthropologie*, 3rd ed. (Paris: PUF, 1966), 365–66.

77. Ibid., 382.

78. Ibid., 386.

79. Ibid.

80. Ibid., 365.

81. Ibid., 379.

82. Claude Lévi-Strauss, "Introduction à l'oeuvre de Marcel Mauss" (1950), in Mauss, *Sociologie et anthropologie*, xiii.

83. Henri Lévy-Bruhl described the position of sociology in France in the early 1930s: "Chairs of sociology are quite rare. They are absent from the law faculties. There is one in the faculty of letters at Bordeaux and another at Toulouse, but there are no others in the provinces. Paris is somewhat better equipped. The Sorbonne has one; there is, besides, a course of sociology at the Institut d'ethnologie. The Collège de France has a chair of social philosophy. Finally a course in sociology is given at the Institut catholique and at the École des hautes études sociales" (Henri Lévy-Bruhl, "France, Belgium, and Romantic Switzerland," *Encyclopedia of the Social Sciences*, vol. 1 [New York: Macmillan Company, 1930], 251).

84. Célestin Bouglé, *Humanisme, sociologie, philosophie: Remarques sur la conception française de la culture générale* (Paris: Hermann & Cie, 1938), 37.

85. Paul Nizan, *Les chiens de garde* (1932; Paris: François Maspero, 1981), 97–98.

86. Bouglé, *Humanisme, sociologie, philosophie*, 33.

87. Ibid., 33–34.

88. Marcel Mauss, "La sociologie en France depuis 1914," in *La science française*, repr. in Mauss, *Oeuvres*, 3:438.

89. Interview with Marcel Mauss by Earle Edward Eubank, 144. In response to the same question, Bouglé named Bonnafous, Georges Davy, Georges Friedman, and Henri Lévy-Bruhl.

90. Raymond Aron, "La sociologie," in *Les sciences sociales en France: Enseignement et recherche* (Paris: Paul Hartman Éditeur, 1937), 42.

91. Mauss, "La sociologie en France depuis 1914," 447.

92. Célestin Bouglé, *Qu'est-ce que la sociologie?* (Paris: Alcan, 1907), 167.

93. "In other words, they [the Rockefeller Foundation] think it is more important to try to make people happy than to study the customs and languages of primitives, and presumably rather useless, people. To put it more officially, the Rockefeller Foundation has, as I understand it, declared its unwillingness to do anything further for anthropology. It is quite useless to turn to them for assistance" (letter from Edward Sapir to Marcel Mauss, New Haven, June 17, 1935).

94. Georges Davy, "La sociologie française de 1918 à 1925" (1926), in *Sociologues d'hier et d'aujourd'hui* (Paris: Félix Alcan, 1931), 1.

95. Letter from Maurice Halbwachs to Marcel Mauss, Strasbourg, February 27, 1928.

96. This idea was disputed by Philippe Besnard on the basis of a careful reading of Halbwachs's book (Philippe Besnard, *L'anomie* [Paris: PUF, 1987]).

97. In *Le péril juif* (Algiers: Éditions nouvelles africaines, 1934), Charles Hagel accused Durkheim of being "a public poisoner and propagator of putrescence" (quoted in Pierre Birnbaum, *"La France aux Français": Histoire des haines nationales* (Paris: Éditions du Seuil, 1993), 74.

98. Interview with Marcel Mauss by Earle Edward Eubank, 139.

99. Letter from Alfred Métraux to Marcel Mauss, Hawaii, March 17, 1936.

100. Letter from Alfred Métraux to Marcel Mauss, Hawaii, July 8, 1937.

101. Letter from Alfred Métraux to Marcel Mauss, Berkeley, February 3, 1938.

102. Robert H. Lowie, *The History of Ethnological Theory* (New York: Farrar & Rinehart, 1937), 197.

103. Letter from Marcel Mauss to Alfred Métraux, February 24, 1938.

104. "In this last task [to develop a real comparative sociology], I anticipate a good deal of success for I find the younger people very interested in what I put before them which is a sociology that, even if it differs a little from Durkheim's, differs hardly at all from yours, in method and spirit" (letter from Alfred Radcliffe-Brown to Marcel Mauss, New York, July 22, 1931).

105. Letter from Alfred Métraux to Marcel Mauss, Hawaii, March 17, 1936. Métraux, who attended a class of Radcliffe-Brown's on "sociology as science," said he was surprised "to find many ideas dear to you coming from his mouth."

106. Letter of recommendation in support of Alfred Radcliffe-Brown, candidate for the chair of social anthropology at Oxford University, September 22, 1936. Mauss also agreed to send a "testimonial" for E. E. Evans-Pritchard (to whom Malinowski and Seligman had introduced him after the war), whose publications he appreciated "to a very high degree" (letter of recommendation from Marcel Mauss in support of E. E. Evans-Pritchard, November 13, 1936). Mauss did not conceal his preference: "Of them all, it is certainly Brown I would most like to see in the position" (letter from Marcel Mauss to Charles G. Seligman, August 20, 1936).

107. Letter of recommendation from Marcel Mauss in support of E. E. Evans-Pritchard, November 13, 1936.

108. "We are ancient and eat very little; what we like best is a vegetable soup, a legume (not tomato) + some fruit. We take no wine, no beer, only water" (letter from Lilly Frazer to Marcel Mauss, December 13, 1930).

109. Letter from Bronislaw Malinowski to Marcel Mauss, January 1930.

110. "I am aware of Malinowski's despotism," Mauss would confide to Radcliffe-Brown. "The Rockefeller Foundation's weakness for him is probably the reason for his success. This weakness, attributable to the age and elegance of other Englishmen, those from London and those from Cambridge and Oxford, leaves him a clear field in England, but you can be quite sure that even his young protégés judge him rightly. Such monarchies don't last. His big book on magic and agriculture will surely be a very good exposition of the facts. That's what he excels at. And the Rockefeller grants given to a whole army of ghostwriters he had at his disposal will certainly allow him to do something complete. It's just that next to that, there will be a very poor theory about the magical nature of that essential thing. In the end, he'll write a big book on the functional theory of society and family organization. Here his theoretical weakness and total lack of erudition will be even more obvious" (letter from Marcel Mauss to Alfred Radcliffe-Brown, January 2, 1935).

111. Charles A. Allwood, Duke University; Edward Sapir, Robert Faris, Ernest Burgess, and William F. Ogburn, University of Chicago.

112. Becker, a professor of sociology at Smith College in Northampton, Massachusetts, received a one-year grant from the Social Science Research Council. He wanted to familiarize himself with "the position of Durkheim's school on questions regarding his general program" (in particular, the sociology of cognition) and hoped to have the chance to consult Mauss (letter from Howard Becker to Marcel Mauss, Northampton, April 4, 1934).

113. Letter from Marcel Mauss to Edwin R. R. Seligman, January 24, 1928.

114. Marcel Mauss, "Henri Hubert, 1872–1927," *Encyclopedia of the Social Sciences*, vols. 7–8 (1932): 527.

115. Lévy-Bruhl, "France, Belgium, and Romantic Switzerland," 251.

116. Stefan Czarnowski, "Biens masculins et féminins" (1929); Paul Fauconnet, "L'enseignement de la sociologie" (1931); Marc Bloch, "Les régimes agraires" (1932); René Maunier, "Les peoples mixtes" (1932); Paul Fauconnet, "L'enseignement de la sociologie dans les écoles normales primaires" (1933); Marcel Granet, "La droite et la gauche en Chine" (1933); François Simiand, "La monnaie, réalité sociale" (1934); Henri Lévy-Bruhl, "L'ancien droit romain" (1935).

117. Letter from Célestin Bouglé to Marcel Mauss, March 13, 1930.

118. Letter from M. Schneider to Marcel Mauss, May 13, 1931.

119. Letter from Maurice Halbwachs to Marcel Mauss, Chicago, November 24, 1931.

120. Letter from Paul Fauconnet to Marcel Mauss, December 19, 1931.

121. Letter from Célestin Bouglé to Marcel Mauss, February 1, 1933.

122. André Philip, "Une vue d'ensemble de l'évolution d'une société contemporaine," *Annales Sociologiques*, ser. A, general sociology, installment 1 (1934). At the time, Philip, a professor at the law school in Lyons, was interested in Henri de Man's notions of central planning.

123. In a letter to Mauss, Marc Bloch explained the objectives of his journal: "We don't just want a little 'erudite' journal, in the petty sense of that word. We want it to be serious, that goes without saying, free of all journalism, but with a very broad field, the past as a whole (primitive peoples included) and the present as a whole, and without a narrow conception of the words 'economic and social.' … We will do everything possible to make *Annales* of some service to these 'human' studies, for which *Année Sociologique* has already done so much" (letter from Marc Bloch to Marcel Mauss, January 18, 1929).

124. Letter from Célestin Bouglé to Marcel Mauss, December 23, 1933.

125. Letter from Maurice Halbwachs to Marcel Mauss, Strasbourg, November 17, 1934.

126. Nicolas Bavarez, *Raymond Aron, un moraliste au temps des idéologies* (Paris: Flammarion, 1993), 24.

127. Raymond Aron, *Mémoires: Cinquante ans de réflexion politique* (Paris: Julliard, 1993), 69.

128. "Avertissement," *Annales Sociologiques*, ser. A, general sociology, installment 1 (1934): vi.

129. Mauss, "La sociologie en France depuis 1914," 3:438.

130. Letter from Pierre Marcel (Librairie Alcan) to Paul Fauconnet, January 22, 1937.

131. Series D, economic sociology, installment 1: François Simiand, "La monnaie, réalité sociale"; Georges Lutfalla, "Essai critique sur la détermination statistique des courbes d'offre et de demande" (1934). Series E, social morphology, language, technology, aesthetics, installment 1: Maurice Halbwachs, "La nuptialité en France" (1935). Series C, legal and moral sociology, installment 1: Alfred Bayet, "Morale bergsonienne et sociologie"; Henri Lévy-Bruhl, "Une énigme de l'ancien droit romain" (1935).

132. Marcel Mauss, "In Memoriam: Antoine Meillet (1866–1936)," *Annales Sociologiques*, ser. 3, installment 2 (1937), in Mauss, *Oeuvres*, 3:548–55.

133. Letter from Maurice Halbwachs to Marcel Mauss, Strasbourg, November 17, 1934.

134. Letter from Maurice Halbwachs to Marcel Mauss, Haute-Savoie, September 11, 1936.

135. Halbwachs had been in Strasbourg since 1919, and ultimately had hopes of pursuing his career in Paris. In 1935, when Bouglé was named director of the École Normale Supérieure, Halbwachs was appointed *chargé de cours* in the history of social economics to replace Bouglé. Two years later, Halbwachs was named to a new chair in scientific methodology and logic. His position in Strasbourg was filled by Georges Gurvitch, a Russian philosopher who had been associated with the Durkheimians for a few years. Mauss supported Gurvitch's candidacy to replace Halbwachs: "Mr. Gurvitch is a very distinguished scholar. He has published interesting studies in moral and legal philosophy. . . . He has moved closer and closer to our methods and . . . has increasingly become the sociologist he was implicitly" (letter from Marcel Mauss to "Monsieur Le Doyen," July 2, 1935). Gurvitch's *Essais sur la sociologie* (1938) was dedicated to Mauss.

136. Letter from Marcel Mauss to Miss Rosenfels, January 2, 1935.

137. Letter from Edward Sapir to Marcel Mauss, New Haven, May 20, 1935. Sapir considered Métraux "the most brilliant member of his seminar."

138. For example, a philosophy student named Madeleine Francès was awarded a grant from the Rockefeller Foundation to conduct research on liberalism in Holland and to prepare a thesis on Spinoza's political thought, to be directed by Léon Brunschvicg. In the introduction to her book, she thanked Mauss, with whom she had long kept in touch. Madeleine Francès, *Spinoza dans les pays néerlandais de la seconde moitié du XVIIe siècle* (Paris: Alcan, 1937), vii.

139. In 1934 Radcliffe-Brown was at the University of Chicago and hoped "to be back in Europe soon," but, he lamented, "Malinowski seems to want to take charge of anthropology in England and to not want any competitors" (letter from Alfred R. Radcliffe-Brown to Marcel Mauss, Chicago, December 17, 1934). Two years later, in autumn 1936, Radcliffe-Brown found himself competing with Hoccart and Evans-Pritchard for the chair of social anthropology at Oxford. Mauss was "in an awkward position" because he was approached for recommendations by all three candidates. See note 106 above.

140. Letter from Arnold Van Gennep to Marcel Mauss, Bourg-la-Reine, June 7, 1932. Throughout his life, Van Gennep maintained total independence from the French university system. He held the following positions: director of translations in the Office des Renseignements Agricoles (Office of information on agriculture) at the Ministry of Agriculture from 1901 to 1908, then at the Ministry of Foreign Affairs from 1915 to 1922; professor of ethnography at the Université de Neuchâtel in Switzerland from 1912 to 1915. After again becoming an independent researcher, Van Gennep earned his living by contributing to various journals, giving lectures, and doing translation work (Nicole Belmont, *Arnold Van Gennep, créateur de l'ethnologie française* [Paris: Payot, 1974]).

141. Letter from Danielle Lévi to Marcel Mauss, November 15 [1917].

142. Letter from Henri Hubert to Marcel Mauss, October 17, 1921.

143. Letter from Rosine Mauss to Henri Hubert, January 16, 1919.

144. Letter from M. [Marthe Dupret] to Marcel Mauss, October 20, 1924 (Bibliothèque du Musée de l'Homme).

145. Interview with Marcel Mauss by Earle Edward Eubank, 141. What struck Eubank during his visit was the large number of books in every room of the apartment: "Books, papers; magazines, and books, books, books,—on chairs, tables, and overflowing onto the floor" (ibid.). The American sociologist described Mauss as follows: "A man of middle height, stockily built, and with a shaggy, grizzled, Waltwhitmanesque beard and shock of hair" (ibid.).

146. Letter from Lucien Lévy-Bruhl to Marcel Mauss, August 20, 1934.

147. Letter from Paul Fauconnet to Marcel Mauss, September 29, 1934.

148. Letter from Georges Bourgin to Marcel Mauss, February 3, 1935.

149. Letter from Jeanne Cuisinier to Marcel Mauss, August 9, 1934.

150. Letter from Marcel Mauss to an unidentified correspondent, November 30, 1934.

151. Letter from Marcel Mauss to Charles G. Seligman, November 13, 1935.

152. Letter from Charles G. Seligman to Marcel Mauss, Oxford, February 17, 1937.

153. Letter from Maurice Halbwachs to Marcel Mauss, May 1, 1935.

154. Maurice Halbwachs, "La méthodologie de François Simiand: Un empirisme rationaliste," *Revue Philosophique* 121, nos. 5–6 (May–June 1936): 282.

155. Marcel Mauss, "François Simiand," *Populaire* (April 1935): 4.

156. Marcel Mauss, "Sylvain Lévi" (1935), in Mauss, *Oeuvres*, 3:543.

157. Mauss, "In Memoriam: Antoine Meillet," 3:548.

158. Letter from Marcel Mauss to Marc Bloch, February 20, 1936.

CHAPTER 17
ENOUGH TO MAKE YOU DESPAIR OF POLITICS

1. Marcel Mauss, "La Chambre future: Dialogue sur un proche avenir," *Vie Socialiste*, April 30, 1932, 6.

2. Marcel Déat, *Mémoires politiques* (Paris: Denoël, 1989), 141.

3. Marcel Déat dedicated his book as follows: "To Marcel Mauss, this essay, where Durkheim and Marx stand side by side" (Bibliothèque du Musée de l'Homme, Paris).

4. Déat, *Mémoires politiques*, 278.

5. Letter from Marcel Mauss to "Mon cher ami," November 6, 1933.

6. Letter from Pierre Renaudel to Marcel Mauss, November 13, 1933.

7. Letter from Marcel Mauss to "Mon cher ami" [Léon Blum], May 5, 1936.

8. Letter from Marcel Mauss to Pierre Renaudel, December 6, 1933.

9. Letter from Pierre Renaudel to Marcel Mauss, December 3, 1933.

10. Letter from Marcel Mauss to Marcel Déat, May 27, 1935.

11. Letter from Marcel Mauss to M. Dunois, April 30, 1935.

12. Letter from Marcel Mauss to Marcel Déat, September 18, 1935.

13. Serge Berstein, *La France des années 30* (Paris: Armand Colin, 1993), 92.

14. Raymond Aron, "La sociologie," in *Les sciences sociales en France: Enseignement et recherche* (Paris: Paul Hartman Éditeur, 1937), 42. After returning from Germany, Aron had published a little book titled *La sociologie allemande contemporaine* (Paris: Alcan, 1935; Contemporary German sociology), half of which was devoted to Max Weber.

15. In the words of Célestin Bouglé, in his correspondence with the heads of the foundation (Brigitte Mazon, "La fondation Rockefeller et les sciences sociales en France, 1925–1940," *Revue Française de Sociologie* 26, no. 2 [April–June 1985]: 331).

16. Maurice Halbwachs, *L'évolution des besoins dans la classe ouvrière* (Paris: Alcan, 1933).

17. Robert Marjolin, *L'évolution du syndicalisme aux États-Unis: De Washington à Roosevelt* (Paris: Alcan, 1936).

18. The thesis was published in 1941 by Alcan and PUF. A few years earlier, Robert Marjolin had published "Rationalité et irrationalité dans les mouvements économiques de longue durée," *Annales Sociologiques*, ser. D (economic sociology), installment 3 (1938).

19. Marcel Mauss, "François Simiand," *Populaire*, April 18, 1935, 2.

20. Raymond Aron, *De la condition historique du sociologue* (Paris: Gallimard, 1971), 8.

21. Marcel Mauss, "Les faits," typewritten text, n.d., 1–2 (Hubert-Mauss collection, Archives of the Collège de France).

22. Marcel Mauss, "The Problem of Nationality," *Proceedings of the Aristotelian Society* (1920), in Mauss, *Oeuvres*, vol. 1 (Paris: Éditions de Minuit, 1968), vols. 2 and 3 (1969), 3:628.

23. Letter from Marcel Mauss to Charles Le Coeur, June 21, 1938.

24. In his courses, Durkheim considered socialist doctrines social facts (see Durkheim, *Le socialisme*).

25. Mauss, "Les idées socialistes. Le principe de la nationalisation," typewritten text, n.d., 18 (Hubert-Mauss collection, Archives of the Collège de France), in Mauss, *Écrits politiques*, ed. Marcel Fournier (Paris: Fayard, 1998), 18.

26. Ibid., 15.

27. Ibid., 11.

28. Letter from Maurice Halbwachs to Marcel Mauss, Strasbourg, July 9, 1934. Like Halbwachs, Mauss probably put money in the Banque des Coopératives, a "movement that offered so much hope."

29. Marcel Mauss, "Les faits: Le mouvement économique d'en bas," typewritten text, n.d. [1920], 93 (Hubert-Mauss collection, Archives of the Collège de France).

30. Ibid., 72.

31. Ibid., 88.

32. Letter from Marcel Mauss to "Mon cher ami," November 6, 1933.

33. Letter from Marcel Mauss to "Mon Cher ami," February 11, 1935.

34. Circular titled "Aux travailleurs" (To the workers) and dated March 5, 1934. The request for members was signed by three of those in the provisional bureau: Alain, Paul Langevin, and Paul Rivet.

35. Letter from Paul Rivet to Marcel Mauss, December 22, 1934.

36. Jean-François Sirinelli, *Intellectuels et passions françaises: Manifestes et pétitions au XXe siècle* (Paris: Fayard, 1990), 90.

37. Marcel Mauss, "Déclaration pour le Comité de vigilance des intellectuels antifascistes," typewritten text (1 p.) with letter to "Mon cher camarade" [Paul Rivet], dated March 12, 1936 (Hubert-Mauss collection, Archives of the Collège de France).

38. Letter from Léon Blum to Marcel Mauss, February [1936].

39. Letter from Marcel Mauss to "Mon cher ami" [Léon Blum], May 5, 1936.

40. Letter from Marcel Mauss to Georges Gurvitch, May 15, 1936.

41. Letter from Marcel Mauss to Emmanuel [Lévy], June 25, 1936.

42. Circular signed by Marcel Mauss, June 22, 1936.

43. Letter from Marcel Mauss to Emmanuel [Lévy], June 25, 1936.

44. Letter from Marcel Mauss to Élie Halévy (1936), in Élie Halévy, L'ère des tyrannies (Paris: Gallimard, 1938), 230–31.

CHAPTER 18
THE TIME OF MYTHS

1. Michel Leiris, *Journal, 1922–1989*, edited and annotated by Jean Jamin (Paris: Gallimard, 1992), 296.

2. Letter from Ignace Meyerson to Marcel Mauss, September 12, 1936.

3. Letter from A. S. Szczupac to Marcel Mauss, November 9, 1936.

4. Letter from Marcel Mauss to "Mon cher ami," n.d.

5. Jean-François Sirinelli, *Génération intellectuelle*: *Khâgneux et Normaliens dans l'entre-deux-guerres* (Paris: Fayard, 1988), 459.

6. Henri Wallon (1879–1962) had a doctorate in medicine and another in letters. He came to the Collège de France in 1937, two years after the chair in child psychology and education was created. A Dreyfusard and socialist, Wallon was a communist sympathizer at the time. In 1933 he was named president of the scientific commission of Cercle de la Russie Neuve (Club of the new Russia). His course at the Collège was suppressed by the Vichy government from 1941 to 1944. Wallon was an active member of the Resistance at the time.

7. Letter from Paul Langevin to "Mon cher confrère" [Marcel Mauss], July 7, 1938.

8. Letter from M. Mauss to Paul Langevin, July 12, 1938.

9. Letter from Jacques Vernant to "Monsieur" [Marcel Mauss], February 1938. Jacques Vernant, born in 1912, was Jean-Pierre Vernant's elder brother.

10. Letter from Marcel Mauss to Bernard Maupoil, April 11, 1938.

11. Letter from Marcel Mauss to Edgar Milhaud, November 7, 1938.

12. Marcel Déat, *Mémoires politiques* (Paris: Denoël, 1989), 618.

13. Ibid., 672.

14. Marcel Déat, *Jeunesse et Révolution* (Paris: Jeunesses nationales populaires, 1942), 16. At issue was the text of a lecture Déat delivered in April 1942 to the École des Cadres de la Jeunesse Nationale Populaire (School of management for the nation's youth).

15. Ibid., 17.

16. Letter from Marcel Mauss to "Mon cher ami" [Élie Halévy], February 18, 1935.

17. Marcel Mauss, introduction to Émile Durkheim, "Morale civique et professionnelle," (1937), in Mauss, *Oeuvres*, vol. 1 (Paris: Éditions de Minuit, 1968), vols. 2 and 3 (1969), 3:504.

18. Letter from Mauss in Élie Halévy, *L'ère des tyrannies* (Paris: Gallimard, 1938), 230–31.

19. Célestin Bouglé, *Humanisme, sociologie, philosophie: Remarques sur la conception française de la culture générale* (Paris: Hermann & Cie., 1938), 38.

20. Ibid., 34.

21. Svend Ranulf, "Methods of Sociology, with an Essay: Remarks for the Epistemology of Sociology," *Acta Jutlandica, Aarskrift for Aarhus Universitet* 27, no. 1 (1955): 114.

22. Letter from Svend Ranulf to Marcel Mauss, November 6, 1936. The letter from Mauss was reproduced by Ranulf (1894–1954) in "Scholarly Forerunners of Fascism," *Ethics* 50 (1939): 32. [Translation of Mauss's letter is my own.—Trans.]

23. Letter from Marcel Mauss to "Monsieur le Président," July 18, 1938. In that letter, Mauss was protesting Japanese aggression. On the previous June 3, more than two thousand Japanese soldiers had landed on the southern coast of China.

24. Letter from Marcel Mauss to Svend Ranulf, May 8, 1939. This part of Mauss's letter was published in Ranulf's "Scholarly Forerunners of Fascism."

25. Letter from Marcel Mauss to Charles Le Coeur, June 21, 1938.

26. Marcel Mauss, "Alexandre Moret (1868–1938)," *Annuaire de l'École Pratique des Hautes Études, Section des Sciences Religieuses* (1938), repr. in Mauss, *Oeuvres*, 3:560.

27. Letter from Marcel Mauss to "Mon cher ami," December 11, 1937.

28. Letter from Marcel Mauss to "Mon cher beau-frère," April 25, 193[8].

29. Letter from Howard Becker to Marcel Mauss, March 6, 1939.

30. Letter from Marcel Mauss to Ignace Meyerson, September 14, 1937 (Ignace Meyerson collection).

31. Letter from Marcel Mauss to Charles Le Coeur, June 21, 1938.

32. Letter from Maurice Leenhardt to Marcel Mauss, May 18, 1936.

33. James Clifford, *Person and Myth: Maurice Leenhardt in the Melanesian World* (Berkeley: University of California Press, 1982), 159–60.

34. Marcel Mauss, "L'ethnographie en France et à l'étranger," *Revue de Paris* (1913), repr. in Mauss, *Oeuvres*, 3:410.

35. Lucien Lévy-Bruhl, "Rapport sur l'Institut d'ethnologie, année scolaire 1937–1938," *Annales de l'Université de Paris* (May–June 1939): 262.

36. For example, Maurice Leenhardt, *Vocabulaire et grammaire de la langue houlailou* (1935); Jeanne Cuisinier, *Danses magiques de Kelantan* (1936); Jacques Soustelle, *La famille Otomi-Pame du Mexique* (1937); Georges Dumézil, *Contes* (1937); Marcel Griaule, *Masques Dogon* (1938).

37. Letter from Marcel Mauss to Charles Le Coeur, June 21, 1938.

38. These young French scientists were Marcel Griaule, Anatole Lewitzky, Georges-Henri Rivière, Thérèse Rivière, André Schaeffner, Jacques Soustelle, André Varagnac, and Paul-Émile Victor.

39. Curt Sacs, *Les instruments de musique de Madagascar* (Paris: "Travaux et mémoires" de l'Institut d'Ethnologie, 1938), 28:viii.

40. Letter from Marcel Mauss to Olaf Jansé, May 10, 1938.

41. On that incident, see Didier Éribon, *Faut-il brûler Dumézil?* (Paris: Flammarion, 1992), 176–83.

42. Louis-Ferdinand Céline, *L'école des cadavres* (Paris: Denoël, 1938), 233.

43. Letter from Marcel Mauss to "Mon cher beau-frère," April 25, 1938.

44. Marcel Mauss, "Note no. 1, Programme d'extension et développment de la recherche," February 14, 1938, 1 (Hubert-Mauss collection, Archives of the Collège de France). This was the first in a series of four short notes, probably intended for the minister.

45. Marcel Mauss, "Note no. 4, Statut des chercheurs," February 14, 1938, 1 (Hubert-Mauss collection, Archives of the Collège de France).

46. Marcel Mauss, "Relations of Religion and Sociological Aspects of Ritual" (summary of an English paper), International Congress of the Anthropological and Ethnological Sciences, London, 1934, in Mauss, *Oeuvres*, 1:557.

47. Marcel Mauss, comments following a paper by Paul Mus, "La mythologie primitive et la pensée de l'Inde," *Bulletin de la Société Française de Philosophie* (1937), repr. in Mauss, *Oeuvres*, 2:156.

48. Marcel Mauss, "Le macrocosme et le microcosme," summary of a paper delivered to the Institut Français d'Anthropologie, *Anthropologie* 47 (1937): 686, in Mauss, *Oeuvres*, 2:160–61.

49. Mauss, comments following Mus, "La mythologie primitive et la pensée de l'Inde," 156.

50. Ibid., 157.

51. Letter from Maurice Leenhardt to Marcel Mauss, Nouméa, New Caledonia, September 5, 1938.

52. Roger Caillois, *Rencontres* (Paris: PUF, 1978), 27.

53. Marcel Mauss, "Th. Ribot et les sociologues," in *Centenaire de Théodule Ribot. Jubilé de la psychologique scientifique française* (Agen: Imprimerie moderne, 1939), repr. in Mauss, *Oeuvres*, 3:565–67.

54. Marcel Mauss, "Paul Fauconnet" (obituary), n.d. [1938], 6 (Hubert-Mauss collection, Achives of the Collège de France).

55. Letter from Maurice Leenhardt to Marcel Mauss, New Caledonia, February 17, 1937.

56. Marcel Mauss, "Une catégorie de l'esprit humain: La notion de personne," *Journal of the Royal Anthropological Institute (London)* 68 (1938), repr. in Mauss, *Sociologie et anthropologie*, 3rd ed. (Paris: PUF, 1966), 331–61.

57. Marcel Mauss, comments following a paper by Lucien Lévy-Bruhl, "L'âme primitive" (1929), repr. in Mauss, *Oeuvres*, 2:132.

58. Mauss, "Une catégorie de l'esprit humain," 336.

59. Ibid., 347.

60. Ibid., 361.

61. Ibid., 362.

62. Ibid., 333.

63. Letter from Paul Fauconnet to Marcel Mauss, August 8, 1938.

64. Marcel Mauss, "Fait social et formation du caractère," paper delivered at the International Congress of Anthropological and Ethnological Sciences, Copenhagen, 1938, 4 (manuscript, Hubert-Mauss collection, Archives of the Collège de France).

65. Ibid., 1.

66. Marcel Mauss, "Trois observations sur la sociologie de l'enfance," n.d. [1937], 4 (Hubert-Mauss collection, Archives of the Collège de France, 7). This is a short typewritten text that was to be presented to a congress on the sociology of childhood in July 1937. Because of his poor health and his many obligations, Mauss could not be present and sent a short text, apologizing for its "relative incompetence" (letter from Marcel Mauss to "Monsieur le Président," July 6, 1937). Henri Wallon (1879–1962), a colleague of Mauss's at the Collège de France, was interested in childhood. He held the chair in child psychology and education (created in 1935) and was the author of *Les origines du caractère chez l'enfant: Les préludes du sentiment de person-nalité* (1934). In addition, Ignace Meyerson, a friend of Mauss's, worked on "graphic signs and the child" in the early 1920s, and in 1926 composed an appendix for Jean Piaget's *La représentation du monde chez l'enfant*.

67. Mauss, "Fait social et formation du caractère," 7.

68. Interview with Jacques Soustelle, Paris, November 6, 1989.

69. Mauss, "Une catégorie de l'esprit humain," 361.

70. The "secretary" of the college was to have been Patrick Waldberg, as Waldberg himself indicates on the cover of his *Chemins du surréalisme* (Brussels: Éditions de la Connaissance, 1965). Waldberg also took Mauss's courses at the Institut d'Ethnologie. The sessions at the Collège de Sociologie were followed by a large and varied group that included Alexandre Kojève, Pierre Klossowski, Jules Monnerot, Jean Paulhan, Jean Wahl, and occasionally Julien Benda, Walter Benjamin, and Pierre Drieu La Rochelle.

71. Alfred Métraux, "Rencontre avec les ethnologues," Critique 19, no. 195 (September 1963): 684.

72. "Note sur la fondation d'un Collège de sociologie" (1937), in Denis Hollier, *Le Collège de sociologie* (Paris: Idées Gallimard, 1979), 24 (new edition forthcoming).

73. Laurent Jenny, ed., *Roger Caillois, la pensée aventurée* (Paris: Belin, 1992); Odile Felgine, *Roger Caillois* (Paris: Stock, 1994).

74. Caillois, *Rencontres*, 27.

75. Letter from Marcel Mauss to Roger Caillois, June 22, 1938. See Marcel Fournier, "Marcel Mauss et Heidegger," *Actes de la Recherche en Sciences Sociales* 84 (September 1990): 87.

76. Letter from Michel Leiris to Georges Bataille, July 3, 1939, in Hollier, *Le Collège de sociologie*, 548.

77. See Pierre Missac, "Réponse à une enquête de Jacques Bénet," *Cahiers du Sud* 216 (May 1939), quoted by Denis Hollier, "Mimétisme et castration, 1937," in Jenny, ed., *Roger Caillois, la pensée aventurée*, 73.

78. Roger Caillois, "Seres del anochecer," *Sur* (December 1940), in Hollier, *Le Collège de sociologie*, 575.

79. Henri Hubert, *Les Germains* (Paris: Albin Michel, 1952), 75. Hubert was always opposed to anthropo-sociological studies, and particularly those done by Vacher de Lapouge on the Aryans, which he considered "pseudo-science."

80. Ivan Strenski, "Henri Hubert, Racial Science and Political Myth," *Journal of the History of Behavioral Sciences* 21, nos. 2–3 (1987): 353–76.

81. Hubert, *Les Celtes et l'expansion celtique jusqu'à l'époque de la Tène* (1932; Paris: Albin Michel, 1974), 29.

82. Henri Berr, "Avant-propos," in Hubert, *Les Germains*, ix.

83. Antoine Meillet, *Introduction à l'étude comparative des langues indo-européennes* (1908; Paris: Hachette, 1934). Meillet, a specialist in Indo-European languages (a term he found "rather awkward") refused to speak of "Aryan peoples." "From the existence of 'Aryan languages,'" he explained, "some conclude that 'Aryan people' exist."

84. Émile Benveniste (1902–1976), an *agrégé* in grammar and *directeur d'études* at the École Pratique des Hautes Études beginning in 1927, was appointed to the chair in comparative grammar at the Collège de France in 1937.

85. Marcel Mauss, "Différences entre les migrations des Germains et des Celtes," *Revue du Synthèse*, February 17, 1939, 23–34, repr. in Mauss, *Oeuvres*, 2:573.

86. Ibid., 571.

87. Letter from Marcel Mauss to Henri Hubert, April 9, 1924.

88. Marcel Mauss, review of Georges Dumézil, *Le festin d'immortalité*, *Année Sociologique*, n.s., 1 (1925), repr. in Mauss, *Oeuvres* 2:315–16.

89. On these questions, see Éribon, *Faut-il brûler Dumézil?* 140.

90. Marcel Mauss, "Note," November 11, 1941. This note is attached to a letter Mauss sent to Jérôme Carcopino.

91. Daniel Lindenberg, *Les années souterraines, 1937–1947* (Paris: La Découverte, 1990), 79; Carlo Ginsburg, "Mythologie germanique et nazisme: Sur un ancien livre de Georges Dumézil" (1984), in *Mythes, emblèmes, traces* (Paris: Flammarion, 1989).

92. Marcel Mauss, "Conceptions qui ont précédé la notion de matière," *Centre International de Synthèse*, XIe Semaine Internationale de Synthèse (1939), in Mauss, *Oeuvres*, 3:166.

93. Ibid., 161.

94. See Marcel Fournier, "Durkheim et la sociologie de la connaissance scientifique," *Sociologie et Sociétés* 14, no. 2 (October 1982): 53–67.

95. Mauss, "Conceptions qui ont précédé la notion de matière," 164.

96. Ibid.

97. Henri Berr, comments following Mauss's "Conceptions qui ont précédé la notion de matière," repr. in Mauss, *Oeuvres*, 2:167.

98. Mauss, "Conceptions qui ont précédé la notion de matière," 165.

99. Léon Blum, in *Populaire*, September 20, 1938, quoted in Jacques Bouillon and Geneviève Vallette, *Munich, 1938* (Paris: Armand Colin, 1986), 131.

100. Letter from Marcel Déat to Marcel Mauss, April 4, 1939.

101. Letter from Marcel Mauss to Marcel Déat, April 21, 1939.

102. See A. Bergounioux, "Le néo-socialisme, Marcel Déat: Réformisme traditionnel ou esprit des années trente," *Revue Historique* (October–December 1978): 389–412. This thesis was called into question by Zeev Sternhell, *Ni droite ni gauche: L'idéologie fasciste en France* (Paris: Éditions du Seuil, 1983).

103. Déat, *Mémoires politiques*, 467.

104. Letter from Marcel Mauss to "Mon cher ami," April 17, 1939.

EPILOGUE

1. Letter from Maurice Halbwachs to Marcel Mauss, September 30, 1939.

2. Letter from Maurice Leenhardt to Marcel Mauss, New Caledonia, February 17, 1939.

3. Postcard from Michel Leiris to Marcel Mauss, Algeria, October 11, 1939.

4. Letter from Marcel Mauss to Henri-Charles Puech, November 13, 1939.

5. Letter from Marcel Mauss to Henri-Charles Puech, October 16, 1939.

6. Letter from Marcel Mauss to "Mon cher ami," November 24, 1939.

7. Marcel Mauss, "Lucien Lévy-Bruhl," *Populaire*, March 16, 1939, 4.

8. Marcel Mauss, "Lucien Lévy-Bruhl (1857–1939)," *Annales de l'Université de Paris* 14 (1939), in Mauss, *Oeuvres*, vol. 1 (Paris: Éditions de Minuit, 1968), vols. 2 and 3 (1969), 3:565. Mauss also published a third obituary notice of Lucien Lévy-Bruhl in *Revue Philosophique* 127 (1939): 251–53.

9. Lucien Lévy-Bruhl's *Carnets* would be published in 1949 by PUF, with a long preface by Maurice Leenhardt.

10. Halbwachs, "Célestin Bouglé sociologue," *Revue de Métaphysique et de Morale*, year 48, no.1 (January 1941): 47.

11. Letter from Charles G. Seligman to Marcel Mauss, Oxford, December 9, 1939.

12. Letter from Marcel Mauss to "Mon cher ami," November 13, 1939.

13. Letter from Marcel Mauss to "Mon cher ami," April 17, 1939.

14. Letter from Marcel Mauss to "Mon cher ami," November 24, 1939.

15. Letter from Marcel Mauss to Camille, November 14, 1939.

16. Letter from Marcel Mauss to "Mon cher ami," November 27, 1939. The Australians in question were those he had fought with during World War I.

17. Letter from Marcel Mauss to "Cher ami," November [April] 1940.

18. Letter from Marcel Mauss to "Cher ami," November [April] 1940.

19. Letter from Marcel Mauss to "Mon cher ami," April 2, 1940.

20. Letter from Marcel Mauss to Charles G. Seligman, April 16, 1940.

21. Letter from Marcel Mauss to "Mon cher beau-frère," May 21, 1940.

22. Ibid.

23. Letter from Marcel Mauss to Charles G. Seligman and Brenda Seligman, May 7, 1940.

24. Letter from Marcel Mauss to Charles G. Seligman, April 16, 1940.

25. Letter from Marcel Mauss to "Monsieur le ministre," November 7, 1938.

26. Herman Weil died in autumn 1941 on his way to the United States. Weil, one of Fossey's collaborators and a specialist in religious history, the general history of law, and the history of Semitic law, had become a naturalized French citizen in 1938.

27. Letter from Marcel Mauss to "Monsieur le minister," April 2, 1940.

28. Letter from Marcel Mauss to "Mon cher Raymond" [Aron], May 7, 1940.

29. Letter from the mayor of the fourteenth arrondissement to Marcel Mauss, June 11, 1940.

30. Letter from Marcel Mauss to Charles G. Seligman and Brenda Seligman, May 7, 1940.

31. Letter from Lucien Febvre to Edmond Faral, Saint-Amour [Jura], July 8, 1940. Edmond Faral was the director of the Collège de France.

32. Alfred Sauvy, *La vie économique des Français de 1939 à 1945* (Paris: Flammarion, 1978), 122–23.

33. Letter from Marcel Mauss to "Monsieur le maire," October 22, 1940.

34. Letter from Marcel Mauss to "Monsieur le ministre," September 26, 1940.

35. Minutes of the committee meeting of the fifth section (religious science, École Pratique des Hautes Études, notebook 3, p. 943).

36. Letter from Marcel Mauss to Georges Davy, December 17, 1940.

37. Letter from Marcel Mauss to "Mon cher Hubert" (Schwab), December 3, 1940.

38. Robert Paxton, *Vichy France, Old Guard and New Order, 1940–1944* (New York: Knopf, 1972), 171.

39. This is an undated handwritten note (CXII, Mauss 27A, Archives of the Collège de France).

40. As attested in the letter Albert Bayet wrote to Marcel Mauss in early 1938 to thank him for renewing his membership in the union.

41. Poirier, "Marcel Mauss et l'élaboration de la science ethnologique," *Journal de la Société des Océanistes* 4, no. 6 (December 1950): 212.

42. Marcel Mauss, review of J. G. Frazer, "The Origin of Circumcision," *Année Sociologique* (1906), in Mauss, *Oeuvres*, 1:142.

43. Marcel Mauss, "Critique interne de la légende d'Abraham" (1926), in Mauss, *Oeuvres*, 2:532.

44. Marcel Mauss, "Sylvain Lévi" (1935), in Mauss, *Oeuvres*, 3:542.

45. Letter from Adolf Caspary to Marcel Mauss, September 29, 1939.

46. Letter from Marcel Mauss to Robert H. Lowie, November 1, 1940. Hubert Schwab had a *licence* in science and letters and had taken courses at the Institut d'Ethnologie and the École Pratique, section of religious science.

47. Letter from Marcel Mauss to Edgar Milhaud, November 7, 1938.

48. George Montandon, *L'ethnie française* (Paris: Payot, 1935), 139.

49. Georges Friedmann, *Fin du peuple juif?* (Paris: Gallimard, 1965), 7. When he was offered the chance "to plea for special treatment" so he could continue to practice his profession as a university professor, Friedmann (Gaston Fromentin) refused. In January 1941, he joined the movement Combat. Bloch was barred from the university, but was granted an exemption and continued to teach at the Université de Montpellier. Nevertheless, his refusal to accept the French defeat and his hostility to the Pétain regime would lead him to join the Mouvements Unis de Résistance (United resistance movements) in late 1942. Adam Rayski, *Le choix des Juifs sous Vichy* (Paris: La Découverte, 1992), 278–96.

50. Letter from Marcel Mauss to "Mon cher Hubert," December 3, 1940.

51. Agnes Humbert, *Notre guerre* (Paris: Éditions Émile-Paul Frères, 1946), 23.

52. Letter from Ignace Meyerson to Marcel Mauss, Toulouse, October 24, 1943.

53. See the motion Henri Lévy-Bruhl signed in May 1941 along with the other members of the consistory. Claude Singer, "L'engagement des intellectuels juifs face à Vichy," *Pardès* 16 (1992): 104.

54. Raymond Aron, *Mémoires: Cinquante ans de réflexion politique* (Paris: Julliard, 1993).

55. During his time in New York, Lévi-Strauss worked a great deal, publishing or arranging to publish some ten articles and writing a book on family and social life among the Nambikuara Indians and another on kinship systems. Speaking of the latter book, Lévi-Strauss recognized "The Gift" as his starting point and inspiration. Letter from Claude Lévi-Strauss to Marcel Mauss, New York, October 2, 1944.

56. See Carole Fink, *Marc Bloch: A Life in History* (New York: Cambridge University Press, 1989).

57. Letter from Marcel Mauss to Edmond Faral, March 30, 1941.

58. Letter from Marcel Mauss to "Monsieur le ministre," March 30, 1941.

59. Jérôme Carcopino's interest in the history of religion led him to participate regularly in the activities of the Société Ernest Renan; he became its president in 1932. There he had met Mauss, a member of the society's central committee, in 1935–1936.

60. Letter from Marcel Mauss to "Mon cher ministre," June 24, 1941.

61. Letter from Jérôme Carcopino to Marcel Mauss, June 27, 1941.

62. With the exception of Henri Wallon and Henri Focillon, who were both fired in July 1942 for antinational activity. Focillon, a specialist in medieval art history, went to New York, where he would serve as president of the École Libre des Hautes Études until his death in March 1943. Henri Wallon, a physician and professor of psychology, was a member of the governing committee of the Front National Universitaire under the pseudonym Adrien.

63. Maurice Halbwachs, "Déclaration d'état civil," June 3, 1944 (Archives of the Collège de France).

64. In January 1938, when Montandon was named a member of the Institut Français d'Anthropologie, his candidacy was presented by Paul Rivet and supported by Lucien Lévy-Bruhl and Mauss.

65. Pierre Birnbaum, "George Montandon: L'anthropologie vichyste au service du nazisme," in "*La France aux Français*": *Histoire des haines nationales* (Paris: Éditions du Seuil, 1993), 187ff. William Schneider, *Quality and Quantity: The Quest for Biological Regeneration in Twentieth Century France* (New York: Cambridge University Press, 1991).

66. Louis Marin, director of the École d'Anthropologie de Paris beginning in 1923, was also a politician. During the German invasion in spring 1940, he was a minister in Paul Reynaud's cabinet. *Revue Anthropologique*, which he directed, and the Société de Géographie Commerciale de Paris (Society of commercial geography of Paris), where he served as president, lent their support to the National Revolution, Pétain's collaborationist program under Nazi occupation. Nevertheless, Marin was fiercely anti-German and refused to vote for the armistice in 1940 or to grant full powers to Marshal Pétain. Threatened with arrest orders from the Gestapo, he left France for England on April 1, 1944 (Herman Lebovics, "Le conservatisme en anthropologie et la fin de la Troisième République," *Gradhiva* 4 [Summer 1988]: 3–17).

67. See Lindenberg, *Les années souterraines, 1937–1947* (Paris: La Découverte, 1990), 65–70; Christian Faure, *Le projet culturel de Vichy: Folklore et Révolution nationale, 1940–1944* (Lyons: Presses universitaires de Lyon, 1989).

68. Marcel Maget, "À propos du musée des Arts et Traditions populaires," *Genèse*, January 10, 1993, 95.

69. This was also the case for Bernard Maupoil (1906–1942), a former student at the Institut d'Ethnologie, who became an administrator of the colonies (Senegal, French Guinea, and Dahomey). Relieved of duty in 1942, he organized the resistance network Cahors-Asturies.

70. Martin Blumenson, *The Vildé Affair* (Boston: Houghton Mifflin, 1977), 23.

71. Germaine Tillion, "Première résistance en zone occupée," *Revue d'Histoire de la Seconde Guerre Mondiale* (1955): 11.

72. Michel Leiris, *Journal 1922–1989*, edited and annotated by Jean Jamin (Paris: Gallimard, 1992), 337.

73. Marcel Mauss, "Note sur Mme Merouchkowsky," n.d. [1941] (Hubert-Mauss collection, Archives of the Collège de France).

74. During the Occupation, Jérôme Carcopino, a professor of Roman history, was director of the École Normale Supérieure, then rector of the Université de Paris, and finally secretary of national education. Carcopino was well acquainted with Mauss and a few of his friends, including Bouglé and Halbwachs.

75. Letter from Marcel Mauss to "Cher monsieur," March 11, 1941.

76. Marcel Mauss, "Note sur M. Lewitzky," n.d. [March 1941] (Hubert-Mauss collection, Archives of the Collège de France).

77. "Le musée de l'Homme judéo-maçonnique," article published in *Pilori* on November 13, 1941, and signed by Jacques Ploncard, a former student at the Institut d'Ethnologie (Leiris, *Journal*, 346).

78. Jérôme Carcopino, *Souvenirs de sept ans, 1937–1944* (Paris: Flammarion, 1953). See above, note 74.

79. Letter from Marcel Mauss to Oleg Lewitzky, May 19, 1942.

80. Postcard from Marcel Mauss to Ignace Meyerson, February 3, 1941 (Ignace Meyerson collection).

81. Letter from Marcel Mauss to "Monsieur le ministre" [Jérôme Carcopino], November 11, 1941. Mauss attached a long note to that letter in which he praised his former student and colleague as "one of the most brilliant teachers [at the École Pratique]."

82. Letter from Marcel Mauss to "Mon cher Prache," May 5, 1942.

83. Postcard from Marcel Mauss to Ignace Meyerson, March 16, 1941 (Ignace Meyerson collection).

84. Letter from Marcel Mauss to Ignace Meyerson, July 27, 1941 (Ignace Meyerson collection).

85. Letter from Ignace Meyerson to Marcel Mauss, September 19, 1941.

86. Letter from Marcel Mauss to Ignace Meyerson, April 17, 1939.

87. Marcel Mauss, comments following Robert Marjolin, "Rationalité et irrationalité des mouvements économiques de longue durée," *Annales Sociologiques*, ser. D (economic sociology), installment 3 (1938), repr. in Mauss, *Oeuvres*, 3:249.

88. Marcel Mauss, "Conceptions qui ont précédé la notion de matière," *Centre International de Synthesè*, XIe Semaine Internationale de Synthèse (1939), repr. in Mauss, *Oeuvres*, 3:162.

89. Ibid., 254.

90. Letter from Marcel Mauss to Ignace Meyerson, July 6, 1941 (Ignace Meyerson collection).

91. Marcel Mauss, "Les techniques et la technologie," paper delivered at the Journée de Psychologie et d'Histoire du Travail et des Techniques (Toulouse, 1941), in Ignace Meyerson et al., *Le travail et les techniques*, special issue of *Journal de Psychologie* 41 (1948), in Mauss, *Oeuvres*, 3:255.

92. Ibid., 256.

93. Ibid.

94. For example, the French writer and painter Max Jacob, arrested in February 1944 in Saint-Benoît-sur-Loire, would die on March 5, 1944, at the Drancy holding camp in France.

95. Letter from Marcel Mauss to Ignace Meyerson, December 23, 1942 (Ignace Meyerson collection).

96. Letter from Marcel Mauss to Ignace Meyerson, June 4, 1943 (Ignace Meyerson collection).

97. Letter from Marcel Mauss to "Chère Mlle," May 5, 1942. Mauss complained he was "rather weak after a short but painful bout of dysentery" (letter from Marcel Mauss to "Cher Docteur," March 10, 1942).

98. Letter from Dr. Marc Sardou to Marcel Mauss, November 3, 1942.

99. Letter from Marcel Mauss to Ignace Meyerson, June 13, 1942 (Ignace Meyerson collection).

100. Letter from Marcel Mauss to Ignace Meyerson, August 22, 1942 (Ignace Meyerson collection).

101. Letter from Marcel Mauss to Ignace Meyerson, February 14, 1943 (Ignace Meyerson collection).

102. Letter from Charles Fossey to Marcel Mauss, Monte Carlo, September 13, 1943.

103. Letter from Charles Fossey to Marcel Mauss, January 13, 1943.

104. Letter from Marcel Mauss to Ignace Meyerson, June 4, 1943 (Ignace Meyerson collection).

105. Letter from Marcel Mauss to Ignace Meyerson, July 20, 1942 (Ignace Meyerson collection).

106. Letter from Marcel Mauss to Ignace Meyerson, June 4, 1943 (Ignace Meyerson collection).

107. Marcel Mauss, "Note sur les crises," 1, single-spaced typewritten text, written in 1942 or 1943.

108. Ibid.

109. Letter from Marcel Mauss to Ignace Meyerson, June 4, 1943 (Ignace Meyerson collection).

110. Letter from Marcel Mauss to Ignace Meyerson, March 18, 1943 (Ignace Meyerson collection).

111. According to Lévi-Strauss, this was in a note dated January 1944 (letter from Claude Lévi-Strauss to Marcel Mauss, New York, October 2, 1944).

112. Letter from Germaine Tillion to Marcel Mauss, September 1945.

113. Marcel Déat, Mémoires politiques (Paris: Denoël, 1989), 609.

114. Marcel Déat, "Vers un État juif," Cahiers Jaunes (May 1943), quoted in Birnbaum, "La France aux Français," 237.

115. Déat, Mémoires politiques, 619.

116. See Pierre Bourdieu, "L'assassinat de Maurice Halbwachs," Liberté de l'Esprit, no. 16 (1987): 161–68. See also Annette Becker, Maurice Halbwachs: Un intellectuel en guerres mondiales, 1914–1945 (Paris: Agnès Viénot, 2003).

117. Leiris, Journal, 412.

118. Letter from Georges-Henri Rivière to Marcel Mauss, August 28, 1944.

119. Letter from Michel Leiris to Georges-Henri Rivière, August 30, 1944 (Archives of the Musée de l'Homme, 8601 11 12; Leiris, Journal, 898–99).

120. Letter from Germaine Tillion to Marcel Mauss, September 1945.

121. In his long letter of October 2, 1944, in which he set out the results of his research, Lévi-Strauss confided to Mauss that he wanted his book on kinship systems

to serve as his thesis and wanted his teacher to agree to be its chairman (letter from Claude Lévi-Strauss to Marcel Mauss, October 2, 1944). Completed in February 1947, the book would appear in 1949 under the title *Les structures élémentaires de la parenté*.

122. Interview with Jacques Soustelle, Paris, November 6, 1989.

123. Letter from René Capitant, ministry of national education, to Marcel Mauss, November 21, 1944.

124. Letter from Jean Margot-Duclot to Marcel Mauss, April 13, 1945.

125. Letter from M. Constantin to Marcel Mauss, June 26, 1945.

126. The objective of the Centre d'Études Sociologiques (CES), founded by Georges Gurvitch and Henri Lévy-Bruhl within the framework of the CNRS, was to "promote and direct research in the different branches of sociology." The center played an important role in new research, pursuing major surveys (on Catholicism in France by Gabriel Le Bras, for example, or on the problems of contemporary labor by Georges Friedmann) and hiring "promising young researchers" (Paul-Henri Chombart de Lauwe, Pierre Naville, Viviane Isambert-Jamati, Jean-Daniel Reynaud, Alain Touraine). Edgar Morin, "L'activité du Centre d'études sociologiques," *Année Sociologique*, 3rd ser. (1949–1950; Paris: PUF, 1952), 522. There were many connections between the CES and the former contributors to *Annales Sociologiques*: Georges Davy, Louis Gornet, Georges Bourgin, and others were members. The general secretary of the center was Yvonne Halbwachs, Maurice Halbwachs's widow. On the CES, see Jean-René Tréanton, "Les premières années au Centre d'études sociologiques, 1947–1955," *Revue Française de Sociologie* 32, no. 3 (January–September 1991): 389.

127. Mauss thus found himself standing with members of the editorial board of *Cahiers Internationaux de Sociologie*, whose founder was Georges Gurvitch. Gurvitch, a philosopher by training and the author of books on the sociology of law (*L'idée du droit social*, 1935; *Éléments de sociologie juridique*, 1940), returned to France after five years in the United States (1940–1945), where he had discovered American sociology. Georges Gurvitch and Wilbert E. Moore, *La sociologie au XXe siècle*, 2 vols. (Paris: PUF, 1947).

128. "Avant-propos," *Année Sociologique*, 3rd ser. (1940–1948), 1 (1949): ix. The man behind this "resurrection" was undoubtedly Henri Lévy-Bruhl. The team's secretary was Georges Duveau, who had recently been appointed a professor at the Université de Strasbourg. The team included several former contributors to *Annales Sociologiques*: Georges Bourgin, Georges Davy, Georges Gurvitch, Maurice Leenhardt, Georges Lutfalla, and others. Multidisciplinary in its orientation, *Année*, 3rd ser., secured funding from many researchers in very different fields: political geography (François Bourricaud), psychology (Jean Stoetzel), psychoanalysis (Mikel Dufrenne), anthropology (Pierre Métais, Denise Paulme, Claude Lévi-Strauss, Maxime Rodinson), folklore (André Varagnac), the history of religion (Maurice Goguel, Gabriel Le Bras, Jean Auger-Duvignaud), aesthetics and literature (Pierre Francastel, Roger Caillois, André Schaeffner), and technology (Georges Friedmann, André Leroi-Gourhan, Georges Canguilhem, François and Viviane Isambert, Alain Touraine).

129. The participants in that colloquium were Fernand Braudel, Georges Davy, Lucien Febvre, Louis Gernet, Georges Gurvitch, Maurice Leenhardt, and Paul Rivet.

130. Interview with Louis Dumont, Paris, February 20, 1989.

131. Letter from Marie Mauss to Ignace Meyerson, February 12, 1950 (Ignace Meyerson collection).

132. Interview with Denise Paulme, Paris, February 19, 1989.

133. Circular signed by Maurice Leenhardt, n.d. The session took place on May 3, 1950, at the Musée de l'Homme, palais de Chaillot. The commemoration was organized with the cooperation of Georges Bourgin, Georges Davy, Georges Friedmann, Marcel Griaule, Georges Gurvitch, Gabriel Le Bras, Maurice Leenhardt, Claude Lévi-Strauss, Paul Mus, Alfred R. Radcliffe-Brown, Paul Rivet, and Jacques Soustelle.

134. Henri Lévy-Bruhl, "In Memoriam: Marcel Mauss," *Année Sociologique*, 3rd ser. (1948–1949; Paris: 1951), 1–4.

135. Henri Lévy-Bruhl, "Nécrologie: Marcel Mauss," *Journal de Psychologie Normale et Pathologique* 43 (1950): 318.

136. Faculty meeting of the Collège de France, March 5, 1950 (C-XII, Marcel Mauss, Archives of the Collège de France).

137. Maurice Leenhardt, "Marcel Mauss (1872–1950)," *Annuaire de l'École Pratique des Hautes Études, Section des Sciences Religieuses* (1950): 23.

138. Georges Gurvitch, "Nécrologie: Marcel Mauss (1877–1950)," *Revue de Métaphysique et de Morale* 2 (April–June 1950): 2.

139. Denise Paulme, "Nécrologie: Marcel Mauss," *Anthropologie* 54, nos. 1–2 (1950): 155.

140. Lévy-Bruhl, "In Memoriam: Marcel Mauss," 3.

141. Lucien Febvre, "In Memoriam," *Annales ESC* 5 (1950): 501.

INDEX

CPSIA information can be obtained
at www.ICGtesting.com
Printed in the USA
BVHW03s0902130218
507949BV00002B/122/P

9 780691 168074